In the Shadow of My Truth

by
Deborah Richmond Foulkes

authorHOUSE

1663 LIBERTY DRIVE, SUITE 200
BLOOMINGTON, INDIANA 47403
(800) 839-8640
www.authorhouse.com

© 2005 Deborah Richmond Foulkes. All Rights Reserved.

No part of this book may be reproduced, stored in a retrieval system, or transmitted by any means without the written permission of the author.

First published by AuthorHouse 11/24/04

ISBN: 1-4208-1318-8 (e)
ISBN: 1-4208-1317-X (sc)
ISBN: 1-4208-1316-1 (dj)

Library of Congress Control Number: 2004099711

Printed in the United States of America
Bloomington, Indiana

This book is printed on acid-free paper.

ACKNOWLEDGEMENTS

In the Shadow of My Truth was developed through extensive research and on-site investigation: multiple trips to Scotland and England, excursions to both Belgium and Spain, all carefully orchestrated to properly investigate every site referenced in the book. Academic research began at the libraries of Harvard University and the National Library of Scotland at Edinburgh where I was fortunate enough to obtain a three year Readers Pass. At these libraries I found records: Rolls of the Pipe including Fine Rolls, Calendars of Inquisitions Post Mortem and other translations of surviving documents and compilations that became the basis for validating the story. In addition to these translations, I located original documents at the National Archives in Kew, Surrey England, purchasing images of many including the entire Ragman Roll of 1296 and from the British Library a photograph of an original document and seal of Eleanora Lovaine was also acquired.

During the last two years, I was also fortunate to obtain many rare, antique books as well as a few reprints that have provided excellent sources of information including Chalmers' Caledonia, three volumes; four volumes of the Exchequer Rolls of Scotland; John Fordun's Historians of Scotland; the 1764 publication of the Peerage of Scotland by Robert Douglas complete with a Douglas Cavers bookplate; John Froissart's Chronicles of England France and Spain; Wyntoun's Chronicles; two volumes of The Douglas Books by William Fraser; Duncan's Regesta Regum Scottorum V; archdeacon Barbour's The Bruce; Rev. Joseph Stevenson's Historical Documents of Scotland and Illustrations of Scottish History; Joseph Bain's Calendar of Documents Relating to Scotland in four volumes; compilations of charters and documents of Ayrshire and Moray; Robertson's Index of Charters; Histories of the County of Northumbria; Bower's Scotichronicon; The Roll of Caerlaverock; Syllabus of Rymer's Foedera; Ayloffe's Calendar of Ancient Charters; the History of the Family of Lindsay in three volumes; Maxwell's translation of the Chronicle of Lanercost; Sir Thomas Gray's Scalachronica; and many more sources too numerous to mention. I wanted to be thorough; the book had to be historically accurate, validating what I first learned to be true through the information disseminated by Spirit.

And lastly to compliment my academic research: for the phrases and understanding of Scottish Gaelic and the culture that evolved around the language I wish to thank An Comunn Gaidhealach America for sponsoring the Gaelic Song and Language Week at Grandfather Mountain, NC where I began my studies of that ancient tongue.

In addition to acknowledging some of the many sources used to validate new age data, there were numerous people in Scotland, England, and

Belgium that I would like to thank. In Douglas, Scotland the inspiring words of James Fleming: that I should write the sequel to My Truth, capturing 'the story of the Good Sir James' kept me focused to complete this second of three volumes on my Douglas ancestors. The encouraging sentiment was echoed by his wife Jeanette Fleming, her generous hospitality challenged only once; that fateful warning: 'take care not to lose the tip from my walking stick' as Jim and I departed for adventure, in search of Park Castle, the stronghold of the Good Sir James. There on the banks of Park Burn I promptly misplaced the rubber guard in a bog of sinking mud; barely five minutes out on the trip. The pitfalls of on-site research again occurred during an ensuing excursion in pursuit of Douglas history. Jim had to scurry to find the dockins plant in remedy to my encounter with the nasty nettles. I had clamored through brush to uncover ruins of the rubble and stone walls of the 13th century castle in Douglasdale, sadly surrounded by a budding crop of the attacking foliage. Lessons still in the learning stage I am afraid!

In the Kingdome of Fife, as it was once called, I wish to thank Stuart Morris of Balgonie, Lady Margaret, and Raymond, the Laird of Balgonie for their enduring support and encouragement. I would be remiss to not include their wee hounds, the Deerhounds at Balgonie Castle, rescued hounds from St. Hubert's Hound Sanctuary; several posing for photographs appearing in this book.

In the beautiful Borders region of Scotland, Hilary and Robert Dunlop of Whitmuir, the Garden House in Selkirk were very generous with their time as well as their fine shelf of single malt. They were also instrumental in finding me good sources for local history including Walter Elliot.

In Belgium I relied upon the kind assistance of Daniel van Buynder and his wife Wendy. I felt like a queen staying in their home and will never forget our mad dash around the pertinent sites of Brabant with their three year old son Byron in tow. Daniel's photographs of Courtrai are noted in the book.

There are very many more; Anne, Susan, Peggy, Jack, Al, and Ed; Robert, Rita, John, Arja, Anna-Maija, Suzane and the UBU; and least I forget, Willelmi de Duglas and his wee entourage; the list must end here but could easily continue; thank you all and God Bless.

DEDICATION

To John Barbour, archdeacon, Aberdeen
Without his epic poem *The Bruys* many heroes would be unknown to us

And to the parishioners of Medieval Churches in England and Scotland, especially in these villages and towns listed below; without their loving support these ancient buildings, these standing records to a way of life from centuries ago, would be forever lost to us…..

Berkeley; Bildeston; Douglas; Durisdeer; Fairstead; Ingram; Lanercost; Little Dunmow; Little Easton; Lyne; Morebattle; Ratby; Stafford; Stebbing; Ware; Woodham Ferrers; and Writtle.

AND IN LOVING MEMORY OF

Fergus, Gandolph, and Floyd

CONTENTS

Acknowledgements..iii

Part I   1302 to 1303..1
Stebbinge Park, Muriel Douglas wedding......................................5
Sezincote; the Manor of Lord Lovaine..11
Berkeley Castle; James meets Lord Berkeley and his daughters..............21
Paris; the Douglases meet Scots in exile at French Court....................63
Stebbinge Park Muriel Douglas dies in child-bed...........................110

Part II   1304 to 1307..122
Paris; James and Bishop Lamberton..127
Stirling; Edward I denies James Douglas his inheritance....................147
Bildeston; Eleanora forced to marry Sir William Bagot.....................181
Ericstane; James pledges fealty to Brus....................................187
Methven; the rout of the Scots...209
Dahl Righ; Scots defeated near Tyndrum, James injured...................218
Arran; James defeats the garrison of Lord Johannis de Hastings..........238
Douglasdale; the Douglas Larder..259
Edirford; James defeats Mowbray and his forces 286
Loudon Hill; James follows his king to victory in Ayrshire.................289
Douglas; Lady Berkeley's suitor defeated; Douglas Castle razed............297

Part III   1308 to 1320......................................317
Lyne; James' cousins, Randolph and Stewart, captured for Brus............319
Pass of Brander; James dubbed before the battle...........................334
Douglasdale; weddings of James and Archibald..............................397
Douglasdale; William 9th Lord Douglas born................................409
Douglasdale; John Douglas born..411
Bannock Burn; James Knight Banneret in rout of the English...............460
Douglasdale; Eleanor Douglas born...473
Carlisle; Archibald rescues James during the siege.........................481
Lintalee; James victorious; earns the fur hat...............................489
Arbroath; James affixes his seal to the famous document..................531

Part IV   1320 to 1330 and Epilogue......................539
Douglasdale; Archibald of Douglas dubbed; William born..................540
Wilbrighton Hall; Nicholas de Segrave dies..................................544
Yorkshire; Campaign to Rievaulx Abbey..560
Berwick; Emerald Charter...570
Weardale Campaign...578
Archibald the Grim born..581
Fawdon; Eleanora passes to the Otherworld..................................582
Teba; the last Battle for the Good Sir James.................................594
Map of Scotland..600
Map of England...601
Glossary..602
Who's Who, Historical Figures 604
My Truth A Mist In Time..607

Part I
1302 to 1303

STEBBINGE PARK 1302-Lady Eleanora Douglas widow of the martyred Scottish patriot, William le Hardi, Lord Douglas was turning thirty-four this year and residing in Essex, England with her children. Her beloved husband William had been gone from her four long years. He was a Scottish nobleman executed in the Tower of London; his estates had been seized for his rebellion with William Wallace in Scotland's Wars for National Independence. The widow had been assigned a proper dower from his lands except for the lordship of Douglasdale. This vast barony with its stronghold of Douglas Castle was still held by a vassal of Edward Plantagenet, Lord Clifford. Ellie had recently returned from Scotland. She was traveling there with her three sons in search of her rents and fees from her dower lands from both her first husband Lord William de Ferrers of Groby and her second William, Lord Douglas.

"Ana," called Ellie to her long time companion and maid in wait, "we have another acceptance for Muriel's good wedding, the de Segraves from Stowe are to attend!" Ana was busy with her fair handwork; embroidering a night cote for the bride. The wedding of Ellie's only surviving daughter now thirteen was to take place at the priory of Little Dunmow and the church dedicated to St. Mary, just one mile from her manor in Stebbinge Park. Ana was pleased to hear that Sir Nicky and his wife Alice were coming to the wedding; knowing how much her girl enjoyed the company of her favorite cousins. When Ellie first married Gilley, her second husband named William, she had been in the throws of love; marrying without the license of the king, her liege lord holding her dower lands of de Ferrers. Lord Douglas was eventually arrested for his contempt and remanded to the constable of Knaresburgh Castle, a fortress just one day's march from Leeds in Yorkshire while he sought manucaptor for his parole from that prison.

The charges brought against the Scottish knight involved taking Ellie as his bride without permission of King Edward. Nicky led the contingency of Lady Douglas' kin, including Johannis de Hastings and William de Rye, who came to Lord Douglas' rescue, pledging their lands and person for surety that Gilley would be granted parole until his appearance before the king's council. "My sweet lamb," said Ana, "that he would come I told you so. To return is he from Scotland, in service of his lord the earl." Ellie was ebullient; everyone invited was returning their replies with yes, all were happy to attend this Douglas wedding.

James and Muriel, Ellie's two older children were just coming back from taking their palfreys to Little Dunmow where they visited the grave of William Douglas, the redoubtable laird and sadly missed father. "Father is most pleased about our choice for husband," said Muriel laughing for what she was about to say. "But he fears the performance of his son at that fair wedding; to play the wee Lowland pipes would be a dreadful sorrow to him, this I know," chided Mura to her older brother James. "Whatever do you mean my daughter?" asked Ellie, looking up from her lists of guests and the financial records of her many manors as she worked; the fair steward of this wee clan in Essex as she fashioned herself these days.

Figure I-Part One; stock grazing at Stebbinge Park

James interrupted his sister, not waiting for her response. "That Mura does not want a piper at her wedding; fearful to offend the English nobleman and his dear kin!" said the squire, feigning mockery at her choice of husband. Ana admonished Muriel. "You, the daughter of Lord Douglas to disdain the sound of Scotland's fair music and sweet instruments at your wedding?" she demanded to know. Ellie started to laugh at her daughter's foolish thoughts and silliness. "Our James has so fairly practiced with our Gillerothe that he knows some six tunes or more as promised. We will have the pipers; your dear brother too shall play the fair Lowland pipes. Your sweet and most missed father would have so insisted; as your mother does so now! It is done," said Lady Douglas.

The widow chuckled at herself; sounding more like their father as she used his favorite expression of emphasis while mitigating the quarrel between her older children. Ellie was looking intently at Mura and James; subconsciously twisting William's seal ring around her finger, the signet he used for putting his name to important documents. She wore the ring everyday to remind her of Lord Douglas and whenever she was anxious, she seemed to hold onto it for support. Today she was announcing bold plans and she was nervous. Before Gilley died, he discussed their future goals and strategy for their remaining children. Now she was about to implement the most difficult of those intentions: taking James to Brabant where he would remain for some years, to learn the arms of the country of his ancestors in Flanders. She turned to her oldest son solemnly; almost fearful for the dreaded task at hand.

"Dear James, this lady has so decided: we will go to Sezincote in July after Mura's dear wedding; to stay at the manor of my brother, now to be the young lord of the Lovaine lands," she said. Eleanora was referring the recent Inquisition Post Mortem in the death of her father, Lord Matthew Lovaine. Her younger sibling was deemed his father's heir and future lord; but since Thomas was still in his minority, the Lovaine estates were technically held in ward for him. "Then will this family journey on to Berkeley Castle," Ellie told her son with an air of excitement. "Dear Joan my kin is the lady of that castle, to invite us for some few days and a party there as well with lads and lasses of your age. Your brothers most to come with us, I have so agreed to Lady Berkeley," said Eleanora. The lady of the manor and of that fine castle in Gloucestershire was Joan de Ferrers, sister in law and cousin to Lady Douglas and a close friend as well. Muriel was pouting; begrudging these plans for her brothers. They were going to parties in Gloucestershire; not at just any manor there, but at the grandest castle of the shire!

The ancient stronghold commanded a poetic majesty as it rose above the village, providing breath taking views of the rocky Severn shore, and the panoramic scenery of the surrounding hills and the Berkeley Vale below. Lord Thomas Berkeley was a man of great influence and respect; an invitation to this fair house was a symbol of importance in many influential circles. "That I will be in Castle Cary not to go?" asked Mura enviously. "Some four days hence we come to visit you and Lord Lovel in Somersetshire; this is your mother's good intention," said Ellie. From there the family would leave from Hastings, one of the original Cinque Ports, where they would find a cog to take them to Boulogue the widow explained. The Douglas household was traveling to Lovaine and the duchy held by Eleanora's kin in Brabant to take her son where he would begin his final training before returning to Scotland. James was looking forward to his new independence; staying in Flanders to complete his education would be his first adventure he decided.

Muriel was most unhappy; everyone spoke of Berkeley Castle parties with great envy and she was not to attend. Married life to be most boring for this lass, said Mura to herself, pouting all the more for her pathetic fate. Just then they were interrupted by the wee sons Hugh and Archie running into the great hall. "We are to go to Berkeley Castle," boasted James to his brothers, taunting his sister as was his teasing way. Then feigning great pleasure at the prospect of this party he embellished the story for them even more. "That we will all be greeted in great fashion; ladies to take their notice of our manly ways. Dancing and much merriment to have the three of us, what heaven is this Gloucestershire I do imagine it!" said James. His notorious smirk, quite like his father's, betrayed the exaggerated 'true happiness to attend this gathering' as the squire continued to regale his brothers, tongue in cheek. Mura was furious when she realized she had become the victim of his fair teasing once again. "Make him stop now mother; I do will it so!" Ellie told her that she who teases must expect the same in return. "Your brother only to oblige your own taunting of him," said Ellie.

But Hugh and Archie were in the great hall for another reason and not to listen to Mura's whining they said. The lads were very upset; something had agitated them that they barely blurted out their words together, insisting that Ellie listen to their pleas. "Mother, some news of sadness, most difficult to say," they told her in unison. "Now young sirs, what is your bidding so excited here?" she asked them with concern, noticing their worried countenances and heavy breathing from their running.

Figure II-Part One; Charles of Invercarron or Charlie to his friends; a Deerhound from the household of the Laird of Balgonie

"Shamus, the wee hound has fallen in the courtyard, he stopped moving!" Hugh told them. Ellie bolted from her seat at the table in the great hall. "Where?" she exclaimed in a panic stricken voice. The Deerhound was turning sixteen; an ancient hound for his size and breed. Sir Shamus was the very reason she first met Gilley; a member of the family that he slept in Ellie's bed every night since her husband was imprisoned by the king. Lady Douglas found the wee greyhound in the courtyard most confused and stunned. He got up slowly and walked about but he was very weak. "Hugh, tell your mother most again what happened; James bring the healing box of your father, the noo!" she exclaimed, ordering everyone about just how Gilley would have reacted in such a serious situation. Hugh and Archie both described the hound, that he was running slowly; then suddenly he collapsed and did not move again no matter what they said, as if he could not hear or see them.

Sir Shamus was now walking about; not showing any signs of eating something foul to cause his problem Ellie surmised. Perhaps my dear hound is nearing his end; his heart to give him trouble most till one day it would quit she sighed to herself. She held him in her arms; the once great beast was growing thin with age she noted as she rubbed his belly. "Dear lad, this mother thinks of you most like a son," she told the silly Deerhound as she petted his ears, examining his body for another sign that might be the cause of his problems, "my wee son with the lang hair about, the grey Douglas hound," she soothed him with her hand as well as her sweet voice, holding him to her breast as she sat on the ground of the courtyard.

James brought the healing box of herbs and some water from the well. Ana came right behind him with a tasine with much honey to which James added ginger and some cayenne pepper to the mixture. The wee hound lapped the healing remedy right up. James then carried Shamus into the great hall, making a bed of fine rushes for him with some linen cloth for comfort. By nightfall the hound was himself again. Ellie would take him gently to her bed each evening now; to coax him up most gingerly as she moved him. He recovered and remained his silly self with them for some weeks. To Ellie, something kept this old Deerhound going, to stay with them until after Muriel's wedding as he if knew not to spoil her special day.

The wedding went perfectly; the weather was bright and sunny for this day in June. The bride was radiant and lovely as she was escorted by her brother James giving her in marriage to Richard Lovel to live in Castle Cary, England. The wee lad Archie brought the ring for the ceremony; presented it to the groom when he was told. Hubicus walked behind his brother with the woven cloth of black and grey; carried for this Scottish ritual on a white silk cushion embroidered in azure with the proud name of: 𝔇 𝔘 𝔊 𝔏 𝔄 𝔖; the same one that Lord Douglas and Lady Douglas and the Douglas Chiefs before them used for their wedding sacraments. The only trouble for their day was with the rector who was to perform the ceremony; he took sick. Happily Roger de Clare from Dunmow Major agreed to fill in for the ailing Stephen Notele, as a favor to Lady Douglas to save their wedding day. As Lady Muriel Douglas Lovel and her husband Richard Lovel, Lord Cary left St. Mary's chapel they were greeted by the sweet sounds of the wee Scottish pipes serenading from the porch. Three Lowland pipers played the music of their Celtic ancestors; among them was a squire, James of Douglas. True to his word, the brother learned to play the small pipes, to honor the memory of William le Hardi Douglas, their father now with God.

Figure III-Part One; Interior of St. Mary's Church, Little Dunmow Priory

There was great feasting at Stebbinge Park and much merriment with wine and fresh ale; jesters and minstrels, players in the gallery of the great hall were all lavishly attired for this day. Silks and linens of bright colors draped and wrapped the tables and the benches for the banquet. Many guests were staying at the manor and in the messuages of Stebbinge Park; that everyone was still celebrating late into the night, enjoying the frivolity and excitement of the event. There was much dancing and feasting through the wee hours; minstrels singing gaily, musicians playing dulcimers and flutes, the gallery alive with entertainment for their guests. Lord and Lady Lovel were most impressed by the good fare and great choice of amusements; everything was perfect for their wedding day.

The platters for the dais, the grand table for the lady of the manor and her family with the bride and groom were bountiful with an extensive variety of fare. The same could be said for the other tables of their friends and family, as the cellarers and kitchen servants made a steady stream with food and drink to the great hall. There were de Ferrers and de Segraves,

Lady Isabel and Lord John Lovel, some de Berkeleys too, but not the Lady Joan de Berkeley; this sister in law of Lady Douglas would not attend. The wife of the noble Lord Berkeley in all her many years of marriage would not once venture more than ten miles from the manors of her estate. Ellie understood; knowing as well that they would see this lovely lady in July at Berkeley Castle. The Douglases and their guests laughed and feasted, enjoyed fair quantities of excellent wine and fresh ale; oysters and eels with sticky sauce a favorite of Eleanora; capons, pheasants, hare and wild boar greeted every guest; beans in a thick sweet sauce with onions and some ginger were on every table; breads and cakes in measure of good plenty, followed by a lovely custard to complete the banquet given by Lady Douglas for her daughter and new son by marriage.

Figure IV-Part One; Map of Stebbing; the motte of Stebbinge Park shown center

Many of the guests stayed through to the very end of the festivities. But Young de Ferrers remained there even later. He was found sitting in the great hall the next morning when Ellie arrived to break her morning fast. As she walked by her stepson he rose to greet her. But in his inebriated state he fell backwards, off balance and almost landed on the floor had Nicky not stepped forward to his rescue. "It so fortunate a day for you that my good brother John, your dear father in law is yet in Scotland on campaign," said Nicky to his niece's husband William de Ferrers. "He would have let you fall most perfectly," he teased the youthful, yet pompous lord, laughing loudly at the expense of the sorry knight. Ellie was in tears of laughter as well, hoping to suppress the sound and not rile Sir William; wanting to avoid a possible brawl in Stebbinge Park. Ellen de Segrave, the wife of young William called in his squire to assist him from the hall; bidding all farewell as she left with him. The son and father most the same mused Ellie of her stepson and first husband. The vile and miserable knight, the Lord of Groby as the father was then called, was violent to women and small children when he would drink. As Ellie recalled her first husband William de Ferrers, she also remembered her great relief to become his widow in 1287. Few months later she met her other William, Lord Douglas and fell in love. Ellie sighed wistfully; oh to be so loved she said softly to herself, thinking of her most precious husband, Gilley.

All her guests had taken their leave for their own manors leaving Nicky and Ellie alone to break their fast together in the great hall. She motioned to her cousin to join her; to sit and speak in private as close kin. Lady Douglas and Lord Segrave were dear friends for twenty years or more that only truth passed between them when they spoke. "That you have done so well my sweet cousin for your sorrow and enormous grief," said the kind knight, "to plan this lovely wedding and arrange for dower too I hear." Ellie pouted, "Young de Ferrers to tell most every one he sees of my agreements over lands and manors?" she asked sputtering his name. "Eleanora, we have no secrets from each other, that he knows it well, holding his lands for him in ward that I did some eleven years ago," Nicky allowed. Ellie relented, and shared a smile with her cousin. "He so like his father; to remind me of the horror of those times; I find him so contemptible," she told him. "Pity is more the truth there I do fear," said Nicky. Then he took her hand and held it for some time.

"This humble baron does so wish to speak to you of your dear knight and husband," he said quietly. "So many tales of trouble; pray do tell me what had happened in the Tower," Nicky asked Lady Douglas. Ellie began the story; first to tell him that de Percy tricked her husband, called him to come and answer charges of breaking a covenant of peace just after signing the treaty at Irvine, Scotland. "This lass had begged my Gilley not to go; a trap I feared with my father in collusion for some Yorkshire lands to give de Percy," she continued, telling Nicky of the plot to imprison Lord Douglas under false pretenses. "That they were not content with his staying in the Tower; they trifled with our letters, bid the solicitors to tell me that my sweet William refused my visits and the words of love I wrote to him, so longing for his arms to hold me!" she paused some, crying softly. Nicky held her close to him; a sensitive man, he truly loved his cousin Ellie as well. He told her how very sad he was to learn of the treachery of Lord

Percy and Lord Lovaine, but not surprised. The infamous deeds were as he had feared.

"That I tried to warn you with my letter to you in Berwick five years ago," he reminded Ellie. "This knight had heard foul rumors, Lovaine men at arms in Yorkshire with their lord meeting with de Percy, then these nobles to speak again in Berwick during that dreadful siege." Ellie spoke of the banners carried by de Percy, with the armorial bearings of the Lovaine blue lion and her premonitions of de mischef. "That before that awful meeting with that vassal of dear Edward, I had a dreadful vision most frightening to me," she said. "This lass knew my Gilley should not go to de Percy. We had cross words; he said he had to go to clear his name. My sweet William had so lost his Douglasdale that he had left to him only his reputation for fair honesty." Nicky knew these rogues de Percy and Lovaine for their treacherous scheming; to ensnare such a knight of renown was simple for these felons, rotten and most foul of humor, with no regard for honesty he sputtered to himself. "That your William's adherence to core values and sweet truth would so convict him one day I knew this," he told Ellie sadly. "Would you tell me of his end?" he asked, "Was he so poisoned as I heard?" Lady Douglas was careful to explain every detail of the horrid execution and the torture William endured as if by this catharsis she could heal herself. "My beloved was hanged cruelly," she said. Nicky winced hearing of the barbarous end; one prescribed for those committing treason.

Figure V-Part One; view from the Bloody Tower of Edward I's personal compartment built over Traitor's Gate where William le Hardi Douglas entered the Tower of London in October, 1297

Standing in the doorway of the great hall was James; he had stumbled upon their discussion, not wanting to interrupt, he waited. Then he heard his mother's dreadful words describing the death of his dear father; how the

9

warders thought him dead, delivered the humble knight yet still alive, but mute, to his wife waiting to bury him. "Sweet mother," James began, "you never told me this!" he exclaimed, incredulous that she had kept the awful secret to herself to bear it all alone. Ellie stood up as her son came quickly to her side; they held each other in a comforting embrace for some time. "That this mother could not tell a son or any other; only our Ana knew for she was there to cleanse the body of our laird your father, preparing for his burial." Ellie wept, sobbing openly into the shoulder of her eldest son. Turning now to Nicky, "He could not speak; his voice most lost from cruelty of the hanging, then so racked, his chest impaled with a vile instrument of pain. But as I held him, my Gilley opened his eyes one last time to tell me of his love, he moved his lips to say what words I could not hear but knew. My sweet husband died that day in my arms; he had fooled the gaolers, to bring this lass one more embrace of his dear words of love," said the widow, grieving once again for the loss of her William. James' words were few, but anger was a pale description to their meaning. "My father's suffered end will not compare with theirs that I will so avenge them; I do swear it."

Nicky told them both he was sorry to re-open the wound, a loss so deep within; but he had to know he told Ellie. "This baron is not truly faithful to that king; the others, the Earl of Surrey and his nephew Lord de Percy are the most vile of English knights that I have known," he told them. "I can only say that I am not alone in my position; other barons in this kingdome share my sorrow for the deeds of Edward and these repugnant vassals." Nicky excused himself from their company; he and Lady Alice must depart for his manor in Chrishall he told them sadly, but he would return for another visit soon he promised. The knight held lands in several shires; Chrishall was in Essex, but a half days ride from Stebbinge Park.

JULY 1302-Ellie had met with her attorneys in late June; her estates of dower were still not providing the expected fees and rents. She decided to petition the king as Eleanora de Ferrers and was received on the 1st July. This plea read: for rectification of the demand against her for the balance of the £83 of William de Douglas' fine for marrying her in 1288; his lands in Fawdon most sufficient for this claim. Then through her solicitors for a second time, Ellie made her appearance before the King's Bench some weeks later. She filed an additional plea for the restoration of her dower lands in Scotland for both her former husbands: Lord de Ferrers and Lord Douglas. The widow had journeyed with her household and steward le Parker to Scotland in 1301; perilously few weeks before the campaign of Edward and his muster to advance from Berwick on Tweed. There she found many sheriffs collecting her rents and refusing to release them. The escheators claimed that they were not notified by Edward's government in

Scotland to reseise her dower rents. Ellie was advised to petition the king to tell them again what Edward had said three years before in 1299: release these fees to the widow Eleanora Lovaine Douglas! On July 22nd the king issued another writ to his lieutenant in Scotland. He told John de St. John that this widow had so petitioned for the dower of the first husband de Ferrers seized into the king's hands for the rebellion of the second husband William Douglas. This dower and the other so restored to Lady Douglas, ordered Edward; the fees and rents released as well, the king commanded.

Ellie woke from a deep slumber; the rain made her shudder in memory of the kidnapping from Douglas Castle she endured at the hand of Robert Brus; the fright she experienced she relived each time she heard the sound of water hitting the roof. Lady Douglas tried to calm herself with the present; tomorrow they were leaving for Gloucestershire and the Lovaine manor of Sezincote, a place where she felt safe. But as she rolled over, turning to her beloved Deerhound she knew at once that he would not be going on this journey; he had made another that very night, to be again with William and the others of her children. She held him fast to her; crying now so deeply, sobbing that her body was in spasms. More than when her father died she grieved now; the wee hound who brought her Gilley to her in Ayrshire was now gone. Some in the Holy Mother church would say that Deerhounds don't go to God's Paradise; but William told her that the Celts knew a better Heaven where silly hounds would be most welcome and knights most happy to receive them there as well.

"Ana," cried Ellie, when she saw her at the door of her chamber, "Our dear Shamus has joined my husband most this night," her words disrupted by tears and sobs of sorrow for her beloved hound. Ana called for James; he brought the others. A ceremony was planned for Sir Shamus; Sir David would take care to boil his bones that they would bring him back to Fawdon in the spring; bury him there in the Cheviot hills he loved so much. The younger lads were extremely saddened by the loss; the Deerhound was their friend and playmate. Hugh and Archie cried; James too found his tears most difficult to hide. Sometimes a loss of a beloved Deerhound allows a family to grieve together; the anger of a father's loss had kept them apart, alone in their sorrow. But the passing of their friend Sir Shamus of Douglas held them all as one in their mourning; to heal them in their common loss of their most uncommon brother and dear son.

SEZINCOTE-The entourage of the wee Douglas clan in Essex made good time traveling west to the Lovaine manor in Gloucestershire. They journeyed with carts and horses, one nurse for Archie, Ana, two maids in wait, Sir David, his squires, the Douglas men at arms, Gillerothe and William's squire Patric and valet Henry who stayed on with Eleanora in

Essex. Lady Douglas and her three sons and household stopped at the manors of her kin and priories along the way during their five days of uneventful travel as they made their way from Stebbing to Sezincote. This summer had many changes for the widow of Lord Douglas; one filled with emptiness for all who would now leave to make their way without their mother. Her daughter had married and was living with Lord Lovel; her James was about to embark on his new life living in Brabant, both would be so sorely missed, she admitted to herself.

Ellie had not ventured forth in public in four years; in mourning for her husband keeping to her manors and staying with her children was her chosen life. Now there was another loss, an awful loneliness in her empty bed; the passing of the sweet and faithful Deerhound to make her sadder still. "Ana," began Ellie sitting in the chamber once of her mother Lady Helisant, "I miss that silly hound so; that I can not seem to sleep without him." She sighed, chuckling some at the concept of the loss she was describing. She wiped her eyes again as tears welled even more. "And this day too I most miss my mother; spared was she to see the awful deeds of Lord Lovaine against her special son as she called my William." Ellie sat in silent grief as Ana began fixing her lady's long hair with a lovely comb of carved ivory and a silver initial of *E.*

Ellie suddenly stirred from her sad state to take notice of what Ana was doing. "You found the comb then!" grabbing for the precious gift from Gilley she thought lost during their hasty escape from Scotland four years ago. "Aye, this lass has found it in the packing for this journey," she told her lady. "That I would surprise you when most you needed to think of that sweet day." Ellie held Gilley's gift to her heart, cherished the silver and ivory; her dear husband's kind remembrance on their first Hogmanay, 1289; the Scottish celebration of New Years. "Thank you my Ana," she told her quietly, "this is indeed when I most need to have such fine memory with me."

Just then there was a light rapping on her chamber door that opened slowly revealing the faces of three handsome lads: James, Hugh, and Archie. "Mother, that we have found an abbey to be near us from our riding out today; we did not venture further to so arrive there, but we know where it is, too far to travel just this day," said James. "We were looking over the lands that so surround this wee parish," said Hugh excitedly, as he stuttered some with his enthusiasm. "My palfrey," smiled her youngest son, "so happy is this lad with his new horse!" exclaimed Archie, displaying that precious smirk his mother recognized as Gilley's. "And, no name yet for this noble beast?" asked Ellie, insisting that her son select his own name.

Archie thought for some time; his brother Hugh had named his palfrey after their father, calling him Sir William. "Perhaps to call him Audāx, after our good father most as well," said the wee lad. James smiled broadly, "Your Latin schooling at the priory well used," commended the squire. Ellie agreed; to use the sobriquet of their father William, *le Hardi*, to name his palfrey Audāx was an excellent choice. Ellie was elated; her sons seemed to be enjoying Sezincote as she once did coming here as a child with Lady Helisant. Being in the old manor brought her found memories, she mused. Ellie's sons continued telling her in excited chatter of their day; she initially had to interrupt them as each one was trying to talk over the other. "One lad to speak; not so many all at once." she teased jovially. "First James; please to ask your question." James inquired about the abbey not far from the wee parish of the Lovaine manor.

Figure VI-Part One; Sezincote gate house; the newer 18h century manor house has an unusual architectural design of Hindu and Moslem extractions with a lovely garden within the estate that can be visited during limited hours of access

"That would be the Hailes Abbey that you speak of," said Ellie. "And on the morrow next we will travel to that abbey; a great shrine for many pilgrims to so seek," she explained. She also told them that the monastery was erected after the wee Norman church that sat beside that residence and shelter. They would visit that chapel as she had done with her mother years before. "To pray for the souls of our William and the others of our family," she said. "This religious house a Cistercian order; built only fifty years ago. These good men and priests are the white monks; but most unlike those mischief making monks of Melrose that plagued your father so," Ellie explained, reminding her sons of the tribulations of Lord Douglas with the Melrose Abbot. The abbot was known to the Douglases as the notorious holy man trifling with the water supply of Douglas tenants in Ayrshire; then complaining to Lord Edward when Sir William retaliated, forbidding them use of Douglas Park when they journeyed from Melrose to their Mauchline manor. Those monks and abbot were unjustly protected by the king and caused much disturbance to the lives of Douglases and their villiens in Ayrshire. Ah, but that was when their fair Douglasdale was held by Douglas lairds as it had been for many generations; tenants in chief no longer, Eleanora sighed to herself sadly.

The widow and mother continued with her story on Hailes. "Then once the monastery was completed, the east end of the abbey church was so extended to provide a chevet where a shrine would be erected for the holy relic: a wee vial with the blood of Christ," she explained to her children, describing every detail, to teach them all about the holy place much as Gilley would have done. "The blood of Christ?" asked Archie, bewildered that it still existed for them to see. Hugh told his brother that as with many relics they are deemed to represent the most holy of existence. "Perhaps the blood is something you will see; that it has dried some this lad would so expect," he said thoughtfully. "We worship in good faith that such device is real as our good father often told us." Ellie explained, adding that such stories were handed down from generation to generation; the proof found in the healing that one received from traveling in pilgrimage to the blessed shrine. Lady Douglas was determined to fill the void of their father; to be their teacher, wise parent, and leader, a true moral example. She felt this was her duty, to present her children with the integrity and honor, great character and piousness her husband lived by; to instill her children with his values and truth.

Figure VII-Part One; Hailes Abbey ruins; three cloister arches form the far standing boundary

Lady Douglas had never looked at her role as teacher until this journey. She realized she needed to seek the information herself on the places of interest as they traveled because she was previously unaware or uninterested of such history when visiting with Lord and Lady Lovaine as a child. The priest in the village was gathering some information so she could instruct her sons properly. "Tomorrow will I take you to the church here in Sezincote, part of the Lovaine manor. Then we can take our horses for some more exploring as our father would have done," Ellie declared happily. She looked over to Ana, conveying how pleased she was to have her children with her in Gloucestershire that she might share her past joys with them.

Figure VIII-Part One; 13th century hunting lodge belonged to St. Peter's Abbey later becoming Prinknash Abbey; wonderful pottery is produced at the abbey today

"Mother," interjected Archie. He was upset; reflecting on his grief for the loss of their Deerhound, the faithful companion and playmate. "This lad does mourn Sir Shamus so," he said, looking up at her, his eyes were brimming with sadness; his face held a glum appearance. Ellie told her youngest lad, holding him in her arms as she spoke, that they would find another Deerhound to share their lives; not to replace Sir Shamus, but to help ease their sorrow for his loss. She missed him most herself she told her sons. "That I was just telling our Ana of my cold and empty bed since his passing from us," his mother added wistfully; quietly conveying her own grief for the hound. "That I will find one special greyhound," said James, "to keep you company my mother until we return to Scotland and our Douglasdale; there to have a kennel full of hounds. It is my dream and promise to you," said the squire who was turning sixteen; towering above them with his six feet of height, and still growing. Ellie smiled at her oldest son. He was trying so hard to be like his father; to fill the void of Lord Douglas. "That you will learn the arms of Brabant is my greatest wish now true. Once you return we can speak of greyhounds and our Douglasdale," Ellie said, hoping to ease the youth's concerns as he was feeling the great weight of responsibility for his family at so young an age.

"When are we to go to Berkeley Castle?" asked Hugh. Lady Douglas told them all her plans: to leave in one short week, to travel west and south, to stay at Prinknash held by the abbot of St. Peter's, then on to Berkeley Castle and the manors there. "We will follow most the visit of one called Winchley, the Archbishop of Canterbury: a guest of the abbot when we were most in Scotland." She painted scenes in vibrant detail of the great hunt led by the Archbishop during his stay at Prinknash in 1301. To have him limited so humbly to only eight hounds and four harriers, with just one huntsman and a page must have been a feat she exclaimed!

"This grand hunt the prized expedition for that bishop; much extravagance and flourish he demanded. Holding Archbishop Winchley to such wee limits to have given him foul humors for that day!" Ellie explained; with her well known insights she accurately described the bishop's demeanor. She then told her young sons how a nobleman runs the hunt, taking more than one day for such ventures. "First to set about the harriers to pursue the smaller game that might distract the Deerhounds' chase of prey; this is his good intention for that beginning of the hunt. The day next the prized main call of the Deerhounds would so take place; there would be banners flourishing, pennons flying in the wind, an entourage of many to ride into the forests. They would then release the greyhounds of noble breeding in pursuit of deer and other large quarry," Ellie said cheerfully, caught up in the excitement of the chase as she described it. "Your dear father took me on a hunt when first I met him in Ayrshire. The Douglases used goshawks and falcons most as well; a splendid exhibition for the ladies to applaud that day!" she continued, elaborating on the grand pageantry of Douglas coursing in pursuit of game. "And on Arran most as well my Gilley set the course and led the way while this lass so watched from Lochranza Castle as the hunt took place. Your brother James was allowed to so accompany Lord Douglas on that fine occasion most as well!"

The younger brothers were excited to hear that James took part in a hunt with their father and they asked him to tell them all about it. He explained how William looked at the droppings of the prey to determine their sex and size. He told them how their father drew up the course and what the signals meant as given by the horn the others sounded. Ellie was impressed with James' ability to weave the tales of le Hardi that the wee ones would show interest in the story and come to know about their father. When he was finished she shared the rest of her plans; how they would travel, eventually reaching the shoreline and the channel. "In the late summer then to venture further south to the Cinque Ports; stopping first to see your sister Mura and her lord at their manor in Castle Cary," Ellie said. "Our next adventure to begin when we arrive at Hastings, the port we will use to leave for Paris." Her oldest son's eyes lit up. "Paris first?" asked James excitedly. "That you would have us travel to Brabant; taking your leave to Paris with only Hugh and Archie is what you told this lad," he said confused by the changes in their itinerary.

"The Douglases will now journey to Paris; only then to travel to Lovaine," she proclaimed with a smile of intrigue. "The reason for this exciting change: a knight sent as ambassador to France just three months past, in April," she told them all mysteriously. Hugh and Archie were most concerned. "Are you to find a husband and a father for our family?" asked her youngest son. Lady Douglas and Ana exchanged startled looks, and then began to laugh heartily. Ellie answered Archie's query by shaking her head with a definite no! "This lass is not to marry unless so forced by Lord Edward," she told them defiantly; then she added more quietly, "The memory of your dear father most heavy on my heart."

Figure IX-Part One; view of Pittarrow lands from Laurencekirk, once held by John Wishart, the Baron of the Mearns

Ellie took the opportunity to explain to them the reason for the altered itinerary without anymore suspense. She had received a letter from the bishop of Glasgow Robert Wishart that his nephew and their father's good friend Sir John Wishart of the Mearns was now in Paris; sent by the guardians of Scotland. "The very knight that helped your father rescue me from Fawside castle, to take me then to Kelso Abbey for our wedding," said Ellie happy to recall those pleasant times. She regaled them with the day she first laid her eyes upon John Wishart. "That this lass was most awakened in the early hours of that morning, Ana was so helping me to dress when suddenly dear Elena, the lady of the castle was led into my chamber on the arm of this wild, untamed warrior. Sir John much the shorter man in stature, missing nearly half a foot from the height of your dear father, was yet a frightening apparition to my presence that fateful prime. Ana here will sure attest!" Ellie chuckled as Ana grimaced in agreement.

Lady Douglas drew a picture in words of the knight's haggard and frightening appearance: his long, scraggly red hair darting out from under his battle scarred bassinette, the misshapen beard and huge moustache that all but covered his face making him seem more ominous. Then Ellie demonstrated the warrior's strange walk, menacing and determined. "That he so moved as this, with low long steps, most like a barbarian or wild ape as he charged into the presence of this lass." The wee lads were giggling as they watched her mimic the mannerisms of the long time compatriot of le Hardi. "That your mother was most scared; his scowling voice was low and gruff, that I truly thought he meant to harm us. Until he read of Lord Hugh's good words," Ellie sighed fondly recalling that day. "For then this lass so realized this was a ruse; a raid to kidnap me for marriage!" she proclaimed triumphantly. "He had much patience, that laird of Pittarrow. For when we took our leave of Fawside a wooden chest belonging to your mother was left standing in the field; that Wishart had to so retrieve it!" James went on to explain how he came to know the knight. "The Baron of the Mearns most often came to Douglasdale, bringing news to our father Lord Douglas of our Fawdon," he reminded Hugh and informed Archie who was too young to remember on his own. "Both knights and barons, sharing interests in Northumbria, good neighbors of the lands they once held there in Redesdale and Tynedale."

Ellie continued, telling them that Sir John and other Scots were on a diplomatic mission; to be received in court by the king of France. "We will see some good men of our homeland; nobles that we know; to help us in our quest to reseise our lands to Douglases," she said confidently of her plan. "Will Bishop Wishart be there too?" asked Hugh, most concerned to meet this good man of the see of Glasgow, he told his mother. "William Lamberton will so attend. The bishop of St. Andrews needed most at court for his diplomacy but not the 'bad bishop' as Edward calls our old friend, the patriot Robert Wishart," she explained, "he will stay in Scotland. Then she realized the reason for Hugh's concern. "My son, you will be with the Augustinians working at your studies soon enough," she said impatiently, "That you will be a priest in the see of Glasgow, too soon for your dear mother, I do know it!" she continued, exasperated that he wanted to leave her; after all she sputtered to herself, too many of my children are most moving from my home, to leave this mother most alone!

Hugh came and put his arm around Ellie, hugging her tightly. "Dear mother, your son so wants to stay; but God's calling is most within him. I will leave when it is time, to remain as lang as you will have me," the thoughtful eight year old said lovingly. "It is my pledge and promise," Hugh assured her. "Dear Hugh, forgive your mother her scolding words," Ellie replied. "I have been too worried for my own loneliness to reflect on your true desire and dear need to be of service to our God." She told him that in four years or less he would return to Scotland and have his choice; perhaps to journey to St. Andrews or even Jedburgh, nearer Fawdon for his training in the church; studying both Canon and Civil Law.

"There are many monasteries to so choose from; several priories in the see of Glasgow with Bishop Wishart or perhaps the abbey of Bishop Lamberton in Fife." Lady Douglas assured Hugh that he would eventually return home; it was her promise to Gilley that all her sons would leave Essex someday to rejoin their friends and kin in Scotland. "And when we are again in Stebbinge Park, that you may begin your work with the Hospitallers at their priory farm there; to learn the ways of healing is my desire; to study the gardens they so plant to fill their healing coffer like our father." Then the widow turned to her youngest son. "And for you Archie, it is my desire that in two years hence when our James returns that you will go to Garleton as I told you most before," she said, anticipating the same questions from her youngest son. "Some days this mother's heart is heavy; that our Muriel has moved away from Essex; and now when we return from France we leave one son behind, a guest of my dear kin most a widow as your mother, Lady Agnes of Lovaine."

Figure X-Part One; the beautiful Cotswolds; a view from the hills of Sezincote overlooking the village of Moreton-in-Marsh

The next few days the Douglases ventured forth across the rolling hills of the Cotswolds. They rode in the vale of these variegated lands to learn the Severn way; traveling through the wooded pastures of Gloucestershire. The Douglases discovered tumuli, small circular earth mounds used for burial; they studied barrows, larger earth mounds, like tumuli they were so built by the ancient ones as well. "That many so believe their placement to mark the stars; these landmarks to so tell the story of the movement of the heavens all above us," the widow explained. "These ancient ones of Gloucestershire built mounds; monuments to their gods telling of their power. They constructed shelters on top of burial cairns, burying their dead below. Their simple devices for all to see; the living kept their loved ones close to them though they passed to the Otherworld," said Ellie as she taught her sons. Taking her lads in search for tumuli was new to Ellie. Gilley had been the leader on such expeditions; he found true joy in telling his family about the ancient civilizations, explaining in wonderment about their customs. These stories were the traditions of her husband and she vowed to continue the practice in his absence. As a young lass growing up in Gloucestershire and Essex, Ellie would not trifle with such stories before. But she was Lady Douglas now and vowed to herself to learn about everything so that she could instruct her children properly. The knowledge she sought from the priest in Sezincote was part of her plan; with this information she could share the history of the lands; mirror the teaching ways of Gilley.

PRINKNASH- After arriving at the abbot's lodge in Prinknash Lady Douglas took her sons on an extended trek through the surrounding countryside. She spoke of how the monastery of St. Peter's in Gloucester managed the hunting lodge in Prinknash; explained why many monks found their way there, leaving the monastery to manage the farm lands that supported the abbey. "The Benedictines came to have their monastery in Gloucestershire, given lands from the Giffards, laying the Deed of Gift on the altar in the Gloucester Abbey in 1096," Ellie said in matter of fact tones. "By about the time your father was born St. Peter's held twenty-three manors, an estate of three hundred acres in all, about the size of Fawdon. In 1283 John Giffard," Ellie continued, as she read from the priest's words, "founded Gloucester College, Oxford for the students of the abbey."

There was a custom, she explained to her sons, for noblemen to commend some lands that the monks would pray for their souls in perpetuity. "That we should do that for our father," reminded James solemnly. Ellie agreed and suggested that when they were reseised to Douglasdale the next laird could do just that! Hugh and Archie were becoming bored with the history lessons and suggested that some feasting was their preference. The monks of the lodge kept with the daily activities and ways of the monastery even in the scheduling of their meals, feasting in the mid day; which was now, these younger sons reminded their mother. "Let us return then; this lass could do for some good wine and fine fare herself," Ellie said cheerfully; in truth she was exhausted from all the teaching, answering her sons' many questions. Being both father and mother to these lads; more difficult than one might ever so imagine, the widow sighed softly to herself. The Douglas household stayed but one night at the abbot's lodge in Prinknash; they had too many carts, horses, and children and men at arms to live there comfortably for long; but the generosity of the monks was heartwarming and enjoyable that Ellie was pleased to leave a good donation for their stay.

Figure XI-Part One; windows of Berkeley Castle great hall looking to the inner bailey

MICHAELWOOD, BERKELEY-Eleanora Douglas and her sons journeyed next to Berkeley Castle, home of Thomas, Lord Berkeley and his wife, Joan de Ferrers, Lady Berkeley. In Michaelwood the entire Douglas household was able to stay together; there were numerous buildings afforded them for their lodging. Then came the exciting day when Ellie and Ana, the three Douglas sons, and Archie's nurse Maudie, all rode out for Berkeley Castle in the escort of Sir David and his squires to stay the evening, attending Lord Thomas' and Lady Joan's elegant party and grand feasting that had become legendary in that shire. The widow wore a new surcote but of quiet hues; not yet relieved of mourning for her husband. The cote she wore below the velvet finery was elegant and brightly crafted with insets and trim of gold and purple; allowing for some colorful adornments to her otherwise quiet attire for this special evening. Her sons were draped in such finery as befits young noble lads; great velvet surcotes of blues, greens and reds with hats in contrasting colors of orange and purple, timed in silk brocade of golden hues. James had his hat trimmed in ermine; as a style he mimicked from his father. These Douglas "men" were all handsome; of great stature and good nature, they attracted many lasses to their presence for their rugged grace.

A party at this castle meant the very best of entertainment; many minstrels strolled about; the gallery in the great hall was filled with jesters and noble musicians; troubadours as well were there to walk among the guests and sing of courtly love. The elegant and stately hall was beautiful to behold; each wall was draped with lovely tapestries and painted with bright colors and heraldry of the Berkeley family, the bold red chevrons lining every doorway. The ceilings of the great hall were vaulted and appeared like stained glass paintings overhead. The tables were set around the room to give space for some dancing. These long trestles were draped in tapestries of blues and rich shades of red and gold; covered with sumptuous platters heaped high with venison, capons, goat, porpoises and roasted calf. Every other table had a wild boar upon it; roasted perfectly, ready to be devoured, sitting in the middle of the majestic groaning boards of sumptuous food. The quantity of selection was overwhelming to behold. Pages and squires of the manor were parading through the throng of guests; pouring the best of wines and the fresh brewed ales from the castle cellars.

James' tall, impressive form exuded a noble dignity as he graced the dance floor often, though reluctantly by his own honest admission. His dark, rugged countenance; his deep, jet-black eyes sparkling in the dim lighting of the great hall projected an intriguing and mysterious contrast to the fair skinned and blonde haired English barons feigning ennui boredom to the evening's festivities. The dashing, almost rakish appearance of the Scottish squire seemed to beckon English heiresses to his side. James found himself beset by many ladies including the two daughters of Lady Joan, Lady Alice and Lady Isabel. Both Hugh and Archie were amused by his predicament; so many lasses surrounding their brother; vying for his attentions, seemed funny to the younger lads.

Across the great hall Lady Douglas passed the evening quietly; sitting with her friend of many years, Lady Alice of Hertford, choosing not to participate in the merriment of flirtatious talk or lively dancing. Eleanora was somewhat reticent to accept the company of individual lords or knights fearing to give rise to an invitation to the dance floor or worse, a proposal of marriage; a very likely occurrence to her station and sizable dower, she reflected. Ellie was polite but distant; there was no choice she told herself as any conversation with an unmarried, eligible man might be misconstrued. While sitting at their table the ladies were visited by many guests, some women even brought their husbands, knights and lords of England, vassals of the king to entertain discussions with the Douglas widow. The night was finally winding down some. Ellie had felt besieged all evening by conversations of the Scottish troubles. Everyone was complaining for the high taxes required to pay for the king's wars with few spoils to reward his vassals for their trouble. The affairs of state were ever on the minds of

English noblemen these days. Talk of courtly love and troubadour's fair stories were over shadowed by the discontented gossip of the ever growing costs to satisfy dear Edward in his quest to conquer Scotland; quite a semblance of unrest Ellie mused with no short measure of satisfaction.

Her younger sons came to join her as the hour was growing late. "Mother, our James is most unhappy with his plight," said Hugh. "He seems uncomfortable with so many seeking his good favor." Archie was more to the point. "James does not enjoy false flattery," he told everyone at Ellie's table, smiling his broad grin, his green eyes twinkling in his bemusement. Ellie laughed at her sons' comments. "And where were you both just now?" she asked them. "Were you two not speaking with some ladies of your own?" she chided, knowing they were flirting with the older women of Ellie's age, swaggering their well known Douglas charm, smirking their way to the hearts of her friends and kin. "But mother, your friends know we are but wee lads; these ladies think of our dear brother as a knight so soon to be!" said the wee Archie, much wiser than his years.

Lady Alice was chuckling at their wit and honesty. "Most like your William, they smile at you with those eyes of beauty, and then speak to you in truth that you can only just adore them," said Ellie's childhood friend. "How do you ever discipline these boys, so charming in their nature?" she asked, teasing Lady Eleanora. Ellie was beaming proudly; her children reminded her of Gilley in every way. "Some days I fear they get the better of this lass," she said, "And you are so correct; the Douglas charm of their sweet father, an enduring legacy. That it will be the death of me, I know it!" The music was beginning again. James was forced to dance with not one lass, but three. Taking each partner for some wee time was his solution to his dilemma, not wanting to decide or hurt the feelings of one lass. His last dance was with the fair Isabel de Berkeley; by the conclusion of the music they were both laughing heartily.

James had boldly told her that he was only dancing with her to spare her the boredom of the English knights across the great hall, watching their every move. The young English heiress was surprised that James was only sixteen, his height and size to compliment his broad intelligence deceived her into thinking he was much older than his years. "That these knights are jealous of a lad, a squire most in age, but not in heart" she told him, grinning at his fair deception. "I thank you for your honesty. You have my heart in friendship for all times dear James of Douglas," she told him, meaning every word of it. "And mine too," piped the other de Berkeley daughter, just returning from her dance with a dour English knight. Lady Alice was her sister's equal in looks and allure but dramatically more outspoken than Lady Isabel. And she was not about to have her sibling hold the attentions of this tall, dark and mysterious Scot all to herself. Most of the English lords were of lighter complexion than the squire; their long blonde hair fairly coifed with a perfect moustache that seemed painted on their faces. And none were as tall as James, his great height common to his Celtic ancestors. "This lady has decided, the most fascinating and charming nobleman so here, most known for his true honesty is our dear James of Douglas," she stated openly to the chagrin of her would be English suitor.

Coming round to where Ellie and her friend Alice were seated was Lady Joan, accompanied as well by her husband Lord Thomas de Berkeley. Introductions were made; Lord Thomas commented on the conduct of the sons of Lady Douglas. "My dear wife has so spoken of your many children fondly; to meet some of them in person is gratifying to this old knight and lord," he said as young Hugh and Archibald were introduced. They were now joined by his younger daughter Isabel on the arm of James. "Dear father, a knight to be of renown and fair chivalry," she said boastfully as she introduced her dancing partner to Sir Thomas. "In truth to spare your daughter ennui boredom was my cause to dance with this sweet lass," said James with a teasing glance. "Yes, father, he most saved me this evening from the monotonous flattery of those false suitors, those English knights of vainglory," she replied in mocked annoyance. James bowed respectfully, happy to have obliged the lady, happier still to have this evening most concluded.

Figure XII-Part One; entrance to great hall from the inner bailey

Sir Thomas and Lady Joan invited Lady Eleanora and her sons to join them the morning next; to have a tour of their castle and the lands of their family's vast estate. "We have held these lands since the Conqueror," boasted the baron of Berkeley. "The wooden castellulum, our little castle

24

from that time was paltry in comparison, with its simple wooden palisade for defense. But the shell-keep that holds this great hall quite followed quickly in construction; the necessity for true fortification most required from the early days of rebellion in the Berkeley vale," said the lord known to many as Thomas the Wise; an intelligent and most provident man. "What is a shell-keep?" asked Archie. The baron was pleased to answer the wee lad. "Most towers so built on the top of a motte; this one to so surround the entirety of that mound, too large a structure to so perch it on the top. Our great hall as you can see is very large, over sixty feet long and half as wide it is," he explained, detailing the architecture to Ellie's sons.

The hour was getting late and Ellie made excuses for their exit; to rejoin them in the prime. "Dear Joan so good to see you most again," said Lady Douglas. "That we will have some time to visit on the morrow is most pleasing to this lass. A splendid party, to speak about for many years to come," she said graciously. The esquire, the page, and the wee Archie all made their bows and said their words politely to take their leave. When they arrived at the Berkeley messuage given for their private use, the lads went directly to their chamber, in close proximity to their mother's room. The Douglas 'men' as they fashioned themselves, had one area set aside by wooden screens where the three of them would sleep; Ellie's chamber was across the way where she slept alone. As Ana was combing out her plaited hair there was a wee rapping on the carved oak door that led into this wondrous suite. "The door most open to your entry," Lady Douglas said, knowing her wee sons were coming to say their prayers with her before they went to sleep; their custom now as the family traveled together.

To her surprise James was with them too. "Dear mother, are all such parties boring so as this?" he asked her. Ellie burst out laughing, smiling to her Ana who shared till now their secret: Lady Eleanora's fear and loathing of such affairs. "Dreadful parties are the way of the nobility in England; this fête of Lady Joan most entertaining in comparison!" she chuckled. Ana interrupted Ellie; to tell the lads of their mother's woes when a young lass of Essex not yet married. "She would cry your mother for days before these parties; hoping to avoid attending them, begging her sweet mother to make excuses for her absence there," laughed Ana, recalling Ellie's anxious dread of the Lovaine gatherings. Ana told them that her lady felt as if she was on display sitting on a dower of great wealth for all to see. Ellie was giggling, reflecting her histrionics to avoid such festivities of the nobility.

Then she told them how different it was in Scotland with Gilley; she just loved the Douglas Ceilidhs. "The dancing with the Celtic music was more fun, these affairs in Scottish manors and in castles almost as elegant and extravagant as their Essex counterparts, but very different to the joyful frolic of the Celts." Archie was not at all impressed. "The other lads my age were quiet; they would not speak except in French," he scoffed at their behavior. "My son, the language of the court, both for Scottish and English nobles is French, Norman French," she told him. "You can speak the words and well," she chided him, knowing he preferred to speak the Lallans, similar to the Essex Inglis. "Archie spoke to them in the Gaelic of our cousins," said Hugh giggling with his story. "They would not speak to us at first, 'you are Scots,' they said. "So our wee brother spoke to them in the language they expected from savages," Hugh told his mother with an impish countenance.

Ana spoke up. "These lads told you they could not speak with Scots?" she questioned incredulously. Hugh shook his head yes. Archie told them they were two sons of the de Clares. Ellie knew well this branch of the noble family, distant kin of the Lovaines. "That they should have some manners and so respect your great and noble heritage. Once their family held powerful baronies," she said pointedly; "but faulted for some transgressions of sheer greed, they lost their lands. Now their mother mourns the loss of wealth she may never have. That she chooses disrespect of others, to teach her children poorly; the evidence of such words from children, most saddens me," she said quietly. Ellie told her sons to forgive such prideful verbiage.

After they said their prayers and spoke to God about their father, the three lads returned to their chamber happily. "That Archie spoke to the de Clares in the Scottish Gaelic," chuckled Lady Douglas to her Ana. "M' lady, your sons were raised to take care of themselves; no English lad can permeate the armor of their great wit and confidence." Ellie shook her head in agreement. "That my dear William taught us well; our sons to take great pride in their Douglas blood; most to save them from the shallow chiding of these silly knaves." Ellie realized once again that Gilley's ways prepared them well for manhood. Even the wee Archie *knew* instinctively the correct response to taunting English lads; lessons from a father passed down to the youngest son he barely knew, by means of his good brothers James and Hugh, sharing his stories.

Ellie was angered by the attitudes of the English nobles and wondered aloud if she was hampering her children's scholastic training by continuing to teach them herself. "Perhaps to relieve this lass of the burden of their daily teaching that I should assign a tutor to our lads. Their work at languages most important now; to read in French and Latin so required for their station," she said quietly with an inquiring eye towards Ana. Ellie had already been sending her younger sons to the priory at Little Dunmow to develop the writing skills of a cleric; an idea touted by Father Stephen, one he gave her while planning Muriel's wedding day. She was thinking seriously as well about another suggestion she received. Their kin in Scotland, the de Lindsays, told her of a tutor she could hire.

"Remember so the widow of that Scottish knight fighting bravely at Caerlaverock that he lost his life?" she asked her dear companion. Ana did indeed recall meeting this quiet lady; a woman of a pious nature but with a fair appreciation for good laughter. "M' lady such a choice for tutor of your wee laddies is most perfect; and when such time most comes that we return to Scotland to live again, this lady will be most at home. When yet in Fawdon or our Essex, her loyalties will be quite known to us as well." Ellie agreed with her wise assessment. She then asked Ana about Maudie, Archie's nurse and her wee son Andrew, the same age at five as her youngest son. "Would Maudie so approve if I were to have her Andrew tutored by this lady?" she asked Ana. "M' lady, there is nothing she would want more than that!"

Ellie had her call in Archie's nurse. She happily explained her plan to Maudie: to educate her son with Archie. The nurse was overwhelmed. "It is my dearest dream come true; thank you Lady Douglas," said this Scottish widow; her husband had been a freeholder in Douglasdale before an illness took him to his God. Eleanora told her quite plainly of her gratitude; coming with them to Essex when she had no coinage for her service. It was the Douglas way to do such things. "My dear husband would have so insisted," Ellie said. Maudie and Ana had become good friends and now would be staying in the same household for the remainder of their years, making both ladies very happy. And for a baby nurse as Maudie was joining the Douglas household when the wee Archie was first born; an opportunity to raise her son with great privileges usually reserved for the nobility.

Figure XIII-Part One; Caerlaverock Castle ruins from the great summer siege in 1300

Maudie took her leave, tears of complete joy streamed down her smiling face; my son will learn to read and write the languages of Latin and Norman French, to perhaps someday become a knight as well, she sighed happily.

Ellie continued her discussion with Ana. "That I will write Sir Alex on the morrow; send a messenger to so deliver our good greeting and ask our Lady Elizabeth now of Fife to join our household as the language tutor for our Archie, wee Andrew and our Hugh; obtaining such permission for her coming here as well. It is done," she said. "Our Gilley would be so respectful of our wise selection for a tutor; a widow of a Scottish patriot, with her dower lands in Ayrshire so forfeited for his treason." Ana nodded in agreement. "And one who speaks the Gaelic most as well," added Ana, knowing Lord Douglas' insistence that his children learn the language of their Highland cousins. Lady Eleanora drifted off to a comfortable sleep that night with all her decisions made; her son's tutoring issues resolved.

Figure XIV-Part One; antique engraving of Berkeley Castle in the author's collection

As the Douglases broke their fast the next morning they were surprised to find themselves joined by Lord and Lady Berkeley in the Michaelwood messuage, eager to show them their lands and castle. Soon they were on their way back to the Berkeley fortress to begin their close inspection in the courtyard of the great structure. "Most like our Douglasdale though bigger," James whispered to Archie. "Our three protruding towers extended out to the first stone wall defenses forming more an odd shape than of square or round conformity." Lord Thomas was explaining to Ellie the need for more towers and bigger structures for defense. "This curtain wall of stone does so protect us; but we require housing for the men at arms and sergeants, stations for our guards to so lookout for possible invaders to our home," he told Lady Douglas. "This is a fortress most impressive," Ellie replied, marveling at the expansive terraces below and the deep moat that formed another barrier of defense. "And a Norman entrance of great antiquity and style," she exclaimed, praising the doorway to the inner courtyard. The younger lads were most impressed by their next stop; the dunjon prison, with a wee pit prison below.

"At this moment we hold not prisoners in the pit so there," said a relieved Lady Joan. Hugh's eyes were wide as he looked down the hole that led to the pit. "So dark is it that one can not see," said the lad politely. Lady Joan shuttered. "You would not want to behold such dreadful sights as may be in that grievous place," she told him ominously. Ellie explained to her wee sons that such barbaric places were used for peasants; those who committed crimes of great felony such as murder or stealing of a horse. As they stood together by the other side of this dunjon room above the prison hold James told Archie, "A nobleman like Sir Hugh de Abernathy would stay in such a room as this, but not a pit. He would have amenities of better food and a privy for his confined state." Sir Thomas beckoned all his guests to come with him now to look out towards the lovely church adjacent to the castle and the village just below them. "Once there stood a fine old nunnery there. But they were dispossessed by the Conqueror, tales of scandals and de mischef caused them to lose their heritage; the manor was then given to his favorite vassal, Roger de Berkeley, my dear ancestor, predecessor to my status as the lord of Berkeley manor," he explained magnanimously.

Figure XV-Part One; 14th century door within the ancient Norman portal, shown here lower left entrance from the inner courtyard

After several hours the Douglases took their leave of Berkeley Castle and returned to Michaelwood where the rest of the Douglas household was staying at the Berkeley messuage. They brought with them stories of adventure they would later share with their sister Mura when they visited her in Castle Cary. The next day and their last in the vale of Berkeley Ellie planned an outing with Lady Joan; her sons would travel with them and then venture off with Sir David for some 'manly exercises' with weaponry. The family rode through the whole of Berkeley manor it seemed, traveling west towards the Severn that led into Bristol Channel. To ride and talk and feast on smoked fish, sweet cakes and wine this day was Ellie's cherished plan. For her three sons Sir David had a different agenda; to drill the lads in their archery; then to train them to run their horses at targets, tilting the rings was what he called it. The knight would teach them using the Berkeley chargers from the manor for such purpose; Lord Berkeley stabled over two hundred horses they were told. Ellie enjoyed watching her sons in their forays of combat; Sir David was kind to them but strict in his ways, enforcing high standards for their achievements. Gilley would be pleased with his fine instruction for these Douglas lads she thought.

Figure XVI-Part One; St. Mary the Virgin Church, Berkeley; sadly in need of great repair the parish church is making an appeal for funds; the extraordinary examples of medieval paintings and other decorations covering the inside walls make the survival of this Minister Church a must

Lady Joan was always at ease with Lady Eleanora; but she was saddened for her too this day; the great loss of William Douglas was such a burden to her widowed kin. "Tell me Eleanora of your sweet Scottish laird; I have heard so many fine words of him from our dear cousin in Hertford, Lady Alice." Ellie thought for some time of what to say. "That this lass is able to so speak of him without tears to fill my eyes," she began. "Our dear friendship has so helped me these last days, to know that I will be able to continue now alone without my Gilley," Ellie said. "Widowhood most frightened me. How could I raise these children without their dear father was my true concern and fear."

Lady Berkeley asked if she considered another marriage. Lady Douglas shook her head 'No!' most fervently. "That you may be forced to do this, marry as reward to one of Edward's vassals, with your dower lands of great value and so held by the king," warned Joan. "This lass most fears such constraints; hoping that one marriage so arranged would be the last!" she said painfully, remembering the terror in her life, just thirteen and married to the brother of this lovely woman, the antithesis of her demeanor and fair morality. Joan spoke quietly, in confidence. "A dear friend and kin has told me of her son," she said carefully. "Her husband is now passed; she has most the same problems as you have with dower rights; so tangled with the debts and mortgages of her late husband, though none reside in Scotland." Lady Joan told her sister in law.

Figure XVII-Part One; medieval wall paintings and decorations at St. Mary the Virgin Church, adjacent to Berkeley Castle

Ellie was adamant; she could not think of sharing her bed with another man, her Gilley spoiled her so for others that might seek her company. Then Joan smiled, and told her more of this English knight and soldier, a vassal of the king first in Gascony, a year later then in Scotland fighting bravely at Falkirk. "That he would be most happy to have a wife in name only," she admitted with a hint of mystery. Ellie knew of Gascony; her William was to be in that retinue with Edward. And Falkirk, that great rout in July of 1298 meant that Scottish nobles held in the king's Tower were redundant; their execution or murder by de mischef more probable following that grave slaughter of the Scots; another reason Ellie held for William's swift end in that Tower.

But as Lady Douglas came back from her brief reverie, realizing those days were gone now from her, she looked over at Joan with a quizzical grimace. "What ever do you mean a wife in name only?' she asked. "How would a distinguished soldier benefit from such a marriage; does he have issue from another wife?" she asked, curious for the answer. "No, that there are not wives or children to so complicate this story," said Lady Joan. "This strange man does not so mirror any lord you might have known, most different from your poet knight Lord Douglas," she said quietly. "The pain of this dear Lady Isabel de Grendon, now Lady Bagot, so difficult for me to share her words of sorrow with you." Lady Berkeley paused to wipe her eyes of tears; she was feeling so sad for Isabel. "Her younger son is Ralph, named most for her dear father Ralph de Grendon a soldier of renown; the father was a banneret and lord of some fair note. Young Ralph is most already betrothed, to become a knight and husband in some few years, living now in Northamptonshire. But William, the elder son and heir of her dear husband is," her words faded. Then she blurted out her secret. "That he prefers to bed a man than take a lady in his arms, most disturbing to his mother and this lady," Joan allowed, admitting she was confused by the ways of the soldier. Ellie was stunned; she had never known of such a man.

Lady Berkeley was determined to go forward with her plan; to encourage her late brother's wife, now the widow of a romantic, loving knight, a true and honest laird; to marry this son of her dear friend was perfect in her mind. "That you could then be free of Edward as your liege lord," she reminded Lady Douglas. "And you would have more surety of income," Lady Berkeley continued, encouraging her sister in law to consider this endeavor. "And such a husband he would be, most never home; a soldier in service of King Edward. Sir William serves now in Scotland most again; these two years past in the retinue of Robert Fitz Walter. Ellie wanted to know about the Bagot mortgages on their estates; she was curious at the prospect knowing any day she could hear from Edward of a license he might grant to a loyal vassal.

"Does this William know of his mother's devices, to find him so a wife that would agree to such an arrangement?" Joan nodded. "That this lady has so spoken to him; he is most willing to meet with you when you are ready, for he will wait he told me," she said, confident her idea of matrimony for Eleanora Douglas and William Bagot, miles, would serve them equally and well. And he truly needs the fair mind of the steward Lady Douglas, Joan de Ferrers reflected; so poor was he with coinage, managing his estates. "Add to this then please, his family lands are in Stafford; his mother's family is so in Derbyshire, known to us as kin, once marrying with the de Ferrers as well you see" said the fair matchmaker Lady Berkeley.

Ellie thought for some time before responding, then seeing her children return, climbing the banks of the Severn from their afternoon of training with Sir David, she spoke very quickly. "Not a word of this in front of my dear sons; they would not understand at this early time this lady's need to rid herself of Edward and his lordship of her dower lands," Lady Douglas cautioned, whispering so only Joan could hear. Seeing her lads approach she changed her voice to hide her sentiments; speaking more audibly so they could overhear her conversation. "First that our James will go to Paris with us; he then will stay with the widow Agnes there in Brabant, my kin, friend of my late mother most as well. Our plan to so request a plea with Edward to repledge our Douglasdale to James; then our family will so return to live in Scotland. This is my dream and hope," Ellie said confidently.

Figure XVIII-Part One; effigy of Sir Thomas Berkeley, grandson of Joan de Ferrers, he died in 1361 with his second wife Katherine, St. Mary the Virgin church, Berkeley

Archie was running fast up the wee hill where his mother and Lady Berkeley were sitting; enjoying their repast and fine wine as they seemingly chatted on about the parties at Berkeley Castle. "This lad to hit his target most on center," he shouted as he ran to tell Ellie of his great prowess at archery this day. "James and Hugh, is this true," she called out, teasing her young son. "Did our wee Archie hit his target?" Sir David was catching up to them and he responded with untypical exuberance. "This knight has never seen so keen an eye at so young an age," he said of the youngest Douglas son. James was laughing; he was impressed as well, "Our dear father held fair competition to our brother; now we know the one to carry on his reputation of great skill in this endeavor!" Hugh told Ellie he too was accurate this day; a great hunter to provide them food for their larder was his promise as well. "Dear Eleanora, how fortunate to have Sir David and three noble knights to be, so endowed with great talents and good ambition do I see!" exclaimed Lady Joan de Berkeley.

As the Douglases began their return to Michaelwood the sons were too involved with stories of their day to take notice of their mother's parting words to her dear kin and friend. "My answer is no this day; for I will need some time to think on this proposal," she said thoughtfully. "Tell this good English lord that we will first make our plea of Edward for Douglas lands reseised. In two years hence will we most know our fate in that cause; an answer to his proposal will not come till then," she said clearly. Lady Joan smiled in her whispered reply. "Either you will be in England as Lady Bagot or in Scotland as Lady Douglas some two years hence. My prayers are with you always Lady Eleanora; so much pain to have experienced, too young a lady for such sadness," she told her friend of over twenty years, knowing well the suffering of this young widow in her life.

Figure XIX-Part One; Bath Abbey and Cathedral

BATH, EARLY AUGUST-Lady Douglas and her household traveled south to Bath Abbey; not knowing many in this shire she decided to avail her family of the abbot's lodging. Abbeys were endowed for the very purpose of aiding travelers to come and stay she reminded her children as she explained where they would lodge next. Payment for a monastery's hospitality was not required; but Ellie always insisted to leave coinage where she could. "This abbey is quite old," she told her sons. "First this site was most a nunnery; then to become the home to Benedictine monks." The Hospitaller or guest-master, as Ellie called the monk in charge of welcoming the Douglases and other guests that happened to the abbey, was most gracious to them. He took the children and Lady Douglas on an inspection of the grand monastery and the cathedral not yet completed. "This abbey most became a cathedral-priory two hundred years ago, after it was sacked by invaders to this town of Bath and refounded with a new community of monks," he said, telling them the details of the history.

"The life of Benedictine monks is hard; but not the same as the white monks of the Cistercians," said the friar, wearing the black robe and cowl of the order. "Our life includes our prayer and work; but rewards by feasting every day on many sorts of fish, vegetables and pastry with many cheeses to be followed with much wine and milk to drink as well," he boasted of their fare. Hugh enjoyed his feasting and fresh ale more than most the lads his age; he asked the monk why all the fuss for table menus. "Some orders forbid their monks to eat of flesh or fish; only the infirm, sick or old ones are allowed to eat of meat," he informed the lad. Archie wanted to understand what the monks did all day. "We devise a day of prayer to serve God," the guest-master said.

He explained that three hours of prayer were set, three hours most apart; Tierce was the first service of the day; Sext and None the second and third services of the day. Tierce was followed by mass where lay people like the Douglases were allowed to come and join the monks but only in the nave of the church. James was very interested in learning of the monastic life; not for himself, but for his brother Hugh. "Does a monk live out in the community?" he asked the Hospitaller. "Only the Dominicans have priests so allowed to preach in the village and to live among the citizens there," the Benedictine monk replied.

Hugh told the friar proudly that he aspired to serve God, perhaps in the see of the Bishop of Glasgow he added hopefully. The older man looked fondly on the Scottish lad with the excited stutter, a boy with his birthday in three short days he was informed. "A noble choice for one so young," he said warmly, "but I can see from your fair countenance that you are so determined in your calling. What prompted you to so desire to serve God, so tender in your age, just eight," asked the caring monk. Without a stutter or hesitation Hugh told him. "That I would offer to serve God most dedicated a priest to be. To pray for my dear father's soul with merit to my words; this noble knight most lost to us too soon," said Hugh quietly. "My humble prayer to God most every day: that this lad to be welcomed most in Heaven for his pious work; to join Lord Douglas in that paradise," he added poignantly, telling the churchman as well how much he missed his father.

Ellie was standing next to her son, and reached around him to hug him for his touching sentiment for her Gilley. "A noble cause," she whispered in his ear, "so proud is this mother of her son," spoke the widow of William Douglas, kissing the lad on the cheek. Archie was further ahead of them; exploring the wee chapels set apart by wooden screens along the outer walls of the old abbey. "Where is the shrine?" he asked, running back to their side. "And the pools to bathe in; for they are not in here, this lad has looked most everywhere to find them!" demanded Archie indignantly. He was searching for the Roman Baths he mistakenly thought were in the abbey. Ellie chuckled to herself; her wee son was again upon her to break the tension of Hugh's poignant words in memory of Gilley. "Dear son, your mother will most take you to the healing waters of the baths on the morrow! And later will I so explain the beliefs of ancient Romans and the Celts who gave great credence to their many gods in worship in the ancient temple just near here," she said. Ellie was shaking her head in wonderment; how could these three sons be more different yet so alike, she mused?

Figure XX-Part One; the ancient baths were remodeled with new stairs in the late 13th century; photo courtesy of Susan Shane

The next morning the Douglases were exploring the roman baths. The King's Bath was restored for use in the thirteenth century. Small alcove steps were put in place so bathers could sit on the steps, talk or contemplate while soaking their feet and legs in the healing waters. They could also wade in the depths of the ancient pool. The strange, yet holy spot was reconstructed over a series of hot springs and an older temple with bathing pools built by the Romans. "They called this place Aquae Sulis then and it was supposed to have spiritual powers of enormous benefit, even to prolong one's life. Women were not allowed to bathe alone with the men; but there were hours allowed for them to enjoy the sultry healing waters of the shrine," the mother explained. Ellie also told them that she and William had planned to come here; to seek the ancient ones, Minerva for the Celts is what he told her of the gods and goddesses that once lived here. During the early morning hours the pools were empty of visitors to the King's Bath; the Douglases could all go in and walk around to see it. Ellie shivered as she felt the great energy of the ancient temple; the mysterious vapors coming off the water as it slowly rippled through the giant spring fed pool. This is an eerie site, primed for strange occurrences, she surmised, as she walked into the sacred chambers once held by the ancient ones.

Figure XXI-Part One; the healing vapors of the baths

"You can see through this water," said Archie, motioning to the bottom of the pool, "that I do see myself as well when I look in it." James told them of Gilley's words; the Celtic belief that one could see to the Otherworld through such bodies of water. "Perhaps to see our father?" asked Hugh, hoping the sacred pool of the temple would help him in his quest. Ellie told them they could all return together when younger men were permitted use of the pool; she would go herself for healing in two hours, the time allotted for ladies in the King's Bath. Many nobles came to Bath she told them; they went on pilgrimages to receive the blessings of the ancient ones; restore their health through the magic of the vapors and heated waters. These were the ancient baths of the Romans built in a temple of sumptuous splendor for their gods; now used by mortals in this King's Bath built over the ancient foundations. James vowed to return here to this sacred place one day. Ellie looked at her oldest son, "Your father was once here in this mysterious shrine; somehow I feel him close to me this day, that he must be with us, watching over our wee clan," she said softly. Her son nodded in agreement; feeling his presence as well in this strange place of antiquity.

CASTLE CARY, 7TH AUGUST 1302- Lady Lovel greeted her mother and three brothers with charged enthusiasm; beaming excitedly at the arrival of her Douglas family. Mura sorely missed all her loved ones since she came to live in Castle Cary with her new husband. "Lord Lovel was most called away on business of the king. So happy is this lass to have some company at last!" she exclaimed. As she kissed her brother James she said most sheepishly, "Even your dear face is comfort to this lady of the manor; I missed my older brother for his teasing." Muriel's loneliness was very evident today. Lord Lovel had served his time in Scotland; he would not return there for some seven years to come. This day he had some feudal business that called him most to Sparkford; a manor that the Lovels held for generations, since 12 Henry II Muriel told them, meaning the twelfth year of that Henry's reign. "My lord the baron would most return in two days hence he promised. But he will miss our party," she stopped abruptly realizing that she was spoiling the surprise for Hugh. The shy lad grinned at his older sister. "Mura, you were never one to keep a secret," he teased her. "But do not worry for I know when my birthday is to so arrive." Hugh was laughing happily at the prospect of a celebration planned in his honor.

Ana was coming into the great hall of the Lovel manor; she brought with her a little gift of fine embroidery for her favorite Douglas daughter. "Oh my Ana," said the wife of Lord Lovel; a young lass, not yet fourteen. "You remembered your sweet promise. This handwork will so adorn my surcote nicely," she cooed. Mura hugged and kissed her friend and second mother as she called Ana. Ellie was pleased to be in the home of her daughter; a place where they could feel comfortable and relax as families do with one another. "Tomorrow we can take our palfreys to ride about the Lovel lands," Muriel told everyone. "There once was a lovely castle here as well; but it was so destroyed." Just then Sir David came in the great hall with their Douglas men at arms and his good squire. At this very moment Ellie remembered she chose not to write Mura about Sir Shamus. "Come sit here," said Lady Douglas, anticipating her daughter's next concern. "Just days after you left Stebbing, this mother woke to find our Deerhound sleeping that deep sleep; he had passed to the Otherworld most in the night," she told Mura with a deep sadness in her voice. "He went so peacefully as we most pray to do, joining now our father, our wee Amy, sweet Martha and dear John, with baby Douglas and my precious mother, all there in the paradise of God's good Heaven, to wait for us to join them one sweet day."

Muriel's face was flooding with tears; the wee greyhound, her first friend was gone to the Otherworld of the Celts. She hugged her mother fast to her; the mourning for one wee hound allowed this girl the grieving she so denied herself at her father's passing four years ago. She sobbed, shaking deep within her body, almost uncontrollably into the breast of her mother. "My noble friend most gone," she sighed at last. Everyone else was crying by now; the tears they shared in mourning the loss of that noble Deerhound strangely helped their healing; repairing their broken hearts from the deep sorrow felt by everyone in the Douglas household. Their solace was to know that Sir Shamus and Lord Douglas were walking Heaven's forests, together most again. "That we should have some feasting and some wine; the squires and the Lovel men at arms were most successful in their morning hunt this day," said Lady Muriel wistfully, trying to compose herself to entertain her family. She showed Ana to her mother's chamber for her stay; and her brothers' rooms close to their mother. "Dear James, a room for you to so enjoy; that once you had some lovely curtains for your bed, so shamefully taken from us when we were kidnapped by Earl Robert from our castle. That dreadful day in Douglasdale," she shuttered to remember that frightening assault on an undefended Douglas Castle five years ago. "Now you may have this lovely tester bed and chamber for your comfort."

Her brother was overjoyed by her thoughtfulness. He had all but forgotten his eleventh birthday celebration and the gift of a private chamber all his own to have his father's old bed with newly embroidered bed curtains that adorned it. "To so relive those days," he told her. "To have this chamber of your fine manor Mura for my stay is most pleasurable to this humble squire," the grateful lad conceded. Ellie detected a great change in her daughter's demeanor; the taunting and teasing that dominated their past behavior went missing from the sentiments the siblings exchanged today. Is it most the marriage for this lass that helped improve her temperament, or are there other reasons for these deeds and thoughts so new, wondered Ellie.

That evening she asked Ana her opinion on the matter; the strange behavior of Lady Muriel Lovel pressed upon her mind. "That she must realize now in good conscience, better to have a teasing, honest lad who loves her most completely through her faults as well, like her brother; than a lord most consumed by rents and fees to so collect, leaving his new bride to often wait on his return," said Ana; disappointed to see her wee Mura frequently abandoned in her new home. "The absence of attention for our lass; to cause some trouble here I do expect," sighed Ellie. "That he was not violent to her my concern; most like Lord de Ferrers I feared him so to be. But to be ignored and left alone; most like a widow to this lord without the passing and good sorrow. Perhaps he will come around some soon; that I do pray so. Our Gilley often said a love left so neglected but withers up and dies," she sighed.

James was lying on his bed awake and thinking of the times in Douglasdale when Lord Douglas was alive and Scotland was their home. He heard a soft knock at his door and saw Muriel quietly enter his chamber. "Dear brother that you are yet not sleeping?" she asked him. James sat up and bid his sister to sit down on the grand bed she prepared for his good use. "Mura, what troubles you so?" he asked. "Do not worry, this bed is of great comfort, a splendid bed that you so thoughtfully arranged," James continued, teasing her some as was their way, accentuating his slight lisp that she found so endearing.

Figure XXII-Part One; Tester Bed; the Bloody Tower, the Tower of London

"It is not your comfort that concerns me so," she began then corrected herself fumbling for the words. "That I most mean of course your," she abruptly stopped, being interrupted by James. "Dear lass something is so wrong, what troubles you to come here and accept the good ridicule of your favorite brother?" he smiled, hoping she would not cry; not wanting her to be unhappy from his words. Muriel just put her arms around his neck and sobbed deeply into his broad chest. "Oh James, Lord Lovel is nothing of our father. He sleeps in the laird's own chamber most alone; to come to my bed just eight times that we have wed, three nights in the first days of our marriage, then five the next ten weeks," she told him, weeping even more through her words, then stopping for a breath only to begin again. "That this lass must seem quite homely or most boring to her husband is what I fear," Muriel poignantly admitted.

40

James held his sister close to him for some time; he had never seen her so demoralized. "Our dear father often said about his oldest daughter: the very image of his dear wife and love for all the ages, as fair a Scottish lass as ever he had seen." James spoke softly, forcing her to stop crying and listen to him. "And our father never lied to please us with words of false flattery," James said to convince her that what he said was true. "Do you love this lord?" he asked his sister with all sincerity. She told James she believed that she could love this man; but their father told them all that true love was in the sharing ways of living together, with a common purpose.

"This loneliness more than this lass can entertain much longer I do know it!" she explained. She worried for a lonely life she confided; to live alone without a simple word or touch. "Worse than a dagger through my heart, so neglected is this wife by her husband" she declared mournfully. Mura was deeply saddened by her life with Lord Lovel and she made her older brother very aware of her plight. James paused and locked his eyes with hers. He told her very seriously, "You must tell our mother now most quickly." Then he cautioned her. "The more to wait; the longer to suffer is my fear for you dear sister." He then kissed her on the top of her head. "Promise your brother you will speak to Lady El on the morrow, most before the celebration for our Hugh." Muriel wiped her tears and held her brother's hand. "Your words to be most true; I thank you for your honesty of counsel this night," she said feeling more composed. Mura was deeply touched by her brother's concern and as she left his chamber she felt grateful knowing someone cared about her. Just imagine she sighed wistfully said to herself, it is our James to so rescue this lass with his love and tender words.

As the Douglases broke their fast the next morning Mura made good on her word to her older brother; she asked for time to speak with Eleanora in private; to meet with her later in the withdrawing room of the manor. Lady Douglas gave a knowing glance to Ana, then to James. "This mother is most aware of your concerns here, grateful to your trust to counsel you in this sad matter," she replied. "You know?" Mura asked her mother with a furled brow emulating her father's grimace. Ellie shook her head yes. "More words to say most later. Know this; a mother so observes her daughter well, to see our Muriel with her brother James most at peace and not to quarrel," teased Lady Douglas, "that something must be gravely wrong!" Muriel and James began to laugh; their mother chuckled as well. Humor was the first remedy to heal their Muriel this day.

Later they adjourned to the withdrawing room to discuss Mura's marriage just two months and few weeks old. "Mother, most perplexed is this lass," she told Ellie. "That he is unlike our father in his ways. He comes to my bed most infrequently; your daughter most to sleep alone, not even a wee hound to warm her bed," she sighed. Eleanora comforted her daughter and beckoned Ana to come join them in the discussion. "That this man has lived without a wife for some lang time," she began counseling her only daughter. "His ways are most like other English lords; this truth your mother had so tried to tell you before you married him. Noblemen and knights of renown are most concerned for heirs and lands to so support their households." Ellie sighed; Mura would not listen to this warning before and now the marriage was complete; troubled as she feared before they wed. Dear William, she said in silent prayer, what shall I say to our sweet daughter in her time of need? Then she had an inspiration; perhaps a son or daughter or twenty children, as her Gilley had planned. To raise and love her children was the answer for her Muriel, she knew it now!

"That you have so consummated your marriage as I spoke to you?" asked Ellie. Mura nodded yes. "The first night he took his pleasure in much haste she whispered to her mother. Ana was agitated; she asked Mura if she had cycle since her wedding day. "Yes, two have come; this third one is not due for some few days," she told them, her eyes were tearing for her sadness of a marriage bed that was cold and lonely. Ellie told her daughter of her painful life with Lord de Ferrers. As she finished Mura spoke up. "Mother, he does not beat me; he ignores me, as if I was not there he talks most through me," she said pitifully. Lady Douglas went to her daughter and hugged her close and hard. "Dear lass, that some day I shall share with you the writings of my poet knight your dear father," she said soothingly. "A rare essence that special laird was he; so gentle with his big hands, so healing in his touch when he held this lady like a child most sitting in his lap, as he rocked me so to sleep. There are few noblemen so like him," she whispered quietly.

Lady Douglas paused for a moment before she asked her daughter her next question. "Could you love most your children to fill the void of a husband's love not there?" she inquired. Muriel thought for some time. "That I would try so," said the childlike lady of the manor. "Good. When first you know that you are with child, have your husband send you home to Essex," Ellie responded. "That I will meet with him on this good matter; the priest of the church nearby as well should know my choice." Mura was noticeably cheered; she could be in Stebbing with her brothers and her mother for the lay-in. "It is done then," said Ana, pleased with Ellie's decision and good counseling. Their sweet Muriel, this Lady Lovel, would be home to have her child chuckled Ana aloud.

Later that day the Douglases held their party to celebrate Hugh's eighth birthday. Lady Douglas beckoned everyone to the great hall; with Lord Lovel on the business of the king this manor was hers today, she mused. "Now," began Lady Eleanora, "this occasion is most special; a day when this mother by God's good grace and your father's good hands gave life to our dear son and brother, our Hubicus." Ellie recalled the day; riding to the de Ferrers manor of Ware in Hertfordshire; utterly exhausted yet believing her lay-in was in two months or more. "I had just given the reins of my mare to the farrier's groom when I felt the pains that followed with your birth dear Hugh in two wee hours; in such a hurry to be born my son!"

James told the wee laddies of the sadness that had just preceded them; the passing of their dear sister the sweet Martha, lost so in the moat at Woodham Ferrers, trapped in the secret passage that led to the old priory, she fell in, passing to the Otherworld most quickly. "Our father took our Hugh first to the Benedictine Priory that was most part of this Ware manor; to christen you himself as was his practice for the others most as well," Ellie continued glowingly as she spoke of William and his ways. "And as with the Celtic traditions, your father in the christening most held out the left hand of our son; the unblessed one for a warrior," she chuckled knowing Hugh defiantly became the only Douglas lad to hold his right hand in preference to the left in his training at arms.

Figure XXIII-Part One; Woodham Ferrers Hall, the main manor house held by Eleanora Douglas; painting by artist Marguerite Connolly Beachmont, Massachusetts

Ana shared her stories of Lord Douglas with the household. "Our dear Lord Will, the midwife for all the births of Douglases including all of you so here this day," she boasted proudly; then her words drifted some, unable to speak of baby Douglas that passed one year after Archie's birth. With Ellie gravely ill and Gilley yet alive, but held in Edward's Tower, their good healer and dear father was unable to attend that last birth that it ended in much sorrow. "With every death comes a birth is what our father told us of the beliefs of the Celts," explained Ellie. "This was never more true then on this sweet day your dear birth my Hubicus; a mother in much sorrow so in need of your loving smile to fill the void of our dear loss of Martha."

Figure XXIV-Part One; Woodham Ferrers village

Ellie brought out four wee scrolls of parchment; all tied neatly in silk ribbons. "That this occasion marks our last time that we are most together for some years," the widow began her speech of ceremony. "With my best hand have I now scribed this writing of your dear father, given so to me when he proposed his marriage to this lass," spoke Ellie solemnly. "Muriel, this one is for you; perhaps to read one cold winter's eve to your fair husband," she suggested. Turning to the lad who was celebrating his day of birth this 8th of August she said, "My son who shares his fair direction with the Austin canons; the same words of our dear Gilley for you as well." She gave Hugh his scroll and Archie his as well though knew he could not read or comprehend the meaning just now. He would soon enough she mused. "Dear James, my only child not born of me, but as close as any so conceived," Lady El said, smiling with pride for her eldest son. "Soon to take your leave as well, your sweet scroll here the same as the other three, My Truth, so written by my poet knight and your dear father. His words to guide his children from the Otherworld where he so waits for us; this writing served this lass and her good knight so well, that they will do the same for you my beloved children is my prayer this day."

Lady Douglas asked James to stand and read the words of one named William; and he did. As others of the Douglas household entered the great hall of the Lovels' manor, Sir David, Gillerothe, Patric and dear Henry all, they too would listen to the noble truth of their redoubtable Lord Douglas.

My Truth, the Core Values of Sir Guillame de Duglas, Chevalier:

1. One must always be faithful in the vows of marriage.
2. One must be honest in the relationship, tell the truth in all ways and in your actions.
3. One must be respectful of the other person, do not hurt them emotionally, physically, or Spiritually.
4. One must have a purpose together, that will make a common bond between the two people.
5. One must always be a partner in the relationship, take care of the other person, but not so as to control their life experience.
6. One must be careful to be less demanding than instincts would dictate, but demanding enough to maintain a balance, harmony and personal level of expectations, keeping your standard of conduct high.
7. One must never commit acts that would violate conduct in the laws, such as thievery, adultery, murder, or other crimes against the laws of the kingdome and God, except in the climate of war, that would jeopardize the state of well being of the partnership and family.
8. One must maintain an identity within the relationship.
9. One must act respectfully at all times in the public eye, but behind closed doors of the bed chamber one can act privately in a playful, provocative manner of fun, frivolity.
10. One must celebrate dates and events all the time to keep the relationship in the forefront of existence.
11. One can maintain harmony by always being on time and being positive in mind, and always in the bed chamber, as it is not a place to argue and be sullen.
12. One must be in the moment always, keep the relationship in view, if something in the future or past takes prominence, one loses a little on life.

13. *One must be kind, thoughtful and take interest in what is important in the other ones life; be a partner at all times, ever wary of being a partner at all times.*

14. *One must be a source of strength for your partner's weaknesses or worries, and concerns, provide advice when solicited but not unmitigated criticism; provide help when asked, never owning control of another's life.*

15. *One must be prepared to intervene with your partner with others if the partner breaks with core values due to over-indulgence and other detracting behavior.*

Not a word was spoken as James read from his tiny scroll. And when he had concluded there was not one dry eye among the household of this kind and most loving laird, William le Hardi Douglas. Ellie broke the silence to add the words he wrote to her at the end of *My Truth* in the forests of Ayrshire that February of 1288:

To my dearest Ellie, these truths are mine and I would pledge to you these words with all my love, Gilley.

"I share with you these sentiments my children, my Ana and good Douglas men as well; that you should know of our great love that has yet endured. This lady most blessed to have her children with her; that each day they so remind me of my husband and his good ways," she told them all most honestly. Then she asked James to make the presentation of his gift for Hugh. As the esquire went to retrieve another of Gilley's writings, a wee scroll as well, Ellie gave her son his present from her. "Your peaceful ways, to seek the truth and preach God's word among the good citizens of our fair Scotland," she began carefully, "to become a priest does not mean my son that you should go undressed as your father would have told you were he here this day." Ellie gave her son a dagger she had made from the sword of his namesake, Lord Hugh, uncle to this lad and older brother of her husband. The wee Hugh smiled broadly. "This sweet dagger to be most treasured. Were it only to fillet a fish is my dear prayer this day; but if I must so use it, may it be God's will," he said cheerfully, admiring the blade and its fine well balanced grip.

James was returning from his chamber; bringing with him the scroll he diligently copied for his brother Hugh. He brought another copy for his brother Archie, surprising Ellie with a gift for the wee lad too this day. "That I would not be here in England for the Hogmanay this year," he told his mother, anticipating her question of so early a gift for Archibald. "I made them most the same in my good hand as you had this lad so do, to give these scrolls of our dear father to both my brothers on this day." Then turning to Sir David James pulled out a third scroll, then a forth for his mother as well. Grinning his well known smirk, he told them all proudly of his laborious effort. "That this lad has been most busy; to write by the wee tapers of the evening, hurrying so to finish them in time!" Ellie was very touched; she rose and hugged him hard, kissing him on the cheek. He feigned a flush of self conscious pride only to receive the chiding of his youngest brother Archie. "You did not shun the kisses of one Lady Berkeley with such embarrassment!" grinned the lad as he taunted James.

Mura was stunned, "Lady Berkeley, which of those fair lasses did so kiss you?" she demanded to know. Ana and Ellie exchanged knowing looks, surprised by news of kissing at Lady Joan's good party. Archie told her that both Lady Alice and Lady Isabel had tried so to kiss their brother; but only the latter so succeeded. "She is the talk of the shires in these parts of England; the most eligible of all the ladies in that county; an heiress of such beauty to but attract the noblest of knights; to vie now for her hand in marriage," marveled Muriel. "Mura, she is not the beauty of my sister," he told her plainly, "but she is much the tease you are and more!" he chuckled.

Then in his serious tone he continued to speak of the English lasses. "That she prefers to toy in pretense for the lords and knights is just her way; this lad most honest to so tell her his true age and landless station," James said. "That I most prefer a Scottish lass is my truth; but first to become a knight and Lord Douglas, then to find a wife is my good intention!" Muriel was laughing at him by now; an old spark was returning to her demeanor. "My brother, the chivalric knight to so become; sought after by English heiresses, fought over by the fair ladies of Berkeley Castle," she teased James. "That you are feeling more yourself I see!" proclaimed the squire mockingly, feigning his disdain for her words. Ellie and Ana exchanged glances again; the Douglas children had returned to their taunting and teasing ways; mercilessly berating the other.

Ellie picked up the second scroll, reading to herself the words of her noble knight. Then she began to recite from it; pleased to read the words of her dear William to her Douglas household.

The Art of Chivalric Warfare...as it is commonly done in our dear Scotland, most pertaining the time of 1270 to 1291 in which these words are so written; all matters are handled with the utmost care and concern for the code of conduct in battle. William de Duglas, miles

1. All Knights are subject to the codes of conduct in battle and tournaments

2. Utmost and careful presumption of battle to attain the highest order, highest good

3. To best the opponent in skills of combat not in the demise of trickery or chicanery

4. To be the best one can be in the common transcendence evident of their skills

5. To conduct ones activities with honor at all times

6. To abide by one's sworn oaths and allegiances to God, Lord, and Self

7. To adjust to the confines of a certain battle but only in the type of combat as a horseman, schiltron, foot soldier, or other combatant as directed by the Lieutenant of the Lord or leader that one follows

8. To outwit, out flank, out perform your opponent in skill and physical prowess

9. To protect and defend the lives of your fellow Knights

10. To protect and defend the lives of women, children, elders, and the infirm

11. To be respectful of ones opponent and allow for fair combat that would not forego the allowance of the opponent to cross a bridge or other wise prepare for the combat event, on fair, equal footing

12. After the conclusion of battle, take prisoners as possible and allow for the sworn allegiances of former foes, the dignity of combat to decide their demise or survival of those formerly in opposing battle placements; this allows for sworn surrender or retreat with dignity and the protection to do same from the battlefield

13. Chivalric dignity at all times is expected and demanded

14. Victory comes from cool heads in battle with courage brought from experience and readiness in training. Always be ready to fight and fight bravely

15. Always go into battle with the blessing of God; Prayer is as important as the armaments and protection you wear

"Thank you Lady Douglas and our James," said Sir David, "That this knight had wanted most a writing of these fine words when first you read them some few years ago, just returning from our ill-fated Tournament in Newmarket." Ellie started laughing, remembering well their adventures in Suffolk; running from the sheriff of that shire, who was in search of participants from that outlawed tourney. "Our next tournament should be licensed by the king," she chided him, "and in Scotland, is my fair desire!" Ana was helping the cook and the cellarers bring in the platters of food with their wine and fresh ale; pleased to see her family happy in their celebration. The worried look from Muriel was gone from her countenance. Ellie invited everyone, including Gillerothe, Patric and dear Henry to come join them in the feasting. "An event of great pleasure for this lady that one and all should join with us this day," she told them. James poured wine for the ladies and himself; fresh ale for the wee lads and others as was their preference.

Ana took her wine and made a toast. "To Lord Will, that he most shares in our good pleasure this fine night, smiling down from Heaven as he sees our celebration." Everyone was pleased to join in the toast to Gilley, when suddenly there was a very odd occurrence that was obvious for all to see: the tallow torches in the great hall, though burning evening low, had hours more to provide their light. Yet they all went out at once! Eleanora looked about for a fair draft of open doors or other reasons for their dimming. Ana scurried for a taper from the fireplace to light a candle; once brightly lit the great hall was now dark save for the coals of glowing embers in the fireplace. Hugh was the first to speak, breaking their silence from the strange event. "Our father most has spoken this fair night," said the lad, as he began to laugh at the thought. "It is done," said Sir David, believing every word of it! The celebration had ended on a high note; everyone was chuckling or giggling, knowing that the Otherworld had spoken: Lord Douglas was most with them in Castle Cary.

ASSUMPTION DAY OF THE VIRGIN MARY-Lord Lovel was finally returning to Castle Cary and happily greeted his wife's kin in the great hall of his manor. This lord was not an unpleasant man; just one unable to communicate his thoughts and emotions, especially to a lady. Aloof and abrupt, the fair way of English noblemen, was Ellie's strong opinion of her daughter's husband. She met with Lord Lovel in the withdrawing room and spoke quietly to him of her wishes for Muriel. "Be assured we will send the Lovel men at arms to escort my dear bride to her mother's manor in fair Essex when that happy day arrives and she is with child. That very plan is most this knight's desire," concluded Richard Lovel; pleased to have that worry of a lay-in for his wife sensibly resolved by Lady Douglas. In six short months Lady Muriel Douglas Lovel would make her journey to Essex; preparing for her lay-in and the birth of an heir for Lord Lovel and his fair estates.

The next morning as Ellie and her daughter broke their fast the mother told her daughter of their plans. "That Lord Lovel has most agreed to send you to us with an escort of Lovel men at arms to Stebbing Park," Ellie announced cheerfully. Muriel was relieved; being home for the lay-in, staying in the company of her Douglas family was a prayer perfectly answered for the lass. "And you are leaving on the morrow?" she asked. Ellie told her that they must hurry on to Hastings. "Or most some other of the Cinque Ports if we can not find a cog to so transport our Douglas household with our carts and horses; thirty in our number now as well, all to go to Paris," she said.

"Mother, that this lass has not before so said," Mura spoke quietly. "Your good counsel is most wise and comforting to your daughter. Perhaps to listen better those lang months ago would I not be here," she confided. Ellie told her that most first marriages were arranged by the families, a wee lass to so marry an older lord. Lady Douglas could not accept that for her daughter and turned down other offers for a marriage contract. But when Muriel insisted on this match; she relented and allowed her so to wed Lord Lovel. "That we all do make mistakes; part of our good learning in this life. A mother never wants her children to so suffer their poor choices. I am always here for you, my only daughter, most loved you are by this humble lady," Ellie quietly conveyed her pleasure as well that Mura sought her help and advice in her dilemma. The child bride put her arms around her mother as she whispered. "So surprised am I our words so centered now between us; to love you and to feel the great kindness that you share with me so helpful now. Thank you dear Lady El," using her father's favorite term of affection for Eleanora.

For their last day Lord Lovel took them for a ride around his manor; told them about the Norman Castle that once sat at the foot of Lodge Hill. "Only the ruins of that fine fortress now remain," he said, "having been destroyed in 1153; besieged twice in Stephen's reign." Sir Richard continued to tell them of his grandfather, grandson of the Baron Lovel who followed King Stephen, choosing to support this lord near the end of the civil war. "The castle there was built of Norman construction, some eighty feet square from the writings," he explained.

Archie wanted to know if it had a moat and how it was destroyed. "Our manor house so sits near the old ruins with the moat most visible," said Lord Lovel as he motioned to the body of water near the footings of the hill. "The moat was shallow; wider and longer than it so appears today. The rival lord from Gloucester set fires to the castle; razed it to the ground," he told them; elaborating on the fortress' history. Lord Lovel continued to share the heritage of his family and their lands; as he spoke he realized the Douglases held true interest in his stories. "The Lovels and the de Carys married;

joining the lands you see of this fine manor." Muriel spoke up, telling her brothers that the carucates were mainly plowland; with half or more retained now by the Barony of Castle Cary and the lord her good husband. "We have some woodlands too; but nothing of your fair wood farm in Essex Mother," said Muriel, surprising her husband by her keen knowledge of the estate. "We have most as many plows as smallholders too," she boasted. Ellie knew at once that Richard Lovel had not realized that her daughter held her mother's skills to understand the finances of a lordship; the wee Douglas steward as William often called her might one day apply to Muriel as well, she chuckled to herself.

They said their goodbyes and expressed their gratitude for the comforts of their stay in the sunrise of the prime; the Douglas household was leaving Castle Cary with their Muriel better for their coming there. Their sister was certainly more content with her life; eagerly awaiting the opportunity to join her family when the time came for her lay-in. As the grooms brought around the horses for the family Muriel went to each one; kissed her wee brothers, hugged and kissed her Ana. As she came to Ellie she put her arms around her and hugged her hard, holding her close for quite some time. "Thank you for every word and deed dear mother; that I will see you most in Essex in some months is my prayer this day," the young girl admitted.

"And dear brother that you will most remember your favorite sister, this I have for you," she said holding out a pair of iron lances suitable for the ends of wooden shafts to carve and hold as weapons she told him. "Sir David said that your will most require these in your training there in Lovaine." James smiled in his appreciation for the gifts then took Muriel aside to whisper in her ear. "Your older brother loves you, believe these words so truly meant; remember most you are a noble Douglas. Send for this humble squire that you need assistance; promise so Mura," he said gently. Muriel nodded. "And most happily will I do just that!" and she kissed him on the cheek; this time he kissed her back the same. "That this squire will hold you to your pledge!" he said, turning to mount his palfrey. "To stop once more at this fair manor when I return from the Lovaine," he vowed to Lady Lovel and her husband, gallantly doffing his hat.

The Douglas household traveled for several more days; staying at priories and abbeys along the way. They had journeyed towards Salisbury before turning south; stopping at Amesbury Abbey so they could visit Stonehenge. "Your dear father so often promised this lass to come to Wiltshire; view the great stones so laid out by the ancient ones; a tribute to their gods who taught them when to plant their seeds; what crops to grow in the ground," Ellie explained. She told them that Gilley wanted to bring his family to see the master-builders' work in Amesbury. "Though coming somewhat north again to so arrive here; our journey was most worth the trouble." Archie and Hugh were running between the great stones; watching the result of the sun peaking through the archways. "How are such figures so constructed?" James asked. "And what about this center one so lying flat; is that an altar?"

Figure XXV-Part One; Stonehenge; a temple to honor the gods of the ancient ones; stones in nearby Avebury were feared; systematically buried in the early 13th century

Ellie was eager to answer her son's questions just like Gilley would have done. "Your father so told this lass it was a stone most standing tall in the center; not lying on its side, a symbol of fertility for all to see. The ancient ones believed in all their wonderment that to leave a legacy of children upon their world would court the special favors of their gods." James wondered aloud if that is why their father wanted twenty children; was the matter one of Celtic prowess or some other reason? Ellie chuckled as she looked over at Ana. "My Gilley was a true Celt in every way; though such intentions for his legacy seem tempered by his one desire and five senses I should say!" Then she remembered another monolith in Scotland; one more obvious for its symbol of propagation and fertility. "Perhaps when we so visit in our Scotland will this lass so take you most to see the ancient stone in Clackmannan; a sacred place where kings were crowned centuries ago," she promised her younger sons who had just returned to her side. After spending several hours at the temple of the ancient ones the Douglases returned to Amesbury where they stayed the night.

ROMSEY-Ellie was not very familiar with these shires on the southern coast. Except for Monmouthshire to the west where Johannis de Hastings and his family lived, she was unaware of any other kin residing in this part of England. On the forth day they planned to stop at Romsey Abbey, a fine nunnery in Hampshire where the abbess afforded a wonderful residence for travelers, so Ellie had been told. But before they arrived in Romsey the weather which had cooperated to this point took a turn for the worse; the showers falling only during the night as they traveled continued long into the day now. As the steady rains soaked their super tunics the rivulets of water turned smooth, passable gates to cart paths of deepened ruts. When the winds blew, the rain was stinging on their faces; blinding them as they tried to see ahead where they were going. Their carts were barely moving; they had to stop every few feet to remove the clogging mud from the wooden wheels.

Figure XXVI-Part One; King John's House Romsey

And the horses were exhausted as they pulled the heavy load of goods up and down the hills; slogging in mud track crevices that once were roads before the rains washed them away. The Douglases arrived at the abbey nearly drenched; happy to see the smiling faces of the Benedictine nuns that welcomed them. While the Abbess Philippa de Stokes was away from Romsey another of the nuns took her place, welcoming travelers and pilgrims to stay at the nunnery. This gracious lady invited the Douglases to stay in the abbess' special hall known as King John's House; private accommodations a few steps from the abbey church. Ellie was pleased to so accept she told the sister and made a generous offering to the nunnery. The nuns took their rain soaked clothing to dry and brush away the mud and soil; promising to return them before the Douglases broke their fast the next day.

The warmth of the fire and the good hot food soothed the weary travelers and renewed their energy that Eleanora and her sons heartily accepted a tour of their surroundings. Their curiosity in tow, the Douglases were eager to learn of the history of the Benedictine convent. The holy edifice and cloister were very old and boasted the finest church of any nunnery in England they were quickly told. "Known in all the shires, Romsey Abbey is the most desirable place for noblemen to send their daughters to so educate them," Ellie explained to her sons; giving many details about the fabled residence where nuns were taught the word of God. The sisters escorted them throughout the abbey, then into the church; pointing out the special appurtenances and many features of the buildings. "A Lady Chapel was most constructed at the East end some one hundred and sixty years ago," said their guide as they entered the sanctuary.

Figure XXVII-Part One; medieval floor tiles, St. Mary the Virgin Church, Berkeley

The fine details were amazing to behold. James was impressed by the fascinating floor tiles brightly painted in many colors with Crusaders performing their deeds of valor. The exceptional pillars in the chancel aisles related elegant stories of ancient kings and beautiful angels. Outside the west wall of the south transept was one of the Romsey Roods; an ancient sculpture that dated to Roman times or earlier, the Douglases were told. Hugh marveled at the rood, "That this dear sculpture is most one whole foot higher than our James and near six feet high is he!"

The first rood depicted the crucifixion and was on the south transept adjacent to the magnificently carved abbess' doorway, while the second was in St. Anne's chapel. Outside the abbey one could see the quiet views of the old village and the banks of the River Test but a short walk from the church. As the Douglases made their way to Abbey Waters, the quiet and serenity of their surroundings was delightfully interspersed with the voices of song birds flocking to the waters edge. Ellie was full of enthusiasm for the moment as she turned to Ana; should this lass so tell the story, she asked with her impish grimace giving away her desire to share the tale of an abbess worthy of remembering. Ana laughed out loud. "Please do tell us M' lady," she answered, smiling at the lads in anticipation of the tale their mother was about to share with them.

Figure XXVIII-Part One; Romsey Abbey, the abbess' doorway, Norman entrance adjoining the south transept; nearly life size, this Saxon rood stands over six feet high; now protected under the vaulted awning to the right

Lady Douglas began weaving a suspenseful saga that would have made Gilley proud; her eyes twinkled in delight as she told her sons the history of the holy woman who once lived in the monastery. "Long ago there was an abbess named Ethelflaeda, a saint for whom the abbey church is now so named: St. Mary and St. Ethelflaeda," said Ellie, a true storyteller at heart now. The sister who was showing them the abbey smirked a bit as well; the story of their sainted second abbess was often heard throughout the land and known to many. Ellie told them of this holy woman's father the king and how she became a nun then most a saint. "This Ethelflaeda was known for her work of miracles; to read the Scriptures in the dark of night by lights glowing from her fingertips. Most as well for her acts of sanctity, chanting Psalms whilst standing naked in the River Test at night," Ellie said with feigned detachment; "a pious woman, with unusual methods to so raise her words up to the Heavens!" "What did this abbess do in the winter?" asked the wee Archie; exercising the taunting wit of his brother James these days.

"Archibald Douglas enough with your words; to so beleaguer your mother!" the exasperated widow admonished her youngest son.

Figure XXIX-Part One; Saxon rood in St. Anne's chapel, Romsey dates from 960

Looking immediately at James, "No words to come from you this day," she warned him. James suppressed his amusement; giving her that well known smirk like his father often did. "Dear mother, pray what did this abbess," he started to ask, but could not continue as he was roaring in laughter. Ellie was chuckling by now; tears welled in her eyes. She could not resist the ways of Gilley that James now portrayed. Ana too was laughing. "Most like your father with your teasing manner," Lady Douglas scolded her oldest son. "My irreverent sons to be the death of me most yet," she spouted.

Then suddenly, and much out of character for her middle son, Ellie was interrupted by Hugh. "That my brothers have so asked their question, this lad is ready for your scholarly reply. I stand so here; demanding the answer for our humble and most respectful query," he told her jovially, a bold departure from his normal habit and quiet ways. "A conspiracy I do know it now; no more history for my sons to hear this day." Turning once again to the sister in charge of the fine nunnery she said, "Thank you most for showing us this lovely place; your graciousness and patience out do mine!" Lady Douglas was motioning her children to take their leave and they returned to King John's Lodge.

"Were all the abbesses like Ethelflaeda?" asked Hugh. "Perhaps to know that the last abbess was a wealthy heiress; a daughter of a powerful family that she made her own rules to vex Archbishop Peckham whose position it was to monitor the convent and its spending." James wondered how the abbess seemed to obtain so much power. "This Alice Walerand was a great lady and expected to be deferred to in the dignities of her position; an abbess was truly the lord of the manor," Ellie explained. Then she began to tell them the silly stories of the abbess known as Alice; her proclivities to the extreme. "She filled the convent with her pets; monkeys and dogs and other animals. To the dismay of her overlord she hired stewards and spent funds without his approval. A headstrong lass with an appetite for splendor that was unseemly to the bishop; they were forever quarreling." Lady Douglas chuckled as she recalled the strange rumors of the nunnery to her sons.

Figure XXX-Part One; River Test adjacent to the present site in Romsey of the existing nunnery or monastery, terms used interchangeably in medieval times

HASTINGS- Hastings was much like the rivaled port of Dover and was not a marsh port so typical in England. Hastings owed its port or series of port-outlets to the clefts eroded by small rivers. "In the year this lass so traveled first to Scotland this coastline was completely changed by the vicious, terrifying storms that seemed to never end. The king's prized port of Winchelsea was destroyed; Hastings Castle partly crumbled, the outer walls of that massive fortress fell helplessly into the seas when the cliff supporting it collapsed into the waters below," Ellie told her sons.

"There is Castle Hill," she said pointing up ahead to the large cliff on the far side of the river. There so majestically sat the enormous castle built on the east side of the vast projecting land mass, made of sandstone. James was impressed. "That is the Old Roar then, is it not?" he asked Ellie as he motioned to the river below them that separated the grand cliffs and continued down to the priory. Ellie told him yes, but that the river too had changed. "White Rock is most eroded now, more so than before; that it gave great shelter to the town below," she sighed sadly, recalling Hastings in its majesty so long ago.

"Mother, what makes the Cinque Ports different from the rest?" James asked her. "That they have a distinctive charter granted by the king, that Edward treats them with special favor most as well," she explained. "My father Lord Lovaine would tell us, to seduce lords to so take on the challenge of these ports they were granted privileges of the king: Right of Tol and Team; to tax and toll, with many more such grants to their good government," she explained. Ellie also described the booty the lords of the ports might claim; that any goods that fell overboard in their waters would become property of the nobles to recover at will. "The right of flotsam and jetsam and ligan is what they call it," she said proudly; delighted to share her knowledge of the ports and happy that her children were asking all these questions. Hugh looked to their knight and escort as he sat on his tall palfrey staring over the cliffs and asked him inquisitively what he thought of the rocks, if they were somehow different.

Figure XXXI-Part One; view of the Ladies' Parlor from Hastings Castle ruins; first approved tournament site in England after the Conqueror arrived 1066

Sir David reflected thoughtfully then told the lad that the great cliffs were indeed smaller since last he came there some twenty years ago. "At least a half mile, a little less perhaps, those cliffs so reached out among the seas," he told them. Now the damage that began in 1287 cast a shadow to the future of the majestic port; the clear rival of Dover he would tell them all, in shipping and in population too, before those terrifying storms. "But Dover has lost her beauty most as well," said Sir David. "The French king attacked and burned it to the ground some seven years ago." James thought for quite some time about that devastation to Dover and added, "Like our Berwick, these ports of sea are very vulnerable to attacking and willful invaders." As the Douglases made their way down to the priory they looked out at the seas that would take them to Boulogue. "How long will it take us now," asked Archie, bored with Hastings, he was ready to see Paris. Ellie told them in one week and few days they would be in that city. "Meeting with at least one Scottish noble who was there; John Wishart, while the others may yet be arriving one by one, to make entreaties of diplomacy with King Philip," she reminded them.

Figure XXXII-Part One; much eroded cliffs at Hastings

"To speed our travels to that place, we will send our carts and some belongings not needed for our stay in the Ile de la Cité, to Lovaine with Lady Agnes." she explained, thinking somewhat wistfully: James will make his life and do his studies there for some years. Eleanora composed herself and told them of her plans for a pilgrimage in Boulogne. "We will take our rest for one day then to visit the shrine of the Virgin of the Sea; from once we take our leave of Boulogne in six days or less we will be in Paris," she said more gleefully. Ellie was looking forward to their stay in Paris; to remain in one place more than just a night or two.

"This lass to buy herself some silks and velvets; surcotes and cotes to have the tailors make in colors grand and vibrant," she chuckled, happy at the thought of shopping in that fine port. Sir David asked Ellie if she had ever been to France before. "The closest port was Antwerp for my longest journey; to see our kin in Lovaine the purpose of our travels there," she sighed remembering that voyage with her mother and Lord Lovaine. Ana was excited as well she confided to Ellie; to be in Paris was a grand adventure, one of so many that she had never even dreamed to take growing up in Groby as she did.

As the sun rose brightly on the harbor this warm morning Lady Douglas and her oldest son with her knight Sir David traveled with their men at arms to meet with sea captains. How lang ago Ellie thought dreamily to have sailed from Irvine to Dublin then to Mann; that Gilley had arranged so with Captain Gregg on his good cog. Now Eleanora was left to so prepare her household for their voyage alone, without her husband. A good sailing ship would have a crew of twenty; her wee household and their horses with their two carts would take a large ship to carry them to France.

Figure XXXIII-Part One; Hastings Castle ruins

"Your father told us once before that taking horses was most foolish on lang passage; each horse requiring the room of three Douglases he would say," Ellie continued, knowing James had forgotten sailing to the Isle of Mann when he was only two and some few months in age. "That this voyage is most forty miles or less; the horses can so travel with us. Even your Fortis at his advancing age can go on board the ship; that we will rest as well before we journey further." Lady Douglas went on to say that she had not the patience of her William to arrange their journey differently with horses and new carts in France; it was too difficult to do. James told her that he was pleased with her plans. "Most the means of our good father, perfectly devised," he marveled at her work preparing for this adventure, going to Paris then continuing on to Lovaine.

The captain she selected was the brother of a monk at the priory; a Hastings youth who knew the coastline and the channel waters perfectly. This ship's owner cautioned her however; the journey after that to Flanders he told her might be dangerous. Ellie and Sir David listened intently to the story of the old sailor about an uprising in Courtrai. "The Battle of the Golden Spurs was what they are calling this great revolt; a massacre of the French feudal host on the 11th of July just passed," he said ominously. "More unrest and confusion so exits there; lawlessness, as so often follows such insurgencies, now prevails," he warned the Douglases. Eleanora expressed her concern, but nothing would delay them now she told them, so close they were to the end of their travels. Sir David knew well enough that trying to compel this lady to reconsider traveling to Lovaine was futile; she had decided and nothing would deter her in her plans now.

Figure XXXIV-Part One; church of Our Lady in Kortrijk where after the battle the Flemish soldiers displayed the golden spurs of fallen French knights as trophies; today replica spurs are interspersed on the ceiling with the lion rampant of Flanders in memory of the battle; photo courtesy of Daniel van Buynder, Belgium

Captain Thomas promised them that his cog would carry the household and their goods and horses safely to the port of Boulogue. On the day next they would sail unless the weather changed their course Captain Thomas told her. "It is done," said Lady Douglas. She made the contract, paid the required fees; showed license for her travels then rode home to tell the household of their approaching departure for France! Riding back to the priory she thought of Gilley; how they had planned to leave for the Flemish province with their family in that summer of 1297. Why had he been so stubborn, she mused? He insisted to meet with de Percy, to defend his name, protest his innocence only it was a trap set by that contemptible vassal of the king and it changed their lives forever. Gilley never made it back to their manor that day in July. He was arrested by de Percy; imprisoned on false charges, held in irons and fetters to further demoralize him. Some six weeks later he would sail, but for London, not for Flanders. He was then tragically admitted into the Tower of London on the twelfth October, one day before her twenty-ninth birthday in 1297; to never see his Scotland again.

James had been riding his palfrey beside his mother. Looking over at Eleanora he realized she was back in Scotland in her thoughts; her face taking on a wistful countenance. "Dear mother are you perhaps thinking so of father?" She nodded. "That we were but few days from sailing to this country now before us; to be rid of Edward's treachery, free to live our lives at peace as exiles then in Brabant," she told him. "This son misses his father most as well," he told her sadly. They rode in silence until they reached the priory; savoring their memories of one named William.

Figure XXXV-Part One; 'town hall' in Antwerp, Belgium; a former medieval port

BOULOGNE SUR MER FRANCE-The Douglases arrived on Friday at Porte Neuve by the cathedral; by the Thursday next they would be closing in on Paris, Ile de la Cité. This day the widow and her three sons were going to do a pilgrimage to the Cathedral of Notre Dame and the Virgin of the Sea. There were many inns and hospices in Boulogne; pilgrims were prosperous to the businesses and monastery of the port. Ellie gave them each some coinage to purchase souvenirs made by local craftsmen; wee badges to commemorate their stay or candles to burn in their chapel at home in Essex. Lady Douglas made donations to the cathedral, requesting prayers for her mother, four wee children passed and her sweet knight, all now with God. These Scottish visitors were welcomed whole heartedly into the grand church; as they entered the nave, they were greeted by a guide for the cathedral who related the strangest story about the statue of the Virgin Mary that came to rest in Boulogne.

The priest was eager to share the tale, recite the fabled legend to these eager listeners. How these Douglases enjoyed exciting stories from history he marveled as he watched their interest grow with each word. "When St. Omer was a bishop nearly some seven hundred years ago a mysterious boat appeared in the estuary of the River Liane. This vessel came to us without oars, sails or sailors," marveled the good son of the Notre Dame Cathedral.

Archie started to ask a question then he caught his mother's eye, waiting to subdue him should that be required. He had been warned: to behave in this esteemed sanctuary, a good ambassador of Scotland now in France. "Did anyone claim the statue later?" asked the lad in his most serious tone. "Not for near some seven centuries has one yet to so appear!" exclaimed the priest.

The Douglases then went around the grand walled city; toured the ramparts constructed for the protection of the village and its people. The eastern corner of city wall that enclosed the vast port held a grand chateau. There were hospices as well that served the sick; every level of society moved about freely in the well protected port. "This castle reinforces the defensive walls, built by Philippe Herepel the Count of Boulogne, some seventy years ago," Sir David told the lads as they walked through the city. Hugh noticed that the buildings and the surrounding stone edifice were almost square. "So strange to see this for a city, so perfect now in shape; is there a purpose for such conformity?" he asked searching for a meaning to their ways.

Ana watched her girl respond; marveling at her ways of teaching, learned from Gilley's fine example. "What shapes do you recall that so appear as this?" she asked him. Hugh thought for but a moment then he told her. "A fort," recalling the ruins James showed him in Northumbria. Archie asked out loud, "That once this was a fort?" Ellie nodded smiling at her wee sons. James told his brothers more stories of the Romans when they came to France then to England and further north as well into their Scotland. Passing on the teachings of his father, the lad proudly shared his knowledge with Archie and with Hugh.

PARIS- Upon leaving Boulogne, the Douglases journeyed swiftly, all on horseback with their destination just before them: Paris. Half their household was traveling north with their wee carts and some supplies to the manor of Ellie's kin in Lovaine, taking their time and guided by some men at arms sent by Lady Agnes for this purpose. When the carts and possessions arrived in Lovaine these guides and men at arms would be sent back to rendezvous with the Douglases in Paris so they might return everyone to Brabant in a well guarded and expertly guided manner. Such travels in these times of great unrest required extra measures for safety. The smaller remaining group left to journey without the cart horses and half of their belongings were able to move very quickly toward their destination. The Scottish family was brimming now with excitement. Finally arriving in the fair city they were ready to explore the Left Bank and the Right Bank; while planning to stay on the Ile in the domiciles of the French nobility.

Ana was the happiest of all; to finally reach the city of her dreams, once her most precious desire when a wee lass had now become a reality. She marveled at the cathedral, also known as Notre Dame, with its great majesty and wondrous stone carvings. Sir David knew this city well and he was able to tell them of the way it was devised. "The Left Bank is for the University of Paris, the educational center of all of France. For the Right Bank there is established the merchant sector; where this knight has seen some fine tailors and fur hats," he teased, remembering the penchant for such finery of one laird and one Douglas son named James. "A fur hat most to find, sure aye," said James making Ellie chuckle. The son's well known mimicking of Lord Douglas and his fair extravagances of apparel made Ana laugh to recall those fond days when William le Hardi was with them.

Figure XXXVI-Part One; Bruges monument of the Battle of the Golden Spurs; the definitive battle for Flanders caused unrest in the surrounding countryside

"On the morrow we will meet with Sir John Wishart and the other Scottish nobles if they have arrived. Perhaps to see our Bishop Lamberton," she told them. James asked of the others who might be coming to Paris. "Another to so attend, the Steward your good uncle is my fair guess," Ellie said, remembering that Sir Alex now held the Steward lands in Ayrshire, forfeited by Sir James for his rebellious ways. The wee lads were very excited in their anticipation to meet with others that knew their father; friends and kin who could tell them more stories of his valiant ways and redoubtable courage. Lady Douglas always included her children for such meetings; Gilley had insisted that the wee ones, sons and daughters both, were an important part of their entourage. He also felt such situations afforded them the opportunity to learn the ways of government and court, even at their young age.

Figure XXXVII-Part One; hospice of Lovaine dating to the 13th century; good example of a medieval hospital

    Before the Douglases were to meet with the nobles from their homeland they visited the exquisite edifice Sainte Chapelle. "The construction of this beautiful church was completed only fifty years ago," said the priest and guide. There were two chapels here they discovered: one was for the king and the Royal Family. The lower chapel was for the servants of the king. "This great sanctuary built to hold the Crown of Thorns as well as a piece of the True Cross," said Sir David; feeling more a member of this wee clan from Essex as he showed them Paris. The upper chapel they peered about to see, finding the beauty of stained glass on all three sides. Eleanora was taken by surprise; the splendor of its odd design created an incredible illusion: a ceiling that appeared to float above a sea of glittering stained glass. "The most magnificent chapel this lass has ever seen," she exclaimed and Ana readily agreed with her.

    Lady Douglas, Ana and her knight with their Douglas men at arms finally arrived to meet with her friends and kin, Scottish nobles on a diplomatic mission in France. They had in tow a squire, a page, and a wee knave of five firmly in the grasp of his good nurse. The Baron of the Mearns was somewhat older Ellie noted but his familiar face and a new broadness in his chest like Gilley's made her laugh and feel relaxed. "The good food and wine of France most agrees with you," joked Ellie, happy to see the dear friend of her husband once again. "Lady Eleanora, dear Ellie a fair sight to see at long last; come sit, we have a feast so set for your arrival, much wine and fresh ale as well," he boasted. "You might recall the messenger from Fawside, our Sir David," reminded Ellie, referring to the day thirteen years ago at Douglasdale when the old baron first heard of Gilley's plan to kidnap and marry her without the king's license. Sir John, smiled and beckoned the knight to his table. Then he turned to look at James; tall or taller than this humble knight; mused the old baron. "The image of le Hardi, though without the manly chest," he teased the squire, gesturing to the girth that surrounded his own frame.

Then the Scottish laird turned to the younger Douglas sons and smiled broadly. "That you are Hubicus; I knew well your uncle and namesake when he was Lord Douglas," said Sir John. Before he could say another word to this middle son he was interrupted; the five year old had broken free and was running from his nurse. He stopped directly in front of his father's friend and bowed as Ellie had painstakingly taught him. "Archibald of Douglas sir," said the youngest son of le Hardi. The Baron of the Mearns grinned. "You most certainly are a Douglas and bold as le Hardi too in your ways, sure aye as your father most would say, sure aye!" he chuckled; taking great pleasure in seeing the family of his old compatriot. Ana and Archie's nurse took the younger sons with them to the courtyard of the elegant manor house; the sun was shining, a perfect day to run off young children's energy outside. James and Ellie joined the others in the feasting. Surrounding them on the walls of this exquisite great hall were many tapestries with many colors, much brighter than the ones at Berkeley Castle. And the utensils on the table were all of silver, with wooden bowls instead of the bread bowls used in manors back in England. Old friends began to arrive in the great hall, including the good bishop. "That you are here pleases this old Scottish patriot; living most in exile for some time I fear," said William Lamberton. "What are your plans?" he asked James and Lady Douglas.

Ellie told the Bishop of St. Andrews that the Douglases were on their way north to Lovaine; her squire son would leave her Essex household for some years or more. "To learn of the arms of this good land; James will study in Brabant staying with my kin the widow Lady Agnes of Lovaine," she explained. William Lamberton shook his head approvingly. "That we may well be here in Paris when you have completed most your studies please come see this bishop. There is room enough to serve in my good household when we return to Scotland, should that please you," the prelate offered graciously as he elaborated on his suggestion.

Ellie was thrilled with the bishop's idea; extending an offer for such a fine position, one of great stature for a squire. Lamberton wished to have James take care of his knives and weapons he told them. A generous proffer for the interim until they were reseised to the Douglas lands, James reflected. "Thank you for that consideration bishop," the squire replied. Ellie reminded William Lamberton of their intentions to return to Scotland. "In two short years that my son will plea for seising to his rightful inheritance, to pay his fine and pledge his fealty to the king; to restore the barony of Douglasdale to Douglas lairds." The bishop shook his head, "That last year when we last met the English king so favored me; in this short time has this bishop lost his favor. Perhaps by then to have regained approval," he chuckled realizing the frivolity of favor to this lord paramount. "You have my promise to so help you in that quest."

Figure XXXVIII-Part One; view of Avoch village from Ormond Castle motte; a monument to Andrew de Moray, squire and son of Sir Andrew commemorates the North Rising, a ceremony held annually there on the last Saturday in May

Sir John begged Ellie to come sit on the dais, on the bench next to him beckoning James to join them there as well. "Tell me Eleanora, what was the truth of le Hardi's imprisonment and murder as I hear it from de Lindsay?" he asked the widow. She recounted the story of the collusion of de Percy and her father; "to satisfy two miserable and most despised of men in their greed and heinous revenge against the kindly knight, my dear William," Ellie began. "That my father so denied a daughter her true love; wanting my sweet Gilley in Edward's prison not sufficient vengeance for that lord. To have him murdered for a crime he did not commit, most treacherous an end for these vile felons to so cause; these scurrilous vassals of dear Edward."

Lady Douglas spoke with anger seething in her every word as she continued to tell Baron Wishart in exact detail the tragic series of events. She also reminded him of the passing of the doom on Sir Walter de Percy in 1289 that began the de Percy feud with the Douglas Clan. Bishop Lamberton interrupted her; telling them that he also remembered this de Percy knight. "That ignoble vassal of the king; to marry the widow of my kin Walter de Lindsay without license; he paid little fine for it I do recall," the bishop said grimly. Lady Douglas shook her head ruefully. "That we were told by Lady Eugenia, relic of dear Andrew de Moray, her husband too so met his grueling end in the White Tower. Within some weeks of Gilley's execution the same fate was Sir Andrew's most as well is what we heard," said Ellie.

Sir John could not understand why those good knights had to meet their deaths when they were prisoners already in Edward's Tower. Ellie explained that as long as William remained alive he might be released on mainperson of her cousins as before. "Most did those vicious lords so fear this lady of Lovaine and Douglas; to most free her husband; that the truth of their conspiracy would find the light of day to Edward through my kin or friends at court," she said. The Baron of the Mearns listened carefully; her words were true he reflected. The long time friend of her husband knew well that Ellie had posted bail successfully before on behalf of William; in fact it was twice before the baron realized upon reflection. Surely she could have maneuvered his release a third time; making her pleas to Edward through Nicky de Segrave and Johannis de Hastings the competitor, good knights of renown and powerful vassals of the king who would intercede on her behalf, Wishart mused. Ellie wiped her eyes, remembering the tragedy of losing Gilley. She told the baron and the bishop that she never foresaw the whole of de Percy's plan; the extent of his conspiracy and his compulsion for revenge. And the sad results still overwhelmed her.

Lady Douglas admitted that she had underestimated their wrathful power, until the fate of one Andrew de Moray was revealed to her. "This laird and Douglas kin, then the Justiciar north of the Forth, was the same knight who hunted down de Percy in 1289," she elaborated sadly. "That murderer of my own sweet cousin, the young Earl of Fife, was a felon sure!" She continued her story, reminding them that Walter de Percy had been turned over to Lord Douglas by his cousin de Moray; to pass the doom: beheading was the decree from the Baronial Magistrate. "Now de Moray too was dead in the Tower; so suddenly, just after my sweet William met his end so cruelly there. That these villains stole from us," her words had grown inaudible as the widow began to cry, "the last year of his life, to trifle with our letters; to tell me lies, his false refusal to accept my visits at the White Tower. We lost forever that dear time together," she sobbed openly now, deeply into James' chest as he held her up. Baron Wishart apologized for his questions that saddened her. Ellie wiped her eyes and made her excuses as well. "That this lass so thought to be most through with crying for my Gilley," she said to the kindly knight; embarrassed for her tears of sorrow. "The agony to have him most alive and kept apart by ruse to not see him; to lose him twice, first by their conspiracy, then again by his sad death," she explained to their old friend Wishart. The widow was trying desperately to convey the horror and devastation she felt from de mischef and the foul deeds of Lord de Percy and her father.

James told baron Wishart that their family would one by one return to Scotland. "We so plan to live again, most as a family, on our Douglas lands," he said; his words more a pledge than a statement. "Our dear father met his end because of greed of one and dishonor of another. We will avenge his death; first to ask the invaders most politely to leave our lands, then evict them all quite violently if they so foolishly choose to stay." The silence on the dais was deafening. Sir John realized another patriot would be returning home when James completed his studies in Lovaine. Baron Wishart stood up from the table. "Come James, Sir David, you too should join us as well to watch," said the Scot, offering his arm of escort to Lady Douglas. "A good time to assess our skills as Scotland's sons to return our kingdome most to Scots," he said boastfully.

In the courtyard was a pell; by the far end near the stables was the contest lance the rings, competition to test one's skills at tilting. The baron had some horses saddled and a wee event was devised with others in the courtyard. The skills of a Douglas squire were now observed by all; his mother knew at once that Sir David's training of her son was excellent: James had great success this day. An English knight to train a Scottish squire; would it be to kill the English invaders of his homeland, she pondered? The irony of war, most confusing to this mother Ellie mused. Archie was sitting beside her as these informal games took place, "Mother, when will this lad be allowed to so compete?" he asked her. Ana was chuckling. "Good that he is the youngest and the last of your dear sons," she said. "Doubtless that another like our wee Archie would age his mother another twenty years in just his one!"

Ellie quite agreed; Archie was like Gilley and her James; wanting to be grown knights at the age of five. Hugh was riding his horse to lance the ring on the wooden shaft, blunted and without a blade made for play and games of competition; to test the skills of pages and of squires while not risking injury. This lad had the Douglas build and good coordination; combined with natural skills he too could become a knight if he so desired. Ellie had insisted that Hugh learn the skills of a page his age; then he could be a knight or a canon, whatever Hubicus desired, he would have a choice and not be hampered by his early schooling. The old Baron of the Mearns was pleased with what he saw: Lady Douglas had continued the education of her Scottish sons in the arms of Scotland and of England, with plans to train in Flanders all arranged. "You have done well by these good lads," he told her happily. Ellie smiled broadly. "It is my desire that my sons have every opportunity that William would have given them. Even my Hugh who seeks the church for his life's work must know how to buckle on his armor like a baron of the realm, most like your dear uncle and good patriot, Robert Wishart," she teased knowing the Bishop of Glasgow for his determined ways.

Sir John could not contain his laughter. "That good bishop will one day yet get us all in bigger trouble with dear Edward," he said. Ellie admitted quietly, "I do pray so." With a knowing glance she said her words again. "I do pray so." As they made their way back into the great hall of the French manor Ellie started to ask about the news from Scotland. Then she suddenly stopped herself to tell him what she heard about the uprising in Courtrai. "Do you think it safe for us to travel through Flanders now?" she asked the baron. Wishart told her to avoid the river region of Courtrai, travel south and they should not find trouble along the way. "Will that defeat of King Philip affect our Scotland?" she asked the baron and the bishop. Lamberton said he was not sure; but such a possible alliance of Flanders and Edward would change the balance of diplomacy, alter the support of others who might take Scotland's side against Edward. "Time will tell us; we must wait to see as events unfold. Clearly this revolt was poorly timed for Scotland as it could weaken Philip's resolve," said Lamberton quite ominously.

Ellie told Sir John of their travels through Scotland, weeks or days ahead of Edward and his campaign last year in 1301and what she had heard since that time. "That when *lord paramount* stayed in Scotland for the winter it was at great expense to his treasury. English lords are grumbling for the cost of his wars; leaving Essex barren of grain and those to farm it," Ellie told Baron Wishart. "Our people grow weary of the wars now too," he told her. "But not my uncle; he like Wallace has the heart of a patriot that will never quit." Ellie asked about the Bishop. She recounted the story of how Robert Wishart let her family stay at his Castle Torres in Carstairs, waiting William's release from Berwick in 1296. "That the sheriff of Lanark, Sir Walter Burghdon is now constable of that castle, appropriated by Edward for the crown," said Sir John, "now the center of the sherrifdom." Ellie was stunned. Lanark was large enough to require its own sheriff so she asked him why.

Wishart explained that most of Lanark was wasted by the years of wars and English occupation; any activity in that area might meet face to face with the Scots' own sheriff Walter Logan. Ellie recalled the knight and friend of Lord Douglas, who pledged his fealty to the king at Edinburgh with William in June, 1296. "Lady Willelma told us of the confusion with a sheriff for the Scots in the same shire so controlled by the English with escheators both to so collect their taxes," said Ellie. "A terrible circumstance," he said. "Yet the English are most bothered by the bands of marauding patriots; to so distract their garrisons on full alert most through the day and night." She told him of the orders to the escheators: to expand their quest of English shires to raise the money Edward owed to the Welsh troops. "And then too came writs from this king to earls and lords to so provide for castleguard men at arms," she continued, elaborating on the grievances she heard most recently at the wedding of her daughter then at Lady Joan's party at Berkeley Castle.

Figure XXXIX-Part One; view from Carstairs village kirk towards the site of castle Torres, once held by the Bishop of Glasgow

"Young de Ferrers has not so sent the men requested from other notices of Edward; this castleguard system is failing most as well, with many marked as simply 'not yet come' and when they do arrive they leave most suddenly; desertion is frequent from the garrisons." she explained to the Scottish patriots. Ellie had more news to brighten Wishart's hopes for a free Scotland. "That they can't hold a full complement of men at arms at most castles; stores of food go missing, the retinue without their draw for pay," she plainly told them. Ellie made it very clear that the raids on provisions by the Scots were having a dramatic effect on the garrisons and their morale; without food and other supplies some were simply leaving their posts, going home. "And of course you must have heard about the troubles at Berwick, the wages promised by dear Edward not forthcoming?" she asked them. Lamberton was now listening intently to the conversation. "How is it that you know this?" he asked; not waiting for an answer he continued. "And tell us more about Berwick; that is the king's stronghold in Scotland and important."

"My kin is Sir John, Baron de Segrave; his retinue most known in Scotland under banners of dear Edward," she said. "Dear Sir John," speaking to Wishart directly, "you might recall his brother Nicky, Sir Nicholas de Segrave, who gave surety for Gilley, when Edward seized your lands and ours in Northumbria?" Wishart told Lamberton he certainly knew of this cousin; he had first hand experience with Edward's retaliation for Ellie's rescue from Fawside Castle. Wishart's lands near Redesdale and his manor of Monilawes, part of Wallington in Tynedale, were confiscated by Edward until Gilley appeared in the king's council to plea and pay his fine for marrying Lady Douglas.

Figure XL-Part One; Fawside Castle; site of the raid of the heart as le Hardi termed it, with his accomplice Wishart in 1288; Eleanora held lands in nearby Winton

"Did you know that when my lands were seized into the king's hands, that le Hardi's old enemy Gilbert de Umfraville sold them to Sheriff Knut; the very one who took you all to Knaresburgh's good prison?" asked the baron as he reflected on those wild years of their linked histories. Ellie was not surprised to hear that the Lord of Redesdale was mixed up in dubious concerns and false charters. "We filed a plea to have these lands restored and it was finally heard some four years later," said Sir John. "And fortunately for dear Gilbert, the courts awarded us reseising of the manor," he chuckled boastfully. Ellie told him of her problems with Fawdon and other Douglas manors of le Hardi that were given her in dower. "That Gilbert does so make his rules and laws in Redesdale; to ignore the king's writs!" she exclaimed, her frustration growing with her every word. "Just like my Gilley and his father, this lass is constantly in the court of Newcastle with requests and pleas for reseising to our Fawdon."

Lamberton wanted to redirect the discussion to Ellie's knowledge of the English in Scotland. He asked Wishart what else he knew of her kin. The Baron of the Mearns explained that these de Segraves were the same powerful family Lamberton had heard about in Scotland. Kin to Eleanora, Sir Nicolas was castellan of several Scottish castles long after providing mainperson for le Hardi. "This knight Nicky is my favorite cousin; sadly was he at Berwick; in service to his lord at the siege of Caerlaverock most as well," Lady Douglas went on to say. "He told me plainly of that dreadful Nithsdale battle. Of the same barbarous tactics of the butcher king most as well, that he refused the Scots' surrender. Most like Berwick, dear Edward put many brave survivors of that siege to the sword or worse: the rope for hanging." Ellie's words of indignation toward Edward Plantagenet were coming quickly; she was biting back the tears thinking of the innocent lives taken by the vicious murdering king. Quietly she told these good Scots her true opinion. "Many English barons have been tortured by the wanton slaying of their brutal lord," hinting correctly that many nobles were in secret revolt to Edward, waiting for their moment to take action; stop the frivolous wars and killings of good men on both sides of the borders.

William Lamberton and Sir John Wishart were impressed; convinced of her honesty, they were very interested to hear more of what this lady knew. They begged her to continue. Lady Douglas provided them with great detail about Berwick, the administration's fears of a revolt with no one there to garrison the castle. "In August of last year there was an angry uprising, a mutiny is what they called it," she told these patriotic Scots, "of foot crossbowman and the archers of the castle." The wages promised by the king himself in July to pay the garrison did not arrive and when they did, only the men at Berwick were paid; the garrisons of Jedburgh and Roxburgh did not receive their pay she told them both directly. "My kin the de Hastings were the constables of those castles, writing Edward of their discontent." Eleanora said that she had heard the king became most worried; the center of his administration in Scotland was in disarray without food and wages. "He feared for his hold on this kingdome, our dear Scotland, is what they said," disclosed Lady Douglas, using the words she overheard at Berkeley Castle.

Sir John and the bishop exchanged looks, stunned to hear this widow knew so many of these English knights in Scotland and of the business of King Edward in their homeland. Ellie mentioned to them that another cousin was Johannis, Sir Johannis de Hastings. This English lord also pledged surety for le Hardi with Nicky and two other knights well known to Edward. "My dear kin is the very Lord of Abergavenny; the competitor in 1291,"

Ellie informed them. Both Lamberton and Wishart understood now how the widow might come to learn so much. Sir John de Hastings was one of the claimants to the crown of Scotland during the interregnum; putting forth his pretence to Scotland's crown that the kingdome was truly an earldom to be divided into three lordships, one for each remaining competitor. De Hastings' claim was summarily dismissed but the ignominious proposal was then championed by Robert Brus, grandfather of the Earl of Carrick. Until that point, there was a stalemate. But when Brus put forth de Hastings' idea again, he was promptly deserted by his own auditors and supporters including the Bishop of Glasgow, Robert Wishart and James the Steward. They quickly abandoned him and threw their support to John Balliol, turning the tide in his favor. King John was made King of Scots only to become the vassal king to Edward Plantagenet not long after.

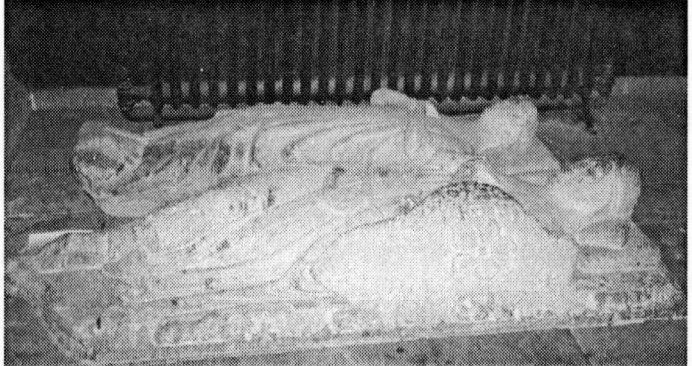

Figure XLI-Part One; effigy of Gilbert de Umfraville and his wife at Hexham Abbey; Gilbert was a constant aggressor trying to steal Fawdon from the Douglases

Ellie realized that the baron and the bishop might want to hear more of Johannis' deeds to date. She told them that he signed the barons' letter to the Pope last year and was now serving as the seneschal in Gascony. Wishart was chuckling; he remembered when le Hardi first told him he fell in love with a nineteen year old English widow with the astute mind of an able seneschal; only later to discover she had many friends and kin at court in England, with a handsome dower as well. The bishop was not convinced that her words were exactly true however; he wanted to learn more. "And of the other de Hastings in Scotland, you say they are your kin as well?" asked William Lamberton, though guessing at the truth as he posed the question. "Richard and Robert de Hastings are brothers, my cousins; last known to this lass in charge of garrisons at Jedburgh and Roxburgh respectively. Is that not correct?" she asked the bishop quite innocently. Wishart smiled broadly, knowing that she was absolutely accurate; Lamberton was shaking his head in the affirmative, surprised by the validity of her information. Ellie did not stop there; she went on the enumerate the size of the castle garrisons in the shire, even knowing the number of armed foot in Jedburgh. "Our little spy in Essex," said Baron Wishart, "Lady Douglas, it is time for you to spend more time at parties of these English knights and their ladies, to send us more good words of cheer of England's strain to fight the wars for Edward. Ellie started laughing. "Parties are what this lass does loathe the most and so avoids completely. Were I to so accept their many invitations they would suspect me sure, aye!" she chuckled.

Eleanora asked them about Balliol returning to his estates in France and of the proposed truce. Sir John told her of the great diplomacy of William Lamberton. "That this bishop has so achieved; the truce of Asnières between the English and King Philip of France will so include the Scots in this agreement for their peace. We held a Parliament in Scone some six months ago to discuss this progress with our negotiations with the Pope," said the Baron of the Mearns. James had returned to the great hall leaving his wee brothers to attend to the horses with the farrier and grooms. He was making his way to his mother's side, curious to learn of their discussions, hearing these nobles speak of Scotland. "As for King John, these French were growing most in number for their support of him as the true and rightful king of Scotland." James exchanged a glance with Ellie, sharing her disdain for the weakened king, stripped of his kingdome, defamed by King Edward. But Lamberton assured them that this support would only succeed to strengthen their position with the Pope. "Perhaps to buy us time for more patriots to rejoin our cause," said Sir John. Lamberton added though that the defeat of Philip in Courtrai might hamper the French position to support the return of Balliol. "It is too early to predict the effects of that insurgence; but it might not bode well for Scotland is my fear," said the Bishop.

James wanted to discuss the details of that battle with Wishart. "How is it that these armed horse, these knights following the banner of the French king could lose so badly to foot of Flemish pikes, with their very backs to the river and no place for retreat?" he began. "When at Falkirk the same strategy so failed with schiltrons; what was the difference in Courtrai?" James wanted to know from Baron Wishart. This seasoned warrior, a knight since the days of Alexander did not know the details of the battle of Courtrai; but Sir David understood and answered for him. "At Courtrai these foot were fighting for their homeland as were your Scots at Falkirk. They took up a position on the front, a location protected by boggy ground and ground water from the River Lys. The Flemish soldiers prepared well for their fight; digging pits to so contrive a smaller battlefield that would cause the French armed horse to become stuck in their attack. Even with the protection of crossbowmen, these chargers and their knights fell perilously to their quick death as the Flemish pikemen held their line," he said carefully drawing the picture of the battle scene.

Sir David continued to discuss the battle plan at Falkirk in more detail. "Though this knight was in England and only heard of this from others, Edward's strategy was to split his army into three divisions; two would attack while he held back the third; to approach the flank of Wallace's position." The de Ferrers knight took some spoons and his dagger to represent the Scottish archers and the knights; with four small wooden bowls he identified the schiltrons, the deadly circular formations of the Scottish pikemen. Wishart began to tell James where the English army gained its success. "To have the English bows attack the Scottish pikemen at close range; these brave men of Alba held formation, only then to be attacked by the charge of knights, through the paths of fallen Scots killed by these archers." James reflected a moment before he replied. "So the difference was in the preparation of the battlefield, shrinking it to a size in fair advantage to the smaller Flemish army. They gained victory as well with the failure of the French king to so respond with a more flexible attack; a combination of arms," James postulated. "The arrogance to believe that knights could grab victory when fighting against only armed foot and Flemish pikemen seemed to be their folly most as well," he scoffed rhetorically. The Baron of the Mearns smiled approvingly. Sir David nodded as well, knowing his student-squire, this knight to be, understood very well indeed the strategy of battle.

Figure XLII-Part One; Groeningheveld gates; site of Courtrai battle field, an open plain, moors set between two small streams; the Flemish army held this position against invading French forces; photo courtesy of Daniel van Buynder, Belgium

James asked about William Wallace; how devastated he must have been after that dreadful defeat at Falkirk. "Wallace truly blamed himself for that great loss. But he did not give up his fight for Scotland; turning to diplomacy to help his beloved kingdome. That he came here for letters from King Philip IV, to take to the papal court," said Wishart, "this humble knight does so believe that letter to King Edward sent by Boniface was the result of the hard work of that good patriot; as well as with the Scottish bishops including one we know so well," he went on to say, acknowledging Lamberton's efforts.

"Did you know this Wallace?" asked the baron. James told them of the times when William Wallace came to Douglas Castle and how he met this honest man on his second visit; bringing wounded to be treated for their injuries, after the raid on Sanquhar Castle and Durisdeer. "My father spoke of Wallace as a true patriot and a man of core values; one that he could trust," said the squire. The bishop wanted to know what other men in Scotland le Hardi believed could be relied upon. "Besides the good baron here," pointing to John Wishart, "There are two: this baron's Uncle Robert, the good Bishop of Glasgow and our Uncle Alex, Sir Alexander de Lindsay; none of the others remain alive," said James sadly, thinking of his kin the de Morays, both Andrews now with God. Ellie wanted to know about the guardian of Scotland and who was controlling Ayrshire. "Lands and fees of my dower have not been forthcoming from that shire or any other most as well" she told them. "Dear Edward," she said mockingly, "has ordered John St. John some weeks ago to secure my dower, repledged to me three years ago. Though the lands were most reseised, few rents and fees have come of it!" Lamberton shook his head, with a pained grimace he told Ellie of another sad circumstance. "That you will have to file another plea; word so came two days passed, John St. John is dead."

Ellie wanted to cry. She dreaded having to make appearances before Edward, to get what already was hers to have. And now she would have to start all over again. Wishart noticed her sad demeanor. He decided to tease her recalling le Hardi's way with her those many times he saw them in Douglasdale; once in particular when she was about to have a fit of pique. "Simon Fraser has taken it upon himself to secure that region for the Scots," taunted the baron, his eyes twinkling for the ruse. "Most since the time he heard that the Lady Douglas was invading Ayrshire in collection of her rents," he said, laughing through his words. Ellie had to chuckle; she giggled at the silly thoughts. Then seriously the baron told her more news of Ayrshire; that after a siege at Ayr and the words of the Pope and French in support of Balliol, the Earl of Carrick was now back in the English camp. "He could not wait another day; to surrender to the same John St. John; it was now some seven months ago. With him went the earl commander of the Carrick army," he said ruefully knowing the many men that only an earl could call to muster would now be lost from the rebels' cause.

Wishart's words were suddenly interrupted; from behind her, Ellie heard a familiar voice. "The Douglases have now invaded France I see," said the Steward who just this day arrived in Paris himself. James turned around to face his uncle, his birth mother Elizabeth's brother for whom he was named. Greetings were exchanged; Ellie and her son conveyed their sympathies for the loss of John, the brother of the High Steward, at the battle of Falkirk. Sir James spoke softly to the widow of his great sorrow. "The loss of William was most devastating," he conveyed to her. "Both to us as family and to our Scotland," he continued, praising le Hardi for his patriotism and valor; a martyred warrior. Ellie bowed her head and thanked him for his kind sentiment.

Turning to his old friend Wishart the Steward feigned a menacing grimace. "That you have the courage to speak of the Earl of Carrick in the presence of this lady?" he teased. "That Brus was the very one to carry off our Lady Douglas and her children from their home of Douglas Castle!" The Baron of the Mearns turned to Ellie with a mischievous grin. "First you are so kidnapped by le Hardi and his brave accomplice, this humble knight, to take you from your castle in Tranent, hence to Douglas Castle; then to be removed the same way you arrived from that very castle by Earl Robert? You live a fabled life Lady Eleanora!" bellowed Wishart.

James said he still carried the proof of that malicious deed; pulling out the Carrick silk left in Douglasdale by the invaders who sacked the castle. "Here is the pennon of Earl Robert," boasted James. Ellie was surprised James still carried that wee banner. The Steward was startled as well to see that silk with the armorial bearings of Brus, remembering the day when Lord Douglas first found out about the kidnapping of his family; informed at his Ayrshire campsite by Sir Andrew his seneschal. The Steward began to speak; he had a noble bearing for a wee round man of below average height with wild reddish hair and sparkling green eyes. More than anything he fashioned himself a great storyteller; this was his opportunity, his eulogy of William le Hardi Douglas and this knight's last stand at Irvine Water. "We were all encamped at Knadgerhill and le Hardi was heading for our tent, to tell us of the Carrick earl's siege at Douglasdale. With his brow furled in that menacing manner most known to all of us, he arrived to do battle." Sir James chuckled to remember the redoubtable laird and his fiery temper when crossed by others.

"His huge form cast a shadow at the door of my tent, his face contorted by his anger as he entered, he flung down that Carrick pennon, to land in my lap. Standing there, he growled, his words so caustic, the audacity of this coward knight to come with fire and sword to his castle when he knew that we were here in Irvine waiting for him to make up his mind to join us or stay with Edward! Side by side le Hardi stood there with Wallace, they were about the same height you know," he said as an aside, " and young de Moray too the esquire, each one standing on either side of Sir William. Lord Douglas expressed his outrage with Earl Robert for his foul deed." Sir James painted quite a scene for his audience describing the threesome, those noble patriots in unison, seeking revenge against the earl. "And a nightmare to Earl Robert should he come upon these warriors at this very moment!" said the Steward. "We feared most truly le Hardi would run him through right there and then had he found him in our camp!" Hugh and Archie had finished helping the grooms with their horses; they had joined James and Ellie and were listening intently to the story of their father Lord Douglas. Hugh's mouth was open, in awe to hear these words not remembering his father for his temper. Archie was impressed; his father was a man of courage, a true hero in his mind.

The Steward continued his tale. "When le Hardi took his leave we begged our God to send Earl Robert first to us when he arrived at camp, so we could warn him of this knight's desire to meet his deed with the point of his sword." As the wee sons of William listened the knight began to embellish his words for them. James the elder told them of their father in the true spirit of a man: a legend among knights for his adherence to core values; a man who never understood why others would deceive or commit foul deeds, the undoing of this brave patriot in the end he told them all.

"And what most happened then?" asked Archie, excited to hear more. The Steward told the lads that the Earl of Carrick finally arrived at Knadgerhill and came to see their Uncle James before he saw the other lairds encamped at Irvine. "Warned him, armed him with the words that Lord Douglas used himself, to run him through; then to ask the reason for his evil act." The young earl told the Steward that he had taken Lady Douglas not to Edward as the king had requested him to do but to her manor in Ayrshire. "Robert Brus told us not to worry; he would go to le Hardi's tent and put himself at the mercy of that baron, for now he was staying most with us, a rebel to the king," said James the elder.

"Did our father raise his sword to the earl?" asked Hugh earnestly. The Steward shook his head no. "Your father was a wise and moral man; a knight of renown. He told Robert that he should re-examine most his view of life; to learn the truth, God's own truth most in him, here in his heart. That was one of your father's strongest beliefs; one we as friends and kin knew most by rote: God's own truth, known to us in our hearts," he said again, sighing softly, remembering his noble brother in law, the frequently headstrong but always honest, William le Hardi Douglas. Ellie's eyes were closed, her mind was on her husband; the greatness that he held inside of him. Yes, she held that truth now within her, here in her heart, closer to her now when his friends and family spoke their memories of him, she assured herself.

James Douglas collected his thoughts, he too was reminiscing about his father. When the story had concluded he told his uncle how impressed and grateful he was to hear such fine words about Lord Douglas. James the younger introduced his brothers to Big James as he once called the Steward. "This cheerful laird is our Uncle James," the squire told his siblings. "The sometimes landless and titular baron of Ayrshire, the High Steward of Scotland; for now he is in between his pledging and reseising to his lands; dependant on the whim of Edward for his favor at court." Hugh was his reticent self, most reserved and polite. Archie introduced himself, "Archibald of Douglas, soon to be a page in the house of Sir Alexander de Lindsay of Byres, Barnweill, Crawford, Luffness," he proudly rattled off the names of the baronies; then correcting himself, "or of Garleton if Edward is yet most stubborn." The Steward scoffed sarcastically; adding some manors of his own to Sir Alex's holdings. "And the Kyle, of Ayrshire most as well; that Edward gave him Steward lands for my rebellion," he said distastefully, recalling le Hardi's sentiments for the despicable lord: that pagan despot king as Gilley called him.

Ellie shook her head wearily; the energy of the five year old was trying to her. "Come here my son," she begged him to take her hand. But Archie was not coming; he had to make his bow first, which he did. With much fanfare and a huge grin he finished with a flourish. The Steward noted that Lady Douglas had her hands full. "Three sons of le Hardi, my wife Gelis would not have envied you!" said their uncle. "She thought one such man to meet was one too many for his boldness, but three more of his disposition?" chuckled the Steward, to ponder her dilemma.

Baron Wishart wanted to know if Archie was really returning to Scotland to stay with the de Lindsays. "His words are true; his God father Sir Alex has agreed to take my son into his household for the start of his good training to so become a squire then a knight," Ellie replied. "This was the wish of my dear Gilley and my pledge to him as well that our sons would return to Scotland." Then she added it was her prayer as well; to live again in that kingdome of the Celts was her dearest wish. Baron Wishart, James the Steward and Bishop Lamberton all knew le Hardi for many years and well but they did not know Lady Douglas except through casual acquaintance and the good words of a loving husband. Today they were seeing evidence of why Lord Douglas was so devoted to this Essex lass; she held for his core values. And she stood for the love they shared; inspiring their children, encouraging them to become knights of renown and return to Scotland; keeping a promise to her late husband.

The feasting was beginning; the gallery was filling with musicians for the first entremet of entertainment. Ellie joined the Bishop, the Baron, and the Steward on the dais with her son James; Archie and Hugh sat on another table with their nurse and Ana, Gillerothe and the others of the Douglas household that were allowed to eat with the family. It was a small group; and everyone felt comfortable in talking freely, complaining most of Edward and his English occupation of their country. As the night progressed the music seemed to fade; the Baron told them of all the things he missed the most by being there in France was the fair music of the wee pipes. "Do you play?" asked Ellie.

Figure XLIII-Part One; the ruins of Garleton Castle; once a de Lindsay manor

Old Baron Wishart growled yes, as most knights he learned to play an instrument, "but never like le Hardi played the small pipes," he sighed. The Steward volunteered his talents if there were others to join him in the gallery; he could play the dulcimer. "Gillerothe, did you bring your wee pipes?" he asked him, recalling the times in Douglasdale when they had Ceilidhs where he would play. The old vassal of Lord Douglas smiled broadly; of course he brought his pipes! Then Ellie volunteered another James to join them, "Our son played for dear Muriel's good wedding," she boasted. "Much the piper like my husband taught by Gillerothe just the same!" James and Gillerothe left the hall, returning quickly with their Lowland pipes. These three generations of Scots headed jubilantly for the gallery of this French domicile; to bring a little of their Celtic music that would fill the hearts of these exiled patriots of Alba. There were few dry eyes on the dais when the Lowland pipers and the Steward on his dulcimer had finished their playing for the night.

The Douglases were up early the next morning; they were going to explore Paris and the Right Bank. Ellie planned to do some shopping; to buy gifts for everyone in their household and for Muriel as well. On their way Sir David pointed out Notre Dame Cathedral and explained that once there was another sacred site there; a temple built in ancient times to celebrate the god Jupiter. The family stopped to pray at the cathedral and explore it as well. Everywhere they traveled now they would discover history and stories of the ancient ones that lived there before. This became their standard; to learn and study when they journeyed to new lands, their Douglas family tradition that began with Gilley fourteen years ago.

Once inside the beautiful cathedral Ellie pointed out the exquisite rose patterned stained glass windows comprised of thousands of tiny pieces of colored glass. The style was described at rayonnant; from shimmering hues of small shapes placed together they formed rays of brilliant colors, depicting stories from the Bible. In the spectacular north rose of Notre Dame was a scene of the Virgin Mary and Jesus in the center; diagonals of color fanned outward from there forming three rings of iridescent shades of primary colors that became pictures of prophets and kings of the Old Testament. Of all the churches they had seen this architecture impressed Hugh the most. "To make such beauty must have taken many years," he spoke in wonderment as his eyes became lost in the blaze of colors and artistry of the exquisite windows.

Figure XLIV-Part One; Notre Dame Cathedral, Paris; photo courtesy Amy Fitzgerald

The family was staying in the very southern part of the Ile de la Cité near the cathedral. From here they would ride their palfreys north today. They went past the Petit Pont, the bridge that led to the Left Bank, continuing on the Rue de Marché Palu until they came to the Grand Pont that spanned the northern branch of the Seine to the Right Bank. "These bridges were once all stone," Sir David explained, "when the last time this knight was here; such structures date back to Roman times," he told the children. "But the devastating floods of 1296 destroyed both bridges and many houses as well; the snows and ice continued to inundate the city and the Seine did not recede for three months or more." Ellie was surprised to learn about the floods in 1296 and hearing about that dreadful year made her shudder. "These wooden bridges were built in their place?" asked James. Sir David nodded yes; the ferry service was all they had to travel back and forth between banks during the construction, or so he had heard.

"Look Mother below," said Archie excitedly. "Wee lads are bathing!" Ellie chuckled. "On hot days as this, it is common," she told her son. The Seine was alive with activity: from the banks or from small boats there was fishing for pleasure and some for business; merchants' vessels were being escorted to the toll houses on the Petit Pont as they brought in food and wine to the island city. Pleasure boating parties were relaxing or engaged in animated conversation, while passing under the Grand Pont traveling down the Seine. This large bridge was exhilarating to travel across Ellie noted; the huge arch at the center was very high to allow boats to pass under it and provided astounding views to the myriad of activities below. Archie was delighted to 'ride his manly horse,' meaning Audāx; traversing the huge structure as he sat high in his saddle he conveyed an air; proud and ebullient. "Oh Mother, look; a portcullis is it not?" he asked as they came to end of the bridge where they would enter the Right Bank. James told him that the fortified gate was very similar in design to the one at Douglas Castle.

As they entered the market center they had to stop as a paveur was laying some stone, or paving for the main street. While they waited for the street workers to make their repairs James asked his mother about the government of Paris. "Who runs the city?" he inquired. "Several hundred years ago a provost was chosen to so lead them," Ellie told them, noting that this method of rule was specific to this city and not practiced in Scotland. "They formed guilds to protect their work or trade and the king issued them specific charters. Paris is not ruled directly by this king; the provost that I spoke about holds the power for this government." The political and ecclesiastical centers were on the Ile de la Cité, while the educational institutions rested on the Left Bank, where they mainly spoke and wrote in Latin Lady Douglas explained. In front of them now was a very long and narrow carriage transporting passengers to do their shopping. Because the cart paths of the Right Bank were so narrow the horses drawing the wagons were hitched in tandem; one horse in front of the other. "Better to ride a horse I think," commented Hugh, seeing the perspiration on the foreheads of the passengers in the crowded vehicle. The streets reverberated with sounds;

clerics singing on the river could barely be heard above the din of horses' shoes clanking on stone cobble or wooden planks and the clamoring voices of the merchants hawking their wares.

The sun was shining brightly and the day promised to be filled with fun. Eleanora intended only fond memories for her James during the remainder of their stay in France; these would be their last days together for some years. Riding through the cart paths Ellie was recounting her spending to date; figuring out her expenses and available funds for today's adventure. The inheritance from Helisant was barely touched she reflected; leaving ample coinage for their extravagances. Everyone would satisfy their wants of purchases today Ellie vowed to herself. The clip clop of horses' hooves on the pavement gave a melodious sound to their travels. They passed many different kinds of merchants; fashioners of metals: gold, silver and copper were on the bridge; the forges were found on the other side of the river they were told; that is where they could find merchants selling armaments that could be fashioned on an anvil.

The Douglases continued to ride their palfreys through the narrow streets on the Right Bank; arriving near some interesting shops they dismounted to walk, to visit the merchants one by one. The lovely aromas of freshly baked breads and the pungent smells of potages of meats and fish cooked with fresh herbs and spices filled the air as they walked through the centers of trade. "Look, a monkey," cried Archie as they passed a shop where a woman was winding wool, with her pet monkey sitting beside her. "Such pets are common in Paris," said Ellie. "And no; we are Scots, sheltering only animals that earn their keep," she said anticipating his next question; desiring such a pet for his very own.

The streets were crowded; a muleteer was leading his burden beast to the next shop, prodding it as the mule wanted to stop. But stop he did; much to the chagrin of his keeper the animal sat down in the middle of the rue. Lords and shopkeepers were conversing under brightly colored awnings that decorated the fronts of buildings; children of many ages were being led or chased by their nurses running through the gates, cobbled streets, as wee hounds and harriers and odd breeds of small dogs the Douglases did not know were playing or scampering through these rues, then waiting outside of the butcher shops and fishmongers to beg for food. Ladies of the manors were assisted by their servants, going from merchant to merchant to purchase their needs for the day or to shop specifically for colorful silks and precious velvets for the elaborate parties on the Ile de la Cité.

The Right Bank was thriving with activity; everyone felt the excitement, and the Douglases were enlivened, so many things to see and do! In front of one shop there was a man holding a hooded falcon. Sir David told the lads that pet birds and birds of prey were a big business on the Right Bank. Ellie had always admired goldfinches and stopped to take a peak; interrupted by her wee son, "No Mother, we are Scots, such birds don't earn their way," Archie teased her. Ellie giggled, knowing she walked right into that remark from her youngest son. Their horses had been secured away by their men at arms; taken to the water troughs where several petite rues or wee paths converged.

Some of these passageways that led from the main rue were of stone and rubble others were of wood built over dirt paths through which the waters of small streams flowed. These small water ways had raw sewage in them and during the heat of the day were unpleasant to be near. And as they made their way down the streets they passed a man with a sheep slung over his shoulder on his way to the slaughter house. The smell from the carcass and from the remains of other animals made the younger lads gag. They had seen animals killed before on their manors but leaving the decaying remains piled in heaps, lying in the sun made for a wretched stench that turned their stomachs. This was Archie's first experience in a bustling marketplace; he did not like the smells of the waste water or slaughterhouse and the wee rodents all about, even in the daytime made him pine for the expansive countryside of Essex he told them. "And the hoot of the owl?" teased James, knowing his younger brother was once afraid of them.

Archie assured James he was older now and not scared; then he turned to Ellie to ask more questions. "Mother, do so many people live in so small a place as this in our Scotland?" he asked. Lady Douglas had not heard him; she was just entering one of the tailor shops, spying some bundled rolls of brocade in green and gold displayed in the doorway. James answered his brother's queries instead; telling him that Berwick once boasted of such great business of trade, a leading port for wool and many other wares he said. "But after the barbarous siege by Edward, the burgh has held but of a fifth of its old glory. And the same of its inhabitants, most had been killed during the invasion and replaced by English moving in, to leave there most quickly too," he told the lad. Sir David and the three Douglas sons continued to the next shop; a blacksmith was making small weaponry and all of them stood to watch with great interest.

It was not long after when Ellie and Ana and Maudie, Archie's nurse, had rejoined Sir David and his entourage. The knight helped distribute Ellie's packages to be carried by their men at arms. Lady Douglas was exuberant; proudly leading her wee clan through Paris and the Right Bank; later she would take them to the Left Bank and the shops on the Petit Pont she promised. They were shopping merrily in every emporium through the district. As they made their way through merchants' rows and shops, Ellie continued her history lessons for her family. "The Romans, the ancient conquerors that came to Paris and later to our Scotland, left a legacy of new buildings here. they built vineyards, baths and amphitheaters in those early days," she told them, explaining in great detail the city's historical past.

Archie gave her a quizzical grimace. "What is that, *amphi-?*" he wanted to know. James happily responded; telling his younger brother all about the ancient arenas where great gladiators would fight lions, sometimes other men in the Roman amphitheatre. Hugh was stunned; men were once fighting great creatures as well as each other here, he questioned? James told them all about the great lions from Africa. "Kings and princes so collect these beasts to grace their castles and great estates in testimony to their own manly ways," he chuckled. Then he smiled, remembering the times when Gilley used to share such stories with him; elaborating about his adventures during the Crusades; places where he traveled on his way to the Levant.

Hugh asked James many more questions about the Roman gladiators. "Have you ever seen a knight fight a lion?" The squire told him no; he only heard about such contests from Lord Douglas, in stories that he told him. Ana was chuckling; telling Ellie how pleased she was to see that James was responding to all the wee lads' inquiries. "That he would ask his father about everything," she recalled, thinking especially of those early journeys when the Douglases traveled to Dublin and Mann or to the Highlands of their kin in Morayshire. Ellie smiled and added, "And Gilley would most answer him; so many things that my dear husband knew about. When James would ask him to explain, this lass would be most eager to hear his good response; to learn from Gilley while he taught our James, sharing vast knowledge from his travels and life's experiences." She sighed; recalling the teaching ways of William.

This day found Sir David and his squires partaking of the grand offerings of the Right Bank as well; enjoying the vast marketplace as they attended Lady Douglas and her family. The old warrior favored escorting his surrogate family through France; the Ile de la Cité, the Right Bank and the Left Bank were favorite haunts of the English knight. Only Archie seemed to disapprove of Paris; Right or Left Bank he did not care for either he told them pointedly. Sir David took James and Hugh with him to find a special currier that dealt in armor.

Ellie and Ana were going with Archie and his nurse to find additional tailor shops; to search for more silks and lovely velvets with ermine for Ellie. The youngest son of Gilley was beside himself; he wanted to go to currier merchants and purchase leather sword belts and armor with his brothers. Ellie had other ideas; he was to have a surcote and a matching hat she told him. "Will the hat be of fur?" he inquired, now showing some interest in the tailor shop. Ellie threw a knowing look to Ana; then she told him most politely that wee lads received fur hats when they became a squire if they were lucky and not one day before!

Later the family reunited to make their way together to the other side of the island, crossing the Seine, going towards the south and east they went through another portcullis and by the many shops of the Petit Pont. Under each bridge there were mills that provided the flour for the city. "That mill is owned by the brethren of the Temple," she pointed out to her sons, as they admired the attire of some of the warrior monks standing outside. At the end of the bridge was a toll booth or a weigh station; all goods entering the city had to be taxed by weight or quantity, Ellie carefully explained.

There were swine herders and boats carrying wheat or fire wood; all these goods had to be imported for use in Paris, Sir David told them taking turns with Lady Douglas to answer the wee ones' questions. The biggest business seemed to take place along the paved streets where young lads were carrying buckets of water on poles. Archie was busy talking when he should have been looking forward; paying attention to where he was going. Had it not been for the swift action of Hugh to grab his brother he would have walked right into a swinging bucket full of water. James chuckled; the wee lad gave his older brother the furled brow of Douglas discontent for his laughter. Quietly, when the older brother moved ahead of them Archie thanked Hugh for his courtesy; the younger sons were on a temporary hiatus from their usual sibling rivalry.

Their next stop was an apothecary; Sir David told them that there were several such shops along the way there with many doctors, practicing physicians who carried their trade to the streets, treating patients as they came upon them for a fee. Hugh was mesmerized by the herbs and medicines being produced by the grinding of pestles. Cures and remedies were being hawked by these merchants just as readily as peddlers called out patties and pastries for sale. Ellie purchased some eel patties; the children had ones of pork which were spiced deliciously they said.

Ana had some pastries with soft cheese and one with custard that she gave back because it was not too fresh. "One has to be most careful with such things," she told the wee ones. They all ordered fruit pastries from another merchant three doors away; in a shop, not selling from a cart. "These are much finer, aye," said Ana. Then a shopkeeper called out "Beggar," to a shoeless man hovering in a corner where the building walls met. "Take this bowl and finish it," he said. Hugh was touched by the generosity and to another man he put part of his pastry in the begging bowl. Such impoverished people were not found in Essex or in Scotland he mused; at least not in their wee villages, the manors of their mother.

Paris and the Right and Left Banks were filled with many prosperous people. But they were also occupied by less fortunate folk; beggars including lepers who would stand apart from the crowds, their bowls put out as well for charity donations. Pilgrims who came to Saint-Jacques were offered food; breads, cakes and any other morsels that shopkeepers had left over were gathered and given to them freely. "It is considered necessary to be charitable to such pilgrims," explained their mother, "they are all to be treated with much kindness." And Sir David added, "Those who provide these pilgrims lodging are to be blessed with the visits from St. Jacques and the Savior for their generosity, or so the stories tell us," he said proudly; the older knight was pleased to provide them with tales of his own teaching to take home with them to Essex.

James was lingering behind them; bothered by the unrelenting teasing of a blind beggar. His father had always told him to show compassion for those less fortunate. He went to the sightless man and put a wee coin into his hand, whispering the value to the man so he would not be cheated. "Take this back to the hospice and know that you are one of God's special children," he said referring the Champ Pourri that had been established by France's Crusader king to house the blind. Just then an older woman came out of a nearby shop and led the blind man away; she was his wife. When she saw the coin she came back to thank the lad and told him she would say a blessing for him at the church that day.

The Douglases ended their excursion and extensive shopping exhausted yet cheerfully contented with their exploits. James had a new gambeson that would be delivered to him by tomorrow next before they departed for Lovaine. He also ordered a hauberk, fitted to him this day as was required; but it would not be ready for some weeks. He told his mother that the currier would send it with some other goods to the manor of Lady Agnes. "We found a special sword belt with long straps and buckles for adjustment that you can give to your brother Thomas," said Sir David.

Lady Douglas examined the fine leatherwork purchased as a gift for the new lord in minority of the Lovaine estates. "The crafting is of high quality and the carvings are most intricate," she said, complimenting her knight for his selection. "And those gauntlets," exclaimed Ellie as she looked at Sir David's hands. "They are new as well? This lady will make a gift of them," she informed the knight, giving him the coinage. Sir David was somewhat embarrassed; he had not expected gifts in Paris. He thanked her quietly; knowing it was her way and William's too when he was alive to be so generous.

They were all returning to where their men at arms held their palfreys. Ellie was looking over the pack animals, amazed at the number of large parcels and baskets containing smaller packages that were now tied to their backs. "And what did you buy?" she asked turning to Hugh. Of all the Douglas men only this middle son was right handed like his mother. James and Archie favored their left hands in both writing and in weaponry like le Hardi, requiring an adjustment for Sir David in his training. Hugh proudly held out his new prized possession; an odd acquisition for a youth dreaming only to serve his God and the Holy Mother Church, he had purchased his first sword belt today. "With lots of room for growth," Sir David assured Ellie. "My wee warrior monk, most like the Bishop Wishart," she teased her Hubicus, and he laughed, smiling at everyone, delighted with the prized 'war belt' as he called it. Archie had been lagging way behind his mother with his nurse; a long day it was for the wee lad. He was very tired and had been walking slowly until he saw the pack horses with their purchases from the tailor on top of one basket. He ran and grabbed his special prize from the basket contents.

"Look, a fine hat to match my surcote!" he exclaimed to James and Hugh." See what mother bought for this lad!" he announced proudly. James remembered his first hat that Ellie and Ana made him 'for Parliament' as he liked to say then. He made a fuss over his brother's first adornment, knowing it was a big event for the lad. "That's one fair hat Archie; there now, let me see it on you," said the squire. "Look at this Hugh, a fancy chapeau for our dear brother." Hugh said he was quite impressed; telling Archie how much older he looked. "Most the age of a page, would you not agree James?" he asked. James concurred most heartily. The Douglas lads were laughing and sharing and enjoying all their treasures, happy with their day in Paris as they took in the many fine establishments on the Grand Pont, the Right Bank; finishing their day's adventure, acquiring much booty at the Petit Pont as well.

Ellie was admiring Hugh's new sword belt and she was pleased to hear they had coinage still remaining, that they returned to her. "That fair shopping has never before so happened!" she exclaimed knowing that if William were alive there would be many more purchases and not one p. remaining! Ana was pleasantly surprised with a gift from her girl; Ellie had bought her some fine cloth for a surcote; some good trim of brocade for the sleeves, with a remnant of velvet for the insets. An extravagance Ana protested, trying not to accept the gift; but Ellie would not hear it. "It is done!" Eleanora told her and Ana knew she meant it. Hugh rubbed his hands over the material, feeling the quality of the cloth. He really loved Ana and was happy his mother bought her something to remember Paris. "Oh Ana; when we go to St. Mary's most on Sundays, what finery will you have to wear!" he said happily. "And look Hugh, this is what I found for our dear Muriel!' his mother boasted. "This fine silk of the color blue she fancies most and some fair velvet for the mantel; what brilliant hues and fine quality of goods; a grand variety to so choose from in these dear shops," Ellie said; impressed with all the lovely things she found.

LOVAINE BELGIUM-Lady Agnes had sent her best men at arms and two knights to escort the Douglases from Paris to Lovaine; a contingency almost unheard of for such a wee journey. But she was not taking chances with her kin; dear Eleanora with her sons and household were not to be molested by the insurgents of Flanders she vowed! When these brave men of Brabant arrived to join the others of Ellie's men at arms, they made a fair army of travelers, heading north from Paris for Lovaine. It took almost one week for the entourage to reach Flanders and the manor of her kin. "Dear Agnes," cooed Ellie relieved to arrive in Lovaine at last, "how many years has it been?" Too many she was told by the gracious lady of Brabant. Lady Agnes was a short cuddly woman; her ruddy face beamed with a broad smile that warmed the room. She loved children though all of hers were now grown. "Come here," she said to the wee lads, "let me take a look at Lovaine men from Scotland!" she exclaimed. And to James she said, "You must be my new squire." She eyed the tall, raven haired youth up and down and then turned to Ellie with a playful grin. "You only told me he was tall and strong, with a good head on his shoulders. You didn't say he was handsome as this!" she chuckled.

Figure XLV-Part One; the canal surrounding the city of Lovaine in Belgium

Ellie introduced her household and thanked Lady Agnes for the escort. "This lass was worried for our journey through Flanders after word of Courtrai came to us," Lady Douglas confided. "There now dear Eleanora, you are safe with us in this manor. And the count's men at arms are nearby; no one will dare come here to do us any harm," she boasted. Lady Agnes showed everyone around and bid them all to take of feasting and some wine, with bountiful portions of fresh ale that the children could enjoy. "Tomorrow James we will introduce you to the rest of our good household. At the duchy manor house and castle there are daily games of tilting and others that you may have seen; or so this lady has been told," she pleasantly informed him. The Brabant lady was indeed looking forward to having a handsome and polite young man around the manor house again. "Eleanora, how fortunate to have two sons remaining; that with my only son most married now and at his manors I am quite alone," she sighed. James told her that anything she might need doing to let him know.

Lady Douglas rode the lands of the manor early the next morning with her sons; to show them the estates that she once visited with her mother Helisant. They had a fair escort of Lovaine men at arms to take them everywhere; no reason to take chances she decided. Lady Douglas told them about the history; the Duke of Lower Lorraine, known as Godefroid I, the Bearded Count of Lovaine and Brussels, from whom the Lovaines of Essex were descended. "And his successors were known with these brave names for their noble ways: 'the Warrior' and the 'Magnanimous' and 'le Debonnair," she said proudly, "followed then by John the 'Victorious'. His son John is known as the Pacific and is the Duke of Brabant today. He is a wise ruler; bestowing liberties upon his subjects is what Agnes has so told your mother."

Figure XLVI-Part One; Lovaine, Belgium is the ancestral home of Eleanora Lovaine Douglas; this ancient cathedral sustained the onslaught of the Third Reich in WWII

Pausing briefly to catch her breath, Ellie related the sad story of a tournament that occurred eight years ago; "John the Victorious my kin had married one of King Edward's daughters," she began. She was careful to explain about the round table in Bar-sur-Aube that had been called to celebrate the marriage of another of Edward's daughters to the Duke of Brittany, the Duke of Brabant's new brother in law. "This John was most experienced; over seventy tournaments in England, Germany and France had he so attended, to die at his first encounter with a French knight," Ellie said sadly. The king of France was opposed to tournaments; unlike King Edward he would not participate or host them the Douglas lads were told. "This squire has much to learn of the arms of France," sighed James; unsure of a monarch who disdained such entertainment; protested regulated jousts for his knights as beneath one's dignity.

Figure XLVII-Part One; Lovaine Belgium

The days flew by and too soon for Ellie it was time to say goodbye to James; to leave for Essex from Antwerp was her plan, as she sat thinking in the great hall of the manor of Lady Agnes. "Because of the hostilities, the Battle of Courtrai, do I pray to sail from the larger port directly to our Essex," she said speaking to James; but she was distracted by the thoughts of leaving him alone in Brabant. The Douglas squire was feeling the exuberance of youth beginning a new journey in his life tempered with pangs of loneliness for his family. "Mother, that I will miss you most as well," he said, knowing her thoughts from the grimace on her face.

"Always remember us, this mother too," she began. James chuckled. "Dear Lady El, you believe that I could ever forget our years together, those happy times we shared with father?" he asked, amused by her silly thoughts. "Know this: I hold the memory here within me; etched so permanently most like the stone carvings of the ancient Celts. When this squire returns you will see a man of great resolve to return his family to our rightful inheritance. Douglasdale will be ours again dear mother; this lad does will it so!"

Ellie's eyes carefully surveyed her son; in six months he would be seventeen, almost the age she was when she first met his father in Ayrshire. James had been her main support these last four years since her husband lost his life in the Tower. Now he would be separated from her for at least two years or more. "How selfish of this lass to think only of herself," she said, rising to hug him close to her. "That you would miss us most as well, I had not thought of it," she concluded as her tears told of her anguish for the parting. "That you will have your Fortis with you to remind yourself of those days in Douglasdale," Ellie whispered to him hopefully.

Figure XLVIII-Part One; Steen or stone castle in Antwerp was once the entry point for the medieval port

ANTWERP-The ancient port of Antwerp was further away from England but safer than Bruges since the hostilities in Flanders began. The port was actually a margraviate or border province on the River Scheldt. There was an abbey there, St. Michael's Abbey on Caloes that the Douglases explored, continuing again their education of such places. They did not stay at the abbey; they stayed with Lovaine kin of Agnes in that city, near Steen Castle that was the gateway to the port on the river. Ellie was planning to say her goodbyes at Lovaine when Lady Agnes announced a change of plans: James would accompany the Douglas household on their journey to Antwerp after all. Lady Agnes needed some men at arms for her son's travels to Calais, so James the squire was now part of the Lovaine escort party for the Douglases.

Sir David took James and Ellie down to the meet with sea captains; to find a suitable cog for the family's journey. The sun was shining brightly over the harbor; the smell of salt air refreshing as they rode down to the shoreline; the docks were crowded, bustling with activity. Ellie was hopeful she could find a ship sailing to Essex that would land them closer to her manor. But they were disappointed; discovering they had little choice in vessels or destinations. All the cogs in Antwerp were sailing for one of the Cinque Ports; or some other destination, too far north up the eastern coast of England. The larger cogs they required seldom sailed to southern Essex they were informed; most of those ports were very shallow and could only be used for small fishing craft. So now they wearily went from ship to ship, looking for a suitable cog that was large enough to carry their entire household across the channel. James and Sir David spoke for sometime with the owner of one of the last vessels on the docks; a man from Hythe. The Captain's pleasant manner and concern for their needs persuaded them: the Douglas household would sail homeward with him.

Captain de Lacy was an experienced sea captain; and his cog was the size they required and well built. But unlike the other large vessels originating from the Cinque Ports, those from Hythe were never called upon by the king to be part of the royal fleet. Hythe like Hastings was an original Cinque Port, receiving its charter from Edward in 1278. The English king used the larger sailing ships from these ports through an agreement in their charters called *Ship Service*; put to wide use during his wars with Scotland. These consigned Cinque Port cogs sailed frequently between Berwick on Tweed and England. But because of an unspoken agreement with the Lord of Saltwood, his manor residing within the Hythe port, it seemed that these ships were overlooked for Ship Service. Ellie was very happy to hear this; breathing a huge sigh of relief. When Lord Douglas was a prisoner at Douglas Tower in Berwick Castle he was put in irons, transferred to the hold of such a vessel; removed forever from his Scotland. He sailed south to the Thames and was then taken by barge to the Tower of London where he met his untimely end. Ellie was never sure of the name of the English cog that took him from her that day; but she knew for certain now that this de Lacy ship was not the one.

The jolly little Norman sea captain was very pleased to transport the travelers back to England; assuring the Douglases that he had the extra room required for their horses as well. Ellie paid her fare, showed her license for travel and then mounted her palfrey for the ride back to the manor. It is done she mused; soon they would be home in Stebbinge Park. James and Ellie rode their horses up the hill from the coastline saying little to each other;

knowing this was the final day together for some time. James broke the silence first; to quietly assure her that he would work diligently at his studies and his training at arms. "And you will receive regular reports in letters that I will write," he said, trying to cheer her, the only mother he ever knew. "And I will keep you well informed of the family and when I can, the words of Scotland will I send," she promised faithfully.

James continued talking; he wanted to share his thoughts with her as he began this new life on his own. "Mother, this lad is most grateful for these fair arrangements made on my behalf and for the coinage given me most generously by your fair self," he began. "That it is important for you to know my true feelings; this lad is most excited about training and studying in Lovaine," James admitted, but he had more to say and Ellie let him go on without interruption. "Before this squire does return to Essex will I find my way to Paris for some time as well," he told her, pausing to look at her most poignantly. "I need to know if this son is the measure of le Hardi; do I have his courage, will I act with honor when so challenged, living on my own?" These were the deep sentiments of his heart he told her.

Figure XLIX-Part One; Hythe is better known today for beautiful beaches than the bustling Cinque Port of medieval days

Lady Eleanora smiled at her son; she expected nothing less and told him so. "Thank you for your honesty of words dear James; but do not fear you are indeed the measure of one named William. This mother does so know it!" she praised him, beaming in approval as she spoke. As they arrived at the manor house near Antwerp Hugh and Archie were scampering out to greet them; running hard and laughing. Maudie's son Andrew was with them too today. "Did you find a sailing ship?" asked Hugh. Ellie nodded yes. "Perhaps this lass will stay in Lovaine," she teased, suggesting that if James wanted a challenge he should return to Essex with the wee ones leaving her in Flanders. James chuckled at the last suggestion. Having bared his truth on their ride back he was quite relieved and in a jovial mood. James picked Archie up and swung him wildly, high over his head. "You best behave while this squire learns his training. Our mother will be sending me reports; should I hear discontent with actions of one wee Archie will I return to Essex swiftly! You will answer to the point of my sword!" he threatened with his silly smirk. Archie demanded that James put him down, "the noo!" he shouted. "When you return will I be a page and taller than my brother; you will pay for your sorry words this day," he snickered, taunting his older brother, daring him to pick him up again, standing there defiantly with his hands on his hips.

Figure L-Part One; the ancient port of Antwerp

Ellie interceded, standing between her sons she was chuckling to herself as she spoke her words, laughing at their feigned quarrel. Hugh was acting silly now as well, taunting James that he might pick him up, which he would have had not Ellie stopped him. "Kind sirs, this is neither the time nor place for these antics, we are guests in this good manor," their mother said as she begged them with her eyes to stop their playful sparring. "Oh mother, this lad recalls when our father would so pick you up and you would call him *Sholto Beast*," James teased, reminding her of those happy days. He walked at her side going into the manor. "I remember most when our father held you high over his head, roaring in laughter at his prize," he said with animated tones while laughing with her. "And you would giggle, then as quickly feign your indignation as he carried you off!" Ellie chuckled as she threw her son a knowing smile. "I miss that noble knight most when I think of his silly ways," she sighed. "There will never be another like your father for this lass," she assured him.

Then James stopped her and turned her round to face him, speaking his words very slowly, solemnly he said, "Promise me: you will never re-marry; at least not until this squire makes his plea with Edward for our lands reseised." Ellie nodded, "That pledge I make most happily," she told him, smiling proudly as she spoke. Lady Douglas never wanted to marry again;

William was her true love for all eternity as she told her husband often when he was alive. Her only fear was Edward; this king yet held her dower that he might force a marriage to reward a yeoman for his service. Ellie's intentions were to prolong her widow's mourning; growing older, returning to Scotland with her sons might eliminate the king's control of her or a knight's desire for her hand. And the longer she waited the more widows there seemed to be in England. These heiresses without husbands were growing more in number with the wars; men of lower station could have their pick among noble ladies with fine dowers, she mused, happy with her plan so far to avert another marriage.

STEBBINGE PARK OCTOBER 1302-The drudgery of travel lasted another six days until they finally arrived home at their manor in Stebbing. Ellie and her wee clan of Essex were greeted by a smiling Lady Elizabeth; the Scottish widow who came to tutor Hugh, Archie and Maudie's son Andrew. Everyone had stories to exchange as the cellarers and kitchen servants brought out a fine feast for everyone to enjoy. "The good de Lindsay men at arms went on hunt most yesterday; hoping you would arrive home soon," said the Fife widow. Lady Elizabeth was happy to have joined the Essex household she told them proudly, as Eleanora extended her greetings to the latest Scottish member of her Stebbing family. It was good to be back home even if it was England, Ellie mused. The lady from Fife brought with her some news of Scotland from the de Lindsays. "Here is a wee letter," she said with that broad accent of the highland clans. Elizabeth came from Elgin, kin to the de Morays but was living in Fife as the widow of her knight who had kin from that shire. Her patriotic husband found his way to Dumfries but to loose his life in the siege of Caerlaverock.

Ellie introduced the lads to their new tutor. Then Elizabeth announced she had a gift for Lady Douglas from Sir Alex; excusing herself she returned with a wee pup, a Deerhound but twelve weeks old and growing! Eleanora was thrilled. "Dear Alex, that he remembered most my birthday," she said surprised as she read his letter. Then she recalled that his birth was celebrated about the ides of April, the same week as her Gilley's day while Lady Alice de Lindsay celebrated hers near the ides of October just like Ellie's birthday. This odd occurrence gave the families reason to so celebrate their special days together, gathering every year to have a Ceilidh when they were living in Scotland.

The lads were cuddling the wee hound when Hugh spoke up, "What ever shall we name him mother?" he asked. Eleanora knew at once. "We will call him Lindsay for that kind family who gave us our new Deerhound and he will sleep with me!" she chuckled, pleased to have company again in her bed. No one celebrated birthdays that she knew except Ana and herself until she met William; he was the first laird she ever encountered to plan feasts and to have gifts in honor of that day, or any other such event he could think to celebrate. She gazed sweetly at the pup; her very own hound. "This sweet laddie is indeed a cherished gift today," Ellie said, glowing with delight. How thoughtful of the de Lindsays to recall William's ways, with a gift for her special day Ellie mused. "This lass to work with the groom so now to train you!" she sighed happily at the thought of such pleasant amusement for herself.

FEBRUARY 1303-A letter sent from Lanarkshire at Christmas had just arrived at Stebbinge Park; a sad message from the de Galbrathes of the passing of Lady Willelma, her late husband's older sister. Willa's daughters were fighting Edward for their inheritance; having to prove their relationship as heirs and validate their ages. They asked Ellie if she would write and swear for them so they might share in their parent's manor of Dalserf given in freehold from their great grandfather the Comyn. Ellie made her plans immediately to meet with her solicitors the day next. "How sad that all we are most able to do for these dear lasses is but to attest to their birthrights to that patrimony," she said sadly. "Dear Willelma, a sweet woman; a lonely widow too for all these years after her good husband left this world so long ago," she cried some now as she spoke her words. "All that knew our William are most gone," she sobbed to Ana. Then she remembered Gilley's hopeful words said long ago, the beliefs of the Celts: with a death comes a birth. Perhaps to have some good tidings of a wee one; this lass does need some words of that, she sighed, wiping her tears dry.

Two days later Ellie was in the great hall reviewing her accounts with her steward John le Parker who had just returned from Scotland. "These fees are barely one in five the settlements of six years ago, they keep going down and never to regain their former value," she protested sadly, wondering what she would do for sustenance in the year to come. Le Parker told her of the devastation; the many tenants that fled, with few men remaining in Ayrshire or Wigtonshire to work the lands. In Berwick and in Fife there were some rents that he collected. "Not much has changed in Scotland since two years ago when we traveled north together," Ellie stated flatly, frustrated to realize that her work these past twenty months, meeting with lawyers and making pleas to Edward's chamberlain had all been in vain. "Your lands near Craig Douglas are deserted most as well," her steward said ruefully, speaking now of the dower lands she received from William le Hardi. "The English control much land in the Borders, building a peel in Selkirk for their garrison," the accountant explained. "But the Scots still hold for many loyalties near the Forest; and they are collecting fees if there are some to collect." Ellie knew she would have to watch expenses now and return to court to beg again from Edward for her dower.

Scotland was going through another turbulent change; Edward's control would grow in the next twelve months to where most of the nobility came to terms with the king and submitted to him. On the fifth of March "the evil bishop" as Edward called the Scottish rebel, made his declaration of reluctant submission: that he held his temporalities of his see of Glasgow from King Edward, Lord of Scotland. This revolting admission, to kiss the gospels and make his pledge to the butcher of Berwick did not come easily for that great patriot, but rather with an aching heart; or fingers crossed in his pledge of fealty. Bishop Wishart was temporarily in the English camp it so appeared; his armor tucked away in a war chest for three more years. William Wallace just returned to his country from his journeys first to France, then to Rome. He must have been disheartened to hear that Bishop Wishart and many others had come to pledge their fealty to that pagan king, the enemy of Scotland. Edward was sending his lieutenant Sir John de Segrave north to Edinburgh; perhaps to prepare for another English invasion in the spring; to seek out any resistance from rebels and suppress it.

Figure LI-Part One; the back steps of Glasgow Cathedral where Bishop Wishart was purported to have held meetings with William Wallace

On the way north Edward's vassals and their large army encountered a band of Scots led by Simon Fraser and the Comyn; Wallace too was believed to be with these brave patriots. Ellie received word in Essex from the de Lindsays; the Scots won a great battle at Roslin. The foul rumors of that encounter with the Scots told that her kin Sir John de Segrave was fearfully wounded. The words written said the knight was left for nearly dead by his men and captured by the Scots that very day. From his phrasing of some passages in the letter Ellie realized that Sir Alex was back in the rebels' camp. "Ana, our Alex has rejoined the cause for Scotland's freedom though not openly," she sighed, concerned for him and for her wee son, the page she planned to send to Scotland in service to his God father. "What should we do about our Archie?" she asked worried to send him to the de Lindsays now. "Were Edward to discover Sir Alex's disloyalty he could seize of the remainder of their Lothiane estates and their Barnweill most as well. Our wee lad to be right there in the middle of the war, at the mercy of dear Edward!" spitting out the tyrant's name as she said it.

Lady Elizabeth was coming in from the withdrawing room where she just finished the language lessons with the three lads for the day. She had overheard Ellie's concern about Sir Alex. "Dear Eleanora, fear not, Sir Alex will always prevail; he has a golden tongue much like his kin William Lamberton, to free himself most often from the ill will of that pagan Edward," Elizabeth said trying to comfort Ellie. "And you know most truly that today's enemy of Edward becomes the next one to pledge his fealty to that king. It was you who told me our dear patriot and good friend Bishop Wishart has now come to so submit." Ellie decided she would wait to reevaluate the situation in a year; things seemed to take their turn in Scotland most every day. When will this unrest end she wondered to herself? She continued to read about the Battle at Roslin as the Scots were proudly calling the rout of the English and the part now written by Lady Lindsay. "And the gossip tells us the true reason for that invasion; a de Segrave knight, Sir John, was most in search of one fair lass: Margaret Ramsey, sister of that laird of Dalhousie," Ellie continued to relate the story to the ladies, all of whom were now very interested and excited to hear of romance and courtly love!

From the words of the lady from East Lothiane and Ayrshire, Eleanora regaled them with a great tale of intrigue and chivalry; the fair Margaret had consented to marry Sir Henry St. Clair, apparently turning a snub to this English knight who was whispered to have some interest in her wooing. Ellie told them that Lady Lindsay must have it wrong; Edward's lieutenant and her kin Sir John de Segrave was already married and nearing fifty. "Perhaps he means to say the young knight, Nicky's son, the one our James was squire to at Newmarket three years ago?" Ellie questioned out loud. If on the other hand the knight in question was really Nicky's brother John, Ellie would not be shocked. Sir John was nothing like her favorite cousin. Nicholas was a moral and truthful knight; redoubtable like her William; likely to end up on the wrong side of Edward someday, she reflected.

"Tell us more," the ladies giggled, begging her to continue; thinking of the handsome Scottish knight St. Clair rushing into battle to defend his country against the invading forces of de Segrave and the English suitor of his betrothed. "This tale she refers to is sheer gossip," Ellie said to Ana and Lady Elizabeth. "They have the wrong lady in this story too I fear." Turning to her tutor from Fife she asked, "Is there a Lady Margaret Ramsey in Bonnyrigg?" Lady Elizabeth was unable to confirm the lass' name. "A sister of this laird of Dalhousie does reside there or so I thought but she was much younger than the lass Lady Lindsay has described. Perhaps to be a niece?" she suggested. Ellie was unsure; she remembered now that her dower lands residing in Glencorse were nearby; perhaps a word from John le Parker might come that would confirm the story of their neighbors. Ellie continued reading; concentrating on the relevant story of the battle. The Scots mustered hastily at Biggar. "But were clearly outnumbered three to one by the English army that was approaching from the south," she continued telling them. "Simon Fraser, the Red Comyn, the Fleming of Cumbernauld, the Knights Hospitallers near Linlithgow, all; the Scottish lairds were calling out their men at arms to join them in the muster, to buckle on their armor and thwart the English army that was advancing."

Ellie read with more excitement as the tempo of the writing increased in intensity. "These brave patriots rode all the way from Biggar where they mustered, moving north and east towards Bonnyrigg, traveling the entire night," she read with praise in every word for these Scottish heroes. "They must have been exhausted and hungry when they arrived," sympathized Ana as she continued to listen while Ellie read. Ellie looked up from the letter. "It seems there was not just one but three battles that were fought and won that day," she declared. "Most amazing these brave men to fight so hard; when riding all that way," sighed Elizabeth. "Where they get their strength I do not know," she said in awe of the brave Scots' tenacity and courage.

"Sir John de Segrave and his brother Nicholas," Ellie let out a scream when she read with utter horror that her beloved cousin Nicky was at the battle. Her heart was beating furiously, fearful for his life! Lady Lindsay had written that John de Segrave was wounded badly; no word came of Nicholas who was apparently coming to the aid of his injured brother. Ellie kept reading; apparently both the de Segraves were freed; ransomed she conjectured, though she did not know what happened to the other fourteen English knights taken that Sunday in the battle. "A knight named Neville led a second English brigade," Ellie related to her focused listeners. "Perhaps he came to rescue the injured de Segrave?" Ana said, putting forth her theory on the matter. Elizabeth asked if there was any word about that Lady Ramsey and her knight.

Ellie went back to a different part of the letter. She read through it and then proclaimed aloud, "Sir Henry and Lady Margaret are expected most to marry the fair rumors so proclaim, at the St. Clair stronghold near the battle site, known as Rosslyn Tower," Ellie advised them. She put down the letter now, sighing with relief as she had read through every word and found no further mention of problems for her favorite cousin Nicky. The identity of the injured English soldier however was still a mystery; perhaps confused by the presence of two such knights named John de Segrave, Ellie surmised. The rest of the ladies at the table were concerned for more frivolous matters; gushing over the story of a knight winning the hand of his fair lady. "This lass does know that tower house near Bonnyrigg, and Dalhousie Castle," said Elizabeth. "But such surprise to hear that one Henry St. Clair had joined now with the Scots. He was sworn to Edward last we knew," she told Lady Douglas and Ana. She further questioned the credibility of the tale while raising several other concerns. "From all our dissensions for the truth of rumors here; let's hope they won the battle!" chuckled Ellie. She was still intrigued about the scorned knight's identity, wondering which Sir John de Segrave was wounded in love and which one fell in battle. "And my dearest kin, that he comes home safe of life and limb," she prayed aloud. "Dear St. Bride, watch over my sweet Nicky."

Figure LII-Part One; Dalhousie Castle; the 13th century keep houses elegant theme rooms in this lovely castle-hotel today, with Falconry demonstrations on the grounds

"That was one beautiful story," said Ana, wiping the tears from her eyes. "Whoever the lady and her knight were, it makes no matter to this lass; I do love to hear a tale of love to so prevail, aye." Oh, to be so loved Eleanora said softly to herself, remembering her dear knight and how good it felt to cuddle into his manly chest. Weeks later the Essex Scots were informed that the story of their countrymen's victory at Roslin was indeed true; the valiant efforts of the patriots were reported and quickly in Paris and in Flanders too. It was confirmed that Nicholas was there at the battle and was not injured; his brother though badly wounded yet survived. But the story of courtly love and suitors scorned seemed yet to be a fable.

The Scots' encounter with the well equipped English army of armed horse and foot was a great success because of the gutsy determination of a makeshift group of Scottish freemen: farmers, sheep herders, tailors and merchants, warrior monks and a wee number of brave knights of Alba producing a tale that ignited the hearts of Scots everywhere. These heroic stories of brave patriots flew fast in the night to those living outside their homeland; arriving in the Ile de la Cité and Lovaine at the same time, just two weeks after the battle of Roslin was fought and won by Scots. James began a letter to his mother telling her of the conflict while Bishop Lamberton completed his congratulatory message to the Comyn after hearing of the rout. "Be of good heart," wrote William Lamberton, "for God's sake do not despair!"

APRIL 1303-A messenger from Castle Cary brought good news to Stebbinge Park; Lady Muriel Lovel was with child and would be returning to Essex to have her baby. Ellie was elated; a new Douglas in the family, a grandmother she would be at thirty-five! Just then Archie and Lindsay came running through the great hall, Hugh was lagging behind them. The three had just returned from the short ride to Little Dunmow Priory. "Father would be how old now?" asked Archie as he sat down next to Ellie at the massive trestle table where she sat reviewing the accounts of her manors. "He would be fifty-three, in three more days," she said. "That means that our James is now seventeen as well." Archie said that was old enough that his brother might get married. "Perhaps to find a fair lass in Paris for his bride, do you believe that could happen Mother?" he asked excitedly at the prospect. Ellie chuckled at her youngest son. "Archibald, he has only two things on his mind most now: to train as a knight and to become Lord Douglas. There is no room in his life for a lass."

Then she looked up at him, wondering aloud; "Where ever did that thought most come from Archie?" Hugh was laughing so hard, trying to contain his amusement as he went to sit down at the table to eat with them. But he was not chuckling because of what Archie had said; the lad was in hysterics because at just that moment the wee hound grabbed part of the half loaf of bread Archie was putting in his mouth. "Stop there you thieving hound!' said the victim of the crime. But Lindsay was already running away at high speed with his ill gotten gain; not stopping until he devoured his prize. "Fortunate for you lad that was not your mutton that he stole; there is more bread here for you," Ellie said motioning to the platter in the center of the table. The mother cautioned her son to be more careful, to pay attention to what he was doing. "Wasting food on the hound who eats quite well already is a luxury we no longer have," she scolded him some more, worried for her rents that were no longer coming.

Lindsay was returning to the hall; wagging his tale, hoping for more spoils at the table. "You sir have had enough this day!" said Archie as the Deerhound slinked back under the table. Ellie shared her good news with her sons. "Our fair sister is to come and stay with us," she proudly told them. "This mother is a grandmother to be, you sirs will be uncles of the lad or lass!" Hugh thought the idea was humorous. "Old Uncle Archibald," he teased his little brother. "How long will it take Mura's lad or lass to say your name, not like mine of Hugh," he taunted him. Archie was through being patient, his hot temper was roused; no one could tease him for his name. He stood up from the table taking umbrage to that taunt. He called a challenge to Hubicus; a contest of archery he suggested to settle their quarrel.

"This lad is no fool," said Hugh, "that all of Essex knows your prowess with that weapon. We'll have a contest of lance the rings," he told his brother. "This lad will inform Sir David of our competition," he said as he turned to find the knight in the courtyard of the manor. Archie stopped him; he was adamant, they were going to compete at archery he insisted. The wee lad not quite seven furled his brow like le Hardi and told his older brother clearly, they would compete by bow and arrow, his choice to have! Ellie interrupted her sons fearing this teasing had gotten out of hand. "There will be no competition this day good sirs; tomorrow I will call a match for both my sons, so that you may settle your disagreement: both archery and lance the rings will we have. For now it is the close of day with little light; someone would get hurt. It is done!" she told them, giving them the choice now to either have their meal or be off to their chamber. She wanted no further arguing between them. Ana was chuckling as she joined the family in the great hall. "Good knights to be, save your battles for your enemies; spare your mother more worries," she told them.

The lads ate in silence then one by one they departed to their chamber for the night. "Our Archie has the temper of our James," said Ellie. "He is most ready to have it out for little reason." Ana told her that he was just at an age; his stature was large for seven and he most wanted to be a man, grow more quickly in size; to become a squire the noo! "The youngest son is always the one to spout off most quickly," she told her girl, reminding her as well of William's temper. "My Gilley reserved his temper for Edward and the Melrose monks," she chuckled, knowing that his mother Martha must have had her hands full with his impatient temperament when he was Archie's age. Ellie suggested that perhaps Sir David should work them harder. "That they will have little left to fight each other at the end of the day," she said, devising a plan to contain their rowdy behavior.

Two weeks later Lady Lovel arrived with a nurse, who was as well with child and two maids in wait, escorted by some Lovel men at arms. Muriel was aglow with the anticipation of becoming a mother; she proclaimed her lay-in would be somewhere between the English quarter day of September, meaning the 29th and her own birthday, All Saints Day, the first of November. "Mother, you were so correct; this lass is most delighted to be with child and plan for the life of my own son or daughter," she cooed. "Your daughter loves her lad or lass most already," she told Ellie, genuinely happy that she was carrying Lord Lovel's child. Ellie told her that she had never seen her daughter more exquisite. "You are most jubilant!" said her mother. Ana was entering the great hall, hearing all the commotion she couldn't wait to greet her favorite Douglas child. "Mura," she said, beaming when she saw her. "Come here and make this lady happy." Ana chuckled as she hugged her wee lass, how good it felt to have her girl home again.

Archie and Hugh came running in to show their sister their new greyhound. "Lindsay is his name," said Archie. Then the wee knave did something very strange, he went close to his sister's belly where she carried her wee child. "Archibald, you may say Archie if that's too hard, I am to be your uncle," he said proudly. Hugh told him not to bother. "Hugh is a natural name to say; this lad will know my name first!" he declared, running out of the great hall with the wee Archie close behind followed by Lindsay, barking wildly. "What nonsense is this?" asked Muriel, not knowing what to make of her brothers' words and silly antics. Ellie and Ana were laughing too hard to explain at first. "That our Hugh has incited Archie to a feud. He told him that your child would not be able to say his name," chuckling as she told her daughter of their silliness; insinuating that Archie was taking the teasing to heart. "Younger brothers are most trying sometimes," said Mura, attempting to be a grownup lady though she was only turning fifteen herself this year.

Ana showed the lass and her maids in wait the chamber Ellie had prepared for Muriel in the rear of the manor; the lay-in would be across the hall, adjacent to the lord's chamber where her mother stayed alone with Lindsay. In the lovely alcove was the Douglas cradle; Gilley had the farrier turned wood-master first carve it for the birth of John. Now it would serve another generation of this noble family. The lovely carved box was almost three feet long, suspended now by two wooden posts that were intricately carved and gilded. No longer a floor cradle with foot rockers it was newly painted as well with cherubs on the sides with the Douglas arms on each end: a shield argent, with a fess azure surmounted by three mullets in chief.

"Oh mother, your fair painting here," said Muriel excitedly as she examined the new decorations on the sides of the old cradle. Ellie told her that six years of storage and no use, the cradle had required some refurbishing. "Your fondness for my cherubs so inspired your mother to recreate them on this cradle for your lad or lass," Eleanora said proudly. Ana had placed some linen cloths in the cradle with the Lovel coat of arms embroidered on the edges and the top. Muriel was brought to tears when she saw the delicate handwork on the linens. "For my own sweet child," she said poignantly. "Thank you Ana, and dear Mother for your thoughtfulness; the lovely cradle most appreciated by this lass, no words can so describe my joy to find these loving gifts," she said in a voice almost inaudible.

Eleanora was in awe of the young lady standing before her; Muriel had become a loving mother to be, a truly happy person with her anticipation of this birth. What a miracle Ellie mused; a true gift that an angel must have so transformed my daughter. Dear Gilley, thank you for your counseling that day in Castle Cary she said under her breath. "And what of your dear husband?" asked Ana. "How is he and what are his thoughts about his heir to come?" Ellie wanted to know. "If that laird to hold for half of the excitement of our Muriel; he is most delighted!" she teased her. "Oh Lord Lovel is quite pleased; he is writing his will, planning his estates in anticipation of the birth of his first heir," Muriel responded. Elizabeth was coming down the passage leading from Mura's chamber. She was eager to meet Lady Lovel and hear of her life in Castle Cary. Introductions were made and Muriel chuckled when she heard of this lady's day attempting to tutor her wee brothers in their languages. "Since these lads were told they would be uncles to your child; all we most hear is the name your wee one will say most first!" she explained in her frustration. Her lessons were being ignored she went on to say. "Much beleaguered is this lass; their taunting ways with each other these last weeks will be the death of their tutor," she exclaimed, feigning her indignation to Muriel.

Mura was chuckling to herself, she missed these silly lads. "Perhaps if I were to help with their instruction," she offered. Elizabeth welcomed her assistance and they agreed to go over the lessons this evening in the withdrawing room. "Do you have some wooden tablets?" Mura asked the tutor. "That we could have use for two; till now we have only had my one with a parchment carta or sheet for each lad to so write upon. Do you have some more then?" she asked. Muriel volunteered her own tablet from when her mother tutored her with James. And then she told Elizabeth where they could find a second wooden tablet; among the things James stored in their father's old chest. Lady Elizabeth was delighted; the lads were smart she told the ladies. "That they require much stimulating in their learning is most new to me," she acknowledged. Ellie told her that anything else she may need to please ask her for it. Mura was delighted to be of help; her attitude had changed since she left Essex. Her life at Castle Cary enlightened her to 'the real world' as Ellie had so prophesied. Now this Lady Lovel was appreciative to be needed; excited about an opportunity to assist their new tutor.

Later that evening Elizabeth and Muriel were commiserating in the withdrawing room. Mura had brought with her two books, one of Latin and one of Norman French and two small wooden tablets. "Good that you thought to bring that taper," she said jovially. "This lass had not one hand free to carry it!" Elizabeth was pleased with the wee boards Mura gave her; knowing she could use them with the parchment she had. "This will most assist the lads when they write," she told the lass, praising her for the idea. Then Muriel began to show her the books she had. "Each one contains some verse and rhymes, some prayers and an alphabet of the language. Father brought these back from Edinburgh for us," she said as she gave the Latin book to Lady Elizabeth to review. "As you can see, they are the very latest even for this day," boasted Mura. "See here, the 'W' does so appear," referencing one of the letters that was not part of the original Latin alphabet of twenty-two characters. "Our father used his 'W' on his signet for William, *Sigillum Willelmi, dominos de Duglas* is what he wrote for it," Muriel explained, as she described the seal that William used for authenticating documents; his device of signature. "Father insisted we learn the alphabet that includes that letter, a modification for the Lallans or the Inglis languages he told us."

An excited Lady Lovel rose early to break her fast during prime; joined now by Ellie and her wee hound. "Take care that this poacher does not steal your food; most like our Shamus in that way, but even more unruly without William's growling voice to subdue him," warned her mother as she gave an admonishing look to Lindsay. "What is that odd crunching noise; that the hound does gnaw on meat-bones so early in the prime?" asked Mura as she peered under the trestle table at the Deerhound. Ellie chuckled. "The wee hound and his peculiar habits; to bit his toe nails when they grow too long." Lady Lovel wrinkled her nose. "How perverse; to have the hound making those noises while this lass most tries to break her fast." Ellie sighed. "Your mother will ask our grooms to attend to Lindsay most this day," she assured Mura; noting her daughter's touchiness. Perhaps it is the lay-in due to cause her mood; a Deerhound was prone to such antics; it was just his way Ellie reflected with amusement.

"Mother, are you perhaps to ride to Little Dunmow this day?" asked Muriel. She wanted to take her palfrey out to visit William's grave at the priory and was inviting her mother to join her. "Why was father not buried inside the church of St. Mary's there?" Mura wanted to know. "The Lovel family ancestors are all buried in the vault beneath the church or in a tomb in the chancel near the altar." Ellie sighed sadly, remembering every detail of that dreadful day when she had returned from London with her knight's body to arrive at Little Easton.

"Father Paul greeted me so sadly; those cruel words of Lord Lovaine, forbidding burial of my sweet husband in our family's church," Ellie said. "My only solace was a priest of St. Mary's Church at that Dunmow Priory; the Augustinians would accept him there, for a wee demand of fee for our father's burial," Ellie explained as her voice began to break with emotion. She added, "A stone feretory was provided by Father Paul to give more permanence to the burial." The widow paused between her words so she could be heard, as she was crying softly. "This coffin would protect the shrouded body to reside outdoors; not in a marble tomb like his Douglas ancestors in the Douglas Kirk," Ellie scoffed. Muriel was caught in her own reverie before she responded, quietly and thoughtfully to her mother's sentiments. "When it is my day to join my father, I shall want to be entombed in that very place, outside."

Ellie was startled by the request. "As young a lass as you, thinking of burial and the Otherworld with your full life in front of you!" gasped Lady Douglas. "Where ever do these ideas so come from, Muriel?" she asked, confused by her daughter's preoccupation with such thoughts. "Lord Lovel was discussing where he would be buried; writing out his decrees and benefices of inheritance for his will. Did father have such a document?" Ellie nodded, "Of course; but alas his lands were forfeited; the church can not enforce what is no longer ours to have; for not just lands did Edward seize of Douglases, but all chattels and crops growing did he take, to sell for his profit," Ellie said ruefully, looking down at her hands she tried to ward off the tears. Muriel realized her mother was back in Douglasdale with her sad memories. She sought to 'semisouneth' her as William would have done; to call her Lady El when she was emotional then speak his words most quietly to becalm her. Muriel rose and gently put her arms around Ellie's shoulders. Mother and daughter held each other for some time and without a word they made their way out of the great hall, arm in arm, to the stables for their ride to Little Dunmow Priory.

The spring became summer with the solstice; Ellie had decided to remain in Essex, the lovely weather brought comfort of clear evenings and warm sunny days as the seasons melded together. With her daughter's visit to Stebbinge Park Ellie would not travel to Fawdon now; she had planned to take the bones her beloved hound Sir Shamus for his burial there some weeks just passed. She asked Sir David if he would venture out to Northumbria instead; to look after their manor and speak with Sir Thomas Chaunceler, William's vassal in the parish of Ingram. Her knight responded without hesitation; he would be most content to go there.

Sir David was looking forward to a journey and some adventure that only traveling could provide. He was ready to leave the morning next if she so desired! "Pray too, so tell that Douglas knight Sir Thomas and the servants there of our decision to journey north to Fawdon after the Equinox of spring, the next," she said pleased to have him travel in her place this year. "Would le Parker require escort north that he might take his leave of Essex too just now?" asked this thoughtful knight, suggesting that it was coming time for Ellie's steward to return to Scotland in search of rents. "To travel so with us might spare him much concern," he added. "What a perfect idea," Ellie replied, pleased that he had thought of it. "And you may stop along the way at the Yorkshire manors of my brother, Fryton and Syston. A fair report of those bovates and messuages would be most welcome," she ventured to say. "It is done!" And with that, it was decided that Sir David would travel north, leaving in three days.

Figure LIII-Part One; lambs at Arden House, Belsyde Farm Linlithgow

The warm days filled the pastures with colorful floral hues; the tall grasses left growing for feed rustled in the gentle winds that danced across the fields. "Look at the wee lambs," said Hugh, laughing at their silly play. The lads were riding their palfreys to the priory school, enjoying the coolness of the summer morning. "How large they have grown in so short a time," he said with all the wonderment of his innocence. Archie giggled too as he watched them run and roll each other over in the pasturelands. "We had better hurry if we are to arrive by the prime," he said referring to their late departure from Stebbinge Park. The priest had scolded them last week. "Not to come there most late again!" Eight in the morning was prime for Archie, but not for the priest who wanted them there by seven. Hugh told his brother not to worry, the sun was rising earlier and they would be prompt. Gillerothe was their escort today and he too concurred. "A tidy arrival for you lads, sure aye!" he chuckled. Their schooling at Little Dunmow Priory began some weeks ago for Hugh. Most nine year olds in Essex of noble birth were attending lessons at a church or priory and he was no exception. Archie was only turning seven this year but like James was precocious; with much persuasion from Lady Douglas the priest allowed him to attend with his older brother. "As long as he maintains the standards, he may stay," the priest stipulated to this arrangement.

JULY 1303-Muriel and Ellie were working on swaddling cloths in the withdrawing room when the lads and Lindsay were returning from the stables. The large oak door of the manor slammed shut with a thud.

"Mother," called Archie curtly. "We have some business with you," he shouted, as Hugh went looking for Ellie, finding her in the chamber off the great hall. Archie was his impatient self. "Father Stephen wants us to take our lessons in the later part of day," he told her. Ellie looked up from her handwork inquisitively. "Why would he demand the change? The prime is best the time for school," she told him. Hugh explained that two other lads were coming to that school and they were older. Ellie was irritated; the priest was making decisions without consulting her. "Your mother will speak with him on the morrow. You will not have school that day. Perhaps now a different solution is required; that Father Paul might school you both in Little Easton," Eleanora told her sons. She had spoken with her father's widow after church the other day. Lady Maud was going to school her stepson Thomas, Ellie's half brother, with Father Paul and she encouraged Eleanora to do the same.

Figure LIV-Part One; Little Easton church

The next day Ellie and her men at arms rode out towards the manor of her family; to speak with Father Paul at the Little Easton church. Her old priest and long time friend was delighted to have Hugh and Archie join the lessons with young Thomas. Ellie was elated, "You have always held for me when ever this lass was in need," she said graciously to one of her favorite clerics. "I do thank you most again," she told him as she mounted her jennet to journey on to the priory. "I will so inform that priest of my decision; on the morrow next my sons will be in your school in Little Easton!' she proclaimed, satisfied with this new arrangement.

At the priory Ellie told the good rector, Stephen Notele of her decision to transfer her sons to Little Easton; the cleric was relieved he told her. His new students were much older and he found his patience wearing thin with the younger boys. "Perhaps this father has much to learn of working with younger children," he admitted. "Most grateful to you Lady Douglas for your kind understanding," he told her. Ellie breathed a sigh of relief as well; her sons would be studying with her brother with one of her favorite priests as their instructor. And the cleric at the monastery was satisfied as well with the decision. She stopped for a moment to visit with her William, his grave at the priory, before returning home. "Dear Gilley, I see your good work here today," she told her husband in Spirit, to thank him and God; knowing that they helped her smooth things over with the Austin canons as she moved her sons from that school to the other in Little Easton. We have all done well today she said to herself.

When Ellie arrived back at Stebbinge Park she was greeted by a very agitated Ana; pacing in the great hall waiting her return, running back and forth to Muriel's bedside. Ana was seldom nervous; Ellie became alarmed immediately that something dreadful must have happened. "M' lady, this lass is most unsure what really is the matter; it is just a feeling that I have," she said, hesitating with her words. "Our Muriel has taken ill; she is in her chamber. That this problem came to her so suddenly is what is most troubling," admitted Ana. Guiding Ellie to her daughter's side, she shook with fear. Eleanora sat on the edge of Muriel's bed. "What has happened dear lass, tell your mother and don't leave out a word of it," Ellie said, her voice quivering with worry for both the mother and the baby that she carried. Muriel was unable to tell her much; she was unclear in her thinking. Then Ellie put her hand on her daughter's forehead. "A fever do you have!" she exclaimed. Turning to Ana she told her to find the physician and the midwife quickly. "Have Patric and our Henry ride to Dunmow, the noo!" she ordered. "Bring me a tasine and William's healing box."

Sharing her concerns Ana went quickly about Ellie's requests. Muriel was experiencing a problem with this birthing too early; most like Ellie did five years ago in Woodham Ferrers. Oh that dreadful time, sighed Ana to herself, remembering so sadly when baby Douglas passed to the Otherworld almost taking Ellie's life as well. "Oh dear St. Bride," she prayed to the patron saint of healers, "please spare our lass and the grandchild too of M' Lady who has suffered all too much in this life." Ana made her way out in the courtyard, wringing her hands and saying prayers. She saw William's squire Patric coming from the mews and gave him Lady Douglas' request for him and Henry to ride; find the midwife and the physician. The squire saddled two palfreys, called Henry and they were hastily on their way. Ana now came to the small building that held the kitchen. As she entered through the tiny arch of the wee doorway her eyes met those of the cook. Ana dissolved in tears, her worries were too great to shield from others now. "Another loss would be too difficult for this family to endure," she said as shook her head sadly; burying her face in her hands she sobbed uncontrollably, sinking onto the bench near the fireplace.

The cook had served Lady Douglas when she was still Lady de Ferrers and he knew Ana just as long a time. He had never seen this lady so upset and all he knew to do was hug her. "Our Muriel is ill; something is very wrong with the child she yet carries within her sweet self," moaned Ana. The cook brought the tasine Ana requested and offered to take it to Lady Douglas himself if she wanted. Ana shook her head no as she wiped her eyes. "Not a word of my silly crying to anyone, promise me!" she insisted, and then she left quickly to bring the soothing liquid to her girl. She grabbed Gilley's healing box from where they kept it near the cellars as she made her way quickly out of the building. At the doorway she stopped; examined the contents and realized they would likely need to replenish some of the herbs. Ana asked the cook to find some rosemary. "The noo!" she exclaimed.

Lady Elizabeth was still in the withdrawing room with the wee lads; teaching them of French and Latin, unaware of the malady of Lady Lovel. Ana ran by the closed door to that chamber, clutching the healing box and holding the bowl with the tasine most carefully. She hurried off to Muriel's chamber at the end of the passageway. Ellie had taken some linen cloths from the garderobe and was wiping the lass' forehead with some cool water. "What else are we to do?" she questioned Ana, hoping for some suggestion to ease her daughter's suffering until the physician arrived from the larger village of Great Dunmow. Ana was beside herself with concern and knew of nothing more to do but pray and that is what they did together in the dimming light of the chamber. Muriel was fading in and out of unconsciousness, mumbling some words that were imperceptible.

The physician arrived as did the midwife; Lady Elizabeth came to see if she could help as well now that lessons were over for the day. The physician advised them that he dare not bleed the lass for her young age. Then he added the dreadful news: he felt no life for the child that she was carrying. "Some tragedy has taken that infant, is my suspicion," he told Lady Douglas, "and is most the cause of this mother's illness too I fear." He instructed Ellie to administer pennyroyal, to diminish the fever while it would assist the mother's body to expel the body of the deceased child. Ellie was starring at the man; unable to believe what he just told her. "This can not be; God can not be taking my grandchild. So much as He has taken from our family, this would never be God's will!" she told him adamantly. "You certainly must check again for signs of life," she instructed him. Ana was incredulous as well as tears fell helplessly down her face. She turned away from everyone, that they might see her crying. Ana was falling apart, unable to control her utter sorrow, devastated to believe that Muriel had lost her baby.

The next words Ellie heard as if she were standing far away, down a long corridor. A nightmarish grip of raw fear engulfed her as the physician spoke again. "Your daughter too may not recover, prepare yourself for I have never seen such illness come so swiftly and so strongly without that terrible result," he spoke his words most grimly. The chamber about her began to whirl; the air was caught in her throat, not reaching her lungs. Ellie could not breathe; she reeled and fell against the physician. Had he not caught her with the help of Lady Elizabeth, Eleanora would have fallen to the floor as she fainted. When she awoke Ana was holding her hand and she was lying on the bed in the lord's chamber. Ellie spoke with true determination. "This is a dream, nothing I have heard just now is true, I swear it must be so," she said as she gritted her teeth in relentless denial. But the look of complete despondency on Ana's face told her otherwise. God had taken another child from this mother; this time he took her wee grandchild not yet born.

Figure LV-Part One; effigies and ancient font at St. Mary's church Little Dunmow Priory; the high archways once led to the priory

Lady Douglas was angry; she could not despair, she was too infuriated with God. "Ana," she said with her teeth clenched, "we will not allow our

Muriel to so die!" The widow asked if the physician had left. Ana told her he was in the kitchen preparing some tasines; one with tansy, another with pennyroyal to administer to Mura for her fever and to begin the purging from her womb. "We will sit with my daughter day and night, never leaving her side as you so did for me when this lass lost Baby Douglas five years ago. She must live," said Ellie still unable to believe what was happening around her. The physician was slowly making his way down the dark and quiet corridor; the servants were lighting one of the tallow torches to illuminate his way. Lady Elizabeth had taken Hugh and Archie to the great hall for their meal; the Deerhound was also with them. Lindsay was pacing; he sensed something was very wrong. The hound had been chased away from Ellie's door to her chamber, and he was confused; forbidden to remain at her side as was his custom since arriving at the manor some months ago.

Ellie was still a little woozy; Ana offered her arm and she took it, making her way to Mura's side. The mother sat cautiously on a wee bench next to the bed, with little emotion she asked the physician and the midwife who had joined them what they planned to do to save her daughter. "First we have this good tasine," he told her. "That we have also prepared some Althea crushed with a little sage and warmed here in some olive oil," he showed Ana and Ellie. Then he took some of the mixture and applied it to Mura's forehead. "For fevers, that when she awakes she should be better," he said hopefully. Then he instructed the midwife to assist the ladies; giving Lady Lovel the tasine he had prepared. The midwife spoke very quietly to Ana; telling her that the cook was going to bring another concoction for their Muriel; pulverized pennyroyal with some honey in vinegar, to see if they could help her drink this liquid and accelerate the purging she required.

"Is that all we are to do?" asked Ellie, demanding to know what else they might devise to heal her daughter. The middle aged physician could not offer much solace; he told her that first she must be awake to consume her medicines that he prescribed. "On the morrow will I come; to check upon her progress from this night," he said with little hope for them to cling to from his words, a look of solemn resignation on his countenance. Lady Elizabeth was just returning to the chamber. She was walking very quietly, having brought the lads to wait in the withdrawing room for her word that they might visit with their sister. Their tutor arrived just in time to show the physician the way out of the manor house and to the stables to find his horse left with the farrier. "Come this way," she offered leaving Ellie and Ana to speak with the midwife alone. This lady held some great experience she told them; but never before had she seen a girl with so many complications of a fever and unconsciousness. "We must help her to wake somehow while breaking the fever most as well," she told them. Ana knew this from the time she nursed Ellie; the next few days would be critical, if Mura was to live they would know by then.

By the second day Muriel had stirred and opened her eyes. Ellie had stayed up with her the entire night. "Mother," she gasped weakly, "what has happened to this lass?" she said unaware that she had lost her baby. Ana came in just then and quickly brought Ellie the other tasine the physician left. "Muriel, you must listen to your mother and Ana; you have to drink of this." Muriel was a perfect patient, but she was drained of any strength and would slip in and out of consciousness to a dreamlike trance. Later that same morning she was awake briefly and spoke some words to Ellie. "What a comfort to have you here," she said, smiling sweetly, squeezing her mother's hand. Ellie sighed gazing into Mura's fair face; more a wee lass than a married woman who just lost her child she reflected. Ana brought in her younger brothers Hugh and Archie; both lads were very still, afraid to startle Muriel. They were also confused by the awful circumstances of her illness, so very much afraid that God might take their sister. Perhaps their good behavior would make God reward their sister with good health they speculated hopefully.

Figure LVI-Part One; model of Little Dunmow Priory in St. Mary's church; the final resting place for William le Hardi, his daughter Muriel and grandson William

Muriel was not completely alert or cognizant of the words they spoke; she would have realized they knew something was very wrong with her had she been fully awake. All day long people passed in and out of the chamber; not much change in Muriel's condition they were told. Ellie was going on her second day without sleep when Ana persuaded her to rest some in her room. As she lay on her own bed, the Deerhound slept on the floor beside her. "What shall we do?" she cried, exhausted by the days and nights without sleep herself, worrying for her only daughter's health and very life. Ana had no answers; she could only think to pray and she did that often while Ellie stood vigil for Mura. Two days later Muriel was with God; to be buried beside her father at Little Dunmow Priory. Nothing could be said to Ellie to bring her out of her depression; her hope and joy for a Douglas grandchild had ended in wanton tragedy. How many more of my children must die before this mother; what has this lass so done to anger God?" she asked Father Paul who buried her third and last surviving daughter, not yet fifteen.

    A letter arrived from James this day and stayed on the trestle table in the great hall of the manor, unopened. Ellie and her Deerhound remained in her chamber. That night Ellie began to write two letters: one to James and one to Lord Lovel. Hugh tapped on her door and let himself in her chamber. He poignantly came and put his arm around his mother; nothing more could be said, the loss of both his sister and the child she carried was more than unbearable. "God has for us a special place, one where we will no longer suffer," he told her quietly. "For you dear mother have most earned your place in His paradise; for now so many times over," he said feeling helpless, unable to justify the passing of his sweet sister and the child she carried within her. Eleanora held her son to her; but no more tears came. She was numb and angry at a contemptuous God for taking her only daughter, stealing a grandchild she would never hold to her breast.

    Archie entered his mother's chamber now as well. His head was down and his eyes were filled with tears; he showed her a small parchment with some words in Lallans. "Some verse for our sister," he said, his eyes looking at the floor. Ellie was sitting on a bench at her writing table and she took the poem from him, still gripping his hand in hers as she read aloud:

    Most missed and loved
    Your smile remembered
    And eyes like a dove
    Our hearts are stricken

    Tell our father we miss him Mura
    John, Amy, Martha, Baby too;
    This lad will see you in Paradise

    Yours faithful and true, Archibald Douglas,
    Loving brother to his dear sister now with God

Ellie read the poem again to herself; my poet knight to be most like his father, she said quietly as she held both her lads to her. "Thank you my sons for your loving thoughts," she praised them. Ana had been standing at the chamber door and heard her girl read the verse; she was very moved by Archie's words and came to put her arms around them all. "Hugh is very sorry he has not learned of healing to save our sister," he said apologetically. Eleanora shook her head fiercely, no! "This is not your doing," she told him. "Our Muriel most told this mother she was never happier than when she thought of lay-in with this child. When that was not to be our sweet sister wanted most to join her wee one," she told them adamantly albeit sadly.

"And they will be together in Heaven?" asked Hugh, recalling the teachings of the church that said a still born child would not be baptized and was not welcome in God's paradise. "Your father has so taught us different ways," Ellie said quite plainly. "My grandchild, your nephew was christened by this lass as your father would have done. Our Muriel is in Heaven with her father, sisters, good brother, and her son; it is the way of the Celts and our Douglas clan," she told them, contradicting the gospels preached in Essex. "Our heritage is Scotland. We will follow the ancient teachings and accept that God has taken our Muriel and her son William as I named her lad, to the Otherworld, to begin again another life," Lady Douglas explained, persuading herself as well as her sons the merit of such traditions.

KILDRUMMY 9 OCTOBER 1303-In the Scottish castle of Kildrummy once held by Gilbert of Moray, kin to William le Hardi Douglas, Edward I was holding court; granting favors to his vallets and other favored subjects. On this day a noble and loyal soldier of unquestioned bravery appeared before his lord Edward Plantagenet seeking the license of an English widow. John de Wysham was the king's long serving yeoman. He sought a long due, just reward for serious personal injury suffered in service to his king at Stirling Bridge in 1297. For this end he planned to elevate his wealth and status at court. Sir John chose to marry an Essex lady, a woman he met briefly at the Tower of London while in the constable's service recovering from his wounds. He noted that during these troubled times, the young relic of William de Ferrers, a tenant in chief, behaved in the most circumspect manner even in her tragedy, leaving the White Tower with the body of her second husband, a Scottish knight found in rebellion to his king.

Five years had passed since then; certainly she was eager to marry a good English soldier of unquestioned loyalty, he mused. Sir John de Wysham planned to become her husband and lord of her dower estates in both England and Scotland; to satisfy his need to rise in social prominence within the realm. Edward granted him license; commanded his chancellor

William de Grenefield to issue letters under the Great Seal in favor of de Wysham for the marriage of Eleanora de Ferrers, if she wishes to marry, Edward added, knowing the answer might well be 'no'. The grateful soldier was making his way homeward to England; he would bring a copy of the document with him and meet with his solicitors to issue a letter to the widow and begin the process to make her his wife. Once done, the vallet was to return to the king's retinue where he would be reassigned to Berwick Castle he was told. Perhaps this lady would so enjoy to take her leave of England to join her new lord and husband in Scotland; he grinned, savoring the prospect. This I will so propose in my letter he decided, pleased with his plans.

Figure LVII-Part One; ruins of the imposing fortress of Kildrummy

STEBBINGE PARK EARLY NOVEMBER-Ellie and her Deerhound were just returning from Little Dunmow Priory; Gillerothe and Patric were following politely behind her, allowing her the privacy she needed. The widow was visiting the graves of three Douglases; her dear knight Gilley, their oldest daughter Mura, and first grandson William. She carried an unbearable weight these days; a loneliness that lingered in her heart and made her cry without provocation; for no special reason tears filled her eyes and ran down her face uncontrollably. Her nose was always stuffy and her eyes were forever red it seemed to her now; my dreadful destiny she whispered poignantly to herself, to forever carry this mourning in my heart.

Ana was in the great hall, pacing back and forth eager for her return. She was growing concerned for Ellie's well being; her girl was losing weight and enjoyed little food these days. And now another matter was before them; a messenger from a solicitor in Oxfordshire with some documents of importance from his knight he informed them. As Lady Douglas entered the great hall of her manor she was greeted by Sir David who was seated at the large table with a man that Ellie did not recognize.

Figure LVIII-Part One; Monty of Balgonie, a harrier makes himself comfortable in the great hall window seat of Balgonie Castle

"This is Henry the squire to Sir John de Wysham with a message from this English knight for you Lady Douglas." The Deerhound was scampering through the doorway to the great hall as Gillerothe and Patric were returning from the mews. Lindsay bolted to the side of the English squire. Then the hound strangely stood up on Henry's shoulders putting his full weight to the intruder to frighten and disarm him. Ellie was stunned with the Deerhound's actions much out of character and ordered him to retreat as she seated herself in the lord's chair at the head of the table. "Lady de Ferrers," began Henry. He was quickly interrupted. "***Lady Douglas***, kind sir; continue," she said bluntly. "Are you not the widow of William de Ferrers the father?" he asked. Ellie nodded. "My sons coming now," she began, motioning to the doors opening to three lads returning from their schooling, Hugh, Archie and Maudie's son, "would be most apprehensive should I renounce their father and use the name of my first husband," she said with a frozen stare.

The squire began again and told her that he held a copy of an important document from the king's chancellor and a letter from his knight Sir John de Wysham and one from the solicitors of that chevalier as well. Ellie sat in utter horror; what next she wondered? She first read the letters issued under the Great Seal and shuddered when she read out loud, "granting license to marry Eleanora de Ferrers, if she is willing," The widow was flustered;

Hugh grabbed for the document and read the words himself. "You are not to marry mother! Archie and I forbid it; James would so agree," Hugh stammered. His mother interrupted him and flashed a look at Archie to cease his anxiety as well. "Kind sir, there must be some mistake. This widow is still in mourning for her knight and husband as I am so allowed. Advise your lord that I thank him for his kind words but this widow is not available to give her hand in marriage at this time," Ellie told him politely but firmly.

Figure LIX-Part One; ruins of Berwick Castle; the stately structure demolished as if to insure that Berwick on Tweed would never fall into the hands of rebellious Scots

"My Lady, that you have not so read the proposal from my lord Sir John," the squire said handing her the letter from de Wysham. Ellie told him that no proposal could be entertained at this time; her young sons were most on her mind, not a husband for her bed. "You might stay the night; Ana please provide him provisions from the kitchen and some wine as well," she offered. "On the morrow will I have a suitable response for Sir John de Wysham, miles." Lady Douglas rose from her seat and instructed the cook's assistant now coming to the hall to bring her food platter and wine to the withdrawing room where she would be. Ellie headed for the slanted desk where she maintained her financial records and kept her writing parchment and seal. Muttering under her breath the widow grabbed a tallow candle and lit it defiantly, bringing the taper to her desk so she could write her response immediately. That pagan despot selling me like chattel to his vassal, rewarding a soldier's service with my dower lands and hand in marriage; not this lass for an English yeoman of the king I vow!

A light tapping on the door to the withdrawing chamber announced the arrival of Hugh and Archie with Ana carrying her platter of food. "More wine for this lady," Ellie demanded curtly. She was almost snarling in her commands when she caught herself. "Oh my lads, this mother is most sorry," she apologized. "And Ana too; that this latest demand of that ruthless king has met with my ire that I do take it out on those I love the most." The door swung open again and in bounced the silly hound; he too was concerned for his mistress' well being and would not being shut out. The Deerhound had learned to open a closed door; his latest accomplishment tickled Ellie no end. "Come here Lindsay," she called heartily, amused with her hound's entertaining ways. "Our dear Edward is going to be most disappointed with his plan. I will write one letter of condolences to Sir John and another to our James; that he might hear about this latest travesty by accident, to abruptly end his sojourn in Brabant, coming to my aid, all for no need."

Archie was not sure how this idea of marriage all came about; he was belligerent and angry and wanted immediate revenge. "That this lad should run this squire through is my desire," he spouted in disdain for Henry's hand in the matter. His mother told him not to waste his thoughts on the vallet of the English knight; she had no intention of marrying anyone ever again, unless le Hardi found his way back from the Otherworld she told him. "This lass will leave this world a widow of Lord Douglas." Hugh wanted to know more about the offer of marriage so Ellie picked up the knight's letter and began to read to herself. Her rage rose to a boil when she read Wysham's misguided proposal: that she could travel to Scotland and stay with him in Berwick on Tweed!

"Ana, come look," she laughed sarcastically, seething in wrath. "That we could journey together as lord and lady to live in Scotland near your other manors when this knight returns to his assignment at Berwick Castle. Berwick Castle indeed!" she blurted out. Ana was thrilled to see the old independent spirit return to Ellie's demeanor; her moping about, her disdain for eating had all but vanished with this latest challenge from dear Edward. "My lass, another husband, more time to spend in Scotland, this is not of your liking?" she teased. Ellie flashed her dark eyes in defiance. "My oldest son will some day deal with Edward and in his way; for now we will wait the return of our Lord Douglas," she said referring to James. Eleanora Lovaine Douglas wrote out her response; she was polite and caring but resolute in her decision to remain unmarried, the widow of her only love, William le Hardi, her dear Gilley.

Part II
1304 to 1307

PARIS JANUARY 1304-James Douglas set out on his aging palfrey Fortis for the Ile de la Cité; the second time in as many years. He had been serving in the house of Lady Agnes in Lovaine for the last sixteen months when the lady took ill and passed before the feast of St. Stephen in 1303 to the Otherworld. Her son was now lord of the manor and though James was made to feel welcome to continue his service as a squire in that household he decided the baronial change was the perfect incentive to leave for Paris. He had been careful with the coinage that was Ellie's gift to him just before they said their goodbyes at Antwerp. Very little was taken from this squire's coffer; his intention was to spend his savings in Paris. James was not traveling alone. He was riding in the company of one knight and two Lovaine men at arms from the manor at the insistence of his mother's kin. The times were too unsettled to travel alone he was told; so this small party set out from Flanders in January to arrive in a few days in Ile de la Cité.

His Lovaine companions were picking up goods at Boulogue for their lord; but first they were taking James to Paris, a well appreciated task the young men acknowledged! The small caravan of riders and pack horses had made good time; the cart paths were firm as precipitation was scarce these past weeks. The horses were carrying little as well to slow them down for this part of the journey except for some half empty baskets containing small goods and James' wee war-chest, a medium sized wooden box that held all the worldly possessions of the squire. As he rode he thought of the weeks ahead, what he might like to do in the city. That I will require a place to stay, he reflected, and a refuge with some security to protect the few armaments this squire has acquired. Perhaps to seek in some weeks the household of the noble Scots at the Court of King Philip: Bishop Lamberton and Baron Wishart, he decided.

"To the Left Bank with us James?" the knight asked, wondering if the lad had decided to accompany them to the more accommodating sections of the city; where men could seek the social pleasures, finding fair entertainment and good drink. "Lead the way Sir Roger; this squire is ready for some excitement before returning to a household for employment," he said jovially. The three young men from Flanders had been in Paris many times; they promised to show the Scottish squire their favorite haunts. "What do you know about the city?" asked Sir Roger. James told him about the touring he and his family did; shopping the Halles, the King's Market on the Right Bank; strolling the bazaars, venturing into the shops of craftsmen.

"On the Ile de la Cité we visited the cathedral of Notre Dame and my favorite, Sainte Chapelle. Ah, the golden capitals pointing in majestic formation to a ceiling painted like the skies; magical streams of light dancing about in bright hues from stained glass walls," he sighed recalling vividly the beauty of the upper chapel. "The poet knight to be," teased one of the squires. "That would be my father, not this lad I am afraid," said James in quick retort. "There is only time for such thoughts in Paris; not Scotland," his words trailed off, thinking of when he might return to his homeland, of what he would find there when he did. "Did you see the relics behind the altar at Sainte Chapelle?" asked one of the others. James said that his mother had insisted and how impressed he and his brothers were to gaze upon the remnants from the crucifixion of Jesus. And how angry he had been to think that Scotland once held such relics until Edward I stole the Black Rood from Edinburgh in 1296.

"Then you have not seen the colleges?" asked Sir Roger changing the subject to more lighthearted affairs. James shook his head 'no'. The knight told him that tonight they would partake of the student's life. The travelers would hear some discussions over much wine; join in debates with students studying at the many colleges such as the College of Theology or the Faculty of Arts. "There is much fun to be had on the Left Bank; even during the winter they have games of competition on the Pré-aux-clercs, the lawn reserved for such team activities of good times," he said jovially. "This knight was once one who wore the tonsure and studied at the college," Sir Roger told them all proudly. "No such shaving of this lad's hair to attend a college for study," joked James as he pulled out the long mane of raven locks from under his hood. The younger boys were laughing; they knew that the ladies living near the Left Bank would prefer the long, curly tresses of James Douglas to the short cropped tonsure; the shaved, bald head of the students. "James has his eye on some entertainment of a personal nature," joked one of the boys. The squire shook his head, denying the suggestion. "Not for this lad; I have had my fill for some time," he teased them.

Living in Lovaine only some few months the young Scot went missing late at night as was permitted as long as he returned in the morning for his chores. He became a frequent visitor to a small toft, a sub manor of Lady Agnes. A widow named Matilda, a young Flanders lady, lived there with her infant son. One day she was returning from the village walking along the cart path leading to her land and dwelling house; her horse had come up lame and she was forced to walk with her young son in her arms to do her shopping. James happened upon the widow and offered his services and his palfrey for the journey. They rode his horse to her home and became fast friends. It was not long before the squire would stay the night; leaving in the early hours of the morning to begin his responsibilities at the manor house for Lady Agnes. The other squires he worked and trained with at the manor teased the Scot for his fast work at finding good company. "My father had told me often; when in search of a good lass, make sure you tell her true who you are inside here," pointing to his heart, "and where you will be when comes the spring, sure aye," said James. And that is exactly what he did; Matilda knew he was not staying in Lovaine. She welcomed him for his honesty; offering him 'her generous hospitality' the squire told his friends at the manor.

"There up ahead now is the tavern and the lodging where we will stay," said the knight as the travelers rode down the narrow dusty paths through the throngs of people. On this side of the Seine the rues were still made of packed dirt for the most part; lined with narrow houses built four stories high. Most of these living places had little gardens on the land behind the buildings for growing vegetables in the warmer weather. Their lodging would be above the tavern: one large chamber; crowded but clean with room for several boarders at a time to stay there. "The accommodations are modest but quite safe for us to so reside; comfortable enough to remain here some days as well," Sir Roger told them. He introduced each of the squires to the innkeeper and his wife. Their daughters helped in the kitchen or in the tavern James was told. "A Scot?" asked the innkeeper knowing the Lovaine knight to bring many friends to stay in his lodging, but never one from Scotland. "His mother is kin to the lord and our James has been staying there with us to learn the arms of Brabant his intention. Most well he did that too, this knight can so admit," responded Sir Roger chuckling aloud.

"We have horses and mules; your stables to have space for our animals?" asked the knight. He was told that whatever he needed could be supplied. "Not many come to stay most recently,' sighed the old Frenchman. "The cost of everything is rising rapidly; we are beseeching the king to return to the currency of dear Louis. But he delays it; tinkering with the valuation to put good businessmen like this poor innkeeper much in debt," he scoffed at the treachery of King Philip to pay for his wars by tampering with the exchange rates. "These days it seems most kings are scurrying to pay for wars they can not so afford," sighed James, feeling the futility of a king's military campaigns; knowing how unnecessary it was to wage a war in Scotland he said to them, "Only a foolish king would continue his oppressive ways there; his spoils are valued at but half or less of their true worth in Scotland now. His nobles at home in England are scampering about to mortgage their estates to pay off their debts of his campaigns," James ruefully told the tavern owner. "There are many Scottish squires residing in Paris," said the innkeeper. "They serve the nobility of that country; though we hear many are traveling home, returning from their exile very soon."

James was surprised to hear that news; he wondered why. "Was there most a truce called?" he asked. "No," said the Frenchman, "the lack of peace extended to the Scots has beckoned them home; the English king to allow some in exile to return to their homeland, while banishing others who will most likely take their place here in Paris," he sighed. The squire realized he might have to limit his dallying on the left bank if he was to join Wishart and Lamberton before they sailed for Scotland's shores, if they haven't left already. Sir Roger noticed his change in demeanor and inquired if James needed to alter his plans. "The celebrations of my independent state will so continue," proclaimed the lad. "Leaving Paris will have to wait!" he boasted. But he was concerned; James did not want to lose the opportunity of meeting Lamberton again. He decided he would take a day to ride alone to the Ile de la Cité; visit the Scots at Court and inquire about the situation in Scotland.

The days passed quickly for the merry group as they traveled the rues of the Left Bank; finding taverns packed with good conversation and games of chance if they so desired. Most of the students were prone to debates, confining their discussions to academic topics. No one seemed too thoughtful or informed on the political developments in France or in other countries; for these intellectuals their world was the college. The University of Paris comprised many colleges and it went a long way to establish a new social order in France: the emergence of the studium, joining the powers of kingship and the church. These scholars asserted themselves to gain control; established themselves not unlike the teachers of a trade. These masters taught apprentices and formed a guild. The effect was control of the university in what would be taught as well as how, when and by whom for all teaching at the colleges. In every tavern where students ventured there were boisterous arguments on the teaching authority and academic freedom. "Their concerns are lost to this lad," said James, weary of the chatter of men who knew nothing of the real world, as his mother would often say. Sir Roger agreed; the scholars could lose themselves in books. "And the city could wash away in flood or the sky fall from its perch…or a pretty woman could walk most by them and they would not know it!" he proclaimed, laughing at these silly fools as he called the students and their teachers. "That isolation is why this knight left the University for a *Better Life*."

"There is a play to be given on the Ile tomorrow; on the steps of the cathedral," said one of the squires. "Would you want to join us?" he asked. James thought that he would like to learn of such entertainment and agreed to meet them there later in the day. "Tomorrow is your last day then?" asked James. Sir Roger told him that the ship was due in Boulogue three days or less; they would have to ride long days having stayed much later in Paris than they originally intended. "This knight is going to play some games of chance this fair evening hour," he told the younger squires. "Do you wish to try your hand at it?" he asked the Scot knowing the others would try. "That I would watch some; but gambling is not something I would do," he told him. "Fair competition for skills of limb and sword would be my choice; to share in games of chance or luck for coinage is not my preference," he told them. "For one so young, how is it that you found a core of truths to guide you?" asked the old Frenchman as he poured them more wine. "My father wrote for us his truth; the values he said were God's own truths held here in our heart," James explained, showing them the parchment. "Our mother copied it for her children in her good hand; each lad received a copy of *My Truth*; it was as if he spoke to us from the Otherworld. To break covenants with this parchment would be to turn my back on my father's love," he explained thoughtfully.

James rose early in the prime; taking Fortis over the Rue St. Jacques to the Petit Pont as he traveled from the Left Bank crossing the Seine into the Ile de la Cité. He realized how eager he was to hear the accent of the Scottish nobles. The vernacular of country French in Normandy and Brabant was almost grating on his ears and the Latin and Norman French spoken on the Left Bank seemed stilted to him. The name is '*Duuug-las*' he would say, trying to accentuate the syllables; correcting their pronunciation of his family's noble name; but they seldom said it properly. "Oh to hear the fair Lowland pipes and Baron Wishart speak his Gaelic," he said out loud, smiling in gleeful anticipation of his arrival at the royal domains where the Scottish diplomats and exiled nobles were staying in Paris. When he was announced in the great hall of their manor house he was aware of a change in the demeanor of the Scots.

"Our decision to return is not of our liking," explained Lamberton, and then in hushed tones he told the squire that he was gravely disappointed by the disposition of King Philip. "The Auld Alliance that we all supported in 1295; your father too," he added, "and agreed with France to have, seems to be a treaty for Scots to fight for France; but not for the French to help us in our hour of great need," he sighed, becoming more audible as he drank more wine. "We gave our assistance to this king of France by raiding England in the north then, nine lang years ago. The fair result of these actions sought to stir up Edward, to then move upon our Scotland," the bishop said angrily. Then turning to look the squire in the eye, "You were there in Berwick in 1296?" he asked him, knowing le Hardi was the garrison commander during the invasion by King Edward. The squire nodded his head sadly yes. "We waited for these spineless royals to return our help in kind; but that was not to be," he said wistfully, making a good speech of his misery.

James told Bishop Lamberton that the king seems busy with the uprisings of his own in the provinces. "And for the expenses of his wars, he manipulates the coinage, so this squire has been told by many innkeepers and shopkeepers in this fair city. The cost of services and goods is fearfully high in Paris," complained the Douglas squire. "The true example of a foolish king I fear," said Lamberton with genuine disgust. "Are you here for to accept my offer for employment?" he asked, changing the subject from the woes of failed diplomacy to his return to Scotland. "Yes, if that offer still stands, this squire would be most happy to accept," James told him, grateful for the opportunity and relieved as well. He had been counting his coinage earlier that day and was surprised to find very little more than passage fees for himself from Boulogue to a Cinque Port. Sailing fees for Fortis and traveling expenses for their journey home through England had been spent in the taverns on the Left Bank.

"Good that you accept," said William Lamberton. "We will be leaving this dreadful country in two weeks. You may sail with us to Berwick, if that's your choice, your passage will be paid as one included in our household," he continued thoughtfully, remembering that this son of William Douglas was without his lands and income. James then told him about the last two letters he received from his mother, telling of the death of his sister and her wee son. Lamberton's face turned ashen; Lady Douglas and her family had suffered so much already he mused. "I must travel first to Essex as I promised; dear Edward has yet tried to award his yeoman license to so marry our mother. His decision poorly timed coming some few weeks after the loss of my sweet sister Mura and nephew William," James said while shaking his head in disbelief; there was just too much sadness for Eleanora to bear alone during his absence he reflected. "My mother plans to journey north to Fawdon then to her manor in Ayton is her desire," referring to her dower lands that were near the bishop's holdings in Berwick.

"Perhaps if there is a ship to take, but to travel only half the way," he put forth hopefully. The bishop thought for some time then came up with an idea. "Return here in some ten days; we will book our ship most then. To find us one good cog to sail that will assist you to Essex," he assured the boy, feeling a great need to help his kin, the nephew of his cousin de Lindsay. James thanked him for this kindness. "This squire has a palfrey and my wee war-chest too," he smiled sheepishly, knowing he had no choice but to tell the bishop everything he needed to sail home with to Essex. The diplomat was not concerned; the lad was earnest in his desire to return to help his family first, a good sign and one he would have expected from le Hardi's son and Lady Douglas' as well. "When you come to Berwick we will put your good skills to work my squire," he said more like a father than employer. "Will you do this bishop the honor of your company for some feasting and more wine?" he asked. James' empty stomach rumbled loudly, giving Lamberton his answer before the lad could respond in words; while the squire just grinned at his new benefactor.

As the kitchen servants were bringing in platters of food another of Lamberton's attendants announced the arrival of an English knight seeking counsel with the Bishop of St. Andrews: Sir Nicholas de Segrave. James looked up from the table both surprised and excited to hear the name of his mother's favorite cousin; but what is Nicky doing in Paris he wondered? The bishop told the servant to delay the English lord some few minutes, then to bring him forward; to set another platter of food for the knight as well that he might join them. "By your countenance I see you know this vassal of dear Edward," speculated Lamberton. James reminded him that Nicky was kin of Eleanora and had been one lord of four who provided manucaptor for his father in Knaresburgh; pledging surety of mainperson for William le Hardi in 1291. "My father had most said of the English knights he knew, Sir Nicholas is one of his own temperament and core values most as well." Lamberton chuckled. "The very disposition of Lord Douglas; the Steward would so agree having supped with him on his first visit not lang ago. For de Segrave's word and reputation of renown, your father's sentiment is highly trusted here."

The bishop then described a curious situation; Nicky's growing sympathy for Scotland and desire with other lords to end the drain on the English treasury of further wars. This matter had brought him to the dwelling of Scottish nobility in Paris for some discussions in secret. The reason for de Segrave's recent arrival in France was unrelated to the cause of Scotland although strangely well timed. These brave patriots, battling Edward with words and faith, were feeling the brunt of failed diplomacy; the wayward knight's presence breathed some hope into their hearts. Nicholas de Segrave had some personal dilemma of redress involving another knight named John Cromwell that took him from the muster of Edward's last campaign in Scotland to the Isle de la Cité. The business with the scoundrel Cromwell was not yet settled; the cowardly lord had so far refused the rendezvous in France, so Nicky was planning his sail back to England. Soon he would leave for Dover to return to his manor in Stowe, he told the bishop.

The clank of spurs and sword, the din of metal glancing off metal resounded, characterizing the brisk, strong walk of an ever impatient warrior entering the great hall of the manor where the bishop was feasting with his new squire, James of Douglas. Sir Nicky as James greeted him was finely attired; the exquisite and emphatic supertunic of brilliant blue brocade with gold trim swung daringly from his broad shoulders, his long blond hair somewhat carelessly disheveled gave him a rakish appearance of a determined malcontent. The severe grimace turned into a broad grin as the

English lord recognized Ellie's stepson, the heir of William le Hardi. "Greetings to you James, you too good bishop, surprised am I to see you here. Were you not in Brabant, to serve as squire in the Lovaine household there?" he asked.

James grinned, knowing his more developed and still growing frame had impressed his mother's kin as he stood to address the dashing chevalier. The squire was now the height of de Segrave though without the manly chest of a knight with several campaigns under his belt. He greeted Nicky jovially and explained his presence in Paris. "And Eleanora, pray how is my favorite seneschal?" he joked. James shook his head in disdain for what he had to share with Nicky. "Another loss of great sadness for that lady; my dear sister passed to the Otherworld for a tragedy of the lay-in," he said quietly. Nicky bowed his head in utter disgust. "That this humble cousin did not know; being on campaign in Scotland has kept me from a visit to her Stebbing manor," he admitted with a woeful countenance.

James then told de Segrave that Eleanora was faced with another dilemma within a few weeks of Muriel's passing. "Perhaps God's gift; to rile her ire and take her mind from the mourning," he conjectured. "That Edward had decided she should marry; promising his yeoman her estates in dower by issuing license for her marriage, yet without consulting the lady first," James said as he laughed sarcastically for the happenstance. "Do I know the unfortunate knight who must now encounter her well known wrath; considering her as chattel in the matter?" Nicky questioned with his characteristic bravado. "One foolish lord to be, Sir John de Wysham; that he tried most to persuade her with the sweet promise of a life returning to live at Berwick Castle," James replied, his face revealing the irony of the suggestion. Ellie's cousin winced when he heard the words; to return to Berwick on Tweed after witnessing the slaughter of her friends six years ago in that very burgh would be anathema to Eleanora. "What was this foolish fellow thinking?" Lamberton interjected aghast for the very thought; at every turn Lady Douglas seemed beset with trouble and controversy, he mused.

More wine was poured and the feasting continued. Nicky became more relaxed and began to relate his tale of contempt for the Cromwell knight and his dilemma of temporary exile in France. Sir Nicholas told his story with complete honesty: both knights with their men at arms had arrived in Scotland for the campaign with Edward. Cromwell was agitated that de Segrave, the long time lieutenant of the Earl of Hereford, would hold as knight banneret over him and his men Nicky explained. In retrospect it seemed that Sir John had planned the altercation all along; to challenge him to a duel. "That this knight so holds for his core values," Nicky groused, "most like your father le Hardi in his fiery temper when so challenged, to be my end some day I know it" he sighed as he explained in earnest his preposterous situation. "Shamefully provoked was this impetuous lord," he chided himself out loud. "This Cromwell in his most contemptuous words so decried my honor and challenged my very manhood; that he so insinuated most directly that this de Segrave knight was close and personal in his relationship first with my lord de Bohun, then too with Prince Edward's long time friend and companion, Piers Gaveston," he said in utter indignation as his voice grew louder and his brow furled in anger.

Lamberton and the Douglas squire understood at once what de Cromwell was hinting about: he publicly accused Nicky of holding preference for a man rather than a lady in his bed. The pretty blond tresses and fine facial features of the English knight could be misleading but were hardly indicative of an effeminate nature. De Cromwell's invention was truly a preposterous allegation for any that knew de Segrave personally, but surely one to pique his ire quickly they both knew! James ignored the foolishness surrounding the ruse of challenge. Instead he asked Nicky why he came to France to settle the feud. "That I must vindicate my truth; so provoked in duel most outlawed now in England. I made my way to Dover but was not permitted passage to leave for France," he said gruffly.

Nicky told them both that because of a royal mandate during war times, departing England with men at arms and horses was forbidden for a knight. "That I most slipped through their grasp quite secretly; the warden of the Cinque Ports most devastated by my fair escape," he boasted. "When in three months or fewer, perhaps to have received my just due and victory from de Cromwell by then, this humble chevalier will have to face an angry Edward returning from campaign; for I will be again in England," he admitted sadly. James realized that his mother's cousin was very much like le Hardi; doing what was right to defend his name and honor without considering the grave consequences of his acts. "It is no surprise to this lad and squire that your ferocious demeanor in defense of your core values holds great esteem with Lady Douglas," the squire chuckled.

Later that day James arrived at the cathedral steps to view the play with his friends from Lovaine; he was his jovial self again they noticed. "Where's the scowl that has hidden your face these last days," teased one of the squires. He laughed and told them of the bishop's offer of passage home and employment in Scotland. Sir Roger was very happy to hear about his good fortune; James was a serious youth on a mission he mused and he wanted to see him succeed. The Scot admitted now that he was scarce of coinage but Lamberton's promise had renewed his spirits: in two weeks he was going to be in England, on his way home. "Paris nights are too rich for this humble squire's coffer," he laughed. That night James returned to the tavern and spoke with the innkeeper about continuing his stay; perhaps to work for board not wages was his request. The old Frenchmen told him he had no work but that he knew the stables of the college could use a groom to assist the farrier. "Would that be of interest?" asked the innkeeper. James told him such employment would be perfect; working with horses was something he enjoyed and he could board his Fortis there as well.

The innkeeper told him to be downstairs in the prime; the farrier was his brother in law and was coming by for some of his wife's porridge and sweet cakes as it was Saturday. "You can stay the night," he told James, "on the morrow you may move yourself to the stables," he said, generously offering the squire lodging without a fee. "Oh, but this lad will pay you for your bed and board this night; there is plenty here for that," he told him as he pulled out some coinage. "But I do thank you so for your fair offer," he smiled, thinking how nice everyone had been to him since he was living alone, away from his family. Everywhere James went people seemed to go out of their way to assist him. Sometimes he felt as if his father was there, watching over him, making sure that someone would offer help when he needed it most.

The next day the farrier met with James and they formed an agreement; for the next week he would live at the stables and work there as well. Fortis and his wee war-chest would be welcome too. My good fortune so continues he reflected. The time he worked at the stables allowed the innkeeper's brother in law the opportunity to travel to one of the ports on the Seine where prized palfreys were being unloaded from a barge, a short trip for the horses from an estate in Normandy where they were bred. "This is a gift to me from God," he exclaimed, "two palfreys to train for a nobleman who has arranged with me a purchase. That when he is to return to Spain he will leave one horse with me for my trouble," he said jubilantly. "That I could find such horses and time to train them was my worry; the first concern now satisfied by your arrival here," he told James.

The days were long hours for the lad; many horses were kept at these stables requiring a great deal of strenuous effort. But the squire didn't shy away from his assignments; he was happy to have found some work to pay for his bed and board and for his Fortis too. He had never given much thought to all the expenses required for his daily living; he had not held the responsibility for the care of others as well. His father and mother managed the family income; only that one year when William was first imprisoned in the Tower when Ellie held Woodham Ferrers alone for their sustenance did they worry about coinage. "Dear Fortis," he said out loud as he brushed down the palfrey, "how many adventures do we have together now?" Then as if to answer for his noble horse, "None lately in our Scotland; that we must so return there soon enough, in a month or less," he promised his long time friend. James began to reminisce about the first time he looked upon the noble animal. That morning of his forth birthday; he and the foal were about the same wee height then, he recalled. He smiled to remember those days in Douglasdale. And then his mind wandered to the time he tried to jump his palfrey and was unhorsed; breaking two teeth and cutting his lip in the process, giving him the slight lisp that now endeared him to the ladies. "From bad fortune comes some good," he said prophetically.

FEBRUARY 1304 HARWICH-James was pleased to be sailing today with the bishop's household; stopping first in Harwich a northern port in Essex, the ship would continue up the coast to Newcastle upon Tyne before stopping at Berwick. The cog they found to take them was enormous; room enough to secure all their horses and the many carts of the bishop's entourage. James was in charge of the horses down below and stayed with them most of the three days it took to make Harwich, the home of the captain of the vessel. "That I should make that stop and let my good wife know where we travel next," he said jovially. The ruddy faced seadog was ebullient to gain such noble passengers as Bishop Lamberton and the grand household of the See of St. Andrews; pleased to stop in Essex first before taking the voyage north to Scotland. Fifty two was the number the bishop gave him plus nearly forty horses and many carts. William Lamberton stayed in the castle of the cog while James found himself below the deck; quite a change from his usual mode of travel as the son of Lord Douglas. But alas this day he was a squire only, in the service of another noble household; not the heir of Douglasdale. A humbling experience he would recall for many years to come.

Figure I-Part Two; Harwich is an active port city today

The sail to Essex was rough going; they were becalmed and didn't move much one day. Though the crew rowed their oars all night the currents flowed against them; so little progress was made until the next day when surprisingly the winds off the coast propelled them in good time to Essex and the harbor that was the home for the captain of the cog. Harwich was a typical small English village on the sea. The old cart paths were set in a grid-iron pattern with the main roads going north to south connected by wee alleyways to break the winds that cut across the shorelines. The old church was built around 1177 and was a resting place for Crusaders on their way to the Holy Land. James considered staying there the night but they landed at the docks in the prime; giving him a full day to travel. The squire said goodbye to the bishop, promising to meet up with him at his manor in Berwick before April. He led Fortis off the cog; hoping he would adjust to being back on land that they could ride out of Harwich in a few hours.

While James broke his fast over a bowl of porridge and some ale he read his mother's letters with the names of the Lovaine and de Ferrers manors in this region of Essex and a rough mapping of their locations. "Frating," he said aloud. "We will travel to that manor but a half day's ride from here; with one lang day's travel yet remaining to arrive at Stebbinge Park!" he exclaimed, telling Fortis that he would be home in his own stable by the next night. It felt good to return from France and Brabant; even if this was still England, he chuckled to himself. Then sadly he thought of his sister Muriel, the letter she had written him in Lovaine; her joyful plans to become a mother. And the devastating news some months later; Muriel and her wee lad were now with God, buried at the priory next to his father. His thoughts wandered to his mother; how she could have coped with another tragedy, losing not just a daughter but a grandson too.

As he rode through the cart paths of Essex he wondered what effect the passing of their nephew William and their sister had on his wee brothers as well. While James continued his journey through the countryside he recalled better times when the entire household traveled from Douglasdale; a family under the banners of Lord Douglas. They journeyed each year when the winter snows subsided; riding south from the Scottish Lowlands through Northumbria and Yorkshire then further south again into Essex. Ellie's English manors resided mainly in this shire; their lord and father when he was alive presided annually over the feudal business as was required. How carefree those days seemed now. He had little to worry about then as William was always there to guide him, to provide for his every need. Now his loving father, the victim of Edward's treachery was lost to them forever. James scoffed as he reflected; this barbarous king was not satisfied with the death of William le Hardi. Edward wanted to destroy what little family they had left; force Lady El to remarry an English soldier, rewarding his yeoman campaign in Scotland with her dower lands! This lad will return his family to our rightful lands; I do promise so my father!

Making the last turn from the Frating mains to the manor house of the de Ferrers estate, he suddenly pictured the silly face of his youngest brother in his mind; Archie's serious attempt to mimic the squire. The thought of that impish grimace made him laugh out loud. "Fortis, our wee brother will be surprised to see how tall this lad has grown!" he chuckled thinking of the petulant lad of six, no eight years old! Archie was the age of a page; and would be going to live with the de Lindsays this year; that's right he recalled, his mother had written him of her plans. And our Hugh will be most ten this year he said to himself as his dismounted from his palfrey; in four years or less he will be living the life of a student, studying for the church perhaps at a monastery in Scotland he mused.

When James entered the manor house he was greeted by some de Ferrers servants he did not know but they were eager to meet him as Ellie sent a messenger that he might be staying there on his way home to Stebbing. "Most welcome you are!" chuckled the old woman who seemed to be running the manor house as she motioned to the lad to come inside. "We are excited to have one of Lady Eleanora's sons to stay with us and one so handsome as you," smiled the cheerful lady, a long time member in the de Ferrers household at Frating manor she introduced herself as Isabel. Her husband was the farrier she told Ellie's son. "And our boy John is now the cook and cellarer," she boasted, speaking her son's name proudly.

The woman was delighted to have this young visitor come to stay with them for the night. "That you are traveling very light for someone just returned from two years in Brabant, or was it France you were staying?" she asked James. He told her about his time as a squire at the manor of Lady Agnes and then how he found his way to the Ile de la Cité with his friends from Lovaine. "After some few weeks in Paris, the prices of good food and drink to rise higher every day, my wee coinage was most spent," he grinned as he told her of his travails in France. "This lad decided quickly to return to Essex. My wee war-chest has traveled on ahead of me with the good bishop in whose household I will serve as squire in Scotland," he told Isabel, sparing none of his story to share with the good woman.

James was polite and unassuming, thanking everyone profusely for their kindness. But in his mind he was elated; a squire residing in the hold of a cog by morning; a young lord of the manor by the afternoon. Fine work for this lad today, he congratulated himself; pleased to partake of noble graces once again. Isabel brought him some salted fish to begin his feasting with newly baked bread and some delicious beans with onions in a thick sauce spiced with cloves and ginger; instead of ale that he was given by Lady Agnes this lady poured him good wine. Her husband came in the great hall of the manor house to speak about the lad's horse. "A fair palfrey you have there son," he said. "Let me take him to our mews; we will groom and feed him for you." James thanked the farrier and told him that Fortis was on board ship for three days; he was concerned that he might have some ill effects from the voyage.

"How old a horse?" he asked then he seemed to answer the question himself. "By his teeth I would guess him to be twelve, perhaps thirteen but no older," the farrier speculated. "My Fortis will be fifteen this year," he grinned, knowing the good care he had given his palfrey made him appear younger than his years. The farrier assured the boy that he would keep an eye on the horse, but he doubted any trouble would come from so short a sea voyage. With everyone looking after his needs there little left for James to do but to enjoy himself; eat heartily from the platters of food being placed in front of him and wash down the sumptuous repast with some excellent wine. The last two years of living on his own, working in the service of other nobles was a humbling time for the squire. He did not look forward to returning to Scotland under the employment of the bishop; but the choices before him were limited. William Lamberton was paying good wages for his work, a fair and generous man; offering a notable position for a squire: to look after the knives and armaments of this nobleman was an honor for a landless youth. Perhaps he would not have to wait long to be presented to Lord Edward; make a successful plea and fine for the repledging of Douglas lands as the heir of his father. He dared not think of that prospect for very long; such a plan might take him a few years to accomplish, he sighed.

Figure II-Part Two; Frating Hall gates leading to the former mains of the manor

James wandered out to the stables before retiring that evening. Fortis had eaten well and seemed his normal self the squire noted. This gentle life was easy to adjust to he mused. Perhaps to stay another day or two at Frating he chuckled to himself; knowing quite well he would not tarry longer. His age of majority approached and Ellie's protection writs for his safe travel expired soon. James had to take his leave of England before the spring. And he knew he had a promise to keep with William Lamberton to repay him for his passage from Paris to Essex. The squire made his way through the great hall and down the corridor to the sleeping quarters. He was given one of the family chambers; one of the closets off the main hall leading to the lord's chamber, screened for privacy by elaborately carved wooden panels that reached half way up the higher timber and stone walls of the manor house. The fine tester bed was of a large wooden frame with heavy red and purple bed curtains trimmed in fine embroidery of greens and yellows. These lovely bed clothes were recently brought out of the storage chests in honor of the noble guest at Frating, Ellie's son James. The cook's own son was a lad of eight and he was waiting to help the squire prepare for bed. He took the gambeson and leather hauberk as well as his cote and surcote. "These will be ready for you on the morrow," said the lad proudly. "Is that the night then?" he asked James. Thank you, nodded the Scot; everything was well, well indeed he sighed happily to himself; the laird of the manor, for this fair night at least he said happily to himself.

With a full belly and some provisions packed for his journey he rode westward to Stebbing. He had a lang day's ride ahead of him; but he traveled light. Most of his armaments and other possessions went with his war-chest to St. Andrews with the bishop's entourage. He wore one sword belt and packed the other; carried the dagger and shield of his grandfather, leaving two knives and a war axe that was his Uncle Hugh's in the chest that traveled with Lamberton to Scotland. For some reason he felt compelled to leave the bishop something of value to insure his return to that household. The weather turned a bitter cold as he rode further in the day; the winds picked up, making an eerie howling sound as they whipped through the trees of Essex's forests. James looked down to the valley below from the cart path and saw snow starting to fall in the distance. They had two more hours of travel if they were to arrive at Stebbinge Park this day. The youth pulled his hood down to shield his face and closed his supertunic around him more tightly; they would ride on he decided. Fortis seemed to thrive in the cool air of the coming storm. At the very least they could make it to Fairstead James surmised. That village was part of another de Ferrers manor; a messuage there as well was held by Sir David. This knight serving in his mother's household held lands only a few miles from Stebbing and would surely welcome him as his guest in Fairstead if that was required.

The snow subsided some when James rode through the village that was the de Ferrers manor; it had been only threatening snow along the way with flurries here and there and no accumulation. He knew now that he would make Stebbinge Park tonight; traveling from Fairstead would be easy as he knew the way from here. What a surprise for the wee clan in Essex, he joked, grinning in anticipation of his unexpected arrival so late in the day. James and Fortis kept riding; both seemed to sense the excitement now as they passed through the familiar village, messuages and tofts to Stebbinge

Park. When they made the hill to Ellie's manor house both horse and rider seemed relieved; home at last from their adventures in Brabant and Paris.

Quietly the squire took his horse to the stables; the farrier was just getting ready for bed when he peered out around the stalls. His face lit up when he recognized Ellie's oldest boy. "James is it?" he asked, grinning ear to ear at the youth who had grown so tall the two years he had been away. "So cold a night as this to be out riding for your pleasure," he teased the squire. "Here, let me take your Fortis." Then he noted how well the palfrey looked and chuckled. "He appears to have aged not one day since I last saw him," the old Norman farrier said quite pleased. "My mother and my brothers are they about?" he asked. This little man with the ruddy face and bushy white eyebrows nodded and smiled. "The wee ones may yet be in bed as they have their lessons tomorrow with Father Paul," he told the lad. "Your mother will be awake; but in her chamber by this hour." The squire nodded and extended his thanks for the information. "Good then; this lad appreciates as well your care in settling Fortis for the night," James told him as he turned to leave the stables; eager to get inside and see his family.

Figure III-Part Two; Fairstead manor church with medieval wall paintings discovered during restoration

To his surprise no one was in the great hall; he crept quietly up to the second floor and down the corridor past the screened off section that made a chamber for his brothers. The lord's chamber had a heavy carved door with hinges that came straight from the wall; without a doorframe it would creak and squeal when he opened it. James rapped lightly on the door, no response; he released the latch and went in the room lit only by a waning taper. Suddenly he was face to face with a growling Deerhound; leaping from the bed to the door in one swift move Lindsay was ready to subdue the unknown intruder! Ellie bolted up from her slumber. "Who's there?" she demanded to know simultaneously grabbing for the dagger she kept under her bed.

James was laughing, "Mother tell your savage beast to take his feet from my shoulders," he said in jest, staying motionless so as not to hurt the hound or himself. "Oh James, to look at you!" she exclaimed. Putting down her weapon she ran happily to his side. But Lindsay still held the lad fast. Ellie was chuckling herself now as she commanded the Deerhound to let his captive go. "Down Lindsay!" she said sternly. The wee hound quickly obeyed her. "I remember now you said you had the hound," he chuckled. "This lad should know you would have held him here in your chamber," he teased her. "Come here, in the light," she ordered him, with a silly smirk of her own as she eyed her son. "You're the very image of le Hardi!" she gasped praising his fair appearance as she hugged him hard. "About as tall as your father too," she guessed. Then noticing his thinner torso she teased him, "But then there is no manly chest protruding over your sword belt here." Ellie was giggling like a wee lass; she seemed giddy almost as she couldn't believe her James was finally home.

Figure IV-Part Two; Stebbinge Park, the lovely drive framed by shade trees

"Have you stopped first to see the wee ones?" she asked him. He shook his head and told her no, he wanted to find her first. "Mother, this lad is so sorry you had to face the loss of Mura and our wee William without me," he said sadly. "I cried some most everyday to think of you and Ana staying with our sister in her last days." Ellie's eyes welled with tears; only James and Ana shared the many years of memories she had of her first child with William. Shaking her head in disbelief she told him how she felt. "This lass was sure she would recover; our family could not bear another tragedy I told God! Then our beautiful Muriel was gone and her William too. A precious lad he would have grown to be had he but lived," Ellie despaired. James realized as she told him the details of the tragedy that his mother had christened a child that died in the womb; something that was forbidden in the church. How like her to do this; much like William would have done to insure the laddie's burial in consecrated grounds with his grandfather and mother, to celebrate a Celtic promise that all will travel to the Otherworld. "And what of Lord Lovel," he asked, wondering how the widower handled the death of his wife.

Ellie explained that she had written him first that Muriel was very ill and would probably lose the child she carried. The messenger she sent returned with word that the lord was away on business of the king. "He did not come for the funeral; though de Ferrers and his wife Ellen came from Groby to attend as did my brother Thomas and his stepmother Lady Maud," she admitted angrily; offering her disdain for the absent widower. Just then the door opened to Ana. "Hearing some excited talk, this lass was hoping to find her James here," she told him happily. "Welcome home dear lad, we missed you so desperately," she sighed. The squire hugged her with his strong arms. "Thank you for being here when this humble squire was in Flanders; reading of that tragic news I wanted to return home most then," he told her poignantly. Another knock at the door; Hugh entered the lord's chamber to greet his brother. "The height this lad has gained, you have grown some and more," marveled James at Hugh's tall appearance. "And where is Archie?" he asked with a mischievous grin. Hugh beckoned him to follow quietly as the younger brother was fast asleep.

James went into their chamber; slinking in the room with stealth-like agility. He drew himself up to stand in the darkest corner so he was barely visible. Then James spoke in the deepest and most mysterious voice that he could summon. "Archibald Douglas; Archibald Douglas," he said eerily. "Wake now from your slumber to meet your maker!" he declared ominously. Archie sat up; wondering if he was dreaming. James repeated his words. "Who's there?" the wee lad demanded to know; his voice yet groggy as he was half asleep. "It is I Jacobus; your brother!" James declared using the Latin word for his name as he leaped out of the darkness to grab the lad and swing him high over his head. The two started their normal playful fighting and verbal abuse; Archie was trying hard to free himself but his brother held him fast. "Not this time wee one; your brother still is bigger and much stronger." Archie was too tired to fight; he finally relented and surrendered. "How was Paris?" he asked, wanting to hear all about his older brother's adventures. James began telling him of the plays on the Ile; the taverns where the students debated academic freedom night and day. "And the fair lasses; did you kiss a lady in Paris?" he asked, wanting to know James' views on courtly love in full detail. James told him that he was not impressed by the French women; he met a beautiful widow in Lovaine however. "With eyes as fair our sweet mother's" he said fondly, remembering the lass for her milky white skin and full bosom most as well, yet nursing her wee son. "Tomorrow will I tell you more; but for this night you must get your sleep." James ordered playfully. It was a wonderful reunion; everyone felt better having their squire home with them again.

The next morning Ellie and her son talked over porridge and ale reviewing their plans. In one week they would leave for Scotland it was agreed. "Archie will be thrilled to hear that we are to journey north; he thinks that when he leaves Essex to live in Scotland he will be leaving his schooling behind as well." Ellie chuckled as she reflected on his reticence to study Latin. "Much the same sentiments as one Douglas squire," she teased James, his own reluctance to learn the language well known in the family. "And our Hugh?" asked James. "How does he enjoy the scholarly endeavors of Little Easton?" His mother explained that little had changed; he loved to learn and study. The wee lads were most night and day with their likes and dislikes she told her oldest son. Lady Elizabeth was entering the great hall and Ellie introduced her to James. "A tutor for the wee Archie; my condolences madam," he offered facetiously.

Figure V-Part Two; Fawdon Farm on the site of the old manor of Fawdon

"And dear Lady El, how did the wee ones fare when they heard of Edward's plan to sell you off like chattel to his yeoman?" James asked in earnest, referring to the license Edward awarded to Sir John Wysham to marry his mother. Ellie flashed an angry look of disdain for the pagan despot as she called the English king. "Our Archie had to be subdued; to run the squire through and then was his plan! And the lad was just the one to carry the message for his knight!" she chuckled. "Poor fool this Wysham; that he offered me the bounty of Berwick Castle for our stay in Scotland," she sputtered. The son and mother exchanged knowing looks; how ever long they lived both knew they would always remember the sight of Berwick's good citizens hanged en mass; the surrender of the castle and the broken truce that followed with the agonizing slaughter of their friends and countrymen at the hands of Edward Plantagenet. James bowed his head and spoke solemnly. "This squire is most frustrated; his plan to be reseised to Douglasdale can not be delayed. That you should be compelled to so remarry is my horror and disgrace. My pledge to you; such ignoble deed will not take place!" he told her quietly. "Thank you James; I pray for that as well."

Figure VI-Part Two; interior of St. Mary the Virgin church, Stebbing; the ancient wooden chest is similar in design and size to the one James Douglas might have used for his worldly possessions; his wee war-chest

James and Ellie discussed the strategy for their journey to Scotland. James would join the bishop's household in Berwick; Lamberton had promised to take him before the council of the king within few months wherever he may be, to make a plea for his inheritance. "And this lass will stay in Ayton; or if the bishop moves his household back to the St. Andrews, we will move accordingly to Leuchars," she proposed. "Mother, would you take Fortis with you?" he asked, knowing now that the expenses of maintaining a palfrey would be too dear for a squire already in debt for his passage back to Essex. Ellie shook her head no. "That you must have a good horse for your own use," she told him. "This lass will provide the coinage that Fortis so requires for his keep. And when you are Lord Douglas, are you to grant this lady a wee income for her dower and a frail bench by the fire in your great hall at Douglas Castle?" she teased him, feigning paltry bearings as she begged sustenance from her son. Ellie knew James well; family was family to him as le Hardi had taught him. Coinage was to be shared; Douglases looked after one another. He grinned widely as he acknowledged her ploy. "Checkmate Lady Douglas," referring to the term in chess when one had bested his opponent. Ellie giggled, "This lass wants to challenge you to a game of Merels; to take advantage of this streak of luck!" she said with an engaging smirk.

FAWDON MARCH 1304-The Douglases were greeted by Sir Thomas as they arrived at Fawdon. They were staying in the dower house of the manor; the fortified house that once was used by the steward of their Northumbrian estates as well. The tower house was yet held by de Umfraville; until the retirement of le Hardi's debt for their fine of marriage Eleanora had been told she was only entitled to this dwelling for her dower and use. But it was still their familiar home in the Cheviot; the Fawdon Burn flowing freely nearby reminded them of the days when Lord Douglas and his family waded the waters to cool themselves from the summer heat.

Figure VII-Part Two; the Clinch marked the southern boundary of Fawdon manor; the remains of a fort there are shown center; residing less than a mile from the farm today

Sir Thomas was pleased to tell them of his successful hunt the morning last; their larder was quite full he boasted. Ellie invited her husband's vassal to join them later for feasting with her family. As she entered the great hall she was delighted to find the knight's servants and cook busy preparing food for their arrival this day. Sir David leaned his head into the doorway and begged the lady join her children for some few moments outside. He led them solemnly back by the wee gardens, protected by the low enclosure built behind the stables. Lindsay was romping along with them as the small procession of Douglases followed the knight. Sir David stopped abruptly. "Sir Shamus lies here among the herbs and special plants Lord Douglas used in his healing," he said quietly, pointing to the beautiful garden, the sweet resting place where he buried the bones of the noble Deerhound.

Everyone bowed their heads in great respect for their wee grey friend and said some private prayers. It seemed a lifetime since they were here with Lord Douglas and that silly hound Ellie reflected as she looked wistfully at Ana. Once the family numbered seven with the hound; with young Hugh not yet born, but carried by his mother they would have counted eight. Now they were four; so many Douglases had passed to the Otherworld in these last ten years Ellie realized sadly. Bowing her head as she walked deep in thought, she headed back inside the messuage to wine and feasting with her guests and family. James spent the rest of the afternoon riding the boundaries of the manor with his brothers. Tomorrow they would busy themselves for an entire day of finding old forts and stone circles; searching for the Celtic settlements to explore. Now that his brothers were older they were more fun to lead around; to teach them of the ancient ones as Gilley once did for him. Lindsay accompanied the lads as they rode their palfreys to the marches of the manor. Much like Sir Shamus, Lindsay enjoyed the Cheviots, a Deerhound paradise, James allowed as he watched the silly hound run and play with his Archie and Hugh in pastures of the Breamish valley.

In the great hall of Fawdon later that afternoon Sir Thomas sat down with Ellie; over wine he began relating the reports coming from Scotland. James was returning from his *scouting patrol* as he likened his perusing of the manor. He and Sir David came to join Ellie and the Douglas knight; eager to hear of the activities of the English and the Scots. "Where are your brothers?" asked his mother. James let her know that Hugh and Archie were nearby, in the lower pastures running with the Deerhound and two squires that accompanied them from Essex. "There are grave rumors about," began Sir Thomas ominously. "The king had stayed the winter; the Scots hold for the north of Perth." The knight went on to explain about some curious military efforts; the secrecy surrounding a wee band of highly trained marauding men at arms. "Led by John de Segrave and the Clifford, this small retinue drew foul rumors for their fearful expeditions," Sir Thomas allowed. "Stories so abound that Scots have failed to impenetrate this small force; no spy imbedded to report on their activities. They travel by night, skulking in the shadows to flush out higher game," le Hardi's vassal said as he described this strange and sinister mode of warfare.

James knew at once what this was about. "Chevauchées" the squire told them. "A woeful band of men at arms to route out the most formidable foe; every man is known to the other, spies or strangers are found out before they do damage telling of their whereabouts or numbers," he said grimly, having heard of such ruthless bands of wanton killers while in Flanders. "But the words to come this morning are most devastating to our Scotland," Sir Thomas told them all, shaking his head sadly he shared what he heard from Peebles. The Northumbrian vassal of Lord Douglas explained the situation to them in grave detail. The Guardian of the kingdome was the Comyn; he was trying for a peace with Edward while other patriots like Simon Fraser and William Wallace were refusing to submit. "These two brave leaders had proved themselves elusive to these English *Chevauchées*," he said using the term James provided.

Figure VIII-Part Two; Fawdon Dean, looking towards Ingram

"De Segrave and de Clifford had not found the rebels until their betrayal by a Scot we believe to be from Musselburgh," Sir Thomas said with disgust. "At Fraser's Happrew these English marauders revenged de Segrave's rout from the year last." Then it occurred to the Northumbrian knight that the Douglases might not know about the Scot's great victory last year. "Sir John de Segrave, the year last suffered a decisive loss at Roslin. Have you received some word of it?" he asked them. Even Ana spoke up as she came into the hall; telling Sir Thomas cheerfully that she knew all about that glorious victory for the Scots! He then added, with some hopefulness, "Though the loss was most terrible near Peebles, we have heard the Scottish leaders so escaped their capture." James was concerned for the safety of Wallace and Fraser; saddened to hear of the betrayal of their whereabouts. "What brave men they are and true," he told the knight. James then explained how their brilliant victory at Roslin reached the shores of Normandy and Flanders quickly. "Those daring Scots," he chuckled, "riding the night to do battle with the English; a thrilling tale of great courage!" he praised the rebels.

ST. ANDREWS-After some few days taking their rest and enjoying their Fawdon as a family together again, the Douglases removed themselves to Berwick and Ellie's Ayton manor house. They were told that William Lamberton was at the castle in St. Andrews, so they journeyed immediately on to Leuchars in Fife. James rode out the next day to join the household of Bishop Lamberton; arriving by April as was agreed. A Parliament was being held there by King Edward. The weeks that followed were filled with new responsibilities for the squire. James earned the respect of William Lamberton for his diligence in service to his laird and the confidence of the bishop as well. When Lamberton sought a faithful ear to hear his woes with Edward, he looked for the Douglas lad alone to listen to his complaints. James was circumspect and quiet both in word and deed; always pleasant and humble dealing with the others of the household but known to be closed-mouthed. The bishop viewed the squire as the replacement of his father in Scotland's fight for freedom; perhaps to be Lord Douglas soon, he hoped as well.

Figure IX-Part Two; St. Andrews Cathedral and Abbey ruins

    Both the bishop and his squire were in the great hall together breaking their fast. Lamberton confided to James that he was preparing to venture west to Stirling in some few weeks. "This bishop has some business in that royal burgh," he sighed with some disdain. "Once returning under dear Edward's safe conduct from France, have I sadly found much has changed in our Scotland." He explained how almost every one of the magnates had surrendered to Edward, except for de Soules who remained in Paris; preferring exile in France to living in a Scotland under Edward's rule. "Wallace, that brave patriot, is still defiant but Simon Fraser may have come to Edward's peace as well," he admitted, frustrated with the current situation.

    Lamberton told James of his need to appear before Edward, to pledge his fealty once again; having avoided such contrivance at the Parliament just concluded in St. Andrews. "To arrive in June is this bishop's plan," he told him ruefully. "You will accompany me, as my squire, a member of my household. But should there be an opportunity for a plea with the Berwick Butcher," he paused to emphasize the vehemence of his words for the English king, " to fine for your Douglas barony I will so arrange it," he promised, assuring the lad that he had not forgotten the squire's true reason for returning to Scotland. James respected the Bishop of St. Andrews for his political cunning and trusted his instincts fully in the matter. "When you so inform this humble squire that the timing is most right; I will take your lead most gratefully," he told his benefactor; his heart racing at the prospect of having the Douglas lands reseised to him.

Figure X-Part Two; St. Andrews Abbey and Cathedral viewed from the bishop's castle

James started to take his leave of the bishop, opening the heavy oak door that led down the corridor, to the courtyard leading to the abbey entrance. But Lamberton beckoned him to return and close the door; to come nearer that he might have a word of some importance with the lad. "Were you to become Lord Douglas," he said softly, "your father's inheritance repledged to you as rightful heir; on what side would you then reside?" he asked. The bishop was wondering if the lad would be Edward's true vassal or a Scot, waiting for the proper moment to stand in rebellion like le Hardi. Lamberton looked squarely into James' eyes, hoping to discern the truth in his response. Without hesitation James replied with an acrid humor. "My father lost his life in the Tower; 'hanged cruelly' on the orders of one pagan despot king," he scoffed, vitriol seeping through his every word. "Before this lad had left for France he was not sure of his allegiance; to become Lord Douglas and support his family was his lone intention," he sighed.

Taking in a deep breath that he might continue, James spoke in tempered tones. "This grieving son will never rest until that brave patriot's dreadful suffering is so revenged." James' eyes were drawing smaller; becoming dark with rage of foreboding intensity. He looked away from Lamberton to compose himself; the intensity of his emotions was causing tears to fill his eyes. I will not allow myself that release he said under his breath. The anger and determination that few men have ever truly felt all but dried his eyes; allowing the lad to continue, telling the bishop his view of Scotland's political situation. "The surrender but a temporary setback for our kingdome; the degradation of our good citizens by these unholy men with tails will not continue," he predicted with true conviction. "This Douglas squire will never hold for Edward in his heart, but always for our Scotland," he declared. "The invaders will be asked to take their leave or die for their foolish ways to stay here. Douglasdale will hold for Douglases; or be razed." Then his ominous words trailed off; a heavy silence enveloped the chamber for some minutes. "Welcome home James," said the bishop, nodding his concurrence with the lad's patriotic sentiments.

STIRLING MAY 1304-The Bishop of St. Andrews arrived in mid May in the royal burgh of Stirling; a siege of Stirling Castle was underway. The courageous Scottish constable of that castle was fighting for his country and would not give up until he heard from de Soules he informed the English king. This tactic of William Oliphant was but to delay the inevitable; many Scottish lairds of the former Scottish government were in Edward's army attacking the fortress. Three months before this final battle, the king had ordered Greek Fire sent from York for the siege of the Stirling stronghold: a horse-load of cotton thread, one load of quick sulfur and another of saltpeter with a load of well feathered arrows. Now he wanted to try another weapon: the ominous siege engine designed especially to destroy castle walls: War Wolf. Forty carpenters worked feverishly together to build the massive structure. Lead from the surrounding churches was seized on the king's orders to secure the counterbalance of the giant catapult. When the massive siege engine was complete weeks later, the king would have his weaponry *masterpiece* as he called it, to be delivered to Stirling for the last stand of the Scots.

Lamberton pledged his fealty at the abbey in Cambuskenneth within days of his arrival; his temporalities were restored to him. Several days later the bishop was making his way into the abbey on another mission; to bring James Douglas before the king that he might submit as well; be reseised to Douglas lands. As the squire and his laird walked down the long corridor to the hall where Edward was receiving nobles for their requests, the two Scots were engaged in light conversation. They continued their discussion as they were winding their way through the passageways, dimly lit by tallow tapers, presenting an eerie atmosphere of foreboding to their work at hand. It occurred to James that this abbey was the very one to first house a piece of Scottish history, safely hidden from Edward's grasp. He reminded the bishop of the story of the nobles who stole the coronation stone: the Stone of Destiny, to hide it before Edward invaded Scotland. "Do you know the whereabouts of that stone now?" the squire asked him. Lamberton gave the lad a quizzical look, "You knew of the *exchange*?" he asked, meaning the plan to steal the real stone and substitute another from Perth.

Figure XI-Part Three; Stirling Castle is in the care of Historic Scotland

James told him yes; explained that his father revealed the details of that ruse to both him and his mother the night he returned from Parliament. He described their predicament to move the stone in secrecy, hide it in Cambuskenneth at the abbey while the Abbot was away. A tale of great daring and suspense of intrigue; James was pressed to continue. "Then to replace it with one most similar though not from Egypt but from Perth," he chuckled, almost whispering as he recalled the story. Lamberton was curious now as well; who moved the stone to Perth he wondered and where did they hide it? James said his father gave him names; but he had since forgotten them, suggesting that Bishop Wishart surely knew. "Ah yes, the culprit's seal upon this noble act of conspiracy; most surely would he know where they took their precious cargo," William Lamberton offered, chuckling as he recalled the devious plot of Robert Wishart to save Scotland's precious Stone of Destiny from Edward's grasp.

Their thoughts turned back to the day at hand; Bishop Lamberton was leading the way now; his mantel flowing behind him as he nobly entered the hall where they would be presented to the king. The English lord was expecting the bishop and had him ushered in immediately. Lamberton did his bowing; made his words of respect to Edward; that he begged 'my lord the king' to grant a second request: to hear from another Scot desiring to pledge his fealty. The bishop pleaded with his overlord to hear this squire. "He but craves to tender homage and fine for his inheritance," he said forming his words carefully to not disrupt the quiet mood of the quick tempered despot. Edward asked who this Scot might be. William Lamberton stepped forward; told him it was his eighteen year old squire now with him. "My lord, the lands he seeks are in the lordship of Douglas," he said a hint of noble bearing to this claim. James was standing beside the bishop; not to speak a word until he was directed as agreed. His tall stature was only compromised by a bowed head, a pretense of respect for the English king.

Figure XII-Part Two; a painting of the Stone of Destiny by Marguerite Connolly; the Coronation Stone stolen by Edward I was returned to Scotland in 1996 and is in a secured vault on display at Edinburgh Castle where no photographs are allowed

"This young nobleman seeks only his inheritance as his father was once the lord, to hold in chief of the Douglas barony," the bishop explained quite calmly, hoping for a similar response from the king. Edward's demeanor erupted to a wrath that could not have been anticipated. The self described pillar of benevolence and good will responded in a vile and ungracious manner. "That his father was so many times forgiven; to again take up rebellion to this king, the most generous of lords. He died for his felony in my prison; his life taken for his treason!" said Edward, giving no chance to be misconstrued he continued to spew his venom; his abject hatred for Sir William Douglas. "For the youth, tell him that Edward is his father's rightful heir. And these lands have I given to my most worthy and noble vassal, the loyal Clifford. And his they shall remain," he concluded; dismissing Lamberton and his squire Douglas with a debasing gesture of true contempt.

James was solemn as he and Lamberton left the abbey. The proud son of William le Hardi a Crusader knight of renown was not cowered by the response of insipient rage; not humiliated by this ruthless lord. James was empowered by the fool hearty words of the English king. "This decision is God speaking to me," he told the bishop quietly. "Now, when the time is right will this lad renew his father's fight and Douglasdale will be restored to Douglas lairds," he vowed with stern resolution. William Lamberton believed every word of his squire; telling him that what their kingdome needed was a king; a Scot to lead them in their fight for freedom. James responded quietly that "whoever that brave man turns out to be, this lad will surely pledge his fealty and his very life to him, sure aye." Lamberton excused himself; hurried off to another meeting, and strangely he went alone. The squire joined the others of the household; a youth turned inward with his thoughts, a new strategy he must now devise for himself and his family, he mused. James wanted to despair; to cry out in anguish. But his anger held him silent; only his mother could comprehend his feelings fully; perhaps too his friend Matilda in Lovaine, but she was far away.

Figure XIII-Part Two; Cambuskenneth Abbey ruins

STIRLING CASTLE MID JUNE-The self proclaimed *compassionate king* declined to entertain the surrender of Oliphant and the garrison at the castle, knowing his war machine was on its way to Stirling, arriving in late June. Edward *generously* proposed that the brave Scots occupying the fortress should remain at their posts, to keep on fighting so he could use his military might upon them for the final battle of the war: the taking of Stirling Castle. The huge wheels turned; the massive instrument of destruction creaked ominously towards the symbol of Scotland's last stand against the English despot. Edward prayed that morning at the abbey; he prayed in a chapel everyday; bringing a portable one on campaign with him as well. The Butcher of Berwick thought himself a pious man; as long as God agreed with him. Though he never proclaimed those sentiments aloud, he reserved such imperious thoughts for his own wise council. War Wolf was seen coming in the distance; making the turn to move across the village below the castle. The cruel king would have his fun with his war machine this day.

Figure XIV-Part Two; Stirling Castle was an impenetrable fortress that commanded an imposing view of the surrounding countryside

Behind the trebuchet came large carts carrying huge stone cylinders of incredible weight, too heavy for a man to carry at nearly three hundred pounds each. One at a time these tremendous balls of destruction would be placed in the catapult. On the command of Edward the throwing arm would be released and hurl the stone a great distance, further than an arrow travels from the finest bow. Menacingly this weapon spun its cargo into flight, untouched and unobstructed, the stone glided forward as if in slow motion. The castle garrison watched in dread, paralyzed in horror as the rock buried itself deep within the castle walls, boring holes, crushing stone to dust. The huge bucket swung back into position; the base of the massive siege engine bolted backwards, slamming savagely back and forth. The deafening noise of the wooden basket clamoring to and fro as the cargo silently propelled towards the castle walls was the only sound they heard. So final in its movement; the silence surrounding the clanking trebuchet was eerie as it rocked on its wheels from the momentum of the action. Then suddenly there was a huge crashing boom! The stone cylinder had reached its target and smashed the stone of the fortress wall to fragments of sand.

The king watched his grotesque fantasy fulfilled. The fun now over he turned to leave; his lieutenant inquired as to the garrison. With an indiscriminate wave of his hand Edward permitted the defeated Scots to capitulate. The brave Oliphant, constable of the castle finally surrendered and began the lang journey to London; to end up on a barge at Traitor's Gate as he was admitted to the Tower of London. On June 24th in the year 1304 the war was over; Edward was king of Scotland. It was not until ten years later that the ignominious siege was finally revenged and a battle fought at Bannock Burn with the fortress of Stirling looming in the background that would overturn Edward's victory, his stranglehold on the Scots.

Figure XV-Part Two; a medieval siege engine on display at Caerlaverock Castle, a site managed by Historic Scotland

The Lamberton household returned to Fife and the Bishop's see of St. Andrews in late June. James planned to ride to Leuchars to tell his family the king's decision as soon as he was given leave to do that. But what then he asked himself? What should they do for income; how could they live together as a family again? This sad defeat marked the first of many battles in his quest for his inheritance. What James did not know was that it would take him sixteen years of relentless toil to reseise Douglasdale to Douglases again, to hold a charter as the laird for his family's baronial estates. As the squire groomed Fortis in the stables, his mind turned to that devastating council with Lord Edward; his thoughts churned over and over within him: where do we go from here? James continued to consider his options during the ensuing weeks that followed his appearance in Edward's court at Stirling. But there were other events yet unknown to the squire that had taken place in very same royal burgh. The meeting between one bishop and one earl would chart James' course for many years to come; that June 1304 marked both the beginning and the end of Edward's reign in Scotland.

About the same time Lord Edward was being entertained by War Wolf Bishop Lamberton was meeting with a nobleman from Ayrshire. He sought to make a secret band between himself and the Earl of Carrick who had come to Stirling to pledge his fealty once again to the English overlord. Brus' father had recently died; leaving him to seek his inheritance. Besides the lands, this Robert Brus was now in line for the throne; an heir to Scotland's king Alexander III should the need arise. For this and other reasons Bishop Lamberton entered an accord with Robert Brus; a solemn bond of mutual friendship and support. Under this agreement each would protect the other from all enemies under penalty of £10,000. Nothing was explicitly spelled out; there was no mention of a revolution or a kingdome to take back from an English despot, the penalty alone sufficient evidence of the serious nature of the secret band.

Figure XVI-Part Two; Urguhart Castle Loch Ness, display of stone spheres or cylinders, eight to fifteen inches in diameter, that could be used in a Trebuchet or similar medieval siege engine

LEUCHARS-Hugh and Archie were returning from the mews when they saw a rider approaching they realized was their older brother on his Fortis; but he was not brandishing the bravado of success. James waved a greeting to them as the lads ran in to beckon Eleanora to come quickly; the squire had returned from Stirling. Ellie and Ana dropped their embroidery hurrying to the doorway of the great hall of the de Ferrers tower house; but from the look on James' face they knew the council with the king did not go well for him. "James, what has happened to so sadden you my son?" Ellie asked as the lad dismounted his palfrey, giving the reins to his brother. Hugh and Archie exchanged worried looks; they had never seen the squire this dejected before. "Come Lindsay," Archie called to the Deerhound. The younger brothers silently returned to the stables with the hound and Fortis in tow; to commiserate on their fate before them.

Ellie put her arm around her son and told him not to worry. "That God puts challenges before us for our learning as William so often told us," she said gently. "But Mother, that we have suffered so much already," he said, agonized over this latest defeat. "This lad is so devastated; Edward's arbitrary decision is unworthy of a king," he lamented. Arm in arm these doughty Douglases made their way into the tower house. Ana was bringing wine and had ordered platters of food for James to be brought from the kitchen.

Figure XVII-Part Two; Leuchars Castle ruins comprise a doocot and motte

Ellie hugged him hard and felt his tears fall lightly on her face. James began to tell her of his times in Flanders; how he met Matilda and told her of his brave father. "And when I was most through describing his torturous end I realized that I would never hold for Edward. Years ago my first thought was to only be Lord Douglas like my father and grandfather before me," James rambled on sadly. "Perhaps that king has done this lad a favor rendering this cruel decision," he said, the heaviness in his heart reflecting in every word he spoke. Ellie told him that she was proud he had to courage to face Gilley's murderer. "This lass is frightened every day to think that soon will I so come before this king again; to beg for my dower in Scotland and Northumbria."

The younger lads were returning to join them in the great hall. James' mood was not much improved but at least he was talking Hugh noted. His older brother was prone to silence when upset or angry, until he thought his way out of his dilemma. Archie was bolder; he came right out and asked the question Hugh had on his mind. "Did Edward so refuse your fair request?" James nodded yes. "And said our Douglasdale was to remain in the possession of his vassal Clifford," he growled viciously; exhibiting the effects of much wine on his very empty stomach. Lindsay sat down next to James and put his head on the squire's knee instinctively. James broke into a wee smile; silly hound he said silently, petting his ears. "What do you suggest we do?" he asked the Deerhound. "Nothing between those ears but a hollowness; now is there?" he chuckled some. Ellie suggested they should sleep on their problems. "To decide our strategy on the morrow," she said hopefully. But James was hearing none of it; they were going to have to face this fatal blow the noo! Their hopes and dreams shattered once again by that pagan despot he sneered.

James explained the situation in Scotland; he told his mother that the war of rebellion was all but over. "Scotland is at peace; except for Wallace and his brave men. Perhaps this lad should join now with that noble patriot like our father," he sighed knowing the futility of that choice. Without a Scottish government or Guardian to back the Scottish cause, Wallace and his followers were finished. James told them he would stay with Lamberton; repay him for his kindness and the passage he paid for the lad to return from France. "Perhaps now Mother you can ask de Ferrers to exchange dower lands in Essex for ones in Scotland," he allowed. "Then you can return to live here; to be near all of us again," James suggested poignantly, hoping to keep their family together. Ellie and Ana liked that strategy; when she returned to England she would set up a meeting with her stepson William she agreed. "And will you assist le Parker with our Douglas dower lands in Scotland?" she asked him.

James' face brightened. "This lad had most forgotten the other manors we so hold," he said, some joy returning to his countenance. "There are lands near Selkirk in Craig Douglas; several manors in Ayrshire, with the one in Livingston as well," he chuckled, shaking his head in disbelief that he had not thought of the other family charters being so focused on the Douglas barony. "And Lord Hugh's lands in Hartwell and Kirk Mychael," Ellie reminded him. "That we burned some of those charters as your father so directed us to do, this lass can not recall many others of those smaller estates," she sighed knowing that the only one who was still alive to recall the lands might be James. He assured her that he would have plenty of time to remember the locations of the Douglas strongholds, "The one in Traquair comes to mind as well," he added. The Douglases were proving to themselves again that together they were never without resolve. "Perhaps we will surround the Clifford," he chuckled at the thought, "and scare him from our lands." Hugh and Archie were laughing with him now; Ellie and Ana too found humor in the sentiments.

Their discussions continued long into the night; concluding with the last glimmer from the tallow torch near the fireplace of the great hall. Ellie had gone to her chamber to retrieve the charter chest and review the lands she could expect to retain as le Hardi's widow along with the de Ferrers manors she also held in dower. As Ellie pulled out the remaining Douglas charters she came across one with Gilley's seal dated March, 1297 when he was still

Lord Douglas. Curious she untied the deed and read out loud to all of them. "Willelmi, Lord Douglas, greetings. For his service to his laird and father, from lands now held of Willelmi de Douglas, miles from his king in chief and others so in freehold, does he so grant to his eldest son Jacobus of Douglas in freehold and for him and his heirs forever," Ellie gasped recalling now when she and William decided to give the Lothiane manor in Glencorse to their son. James looked at her utterly amazed; once again his father was coming through from the Otherworld to let them know he was there and to help his family when they needed it most.

Figure XVIII-Part Two; ruins of the bishop's castle at St. Andrews, not far from the old de Quincy manor held by Eleanora Lovaine in Leuchars

Archie asked about the lands; where they might be. Ellie smiled as she recalled the first time she and William visited the estate with a very young James in tow: *'Are these lands to be of James?'* the wee lad inquired. *Gilley then informed this son that he must wait, for now Willelmi was Lord Douglas and the lands were his!* She then shared the rest of the story with everyone. "Our James the heir apparent was undaunted; *'This lad will so require a better castle for his use!'* this son informed his father. That my William was most stunned; warned this lass that there was a usurper to our kingdome in our very midst!" Ellie chuckled. "That these carucates were in the Mid Lothianes and held some of the best farmland in all of Scotland," she reminded them as well.

The squire was beaming with sheer joy. "No longer am I a landless youth but a freeholder and knight to be!" he exclaimed happily. James took the charter and began to read through the description of the lands. He noted the year recorded; recalling the secret meetings in Carstairs where Bishop

Wishart was organizing rebellion against the English king. Over and over he read the deed and marveled at the date: March 1297. The significance of the of the month and year on the document was that it was sealed and witnessed by his Uncle James the Steward, Alex de Lindsay and John Steward well before the 10th of June in 1297, when Edward issued his writs seizing William's lands for his rebellion. The deed was valid!

Figure XIX-Part Two; view from Glencorse manor lands

"It is not the size of Douglasdale but a beginning none the less," proclaimed James. Ellie kept saying how happy she was; having forgotten all about the Douglas manor in the Lothianes that was part of Lord Hugh's estates, dowry lands from his marriage to Marjory de Abernathy. Archie and Hugh were thrilled; they sensed this discovery was the beginning of something extraordinary; excitement filled the air. Even Ana was astounded. "That our Sir Gilley so speaks again to us," she marveled. Their emotions ranged from overwhelming devastation to complete elation in just a few hours; the enthusiasm stirred everyone, keeping even the younger brothers very much awake. So a little more good news would not deter a bed hour already missed their mother concluded.

Ellie told them that since the war was all but over, she would now take Archie to the de Lindsays before leaving Scotland. The wee lad's face lit up in a huge smile, "This lad to stay in Scotland?" he asked hopefully, fearing he heard her words incorrectly. Lady Douglas told her wee son that she could not afford another journey north without more income. "That you should go to the Lothianes now that Scotland has made her peace with Edward, my Archie can so safely stay here," she said softly. Hugh asked about when he could begin his studies in Scotland. "You will so attend your schooling in the monastery in four more years or less; your age can not advance quickly enough for you my Hubicus?" she chided him good naturedly; reminding her son again that to begin his schooling there he must be thirteen or older. "Much as Bishop Wishart has so informed us," she concluded.

James was very pleased; they had a plan, some hope for the future. But he was not to relent on Douglasdale he told them. "That dear Edward will not live forever; another king might find for Douglases again in that barony of our dear father and Douglas ancestors for many generations of our noble family." Ellie smiled with pride at her son's resilience. "Or the king could have a change of heart," said Hugh hopefully. "Such a man has no heart and therefore can not change it," said James sarcastically. "A noble thought dear brother, one that should not be wasted on that tyrant." Ellie asked her son when he was to return to St. Andrews. He told her on the morrow; the bishop was returning then to Berwick.

"More plans for this household," she announced. "We will leave the day next for Athelstaneford and the de Lindsays. In one week we will be returning to Ayton, then home to Essex with my dwindling clan," giggled Ellie. "And within few weeks of my arrival there will I meet with de Ferrers is my intention," she said confidently. James reminded Ellie that he had another problem. Fortis was growing older and James would be getting another horse for his work in the bishop's household traveling often as they did. He could not expect his mother to support the palfreys of both her sons. "A sad admission for this squire," he told her. "Even if my rents from Glencorse could be collected, the fees would not be sufficient," he explained. This time it was Ana who had the solution. "Perhaps Sir Alex will keep Fortis for you lad," she suggested. Ellie said that was a brilliant plan. "Sir Alex will of course take Fortis, and Audāx and the wee Archie most as well. It is done!" she exclaimed using Gilley's words for emphasis.

HOGMANAY 1305-Ellie, Hugh, Ana, Sir David, Lady Elizabeth and the rest of the Douglas household gathered round to hear Ellie read from James' letter that had just arrived from Scotland. He told them that he was recently seeing Archie at the de Lindsays in the East Lothianes; enjoying a visit with Fortis as they rode the countryside together like old times. James informed them that a visit to "my wee manor" meaning the lands he held in Glencorse, was a good beginning; perhaps to put some much needed coinage in his dwindling savings, but not for some many months or years he said sarcastically. His letter rambled on about many subjects and then it turned to Archie. "Our wee brother has a lass," he informed them jovially. "The twelve year old daughter of Uncle Alex is most fond of our Douglas page; he enjoying of her company as well; the strangest lad and lass this squire has ever seen together!" James told them that Beatrice mothers the page and Archie taunts and teases her in return. "True love is what I see here," Ellie said as she read James' words out loud to them, chuckling at the thought of Archie enamored of the de Lindsay daughter.

Then his letter turned to the more serious subject of the war; specifically to Wallace. "A very tragic story is so concluding," James wrote sadly. "This once revered patriot is to be most hunted down like a wild animal. Our dear uncle with some other noblemen so commanded to the task; ordered by Lord Edward to find William Wallace and turn him over to the English garrison," he said, describing the foul rumors he heard from Bishop Lamberton. Sir Alex was making his journey to find Wallace for the king; "exhibiting the tenacity of Douglas men, the likes of that noble knight Sir Shamus of Douglas." To anyone who knew the Douglases and their late lamented Deerhound, these words were silly and confusing, but James was cleverly disguising the truth of the situation for his family alone to understand.

Ellie realized they had to read between the lines; in case the writing fell into English hands her son was sending a hidden message. She was chuckling as she explained that when James wrote: *that noble knight Sir Shamus of Douglas;* he meant his words in jest; inferring quite clearly that Uncle Alex's *search for Wallace* was for appearances only. After all, the good Sir Shamus was but a noble beast with little more than flax and fluff between his ears she giggled. Ellie went on to elaborate. "It was widely known that Edward was furious with de Lindsay having dubbed the knight himself; his family's English lands in Suffolk now in forfeit for his disloyalty. To have ordered this honest knight and others to hunt down William Wallace was a most debasing and tragic deed," Ellie explained.

Every sentiment was very apparent to Lady Douglas as she read from the letter; she could even see James' grimace in his words *the most noble and generous king* as the squire referred to Lord Edward. Ellie understood his sentiments. She realized instinctively that Lord Paramount was committing a grave error in not forgiving the Lanark Rebel with the rest of the Scots; his treason was not any more than others who fought the English. James feared for Wallace's welfare; worried that he might fall into Edward's custody to meet a treacherous end in the Tower like Lord Douglas. As Ellie sat reading she felt a raw pain in her stomach; that gut wrenching distress and ache of bitter sorrow she knew too well. To think that another brave knight might suffer like my dear husband, she cried silently to herself. "Our Uncle James the Steward has been refused safe conduct now to Scotland; prohibiting his return from Paris until that noble patriot and friend of our dear father is most found," James concluded ruefully.

The next morning Ellie was breaking her fast in the great hall; writing to her son as she consumed her porridge and ale. She was intent on answering James' letter quickly. Her plan was to send a response along with the gifts she had for him and Archie with some of her Douglas men at arms who were returning to Scotland in a few days. "Ana, Hugh, come here," she called to them. "Are there any words you would like to add to my own?" she asked them both. Hugh urged his mother to write James and inquire of what he knows of their dower lands in Scotland. "From both Williams," he suggested. "To so determine if you should make more pleas with Edward," the lad suggested; hoping she would obtain a writ for Edward's chancellor in Scotland, William of Bevercotes. "And for his lieutenant there as well," said Ellie, "That he should be the king's own nephew John of Brittany; perhaps that he might assist our cause." Ellie thanked Hugh for the good suggestion and added those sentiments in her letter.

Figure XX-Part Two; Stebbing village today near Motts Cottage

    Then Ana approached her privately; told her quietly that she needed to warn her son of difficult times to come; her rents were barely putting food upon their table. Ellie sighed deeply; she knew what Ana meant as she held her private council these days. Lady Douglas was seriously considering the proposal of William Bagot; to free her from Edward's overlord. Perhaps as well, the knight might provide her additional sustenance; coinage to send Hugh to a college or perhaps a monastery for training in the church as was her plan. But to tell her oldest son that she might have to marry to meet her debts was excruciating to the widow. "Our James is very proud; he will blame himself that we might have to do this. And even though this marriage would so be in name only, this lass does have to marry with a license and a ceremony in the church," she said ruefully. Ellie was shaking her head in despair for the painful acceptance; her inability to continue without some income from her dower lands. De Ferrers was gravely in debt; his estates were heavily mortgaged. Other nobles who might have purchased some of their lands were held of empty coffers, drained from Edward's wars. Most everyone was owed payments for their service in Wales or Scotland and the Royal treasury was depleted, unable to meet the obligations due the English lords.

On a separate parchment Ellie began one of the most difficult letters that she had ever written; even the letter seventeen years ago to Gilley describing her situation carrying his child and yet unmarried was much easier than this missive. She began to write but the tears were overwhelming her countenance as she put down her words in ink.

Dearest James,

With an aching heart does this mother so admit her sorry fate; to have fought with Edward for my dower lands and rents has been most lost on everyone save you and Ana. And now do I so confess an empty coffer for my trouble with demands from the king to pay for the fine yet owed of our dear William some fourteen years ago for our trespass of marriage.

Having visited again with my solicitors this lass has so decided to come before the King's Bench the week next to plea with Edward to release me from this fine once more! Your mother will not relent; but for the present all my rents in England have been held by the escheators for payment of that fine. A decision of much pain and many sleepless nights has now been rendered; your mother begs of your sympathy and understanding heart that you might accept my plan of last resort.

Lady Joan de Berkeley has a friend Lady Bagot. This sad woman wants her son to marry; though in name only. His name is Sir William Bagot of Staffordshire.

Ellie continued to explain to James her arrangement with the knight. He would give her lands and much needed income; hold her dower as lord. She provided her son with every aspect of the agreement; their marriage of convenience as she termed it. Lord Bagot promised to execute every action she requested with her estates. Then Lady Douglas made her final plea to James; this marriage would give her freedom from Edward; as the wife of William Bagot the king would no longer be her liege lord.

She begged her son to forgive her; the choice was more than difficult. "Your good council is most sought," she told him. Eleanora was at her wits end. She tried valiantly to convey what it was like for a widow with lands and income held by the king; telling her son that Edward would not relent, that he would see her married to a knight of his choosing should she try to remain a widow much longer. The desperate mother closed her letter by begging James to explain the confusing and trying circumstances of her marriage to an English knight to the wee Archie as well. "That you can visit me in Fawdon or Craig Douglas as this lass will so retain her Douglas manors for my residence alone, as now," she said pleading with her heart that he would accept her plan. "Only to journey to Stafford for required meetings with our solicitors is our plan. And when Edward's nephew, the new lieutenant in Scotland, repledges Douglas dower lands to your mother will I return to live in that kingdome, near my sons; as a family as we most planned," she added, hopeful for his support.

Lady Douglas read her words to Ana and her Hugh. This was the first time Hugh had heard of her decision to remarry. "Who is this man; when did you so meet him?" he asked indignantly. Ellie was startled; she had not expected such a reaction from her Hubicus. She explained that she had met him only once at the office of the de Ferrers' attorneys three weeks ago. "Lady Joan de Berkeley told me of this lord two years before in Gloucestershire. He is not a normal man like our dear father," she started to explain. Hugh was clearly upset; he had never expected that his mother would wed another man, let alone an English nobleman and knight. William Douglas was her true love she had so often told him; what was this marriage all about he wondered? Ellie could see his grim face; she heard the pain in his voice when he spoke to her. "Dear son, that you are sadly damaged by this mother's actions pains me so," she said. "What else is this lass to do; my lands are levied that there are not rents to so collect," she cried softly as she told him. "Please tell me; offer me another choice I beg of you!" she demanded, breaking down in tears.

Ana interrupted Ellie. "Perhaps to tell young Hugh the entire story," she suggested. The widow was unsure, but Hugh had to know the truth so she informed the lad that she was marrying Sir William Bagot but would never live with him. "As our Archie would forthrightly say, this lass will never share his bed," she explained to Hugh, mimicking her wee son's very direct but often brazen words. "This English knight is not a man who seeks to love a woman; he is a soldier who has never married. This widow of William Douglas has left her heart most broken at Little Dunmow Priory; no man living can replace your father!" she declared poignantly. Hugh sat quietly for awhile and reflected on the situation. He realized that Ellie was not making this decision lightly; she was sacrificing herself in marriage because she was worried about supporting the household, her rents and coinage barely buying staples for the larder these days. Hugh also knew that his mother was desperately afraid of Edward; she would do anything to avoid dealing with the king. "This lad will pray for another solution to our problems here," he offered; hoping for a miracle to resolve his mother's dilemma.

Ellie explained her concerns to her son; told him that she was sleeping very little these days; worrying about facing the king and council in some few weeks to make her pleas. Eleanora shared with Hugh that she was forced to do battle with Edward and his vassals once again; to address the issues of her husband's unpaid fine; to expose the dishonest escheators in Northumbria and Essex who recorded their fine twice; and to reveal the thieving de Umfravilles who were collecting Fawdon fees and rents then stealing them, withholding them from the king though ordered by Edward's many writs to release the coinage. All these problems were weighing heavily upon the lady, she confessed. "Mother, this lad is sorry you must seek these dreadful answers to our problems of coffers most empty," Hugh said sympathetically. Ellie slumped in her chair, sobbing in her relief; at least one son would so forgive this lass for her marriage to this knight, she sighed to herself.

Gillerothe was leaving for Douglasdale with Patric and Henry; he took the parchments from Lady Douglas to take to James who was staying in St. Andrews. "Perhaps to stop in Ayton and look for our squire that he might be at the Lamberton manor in Berwick," she suggested, knowing the Bishop might have returned home for Hogmanay as well. "These are for your family," she said, offering some small gifts for his sister and her husband. The loyal servant to Lord Douglas was pleased by her thoughtfulness and grateful to be entrusted with the letter to James and gifts for the lads as well. "This small shield once of le Hardi you most recognize," she smiled as she gave him James' gift for Hogmanay. "And this dagger is for the wee Archie," she told Gilley's valet, "once of Hugh." Gillerothe broke out his big silly grin, "That I have served the noble Lord Hugh as well M' Lady; such fine armaments I do recognize," he said approvingly of her choice of presents for her sons, the Douglas squire and the page residing in Scotland.

BERWICK LATE FEBRUARY-Ellie was correct to surmise that the Lamberton household might yet be in Berwick though it was nearly six weeks since Hogmanay when Gillerothe faithfully delivered the gifts and letters from Lady Douglas. He did not stay to see the lad read from the parchments or he might have seen a James he would not like. The squire to Bishop Lamberton began reading the letter; the light of the wee candle in the outer tower of the Berwick estate flickered and blew out. James lit the candle again and out it went but there was not draft in the chamber. James' frustration with the candle was stirring him to anger as the words he read from his mother churned in his stomach. Finally he had the candle burning again as he continued to read the dreadful news. His eyes filled with tears; but not of sadness or sympathy, but rather of cold indignation and disgust. How dare she lay this deed upon us and swear in the same breath she holds true to the love of our father, roared the lad under his breath. Full contempt he held for her and her impetuous deed! Tell my brother she says? What sickness has taken the mind of this woman who was my mother?

Figure XXI-Part Two; only the doocot or dovecot remains of the once fair Lothian manor of Athelstaneford, where the Saltire, Scotland's flag, was born; the Cross of St. Andrews appeared in the sky in 832 over the battle field inspiring King Hungus (Angus) and his Pictish army joined by Scots to victory over the Saxon King Athelstane

The next day the squire took leave to ride to Athelstaneford and speak with Archie. When James arrived at the manor he was greeted by Uncle Alex who beckoned him to the great hall of the keep. The anger was frozen on his face; his near violent demeanor was so foreign to the de Lindsay knight that he felt compelled to sit the lad down and get to the bottom of the trouble. James sputtered the words as he told his uncle of his mother's letter. "Lady Douglas is to remarry; her husband to be is an English knight, a soldier of King Edward." Alex de Lindsay was surprised at the news but as he read from the parchment he understood at once; the brave lady who fought so hard for her family, finding herself without income was forced to sell herself in marriage for dower rights. "Your mother," he began, speaking his words calmly, only to be interrupted by James. "Not my mother!" scowled the squire. The door to the great hall suddenly slammed open as Archie came running in to greet his brother. "James," he shrieked, "I saw Fortis saddled by the stables and knew you were here to ride him! Are you just visiting the day then?" he asked.

James said quietly that he came with some news of 'your mother'. Archie was laughing, "What did Lady El do that you have disowned her?" he chided never dreaming that she would ever remarry. Sir Alex interjected,

"Your mother has found herself in dire circumstances with little income coming from her dower that she is unable to meet her expenses of the escheators and your father's debts from the fine of marriage. She has chosen after her seven years of mourning to marry an English knight yet maintain a separate life from him to live in Fawdon and Essex once her troubles with her dower income are so resolved," he explained to his page. Archie was stunned. The thought of their mother the wife of anyone but Lord Douglas was a shock! "And possibly a crime of grave felony," he said, shaking his head in angry disbelief. "It is certainly not a crime," said their uncle almost laughing at the lads' great drama given for what he saw as a simple financial transaction between adults of station.

The Douglas squire beckoned Archie to join him; to ride their palfreys and speak of these sad tidings as brothers must do. Taking leave of the great hall at Athelstaneford James suggested a visit to Aberlady Bay. "To the chapel there; a Carmelite friary built in memory of Sir David de Lindsay, a Crusader and grandfather to the fair and lovely Dame Beatrice," James said, emphasizing the lass' name to tease Archie. "The white friars for their kindness, caring for Sir David when he took sick, were given these de Lindsay lands." The two brothers rode their amblers Fortis and Audāx and crossed the drawbridge over the large moat surrounding the de Lindsay fortress, heading north to the lands of Luffness. As they traveled James shared stories of the Vikings and the legends of Lofda. "A great warrior to have a tomb himself at Luffness; his name once given to the bay," James explained. "That invader to our homeland was a follower of Anlaf or so our father told this lad."

Except for the brief interludes of history, the brothers rode in silence; exchanging few words otherwise until they arrived at the Carmelite chapel. "Let us pray for our dear father," said James, as he dismounted, tying Fortis to a gate post. "And I will pray for our mother," insisted Archie daring James with his eyes to challenge him. The squire's face bore a strained grimace as he suppressed his smoldering rage, but he bit his tongue. He decided not to correct his younger brother on the status of one named Eleanora. When they returned from the chapel Archie was talking away but James' demeanor was not changed. He was still sullen and quiet. Archie knew it was his way when troubled, so he kept talking. "Did you know our uncle was called upon to find of William Wallace?" he asked his older brother.

James told him that he knew that from the bishop that Sir Alex's loyalty, his pledge of fealty to Lord Edward was being tested. "But he is now relieved of that sad duty," said the page. "Where did you hear of that?" asked James. The wee lad told him that Beatrice had confided in him. "Most distressed was this lass, hearing the sad news by mere accident from her mother," he continued. "That I just had to comfort her as we do with our mother when she cries." James ignored his last words about Ellie. He spoke bitterly now, that all good Scots were falling to that pagan despot. "Perhaps the time to come that we Douglas men will take up arms against him," he scowled. "What will they do with Wallace when they catch him?" asked Archie. "He is too smart to fall in their trap," said James, "that he will never be found unless a friend turned traitor so betrays him for coinage or some other trappings." The page thought about what his brother said. "What fool would do of that?" he asked incredulously. Lamberton's squire just shook his head; he could never imagine such a man he told Archie, but then people were always surprising him these days, alluding to their mother's betrayal of their family, her remarriage to an English knight.

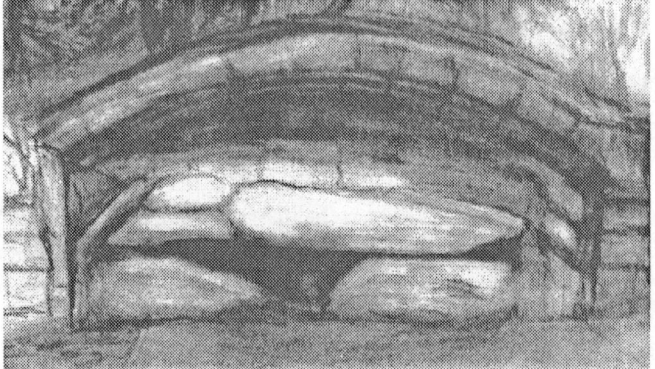

Figure XXII-Part Two; artist's drawing of the much damaged effigy and tomb of a Crusader David de Lindsay at the 13th century Carmelite friary ruins, Luffness manor

    The Douglas brothers mounted their palfreys and rode down the cart paths, through the woodlands without saying another word about William Wallace and his fate. Finally James made the turn that would take them to the dunes and shoreline of Aberlady Bay. "Our father had told me that bodies of water were very important to our Celtic ancestors; that if you looked long enough into the surface you could see to the Otherworld," James reminded Archie solemnly. He tied Fortis to a tree and began onfoot; sliding down the dunes to the bay below he called to Archie to follow him. The lad was hesitant; then he decided to join James in whatever he had in mind. They sat for hours by the waters edge; talking of William and Douglasdale, trying to comprehend the horrible news from Essex. "We can never be a family again," said James with disgust. Archie was crying; his whole world was crumbling before him. His mother was going to be Lady Bagot, married to an English knight; his idol and older brother vowed to never speak to her again for her treason! He was sobbing now; unable to hide his abject sorrow from his brother he bolted up to leave.

James abruptly looked up. "Where are you going? Are you to leave this humble squire too?" Archie cried through his words, his sobs making his speech almost unintelligible. "This is my fault; if father had wanted to stay he would have gone to France with us; now he's gone. He doesn't even come to speak with me anymore in the middle of the night and he most left us the very time this lad was born," cried the wee Archie as he wiped his streaming eyes with the sleeves of his surcote. James got up and went to his younger brother, hugging him hard. "Our father did not leave because of you lad. He was stolen from us by that evil lord de Percy. And he has not to come to visit me in my dreams since I returned to Scotland," he admitted.

Figure XXIII-Part Two; Aberlady Bay, Luffness manor; once a port, silted mud today

Then James let out a gasp. "Bluebells!" he exclaimed pointing to the small patch of wild blue flowers growing on the nearby bank leading down to the bay. "Our mother, your mother; by St. Bride," he muttered. "*She* always said his words: to forever think of him when we saw the Bluebells. And there they are! But too early for those flowers to be growing; something is most wrong here," he said exasperated to think that his father was approving in some strange way the marriage of his lady to that Staffordshire knight. "No, something is very right here," said Archie. "Our father does not want us to destroy our family; we must stick together," he vowed.

James felt the anger within him subside some as he looked over at the small blue flowers. He would be resigned to the marriage; but not approving of it he declared to himself. "Dear Archie, this squire needs his brother; you must never leave me!" he told the wee lad as he held him. Archie hugged him back, clung to him as his sobbing ceased. "James, this lad will always follow you; wherever you are to go, Archie will be there to save you," he said boldly. The squire started laughing, "You save me? It is this noble knight to be who will save your sorry self!" he teased the youth. "Come, let us return to Athelstaneford or you will be in trouble with your laird."

Archie chuckled. "This lad will never be on the cross side of Uncle Alex," he said, smiling up to James as they climbed the hill to their palfreys. "Beatrice loves me," he said with his matter of fact tone. James asked him what he meant; how did he know that? "She told me," Archie said. "And I most love her as well." James chuckled at his wee brother's sentiments. "In love, a page in love with the laird's daughter," he scoffed. "No, she is in love with me and I love her back," Archie said indignantly. "Someday we are to wed and have twenty children for I have told her so!" The squire was nearly bent over in laughter but Archie remained serious and insistent. "One day you will be God father to our children; it is done!' he said, mimicking Lord Douglas, the father he barely knew. It is done indeed said James to himself as he mounted Fortis to return back to the de Lindsay stronghold.

Figure XXIV-Part Two; Bluebells

That night both lads slept in the same bed chamber of the manor; when they woke the next morning each brother shared his story of Lord Douglas as they broke their fast in the great hall with Sir Alex. The father had visited both his sons in their dreams. He always came when they needed him most reflected James. "Goodbye Archie," the squire said as he began the lang ride back to Berwick and the manor of Bishop Lamberton. "Are you going to the wedding then?" asked Archie as his brother turned to leave. "No chance of that!" said James and he was gone. Alex de Lindsay was standing behind his page as he waved goodbye to his brother. "And are you to attend the ceremony?" he asked the wee lad. "I told my father that I would," admitted Archie referring to his dream. "But I should say it will be with a heavy heart," he admitted to his uncle. "A lass does many things to confuse a lad," he ruefully concluded, letting out a deep sigh. Uncle Alex chuckled. "Aye, truer words have not been said my page!"

WESTMINSTER-In mid February Eleanora de Ferrers as she discreetly fashioned herself these days appeared before the king; begging for the settlement of the fine for her marriage to William Douglas. On 18 February the king commanded a writ; a levy of the lands and chattels of the late William de Douglas was sent, to have the money delivered to Westminster immediately; payment for the arrears of the fine for marrying Eleanora de Ferrers will now be settled, ordered the king! With her solicitors in stride Lady Douglas made a clear case; dishonest escheators tried to twice collect her fine. Recording her obligations and William's separately, these sorry knights of the shire sought to take both fines perhaps remitting only one to the king's treasury. With her she brought the Northumbrian assessments for the seizures made to date: £43, 14s, 10d and odd pence taken from their estates including corn and hay from Fawdon. King Edward accepted her findings and receipts. He also released her from the double fine entered in error in Essex in 1291 with a writ he issued the next day. An additional £17 in chattel and rents were seized from her manors of Stebbinge Park and Woodham Ferrers she added in her defense; producing receipts and documents for these involuntary payments as well. The remaining balance owed should only be £40 asserted Eleanora Douglas, proposing that William Douglas' manor should provide sufficient income to retire the debt. Edward agreed; he ordered the smaller, unpaid sum to be taken from the Fawdon rents collected by de Umfraville and releasing her lands from all liens.

Ellie wanted to take her leave of Westminster immediately; as soon as her final request was granted. She was unnerved by all the commotion and activity surrounding the king's court and could not wait to return home to the tranquility of Essex. Everyone there was abuzz with gossip; a feeling of unrest permeated the air as in just nine days Parliament would open to a sizzling trial. A knight of renown, a powerful baron of the realm would submit to king and council for charges of contempt; exposing his lord the king to danger in Scotland by the withdrawal of his men at arms with those of Cromwell to engage in private contest; a duel in France. The English lord surrendering to the king's will was none other than Nicholas de Segrave! Ellie was trying to keep her wits about her; concentrating on her own troubles. There was grave controversy surrounding Nicky's suspected collusion with King Philip of France. His appearance at the royal court in Paris, the very time the magnates of Scotland were also in attendance pressing their diplomacy fueled many wagging tongues. Speculation swirled that the de Segrave knight might be involved in a sinister conspiracy, perhaps a plot of treason was the whispered talk around Westminster. Ellie dared not speak of him to anyone; she was not Lady

Douglas this day but Eleanora de Ferrers seeking her dower. Hiding from her true identity, stifling her instincts to visit her dearest cousin; she had to leave London not knowing his fate. Ellie dared not speculate that her Nicky would be convicted of treason; held in the White Tower to face the same fate as her dear knight and husband William le Hardi. Forcefully the lady suppressed all thoughts of Nicholas de Segrave in self defense. She mounted her jennet and cautioned herself to think only of her own appearance this day before the king, hoping she was successful at long last in securing her income.

Figure XXV-Part Two; antique print in the author's collection of the White Tower and the Thames published May 1830 by Robert Jennings for the History and Antiquities of the Tower of London by John Bayley

As Lady Douglas rode out of Westminster that afternoon she grumbled under her breath, "William, I could just kill you for not paying that fine for our marriage!" And just as clearly as if her husband was riding his palfrey next to her she heard him speak: "Too late." She turned round to ask Hugh if he heard anything. Ellie was sure someone must have noticed that Gilley spoke out loud but her son replied that he heard nothing. She thought long and hard about the words she had listened to until she was absolutely certain now that her husband had spoken aloud to her. The words were clearly his, Ellie mused. Then she softened her thoughts as she reflected on her only love. Lord Douglas was standing behind me this day, to give me strength to face that butcher king; of this I can be certain, she said smugly to herself. Dear Lord Will she prayed; please look after our friend and kin, my sweet Nicky this day in Edward's vengeful grasp.

Hugh rode his palfrey Sir William closer to her to speak in confidence. "Mother, a word with you?" he begged. "Must you so marry that knight, now that you have your rents restored?" Ellie shook her head no! She smiled triumphantly at her son for her success today before the King's Bench. "That I have income now I will not have to marry," she told her son happily. "This lass will so inform that knight in one month or less when my coffers are once more filled with coinage; our larder brimming high with the harvested crops of our tenants." As the mother answered her son she looked intensely at his countenance to assure him of her true intentions. Hugh's eyes beamed in happiness; his face answered her query with a glow of childhood innocence that Ellie so treasured about this lad.

On the 28th of February Sir Nicholas de Segrave appeared before the king. He had returned from France and was staying in the house of Nicholas the archer when the warden of the Cinque ports arrested him. The confinement was short lived however as twenty-one barons of Dover helped him escape. Rescued, he quickly made his way to his manor in Stowe. When Edward returned to England he ordered the sheriff of Northamptonshire to summon Sir Nicholas, Lord of Stowe to Parliament at Westminster in person; to make his plea to the charges and abide by the king's decision.

In full Parliament in the presence of his lord the king and the archbishop of Canterbury, other bishops and many earls and lords of England, Nicholas de Segrave, miles made his submission. He admitted his guilt to the charges of contempt for exposing his king to the danger of his enemies in Scotland by desertion of himself, his army and the men of Sir John Cromwell, since he was considered the aggressor in the provocation. Edward was riled to a point where he was considering a sentence of death. The point of pain for the English king was that de Segrave had deserted England for France; in effect subjecting the kingdome and his king to the dominion of the king of France by bringing their resolution to that court illegally. This grave error Nicky admitted to as well and was remanded to the custody of the constable of the Tower of London, a position once held by his grandfather in 1203.

The council of the king deliberated for three days. The magnates were forced to say that such a deed required the penalty of death but also added that the king might allow himself to be moved by such compassion as to release de Segrave should he find manucaptors. Edward Plantagenet relented; he allowed Sir Nicholas his freedom upon finding seven good men of the realm, lords to pledge of lands and surety; to surrender him and all his lands at the king's will. On the 29th of March these barons of England came forward and Ellie's cousin Nicky was given his freedom the next day to return home to his manor in Stowe. The true story of the affair was never entered into the final records; only the whispering tongues of Westminster spoke near the truth of the events and the knight's interlude in Paris with the Scots.

STEBBINGE PARK-Once again Ellie was to despair; the words of the king, the writs he issued under Privy Seal were slow in their commencement; not yet coming under the Great Seal of the chancellor, the final distribution to the shires was not made for months to come. The Essex escheators still held her rents; Eleanora was bled dry by dishonest knights as sheriffs for the county. Her household larders emptied and by the end of

March she relented; with no other choice known to her Eleanora Lovaine Douglas agreed to give her hand in marriage to Sir William Bagot. The same day Nicky acquired his freedom from Edward's Tower, Ellie began the process to acquire her independence from her lord the king. The loyal vassal of Edward Plantagenet, the friend of the Prince of Wales, Lord Bagot set off from Stafford to fine for the marriage license and on the 8th of April he received the grant from Edward I, king of England:

In consideration of the service of William Bagot, miles, for Eleanora, late the wife of William de Duglas, to marry him whenever she will. Issued by the king on like information

In early June Eleanora met with her solicitors in Hertford to review another legal case they were handling for her. For two years she had been fighting the son and heir of Gilbert de Umfraville in a suit of dower for her income from Fawdon. But the rolls in Northumbria were filed two years at a time; the rents and fines collected by the escheators were not reported to the king sometimes three or four years in arrears. By Ellie's calculations, the heir of Redesdale who held of Fawdon of which Eleanora held from him in freehold for half a knight's fee was keeping her rents, not paying them to the king to retire William's debts. "That I must file a suit of dower once again," she fumed. "This greedy reprobate, thieving from a poor widow," she chided.

Her attorneys assured her that King Edward would act and that he did. He issued a writ from Witley to his vassal and seneschal Richard de Buselyngthorp to take the attorneys of Richard de Umfraville and his wife Lucy de Kyme in a suit of dower by Eleanora, late the wife of William Douglas. The delays in resolving these payments had forced her hand, her hand in marriage that is. The date was set for the middle of October; she would write to Lady Bagot his mother now and invite her to come to Bildeston around the Ides of that month for the quiet ceremony they agreed upon. Lady Eleanora Lovaine de Ferrers Douglas would now be Lady Eleanora Bagot, uxor of William Bagot, miles.

Ellie and Ana were sitting in the great hall of Stebbinge Park with Hugh. Soon the entire Douglas household would enter as they too were summoned by their lady to hear her sad announcement. She told them all that she had finally agreed to marry Sir William Bagot in October; her fight for rents most hers was bringing no coinage for her relentless efforts. Nothing would change after she had married the English knight she assured them; she would remain in Essex and spend time as well in Northumbria, perhaps in Scotland too was her desire. "There will be some guarantee of income now, coinage for our coffers," she told them dejectedly. As this lady spoke to her wee clan of Essex, these long time members of her household with her de Ferrers knight and her men at arms, as well as her remaining son, her eyes welled up with tears of deep sorrow. All the years she stood as Lady Douglas, holding the family together with sheer will of spirit had taken their toll. She was alone; all her seven children but her Hugh were either faraway in Scotland or with God in the Otherworld of the Celts. Her wee Archie was a page in the Lothianes with the de Lindsays and her James was estranged from her; her remarriage to an English knight was too much for him to accept.

Quietly, Ana had gone to each of these loving Douglases, the people in Ellie's household and told them privately what they knew already; that Lady Douglas cried herself to sleep most every night for her loss of Gilley. Sadly now even his name would be stripped from her as well. No one said a word until she was through with her speech. Then one of William le Hardi's man servants spoke. "It is I Gillerothe of Douglas who knows more than any other here how much Lord Douglas loved his Lady El, his dear and loving wife; how sad that good knight would be to know what you are forced this day to do but to put food upon our table. We good Douglas folk are deeply saddened Lady Douglas. But know this; we are forever in your debt, grateful for your kind concern for us all," spoke the elderly valet of her husband.

Ana told her that not one of the household was going to take their leave. Sir David interjected his own words. "Lady Eleanora, for most two decades now has this knight been in service to M' lady. No laird of greater courage would this old knight so find than you; most bravely you have led us all to safety in the face of great personal loss. We are all proud to serve in your household; the name you hold will always be that of Douglas to your wee clan here, no other one will do!" he told her with bravado. They were all laughing, cheered by the good words of Gillerothe, Ana and Sir David. Douglas faces smiled back at their lady. Ellie started crying again but through a grin of gratitude as Hugh came to stand behind her with his hands placed reassuringly on her shoulders. "This lady is most thankful," she said through her tears. "We have all been through so much together; each and every one of you most precious to this Douglas lass," she told them honestly.

SCOTLAND AUGUST 1305-Near Glasgow in early August a travesty of momentous proportions seldom known to good men was taking place in Bishopbriggs. The brave patriot William Wallace refused to pledge his fealty; refuted all allegiance to Edward. While making concessions to nobles the English king singled out the Ayrshire knight for capture. To accept of Edward's peace, Lord Paramount made it the charge of other Scottish nobles like Alexander de Lindsay to find the Lanark Rebel; the name Ellie gave this brave knight when he first came to Douglas Castle lo those many years ago. Sir Alex made the appearance of trying to find Scotland's greatest hero; searching in all the wrong places he was successful in his ruse. But such was not the way of others. Edward Keith of Selkirkshire, brother of Robert Keith a newly appointed guardian of Scotland, was one noble to accept the bait, the writ of pursuit of William Wallace was issued in his name; the manor of Synton was awarded him for his part in the chase. But Keith did not capture Wallace himself; the men at arms in service to the sheriff of Dumbarton, Sir John Menteith were responsible for the outrageous act. On 3 August 1305 Wallace was sadly in custody; held in chains as he began his journey south to meet with Edward's wrath for his enduring acts of staunch patriotism.

William Wallace, the son of Alan and brave patriot from Ellerslie was smuggled out of Scotland by his shameless captors, passing from Sir John Menteith to Sir Aymer de Valence, then to the inimical Lord Clifford of Douglasdale, where he was handed over to Nicky de Segrave's brother John, held at Carlisle tower, then to make his final journey to London. The barbaric deeds that followed were thought to be a good example to any Scot considering rebellion to their benevolent and dear Lord Paramount. While Edward intended to further tame Scotland and bring the kingdome to her knees forever, this vengeful plan it seemed did the very opposite. Each atrocity endured by this good and true man of core values, who held for Scotland in his heart to his very dying breath; seemed only to fan the flame of freedom.

The Lanark rebel was convicted of treason by his judges; one judge was Ellie's cousin Sir John de Segrave. Dragged savagely, unclothed down London's cart paths subject to the callous ridicule of unknowing English peasants, William Wallace was hanged cruelly; drawn on the rack; then hideously disemboweled. When in his lifeless state Sir William was then decapitated and his body further mutilated that many pieces could be sent throughout the land, in grave symbol of Edward's power. Essex saw the gruesome display of body parts paraded through its towns and villages in gory spectacle. Ellie, Hugh and Ana would not venture out of doors for days until they were sure the despicable caravan of carnality had left Essex, on its way north to Scotland.

Lady Douglas found her Hugh one morning writing in the withdrawing room on her slant top desk. He looked up as she came into the darkened chamber lit only by a candle near the inkwell of the writing surface. "Dear son," she asked, noticing the tears falling from his eyes, swollen from sadness. "What troubles you?" Hugh shook his head. "This lad had never known of William Wallace but our James had often told me of his visits to Douglasdale; how he saved our father's life at Durisdeer when I was but a lad of three," he began. Ellie understood; she had been distraught over the news of his capture and execution. The details of his trial and torturous end at Smithfield Elms brought back her own sad memories of Lord Douglas; reminding her of the vivid horror of his sentence, hanged cruelly. All she could think about these days was that awful feeling of helplessness as her precious knight was taken from her seven years ago.

Figure XXVI-Part Two; view of Stirling Castle from the Wallace Monument

"My son, this lady feels the overwhelming grief for that brave knight as if Wallace were our own dear kin," she said softly. "His courage and love for our Scotland, the kingdome of your ancestors makes this travesty all the more bitter to this lass. He was a man most like your own father William; a knight of renown who has paid the final price for his adherence to his truth." Hugh told her that he could not comprehend such violence. "Why must there be so much savagery?" he asked her. "Where is the compassion of this Edward?" Ellie put her arm around her son. "That Edward was pious only when God agreed with him." Gilley's words so often said she shared now with her Hubicus. "Your father so told us that a knight was bred to fight; to do God's work in battle. Our father and now dear William Wallace have fought for what they so believed was right and true, the rights of Scotsmen to their lawful ways; to pay dearly for their convictions," she said solemnly.

As she wiped the tears from her own eyes she told Hugh what she had come to know: it was the wife and children left behind in this world to sometimes pay the biggest price; the painful longing for the return home of their warrior knight that would never be. "That sorrow I feel most every day; it fills my soul with a haunting loneliness, that only seeing my Gilley, holding him again in my arms would end."

Hugh showed her his journal. "This lad most had to write of him; to express my sentiments that it may remove this pain I feel so here," he sighed. The words he had written in memory of that noble patriot, William Wallace were healing to his broken heart he told his mother.

'A truer man has never been to his word and courage; to fight for all of Scotland valiantly without the face of self upon his deeds. The betrayal of this noble patriot will be forever recalled; wretched fools who threw Wallace to Edward's wrath not unlike those who betrayed our Lord that day of infamy, to send him to the cross. Though William Wallace was not the Son of God he is the Son of Scotland. And as our father often told us: Scotland is our home, Douglasdale our Paradise, a true Heaven for all Douglases, sure aye!

Then the young lad added out loud, "God Bless William Wallace now with God." Ellie too bowed her head and added, "Amen."

BILDESTON SEPTEMBER 1305-Eleanora Lovaine Douglas and her Douglas household had descended upon the manor of her Lovaine kin in Bildeston, to the north in Suffolk. Her father's widow had traveled to Sezincote leaving Ellie to have Bildeston for her few guests invited to the quiet ceremony in October at the family's church adjacent to the old manor house, St. Mary Magdalene. As they rode up the cart path past the rolling farm lands of the villeins of the old Lovaine estate, Ellie realized that although she had not been here since her marriage twenty four years before to Lord de Ferrers, little had actually changed; only the old church seemed different with the gated wall now of rubble and stone and a new south entrance added to an existing Norman doorway. Her brother Thomas was at the manor and came out to greet them heartily as they arrived. "Ellie," he exclaimed, "how pleased this lonely squire is to see his fair sister and dear nephew too," he teased Hugh. Ellie's father Lord Lovaine had twice remarried after her mother died; both ladies were near the age of his daughter that some of her Douglas children were born well before their Uncle Thomas Lovaine. Hugh was three years younger than his mother's brother but with his recent growth spurt into the taller Douglas frame, he had outgrown Thomas in height. "Dear uncle, how good of your to greet us so cheerfully," he grinned, making plain his taller bearing as he stood next to Ellie's brother.

"You will be most pleased to know that young Archibald has just this hour arrived," the Lovaine squire said to the surprise of Ellie and Hugh, for he was not to come for another few weeks. Just then a wee page bolted through the huge carved oak door of the old manor house, rattling the hinges barely off as it slammed hard against the exterior wall. "Mother!" he screamed loudly. "Hugh, Ana, everyone, this lad is so happy to be home with his family!" he exclaimed with a smile that practically filled his face. "What brings you here so early?" she asked him, adding the reassurance that she was thrilled to see him. Archie told her that he carried a letter from Uncle Alex that explained everything. "Our uncle was found in rebellion; the king has banished him with six others found for Wallace. For half the year to end March the next, he is to live in exile most probably in France as was his plan," he told them excitedly pulling the parchment with the de Lindsay seal upon it out from under his surcote.

As Ellie entered the great hall of Bildeston manor she was reading Sir Alex's letter, her eyes wild with fear and dread. Sir Simon Fraser had been exiled for four years; Sir Alex for six months read the king's Ordinance. "And is he in forfeit of his lands then?" she wondered aloud. Archie told her that he is not to return home to Scotland until spring. "But you will find it so written here," the lad said as he pointed to the instructions from his uncle. "He will meet with us at Fawdon or another place of our choosing when the snows end; he will then return Archibald to his service should we deem it prudent," Ellie read aloud. She was taken aback by the suspicious tone of that last phrase, *should we deem it prudent*. "There is something more that is yet unsaid," she told them. Then a stray thought raced through her mind from words Sir Alex said long ago: revolution! "Beatrice and her family are to stay in Ayrshire and Uncle Alex knew you would be worried," his words trailed off as Ellie interrupted. "That he returned my son to me unharmed!" she exclaimed happily, drawing the wee lad to her, a big smile on her face. "Two sons to come home to Essex then!" Hugh was happy to have his brother's company as well he said. "This lad most missed his brother," he confessed.

"Does our James know of this?" she asked him, hoping for some more news on her oldest son. "This lad has so spoken with his brother only three weeks past. He is safe to remain in the bishop's household as Lamberton is now a guardian of the realm he told me." Ellie wanted to know if his anger had subsided some. "No," said Archie with his normal matter of fact tone. "James said he will never forgive *my mother*." Ellie recoiled in pain at the reference 'my mother' knowing her oldest son was carefully deliberate in his choice of words. Then Archie added, "But he will seek our love again; it is too lonely for him even in our Scotland. James does not speak the words, but his sad face does tell me of his grief, that he misses his family more than a little I fear." Ellie added sadly, "And his mother misses him the same."

Ellie continued to read of the news from their homeland; many of Gilley's friends, fellow patriots, were coming to pledge their fealty and reclaim their lands. An annual event I fear she said under her breath. "That our friend John Wishart is at long last to return from France," she said happily. What she did not know then was that Edward planned to recoup his losses from campaigns against the Scots devising a new method for them to gain entry to their lands. Beginning a week later in October he initiated a process where nobles could be reseised to their estates by paying over value of their lands of one year's rents to the king; ironically these fees would go into his treasury or be used to repair Scottish castles in his domain that he kept to compel nobles to his adherence. He generously would allow them to pay out only one half of those rents, keeping the other for their sustenance, he told them. Those who Edward trusted least such as Bishop Wishart were to pay of him three years' value or more of their fees and income. The baron of the Mearns Sir John Wishart was assessed four years' value for his rebellion when finally allowed to return from exile.

Figure XXVII-Part Two; Bildeston village; set somewhat apart from the original manor and adjacent medieval church, the village probably moved here in the mid 14th century

    Ana was bringing out wine for her lady while the Lovaine cooks brought food from the kitchen as the Douglases began their feasting, celebrating the return of Archie. Ellie set the letter from Sir Alex aside when she noticed another small parchment in front of her on the table. "What of this?" she asked. Archie looked up with a disgusted grimace. "James had insisted that I bring this letter to you as well," he said grudgingly. "Sorry Mother, it was a pledge I made to him," he said as he looked mournfully to Hugh, then Ana.

178

The letter began formally:

James of Douglas, Saluz, greetings. This humble squire respectfully admits that he can so understand your fears and need to be free of Edward Plantagenet as one liege lord. Yet have you so sadly forgotten you are a Douglas? Do you not recall that sacred ceremony of our Celtic ancestors shared by Lord and Lady Douglas sealed in the blood of that ancient race, was it so very long ago? J pray you reconsider this plan of outrage. James of Douglas will not attend the grave folly you so foolishly contrived. Jf this ceremony of sacrament does so take place you will have made sure your fate to reside in Edward's England for the remainder of your years. Ever more will J remain a Scot to live my days in Scotland; a son without a mother orphaned for your treason to our family. Are you to join the fate of men with tails? J pray not! Repent and call off this travesty.

Ellie was shaking, trying to keep from crying she sat feverishly twisting Gilley's ring on her finger, the seal ring he used for signing documents, the ring she wore ever since he was laid to rest in Little Dunmow Priory. Her eyes welled with tears, sobbing she ran from the great hall and slammed the door to her bed chamber. The wee hound Lindsay scampered after her, scratching at the door trying to open the strange lock. The Deerhound was confused by her actions and began to howl miserably until Ellie let him in her room. Ana wrapped at her door but Ellie ignored her; she came in anyway. "Dear lass, what was said in that letter that hurts you so is only the grief of a lad who has lost his father and now fears he has lost his mother most as well," she said soothingly, hoping Ellie would listen. Sobbing profusely Lady Douglas could barely speak. "Why does he write his words so cold that I am not his mother now; a lad I raised from a babe as my own and truly loved as well?" she asked, shaking in abject sorrow to think this son could despise her so.

"Oh my Ana, if there was only a choice to make; a lass is held to few options when her lands yield few rents. And that I miss my Gilley so! He would know what to say to our son," she cried, unable to stop crying she was choking on her tears. "This lass does so regret to have sent a letter to him; perhaps if I had told him face to face would he have so forgiven me?" Ana held her and rocked Ellie in her arms telling her that no matter how she told James he would not accept her marriage. "The lad has blamed himself I fear that you have made this choice against your will. Were he but able to receive of Douglas lands this circumstance would never have occurred; he knows this to be most true," Ana told her. Hugh and Archie were coming in the chamber to quietly sit on the bed. "Mother, our James is sick with grief that he can not fill his father's absence and support us with our rightful inheritance," said Hugh. Archie told Ellie that he knew James would give up his forced isolation from the family. "Our older brother is most stubborn. He stays with his grief more than anyone this lad has ever known. But he is not of stone," Archie said pleading with his eyes that she listen to him.

Figure XXVIII-Part Two; the Hyde or Hide Lea today near the site of the original Bagot manor house

"He loves you mother and you will see, James will come home to us again," he assured her. Archie told everyone how he and James had gone to Ellie's manors to speak to villeins about their rents. "With charters in his hand as he traveled the boundaries of those farm lands, we rode and rode to each and every tenant. But little coinage did we find and few crops growing in the days we traveled; nothing that he could thus send to you was he able to so find," explained the wee lad. "Except of this," he said as he pulled out a small pouch containing a few silver coins. Ellie was stunned; she had forgotten that James had pledged to look after rents on some of her lands in Winton, the barony of Haddington and Berwickshire too as they were all within close proximity to the bishop's manors where he was staying. She shook her head in disbelief as she counted the rents her sons had collected. "Enough that we can journey to our Scotland in the spring," she told them happily.

"Mother, that squire, my brother was relentless; trying to find of income for your coffers that you would not have to marry," he continued. "He kept some coinage too that he could bring his Fortis with him back to the Lamberton estates," he told them. "That this is true then, he does not refuse his mother?" she asked hopefully. Archie dismissed the question with a knowing smirk; of course not. He then told her about a recent incident in Winton. Archie and his brother were riding through her manors in the Lothianes when they were met by one English knight, "A sheriff we were told; James told the constable that he was James Douglas of Lothiane, the farms of Travernent and Winton of his mother's dower that he must collect to send to Essex." Ellie started to laugh, picturing James in this ruse; calling himself James Douglas of Lothiane, she chuckled to herself. In truth there was another Douglas squire, the twelve year old grandson of Andrew of Linlithgow, who also held the name of James. William le Hardi was the lad's God father; his own father chose the name of James in honor of Lord Douglas' oldest son and heir.

Figure XXIX-Part Two; Winton House; Winton was part of the de Quincy estates that Eleanora held in dower from de Ferrers

Archie continued to regale his mother with their tales of intrigue in the Lothianes. "Our James would appear to them in disguises; sometimes he looked a mere monk in his travels," Archie chuckled as he told the stories of his older brother scouring the farms of her manors for fees owed to his mother. "That dear Edward did so help himself to £25 of my rents from those farms not so long ago," she moaned knowing the king's escheators had taken what they wanted from many manors in Scotland. Lady Douglas bowed her head and cried some more; not just for her quarrels with James over her impending marriage but also for her continued futility in her fight against the English king and his vassals over her dower. Trying to compose herself the widow quietly dried her eyes and asked her sons to join her in the great hall; they would resume their feasting and speak of James another time.

A day after Ellie's thirty seventh birthday and just two days before she was to marry, Sir William Bagot and his mother Lady Isabel de Grendon

Bagot arrived with his entourage of squires and attendants. Another man about his age, a friend they were told, would come as well. This other guest was a knight named Sir William Martyn; arriving the next day with Richard Bagot, the younger son of Lady Isabel. Ellie greeted them all graciously and Ana showed their attendants to the rooms set for their stay. Sir William was a small man, shorter than Hugh, with curly blonde hair and a great mustache which he seemed to continuously groom, sometimes with his fingers as he sat in the great hall and spoke with several of their guests. The future husband of Lady Douglas had very fine features as well; handsome with pretty blue eyes, but not in the rugged Douglas fashion. Archie was stunned when he saw the man who was to be their stepfather and called Hugh aside to say that he was glad their brother James was yet in Scotland. "If this Bagot is a knight of renown in England than the Scots should have no trouble retaking their kingdome," he said with grave sarcasm. "Archie, we need to have peace in our land not war," said Hugh. His brother threw him a look that clearly told him that the wee Archie had other thoughts. "Too long have you been with our James in Scotland that you only think of rebellion," teased Hugh.

Figure XXX-Part Two; site of the former manor hall of Bildeston, across from the church of St. Mary's

"Much longer have you stayed in England to become one of them," taunted his younger brother, pointing to the Bagot brothers and the odd knight who came alone to attend the wedding, adding in a whisper, "men with tails!" Archie had reached a cord; Hugh bolted after him; revenge was on his mind. "No wee page is going to so insult this lad," he shouted as he ran hard, catching up with his brother in the courtyard of the Lovaine manor. The lads were yelling their challenges so loudly at each other, daring to do battle, that their mother heard them inside the great hall where she sat with her guests. Ellie excused herself, fearful they would do harm to one another. She was horrified when she found her sons outside about to do their fighting with knives.

Figure XXXI-Part Two; interior of St. Mary de Magdalene in Bildeston; a beautifully maintained medieval church with many 13th century features

"What does this mother have to do to keep you lads from foolishness as this?" she scolded them, ordering them to surrender their weapons to her. "The noo; this lass does so implore you! Do not fight among yourselves this day." She admonished them sternly for attempting such folly without so much as a gambeson to wear. "Remember the words of your father, the battle waits for the warrior; that you must yet to have your armor for protection, even in such competition of combat for this day!" Then she started to cry. "To quarrel does so hurt this lass, please stop!" she begged them. "Mother do not cry; we were not to do battle," said Archie trying to calm her. "That I must marry," she said in low tones, "is most devastating to us all I know. To help your mother through these dreadful duties she must now perform is my most humble request this day."

By the evening 16 October 1305 Eleanora Lovaine had married her third knight named William. She wore a simple surcote with a short headdress over her plaited hair; there was an elegance of simplicity that held for the solemnity of the event in all its many ways. After their vows of sacrament were given, Lord and Lady Bagot went to the great hall of Bildeston manor for some quiet feasting with their guests. When the evening drew to a somber close in some few hours the lady and the lord adjourned to separate chambers; Sir William politely kissed her hand as she withdrew from him.

Lord Bagot was a nice man; honorable to his word he would allow Eleanora her every wish. When they would fine some days later for his inheritance of La Hyde and Patshull and other manors in and around Staffordshire he made a pledge to his wife to acquire lands to leave in trust for her heirs and issue, Archibald and Hubicus of Douglas. They parted on cordial grounds and proceeded to their private estates not to live together as was their intention.

Figure XXXII-Part Two; St. Mary Magdalene, Bildeston; the church is set outside the present day village, adjacent to the site of the old medieval manor

DUMFRIES 10 FEBRUARY 1306-Ellie and her sons Hugh and Archie were spending the long winter of 1305 to 1306 quietly together in Essex. James Douglas of Lothiane as their older brother and squire called himself these days was yet performing his carving duties in the household of William Lamberton. Sir Alexander de Lindsay was still in exile planning to return to his homeland; to what turn in the political wind he was unsure. When on this day in Greyfriars' kirk of the see of Glasgow under the dominion of the "bad bishop" Robert Wishart, a violent and unthinkable act of sacrilege marked the beginning of the *revolution* that Sir Alex only dreamed about during discussions with Ellie and James in 1302. Scotland was again under the tight control of Edward for the first time since 1296. The English rule of law was unlike the Scottish government; high taxes with no manner for redress of grievances against the English king brought a simmering discontent. Sparked by the return of English garrisons to Scottish castles, patriotism was going to raise its formidable head again in the country that Edward so wrongly thought had ceased to exist.

A meeting with Robert Brus and John the Red Comyn of Badenoch was taking place. Robert Brus was there with a proposal to this laird, the head of one of the most powerful families in all the realm and the nephew of their last king, John Balliol. They both held claims for the crown of Scotland; the Comyn's perhaps the stronger of the two. John Comyn had lands and wealth and following; but he was a failure. Scotland for all his trouble was yet again in the tight grasp of Edward Plantagenet. It was time for revolution; there was no other way. And Robert Brus was ready with his words and deeds to follow; to give the laird of his own great holdings for the Comyn's support of Robert, King of Scotland. Apparently Sir John did not take to the idea; an argument arose, the once sole guardian spoke of Brus in treasonous terms; threatening to reveal his evidence to Edward. Robert's temper erupted violently at the threat; he stabbed the coward near the high altar of the kirk. The stories that followed varied; one John de Lindsay was said to have made the deed final. John the Red Comyn, descendent of Donald Bán of Northumbria was dead. Ironically, not since Edgar slew this same Donald Bán in 1097, to drive him from the throne had a King of Scots come to power in such a brutal manner. Now Robert Brus was heading to Scone to claim his crown and kingdome under the shadow of murder.

News of the terrifying deed flew through Dumfries and Galloway. A messenger rushed to the manor of Bishop Lamberton who received him in the great hall. Standing at his side was James Douglas; hearing every word. The Revolution had begun! By the time the Bishop had read aloud the missive James had planned his own strategy; he would take his leave of the bishop to support the new King of Scots. He followed Lamberton to the withdrawing room that he might have a word with his benefactor. The bishop smiled to himself; his squire was ready for the fight, may God protect him and our new king he prayed under his breath. "Here, before you tell me your plans, these are mine," said William Lamberton to his trusted squire. "This coffer must be carried to Earl Robert; it contains the wealth of the Kingdome of Scotland," he said sarcastically, knowing the coinage was barely enough to begin a revolution let alone run a country.

"James, I must have someone that I trust take this to Earl Robert," he told the lad. James Douglas thanked the bishop for his confidence in him. He would indeed seek of Robert Brus on the bishop's behalf. "And for my own good purpose most as well. That I will pledge my fealty to this laird, our king to be," he said boldly. "For as you know, it is my sole intent to restore our family to our rightful inheritance; our Douglasdale to Douglas lairds," said James confidently. "Though too late to spare my mother the indignities of marriage to pay her taxes to the king; this lad to be successful in his plans. And will this squire bravely fight for king and country like my true ancestors and dear father before me. With the courage of one Sholto of Douglas who staunchly came to King Solvathius' aid and put down the rebellion of Donald Bane in 770, comes one James of Douglas to do the same again for Scotland and her king!" he said in his determined low whisper; meaning every word of it.

Figure XXXIII-Part Two; St. Andrews Bay from the bishop's castle in St. Andrews

James took his leave of Lamberton. The bishop had given him a pack horse which he used for his wee war chest, the wooden box that held all his earthly belongings. He saddled Fortis, careful to hide the coffer and its contents from suspicious eyes. James rode out for Selkirkshire and the Blackhouse tower fortress of the Douglas family. These lands near Craig Douglas were part of Ellie's dower; perhaps to be this lad's stronghold he chuckled happily to himself. His plan was to meet with the earl in Dumfries, do his pledging and give him the coinage from the bishop. Then the squire would take his leave of him for some family business; to meet with Ellie who was heading now to Fawdon, as was the plan for Archie's rendezvous with Sir Alex there in March. "Our mother will be surprised to see us Fortis," he said out loud to his palfrey, chuckling as he realized what he said. "Yes Lady El, you are still my mother," he sighed. He had received a letter from Eleanora and his brothers for Hogmanay to which he sent back a curt response but expressed in words that would open the door to speaking to her once again.

BLACKHOUSE TOWER-James found the old tower house deserted but for some old servants of his father that were farming some of the manor lands with their son nearby. They received him well and he was thrilled to be the laird of the manor for the night and he promised he would return again whenever he was in the shire. James also insisted that they remain in the manor, occupy the tower house as they once did for his father. "But know this," he told them, "James is a Douglas holding in rebellion, supporting Robert Brus our new King of Scots," he confided to his father's vassals. These Douglas folk were surprised by his news; excited by the prospect of a true king for Scotland. They told him they understood the needs of the squire as well; thanked him for his honesty and offered their loyalty and assistance. Douglas folk with decades of Douglas service to the laird, they were not surprised by the youth's confession; they too would share his sympathies; le Hardi and his family were most dear and sorely missed in Craig Douglas they told the lad. "That I must leave my war chest here," he chuckled as he told them, motioning to the wee wooden chest. "Some day that fair coffer to grow in size suitable for a knight," he said shyly. His father's vassal offered to insure the chest's concealment; that he might come and stay whenever he had need. And they would tell no one of his visits there they promised. James was grateful to them; pleased with his first day of freedom, one step closer to becoming Lord Douglas.

Figure XXXIV-Part Two; good example of the great hall with window seats and fireplace in a tower; Smailholm

ERICSTANE-James rode his palfrey Fortis down towards Moffat, on the way to Lochmaben to meet Earl Robert. However, the would be king was leading his cavalcade north, making his way towards Glasgow then to Scone where he would be crowned in the presence of bishops and earls and many barons of the realm. When James perceived a camp near the lofty hill at the head of the Annandale River he realized that his journey was complete; there before him was the new King of Scots and his entourage. He rode into the camp and immediately dismounted his palfrey. Recognizing the earl from their encounter nine years before when a younger Robert Brus in Edward's service brought fire and sword to Douglas Castle, James knelt before him; told him who he was and why he made the journey. "Most noble knight and lord my king; this humble squire, James of Douglas, son of William le Hardi, laird of Douglas, does come to pledge his fealty to the King of Scots," he said. Robert had not recognized the youth; the lad had grown in stature to be over six feet tall and some inches he perceived; his dark mane of raven hair flowed in the March wind about his shoulders. He was large boned, his broad squared frame was supported by legs of great size and length; his swarthy skin well known to the Douglas race flattered his deep, dark eyes. He was certainly le Hardi's son thought Brus.

Just then the squire reached under his surcote; giving Robert's companions quite a start. The would be king motioned his men at arms to hold back, perceiving no harm from the youth. Grinning from ear to ear, James brought out a silk pennon with the armorial bearings of Brus upon it. "That your men had left this at our castle our last day in Douglasdale," he chuckled, knowing the earl would at once recognize the telling evidence of his presence there some ten years ago. "You are most welcome to join our adherents to the cause for Scotland's independence," he told the squire happily. "And this laird does so remember one knight of renown who held of this, le Hardi is indeed your father, I am sure of it!" James looked up; interrupting his sovereign's words of welcome. "There is more that I must say my lord," he said speaking plainly without pretense. "That I have come in support of Brus is true; but most as well to pledge my loyalty to a king that can restore this squire to his rightful inheritance, Douglas lands for Douglas lairds, to remove the Clifford from the home of my ancestors is my most true desire," he continued, still kneeling before Robert Brus as he spoke his pledge of fealty. "But no more loyal a squire could one king have than James of Douglas is my pledge to my laird and most noble king."

Earl Robert told the squire to rise; he appreciated the lad's candor. "Such words of fair honesty are what I would expect of le Hardi's son," Brus said. Earl Robert was grinning now himself as he remembered those days at Knadgerhill; he reminded the squire that he met with Lord Douglas in his tent, encamped at Irvine Water. James stood up and laughed as he recalled those days as well. "My father was to run you through then and then he told us," said the lad with a mischievous grin. "And what tragedy that would have been for Scotland's cause this day!" he chuckled.

James abruptly turned his back to the king, walking towards Fortis to retrieve the coffer holding the coinage from Bishop Lamberton. "This fair treasury of Scotland from the good bishop in the east," he boasted, "until this day the good benefactor and employer of this humble squire." Robert Brus opened the wee coffer and smiled broadly; Bishop Lamberton came through as promised he told them. James looked around now and seemed to recognize one in the group, John de Lindsay, the kin of Sir Alex. Introductions were made and he joined the others in their feasting. "Will you come with us to Scone then?" asked Earl Robert, expecting the squire would relish the idea of attending the coronation. James thanked him for the offer, but declined the invitation. He had business with an Essex lady in Fawdon he told the earl. Robert grinned, teasing the lad about a rendezvous with a lass that was more important than to see a king be crowned.

Figure XXXV-Part Two; a Saltire appearing over the Devil's Beef Tub; a location near Ericstane where James met Lord Robert bringing Scotland's treasury from Lamberton

"My mother," he explained with emphasis, smiling somewhat sheepishly. "The same fair lady you have met before," he reminded Robert. "With Eleanora this lad has been estranged since she was forced to marry an English knight just some five months ago," he said sheepishly. "That I have promised to so meet with her and my wee brothers, one a page in the service of Sir Alex, returning soon from exile I do hope," he said to the king. Lord Robert and his new adherent sat together and spoke for some time; they seemed at once at ease with one another, perhaps for the many people they knew in common and the stories they shared together now. James told him of the first time he went to Scone to see a king so crowned. "When Balliol was at that noble site this lad accompanied his parents to see him sit upon the Coronation Stone; to speak the words in Gaelic of his heritage," he said. Then it occurred to James that Robert may know more about the stone being stolen in 1295 and its whereabouts this day. "Was the real stone hidden so in Perth yet found?" he asked Earl Robert. The king to be told him he knew none of this; unaware of any ruse involving the Stone of Destiny.

James began to weave the story of intrigue, much the storyteller as his Uncle James, the Steward. "After Parliament concluded in August 1295, certain magnates of the realm including my dear father, good uncles and de Moray kin were meeting with the Bishop of Glasgow, enjoying his fine wine in great quantity," James began. He told them of Robert Wishart's plan to steal the Stone of Destiny and replace it with another. "The very one that

Edward so took with him back to England was a false stone, the very folly of that pagan despot; to take a copy carved from stone of Perth," James said chuckling at the enterprising bishop and his knights, including one named le Hardi. He continued to explain that they made off with the real stone first to Cambuskenneth, then to a hidden location further north. "The good men of Perth removed the stone from the abbey and its temporary hiding place there, then to take it back to lands in Perthshire some months later. Yet all those brave men to have known the location of our heritage and right have perished, so this lad was told by Bishop Lamberton." Earl Robert was intrigued by his squire's story, recalling now that he once heard of this adventurous tale, but thought it was a hoax. "It was not a story so made up; the good Steward my uncle and my dear father both had told me on separate occasions; their ruse successful, the plot to steal the stone on the direction of that unconstrained bishop was so done," he chuckled, pleased to be able to share the tale with his king.

Robert then spoke of le Hardi; extending his condolences on the passing of that noble knight in Edward's Tower. The squire's reaction was one that would forever stay with the King of Scots. The gentle lad with the slight lisp transformed before him into a vicious warrior with unrelenting vengeance on his mind. "That my dear father stood for core values; his adherence to his truth the cause of his great suffering," he sneered ominously. James stared away from the group, his tone steeled in his determination. "The butcher king lied to my dear father at Berwick, deceived him into surrender then to murder the brave citizens en masse. Then two years later permitted the vengeful knight de Percy his lies to accuse my father of treason; to so steal his very life from us!" he declared. James brought his gaze to meet Robert's; the eyes of madman could not have been more frightening. "This lad does vow to seek his cruel revenge from Edward and every sorry vassal of that very diel that has so conspired to murder my dear father, execute him for his fair honesty." The camp was hushed by the words of the squire; all eyes were upon him as he told the tale of the honest Justiciar de Moray; the fate of the shameless murderers of the sheriff of Dumbarton, Earl Duncan of Fife and Eleanora's own cousin, when Lord Douglas passed the doom

"That Sir Andrew met the same de mischef as my father some few months later," he concluded sadly. The King of Scots realized that his new adherent was on a mission and fortunate for Robert, their enemy was one the same: Edward Plantagenet. James seemed to return to his less formidable self as he looked about the royal camp of Brus' adherents. He started to laugh. "Does this lad so pass the test of fire to your fair group of rebels to Lord Edward?" he smirked, realizing his angry diatribe had lasted many minutes of uninterrupted speech. Lord Robert smiled broadly. "That I knew you were a Douglas lad and true. But this king did not so know you are a warrior most daft as he they called le Hardi!" he exclaimed. Then adding with a boisterous roar, "This King preferring not to face you on a battlefield has so decided: better to welcome you lad to our fight!" And so began their fabled partnership. The humor and warm personalities of a squire called James and a king named Robert seemed to blend perfectly; building a bond of friendship and trust that would be tested; to yet endure, that Scotland would be free again because of it.

Figure XXXVI-Part Two; traveling from Moffat to Craig Douglas, scene in late winter to early spring in the Borders on the winding, romantic A708

After several hours of good company and cheer James begged leave of the King of Scots and his band of supporters. He promised to meet up with them at a given place, in six weeks or less. "For again will I find you, most noble king," assured the squire. "And at your side in service will this humble squire be from that day forth," James promised him jovially. Riding east towards Selkirkshire, he calculated his next move; he needed a faster horse for the warfare that Robert planned. Perhaps to find of the Hobini he mused, the noble little horse from Ireland that could truly out run most any English horse and on any given terrain. James rode the familiar trail to Craig Douglas with a new perspective; for the first time since his father's death in the Tower he was feeling the power of his destiny before him.

The squire from Douglasdale knew that something remarkable had transpired at Erickstane; though he could surely not imagine the significance to come. Once just an ignominious manor on the river Annan Ericstane became this day a place of staggering importance to James, Robert and a nation of Scots weary of Edward's oppression. The squire felt a difference in himself as he and Fortis rode for the Douglas stronghold. He knew some purpose was about him now; a strong sense of God's own truth within him stirred. He was finally to begin that long path he so yearned for: to avenge his father's cruel end at the hands of one pagan despot king named Edward. Passing Cappercleuch he decided to stop to pray and give thanks at the Kirk of St. Mary's in the woods near the loch of the same name. James took some moments to reflect before he entered the sanctuary where once he and his family had worshiped when staying at Blackhouse Tower.

Figure XXXVII-Part Two; St. Mary's Loch

From the commanding heights of the church yard one could see St. Mary's Loch in all her majesty; rolling gently in the brilliant blues of the crisp, clear March day. "That would be the Tweed then," he chuckled to himself recalling the time Ellie thought they were lost and he teased her that every body of water was that very river winding round them, carving its way among the hills. As he looked beyond the loch, he beheld the bright glimmer of the Yarrow as she snaked her way towards the Tweed. Then up through the solemn hills, the bracken braes now bare from winter's punishment he passed his eyes; the clouds shifted above, moving color on the broad slopes in gentle hues of mystery that beckoned to him of an earthly paradise that he knew so well.

The Celtic teachings of his father comforted him now; nature's fragrances of spring to come filled his nose and the warm sun cuddled him against the chilling March winds, swirling on the hilltops, slashing from the rigs to the vale below. James found himself alone as he entered the kirk. "Dear St. Bride, patron saint of Douglas warriors past," he began his words. "That this humble squire before you will have the strength and courage to never look back; to always face forward to the immense task that is my fate," he said quietly. Then sighing softly to himself he continued, adding a special prayer for his father and siblings now with God. He made an offering of coinage as he left the chapel. Making his way eastward, the squire rode up the Douglas Glen towards the tower that would now become his safe sanctuary in that shire. As he urged Fortis down the wee path towards the Douglas Burn, he reflected on his life; forever changed again. James Douglas was in rebellion.

Figure XXXVIII-Part Two; site of St. Mary's kirk near the loch of the same name

FAWDON-Robert Brus King of Scots was making his way north securing fortresses along the way that commanded the Firth of Clyde; these castles were essential to the new nation and her king to keep open the supply routes. His new squire was riding east; not at his side but on his way to Northumbria to take care of family matters long overdue. Ellie and her two sons Archie and Hugh arrived with the rest of their Essex household several days before at the Douglas stronghold in the Cheviot, to await the arrival of Sir Alex and one named James. "Ana," called Ellie from her chamber, "what has this lass done with dear Gilley's signet?" Lady Eleanora Lovaine de Ferrers Douglas Bagot was frantic; she had lost William's ring somehow; faithfully putting his seal on her Book of Hours each night before retiring she could not find it now. Ana came in and showed her calmly where she laid it down. "Thank you my Ana. This lass is so unsettled this day; and unsure of what is coming over me!" she said perplexed by her confused state.

Just then Ellie could hear screams of joy from the great hall; her Deerhound Lindsay bolted from her chamber to join the clamoring noise of excited voices as Ellie and Ana ran behind him down to the lower level of the great hall. There in the light of a setting afternoon sun, in the open doorway stood a smiling squire in full armaments. His height had finally topped at six foot two inches; a manly chest filled out his broad frame as he lang raven locks pushed mischievously out from under his mail coif. Archie and Hugh were assaulting him with question after question. Ellie walked in quietly, not knowing how he might receive his mother, she was afraid to speak.

"Good day Lady Bagot," he began with a strained smirk. Ellie just stood there, unable to look at him, twisting Gilley's ring nervously as was her fashion when she was scared. James walked over to where she stood, then noticed his father's signet was the only ring she wore on her hands. "You still wear the seal ring of my father?" he asked her. Ellie felt the anger rise within her; what did this lad expect? She would always belong to William; no marriage of convenience could change that, Ellie fumed silently. She was indignant when she responded out loud. "Of course this is my Gilley's ring, what other would this lass so wear?" she sputtered, locking her eyes with his. Both of them were too stubborn to look away as tears welled, spilling down the cheeks of both their faces.

"Go ahead you two," ordered Ana, "hug each other and be done with this sad drama in our household, the noo!" James wrapped his strong arms around her and held her close. Ellie was crying hard into his surcote, feeling the warmth of his tears falling upon her nose. She started to laugh lightly from the strain of emotions. "You are stubborn as one named William that you vex your mother so with your anger!" she scolded him, her words muffled as she pressed her face harder into his broad chest. James spoke quietly to her. "Mother, this lad does know sometimes we love so hard it hurts. When your letter came with that chilling news of marriage, my grief turned cold to hate; so sorry is this squire," he said softly.

"Some words I have to share with my mother now," he told her with some hint of bravado. "My own independence has been struck of Edward," he said proudly, holding her out slightly from him that he could look into her eyes as he spoke his next words. "I have pledged in rebellion to Robert Brus soon to be crowned King of Scots in Scone." Bolder still he spoke, while nervously waiting her reaction. Ellie pushed back from him, eyed him up and down with an impish smile. "If I was not sure I so buried that good knight eight years now gone, this lass would swear le Hardi's words most spoken here not yours!" she chided her son good naturedly, feigning her disdain. But Ellie was not good at suppressing her true feelings; her face broke into a broad grin. "So the revolution has finally come and a Douglas knight to be will lead the way, sure aye," she sighed in wonderment of the moment. James was startled. He was sure she would admonish him for his dangerous decision.

Excitedly Ellie called for wine and feasting as she grabbed James' hand and brought him to sit next to her at the large table in the great hall. "Ana, do stay here with me," she motioned for her to sit on the bench next to her. Archie and Hugh were thrilled; their brother was home again and no longer angry with their mother for her marriage. "So tell me of the knight of renown you have so married," he teased, knowing the true nature of her marriage from Sir Alex and the stories of the strange wedding attended by few family members and one knight from Wales, known to be a close friend of the prince. Ellie told them all that Lord Bagot was safely in Stafford or perhaps in Wales with friends. "Having served his last retinue five years ago under the banners of Robert Fitzwalter, he will not return again to plague of you in Scotland," she chuckled. "Was he truly at Falkirk as Archie so told this squire?" he asked. Ellie bowed her head and nodded yes. "Most as my dear Nicky," she moaned. James took her hand and held it; assuring her it was no longer of importance.

Figure XXXIX-Part Two; Fawdon mains buildings now in Branton

"Dear James, that I have missed you so," she told him, her words trailing off as Sir David and his squires were returning. Seeing the amenable group with James seated in his rightful place next to Lady Douglas at the table he realized that the estranged mother and son had resolved their differences. Harmony had returned to the Douglas household. "Good James, how happy this old knight is to see his favorite student," he boasted. James told him that he may not say that when he hears the news he brings. "Earl Robert is in rebellion, to be crowned in Scone in some few days," he told the English knight. Sir David shook his head, he knew in heart this day would come; his squire would soon be a knight, to avenge the murder of his father. "Sure this knight should take his leave and warn dear Edward," he teased. "Then this lass would run you through; then and then," admonished Ellie, as she pulled out Gilley's old dagger that she carried with her. "Mother, whatever are you doing with that weapon so tied upon your person?" asked James, shaking his head in disbelief.

"Our mother feels she must protect her family from the invaders, which side, English or Scot, she has not yet told us," said Hugh in his teasing refrain. "That she might use it on her husband would he chance into her chamber walk," said Archie sarcastically. "Oh hush with you lads. This lady has need of protection; these are fearful times!" she admonished them. Ana said that she had better let her sons do the defending with weapons drawn, chuckling at the sight of her lady brandishing William's dagger, the one Ellie had given him on the occasion of his fortieth birthday. "Forty years and forty more," sighed James as he read the inscription. "This lad does wish he were most here to help us now," he said quietly.

"When are you to return?" asked Sir David. James told him that he would remain in Fawdon for two weeks or more. "By then this lad does hope to see our Uncle Alex. The rebellion was only in the planning when he left in exile for his time. There is much we must discuss." Ellie asked him what she should do about Archie. "Sadly our page should now return to Essex with his mother," James said, looking over at his younger brother. "Until a year, perhaps of two we will have to wait; then when our Scotland is more stable we can have dear Archibald join our force." Hugh was not to leave that thought alone. "Dear Edward should be shaking in his bed with fear most paralyzing: the very thought of one Archie to do battle most against him," taunted the aspiring priest. "Choose your weapon churchman," demanded the lad, "this page will have his honor." James started laughing so hard his eyes were tearing. "Enough of this!" he shouted over their exchange of sparring words. "Save your anger for the English king," he scolded them, looking over at Ellie as if to ask how long this antagonizing had been going on between them. "This lad will leave you home when battle comes," he warned his brothers. "Cooler heads are so required." Ellie was thrilled; the constant competitive quarreling with her younger sons was wearing thin upon their mother. "This lady is most pleased to have her James at home again," she said triumphantly, eyeing her two younger sons with an admonishing grimace.

"Do you know of Sir Thomas and his whereabouts?" asked James. He explained to them that he wanted to find a smaller, faster horse. "Ah, the Hobini is your choice then!" said Sir David recalling their travels to Dublin when he was able to ride that noble horse. "Yes, exactly that horse is of my liking for my purpose now," said the squire eagerly. "Do you know of one in these parts?" Ellie explained that some of the Irish knights and others were forced to sell their Hobini. "That dear Edward broke another of his promises: the Earl of Ulster and his men were never paid; many men at arms were selling goods and extra horses to pay their passage home." She told him that she had seen some near the stables of a manor south towards Whittingham. "The heirs of de Flammerville, the Ryles, do hold of that manor in chief; kin to your father's stepmother," Ellie reminded James. "That I saw some of their men at arms riding Hobini, as we were coming north to Fawdon." James asked Sir David if he would accompany him there the morrow next in search of his new horse; to which he happily agreed.

"And what of Fortis?" asked Ellie. James sighed heavily, "That I must leave him now with you, perhaps to keep at Fawdon with Sir Thomas," he suggested. His mother told him the Fortis was most welcome and surely Sir Thomas would keep him at his messuage while the Douglases were in Essex. "This lady will enjoy a noble palfrey for her pleasure when she comes here," she told him, pleased with the arrangement. "But how are you to buy another horse; do you have coinage?" she asked him. James allowed that he did; not a lot but certainly enough to buy one Hobini he surmised. "That you should have some coinage for your travels," she insisted, giving him of her coffers. James tried to refuse but Ellie convinced him otherwise. "That I must share these fees with my seneschal," she told him proudly, indicating the source was not from her husband Lord Bagot but from her dower rents that James collected on her behalf.

"As once my son so told this lass, the rents you so collect to mean less coinage for Edward's treasury to fight his wars in Scotland. Most now these fees will serve another purpose, dear to the heart of this lass," she announced in more deliberate and quiet tones as she looked around the table, eyeing everyone to further emphasize her point. "To avenge the murder and execution of William le Hardi Douglas!" she proclaimed. Eleanora's demeanor was resolute; her countenance determined as she spoke the words of treason towards her king. James grabbed the coinage with smug decidedness. "This vassal of Lord Robert does so humbly accept these fees to aid the Scottish cause, and purchase this warrior's Hobini!" he declared, sharing in the sentiment of her thoughts.

Another week went by and still there was no word on Uncle Alex. Then finally late one evening Sir David's squire bolted into the great hall to announce the arrival of three men on horseback, the knight was wearing the tabard of de Lindsay he exclaimed excitedly. A tired knight greeted his Douglas kin; grinning ear to ear when he saw James and Ellie interacting as if there had never been a wedding to an English knight. "Sir Alex, have you heard the news then?" asked an excited squire. "Aye, this de Lindsay knight leaves his Scotland and Earl Robert sees his chance," he chuckled, referring to his own family's claim to the line of Balliol and Scotland's throne. "Have you been to him?" asked Sir Alex, knowing the squire was ready to do battle for a king who could restore him to the Douglas barony. James told him that he carried the royal treasury to Lord Robert. "The Scottish Church was generous in her support of the King of Scots, entrusting one noble squire of Douglas with the deed to deliver of that coffer," he boasted of his achievement to take Lamberton's coinage to the king. "And on bended knee this James of Douglas did pledge his fealty to our brave King of Scotland."

"James *of Douglas*; not of the Lothianes?" asked Archie teasingly. The squire shook his head yes. "No time for the work of a steward collecting fees and rents; this lad is set for battle!' he proclaimed. "Why ever did you call yourself of that name then, but for your lands in Glencorse?" Ellie wanted to know not trusting her youngest son's word in the matter. James threw Archie a good natured smirk. "To protect my wee page of a brother," he snickered. "That Archie would not have to fight the English knight in my defense," he said. Then he explained that he was not sure if he was being followed; that Lamberton was being watched, his loyalty most questioned. "That I did feign my knowledge of his household and his name," he continued. Archie then told them of the time that he and James pretended to be English lads. "Our accents and the words we used were clearly Essex Inglis mixed of Norman French," said the page. "That James made up a story of his father's household in service of the de la Zouches."

Ellie was stunned. Her sons were deceiving English knights and sheriffs in the Lothianes as a game; all the while she thought they were safely tucked away on the manors of their benefactors, the de Lindsays and Bishop Lamberton. "My lads with their cunning to get themselves in trouble they would rather so avoid," she admonished them. James told her the practice would serve them well in the months to come where the English would be in hot pursuit of one James of Douglas. The reality of the war became terribly real to Lady Douglas, now Lady Bagot, with the last words of her son; upon reflecting more, her eyes welled again with tears.

"No more talk of war this night," said Ana, seeing her lady saddened by the thoughts of her sons on the battlefield against the English king. Sir Alex then suggested what Ellie was already considering; that Archie return to Essex with his mother for one year. "By then the king should have his forces so allied, perhaps dear Edward will give up and forfeit Scotland," he said with a laugh. "Though knowing Lord Paramount, that would never happen," he added sadly. "But perhaps he will not live to enter Scotland with his armies." Ellie questioned the meaning of that last statement. James told Ellie that Edward was aging badly; sickness pervaded his body spewing foul odors of an illness that does not relent. "Perhaps to meet an ignominious end would be my wish for him," said Ellie. That night they feasted and drank of good wine well into the wee hours of the morning, as Sir Alex's arrival meant that James would take his leave to join Lord Robert any day.

The next day began late for the Douglases and their kin; the long hours of the evening past kept them in their beds most the prime to none of the midday. As they broke their fast the squire told his uncle about his new horse; his plans and strategy in raids that would lead him to Douglasdale someday. "To drive the Clifford out from Douglas Castle is my greatest wish," he said wistfully. Ellie asked them if they would like to join her; she was riding to the Ingram to visit St. Michael's Church there. "So lovely is this newly rebuilt kirk," she said enthusiastically, describing the expansive renovations and ambitious additions including the two Chantry Chapels and a magnificent entrance from the nave by arches piercing through the massive masonry. Then she hesitated. "Perhaps it is unwise for you to go this day," she correctly cautioned. "The new rector is William Reginald; Chaplain to dear Edward and a tutor to his son." James and Sir Alex exchanged glances and agreed with her. "That we are so meeting here is a chance that we must take," said Uncle Alex. "Better we avoid attention to this occasion," added James. Ellie left with Sir David and his squires; realizing sadly that a rebel's life was no longer his to live freely. Someday we shall live in peace; I do pray so, she sighed.

Figure XL-Part Two; Ingram, St. Michael's Church; Fawdon manor resides in the parish of Ingram and once held pasture land in common with the church

    James and Sir Alex decided to take their leave of Fawdon that next day. The goodbyes were difficult; James would be in the retinue of his king and rebel to Lord Edward. There was no way to plan for a time when they all might see each other again. They agreed to communicate through Sir Thomas; the long time vassal of le Hardi, one who could be trusted for his honesty and courage. "This family will so come to Fawdon twice the year. The lovely colors of the Cheviot with the celebration for the birthday of this lass so soon to follow. These are my favorite days to spend in this dear manor," she assured her son. Archie and Hugh said their goodbyes to their brother as well; promising to behave and study their languages with their tutor Lady Elizabeth. This lady had recently returned herself to Fawdon, having visited with kin in Fife, she was pleased to greet Sir Alex and thanked him again for the position he devised for her with the Douglases. "Good to see of you most as well dear James," she told him. "Don't let up on my wee brothers," he advised her jovially. "If they should give you trouble, remind of them, they will answer to this squire for their sorry ways!" Too soon for Ellie the knight and squire, a de Lindsay and a Douglas, patriots of Scotland and adherents of the Brus were riding north to the Berwick to meet with Bishop Lamberton.

Figure XLI-Part Two; Moot Hill where the kings of Scotland were traditionally crowned; in front of the gothic chapel at Scone Palace sits a recreated Stone of Destiny

Sir Alex and his nephew arrived at Ellie's manor near Ayton and sent a messenger to the bishop. Word returned to them to come at once; meet him in North Berwick to take the earl's ferry to Elie, then to Scone. Bishop Lamberton was slipping out discretely to rendezvous at the Abbey of Scone where he would celebrate a pontifical high mass for their new sovereign on Palm Sunday. As James rode his new Hobini north he reminisced out loud with his Uncle and the de Lindsay squires in their party about the siege of Berwick just ten years before. "That Edward came to that royal burgh committing the most unholy of crimes. Now we Scots have a new king to lead us out from under the tyranny of that butcher," he announced with brazen resolve. Sir Alex thought for some moments and added solemnly, "That we pray your dear father and his good kin the de Morays, the son and father both to join with the brave patriot William Wallace; that all smile down upon us this day in satisfaction of our deeds." Amen said James to himself.

Lamberton welcomed his former squire and his kin de Lindsay as they boarded the ferry that would take them to Fife. Immediately James recognized his cousin Andrew, eldest son of the Steward who was being held as a hostage for his father's loyalty in pledge to Edward. The two Scots joked at their meeting under such circumstances; running from the English to see a new king be crowned. The group of patriots traveled quickly once they reached the shores. "A mission from God!" bellowed the Bishop in an uncharacteristic moment as they arrived at Scone Abbey. The King of Scots looked upon them, beaming from ear to ear as he saw the bishop arrive with his entourage including the renown Sir Alexander de Lindsay just back from exile and the resolute esquire James of Douglas. "Behold a noble contingency," growled the 'bad bishop' Edward's enemy, Robert Wishart. He recognized de Lindsay right away and Lamberton of course, but who was this squire? Then looking the lad up and down, squinting through his spectacles he asked his questions. "This esquire does resemble one named le Hardi, a Douglas sure to be. Could this be the wee James in search of Parliament?" he chuckled, recalling an earlier encounter when the youth was but a knave of four with his father at Birgham.

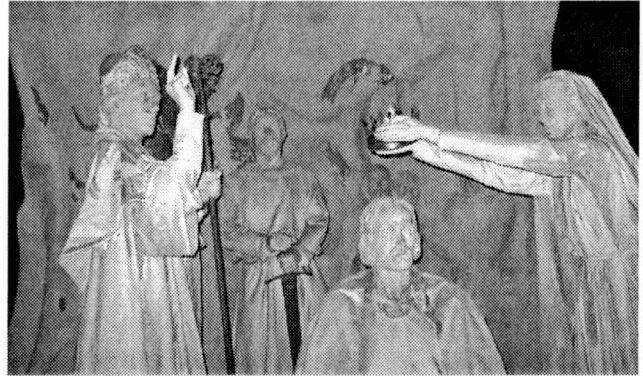

Figure XLII-Part Two; Edinburgh Castle; the Historic Scotland depiction of the coronation of Robert Brus with the Bishop of Glasgow presiding and the Countess of Buchan placing the crown on the new king at Scone Abbey; the countess was a cousin of Eleanora Douglas, the aunt of young Duncan, the Earl of Fife in his minority

"I am more than four and ready," replied the lad in good humor, mimicking his own words said that day as Parliament convened. "Good, good," said the aging friend of his father. "Today you will see a real king receive again his crown in the mass of Bishop Lamberton," he said, subtly referring to Edward's vassal John Balliol with disdain. Then the Steward peeked around the corner; spotting his nephew and de Lindsay he strolled jovially into the hall. "That we are saved; another two exiles from France returning for a fight with Edward!" he declared, referring to James' sojourn to Brabant and Paris and Sir Alex's recent banishment from his homeland. Then the King spoke to James directly. "Your first command from your king; to find the whereabouts of the Coronation Stone!" he bellowed happily. James turned back to the old bishop. "It was your charge to keep with the Steward; I will need your help and strong prayers for success in my search of Perth's good lands," he told them spiritedly. The squire then looked around the great hall of the abbot's lodgings and noticed another churchman that he seemed to recognize; Bishop David of Moray, as he came to be known to the squire.

Figure XLIII-Part Two; Elgin Cathedral ruins; near the Bishop of Moray's residence

At that moment the uncle of young Andrew the hero of Stirling Bridge crossed the room to bellow his fair greeting. "The son of le Hardi you can only be!" he said, laughing heartily in his enthusiasm. "Yet so grown from one as this," he teased, demonstrating the height of a shorter James when a knave of five. "That last we saw you with your family in Moraydale, so young a lad but promising," he exclaimed. James returned a quick retort. "And you my kin seemed to have grown as well," he said indicating the protruding girth of David's middle. "In stature of course dear bishop; your new position with the church since last we met," he said with his teasing smirk.

Then more seriously, James added his praise to Bishop David's recent accomplishments. "That the great scepter and the noble ring; your investiture of the see of Moray wears well on you good bishop." The two kinsmen embraced; both suffering great losses since Edward crossed the Tweed some ten years ago. "Of your tragic loss," began David, referring to William's execution in the Tower. He was quickly interrupted by the squire. "That we will speak of your brother Sir Andrew; some circumstances of his end you must come to know," James told him, intending to discuss the matter of the de Percy conspiracy during their feasting. "Let us take time together following the celebration of high mass for our king," he suggested.

James made his way through the throng of Brus' supporters and found his Uncle James surrounded by many men he also knew. The Steward wanted to introduce his nephew to his friend and kin Sir John de Lindsay; but James told him he most knew the uncle of Sir Alex. Greetings were given and pleasantries exchanged. As the Douglas squire reflected on the gathering he realized he was feeling quite at home with these magnates of

Scotland. Many of these powerful nobles were known to him from his youth when his father fortuitously took him to Parliament; giving him the presence that he held this day at Scone Abbey. The lad was confidant; standing tall among the influential barons, earls and clergy of the realm. The legacy of William le Hardi Douglas, this noble bearing was one of his greatest gifts to his son; the martyred father yet lingering in the shadows of Scone.

Figure XLIV-Part Two; site of Scone Abbey from Moot Hill adjacent to Scone Palace

They all adjourned for the Augustinian abbey church where high mass was said; the crown placed once again in ceremony on the head of Robert I, King of Scots. A proclamation was issued that day; a new king of Scotland ruled the land. King Edward I of England assured of peace in the conquered lands north of the Borders was roused from his bed to shock and indignation when he received the word: Robert Brus was in rebellion and had proclaimed himself King of Scots. He did not wait for the sun to set. On the 5th of April 1306, just one week after the coronation, Edward appointed his cousin and a brother in law of the murdered Comyn, Aymer de Valence his special lieutenant in Scotland; armed him with a great muster of men, to **Raise the Dragon** as he had done ten years ago at Berwick on Tweed. The raised dragon meant to show no mercy; to slay and burn and pillage, to murder all prisoners. Edward the kind and benevolent king was showing his true colors once again. For all those Scots who swore to Brus, Edward vowed revenge. He sent armed horse with fire and sword to waste their homes; destroy their lands and put all rebels caught to their gory deaths.

ESSEX LATE SPRING 1306-Edward issued writs; knights and men at arms were needed for his muster. Sir William Bagot was called to Edward's service; in the retinue of Henry de Lacy, Earl of Lincoln in pursuit of Scots now in rebellion he rode to war. The earl led his men at arms under the command of de Valence in pursuit of Robert the Brus, King of Scots. And for this new insurrection, King Edward needed more knights; Richard Bagot, the younger brother of Ellie's husband, was dubbed in 1306 with Prince Edward and many other young noblemen of England. Sir Richard Bagot too would join Edward's forces in pursuit of James and the titular King of Scots. Surprisingly Ellie had not considered that her husband would be called to muster for Scotland; the shock of his letter informing her of this summons to duty sent Eleanora into a fit of pique. "That I am off to Scotland to bring the nobles once more to Edward's peace," she quoted from Sir William's missive. How dare he take this tone she fumed! Ana was sitting with her in the great hall of Stebbinge Park as Ellie read from Lord Bagot's letter. "Dear lass, he is a warrior; ordered by his king. Of course he should have such feelings. He knows not of your James in rebellion," she offered quietly. Ellie realized soon enough they would know of James; it was only a matter of time she mused. Then what would she do?

When her lads returned from Little Easton from their studies with Father Paul Ellie read them the letter from Lord Bagot. Hugh was stunned; Archie belligerent. "That he should speak of peace as he invades our Scotland?" he asked in indignation. Hugh told his mother that he had not anticipated the husband of his mother going to war against their homeland. That he is not the stepfather of this page, Archie muttered under his breath. "This brother worries so for the safety of our squire," Hugh said mournfully. Archie spouted his concerns differently. "The English knight should hope and pray for luck upon his side; our mother will so be a widow once again if James does find him in our Scotland, sure aye!" Ellie sadly realized her sons were expressing her own true feelings; Sir William Bagot was leading men at arms to do battle with the Scots and she was in sympathy with his opponents!

"What has this lass so done to her family; to tear them apart with a marriage of convenience just to be most free of Edward?" she asked rhetorically. Hugh came to stand beside Ellie and put a comforting hand on her shoulder. Ana told them both that what their mother needed was their support; they must pray hard for James and be considerate of her girl. "Mother," Archie addressed her seriously. "When this Bagot knight is through his life let there be no others for you to marry unless he is a Scot, loyal to King Robert!" he declared, then excusing himself he abruptly left for his chamber. Hugh told her that for once the wee Archie made sense. "A marriage such as this is very wrong to do again," he said softly. "How can one Douglas lad accept a stepfather who carries himself to war to do battle with our brother?" Ellie shook her head sadly and started to cry. "If any harm comes to my son," she sobbed, unable to complete her words. "There my girl, don't cry; my precious lamb, no harm will come to James I promise you," said Ana reassuringly. "And God would so forbid it!" said Hugh.

Figure XLV-Part Two; Little Easton Manor adjacent to the church of the same name

SCOTLAND EARLY JUNE 1306-The Bishop of Glasgow had begged of Edward that he might have hewn trees to repair the bell tower of the cathedral. He was granted his request but the Bishop had a change in venue for the royal timbers. With renewed vigor, the old bishop began his plan. In support of the King of Scotland he ordered that the wood be used to build siege engines. The Comyn's castle near Kirkintilloch was where he put Edward's good timber first to use as they successfully assaulted the old tower. Then the bishop, with one victorious fight under his sword belt, marched his retinue and siege engines east into the Kingdome of Fife. Again the 'bad bishop' buckled on his armor like a baron of the realm and went to do battle with the English, taking Cupar Castle. It was sadly here some time later that Aymer de Valence captured the castle and the noble inhabitant. He ordered Bishop Wishart held prisoner to await Edward's orders. Moving quickly through Scotland, Edward's lieutenant then sought the surrender of another noble bishop and patriot: William Lamberton. On 9th June de Valence received word from the smooth talking churchman; he was then at Scotlandwell in Kinross-shire and wanted to discuss his predicament. Two of Scotland's rebel-bishops were now in Edward's custody. The Bishop of Moray was able to escape the chains of English slavery, fleeing his see to Orkney; to fight another day.

By mid June de Valence with his retinue including the Earl of Lincoln's armed horse and onfoot were venturing into Perth; moving with great alacrity and speed their forces quickly secured the town. His recent success in capturing Edward's favorite dissenters Bishop Wishart, Bishop Lamberton and lately, the good Abbot of Scone buoyed de Valence's spirits.

His powers issued of the king however would not permit him to put the churchmen to the sword. Instead he was commanded to send these brave men into captivity. In shameful chains and fetters these noble prelates were ridden southward to Wessex where they were removed to the dungeon prisons, held in irons there, waiting further orders from the English king. More than six weeks went by before writs were finally issued by Edward to the sheriff of Hampshire. The gallant Bishop of Glasgow was sent to the confinement of Porchester Castle near the Cinque Ports on the southern coast of England. The silver tongued Bishop Lamberton valiantly tried to appeal; he was merely delivering Andrew, the young son and heir of the Steward to Scone as ordered when he happened upon the coronation of Robert Brus. But the band or bond he signed and pledged in 1304 with the Earl of Carrick that was to take effect in this year of 1306 came to light and he was committed to incarceration; taken to Winchester Castle to be held in chains there until Edward relented.

Figure XLVI-Part Two; Cupar Castle on Castle Hill; Robert Wishart's last stand against Edward, 1306 where only ruined walls denote the location of the fortress

    Robert Brus was intent on doing battle with the English. He devised a plan where some of those most trusted would scout of the castles and surrounding burghs to bring back information on the movement of the armies; the stores being diverted to their locations and the fortification of their central delivery point that now was in Linlithgow. James volunteered to go to that palace having kin in that burgh and the Douglas stronghold in Livingston to use as his base of operations for his reconnaissance work if needed. As James made his way south he set his own strategy for arriving at the castle. He would become again a lad known as James of Lothiane; a good grasp of Inglis from his days in Essex, his accent would surely be accepted by the English retinue garrisoned at the castle. And he knew as well that the Lothianes, East or West boasted of few supporters for King Robert; most held of loyalty to Edward.

Figure XLVII-Part Two; Linlithgow Palace; speculation is that one day Historic Scotland will roof these lovely ruins and restore the interior

It was that same 9th of June when he found himself at the stores of Linlithgow Palace. Unloading carts from the barge shipments coming from Berwick was a younger lad much in need of help that day. James went to the young cellarer's aid and through the hour that he helped him, discovered many valuable pieces of information. The constable of the castle was Peter Lubaud he was told. The garrison this day was one knight, fifteen esquires, five hobelars, eight crossbowmen, and twenty archers. "They are sending these stores to help our armies of the earl," the chatty lad bragged of his knowledge. James had told the young lad that he was waiting for some Scottish knights yet loyal to dear Edward. As he turned to take his leave of the cellarer, he heard what he thought was a familiar voice: two Lothiane knights were walking his way; one was his kin Sir Robert Keith.

It was too late to bring his hood to cover his face and being tall with the raven hair and distinctive Douglas looks, he was forced to give great welcome to his cousin. Robert Keith was the heir to many holdings of his father William. Until five years ago this young man was held in Edward's prisons in Cumbria for his rebellion but this day he was in service to the English, receiving wine and grain from the constable to take to his commander. James smiled as if this was the man at arms he had been waiting to meet; to rendezvous as escort for their stores. "Greetings dear kin," said James ebulliently and when Robert went to introduce him to his companion Henry St. Clair, the squire interrupted. "James Douglas of Lothiane," he chuckled, "so called as the only lands this lad to hold for his sustenance, the rents of lands in Glencorse," he said, mocking his diminished status.

"What brings you Lothiane knights here dear Robert," asked James, getting the advantage in conversation; his Inglis and his accent fading as he noticed the cellarer had finished with his chores and left them. "That we are vassals sent by Henry de Lacy; here to bring our stores to the earl's camp." The squire allowed as how he was in the burgh to stay with his cousins, the family of William Douglas of Linlithgow. "Then to visit at Dalserf, late of my Aunt Willelma and her family; yours as well," he spoke in a manner that seemed open and chatty. "How is dear Bernard?" he asked referring to the family of his cousin Johanna de Galbraith, Willelma's oldest daughter who married this de Cathe or de Keith, a cousin as well. Have you seen your family?" he continued questioning the knight. "Sadly with the *riote and rebellion* of the Earl of Carrick, we have not time for visiting with kin or seeing of our friends," said Sir Robert wistfully. The knight suggested that James join them for some feasting once they had their stores loaded on their carts for their lord, Earl de Lacy. James Douglas of Lothiane offered his most hearty acceptance to their invitation.

By early evening the squire excused himself to take his leave. The longer daylight hours of the summer gave him extra time to travel north before he camped the night. When the sun began to rise again he was already on his Hobini riding towards the camp of another earl, Robert of Carrick, now King of Scots. The valuable information he brought with him was relished by his laird. The stores coming by sea meant that the Scots had disrupted the English supply lines by land; forcing them to ship by barge from Berwick. "Good work my Douglas squire," said Robert; then he added with a hearty laugh, "That I mean to say, our James Douglas of Lothiane, loyal English vassal, an Essex lad who speaks the Inglis of East Anglia," he teased the squire. "That you are on the side of Scotland this laird is most relieved!" The king allowed that with the information James gathered he could develop his strategy for the new few weeks. They would break camp the morrow next he said, heading west towards the strength of English army.

While Edward's lieutenant rested in the town of Perth, lurking in the hills was a king who just few months before was enjoying the royal splendor of his coronation in nearby Scone. Robert Brus with his fair contingency of men had made his plans. He decided it was time to do battle with English. On 18th June he approached the town, from the higher grounds of the west.

Without siege engines the king was unable to attack Perth with the deep moats and high walls of protection. Instead his strategy became a simple one: to entice the brother in law of the Comyn to do battle with him. He entertained a message to de Valence but the English commander feigned piety; to do battle with the Scots the day next he claimed. James Douglas was with his king when the word came; he felt uncomfortable with the response but dismissed his uneasiness with his impatience to do battle. "This squire like his father grows weary with the wait for combat," he told his lord the king. Robert was not pleased by the response from Comyn contingency as well. But this was the king's first major battle; his instincts were not sharpened by experience in warfare and he did not suspect the ruse that was put upon them until the rout was underway.

Figure XLVIII-Part Two; Linlithgow Palace, the Peel on Linlithgow Loch

The Scots withdrew to Methven Woods six miles away; the men scattered, relaxing their guard and removing their armor they were the perfect prey for a wily general of pure treachery. Some found their way to Methven Loch to swim or bathe, not far from the pavilion of their king. De Valence mirrored the truth of his lord the king; keeping the peace until the morning next as he promised was not his intention. He showed no mercy; attacked at dusk that very day when the Scots had just settled into their complacency. By the time the word was shouted throughout the Scottish camp that the English were attacking, many brave patriots lay dead or dying; their armor lying on the ground beside them. There was no battle at Methven; there was a rout.

Very few men escaped and some of those that did found themselves in the mountains of Athol with their king; on the run. James was one among them; his little Hobini made his quick escape possible. And in the fray he saw many banners of English knights he recognized; ermine, black with white spots, a bend gules with three eaglets or, the armorial achievements of his mother's husband Sir William Bagot. He dared not think about it, he mused. His suspicions were correct; the Earl of Lincoln and his retinue of men at arms including Bagot were indeed present that day. For his part the Earl was rewarded with the lands of James the Steward. It was just last year the uncle of James Douglas had returned from France and been restored to his Ayrshire lands. Found in sympathy with the titular King of Scots some months later he was again stripped of his holdings; the lands then given by Edward to his loyal vassal Henry de Lacy, the earl Lord Bagot followed into service of his king.

Figure XLIX-Part Two; Methven Loch

The war for Scotland's new king was not going well; but the squire's resolve was his truth: to live and fight again. Robert was still king, alive to take his breath and in command; thanks be to the good St. Bride for that he said in silent prayer. As became his fashion after each battle James reviewed everything that occurred during the encounter in the minutia of detail; deriving lessons from every failure to turn defeat into success as his father had taught him. At Methven the lesson was simple: whenever encamped, post lookouts. From this first failed assault against the English near Perth, James promised himself to never again be so surprised in battle; such clear advantage would not be left to the enemy's devices. Some said he became obsessive in his desire for camp security; strategically posting onfoot while sending forth armed horse to survey the surrounding countryside. This method of scouting became his habit; hard lessons learned from the

Methven rout. This devoted practice served him well in the almost seventy battles that followed.

Figure L-Part Two; site near Methven Woods, south of Methven Castle

    King Robert led his meager group of followers through the mountains. This ragged band of Scottish patriots rode north into Aberdeenshire where they were joined by some of the wives of the king's retinue along with Brus' sister Mary and his other sister Christian who was the wife of Christopher Seton, one his most loyal knights and supporters. It was a short reunion as the English forces closed in, causing the group to once more flee to the hills this time near the mouth of the River Tay. For some days and few weeks the little band of warriors and the ladies camped contentedly in the wee braes and glens, though always moving and hiding; they were on the run. Their course crisscrossed the rugged countryside between Loch Tay and Glen Almond. The traveling was slow but always interesting to James. And he felt his father's presence where ever they journeyed, remembering his teaching ways, the older traditions that now served the squire thoughtfully in the daily challenges of a rebel's existence.

    The wee band of the king's men and ladies made their way to the banks of Loch Tay; finding refuge in places of the ancient ones as the Douglas squire told the ladies. "Such islands were most built for defense upon the waters; to guard against surprise attack, these people, ancient farmers on Loch Tay, constructed sites that jut out into the waters." he explained. "To build an island or just a dwelling of some size," James continued to elaborate, "constructing nearly two dozen such sites on this fair loch." The squire told the ladies how his father had brought him there when he was but a knave. That his words do serve me well when most I need then, the squire mused as he moved towards another hiding place where the Scots would stay the night. They were being led by Highlanders, new followers of Brus, sympathetic to their plight, loyal to the King of Scots. These Celtic warriors had joined Lord Robert after the massacre at Methven where only one in ten of Robert's followers survived that day.

Figure LI-Part Two; the rugged landscape of the Highlands; the wild crags near Glen Almond could be perilous, quite challenging to travelers

James' prowess with a bow and skills at fishing taught at the knee of William le Hardi bode well for the squire in the Highlands. "That my father often told his son, one day your knowledge of such things will be of good benefit. To know the way of the Celts and the ancient ones before them; their understanding of the lands and the bounties so there offered," the lad would tell them. He was of jovial mind; unrepressed by their dire circumstances or what may lie ahead, he was free he told them; fighting for his country and his king. And he shared stories with the ladies; told them the tales his father related so many years ago, in another life it seemed to him now, when a lad could be carefree, laugh and play without the fear that war brings.

"Not since the day we buried my father in Little Dunmow Priory," he began, only to be interrupted by his king. Robert had been sitting alone, though not far from the group of ladies; his brow was furled in deep thought, searching for a solution to their situation. "Le Hardi was buried in Essex?" he asked the squire. "Aye," said James, shaking his head sadly. "That we held of no other choice. It is my dearest wish to bring the bones of that brave knight back to Scotland; to rest again in the paradise he called his Douglasdale. A pledge this squire has so made to him," said James with an air of confidence that he would do it. Robert told him the story of how he happened to be born in Writtle not many miles from there. "That the hunt compelled my parents to first meet in Carrick," he chuckled to recall the tale. "And when years later it was time nearing for that lady's lay-in, preparing for my good arrival, she so insisted to accompany her husband to their Essex hunting lodge."

Figure LII-Part Two; Loch Tay, the site of crannogs and Priory Island where Robert Brus and his followers sought sanctuary from the pursuit of Edward's vassals

Robert smiled broadly as he elaborated on the story; how his mother was an avid horsewoman and would not be denied the glory of a hunt. "But this lad had other plans; their son so joined them then and there!" he laughed as he told of his first day's beginnings in this world. James recalled the manor of Writtle. "My mother, actually my brothers' mother, but she's earned the title many times by me, sure aye!" he exclaimed, boasting of his stubborn ways that she had to contend with from the first day she married le Hardi. "This lass my mother, that she was born in Little Easton and so holds the manors of Stebbinge Park and Woodham Ferrers; we often traveled between those manors, passing Chelmsford and Writtle along the way," he allowed, sharing of his knowledge of Essex.

The story telling squire and the charismatic king were entertaining the ladies with their wit and charm. James told them of his antics as a knave; sympathizing with his mother's dauntless task, he told them how she forthrightly raised him. "That one day this lad should take his rightful place in the noble house of Douglas," he proclaimed her intentions. James told them of his insistence to have a fur hat like his father. He recalled the story of the wee laddie, just four years old, insisting on such attire to accompany "Lord Douglas to Parliament, in business of the king," he chuckled at his own folly, remembering how desperately he wanted to join his father in Birgham. By now the ladies were howling in laughter, forgetting all the inconveniences of their rugged campsite in the mountainous country between Perth and Argyll. They were all fugitives running from Edward's army; in perilous fear of capture. But for these few hours their laughter filled the air and joy was celebrated in their hearts. Those ladies who had children of their own or younger siblings to raise, recalled stories of the wee ones and their antics; that they all wished to have a caring son like James they told him. One of the ladies, the wife of the sheriff of Elgin Sir William Wiseman, shared stories of her own now with the group; to open the flood gates for others to recall more peaceful times with their families.

Figure LIII-Part Two; Crannog Center on Loch Tay, Ben Lawers looms in the misty background on a day in late April, still snow capped from the winter; Robert Brus and his surviving army sought refuge in such sites in their sad retreat of 1306

The gentle youth with the silly smirk beguiled the ladies with his true honesty; his simple praise for his redoubtable father and concern for the feelings and fears of his mother were genuine emotions and they all knew it. He told them of Eleanora's relentless perseverance in training him in languages and speech undone by one impetuous act of folly: to jump his horse in a moment of vainglory, as he framed the misadventure. James began the tale of his misdeed; he smiled warmly as his words flowed, in fond reminiscence of those days in Douglasdale with his family. "This foolish lad had so insisted to jump his palfrey like a destrier, to be unhorsed; to break my teeth and bloody my face, that I am now forever with a lisp that made my mother cry," he sighed. "That misguided step has left me thus; humble before my God that with every word I speak I will be so reminded of this folly." He told them of his father who came rushing to a son's side fearful of some terrible injury from the fall. Instead of admonishing his son, le Hardi consoled him saying, "We each to learn our own way young James; better to do what others more experienced in such matters advise in training for your knighthood." The words his father said to comfort his mother he shared with them as well. "Not all knights are so fortunate in their first battle. To break a tooth or two and not a leg or arm; take heart in this relief of injury," his father told his bride. The lasses were brought to tears by his story. Laughing at his wit; crying with his sentimental tales, these companions of the outlaw warriors grew to respect the daunting lad from Douglas.

Lord Robert was returning from his self-prescribed isolation; he joined the ladies and his squire, to listen to more of the storytelling. Having reflected on the direction the group would venture next, he was in need of less strenuous conversation he mused. The relaxed chatter and sentimental stories brought him back to days he spent in Essex and in Carrick when life's hardships were centered on boyhood concerns. "That as a wee lad I wanted to have a horse for my very own," began the king. "My father had so told me that were I to learn to ride a palfrey, this lad would so receive one for his very own right there and then," he scoffed, telling them that he grew impatient waiting for the teaching and decided to take matters into his own hands. "This lad to steal a horse and ride it was his intention" he boasted.

The lasses groaned; frightened by his words, thrilled by his daring plan, they waited to hear more. "Early in the morning this lad made secret his escape, down the turnpike stairs, out the great doors of the dunjon to the courtyard, silently into stables behind the keep this knave so crept. Quietly I dragged my mother's saddle to where her jennet stood as it was the furthest from the farrier yet sleeping there," he said, continuing to weave his tale of woe and poor judgment. "I climbed upon a chest and finally was this lad so sitting on the horse, ready for his ride! Through the palisade gates I went, riding the marches of the manor, a wee laddie barely five years old. For nearly half the morning maybe more, this knave rode his mother's jennet. I felt the pride of my skills upon that noble horse and basked in the success of the thievery as well," Robert boasted to the ladies. Then he told them sadly, that blessed journey came abruptly to an end; not at all of his liking. "Riding back to the manor of my father and dear mother who should this lad so meet?" he asked looking around the group most sheepishly. "The Countess herself on one of father's palfreys with the farrier and two greyhounds in hot pursuit of one wee Robert!" he told them; noting that he was not permitted such a ride for nearly one whole year from then! With a mischievous grin James jovially added his words. "With such skills within our very midst we shall never want of horse to battle with dear Edward!" he teased. "Aye, a horse thieving king," Robert grumbled good naturedly. "Better than a kingdome thieving Edward," James retorted.

As the afternoon wore on, the king was more a knight in the company of fair ladies and his squires. He told stories of courtly love; he shared tales of tournaments and knights of renown. The laughter cheered his heart and cleared his mind for other things. For the first time since he had been on campaign, Robert Brus was enjoying himself. Ever since the Queen had departed their group before Methven, the king showed signs of melancholy. Now he was animated and vibrant once again. James watched the others in the group as they listened to their king; making his observations, drawing his conclusions slowly and carefully as was his way. He felt comfortable with these ladies following the band of warriors; his only reservations were of Elizabeth de Burgh, the lady sent ahead for safety. That this disdain is an odd sentiment toward the king's own wife he reflected silently.

But James' guarded feelings towards the queen came from careful analysis, not whim. When the squire first arrived at Scone with Lamberton and Alex de Lindsay, the coronation had already concluded some days before. But from conversations he heard of Bishop Wishart, the queen was mocking the Scots for the proceedings. She retired to another chamber in a fit of pique at one point in the day. As the lady made an indignant exit she spoke some odd words, denouncing the ceremonies. "To play at kings and queens," she admonished them. James listened as the old bishop spoke and felt a sadness in his words as he told the others of her outburst. Robert Wishart had gallantly provided robes for the coronation from his own vestments. The royal banner of the last King of Scotland he removed from his treasury where this crafty bishop had hidden it away eleven years before, after that July Parliament in 1295. Now this lady chosen by his king was belittling him for his proud deeds; the work of which would surely bring him to Edward's prisons unless privileged to die on a battlefield in his armor he reflected.

The day next on the hunt James had a morning of success with bow that even he had never seen before. The doe and hare and grouse seemed to rush into his catch that day. And on his travels he found a bounty of berries, wild kale and hazelnuts to add to the feasting. Returning to the camp he found the ladies making bannock as he showed them on a griddle. Their eyes lit up with excitement at the game brought to fill their larder; meat for their table was a welcome sight as well as the sweet berries and nuts to make some special treats. "Much wine to have as well," barked a young squire of Sir Nigel Campbell. He too was just returning; riding up the glen on his palfrey into their camp. His knight was out yet with others in search of game. The lad told them he had found his way to a manor house nearby and made off with a half filled cask of wine intended for a feast that very afternoon he speculated from the crowd of horse near the stables. "One more stray squire unknown to their group would not be so found out; that I was able to so bring this wine to my liberty, from their very grasp!" he told them with glee.

When the others in their retinue returned to camp from the hunt, they were playfully admonished by the ladies for their paltry showing. The fine wine and conspicuous spoils of game the two squires profited this day were a welcome sight to these stern warriors. With hearty laughter and buoyed spirits the men at arms took the lasses' challenges proclaiming a competition of sport for the next day when they would search of game. A great rivalry ensued the next few days; knights were vying for praise and recognition; contriving ingenious ways to increase their spoils of hunt. But it was James, leaning on the teachings of his father for the ways of his ancestors, who brought the fruits of both the land and waters to their larder. Complimenting his skills as a bowman, he relished in his knowledge of fishing from the waterways that ran though the hills and glens that had become their hideouts. He made traps with his hands to catch salmon, pike and eel. No matter what the others in the king's entourage did to compete it was James who won the day with his abilities to harvest of fish or game. The Celtic lessons from the lands the squire learned so long ago in Douglasdale brought flourish to their feastings.

INCHAFFRAY ABBEY- King Robert and his followers never stayed one place very long; they were on the run and remaining in one location could prove deadly. De Valence's men were moving in from the east and from the west as the Scots approached Argyll, kin of the Comyn were closing off the rebels' escape with tenacious pursuit of their enemy, forever on the lookout for King Robert. As Brus reflected on their position he remembered the many horses Sir Nigel's squire had seen days before when he liberated the wine. The king sensed a grave foreboding with the presence of that small contingency. And rightly so; these armed horse were part of a much larger retinue to rendezvous with Edward's sympathizers in search of Robert and his followers. To avoid capture Brus decided to abruptly alter their course of travel; boldly leading his wee army and camp followers southward towards Crieff.

Nearly retracing their escape from Methven, Brus' small band of weary adherents found themselves camped near the Falls of Turret. Little did they know they were traveling under the watchful eyes of some Augustinians loyal to their cause. To the rescue of King Robert's men came these brave priests of nearby Inchaffray Abbey. At the behest of Abbot Maurice the canons regular led the band of rebels to the safety of their monastery on a wee island in a lake. At the abbey chapel, Lord Robert, James and others in the king's entourage, including all the ladies, stopped to give thanks for their safe escape. Here they were all introduced to the words of St. Fillan and told about his healing stones. The Scots were engrossed by the tale.

Impressed by their genuine interest, Abbot Maurice beckoned Brus and his small party to an alcove in the nave of the chapel to gaze upon the saint's relics as he continued to share the legend of St. Fillan. "Wolf cub is what we called that devout follower of Columba," began the abbot. "One such story handed down was this; that as a farmer plowing a wolf attacked and killed his oxen. The next day the wolf returned to help our Fillan submitting to a yoke." The ladies listened intently. James watched with interest; especially intrigued by the relic the abbot now held in his hand: bones from the left arm and hand of the saint. "That he had not light to read from in the night; his left arm glowed in warm hues to provide the lamp he did not have," explained Maurice, the custodian of Mayne, the left arm and hand of Fillan. James shared the tale of the abbess from Romsey who read at night from light glowing from her fingertips. "This lass has never heard of such stories," admitted Mary Brus.

King Robert determined that such a relic was important to his cause. He praised the churchmen for coming to his assistance and deemed that Maurice should join the royal entourage when it was safe; bringing the Mayne with him to aid the cause of Scotland when he could. Abbot Maurice was eventually designated the Chaplain of King Robert for his bravery and dedication to the cause of National Independence and for his fortuitous rescue of the king and his wee army this day.

For the rest of their tour of *innis-abh-reidh*, Gaelic for *island of smooth water*, the Master led the Scots around, following the shoreline of the lake. "To have the best eel in great quantities in these waters," boasted the Hospitaller of the abbey. So much wonderment, mused James. As he later reflected on the day; he found himself more than amazed for the words and deeds of Fillan; fascinated by the miracles associated with the healing priest.

Several days later the Scots were again on the move. With their escort of canons regular from Inchaffray they traveled to the safety of Killin and the wee kirk of the healer St. Fillan. Here the Master showed them the eight healing stones, all of various shapes and sizes that St. Fillan used in his work. "To cure of ailments in different parts of the body," the Augustinian explained. Lady Christian wanted to know about the round stone that appeared to have two eyes and a mouth. "That is the healing stone for headaches," the canon explained. "My brother Hugh would have great interest in these ways to heal with these fair stones of the holy one, a follower of dear Columba," James shared with the canons from the abbey. How incredible indeed that such small pebbles held such power, he sighed to himself.

DAIL RIGH-Within a few days the Scottish army and their king had traveled further west towards Tyndrum. Almost immediately the Comyn spies in that region informed their laird that Brus and his military force were somewhere in an area north of Glen Dochart in Dail Righ, an old Gaelic name meaning the king's field. Once the grouse heather fields used for the king's hunt in early days of Scotland this open green became the site of James' first true battle and the squire's first injury of merit. Early that morning in August when most of the king's followers were yet asleep, the sentries alerted the encamped army of the Scots that a band of armed horse and onfoot were approaching; they did not appear friendly. In an instant young James was putting the saddle on his Hobini and was grabbing for his weapons. He donned his coif and adjusted his mail hauberk that covered his gambeson to just above his knees; but he did not have the full armor of mail for his legs this day; he would have to come of it soon he mused. The rest of King Robert's retinue was equally quick in responding to the alert of intruders. Sleeping in their armor as was their custom since the disaster at Methven, the Scottish contingency was ready for combat in but a few minutes.

The ladies and churchmen were led to safety; taken by some of the squires and onfoot to a remote area of woods secluded from the view of the oncoming force. James took his position behind some of the more experienced knights as he had been told. The combat was horrific; the Scots were badly outnumbered both in armed horse and onfoot. The king himself took on several men at once, but hardly by design. During the battle that followed Robert was unhorsed again, but not like Methven where three times he dismounted against his will, saved only by the valiant recovery of Christopher Seton who fought off the English attacker. This time the king managed to fell his opponents yet remain in the saddle to eventually lead his remaining men out of the near rout of battle to a place of safety.

Figure LIV-Part Two; Strathfillan in the shadow of Ben Lui at Dahl Righ

James rode into the fight without fear; his smaller sword was held in the ready while he carried the small shield once belonging to le Hardi in his right hand. His heart was beating hard; his breath was short and rapid with the excitement of his first real encounter with the enemy. The first attacker reached the squire and engaged him; carrying a sword and larger shield. James was able to parry this first attempted strike with the small shield. Then the squire counterattacked; moved his left hand deftly in a left to left diagonal cut from the high guard position. The English man at arms parried with his shield; the strike glanced off the edge narrowly missing the opponent's elbow. Like his father Sir William, the old Crusader in combat, James' mind moved quickly. He aptly noted the flaws in the training of the opposing squire making him vulnerable to future strikes.

James brought his Hobini round circle; the smaller horse was moving well he mused. Then abruptly the English lad, holding his sword in the ready made a bold move; in this small area he drew his warhorse forward, faster and faster he moved the noble animal. James braced as in the joust to take a blow, holding his shield low; the strike was deftly parried once again by the Douglas squire. Before the opponent made his escape James had counterattacked with a diagonal upward cut aimed at the lower leg of his opponent. The swift flowing movement of his sword, the strong cut perfectly balanced, James moved his left arm almost unconsciously as the sharp blade encountered the soft tissue of human flesh. Seriously injured the squire cried out in agony from the perilous wound. Blood covered James' sword as he withdrew it and oozed down towards the shoulder of the blade, dripping on his bare legs as he returned the old standard to the on guard position.

The young Englishman withdrew the battle for his injuries; leaving James to encounter another opponent. Coming out from behind the lad, riding high in his saddle was a knight. Barely bringing his Hobini around in time to make the parry on the strike of the attacking English warrior, James thankfully felt the thud of the knight's battle axe as it hit the flat of his shield. The air was filled with a thunderous din of clanking iron; swords of Scottish knights striking blows on English shields resounded as warriors parried thrusts. Rumblings of physical exertion came from both rider and horse; snorts of noble chargers encircled the hard breathing of knights in the close struggle of combat. This is surely nothing of the pell or parry with Sir David he reflected on his training; these real contests of life and limb compare to none of that he scoffed.

The knight was better schooled or more experienced than the first combatant James surmised as he drew up his Hobini for the counterattack; the English soldier's timing and confidence created a special aura of perfection that could easily overawe most squires. But not me, proclaimed the Douglas youth as he rallied himself for the fight! He drew his Uncle Hugh's old standard into the on guard; his left arm poised to strike, he moved to make a shearing cut. The older knight parried, using his shield to smash forward; James' hand glanced off the face of his opponent's shield, the stinging sensation traveling up his arm to his elbow. James was angry with himself; he did not suspect the move, but there was not time to think further on his folly; the knight was again in the attack. James parried with the same smash forward of his small shield and the blow was so hard on the knight's hand, unprotected by his shortened cross guard that his right hand was disarmed. Unfortunately for James, the knight carried a lang dagger behind the larger heater shield he wielded. With his left hand he made a lunging slash that cut deeply into the right leg of James. At the same moment the squire counterattacked from the middle guard to cut through to the knight's neck, foolishly unprotected as he leaned forward to lunge his dagger into the exposed thigh of the young Scot.

James' slashing strike cut through to bone unhorsing the knight with the fatal blow. The Douglas squire realized his own injury was severe; a warrior injured in the leg was sadly compromised he remembered from his training. That he must seek some cover among the low growing shrubs in the nearby pine grove he mused. Blood was flowing profusely now from his wound, dripping in warm rivulets down his bare leg. As he rode toward the shelter of evergreens, the old pines of the Caledonian Forest, in retreat he ripped some of the silk cloth of his cote in strips to tie around the gaping gash. James had finally made his way safely from the fray to a wee burn near the River Fillan. Here he washed off the wound and the leg area below to determine the extent of his injury; he also used the cold water to bring himself to a heightened state of awareness. Suddenly from behind him he heard the thundering hooves of an approaching war-horse. Grabbing his sword and shield James wheeled around and stood to parry the blow and run the oncoming horse through in one fluid motion. The course succeeded; the horse buckled from the blow, unhorsing the rider. James was now holding the advantage; though barely standing from both the fatigue of battle and the bloody wound of his right leg.

The combat ensued onfoot; the two warriors exchanged and parried strikes. Then James realizing his strength was waning, the injury taking its toll upon the youth, decided to summon all his stamina for one final attack. He led with his right foot and moved into the ready from the high guard position with his left arm held for the strike. James's size was smaller than le Hardi's but he was still taller than most men at over six feet two inches; his slender physique offset by youthful vigor. He began to make his move on Edward's vassal; the English sympathizer held his shield high, braced for the blow. Seeing his opponent commit, James moved deftly from the high guard to the middle, balancing his body to the flow of momentum. Towering over his opponent James delivered a final cutting strike that slipped perfectly under the warrior's shield. The injured man fell backward, slipping into the burn; off balance, he was unable to counter the final thrust James made to finish him. Staggering back as he withdrew his blade from the abdomen of the dead man, the young squire realized he was feeling weak and light headed as well.

Figure LV-Part Two; behind these drumlins or mounds of glacial spoil lies a kettle hole lochan; Brus and his men dumped their heavy armaments here to assist in their escape

James stumbled as he tried to seek the shelter of the trees. As he groped his way to a hiding place he heard a strange buzzing in his head, a high pitched whirring sound like thousands of bees creating an eerie, frightening cacophony in his ears. He felt weak and shaky; his legs would barely move as he slipped into unconsciousness. When he awoke he felt groggy and he could hardly see. There seemed to be a blinding light before his eyes, holding his lids almost shut though he tried with all his might to open them, succeeding for only a few seconds. The bright white glare was overpowering in its brilliance. What was this he was seeing, an apparition he wondered?

Through the grey mist surrounding the strange luminous aura before him James thought he saw the shadowy figure of an old knight; a huge warrior with a discernable scar running down the right side of his face. But it couldn't be my father he mused as that brave swad is most with God; perhaps I am as well he scoffed half heartedly. The buzzing in his ears returned, louder and more deafening it came, until his awareness faded once again. When James awoke the next time it was Robert Brus who was standing over him. "Are you dead?" the squire asked as he looked up at his king brandishing a wry smirk. Robert told him no, he was very much alive, no thanks to a party of the Comyn's relatives, he groused. "Then so this lad must be as well," James chuckled as he tried to get up from his prone position.

A pained grimace crossed his face. "That I need of help to regain my feet," he said apologetically. Robert beckoned Sir Nigel to his assistance. "Three English dead; two yonder not far from here, one there to your credit I suspect as well," said Robert. "Next time do a little better and don't spill of your own blood," he said feigning a serious countenance that broke into a broad smile. "No need of proper leech-craft," joked the squire, referring to the staggering blood loss, the dark red stains covering his garments. "How did you come to be so here?" the king asked motioning to the lad's weapons and coif lying near his horse some yards away. James realized suddenly that the image of his father dragging him to safety was probably not a dream after all; certainly someone removed his mail coif, then dragged him to this spot he thought. "This lad so saw le Hardi; the knight most joined the fray to bring this squire here," he responded with a grin. "Good that he did that, aye!" Robert said. "That you were nearly overtaken when we rode here," pointing to another of Edward's sympathizers lying dead near the burn, where a battle axe of the king finished his war with Scotland.

An uneasy Robert Brus was mulling over his thoughts later that night in camp. He reluctantly decided the group must at long last split up; the English were in Aberdeenshire as well; there was little time to waste. The Scots had made haste to leave Dahl Righ and barely escaped with their lives. They even resorted to throwing their larger war-swords and other heavy weaponry into the wee lochan of Dahl Righ to unburden themselves in their flight, so desperate was the speed of their departure. The king made the difficult decision to send the ladies to a safer refuge. Alexander de Lindsay with his squires and men at arms bid farewell to his nephew James. He was joining the escort, to ride with the Earl of Atholl and James' cousin Robert Boyd taking the ladies to Kildrummy. The plan was to journey to this castle held by the king's brother, Nigel, with several other knights and their squires, securing the ladies in safety there.

The king's men remaining in camp numbered two hundred; maybe less. They surrendered most of their horses to the ladies and their escorts; planning to head to the Hebrides on foot. James gave up his Hobini specifically to Uncle Alex who promised to get the horse back to Fawdon somehow. "Not to trouble yourself young James; for this knight was raised in Northumbria as a lad. That I can move discreetly in that shire yet unnoticed is well known," he said, chuckling confidently. Sir Alex confided of his plans. He told James that Lady Alice and the de Lindsay children were yet in Garleton; he would dispatch an escort to move them to his manor of Barnweill in Ayrshire. James would miss his uncle; a man he knew and trusted, with an affable manner; a knight who seemed to have as many lives as manors, which were numerous, in his often and prolonged escapes from Edward's wrath. De Lindsay took up arms with Wallace and submitted; went to Irvine Water with le Hardi to surrender again to Edward; took up with Wallace several more times to pledge again to Edward. Newly returned from the specific exile of the Ordinance of 1305, he was again in the retinue of rebels.

The castle of Kildrummy was well fortified to withstand any siege; heavily provisioned the old stronghold would offer the best protection for the women, the king surmised. A fortress built by Gilbert de Moray, Bishop of Caithness, it was a huge structure surrounded by a massive curtain wall and protected by impenetrable towers; even the gatehouse boasted two dominating towers at the entrance. James told his king the story of his family; their kin the de Morays; how the families were similar and very competitive. In the course of the conversation he reminded Robert of the overall design of Douglas Castle the very one that the Earl of Carrick raided nine years before; bringing fire and sword on the orders of Edward Plantagenet to command Lord Douglas to his peace. How the many years and strangeness of circumstances changed their relationship since then, Robert reflected out loud. James heartily agreed. The irony was profound as he considered their tenuous situation; fighting Edward's vassals side by side; a king and his squire battling together for a free and independent Scotland.

Figure LVI-Part Two; Wallace's sword on display at the Wallace monument, Stirling; both William Wallace and James Douglas were well over six feet tall but only Wallace perhaps used so large a sword, though it was much altered since 1305

James continued to regale Brus with stories of the friendly rivalry between the Douglases and their de Moray kin. "That my grandfather so began the building of three angle towers at Douglasdale, to construct as well a stone wall much the same as his cousin Gilbert built his enclosure walls at Kildrummy," he chuckled, knowing the families were always trying to outdo one another; building bigger castles, buying more manors in other shires. "My dear father always laughed at my grandfather's folly; the wooden palisade most out of place with the new splendor of the great stone donjons, two aside the portcullis, the third at the postern. The magnificent angle towers of Kildrummy recreated in their miniature at our Douglasdale. One day I would like to see of Bishop Gilbert's castle, that grand castle of enclosure, sure aye!"

The parting with the ladies had been difficult for many in the group; it signaled not only a return to sterner times with Edward's forces nipping at their heels but also the end to some much needed diversion for warriors on the run. In this distinguished group of ladies that were being convoyed to the safe sanctuary of Kildrummy were Brus' sisters Mary and Christian. They were to rendezvous with the others including the Queen and Brus' daughter Marjory. Leaving the rugged outdoor life for the protective confines of a fortress, Sir Alex and the younger Boyd could not have known they were headed for far greater trouble.

Figure LVII-Part Two; ruins of Kildrummy Castle managed today by Historic Scotland, this view is from the great hall looking towards the chapel

While the king's adherents moved westward, Edward's ruthless lieutenant de Valance and the Prince, Edward Caernarvon were savagely reaping success in the east. The blood bath that followed could not have been imagined. The vicious acts commanded by Edward Plantagenet in the dying days of his reign were unparalleled in the annals of his day for their cruel and merciless vengeance. Edward's vile spewed relentlessly upon the Scots. From mid August to 10th September there was an extended siege at Kildrummy Castle led by Prince Edward, later Edward II. The mighty fortress fell to sabotage; a blacksmith named Osborne betrayed the Scots for a promised reward. He set the grain stores held in the great hall on fire forcing the garrison to surrender to the will of the English king for their lack of provisions. It was said that Osborne received his gold payment justly dealt; poured down his throat like molten lava asphyxiating the traitor there and then.

FAWDON THE IDES SEPTEMBER-Before the siege at Kildrummy began Sir Alexander de Lindsay sent two of his squires with some others of the de Lindsay men at arms to the Lothianes; riding south, one squire took with him the Hobini of James Douglas as they safely made their way along the hilltops under great care to move unseen in their escape. They arrived at Garleton Castle and rescued the de Lindsay household, escorting them to the safety of Ayrshire. Some days later Lady de Lindsay dispatched two letters to Lady Eleanora with one Hobini, to be taken east to the Fawdon manor in Northumbria. The squires knew the way from having been there with their knight not six months before, they assured their lady. When they arrived safely they were greeted by the loyal vassal of le Hardi.

Thomas Chaunceler was eager for information on the war and the whereabouts of young James. "Lady Douglas would be coming north in few weeks," he told them. Sadly they related the story of Methven, which Sir Thomas knew about from others fleeing south to the sanctuary of the Cheviot in late June. The squires told him too of the battle at Dail Righ; how James was injured, but was healing from his wounds. "He most now is on his way to the Hebrides, in the company of King Robert," they told the Douglas knight. "That we are to return to Kildrummy is our plan to support our laird there," continued one of the de Lindsay squires. Sir Thomas was surprised they had not heard the dreadful news. "That Kildrummy has been taken!" he told them. The squires exchanged fearful glances; what of Sir Alex they inquired? Sir Thomas did not know. "That Sir Nigel Brus and others at the castle were committed to the constable at Berwick where they are yet held," he said sadly. "No word of Sir Alex and his fate has yet come to this knight," he said hopeful that de Lindsay had made another of his now famous escapes from Edward's grasp.

TAIN-Before the siege began, Sir John Strathbogie, Earl of Athol, the queen and Marjory Brus had taken their leave of Kildrummy Castle; preceding north and west in hope of reaching the Bishop of Moray; then to find their way to Orkney where eventually they prayed to join the king. The ladies were safely at the sanctuary of St. Duthus awaiting word from the bishop; Earl John took leave of them, to make his own escape by sea. Sadly the ladies were surprised in their hiding by the Earl of Ross; he flagrantly violated the pilgrim's sacred place and captured Brus' wife and daughter, a great prize to ingratiate himself with de Valence. The queen was taken to a manor house in Burstwick in Holderness; young Marjory was taken to de Percy. He deliberately held the girl prisoner awhile before releasing her to Edward. When dear, compassionate Edward passed the doom for the daughter of King Hobbe, it was so vile that he was forced to repeal it. The twelve year old girl was first sentenced to a cage in the Tower of London, with no one to speak to but the Constable of the Tower. On the pleas of the clergy he sent the girl to the Yorkshire Gilbertine nunnery at Watton.

The Earl of Athol, believing the ladies to be safe, was making his escape in a wee cog when the ship was forced to land at Moray. It was boarded by adherents of de Valence and the infamous passenger removed and held, awaiting the king's orders. Sir John was then delivered to the Tower of London and remanded to the constable for his second and final confinement in the White Tower. Ten years before in 1296 Earl John was found in the company of Scottish rebels at the battle of Dunbar; captured and confined to the Tower. Even his Plantagenet blood did not deter his bravery and unquestioned loyalty to the cause of Scottish National Independence. For his unrelenting patriotism he became the first earl in over 230 years to be executed in England; hanged cruelly. The rope was strung around his neck while he was yet still standing on the ground. The noble patriot choked and gasped for breath as he was drawn savagely upward by the swinging rope, to the top of the highest gallows of over thirty feet, as Edward specifically commanded. When the earl's struggle against death was gratefully at it's end, his body was brought down, decapitated and burned.

In the reign of terror that followed Robert Brus' escape during the months of August 1306 to late October of that year, many other brave Scots were captured and executed in the most savage of manners. On 4th August John de Seton was drawn and hanged along with another fourteen adherents of Brus in Newcastle-on-Tyne. Also included in the long list of executed prisoners was the standard bearer of Scotland, Alexander Scrymgeour and Duncan Boyd, kin to Sir Robert Boyd sent with the ladies to Kildrummy. These Scots were hanged; spared only from the drawing in their deaths. Sir Christopher Seton was betrayed at Loch Doon by a Carrick relative; taken by de Percy in that siege the 14th of August and brought to St. John's in Dumfries. The brave and daring patriot Sir Simon Fraser, once a knight in Edward's household, had also been captured and was awaiting his sentence at St. John's as well. Christopher Seton and Simon Fraser, knights were then ordered to the confinement of the Tower of London where they arrived on 6th September. The next day Fraser was drawn, hanged and beheaded, his head set on a pole next to Wallace's on London Bridge. Christopher Seton, the husband of Brus' sister, was given of his sentence: hanged, cut down, and then beheaded.

Sir John de Lindsay, the uncle who once held in ward a younger Sir Alex during his minority preferred drowning in the waters of his Scotland to surrendering into the hands of Edward's vassals. This brave knight and several of his followers rode out into deep waters of Kirkencliff; there near Stirling they chose to pass from their lives to the Otherworld of the Celts. In Kildrummy, the knights and others surrendered to the king's peace after a full month's siege that ended on the 10th September. They were all brought south to Berwick, waiting miserably for Edward to send notice of their sentences. The word finally arrived from the king on 14th October; the sentences for Nigel Brus, Alan Durward, and Alexander de Moray, knights were proclaimed: hanged cruelly, drawn and beheaded. The lists went on and on; only a few Scottish nobles escaped the wrath of Edward Plantagenet.

Alexander de Lindsay, the knight with many lives, having been at Kildrummy during the siege was suspected of once again being the guest of Edward's generosity in Berwick; there just nine years before he was held prisoner by Earl Warenne along with his cousin, Sir William le Hardi. However, the de Lindsay knight enlisted his kin Robert Boyd to make fast their escape through bribe; to pursue unrest in Galloway some few months later. Joyously these noble knights and patriots had slipped from Edward's grasp; alive and well, Sir Alex and Sir Robert were soon back in the thick of battle for Scotland's independence, much to Edward's chagrin. By late summer 1307 Sir Alex became the subject of many entries in the king's rolls of the pipe: horses lost pursuing Alexander de Lindsay, horse killed by de Lindsay; provisions and horses taken in pursuit of Sir Alexander; the lists were endless. Boyd met up with another of his kin: James Douglas. A partnership developed there in Ayrshire for a mutual purpose; ridding Scotland of the English infidels. By September 1307, Boyd like Sir Alex was receiving honorable mention in Edward's rolls; blamed for many destriers killed or chargers liberated by his hand.

The wives and other ladies once in Brus' camp were also taken prisoner at Kildrummy and treated in an unimaginable manner; their sentences unusually cruel. Only the widow of Sir Christopher Seton escaped the king's wrath when taken into custody by the prince's men at arms. Much like the daughter of King Hobbe, she was sent to another Gilbertine nunnery, at Sixhills in Lincolnshire. The other noble ladies were not as fortunate; the Countess of Buchan for her part in the coronation of Robert Brus was sent by the barge La Messager to Berwick. She spent the next four years in an open cage suspended from a tower at Berwick Castle. Mary Brus the sister of King Robert was detained with two of her maids, traveling as prisoners on the same barge as Countess Isabel. They arrived in Berwick in the company of many other prisoners detained by de Valence, including the

Abbot of Scone, his clerk, and several knights and squires. Mary Brus was then remanded to the constable of Roxburgh Castle. She too was confined to a cage. Built of timber and iron, she was held for all to see; allowed only a reprieve for privy and refused communication with any save her English servants. Both ladies remained in English custody for over seven years; some three years before their imprisonment concluded, Mary and Isabel were moved from these cruel, barbaric confinements to other prison cells.

Robert Brus and his declining number of adherents made their way towards the Hebrides in search of a safe refuge. The king was spared the knowledge in his travels of the slaughter that was taking place in the wake of his escape; though he certainly was told of the capture of his bishops Lamberton and Wishart. They should both be safe from hanging he mused; knowing that Edward feared only the Pope in his endeavors and would not execute the prelates. Perhaps this ignorance of the fate of his other followers, the savage cruelty yet unknown to him actually prevented his own demise. That great sorrow and despairing grief would certainly come to Robert later; but for now his resolve to battle forward was not challenged by the knowledge of those tremendous losses of kin and friends at the hands of the pagan despot Plantagenet. Robert Brus was ambling towards his destiny.

Figure LVIII-Part Two; Coalgill near the Park Castle motte

James Douglas was one of the king's remaining followers, traveling with the wee band of men; hobbling along, his right leg slowly recovering from the siege at Dail Righ. The squire had fashioned himself a walking stick, a valuable tool he learned about when traveling on foot with his father one early spring morning, years before in Douglasdale. William le Hardi and his son were climbing through Coalgill near Park Castle; the wee hill was soggy and nearly impenetrable to travel. The father showed the son how to select a tree for its sturdiness and durability; then whittle a staff that would provide strength and aid in their movement through the glen of Park Burn. Le Hardi also showed him how to make a path of woven branches to cross the burn. "The ways of our ancestors will one day serve my son in his destiny," he told James prophetically that day.

"My squire looks more a shepherd in search of his flock," teased Robert as he watched James trying out his lang staff. The lad smiled broadly. "This warrior has seen some better days," he chided himself. "Feeling most long in tooth for so young an age," he chuckled. As they approached the shores of Loch Lomond the king was in a jovial mood for one so closely pursued by his enemies. "Can you fashion us a wee vessel with that knife?" he asked of James, a broad grin coming to his face. "Our Celtic ancestors were builders of such boats," the squire responded. "Though the only one this lad has so seen was sunk near an old causeway, used for passage to the Otherworld," he said with a smirk. "Of that good ship we should most avoid," said the king in quick retort. "But a wee cog would be worth its weight just now," he added wistfully.

Figure LIX-Part Two; view of Park Castle motte adjacent to Coalgill

The followers split up; to rendezvous in short time, perhaps to find a barge or loyal friend to transport them across the loch to safety from their pursuers was the plan that Brus proposed. James hobbled along the shores where he suddenly discovered a sunken treasure, a wee boat. "Dear St. Bride, I thank you for protecting this fair warrior," he exclaimed. He called for help to bring the small craft to the surface; it was certainly sea worthy he determined from close examination. "That this vessel was so left for our wee army," he laughed, suggesting that the gods of ancient warriors were watching over their king, aiding in their escape. "This lad had thought he saw the Otherworld when first to see such treasure sunk below the surface," he sighed. "To the very depths of those darkened lands of ancient myths; to save us in our flight this day," he boasted merrily. Robert was ecstatic with the discovery. He devised a method where three would row over at a time; one to row back and fetch two more. "A lang night and some part of a day to so bring our fair group to safety; but well worth the wait and better than alternatives before us," he surmised.

Figure LX-Part Two; ancient yew tree said to be used during pagan worship and other ceremonies once held at the ancient site where the Ratby Church resides today

"This fair yew tree does portend of good tidings," James allowed, surveying their landing place. He told Robert how his father had told him about the ceremonies of the ancient ones; the magical protection of the yew tree. "When one so sees this sacred refuge, our Celtic teachings most tell us that we are safe from harm, protected by those in the Otherworld. Most like the one near my mother's manor in Leicestershire, the ancient tree near the kirk of Ratby," he added recalling the times he and his family stayed in the de Ferrers manor of Groby Hall. Robert promised the squire that he would be rewarded one day for finding the leaky boat for their escape across Loch Lomond. "These lands where the Douglas and the mouth of Douglas, fair Inveruglas, so meet will be the manor held by one named James Douglas, the glen to bear his name as well," declared King Robert. *Stuc an t-Iobairt* James said silently to himself, mulling over the Gaelic name of their landing place, now the gift in lands from his king. By the time all had crossed they again split into two groups in search of food, unsuccessfully at first. Then they came upon a true adherent of the king's, Malcolm, Earl of Lennox who saved the day. The wee party took refuge for some short time with that laird before continuing their journey westward.

FAWDON EARLY FALL 1306-Ellie and her household returned as promised to Northumbria hoping for some word of James. When they arrived they were greeted by a very grim Sir Thomas. Ellie was frightened, shrieking in a panic of great worry when she realized that James' Hobini was in the stables and James was no where to be found. When Sir Thomas was able to get a word in between her hysterics he informed Lady Douglas, as he called her, of his news of the war. "That Sir Alex had sent his men at arms to rescue his family. Upon completion of that deed, they so returned to Northumbria with the Hobini of our squire, to bring the horse to Fawdon. Here as well, two letters from that household, residing safely now in our Ayrshire," said the knight. Ellie grabbed the letters and flew into the manor house as Ana and her sons followed closely behind. She sat and lit a candle at the big table in the great hall as she began to read from one of the two letters. "With much dismay I write you," began Lady de Lindsay. She told Ellie of their hasty exit from the East Lothianes and the certain worry she had for James and Sir Alex.

Ellie read with dread about the terrible slaughter at Methven; that King Robert was unhorsed and nearly captured. "Save for the timely action of good Sir Christopher de Seton, felling de Mowbray in that battle, or we would be this day without a king to lead us," wrote the distraught lady. Ellie continued, reading aloud that James had been injured at Dail Righ on 14th August. "Yet last we heard from another de Lindsay squire that he was recovering from his wounds," Uncle Alex's wife allowed. Hugh and Archie were stunned; James had taken a serious injury to his right leg and was nearly captured; saved by King Robert and his men. The older son was their role model and hero; to think of their brother with a painful injury and nearly taken by the English was traumatic to the lads. Every word that Ellie read was terrible news. "The brave Bishops, Lamberton and Wishart are both now in Edward's prisons; held in irons and chains in England," Ellie said despondently as she continued reading aloud. Everyone in the Douglas household was sitting on the edge of their seats around the trestle table in the great hall of Fawdon listening to the words of Lady Lindsay. "That we have heard of great tragedy and the vile treatment of our captured heroes," began Ellie; then suddenly she stopped, tears began to well in her eyes. The words 'hanged cruelly' she could not speak; thoughts of her William's tortured execution filled her mind. She gave the letter to Hugh to continue reading.

Hugh began relating the story of the capture of Tibbers Castle in Nithsdale; John de Seton who commanded the garrison of Scots was taken to Newcastle with his men. His dreadful sentence was executed on the 4th of August: drawn and hanged cruelly. Fourteen others from Tibbers were hanged that very day in Newcastle; spared only from being drawn. "One word of note directly from our squires; Lord Richard Lovel was at Methven, and could have been a bannerette," he read, noting that the words were written to Lady Lindsay by her husband, to be sure to tell Eleanora most immediately. Ellie sighed in anguish, her heart heavy with the sorrow. Archie was aghast. "This knight, the husband of our Muriel, to fight in battle with our James!" he shouted indignantly, his eyes wide with anger. Hugh gave his younger brother a look of concern; everything was going wrong it seemed.

Figure LXI-Part Two; Fawdon farm in the Cheviot

"The fate of my dear husband is not known to us," Lady Alice continued despondently telling them all the few details she had heard about the capture of Kildrummy where Sir Alex had joined Nigel Brus defending the castle in siege. "So many times to have escaped of Edward's treachery," Hugh read. Then he abruptly stopped. "Her words do not continue," said Hugh quietly. Everyone was silent; how foolish they felt now; to think that war with Edward would go well and easily when it never had before. "To know de Ferrers travels in the retinue of the earl with my own husband Lord Bagot most in tow; Lord Lovel joining the sorry group as well," Ellie moaned, "all in pursuit of James!" Archie realized his outburst had upset his mother. He told her not to worry, "Our James will think of something; he is the best at strategy and learns quite quickly," he assured Ellie. Ana knew the pain and agony of her girl; she too feared for James' well being; to be crippled with an injury only increased her worries for their squire's ability to escape.

Lady Douglas looked down at the second letter, turning it over, she was afraid to open it. Then she read the words: To Henklebaldicus of Douglas.

"This must be for you my son," Ellie said, questioning the reason for the formality as she recognized that someone had addressed the missive using the more stylized, Latin version of Archie's name for emphasis. Archie looked at the handwriting and realized it was from Beatrice de Lindsay. "My girl has so written this lad!" he exclaimed in a rare moment of glee these days. Ellie looked at him with an admonishing grimace. "My girl?" she asked. Hugh started laughing. "Our page has so fallen for the daughter of the laird," he chided.

Archie looked menacingly at his brother, ready to challenge some competition of weapons when he recalled his pledge to his brother. "That this lad so promised our James not to tarry in a fight; you are spared this day churchmen for your words of great contempt," he scolded Hugh. "This lad loves his Beatrice and she loves him most the same; we will be so married to have twenty children is my plan." Ellie and Ana could not suppress their laughter despite all the sad the news received this day. The very words of Gilley when he first told Ellie of their life to be; on the way to Kelso Abbey, when they were to be married. Ellie recalled his intentions, the words he said as if it were yesterday: *to have twenty children is my plan*, he had confided. "How did you arrive at that fair number of wee ones for your household?" she asked her son. He told her plainly that he discussed it with his father and that's what they agreed upon several years ago. Archie excused himself; to take his leave and read the words of his sweet Beatrice alone in his chamber.

The quiet in the great hall left many to reflect on the life of William le Hardi; the loss of that noble laird into the treacherous hands of Edward was felt by everyone at Fawdon this day. "And now so many others that we know are dead; most savagely," Ellie cried softly. She looked at Hugh. His countenance was dour as he finished reading Lady Lindsay's letter. Sir Thomas began telling them the rest of the news from Berwick; including the fate of the Countess of Buchan, Ellie's cousin and Mary Brus, the sister of Lord Robert, both now in barbaric cages. "How is it that this king holds not of chivalry that he must treat the noble women of these brave knights so brutally as well?" he asked his mother. Ellie was trying to keep herself composed but she nearly fainted from the words; the agony she felt for the lasses now held by Edward was very real to her.

"That fate most dreadful; one sentence for this lass your mother, she feared to so endure some ten years ago. That I soo barely escaped such wrath and torture is what I see from this tragedy," she noted with tremendous irony; her words now muffled in tears of deep fear and sorrow for the wives and lovers of the Scottish rebels. Ana held her tightly knowing Ellie's dread of Edward; made more real now by his unrelenting savagery set against the Scots. "Mother," interrupted Hugh. "This lad would most like to visit with our brave bishop; our dear friend Robert Wishart," he told her. For a lang time he had heard of the noble prelate and true patriot. He was very touched that such a fine man would now be held in chains in Edward's prisons. Ellie thanked him for his sentiment and assured him that somehow she would find a way for him to do just that. While Hugh planned his visit to the bishop, Edward was devising his next punishment for the disloyal churchman. By the end of October, Robert Wishart would be removed to Porchester Castle on England's southern coast. But the change in venue would not deter Lady Douglas. She devised a strategy to both help her son in his quest and also return the many favors bestowed upon her family by that brave patriot; she would send him provisions and kind sentiments with a visit from her son.

AYRSHIRE EARLY JANUARY 1307-Robert Brus had successfully made his way to the Hebrides in search of safety. James Douglas traveled south to Ayrshire; in some weeks he found himself making his trek every few days between the several Douglas manors in the shire. He knew enough to keep moving even though the good servants and vassals of his family assured him he could stay in safety. "That this squire does not want of harm to come here for your kind generosity," he told them. "Know this: as a Douglas laird to be will I one day return to lead us from the oppression of the English," he promised and to a man everyone prayed he would be successful. For centuries the Douglas Chiefs were true men to be followed for their fairness and generosity. The legacy of their leadership was to aid the young heir of Douglasdale in his flight from the long reach of Edward; providing him with refuge, affording him security from de Valence's adherents.

James knew well the locations of his family's lands from memorizing the charters ten years ago as he father had required him to do. Once again the preparation Gilley so diligently demanded of the young man was serving him faithfully when a father was no longer alive to assist him. Many tenements and messuages held by le Hardi scattered the shire. From Girvan to Stewarton, from Carrick to Kyle, small land holdings or larger manors, holdings of Douglas lairds, some inherited, others received in dowry for marriages to Douglas Chiefs; these ancient lands of the Celts now sheltered the young squire from the frightful pursuit of Edward's vassals.

While James was roaming the countryside of Ayrshire, two others of Robert's following had returned to the safety of that county. Uncle Alex, the laird with many lives, finding a way to buy his own freedom and Robert Boyd's as well; escaping Edward's prison through the bribery of coinage. Always one to carry many silver coins upon his person, de Lindsay was able to move quickly with his plan; he paid a fast ransom for each knight and their squires. Before the English guards realized their captives were gone Uncle Alex and Robert Boyd were riding out of Berwick on Tweed, heading west, spurring their palfreys towards Lanarkshire. Passing through Crawford and heading west to Ayrshire, the two knights split up, making their way to their separate strongholds. De Lindsay rode towards Barnweill to seek the safety of his family. He would stay there until Edward seized his lands and forced them to flee south to Dumfries where they remained for sometime.

Boyd was on his way to Cunningham when he ran into the Douglas squire and decided to follow his Cousin James' instinctive lead. The lad was uncanny in the way he moved stealth like through the English lines. "A good stalker of fair game you must be," chuckled Sir Robert as he watched the squire maneuver and stake out the enemy's position. His plan was simple: travel by night, taking refuge in safe places they both knew well; including Steward lands that were familiar and hospitable to Scots on the run from Edward. They planned to stay the winter in Ayrshire; keeping on the move, hiding successfully from both de Percy in the south and de Valence in the north. Within a couple weeks James had led Boyd to all the Douglas strongholds in the shire; first to Auchinleck, then venturing out to Trabboch for some time, south again to his mother's manor near Maybole and his father's Carrick lands and tenement near Girvan.

Figure LXII-Part Two; Auchinleck kirk with a conical hill in the background

"We have another manor near Stewarton," he informed Boyd. "And a larder-full to take from Dreghorn, a manor of de Ferrers, my mother's kin there should we so require it," he allowed. By January the two cousins were becoming restless; waiting for some word from Robert on his return. Before parting company the king and his squire had agreed to send messages should there be some progress; good news to beckon a return to the fight. The foul rumors from every shire were devastating. They heard of many hangings, cruel, barbaric tortures that ended the lives of many friends and kin; a fearful warning to any in sympathy with Brus. But these two warriors were undaunted; their fugitive and albeit landless condition from Edward's generosity, giving their estates and income to others provided them little incentive to do otherwise but continue their fight for Scotland's king and laws.

Johannis de Hastings, the one time contender for Scotland's crown and kin of Eleanora Douglas Bagot was spending a lot of his time when not on campaign on the Isle of Arran. In May 1306 he had been awarded the earldom of Menteith that included Arran and Brodick Castle for his service to Edward. He was expecting provisions within the month; unbeknown to him, the shipments would become a target for interception by a lad he met some fifteen years ago at Knaresburgh Castle. James Douglas of Lothiane, laird of his lands in Glencorse, the spy with the English accent and perfect Inglis spoken like a true man from Essex ventured on a mission of intelligence, this time to the port of Ayr. Here he overheard news of a fair shipment; an expedition with provisions bound for Arran. Three ships were to sail up the Firth of Clyde and put into the shores of Brodick Bay with clothing, grain, wine, armaments, and other general stores for the castle. Knowing the island from the hunting trips he took there with his father, James realized the cogs would be sailing for the shores of Arran on the inner end of the bay where the Rosa and Shurig Waters came together.

Quickly he rode back towards the Douglas tenement in the parish of Girvan to rendezvous with his compatriot Boyd. They excitedly made their plans to place these supplies into the Scottish treasury. The Douglas squire dispatched his messenger, a trusted Ayrshire man that had traveled with them since the debacle at Methven, to the last known location of their king in the Hebrides. "That we should find ourselves outnumbered; the English garrison in tight pursuit, we will have our lord the king to so journey to our rescue," James determined. The Scottish knight agreed with the strategy and they set out to acquire a suitable craft and enlist some crew members for their adventure. It was not long before the tiny navy in service to Robert I King of Scots left Girvan, heading for Arran, halfway up the western coast of the isle. The more obvious route from Ayrshire was from the port of Ayr; then landing near Whiting Bay; this was not to James' liking. The idle talk of English soldiers was of a second garrison at Kildonnan, in addition to the retinue at Brodick Castle. Landing on the southern shore was an easier voyage by sea but could chance their getting caught between two patrols; easily destroyed before their mission had even begun.

ISLE OF ARRAN LATE JANUARY 1307-Lord Hastings was in the company of two knights, several squires and yeomanry enjoying time for sport in the hills of Arran; hunting freely with hawks and leashed hounds his decided passion. Johannis had no idea that his absence from his stronghold while on hunt would prove his folly. Edward's vassal from Abergavenny was a conservative and pious man in his ways; a knight of fair chivalry. He was also the same English lord and kin of Ellie who pledged mainperson for the release of William le Hardi, Lord Douglas from Knaresburgh Castle in 1290. Perhaps somewhat detached, de Hastings could not imagine the unthinkable: a raid upon his fortress in Brodick Bay. It came as an even greater shock when he later discovered the identity of the invader and successful thief: le Hardi's eldest son, James of Douglas!

Figure LXIII-Part Two; sunrise over Holy Isle from Lamlash, Arran

Johannis would later recall once complimenting a younger James not yet five on his fair acts of chivalry; proudly escorting his sister Muriel to the knight, the day the two first met. Now the squire would repay de Hastings' generosity with a venture of his own. The young Scot realized the success of this raid was extremely important and not just for the provisions they would secrete away. It was true the plan was crafted of himself, his strategy the lone device this day; honed of his deft discovery of cargo for the taking. But this event was marked by a more profound significance than the acquisition of goods though badly needed by the Scots. James knew the very act and deed marked a greater significance. He was making a clear and well defined statement of his rebellion. James Douglas, son of Sir William le Hardi, Lord Douglas was openly challenging any Englishman: he who dared to steal the lands of Scots by accepting the spoils from the blood stained fingers of that despot pagan king would be made to pay to the very end of his last possession not excepting his life.

The Scots were rowing hard; moving around the western tip of the island. A huge rain storm seemed to follow the tiny galley; the seas were rough with swells that rose high above the walls of their small craft, bandying the galley about, up and down the waves, hitting the bottom hard with a terrifying thud. Everyone was feeling sick, the tumultuous journey took its toll; but the dozen patriots stayed the course. They bravely traveled across the Firth of Clyde and pulled their oars through the undulating currents. Cold and bitter winds spat blistering sea water at their faces, stinging them, blinding their eyes as they rowed closer to the isle in search of booty.

James of Douglas, Robert Boyd and their crew of loyal Scots landed on the shores of Arran at Machrie Moor, not far from an ancient standing stone. "That I recall this very spot," James told Sir Robert. "My father once so brought us here when visiting with our family, staying further north at Lochranza with my Uncle James and others of our Steward kin," he explained. Boyd knew the isle well himself having hunted with the same folk many years ago. Arriving in the safety of the night on the western shoreline they brought their wee boat to a place of safety. "That this lad will seek to secrete away our tackle, with the oars and rudder to so hide with branches from the greening will I gather; securing all in hiding over by the wee brae there," James said, pointing to the hillside near the shoreline.

Figure LXIV-Part Two; western shoreline of Arran

He then told their retinue to carry the galley to the covering afforded there as well. "To cross the isle just now is not my choice," the lad told their men at arms. "We will take our wait some few miles from here on these shores; for this night and one more." The small group of ruffians made their way silently up the coast towards Imachar Point; then to some small caves that would afford them shelter, become their home until the day before the English ships would put down their anchors in Brodick Bay. James told

Boyd of his last exploration of the caves. "For a lass, my sister Mura was most impressed by the stone caverns," he joked. "The echoes of our voices confused our Deerhound Shamus most as well." James was comforted by the memories of those times spent on Arran with his family. Now this isle would become his first major foray against the English invaders to his homeland.

Figure LXV-Part Two; Lochranza Castle with the ancient fort site looming above

The Scots made camp in the sheltered rocks; bringing with them what would become their standard equipment on future Douglas raids: griddles for their bannock, oats for the flattened cakes they would devour to stave off the pains of hunger in their bellies. The next day brought more chilling rain as the raw winds of winter blew through the shelter of their caves. To keep their minds off their inclement conditions, the Scottish warriors exchanged stories of great hunts, chivalry and Celtic lore. James spoke of his philosophy, the reason for his fierce warrior's demeanor. "That this lad has seen of times in Scotland when we were so free to spend our days most searching happily for the clues to life, words of our ancestors; to speak of lands lost and of souls now in the Otherworld." He shared often of the peaceful days now gone from them. "Where since the final victory so came against the Norwegians at that wee skirmish then at Largs 1263 we were free to roam untouched by dangers from invaders. Our spirits rising with the sun each day; to hold of us the glorious beauty that was our land and freedom," his voice was tranquil as he spoke these sentiments; then abruptly changed to a prophetic snarl. "Until the most despicable of men showed his personage in Berwick, calling himself Lord Paramount, some ten years or more ago," James said bearing a countenance of stern resolve.

He wanted the men that followed his lead to understand his manner and his ways. "That every true warrior so knows," he said sadly, "true peace can only follow victory. No soldier of any merit wants a war. As knaves we train for manhood and our spurs; but in truth not for vainglory but to be most ready for a day we hope and pray will never come." James continued, determining that his words were meaningful. "For we have seen of devastation and the untold death of heroes, men we know to breathe their last, to so leave their lives for the Otherworld; dying in their armor on the field of battle, their final wish fulfilled." No one interrupted the Douglas squire as he continued to speak. "My dear father was a brave knight of renown, broken in his spirit by the treachery of Edward's lies and false truce. He later fought with that daring rebel William Wallace, a knight who held of true passion for his Scotland. That redoubtable laird of Douglas died for his courage and his truth; the truth he held most here in his heart," he told his men. James spoke of the wisdom imparted to a youth who missed his father to the very depths of his soul. As he continued what would become his ritual with his men, he shared his thoughts lang into the night. He told them of his life and good times growing up in Douglasdale, traveling to Douglas strongholds in the Borders, enjoying the family manors in Ayrshire, Galloway, Dumfries, Fife, Berwickshire and their Fawdon in Northumbria as well.

These warriors would become followers of the young Douglas and travel together to reap havoc among the English. Each night before the battle or the raid they planned, he would speak the cause of freedom as he did this day. "The ways of our Celtic past most savagely uprooted, that our course of action to be most spoken to us; to restore that noble bearing to our homeland." He told them that to be true to one's own destiny they must evict the English infidels. "The diel's own invaders to our home, the kingdome of our proud ancestors; the place of our sweet and gentle birth; God's own words to speak so plainly to us, here, in our hearts," James said with a passion that few men could have shared. The ragged warriors of Scotland listened, wanting more; even his cousin Sir Robert was intrigued. He described the vassals of the king who came to Douglasdale, to Ayrshire, and the Forests to reap the spoils of a battered people. "True men with no belief in God or Heaven; for if they so had faith they would never breach the marches for the greed of Edward," he told them plainly.

After the lad concluded, he withdrew himself to sit alone and contemplate the strategy for the fight to come. In the dreary grey of the late afternoon James of Douglas was looking out the mouth of a cave towards Arran's shores. He watched the diligence of a spider carefully making his way up to his web, only to be washed away by the rain dripping down in rivulets from the stone overhang above. Twelve times he watched the relentless spider attempt his feat only to be vanquished once again. Then on the thirteenth try he was successful; James seemed to experience the success vicariously, respecting the resolve of the small warrior sharing his cave. He recalled the words of his father speaking of God's love for his people; how He would lead them in His grace should they but ask. *'He will come to us as a spider, or a bird, or some other creature,'* William le Hardi told his wee son. *'To assure us all that He is here; watching over his flock giving His people courage and hope to so continue.'* Just then James noticed a corbie flying over the hills behind them; the crow was calling loudly as if reminding the squire he must be the inspiration and the leader for his men; that his God would stand behind him with his love and guidance to their victory as well. "Thank you most again dear father," James said quietly to le Hardi, knowing he would hear his son's words, even far away as he was in the Otherworld.

Figure LXVI-Part Two; standing stone Machrie Moor; Arran

    The two lookouts were returning from scouting the area; it was time for some others of their retinue to take their post; to search the far reaches of their camp in case the English garrisons of either fortress might stumble upon the Scots. Ever since the rout at Methven, reconnaissance was a mandatory practice with James; he would never be caught twice, unprepared for English trickery as he was in Perthshire seven months ago. The report from these first two men at arms was good; few people were about; everywhere they looked there was little or no activity. James thanked them for their information and began laying out his plan for Brodick Bay before his cousin Robert.

    "What of this," he counseled with the knight, technically the soldier of rank in this adventure. "To bring our wee army most here," he suggested, indicating a coastal location near the Glenn Dubh. The knight and older cousin reflected on the choice. "Perhaps the shelter of Glen Cloy will serve us better. This knight has been there; staying once at Brodick Castle, this area could afford us view of the fortress and shelter our good Scots from harm," he explained. James liked the suggestion immediately. He was not as familiar with the eastern coast, facing the Ayrshire shoreline. Their final choice decided: to base their expedition from Glen Cloy just two miles from the castle. Boyd's observations were cleverly thought out and the squire told him so directly; publicly praising the knight in front of their men at arms. They concluded their meeting, satisfied with the plan and gathered their retinue for the journey. "It is done," smiled James.

GLEN CLOY-The rains continued to fall; the stormy weather seemed to follow the Ayrshire men as they traveled eastward. By the time the Scots made their way past Loch Nuis, their gambesons and surcotes were soaked through, their mail beginning to show signs of the unrelenting rain. "Perhaps to find some dry clothing on those vessels," suggested James. "To tell our king that we have ventured forth to search of cotes and supertunics for our trouble; not coinage or armaments!' he chuckled. Boyd shared the lad's sarcastic demeanor; being cold and wet, hungry and uncomfortable, their winter travels onfoot were not going well. The Scots marched on; at least they had not encountered any English soldiers James mused; so far so good.

Figure LXVII-Part Two; caves on Arran's western shore

James and Sir Robert arrived with their small retinue in the wee hours of a new morning happy that the woody glen was unoccupied. The Steward cousins conferred on a suitable location for a more permanent camp than the caves afforded them. "There, just above the bed of the Cloy Burn," motioned the knight, indicating the mound that formed the site of an old fort. James noted a circular structure completely surrounded by a single vallum; a stone wall of good defense even in its diminished state. The Scots to a man cheered and roared in triumph as they approached the ancient site finding it just as Boyd remembered yet safe from English intruders. And it had a fresh spring that fed into the burn; it was perfect for their extended use. "There sits Fairy Glen," noted Boyd pointing southeast. "This place of safety is most known as well as the Fairy Mound Fort; Tòrr an t-Sean Chaisteil," he chuckled, speaking his Scottish Gaelic. James nodded; pleased with the knight's selection. The ancient fortress was one he would enjoy exploring when there was opportunity for such pleasure; curiously much the same as the Old Hill Fort near Lochranza Castle, the very one he had explored with his father a lang time ago, he mused.

The Douglas squire looked about; the fair retreat afforded an excellent view of the bay. "Perhaps Queen Elfhame will come to so protect us, her Celtic warriors here; to make us invisible to the men with tails," James joked happily. Being safely hidden in the glen, unbeknown to the garrison of Brodick Castle, was a huge relief he told Robert. "And the rains have finally broken most as well," pointing to the misty clouds rising upward from Goatfell, the island's highest peak. The dark forbidding hues of winter weather seemed to vanish as the warming sun revealed a sliver of red and yellow sky, barely peaking out over the mountain and stretching round to the bay below.

Figure LXVIII-Part Two; Brodick Castle over looking the small inlet near the Rosa; taken from the ferry Caledonian MacBrayne, the low clouds hovering over Goatfell

Lookouts again were posted; the griddles heated up and the Scottish soldiers cooked their bannock. Perhaps to feast on the spoils of the captured booty most tonight the squire mused. He and Sir Robert then took their leave of camp to scout out the bay; search for the vessels expected from the mainland. James and Boyd made their way unobtrusively from their stronghold in Glen Cloy, following the winding shore of Brodick Bay at a good distance, past the standing stone, towards Cladach. They noted some activity upon the horizon of the Firth of Clyde; speculated that it might be the three supply ships headed for the stone fortress held by the de Hastings lord; the stronghold of Brodick Castle. Eager to determine their opposition, the two men crept closer for a look at the imposing citadel. Boyd told him of the tower and its design. Suddenly he remembered that the farrier once kept some extra horses for the garrison in an earth and timber structure near the postern. The enterprising Scots decided to venture forth for a closer look.

It was still early morning and very quiet; the cousins surmised that the men at arms might be out on hunt. What they did not know was that de Hastings had taken most everyone with him that day for sport in pursuit of game, to the other end of the island at Lochranza. Uncharacteristically over confident, Johannis feared little for an attack or an invasion of his island. James and Boyd were making their way into the castle grounds taking great care to go unnoticed as they moved into the outer buildings that once housed additional horses. To their complete delight they discovered little had changed from the days of Stewartd lairds.

Figure LXIX-Part Two; Glen Cloy, the sea mist and low clouds of the prime still clinging to the peaks of Arran

Finding two jennets, some palfreys and a cart horse occupying the stables James joked with Boyd that the English were offering the Scots more equal terms for their planned encounter; leaving horses unattended for their use. "Let us thank them later for their courtesy," he said, quickly saddling two horses as the knight did the same. "Our horse stealing king leads us now, even in his absence," he chuckled. "Fortunate for us the Countess his fair mother is not here; sure she would discover our bold deed of thievery and stop us!" And with that the two men rode off, spurring their palfreys on, each riding a horse and leading one other. The day had started quite well indeed reflected Sir Robert out loud, smiling confidently at James. "Good that you have so visited this fair castle," the squire added. "An excellent beginning to our partnership!'

Upon returning to camp, little time was afforded them to rest; the lookouts reported the arrival of the three supply ships at the inland bay. The warriors were more than ready; anxious to return to Brodick Castle, they rode two to a horse leaving four to travel on foot until more horses could be acquired. James and Robert led their men to a concealed location not many yards from where the English were unloading their cargo. More than twenty men were coming up from the boats; some carrying casks of wine, others heavy chests with weapons. The underwarden of the castle was taking his time checking through the provisions; a careless demeanor of complacency pervaded the dock. The early dawn was quiet except for the slight ripple of the tides and some passing gulls. But suddenly everything changed. Seemingly from nowhere came a perilous, chilling sound: A Douglas! A Douglas! The frightening war cry filled the air with terror and foreboding. The English soldiers were stunned; surprised by the ambuscade. Wherever did this makeshift band of marauders come from they wondered; but there was little time for thought. James and Boyd with two other Scots were riding their horses straight for the ships' men; brandishing their weapons, their shields reflecting anguished treachery as they moved through the glaring sun.

The advantage of surprise caught the English off guard; many were not in full armaments, few grasped the danger quickly to ward off the attack. James moved as if possessed; a demon on a ride for vengeance, Boyd in tandem at his side. Sir Robert swung his mace and crushed the skull of the first man he encountered. Then the squire moved about, guiding the palfrey carefully, knowing the horse's limitations in such confined battles. James spurred his ambler quickly forward; encountering his first opponent as he made a left to left upper cut from the high guard to meet the shoulder of the Englishman; the exchange made the arm dangle as the crushing blow cut through bone. The others of the Scots were meeting with excellent success as well. Some of the ships' crew decided they would fight another day, withdrawing to the protection of their vessels they tried to leave the inland bay quickly. But the ships were undermanned as the land breeze rose to strange and quickened heights. As if the Celtic gods were blowing fiercely from their heavens, aiding their brave Scots to avenge the invaders to their lands, the two retreating cogs were swamped; unable to ride out the sudden gales or land on shore. Their cargo was now waiting patiently to be transferred to the Scottish treasury.

The de Hastings men and others that remained on shore were overwhelmed by the aggressive onslaught of these vagabond warriors. Shrill cries from English victims followed hideous blows of violent aggression. Sounds of metal hitting metal reverberated through the air; the formidable clanking, swords on shields, was heard even above the din of the anguished. Sparks flew in the grey light of the prime. The cogs' men at arms struggled, the underwarden's men endeavored to regain their step; each one was felled, to lose in every battle as the odd contingency of Scots fell upon the English annihilating nearly everyone. James and Robert, now both veterans with raw memories of Methven, were slaying victims without hesitation or mercy. The Douglas squire turned his palfrey once again; readying his horse for another attack. But as he was making his maneuvers he realized a new front was forming, coming from the castle behind them. Screams of the wounded English stirred the few remaining of the garrison; the gates at Brodick opened, the portcullis rumbled upward as the drawbridge slammed down. Horse's hooves beat a drum-like rhythm as they proudly headed for the battle; the de Hastings men at arms yet remaining in the castle were coming to the aid of their comrades.

Figure LXX-Part Two; Brodick Castle, managed by the National Trust for Scotland

James answered their attack with one of his own; the fierce warrior instinctively led his horse to run full tilt right for them as if in the joust. He was a frightful sight as he brandished his sword in the ready, riding faster and faster towards his opponents. As the squire drew nearer his dark countenance revealed the fearless grimace of another great Douglas warrior, the brave Sholto. "A Douglas! A Douglas! he bellowed; his noble family's deafening battle cry sounding in defiance. Boyd looked about and saw the garrison coming for the squire; he too spurred his palfrey forward to attack the armed horse of the castle; the other Scots having subdued the English from the supply ships turned to follow the knight's lead as well. With the battle almost upon them a strange order was given; the English captain called his men to halt, to not engage the enemy. "Return to the confines of Brodick's walls!" he commanded the garrison. Without the satisfaction of combat, as James would later tell the story, the Scots forced the English to retreat to the interior courtyard; the safe sanctuary of the Brodick stronghold.

With little else to do, the Scots helped themselves to the largesse of Lord Hastings; filled the coffers of the Scottish treasury and secured their booty to their stalwart fortress in Glen Cloy. There were casks of fine wine, salmon and smoked meats of many varieties, stores of oats, barley and other grains. James sought to bring horses for their pleasure and burden animals to carry their spoils away to their hidden camp. Boyd looked after the weaponry; offering the young squire his pick of mail and padded surcotes. The lad allowed the rest of their wee army as he called them, to share of the plunder as well; everyone was celebrating this day; far away in the safety of Glen Cloy where they now awaited their king's arrival.

Figure LXXI-Part Two; Glen Cloy and site of old Roman fort above where James led his men to safety with their booty from the raid of the Brodick supply ships

It was some seven days or more before King Robert arrived on Arran at Whiting Bay. With him were thirty or more small galleys carrying three hundred of his followers. Johannis de Hastings had left the isle to round up men at arms from Bute; hoping to punish the invaders for their folly of attacking his provision ships. However he did not return for some time and not before the Scots took their leave of Arran, to rejoin the fight on Scotland's mainland. The isle was strangely quiet as the men at arms took over the small village near their landing site. An old speywife informed the king that the friend he sought "perhaps to be in a stalwart place; known as the woody glen," she offered. He thanked the woman for her assistance and beckoned a small company to follow him eastward to Glen Cloy.

The squire was on patrol of the old fort site when he thought he heard a familiar sound; the king's own signal, the shrill voice of their leader's hunting horn. He ran full tilt towards the campsite when he heard the bleating sound again as it echoed through the glen. James nearly collided with Boyd coming round the corner. "That rugged, raunchy sound could only be the horn of our dear king!" exclaimed the squire. The knight agreed and there was cheering bellowing down from the fort site as the rag tag confederates ran to greet Robert Brus. "Where are the English?" asked Robert. "Mostly dead," said James, "that we have taken of their provisions that they no longer need them."

Boyd told the king that de Hastings had left Brodick to enlist more men at arms for another encounter he suspected. "How many men are you?" asked the squire. "Only three hundred," groused the king. That should be enough James allowed as he beckoned the King of Scots to climb the brae to the ancient Celtic fort. "To see of our secret stronghold," he boasted. "One so found by Sir Robert," pointing now to Boyd. Laughter and good tidings filled the air as King Robert was shown the liberated possessions of the de Hastings. "We shall thank your mother for the kindness of her kin," joked Robert Brus, knowing that Eleanora's cousin Lord Hastings had been given the former Steward lairdship. "Aye, that these were once his goods and he so praised this lad for his chivalry lang years ago; that I will return the favor complimenting his fair provisioning of our army," James retorted, happy to have his king returning to the fight.

They supped on the Brodick provisions and drank from the castle wine; lang into the night the Scots celebrated their reunion. And they also mourned their dead. For until now Robert Brus had not been told of the butchery and savagery inflicted on his followers, friends and kin. James and his cousin Robert Boyd sat apart with their king to tell him. Brus had never known such sorrow; he pained with every word, blamed himself for the treacherous doom bestowed by the demon king upon his adherents and family. Only one who had lost so much could comprehend the king's devastation. James of Douglas understood. "That this squire felt his heart to harden when we buried my father; le Hardi's torturous end and de Moray's murder too, reminding me this very day our battle is most virtuous and right," he told his lord. With plain words these brave Scots shared their sentiments and unbearable loss.

Grief filled the king's heart; tears streamed down his weathered cheeks. Robert Brus began his recriminations; speaking softly that others might not overhear, the king questioned his very intent and act to lead Scotland in revolution. Before he could continue an almost belligerent Douglas blurted out his indignation. "Blame no one but the butcher not the victims of this fair tragedy! Edward broke the truce at Berwick murdering women and children in their beds. The vile pagan, usurper of our kingdome, refused Caerlaverock's surrender for some time and then accepted Scots to his peace and hanged some for their bravery most there. That we must not forget the fight at Stirling Castle; there he set War Wolf upon the fortress, after the depleted and starving garrison most had given up, surrendered to him; yet Edward refused their peaceful end, to wage a siege for his amusement; our beloved and most pious Lord Paramount. Edward sees of Celts and Scots as turds and rubbish. We need our king to lead us; you will find the resolve," James told Brus, knowing the King of Scots already had. Boyd and Douglas left Robert Brus to his own thoughts. After setting more lookouts, James ambled off to sleep in the peace that his king was returning to Scotland; to do battle with the English.

Figure LXXII-Part Two; Whiting Bay with Goatfell in the background

TURNBERRY-Robert Brus was determined to regain his kingdome. He sent Carrick men ahead to Turnberry; to signal the way clear for the king's retinue to land there near the family stronghold in Ayrshire. A blazing fire broke open on the coast line and was mistaken for that very sign Robert sought: a signal fire telling him to land without fear of English reprisals in the area. When the thirty-four wee galleys put to shore in South Ayrshire they were greeted by many frantic Carrick vassals; de Percy was in residence in Turnberry with a garrison of men so large that more than two thirds were being housed in the village tenements and messuages.

Edward Brus turned to his cautious older brother and told the king a decision here was overdue; to take his kingdome now or to forsake of it forever. Robert Boyd was commiserating with James; a look of grave concern crossed the squire's countenance. "That we must decide on this and hurry," he advised, "for it will not be long before we are so discovered here." The King of Scots had other worries on his mind; his two younger brothers were landing in Galloway with two hundred men by ship. What if they were to meet a force of size, being surprised by English garrisons in that shire as strong or stronger in their number than de Percy's in Ayrshire. Robert sighed heavily at the prospect and took his leave of everyone; sitting alone looking out on the waters of Turnberry Bay, down toward Ailsa Craig.

"How many times I came to sit by that old standing stone near my home?" he spoke softly that only he could hear above the sound of the sea rolling to and fro, licking the rocks of the shoreline as the tide receded. "And I in hopeful supplication to our ancestors, that the stone to so impart some ancient vision that would guide me; oh to know their wise thoughts this day!" he whispered to himself. The king reflected on the many peaceful times he came to that sacred spot; a simpler time when he could easily sort out his thoughts and plan his life. Just then, in his silence, Brus was startled to the present by the rustle of breaking twigs and trampled brush as his Douglas squire approached. The titular king beckoned his loyal vassal to join him in his solitude.

Figure LXXIII-Part Two; little remains of the Carrick castle at Turnberry on the Ayrshire coast, north of Girvan

"That this humble squire so remembers joyous times when le Hardi was alive; coming to this very coast where we visited our Douglas manor, my grandmother's fair dowry, her lands near Girvan; Lady El's dower most as well near Maybole." Robert shook his head mirroring the sentiment. James bore le Hardi's manner in his boldness; he was not deterred by social status and always spoke his truth as he was taught. "My lord the king, pray let me tell you of our times on Arran," the engaging youth began. "Of my brave companion in the cave; arrogant and defiant, that for some twelve times this small warrior tried his best to reach his objective; a spider seeking shelter in the rain, relentless in his quest to finally meet success and reach his web on the thirteenth try. Is it not some twelve battles that you have faced and lost whence becoming Scotland's king?" he asked rhetorically. Brus concurred silently as before, but now he was intrigued by story. He motioned the lad with the slight lisp, the youthful squire of an age well beyond his years that he might continue with his counseling to his lord.

Figure LXXIV-Part Two; view of Alyssa Craig and the light house on Turnberry Bay from the site of the standing stone near the Carrick castle

"Then know this my king, the words of my dear father are most true: God so speaks to us, coming as a spider or a bird. The great God of the Celtic people will not desert our good King Robert, but lead him to our victory. Ma's breug bh'uam e, is breug thugam," he asserted, using the Scottish Gaelic of his Highland ancestors deliberately, for emphasis. "If it is a lie as told by me, it was a lie as told to me, the fair words of Arran's St. Eilean. My father's own truth to me and now for you to hear: for William le Hardi Douglas was no liar; that you most surely know joining him there at Irvine Water ten lang years ago. This is my pledge and promise: I tell you true; the kingdome of Scots awaits their brave leader King Robert. Scotland is most yours for the taking majesty," the lad concluded hopefully. James breathed deeply then started to take his leave of the man he knew first as Earl Robert of Carrick. "A Douglas bold and true; good that you are on the side of Robert, King of Scots, ready to do battle with one Edward; my truth for you dear squire!" Brus confided; he also added that he would devise a strategy to take the toune; to rout the garrison from their beds in the village and slaughter them like the trespassers that they were. James chuckled. "This day to rout de Percy from your Turnberry; the next to bring de Clifford to his knees, begging this squire to take back his Douglasdale but to spare his life," he boasted gleefully.

The slaughter of the Turnberry garrison; the laying waste of the village turned much booty for Robert's retinue, growing steadily in number for the rout. Sadly with every victory turned there came a tragic defeat for Scotland. Robert's brothers had landed on the shores of Galloway with eighteen ships and galleys on the 9th of February. Making their way north, Thomas and Alexander Brus with a large contingency, followers of the Lord of Kintyre and others, encountered a Galwegian Chief named Dougal Macdouel loyal to dear Edward. During the battle that followed, both brothers, including Alexander, once the fair Dean of the See of Glasgow, were badly wounded. Only a few of Brus' followers made it back safely to their ships. The others, many taken alive as prisoners, were either beheaded by Macdouel or turned over to Edward at Lanercost to receive their sentence.

Thomas Brus was deemed dragged by the tails of horses in Carlisle, then hanged, and later beheaded. Alexander was sentenced to be hanged that same day, 17th February and then he too was beheaded. These executions in Carlisle, the result of the Macdouel treachery would be dealt with severely, the King of Scots vowed poignantly; the aching heart of a grieving elder brother was turning to hardened resolve. No further grief would break his determination now; Edward must be defeated. "No; *will be* defeated; I do swear it!" Robert Brus promised. "On the very souls of my dear brothers now with God," he said with stern reverence.

Figure LXXV-Part Two; view from a cave in Kirkpatrick Fleming where Robert Brus was hidden in safety by loyal Scots, located on the site of Dunskellie Castle

DOUGLASDALE MARCH 1307-Lurking in the hills of Douglasdale just west of the Douglas Water was a squire leading his wee retinue of just two men at arms, in preparation for an ambuscade of de

Clifford's garrison at the former stronghold of his family. From his vantage point on Hagshaw Hill James of Douglas viewed his homeland for the first time in nearly ten years. "That this Douglasdale is my paradise too my dear father; to be most ours again, I do promise you, sure aye!" he said in a prayerful tone, a low whisper that only he could hear. "That we will move north on the morrow should we have no luck in Hazelside this night," the lad advised his men with a confidant air. "Perhaps to Craigend where there is a cave for safety there, I do recall. To take our view of the garrison from Poniel Hill would be my plan." James remembered the lands well; his father had often told him that such knowledge would someday repay him for his careful scrutiny. The tenements in Poniel were once a gift of the Abbot of Kelso to his grandfather; a point of pride with le Hardi. Now these moorish lands of the string would provide advantage to the squire's lookouts; keeping the alien garrison at bay.

Ever since James could ride Fortis by himself he recalled being with his father Lord Douglas on the hunt or setting traps for fishing. As a family the Douglases would venture about their lands in search of cairns and other markings of the ancient people that first populated Douglasdale. 'Making peace with the old ones gone before us, pledging your faith to the lands of our forebears' James recalled his father's words. How well they serve me now he mused. The lad had conceived his plan for the recovery of the castle. He would drive out the English laird, raiding the castle, annihilating the occupants, as often as it took until the English fled Douglasdale for safer havens. Robert Clifford had held the Douglas barony for nearly a decade; ever since Lord Douglas was remanded into the custody of Ralph de Sandwich, constable at the Tower of London. Holding the estates with little trouble these last ten years, Edward's vassal could not conceive resistance to his lairdship now. "Should he be surprised? This is my expectation, aye; that he will be repelled from Douglasdale my full intention," vowed James to his men at arms.

The squire had devised a strategy to approach one of two trusted vassals of his father. He could certainly expect the support of Sir Andrew de Fleming from Glenbuck, his father's seneschal. But for this venture he would need a more ruthless and wily veteran whose prowess with sword was well recognized. James planned to call upon Thomas Dickson; the valet that was with le Hardi when de Percy seized the laird on false charges of breaking the covenant he made at Knadgerhill. This lang time servant of his father might enjoy the retribution the lad surmised. Dressed in a simple tunic to conceal his mail and armaments, James completed the disguise with a semi-circular cloak of plain cloth worn through in several places; the attached hood serving to cover his raven locks and Douglas countenance. The heir apparent to the family's baronial lands looked more a shepherd; a poor tenant that no one could suspect was the disinherited laird of Douglasdale except for his great height. James was riding one of de Percy's palfreys liberated in Turnberry when Robert's forces lay waste the whole district. The squire and his two yeomen made their way unnoticed across Broomerside Hill down through old Shielings and south towards the farm at Hazelside in the twilight of the evening. "Let us pray that Dickson is still in residence," he chuckled knowing that to find of a loyal villien of de Percy in their midst instead could spell a bit of trouble for his retinue.

Taking no chances as was to be his custom, James had his followers adjourn to a grove of trees nearby taking cover with three horses to wait for his return. The lad would go himself he determined; Dickson would be suspicious of any messenger that he might send, fearing retribution from the English as le Hardi's most trusted and faithful vassal. With a quickened heart, beating hard in anticipation the squire rapped three times on the familiar wooden door. The bar receded slowly on the inside with a painful creak and seemed to take forever before moving ajar. A lad about the age of Hugh peered past the door jam and James caught his breath. Then from behind the young Scot was the curious but familiar face: Thomas Dickson, a little older but recognizable at once.

Figure LXXVI-Part Two; a scene near Hazelside along the Douglas Water with the windmills of Hagshaw Hill in the distance

A broad smile crossed James' face as he ducked into the doorway; pulling down the hood to reveal what words could not have said. "Good Thomas, that I am James." His father's loyal vassal grabbed the lad and all but hugged him breathless. Tears flowed down Dickson's face. "That I knew one day you would find your way back home to Douglasdale," he stammered in his deep emotion. "Come sit, our good mother here will bring you sup to quell the hunger heard rumbling in your stomach there," he joked with the squire. "That I have two good men as well outside, with our palfreys hidden not far from the Douglas Water," James replied knowing his men were hungry too. "Better to bring them inside; hide them from the men with tails," scoffed Thomas conveying his sentiments against the English succinctly.

Figure LXXVII-Part Two; view from the motte and ruins of Douglas Castle, looking just to the left of Gallow Knowe

    The warm food and ale felt good; the welcome was more than James could ever have expected. The Dicksons were a hearty lot and ready for whatever he had in mind. "That we heard from Gillerothe of that most sad and infamous end to your noble and courageous father, Lord Douglas," Thomas told the lad as he sighed for the sad memories. The squire thanked him humbly for his sentiment. "And was it you just returned from England?" James nodded and told him of his times in Brabant. "Stopping first to see Lady Douglas and my brothers first in Essex," he continued. "That she was forced to marry," James said softly. Thomas told the lad that Gillerothe had spoken highly of the lady's courage; having dear Edward as her liege lord was something they so sadly felt, understood as well her requirement to remarry or seek a nunnery. "Then to find Sir William Bagot our mother's husband by convenience in the retinue of de Lacy; that soldier with many others of our English cousins did we encounter so at Methven; most difficult to contemplate a war as this," James allowed. "And now to return to Douglasdale and not see my father here, but an English vassal of dear Edward in his place to turn my heart to stone, with no mercy can I treat these infidels," the squire sputtered, his calm demeanor flashed with anger for the injustice that he felt deep within his soul.

Dickson told James that many others of his father's former tenants would come to his aid should he have a plan. The squire shared his ideas freely round the table as they feasted. "That you know my father often told us all of the success of the Mamlukes with their fair strategy in the late years of the Crusades; to attack in small numbers, rid a fortress of its garrison a few so at a time to wear down their resolve," he reminded Thomas. "Perhaps we can so triumph with such scheme of device." The martyred laird's loyal varlet responded favorably to the tactic; suggesting that he bring some others to meet with James the following evening. "You will stay the night then?" asked Dickson. "Would only the fair walls of Douglas Castle suit me more," he chuckled in reply. Dickson's son offered to look after their horses which James gratefully accepted as well. Thomas asked about the Brus and offered condolences for his brother Neil; and the barbaric treatment of the ladies in their following.

Figure LXXVIII-Part Two; Hazelside

"That sadly two more brothers, the faithful dean of Glasgow dear Alexander and Sir Thomas Brus, both have now been executed; one head resting on the gates at Carlisle, the other on the keep. The English having raised the dragon in their fight will not so relent it seems," the lad offered ruefully. James then provided all the details of the treachery of Macdouel, the Galwegian laird who caused the execution of the king's two brother just weeks before. "So it must be for us then; to return their grace with the same heart felt remorse of cold revenge. No one will be spared; that must be our pledge, just like the taking of Sanquhar Castle," James said, reminding Dickson of the siege he planned there with Lord Douglas ten years before. "That we have no William Wallace to come to our defense should one yeoman live to dispatch an army after us," he cautioned, though somewhat light heartedly to recall that siege of ten years ago when Wallace rescued his father at Durisdeer.

The next evening, one by one, good men of Douglasdale once staying in the company of le Hardi came to pledge their fealty and join the retinue of his oldest son: James, Lord Douglas yet to be. Many of the men the squire quickly recognized at least by name when they were introduced. The last to come was his father's seneschal Sir Andrew. "Though past the age for duel, good Thomas here thought I should come along at least to set my eyes upon you lad," he said smiling broadly. "The very image of Sir William; sure aye!" he chuckled using the old laird's favorite expression.

Figure LXXIX-Part Two; ruins of St. Bride's; formerly known as Douglas Kirk

The squire thanked him readily for his support. Each of his father's vassals offered suggestions and provided information on the size and makeup of the garrison; details on the habits of the captain of the castle. As the following Sunday would be Palm Sunday Dickson suggested that it would be a perfect day for enacting the squire's plan to attack the English when they least expected it. "Perhaps when most are attending at the Douglas Kirk; the services so there for this most Holy day," suggested James. "That I will lead these two good men from Girvan here to linger most outside in the ready; adorned in inconspicuous attire but not to be among the worshipers of that fair kirk as strangers to this dale we could be recognized for our plan. That when all the English are arrived most there will we give the Douglas war cry to attack the men of the garrison." Dickson championed the plan immediately; he volunteered to be one of the first up front near the chancel; to take the captain of the castle was his desire.

PALM SUNDAY-James and the Girvan yeoman were in the vicinity of Broadlea just south of the wee burn of the same name; they could not see Douglas Castle from their position but they could see the procession of some twenty men that comprised the English garrison ride through the outer gates toward the Douglas Kirk. Once de Clifford's men at arms arrived safely at the sanctuary James beckoned his men silently forward. Fording the Douglas Water they quietly approached the village. One of his father's vassals posted as the lookout near the kirk gave his signal to indicate that the entire retinue was present and being seated. Unfortunately in the nave of the kirk a restless warrior took the exchange to mean it was time to sound the fearless, piercing war cry. "A Douglas! A Douglas!" he shouted. The garrison was surprised. None of these men at arms wore their armor to the kirk; though some carried weapons, no Englishman carried his shield. But because of the premature sound to arms, many of the congregation were not yet seated; some of de Clifford's men were able to respond to the attack more readily. Thomas Dickson was the first to be wounded in the close fray that ensued; but not before giving the English commander a taste of his sword.

Figure LXXX-Part Two; Douglas Kirk, St. Bride's is in the care of Historic Scotland

James immediately noticed something had gone awry as the lookout began waving his arms wildly. The Douglas squire spurred his palfrey forward, faster and faster he rode leading his yeoman to do battle in the kirk.

He threw open the large oak door with the carved armorial bearings of his Douglas ancestors. Giving the battle cry again he thrust himself forward, into the chaos and close quarters of the fabled kirk. James held the old standard of his grandfather in the ready, his left arm in the high guard position as he parried quickly with his small shield to counter with a left to left upper cut, that met with the cross bar of his first opponent's sword. James moved his feet with quick agility, blending his body with the momentum of his attack. He turned to meet the side of his opponent's sword and smashed forward with his shield as he parried the blow. The shield was strong; of an ancient Celtic design it was reinforced by a single, long hand bar; perfect for such a tactic. The forward action of his shield worked to numb the hand of his opponent; possibly to have done more damage by the verbal response of the Englishman, he mused. The squire turned his left sword hand aiming the hilt at his adversary; with a single thrust he ended the Englishman's fight for the day.

Figure LXXXI-Part Two; the Douglas Larder raid began from this spot

These close battles were won by mental confidence as well as physical prowess; perfected use of warrior's center of gravity was essential as well. Properly trained, James' back was straight, his feet planted but not heavy in their stance as he moved expertly in one fluid motion beginning with his sword held in the ready, his small shield carried low in the right hand; he now moved to encounter another opponent. James made an initial strike that was not parried; he cut across the man's upper torso down to his thigh. The wounded solder was already off balance and now slipped forward towards the Douglas squire. The Englishman but fell into James second strike; a strong thrust from the middle guard that caused a pulling slash on the man's upper arm and hand. The wounded yeoman stumbled to the floor, tripping over a fallen comrade. The squire used a dagger he held behind the shield and swept across the cheek and down the neck of the shorter man as he slumped quietly to his death. The ferociousness of the Douglas squire's attacks was of a power that seemed well beyond his youthful physique as he transformed to an unrelenting terror.

One of de Clifford's retinue was still unsheathing his sword when James burst forward, moving fast upon him. The sorry knight was not quick enough in his defense as the squire made a vicious cut to the right slashing across his unprotected right arm, cutting to bone, following with a second uncontested thrust, he cut through the throat near the collar bone. Blood oozed down the hilt as he pulled back his sword from the dying victim. James reeled, quickly turning to parry with his father's small shield as another English warrior drew his sword to attack; the blow hit the metal edge of the shield. The squire slowly and deliberately righted himself; moved deftly back to assess the opponent. The clashing thuds of English swords hitting Scottish wooden and leather shields were heard throughout the sanctuary followed by groans and cries of surprise; the stunned men of the English garrison were failing; the outnumbered Scots were routing de Clifford's well trained men. James was focused and his tough training was serving him well. He always brought his sword back to the high guard; in the ready to return a blow, his arm supple not stiff, able to make a shearing cut with the fast blade of his grandfather's old standard.

Soon the victors were receiving prisoners; the few remaining English, yet standing, were yielding in surrender to their savage aggressors. As James was making his way to the nave of the kirk he slowly began noticing that some of his family's funeral hatchments and shields were missing from the walls. The large escutcheon of Willelmi, dominus de Duglas still hung near the chancel to his great relief. Apparently some of our Douglas armaments were so moved in favor of the English laird, he sputtered sarcastically to himself as he came upon an unfamiliar shield; a large banner with the armorial bearings of de Clifford; the checkered gold and blue with a fess of red, now in disarray.

The irony fell upon him in boisterous laughter; he had unknowingly destroyed de Clifford's escutcheon! The once proud banner of armorial bearings was rendered into sheaths of tattered silk and velvet during the siege against the garrison. "So that is what so caught the edge of the old laird's standard," James chuckled. In the excitement of the battle as he first entered the old kirk he had pushed back his body to regain his stance; with his sword in the high guard he became tangled in some sheathing and ripped across the cloth to untangle himself. "That my grandfather was so with me this day as I wielded his sword," he boasted, pointing out de Clifford's armorial bearings. "This lad was forced to fight his way through that sorry shield and banner; the cheeky Or and Azure with the Fess of Gules," he scoffed, trivializing the now tattered armorial bearings of Robert de

Clifford, Edward's vassal, Henry de Percy's kin and co-conspirator; sending William le Hardi to the Tower of London and his martyred end.

James wandered about the kirk and felt himself solemnly overwhelmed by his surroundings. Along the outer walls were the family tombs; the first arched edifice held the effigies of his Uncle Hugh, a knight and warrior favoring the large Douglas frame lying along side the petite stone carving of his wife Lady Marjory de Abernathy. The odd couple, he recalled. As a child visiting the Douglas Kirk James always went to their tombs just to marvel at their uniqueness, to see them lying together under a great arch of simple decoration: Marjory with her small feminine frame barely one third the size of her husband; Hugh, sixth Lord Douglas, filling up the rest of the wall tomb with his massive, life size image. The stone carvings were painted in bright colors of gold, purple and red detailing exquisite robes, marked by the pale beauty of blue with white, the Douglas family arms of three mullets on a chief.

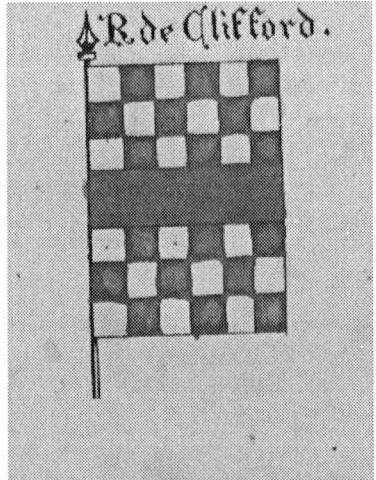

Figure LXXXII-Part Two; armorial bearings of Robert de Clifford as depicted in the nineteenth century translation of the 'Roll of Arms of Princes, Barons, and Knights who attended King Edward I to the Siege of Caerlaverock in 1300' by Thomas Wright

There were other tombs of his ancestors; his grandfather Sir William and his first wife Lady Martha, James' grandmother. The next to last monument contained the delicate effigy of his own mother, Lady Elizabeth Steward, the first wife of William le Hardi. Beside this lofty archway was another wall tomb, yet unadorned, empty and waiting for an effigy that was not yet carved; the recumbent stone image of William le Hardi, seventh Lord Douglas with appointed room for his second wife Lady Eleanora of Lovaine. The bones of the martyred knight were yet at rest in a stone coffin at Little Dunmow Priory. James took a few moments to pray, first at the effigy of his mother Elizabeth, then near the plain, yet unadorned, arched structure that stood waiting the laird's remains, his bones to return from exile in England.

Gathering his wee retinue from Girvan and the good men of Douglasdale, James led the march down the cart path and through the castle gates. The English prisoners numbered few as nearly two dozen lay dead or dying in the rows and across the benches of his family's old kirk. James, Lord Douglas yet to be was returning in triumph to Douglas Castle. The only serious injury was to le Hardi's vassal Thomas Dickson; his son and the former farrier at Douglas Castle carried him home to Hazelside where he stoically recovered from his wounds. Some years later Robert Brus rewarded this brave valet noted as Thomas, son of Richard, with the barony of Symington in Lanarkshire for his service. The family later took their surname from these lands and held them along with the Hazelside farm for generations.

Figure LXXXIII-Part Two; Douglas funeral hatchment on a vault wall in the lower levels, under St. Bride's kirk in Douglas; photo courtesy James Fleming

When the young laird arrived at his ancestral home he was greeted by a servant and the cook, both defiant to his entry, in faithful service to de Clifford. The good Scots had marched across the drawbridge and under the open portcullis. In the great hall they surprised the cook and kitchen helper who were setting out a huge repast for the garrison. "In our honor," James said sarcastically. He had intended to free the servants until they tried to fight the Scots. "Sorry fools, so put down your weapons," he commanded the two men. Their stubbornness ended in their deaths; neither one was a trained warrior and held no mettle against the Douglas squire. James ordered some of the Douglas men at arms to remove the English prisoners taken at the kirk to the dunjon prison of the tower. His Girvan retinue he took with him on a tour of the castle that he knew so well; in search of any English that might yet be in residence.

James climbed the scale-and-platt stairs, counting the steps along the way as he once did as a wee knave. The staircase was unusual for a Scottish tower, designed by his grandfather from one he recalled at a Flemish barony. The stairs led from the great hall to the third floor of the family chambers; he felt his heart lunge with the pain of loneliness that a son feels for a very loved and revered father as he now stood in front of the carved oak door that opened to the laird's chamber. It was almost ten years to the day that a younger Earl of Carrick had brought fire and sword to Douglas Castle, kidnapping Lady Douglas and her children on the orders of Edward Plantagenet while his father was at the Irvine muster for the Scots.

For almost a decade James had been waiting for this very moment, planning this strange mission even then. His last day in Douglasdale, during the Carrick raid, he had secreted away a treasure in a special place located in one of the protruding towers that was accessed through this chamber. In the stone walls was a hidden vault; he prayed it went undiscovered as he made his way toward the castle safe. Ten years ago the eleven year old page quietly slipped past the Earl of Carrick's men at arms who were plundering the castle. He had wrested a small tapestry from the thieves; a gift he helped his father select for Lady El commemorating the anniversary of their marriage. The design was of a castle on a loch in shades of green and blue with two birds in flight.

Figure LXXXIV-Part Two; medieval stone coffin remains at St. Bride's in Douglas, similar to the one that held the body of William le Hardi in the Essex priory

Stepping down the small turnpike stairs that curved unnaturally to the right he descended alone. The unique design was for the advantage of left handed warriors his father once explained. James came upon the small chamber near the mouth of a tunnel to the cellar. Carrying a tallow candle for light the lad peered around the opening, running his hand over the mortar between the stones. "That I know it must be here," he said shaking his head in frustration. "To have come this far," he sputtered indignantly, then in gleeful delight, he shouted "Sure aye!"

The squire moved the loosened, camouflaged stones that formed the hidden opening aside. He reached through the small aperture and pulled out the tapestry wrapped in an old linen cote. Stored carefully inside was a small velvet pouch that contained a gold and silver brooch that he had wrested from the booty secured by the Carrick men at arms; the Celtic brooch with six flowers, primroses that Gilley had presented his wife for their six years together the year Hugh was born. James was shaking with sheer joy, whooping, hollering loudly as he climbed up the stairs two at a time. "Now we shall enjoy great feasting," he boldly proclaimed. Two Douglas lookouts were returning from their patrol of the castle grounds and two others were sent back out in their place; James was ever vigilant for reprisals to their deeds this day. All these men from Douglasdale patrolling for English resistance were former vassals of William le Hardi and knew the Douglas stronghold very well; many having served as knaves in the household or as grooms assisting the farrier.

Figure LXXXV-Part Two; stained glass from the Douglas Castle Chapel on display in the Douglas Heritage Museum; reminiscent of their predecessor Sholto Duglas

In the great hall he sat down in the laird's chair; the very one that once belonged to his great grandfather Archibald. His men were reporting in with cloth sacks containing well earned booty; mostly English coinage, silverware and plates along with armaments, swords, quivers for arrows, stacks of arrows and armor for the twenty men of arms of the garrison. "That we will all partake of this bounty," James told them. "Sharing in the spoils the fair traditions of le Hardi, sure aye!" he chuckled, mimicking his father's sentiments. William's former vassals joined in the laughter recalling the boisterous persona of their martyred laird; his son the heir apparent to his fair and generous ways administering to his loyal Douglas adherents.

Suddenly one of his Girvan yeomen entered the great hall. "Good James, that we have a surprise for you," he boasted leading a noble horse through the great oak doors. The squire was stunned; surely de Clifford had taken his war-horse with him to his other estates he mused; but standing now in front of him was a handsome destrier. "A gift for our laird of Douglas, from the most generous and gracious garrison commander," joked the son of Dickson who had just returned from the village to inform on his father's expected recovery. They feasted and drank de Clifford's good wine; the Douglas men at arms divided the spoils and loaded the sumpter horses for the squire; beasts of burden to take his booty home with him. "Where are you to go?" asked Thomas' son. "Perhaps to Blackhouse Tower for some days," James allowed. "Would you secure this favored seat of the laird; that when I return again to this dale to claim my inheritance, this chair will be most ready for me?" he asked jovially. Thomas' son Richard Dickson named for his grandfather happily agreed to the task. "And what of Park Castle?" James inquired; wondering if any English had taken over the family stronghold where his father William and his Uncle Hugh had lived when William Long Leg, James' grandfather was laird of Douglas Castle.

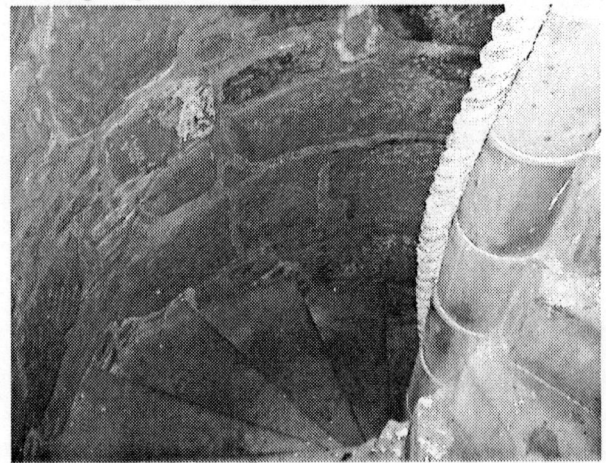

Figure LXXXVI-Part Two; turnpike stairs at Caerlaverock that were built for the advantage of left-handed warriors

Dickson explained that the great rains of some years past had all but washed away the access to the tower house. The English found it too treacherous to secure; too much trouble to rebuild the tiered embankment and only road that was used to reach Park Castle from Parkhall. "That they were so using Totheral not far from here at Needle Knowe; but only when Lord Clifford was most here in Douglasdale." he said. "What of the others of the garrison?" asked the Girvan yeoman. James said forthrightly that he would hold a baronial court and pass the doom the noo! "As before this raid we had so decided that no one of the garrison survives this day," he reminded them. With quiet resolve James rose from his seat at the table and beckoned his men to follow him to the dunjon prison where the remaining

English prisoners were being held. As James began his descent down the familiar turnpike stairs he suddenly stopped, realizing that all his sentries had returned and others had not yet gone out. "Richard that you and three other good Douglas men go now to post the lookout; that we are not surprised here in our work." The squire chided himself; under his breath he faulted the oversight. Consuming too much wine could be my folly; that Douglas Castle is not mine to so secure this day; but only for the visit, he reminded himself.

Walking towards the dunjon prison in the cellars James made an abrupt turn to wander into the older areas of the maze of connected tunnels and vaulted storage areas. He went to the hidden and once locked room his father used for his study of Alchemy and healing. The door no longer bolted he went right in and found the old wand, a Scots Ell in length, secreted away on the back of an otherwise empty shelf. This was same staff that Lord Douglas used for baronial court. "That the English understand not the value of our Celtic ways," he scoffed. With the wand he would mark out the baronial court and pass the doom on the English invaders to his homeland; it was James' intent to do things properly, in the tradition of his father le Hardi.

Figure LXXXVII-Part Two; gates at the west lodge of Douglas Castle with the Douglas Kirk looming in the background on the left

Just as the squire was leaving his father's old healing room something caught his eye; there in the darkness was a glint of something shiny under the bench table built into the wall of the structure. James bent down and found a broken piece of an old bowl his father used with a small pestle to create herb treatments. Then under the shelf lying on the floor he noticed a badly torn booklet of small parchment pages tied together in silk ribbons; the old leather bound book held the reference *viribus herbarum*; resources of herbs he translated in his mind. Reaching back further still under the old shelf he found two rolls of parchment eight inches wide with strange symbols and numbers written in the well known hand of le Hardi. "My dear father's old recordings of his alchemy," he sighed happily; this will I bring for our Hugh to study there with the Hospitallers in Stebbing he decided as he grabbed the pestle William used to make his electuaries as well.

James returned to the dunjon prison. He directed his men to stand aside as he went about the business of creating the baronial court. In the manner of the old tradition once used by the Druids to declare a place of worship, he waved the white rod of magic; designating an area with four corners where the Baronial Magistrate would hear the English pleas. With little other ceremony the lad proceeded; proclaimed the charges and then passed the doom; death by beheading for their treason and conspiracy of person; invading and debasing his family's home and lands, vassals of dear Edward, Henry de Percy and de Clifford; enemies all. If his retinue of followers had not believed his earnestness before they did so now; James was intent on punishing the infidels; permanently removing every last Englishman from his Douglasdale. "There would be no mercy this day, as there was none so shown for Sir William le Hardi Douglas, Sir Andrew de Moray, and Sir William Wallace," he proclaimed solemnly, continuing to list the names of his fallen comrades including the brothers of his king. Then he ordered the sentences carried out.

Figure LXXXVIII-Part Two; well in the courtyard of the castle of the Bishop of St. Andrews, similar to the one within the walls of Douglas Castle

James left the executions to the Douglas vassals of his father; likely their vengeful hearts would enjoy the duty; returning the favor for their martyred laird, an eye for an eye, he reflected. The squire set about deciding how to best demolish the stronghold without completely razing his family's home; giving notice to de Clifford that should he return, James would as well to complete the task. He decided to bring about the palfrey of the garrison captain that had been badly injured at the Douglas kirk; during the fray an English yeoman had run out of the chapel and tried to unsuccessfully flee on horseback. The animal was struck down with a pole axe to the chest. "Bring the wounded ambler most here," he motioned to his Girvan vassals. "That we must taint the water with the carcass of the horse; end his life and poison the well with his fair remains," he directed. Then he motioned to the others to bring from the larder salt to add to the water. "From the grains we can not use, let us bring them to the cellars; the former kitchens and stores of the old earth and timber hall," he allowed. The squire had intended to destroy all the remaining food supplies beyond what was secured for their own bounty. "A larder fit for Edward and his vassals, the deserving men with tails!" he venomously proclaimed.

Figure LXXXIX-Part Two; vaulted cellars at Dirleton Castle provide a glimpse into the past of Castle Dangerous

Returning to the dunjon prison James found the English captives dead; their heads most severed. Their blood flowed slowly in small streams through the old ruts in the earthen floor, collecting in ugly pools across the vaulted cellars; many more to die like this before I will forget of Berwick, James mused. "Bring in the grains and use your pole axe on the casks," he directed. The wine and ale streamed from the broken lids, mixed strangely with the darkened puddles of blood and gelling body fluids. Then the squire ordered his men at arms to set fire to the whole of it and strategically to other areas as well, including the wooden palisade that more than half surrounded Douglas Castle. "That my father had so wanted to replace those suspect walls with stone," he quipped. Richard Dickson was coming back from the stables. He had removed all the horses before but wanted to know if any of the farrier's tools could be of use. James suggested that he secure what ever else was valuable then set the place on fire as well; then he corrected his orders. "This message of destruction is enough for Robert Clifford on this day; should he so insist to rebuild what we have most destroyed, then we will come again to better do it! Leave the mews standing; that this laird will have his memories of his childhood waiting his return to so live here again," he said confidently.

BLACKHOUSE TOWER-Three men mounted on palfreys, leading several pack animals and one destrier, were riding late into the evening from Cappercleuch down through the glen to the Douglas Burn. As they approached the final turn toward the manor lands in Craig Douglas, James abruptly stopped. It was late enough in the day to be dark already but he could see much light coming from the tower house; this was unexpected. He decided to insure that the occupants were not English men at arms who may have stumbled upon the Douglas stronghold. His Girvan vassals hid their horses and posted lookout while the younger squire made his way unobtrusively to the tower house. He stood in the shadows and tried to hear the conversations in the great hall. Then suddenly the large oak doors from the lower level swung open and out burst some quarreling youths with a familiar banter to their swagger. "Halt there," James commanded in his most frightening and grievous tones.

Hugh and Archie stopped in their tracks and turned to find the source of the gruff and ominous voice. From the shadows a tall man in armor jumped forward; the brothers were startled at first then shrieked happily to discover their older brother was the warrior standing before them. Both Hugh now thirteen and Archie almost ten were considerably taller; their hair long and clothing very different from the last time their brother saw them at Fawdon. "That you are here!" exclaimed the squire. "This lad had never thought you might so come. Ellie was walking up behind them with her Deerhound trailing closely at her heels. "Would we miss the birthday of our hero and good son?" she asked. "Mother!" James shouted happily as he ran to embrace her in a big bear hug. "Down Lindsay," he commanded the silly hound.

The Douglases withdrew to the great hall as James summoned his men at arms to join them. "That we feared for your very life," Ellie began. "A lang year and some," she sighed. "We only came to store our goods here," her oldest son explained. He introduced the two yeomen. "From Girvan," he added jovially. "Most near the parish where I met my dear Gilley," Ellie cooed, reminiscing about her first days in Ayrshire. "Welcome, we have a larder full to share in our feasting," she allowed. "Ana," she called out directing her voice to cellars of the tower, "come see our warrior to return!"

The older woman came running up the turnpike stairs from the kitchen; she was smiling broadly, but wanted to know immediately about the injury they heard the squire had at Dahl Righ. "That I might limp some," he allowed with his characteristic big grin, "but that it heals most slowly to irk this squire. For now I have the armor to protect me from such folly." Archie wanted to know what all the booty was about. "We have come from Douglas Castle," James said in hushed tones. Archie's eyes were huge with wonder and excitement. "Did you so take back our home?" he asked hopefully. "That I did, but with few men to so secure it, our wee army here with some good men from Douglas had to take our spoils and leave. But not before we left de Clifford with a warning." James elaborated on the strategy; the attack beginning in the Douglas Kirk ending with the successful taking of the castle. "Then to so depart with our fair home yet standing but damaged for its use to the English," he told them. "Most devised as William le Hardi's plan for Sanquhar; not a member of the garrison survived to tell the tale this day," he assured them.

Then James looked at Ellie. "Dear Mother; a warrior must do of many things distasteful. That only those who have fought in combat, so close in arms to look the enemy in the eye; alas only these soldiers can so understand of what we must do in battle to survive." James said somberly. Ellie told her son that she comprehended his sad meaning. "Le Hardi, your dear father advised this lass to never question of a knight's grave deeds in warfare. Many occurrences of evil do so happen there; brutal and deadly; atrocities of unspeakable accord." she explained to the wee ones. "Our father told me that a sword was most for killing; to always remember that. A knight must know that he faces death in every turn; in each battle that he fights. At Sanquhar my sweet husband was forced to end the life of wee page; a lad most the age of our James then; a most horrific act if judged by men at peace. But one most necessary, I assure you. To spare the life of men at arms in battle they must be bold in their attack; to not think of their deadly actions; to react in rote to their situation if they are to survive." James lowered his head. "Thank you mother for you understanding of the cruelty that so transpired there and in every battle that we fight," he said somberly. "That it was as well in our Douglas Kirk where we began our siege; to break with the sanctity of that Holy place; I am most sorry. Dear God and our precious St. Bride please forgive us," he said prayerfully.

Hugh sadly shook his head; he found it difficult to comprehend of war. And he was also troubled about their family stronghold in Douglasdale. The churchman to be had few memories of Douglas Castle. "This lad so wants to see our home again," he pleaded. His older brother explained that they only sought to drive the English lord away from Douglasdale; burning down the wooden palisade and setting fire to the old earth and timber hall that was the original family stronghold, but not to raze it. "We left the tower standing; the old keep and three protruding towers are untouched for damage. We poisoned the well; meant it as a warning to the English. Should Edward's vassal take his leave of Douglasdale, then we will most return; to secure our stronghold for our use, not to so destroy it," he promised Hugh. Ellie wanted to know how everything looked; the last time they were there, several fires had been set by Brus. The courtyard was still ablaze when Lady Douglas and her children were forced to leave with the Earl of Carrick as his prisoners. "The carved oak scale-and-platt stairs are yet secured there," he assured his mother, knowing how she treasured that characteristic design that dominated the great hall of the castle.

The squire sat down at the table and began to explain more of the details of the raid. He also elaborated on his intention for recapturing their Douglas fortress in the future. "Our father often told us of the times in the Levant; the devices of the Mamlukes so successful with few men to face the large army of Crusaders, well trained and armed, but ultimately defeated by this band of renegades." He told them all about the men that joined in the fight; how Thomas Dickson had called out vassals of le Hardi to aid the squire. "To take our battle to our Douglasdale in our Celtic month of Bran; the famed warrior to help us in our deeds," he boasted.

Figure XC-Part Two; Blackhouse Tower ruins, next to the ford on the Douglas Burn

Hugh and Archie were overawed by the story that followed. James related his tale interspersed with wisdom of their ancient culture. He told them of the history of the Celtic warrior and the month of broom; the weeks surrounding the vernal equinox. "That one Plantagenet king derived his very name from that jaunty sprig, *planta genista;* this lad so knew the timing was most perfect to our quest. From the day when the sun takes charge over the moon, this Douglas squire called for the fierce god Bran and the Alder trees to show us bravery and true courage in our battle most out numbered in our plight." With every detail of the siege; the encounter in the kirk, the surrender of the castle and the pronouncing of the doom, James shared his story entwined with Celtic lore. "To give of thanks that day for our success to the ancient ones; our people freed from the unrelenting grasp of invaders and unwanted guests, our fabled lands liberated from the men with tails," he concluded; sharing with them the teachings of his father.

James rose to search through one of the wooden chests he had secured from the family's castle. He had opened the lid and found the small tapestry wrapped in the old linen. "Lady El, most I have this for your eyes to see," he told her proudly as he unrolled the lovely tapestry he and Gilley purchased for her in Edinburgh ten years before. "That I so thought this lovely wall hanging was most lost from me; stolen by those invaders to our home," she exclaimed as she rubbed her hands over the intricate woven wool of blue and green with gold, and the lovely scene of a castle on a loch with birds. Ana was surprised and asked James however he came to find it. "This squire on that fateful day so thought we would return quite soon; that I secured it in the hiding place of the dunjon tower, in the mortar safe where our father once hid our coinage," he boasted.

Then he handed Ellie the small velvet pouch that was secreted along with the tapestry. "And yet, this fair jewelry was most taken from the sacks of Carrick thieves; vassals of the earl that came to reap the booty of our home." Ellie could not hold back her emotions; tears engulfed her as she slumped back into a chair. "The Celtic brooch of primrose, six flowers to commemorate our years together then," she sighed. Lady Douglas marveled at James' uncanny knack for strange surprises; cunningness that brought her gifts from Gilley, albeit resurrected for her to have again now. She chuckled. Having assumed the brooch and tapestry were certainly lost from her forever, their arrival was truly unexpected. "Perhaps this gift a symbol of our Celtic ways; the many lives so promised us that we yet return again to live undeniable now, that our dear Elfhame has returned to me this brooch," Ellie told her sons. "James, your gifts are truly yours alone; no other could so bring a bigger joy to your mother," praised Ana. "Except for bringing our dear father home again," added the squire with a wistful grimace. Ellie excused herself for a short moment, returning to the great hall with something she had meant to present her knight to be in honor of his birthday, coming of age to his majority.

"Yes and this I have for you as well my son," she told him proudly, holding out the secreted surprise. She beamed in happiness as she presented her son with the silk brocade pouch that held the prized possession of the old Crusader: Gilley's oliphant. "Now it is this humble squire that can only say: Mother your gift is most precious; you yet surprise me with your thoughtfulness," he said as he stood up to hug her to him. Ellie looked at her oldest son and giggled, thinking of how much James resembled Gilley, her own beloved knight; how tall the lad had grown as well. "More than ever are you so like Lord Will," she sighed. "Be sure to have his luck as well that he never lost a battle when he used that fair horn to call his retinue to action. The last time that he used it was at Berwick, warding off Edward's naval contingency in the Tweed, you might so recall?" she asked him. James remembered every detail of that siege and promised her faithfully that he would always use it in every fight with Edward to that same end. James rubbed his fingers over the ornate carving of the oliphant. "It is with great pride that I will carry this dear horn of our martyred father," he said aloud.

By morning James was in the great hall breaking his fast with Lady El. Sadly he told his mother that he must take his leave with the next sunrise; to hide again in the forests was his plan. "Our king is on the run; pursued by Edward's men with hounds and Chevauchées. Till then pray tell me more of the wee clan in Essex," he said longingly. Ellie began with stories of the "evil bishop" their father's long time compatriot Robert Wishart. "That he has come to be in Porchester Castle, most near the southern coast, not far from the Cinque Ports," she explained. "Our Hubicus once hearing of that prelate's fate begged permission to go and see him," Ellie said. Just then her middle son Hugh was joining them in the great hall to break his fast. "Hugh? That you so journeyed to see the good bishop?" James asked, incredulous that his younger brother would dare such travels under the watchful eye of Edward.

The English born son of William le Hardi nodded as he yawned, undaunted by the inference of the king's power. "That this lad has so been in Edward's prisons once before; our God so watched over me most then as now," he said smiling in his innocence. James and Ellie chuckled at the lad's response, recalling the time eleven years ago when a two year old Hugh of Douglas was arrested at Stebbinge Park by the sheriff for being *the son of Sir William Duglas a rebel and a Scot*. Now he insisted upon visiting the friend of his father, Bishop Wishart who was held by Edward in his prison. Robert Wishart had been captured at Cupar Castle in 1306; but not before he had destroyed the garrison at the Comyn's castle of Kirkintilloch with the oaks he begged from Edward transformed into a mangonel; a catapult siege engine. After the bishop was secured to England, Edward ordered him remanded to the constable of Porchester Castle. He was to remain there for two more years, until a Papal Bull allowed for his temporary release to attend church functions with Bishop Lamberton in Vienna.

"This lad so traveled with one of the priests from Little Dunmow Priory; the Augustinian house most the same as the affiliation of canon's at St. Andrews," he reminded James of his time serving Bishop Lamberton there as his squire. "Our mother insured gifts of fine cloth and other goods to trade or use for his stay there; to accompany us on the journey," Hugh explained. James was truly impressed by his brother's determination;

Edward's wrath that he might find out could spell trouble for the lad he said with concern. "This mother interceded; to request a letter from the son of my kin, the canon Stephen de Segrave," Ellie interjected. "Certain to expect an appointment to the very see of that good bishop from Lord Edward; his support on our behalf was well received." Hugh continued with his exciting story; telling his brother how he rode his palfrey Sir William south through several shires, with Sir David and Patric as escorts for himself and the Essex canon. "We finally arrived at the old priory in Southwick before calling on our father's friend few miles away in Porchester." Hugh described St. Mary's Priory and the chapel in the storytelling manner of Douglas tradition. He shared details of the Augustinian house and how it had moved from the castle to its new location further north.

"That we first called at that wee kirk, to seek the blessings of our God to so continue on our quest to meet with the good bishop," he said excitedly. "There in the confines of that sacred place next to the cloisters is a terraced vineyard and cultivation for many small crops growing much like the very vineyard of Little Dunmow Priory," Hugh explained, drawing the picture of the landscape with pure enjoyment for the moment. "Finally the time so came to ride over to the castle; to call upon the constable to seek entrance to the tower that held our father's friend." He described the ancient Roman fort of Portus Adurni; the high walls towering twenty feet about the sea that surrounded the four story tower of the English castle. "One of the protruding towers of the curtain wall held the prison of Bishop Wishart." James was laughing to recall the old friend of le Hardi, the patriot who held the secret meetings at his castle in Carstairs. "That old bishop is one brave warrior to defend our Scotland most like a knight of renown," he told them, "preaching war against Edward most like the kirk does speak of the Crusades." James chuckled to recall the circumstances of Robert Wishart's capture at Cupar: in full armor rather than the robes of prelate.

Ellie elaborated on their ruse: Hugh was dressed in the hood and black tunic of an Augustinian friar rather than a secular priest, with the Austin canon in his normal attire, similar in appearance though made of softer cloth; only the tabard of de Ferrers worn by Sir David indicated an Essex home of these churchmen. She giggled as she described the ruse of Hugh and the canon from Little Dunmow. "We entered the chamber of prelate's confinement most quietly; Robert Wishart greeted us cordially as he vallet announced us as Augustinians from Little Dunmow Priory. The poor lighting of one wee tallow candle made it difficult to see," explained the aspiring canon. "As soon as the constable's men withdrew that this lad lowered his hood and announced: that I am Hubicus, son of William le Hardi," Hugh boasted proudly.

Archie was making his entrance into the great hall and interrupted them. "Ah, the brave exploits of one named Hugh," he said; sincerely praising his brother's good plan to lift the spirits of their father's friend. James told them all how pleased he was with their successful venture and begged to learn more about Wishart; his disposition and condition so he might report the news to 'my lord the king'. "That bishop holds a special place in Lord Robert's heart having granted our king special dispensation for his grave deeds in Greyfriar's kirk," James informed his family. "Our father would be most proud of you as well good Hugh," he added emphatically. The 'churchman' as Archie called his brother continued his story. "That we so discussed his plight," he said thoughtfully. "Our brave bishop would never think to desert our Scotland, to cry 'Saor Alba' more than once, and loudly; most defiant is this prelate," he exclaimed. "Good that the English do not understand our Gaelic," Archie said jokingly, knowing that Bishop Wishart was saying 'Free Scotland'.

Figure XCI-Part Two; Bishop Robert Wishart did not return to his See and Glasgow Cathedral shown above, for eight years after his capture at Cupar Castle in 1306

"His words for Edward mirror yours good James; then he begged for news of King Robert, 'math rìgh' as he so said, continuing to speak the words of our good cousins in the north to confuse the others with us, those he did not know," Hugh told them, pleased that he comprehended the Highland Gaelic to participate in the secret communication with the Bishop. "When this humble lad so told him of the tragic ends of brave followers of the king, we wept together and then said prayers for their souls, holding service with the bishop's Scottish chaplain." Robert Wishart and his three attendants from Glasgow had not known about the others Hugh explained; "whose heads adorn the bridge with Wallace." James shuddered at the words knowing his fate could be the same; as it might have been that day at Dahl Righ. His brother said that he told the bishop about James' injury. "And that soon our Archie will rejoin him there to continue the fight of our dear father."

Bishop Wishart inquired of Hugh's plans as well, Ellie told James. "That he so offered to write letters on his behalf; to encourage him to continue with his studies with the Augustinians." The English born son of le Hardi then revealed the rest of his good news: the Austin canon with permission of the prior Richard of Dunmow offered to teach him, take him further in the studies of the church. "That someday will I return to Scotland, bred for God's good work; a secular canon most to be perhaps to hold a prebend of the Glasgow see. There is one of that see at Roxburgh Kirk so this lad was told; that I could so reside most between our Fawdon and Blackhouse Tower with this endowment," he suggested. Ellie was taken aback; this was the first time she heard of the full extent of his plans. "A mother is the last to know such things," she chided him lightly. "Such strategy seems promising; how did you come to know of this?" Ellie inquired. Hugh allowed that Wishart promised him support to that very end. "The bishop himself spoke of that prebendary; should I pursue my studies as so planned that kirk would so be held by Hugh of Douglas," he proudly told them, hoping his mother would understand his bold intentions.

"A secular canon of the see of Glasgow?" exclaimed Ellie. "Oh my Hubicus, an honor to that end and a way for you to earn a stipend for yourself while doing the work of God you so yearn to do." Archie was through with talking about plans of church life, he wanted to learn more about the battles in Scotland; especially the one near Glen Orchy. "Tell us more of fighting the English," he suggested. "And what happened so in Methven with that rout; how did you escape Dahl Righ most wounded?" James shook his head, responding to the straightforward questions of the wee Archie with a smirk. "This squire will always post of sentinels to watch for de mischef from these English soldiers who boast no need for chivalry," he said, and then looking at Sir David who had joined them, "present Essex knight excepted," he chuckled. "Our king untried in such circumstances of great battles did not set a watch to prevent English treachery. Not believing de Valence would break his word to chance an engagement of sword the night before the battle so agreed upon, we were left defenseless," he scoffed.

James provided many details of the English slaughter of the Scots near Perth. "So many lives to save had we but thought of it; to post the ones to watch, insuring safety as our father would have done," he sighed, sorry he had not thought to be more cautious as well. Then James began telling them of his encounter at Dahl Righ. He described the battle and how he was injured. "The gash was deep but not so bad to unhorse this squire," he said distractedly. "But after withdrawing to tend to my injury, standing near the burn, I was attacked. Winning the battle most again, but finding my strength most damaged in the fight, I staggered back, falling to ground, trying to drag myself to safety. But for my weakness from the grave wound and so many encounters for one yet inexperienced as a warrior, this lad fell into unconsciousness," he told them quietly.

Archie, Hugh, Ana and Ellie were wide eyed and stunned; their hero had fallen in battle and could have been killed! James looked directly at everyone, shaking his head in bewilderment. "The strangest of events to occur most next," he explained. He told them of the bright white light, the apparition that came to save him. "The tallest of warriors, an old knight with a scar running down the right side of his face," he said looking directly at Ellie. She gasped, knowing what he meant; his father had come to rescue him. "This lad recalls most clearly, to be pulled to safety by that strange knight. When I came to consciousness again it was my lord the king so leaning over this squire," he quipped. "I asked Lord Robert if he was dead, his words were decidedly most no!" he chuckled recalling the strange happenings that day.

Ellie's eyes were tearing but she was smiling, "Your dear father most with his son to spare his life that day," she assured them. James agreed. "Never have I been so sure that it was le Hardi till this day, but there is no other explanation," he said still bewildered by the strange rescue. Archie agreed. "Of course it was our father; he would find a way to do it." Hugh's face was aglow in wonderment; the fair work of our hero and Celtic warrior he mused. "That this lass must share her sad news for you as well, about the retinue at Perth," she sighed sadly. "Mother, that I know of the presence of Sir William Bagot, that knight banneret in Methven," James told her, hoping to ease her guilt some. "Never to have dreamed that knight would be called to muster from his service in Wales," she moaned. "Had more harm come to you, this mother could never have forgiven such a marriage, even for convenience of being free of Edward."

The squire watched the widow begin to twist his father's signet ring in earnest; realizing there was great need to change the subject of their discussion and the noo! He rose to fetch some other items he secured from Douglas Castle during the raid two days ago. "Dear Hugh, for your bravery and service to our Scotland," he began with a mischievous grin. "This laird of Douglas most to be is here to so present my brother his due inheritance: the legacy of Sir William le Hardi's experiments and learning of healing." James carefully unwrapped the pestle and the damaged scrolls of his father's work in Alchemy with the tattered leather journal on herbs. "This lad so heard that you were to study with the Hospitallers at their priory farm in

Stebbing, to become a healer in the image of our dear and much missed father," he proclaimed with ceremony and bravado.

Hugh took the pestle and the writings, carefully holding and examining them all; the look he returned to James, to Ellie then to Archie was pure amazement of the good fortune to have found these treasures. "Oh James, a precious gift to have located that old journal and those parchment rolls," the mother exclaimed. "And the pestle too," said Ana remembering the first time Gilley made a special tasine for her lass when she was with child. "And for you, dear wee Archibald," the squire said with a teasing smirk, "this wand of magic, a Scots Ell in length, in the tradition of our ancestors; the scepter to mark the laird's baronial court. You my squire most to be are thus entrusted with this sacred instrument," James said as he presented his father's white wand to the youngest son for safe keeping.

Figure XCII-Part Two; Girvan shoreline looking towards Alyssa Craig; in 1260 James' grandfather William 5th Lord Douglas sat on a jury of peers, all landowners, freeholders in the parish of Girvan to settle an assize

James told Ellie he had some more news of his trying adventures before his raid in Douglasdale. "One chance happening in Ayrshire; this lad so overheard of a shipment going to Arran and the castle of the laird," he said sheepishly. "That these are the most difficult of times," he said to brace her for the story to follow; capturing the supply ships of her kin. "Many times will this lad and the others of your sons here that join with good Robert, King of Scots," James allowed quietly, "find ourselves to take up arms against your own cousins, once the benefactors of our dear father. One Johannis de Hastings, the Lord of Abergavenny, now the laird of that fine Isle of Arran; his castle on Brodick Bay. This fortress was the very one we so attacked reaping much booty for Scotland's wee treasury."

Ellie was both stunned and ashamed; she was feeling responsible for every English knight that came to her beloved Scotland; how could she mask her own allegiances when she returned to Essex she wondered? "This lass is most despondent; my own kin doing Edward's bidding in our kingdome. What am I most to do?" she moaned. "Take heed dear mother, you must guard your own identity I fear," advised James. "And protect these lads my brothers most as well; to send them both to my care when it is safe to do so," James advised. Hugh and Archie exchanged guarded but excited looks; both lads wanted to be part of Scotland's fight for National Independence, serving in their own way. Ellie realized that being a Douglas was becoming a liability in England. She would have to be Lady Bagot or de Ferrers in her business dealings, never to use the name of her beloved William, a traitor and rebel to Edward. And more sadly still, her sons were being forced from her side for their Scottish heritage; fearful of reprisals should they remain in England.

The sun rose early; the brisk cold morning of early spring beckoned them to an early start. James and his two men from Girvan were returning to western shires, to lurk about the hills of Ayrshire in support of Lord Robert this day. Ellie promised to return to Fawdon in the fall, but she was not so sure of making it all the way to Blackhouse. "Coming through the Forest may not be possible for us; but this lass will try to travel through the Ettrick," she promised. Archie was sorry to see his brother go; he wanted to join the squire to fight the English in Douglasdale. "Soon enough will you so be at my side," James allowed. "For now you must insure the safety of our mother to return to Essex," he chuckled. Ana came from the kitchen with some special treats; some wrapped neatly in linen, others stored in old, wee crocs, packed together for their journey.

"This squire will most need another set of armor if this feasting so continues," he boasted. Ellie assured him teasingly that he had some ways to go before he could properly fill out the mail hauberk of le Hardi. "This lad has been keeping our father's good armor most clean of rust, ready for our warrior to fill it," boasted Archie. Hugh interrupted, "And his sword as well, that I have been assigned the task to prepare for your good use of it. I say prayers to dear St.Bride when most I clean it," he smiled. James was heartened by the support of his family; his stay at Blackhouse reinvigorated him he mused. "Thank you all; this squire is ready once again to do grave injury to Edward," he proclaimed as he mounted his palfrey and headed west towards Ayrshire. "That you find this squire several more Hobini for that destrier," he told them having left the horse in the stables of the manor at Sir David's direction. The English knight knew he could easily exchange such a fine charger for several lighter horse when they returned to Northumbria.

AYRSHIRE MAY 1307-James and his growing retinue of adherents had returned to the roam the hills in the western shire. He led his men to his family's strongholds, spending time at each of the several Douglas manors in Ayrshire, though he stayed north of Girvan and only once stopped at Ellie's manor near Maybole. James was generally found making his way from Auchinleck to Trabboch and up north to Stewartoun; but never taking the same path or sequence twice to their travels as they rode the cart paths and old Roman roads. The Ayrshire sheriff was his mother's kin and father's manucaptor, Lord Johannis de Hastings, James' unknowing benefactor on Arran; liberating that lord's supplies at Brodick Castle for Scotland's benefit. The squire was determined not to meet up again with de Hastings; avoiding his constable Sir Robert Leybourn as well, the lieutenant in charge of the English prison at Ayr castle.

The rains had begun to fall; driving hard as the day progressed. The squire was riding alone on a short reconnaissance; he had needed time to sort things out he mused, keeping a fresh perspective on the lands he knew so well to clear his head. But with the flash flooding of the wee burns, the full force of the winds rushing upon the moors, James thought better to find some shelter than to continue fighting the elements in his return to Auchinleck. He stopped at a messuage in Logan; no one seemed about as he ducked quietly into the stables with his Hobini. The building was strangely quiet; not a single horse or other farm animal resided there. Could this manor be abandoned he wondered aloud? Then he heard a stirring; his heart started to beat quickly, fearing what he might find lurking in the shadows of the shelter. Perhaps this messuage was now held by English vassals he conjectured; hoping and praying that he had not just walked into an ambuscade.

The rustling of dried grasses and rushes laid upon the flooring spooked the squire once again. This time he was sure the noise was coming from a nearby stall. "Who is most there," he commanded to know. A small child of barely five or six he suspected came forward; eyes widened in fright, the child began to cry. James returned his sword to the leather sheath on his sword belt and went to comfort the wee laddie. Kneeling down to look the child directly at his eye level, the squire wiped the tears from the dirt covered face of the frightened boy. "Where is your mother wee one?" asked James with quiet concern. The laddie said his mother was out trying to find some food. "Please do not so tell her that you have found me hiding here," he begged, explaining to James that his mother was alone now; his father was with God. "Why are you most here and not in the manor house?" James asked. The laddie said that his mother decided he would be safer hidden from the English, waiting in the stables until she returned. "Too cold and wet this day that I must not go with her," he stammered, beginning to cry again. "What name do you have?" James inquired. "Walter of Logan," he proclaimed proudly.

Just then the barn door swung ajar and a small, slender man nearly a foot shorter than James and wearing light armor entered leading an old palfrey into the shelter. The man at arms was soaked through from the downpour that had not let up since James took refuge in the stables. In the darkness this odd soldier stood frozen realizing he was not alone; when suddenly young Walter shouted out loud. "Mother, come see," he exclaimed, "that this lad has found a new friend." James moved out of the shadows to introduce himself to the soldier who he realized now was most the widow of her late warrior. He understood at once that she felt frightened being alone; scared enough that she disguised herself as a man when she rode about the countryside. "Good lass, a fine son here you do have. That I am James of Douglas, my father once held of several manors near this messuage," he explained. "And are you kin of the Logans who most lived here some time now gone?" he asked her. She shook her head yes, but cautiously as she stroked the long blonde hair of her young son. "What is it that you want here then?" she inquired, still wary though comforted by his Lallans words and a distinctive Scottish accent; she hoped he might be a patriot. "Only shelter from the torrential rains that yet fall upon these moorish lands of our blessed Scotland," he allowed, brandishing the slight lisp that seemed to endear him to her.

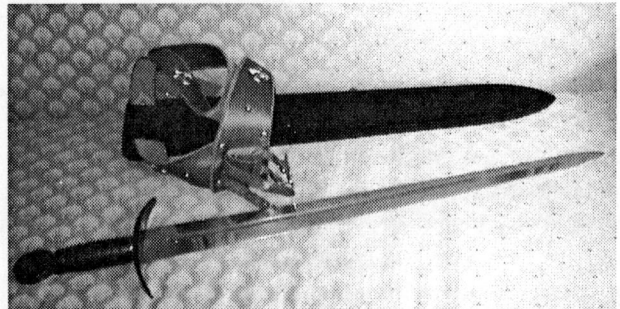

Figure XCIII-Part Two; reenactment-quality replica sword of the late 13th century; an old standard and a leather left handed sword belt with sheath

"My father was William le Hardi; pledging most his fealty to Lord Edward some eleven years ago at Holyrood Abbey with another knight, one from this very shire, most like your son he too was known as Walter Logan." The woman explained that Walter was her late husband's kin and God father to the laddie. "My son's father was sadly killed some six years and more ago at Caerlaverock," she said. James offered his sincere condolences as she invited him to the manor house to share in the small bounty of food she had in the larder.

The three of them ran quickly from the stables and took refuge in the great hall of the messuage, nearly soaked to the skin from their short encounter with the rains and heavy winds that still swirled the courtyard of the manor. They were greeted by an affable, older woman in the kitchen of the small earth and timber fortified house. James quickly noticed that the only fire was in the nearby kitchen; the stores were meager, without any game or other meat in the larder. He offered to help replenish her food supplies in the daylight when the storm should take leave of the region; doing some hunting with his bow. The lady turned away, tears were flooding her eyes. She wanted to trust the squire but the bitter years since her husband was taken from her, falling in that battle there, had brought many soldiers to her home. These English and Scottish men at arms passing through the shire all promised her assistance while disguising their motives that she dared not believe what James said now. Her son noticed her tears and went to comfort her. "Do not cry mother," he coaxed her. "This lad will not allow another to so harm you."

James was profoundly moved by the scene; a woman alone raising her son in the wilds of Ayrshire, the battle ground between the English invaders and the remaining Scottish adherents, trying to provide for her son and household. He understood at once that she would be easy prey to some fast talking soldier with temporary comfort on his mind. "What courage you must have lass," he said quietly. "But that this humble squire does yet not know your name." He looked into her eyes and then gave her a mischievous Douglas smirk. She smiled back realizing that she had not properly introduced herself. "That I am Lady Joanna Logan," she replied, then chuckled as she realized her deplorable appearance. Joanna was wearing a leather hauberk soaked through to her gambeson and her beautiful blonde tresses were packed tightly to her head under a coif of mail. "Permit this lass to so attend to her needs," she said as she took her leave of her guest and son.

Young Walter and his new friend were making themselves useful in the kitchen. James fetched water from the well and brought up some stores from the cellars. Elizabeth introduced herself and told the squire that she was only one of three remaining servants that stayed on with Lady Logan. "With the lands of this once fine manor burned and laid to waste, no coinage for our household to so live on that our lady has only her good word to so repay the others for their meager stores for our larder," the cook and household worker confided sadly to James.

Their kitchen work was interrupted by the arrival of a beautiful woman in their midst; the small soldier James encountered in the stables had transformed to a willowy vision of Celtic beauty. "Mother," exclaimed the laddie, "that you have not so worn that lovely surcote since the winter last," he gasped. James chuckled at young Walter's honest admission. "Does the squire have the honor of your company to sit in feasting?" he inquired graciously. Joanna smiled as her entire countenance seemed to beam in glowing colors of enchantment. James realized he was overwhelmed with her beauty and had to catch himself; there was little time for romance with the war at hand and a king to defend.

That night James slept in the great hall and in the prime as the sun rose he made good on his promise and brought fresh game for the larder. "Dear James," said Joanna, "what comfort that you bring to us in these times of great sorrow." Elizabeth was thrilled with the prospect of cooking up the spoils of the hunt and Walter was beside himself with glee. "A belly full will this lad so have," he exclaimed. "That when this squire is able will I come to see you most again; if I might be granted such privilege," James said shyly as he turned to Joanna. He told her that he must return to the Douglas manor lands in Auchinleck; that he would be making his way between his father's former strongholds, keeping abreast of the English activity in the shire. "And in two days hence will I send of stores from Auchinleck to fill your larder until the next time that this lad will be most able to come in person," he assured her. Lady Joanna thanked him for his generosity. "A Douglas tender and true," she said, a warm smile crossing her face. Then as he turned to take his leave he retuned to her side and gently took her hand in his. "Never fear that anyone will hurt you again Joanna; you know my whereabouts and have only to call for one James of Douglas that I will be most here," he promised; then he rode off.

Upon returning to Auchinleck, the squire sent some of his retinue to take provisions to the widow as he promised. But there was little time for him to reflect on the encounter with Lady Logan, to daydream of what might become of their friendship for once again James was on the move. A rebel on the run he was constantly gathering intelligence of the English presence and any changes in defenses that might be found; the same successful plan he employed the months before, that kept him safe from Edward's grasp. Traversing the shire he avoided the de Hastings garrison and kept them from discovering his whereabouts. James' plan also offered him opportunity to reacquaint himself with more of the countryside of his ancestors. Staying only two nights in any location, James and his men at arms rode by day through Ayrshire, coming upon other Douglas tenants and former vassals of le Hardi; finding many more eager to join up with him. The legacy of the Douglas Larder, the sarcastic reference given to his first and successful raid on Douglas Castle, drew courage for Scots to defy Edward and join him in rebellion.

James gained members to his following wherever he went. He felt bolstered by the many loyal adherents of his father now offering their allegiance to him. The Douglas squire was also gaining self confidence; increasing his knowledge of the landscape; remembering the sheltering glens and wee burns that wound their way through the lands of Kyle Stewart and the wee Douglas manors there. He recalled the words of his father: 'know well the lands of our Celtic ancestors; come to trust your instincts learned from the ancient ones; they will so protect you in your hour of need.' William had always said that the braes and corries of their moorish lands and those of the good forests, 'all will hide you from the aliens should they come to steal our way of life; to warn you most of invaders to our kingdome. You will never be more safe then in the wilds of our Scotland.'

The squire's trained eye continually perused the fells and inspected the dense foliage of the pheasant woods for the telltale signs of English. During such wanderings he spotted some men at arms heading to reinforce the English garrison at Cumnock. Word in the village of Auchinleck told of many soldiers recently arriving there; to forebode a trap being set to capture Lord Robert, James was told. He returned to his manor and rounded up his followers. They rode quickly to rendezvous at the king's camp. James warned him of the foul rumors with descriptions of the army and their leaders sent for the ambuscade. Robert reacted swiftly; taking the advantage of surprise, he called his men at arms to muster and attacked the English camp.

The battle that followed at Cumnock was the reverse of Methven. The very nonchalance and unprepared attitude of the English force, perceiving their superior number and strong position became easy prey for King Robert and his growing number of supporters. James and his Douglas retinue added to the king's armed horse, armed foot and bowman; the element of surprise made their crushing defeat of the English a sweet success. Few men were lost by the Scots while many English men at arms gave of their lives that day at Cumnock. With this huge victory at hand King Robert made himself master of Kyle and Cunningham; commanding the good citizens to pledge their fealty to the King of Scots. But even after killing so many of the garrison and other English in the area, the Scots were yet unable to take Cumnock Castle and left it in tact; taking to the hills to reorganize their forces having word of reinforcements being sent to Kyle.

De Valence reacted quickly to the debacle at Cumnock; he ordered one thousand men under the command of Sir John de Mowbray at Bothwell to move into the region. Excited word of King Robert's successful campaign in Ayrshire resounded; brave tales of cunningness, slipping out of the grasp of the Earl of Pembroke's hot pursuit; pulling off victories in the face of overwhelming odds, pervaded the shire. Each day the king gained more supporters for his cause, stalwart men happier to die in service to a Scottish king than to face inevitable capture and grisly death at the hands of the English; the dragon still raised by Edward. Many knights hiding in the hills found their way to Robert's camp; one well known to James, Alexander de Lindsay rejoined the fight for Scotland's freedom.

With the influx of adherents came new intelligence; the gathering at Bothwell of the forces ordered by Pembroke was made known to them. James quickly reacted with a plan. "That the only manner to so approach the Kyle road is by way of Edirford," he explained. "There is but one track in and only the other side out, narrowing in the ascend; the confusion to armed horse for the marshes and bogs, running either side of the narrow gorge, a wee corrie flanked by areas where no horse could go; to confine them for our attack." He went through every detail; told his king how he planned to pick off the English armed horse both at the mouth of the stone ford and at the end of the pass from their position east of Caprickhill; cluttering the retreat of de Mowbray's retinue with the bodies of their fallen comrades and the carcasses of destriers. Robert was impressed with the strategy laid out by the squire; he readily embraced the tactics dispatching James and sixty horse, mostly his own Douglas adherents with him to an area north near Milton.

Figure XCIV-Part Two; bog lands and probable site of an old whirlpool; now silted up it was once part of the Irvine River near Hurlford; bog green on one side, marsh lands on the other a perfect place for an ambuscade near the adjacent ford

The Douglas squire and his men rode towards the ford, taking their defensive positions to lay quietly above the pass; while the English unknowingly cooperated fully for the ambuscade. De Mowbray rode his charger in full view out in front of his retinue; leading nearly seven hundred followers in all, but not the full thousand de Valence had requested. Into the corrie these English soldiers marched undaunted and unprepared for any mischief, just as James anticipated. The Douglas squire cautioned his men to wait his orders; he would allow de Mowbray to cross the ford and begin the assent. As he watched the English move into his ambuscade he breathed deeply to remain calm, watching ever closely for the procession; for the intensity of the moment he felt that everyone could hear the quickened beats and heavy thumping from his heart; it seemed so loud to him.

Suddenly James blew into his father's horn; the old Crusader's oliphant bellowed in response with ghastly sounds shrieking a warning to the English should they heed it. Then he gave the fierce and frightening war cry: 'A Douglas, A Douglas!' as he led the charge of armed horse towards de Mowbray's retinue. The English were ill equipped for a counter attack; great peril to their numbers resulted as many tried to flee through marshlands that swallowed up their horses. The English lieutenant watched in horror as his proud forces were pummeled. Helpless and confined, the unsuspecting retinue from the Bothwell muster was being destroyed before his eyes. The Scots held with archers, Douglas vassals of Ettrick Forest from Craig Douglas and Traquair, firing down from both sides of the ravine, and at both ends, stopping any escape perfectly as planned.

Figure XCV-Part Two; site of the old ford on Irvine River near Hurlford and the narrow pass lined on either side with bog and marsh lands

The Scots bottled up de Mowbray's retinue in the pass. The war-horses making their way across the ford scattered to the shallow of the stream in a widening area that gave way to James' open attack as he rode his Hobini into the Irvine Water. Charging into the array of fleeing English he carried his sword high in the ready, signaling once again, blowing the terrifying call to arms from the old Crusader's horn James led his men to do battle with the English knights and squires. Edward's proud army was stumbling and off balance from the hot pursuit of vengeful Scots. The clip clop of horses' hooves in and out of the waters reverberated in the background of war cries and the ominous din of metal hitting metal in the fray. James encountered his first knight; a smallish man riding a large destrier; the two exchanged cuts and thrusts that were parried by the other. Yet James noted that the

Englishman appeared seasoned on campaign but was finding it difficult to maneuver his great charger over the rocky bed of the stream; it was slippery for the large animal and the rider seemed uncomfortable the squire noted by his grimace. James turned his little Hobini, reared the animal up making a half turn then another evasive change of course to the right that he found his sword moving in a successful strike, cutting the flesh of the opponent's forearm, thrusting into the abdomen of de Mowbray's stricken adherent.

The English knights and others of their men at arms were no match for James of Douglas; the angry warrior leading his ragtag band of swad defending their homeland. In the confusion of the confining battle, with no place to turn and flee quickly, the Bothwell retinue was forced to battle through the Scots or turn back towards Lanarkshire to fight another day. The Douglas warriors were able to move in and pick off their foes almost with ease. The ravine was filled with the clashing sounds of swords and battle axes, clanking metal followed by the deafening thumps, dull thuds of parried thrusts and cuts hitting leather covered shields; the controlled pandemonium interrupted only by the shrill cries of overpowered English taking mortal wounds. De Mowbray fought his way through the throng of rebels, hoping his men would show courage and follow his lead but few English soldiers did. In the foray, one of the men from Girvan attempted to pull de Mowbray from his horse; his sword belt broke in the struggle, taking with it his sword, not yet drawn in battle. De Mowbray made his beleaguered escape; he never looked back and only stopped when reaching the safely of the English stronghold in Ayr where de Valence was planning a muster. What a sight for the garrison to see, this English knight and lord undressed, his sword and leather belt most left at Edirford. The Scots had another rout to their credit this day.

James and his men counted their number; few were injured seriously, fewer still were lost from the battle forever. The same could not be said of the English; their dead and dying filled the ravine, with body parts lying in scattered fashion; their blood streaming into pools that began to fill the marshes with the darkened hue of death. There was much booty to claim from their fallen foes, mused James. He did his body count; still not the number equal to those lost at Berwick he said coldly under his breath. "At least the spoils are worth their weight," he chuckled out loud. One of the yeomen from Girvan smiled proudly, holding up the trophy of de Mowbray's sword belt and old standard still sheathed within it. "There is much in prize to be had today!" he boasted. Horses, saddles and armor were a luxury to Scottish rebels; for their years of resistance with little prosperity in their homeland, these brave warriors fought with tools of farmers augmented by well used swords, battered shields and leather armor of cuir bouilli. Now they would have battle axes, mail hauberks, fine bassinets with noble palfreys and destriers to ride; a great way to celebrate a victory adding armaments, horses and coinage to their war chests. James as always now allowed his men to split the bounty of the fight; taking little more than his share, while saving some for Scotland's treasury.

LOUDON HILL 10TH MAY 1307-James' unrelenting prowling of the countryside had brought more victories to the Scots. Though only wee skirmishes, these successes were insidious, reeking havoc with the morale of the English soldiers from captain down to the lowly foot, the proud army of Edward was slumping from the harassment of the doughty Scots. James had stumbled upon an unguarded English camp one early evening. Another rout ensued but when de Valence led his men to charge the Scots in retaliation for their deed, they had vanished, ghost like into the mist of Scotland's moorish lands. These were the braes and pheasant woods James knew as a child; traveling with le Hardi through Ayrshire into Douglasdale, Auchinleck to Logan, Muirkirk to Glenbuck and Carmacoup. He knew every ford and gill and his men respected him, trusted his knowledge; put their complete faith in the twenty-one year old son of William le Hardi.

Figure XCVI-Part Two; Loudon Hill, Ayrshire

De Valence had received another one of Edward Plantagenet's scathing letters; the snide chastising of the evil minded king had brought him to a decision: he must challenge the King of Scots to do battle. A date was set; on the 10th of May in 1307 Robert Brus would lead his men to meet Edward's lieutenant and his retinue at Loudon Hill near Darvel. Brus like James learned from mistakes; he arrived some time before that date and began to study the site, the terrain where they would do battle; making plans to elevate the Scots' advantage. Though Robert held of 600 good men this day, he knew that de Valance would have many more men at arms, a good lot of them heavy cavalry. The king and his squire walked the road under the slope of the hill; testing the firm ground and looking out over the expansive battle site. They both agreed that they had to narrow the field; force the English to a smaller line; the strategy of the Flemings at Courtrai. If they dug ditches to confine the attack, they could face the Earl of Pembroke's army straight on and not get outflanked, Robert allowed. James understood at once what they must do. The squire offered to organize the digging of three rows of deep ditches either side, treacherous enough to halt any advance of armed horse; using the morasses on one side as a boundary much as he did at Edirford.

By the late evening of the 9th, the light of day still on them, the Scots had finished their trenches; their toil of digging gave them a good night's sleep, ready to do battle the next morning. De Valance did not disappoint the Scots; he arrived with 3000 men at arms, their approach from Ayr readily identified from Brus' vantage point on Loudon Hill. The front held for the Scots in the beginning using the terrifying force of schiltrons; spears like the quills of giant porcupines confronted the destriers of the English knights. High in the hills where the wee folk, camp followers and cooks not trained in battle, stayed for safety a message was delivered to Lord Robert: more English were arriving; perhaps to be reinforcements from another garrison. Brus was unsure if these armed horse were additional relief; perhaps these English were creating a deception to their number he conjectured to confuse the Scots with the size of their forces. He prayed so.

The king called James and Alexander de Lindsay, the veteran of many escapades with Wallace in the shire; seeking their advice. The Douglas squire offered to go behind the lines and seek the truth of the resurgence. "Many of our kin are in the retinue of de Valence," scoffed de Lindsay. "Perhaps our James of Lothiane can pry the words we long to hear from the mouths of these misguided Scots," suggested Robert, a glint of mischief in his eyes. James mounted his Hobini and grabbed a surcote and plain tunic from one of his men. Before the king could change his mind, he was off; promising to return with words Lord Robert longed to hear. Alex and Brus were chuckling as he rode quickly taking care to go around the battle lines and into the cover of the forest.

Encamped behind the lines were retinues of English knights and knights banneret, many pennons and banners James recognized, even some from the tournament at Newmarket seven years ago. But it was the curious sight of the de Cathe armorial bearings that caught his eye. His father's sister, Willelma de Galbrathe from Dalserf had four daughters; Johanna the eldest had married Bernard de Cathe, bearing him a son and namesake before her death six years ago. Could his kin be in this English retinue? As he maneuvered around the fringe of the enemy camp he happened upon his cousin Bernard with some others of de Clifford's men. The soldiers were waiting word to join the battle in the wave of replacements. James circumspectly beckoned de Cathe to a course of honor. Bernard de Cathe was startled to find James of Douglas in his presence but would not give the lad away. In the strangeness of these wars, there were many unlikely foes: friends, neighbors or cousins, separated only by their forced allegiance to Edward, fearful of his reprisals to seize their lands and income. But James did not hold of Douglasdale; he had no lands known to Edward to be seized from him; his allegiance to Robert was free to give. Bernard was careful to speak with James in private; shared with him condolences for the passing of le Hardi and Willelma. He also listened to the words of his cousin; Robert was failing and he wanted to come to the king's peace.

De Cathe was eager to hear more, so James allowed as he would be favorable to meet with some terms; then his cousin began to share the words he hoped to hear. "Our forces are most moving quickly, to give rise to hopes of reinforcements where there are none," he quipped. "Come meet me here this evening if the battle yet lingers; I will speak with others of greater rank in service to de Valence; offering your pledge and see what comes to that end for you," he proposed to his cousin.

Figure XCVII-Part Two; Loudon Hill; a volcanic formation almost ninety feet high; an excellent defensive location

James thanked him for his offer, promised to meet with Bernard on the morrow and then vanished into the hills; deep into the land of the Celts that protected the squire, escorting him back safely to the side of his true king, Robert Brus, King of Scots. De Lindsay was the first to spot his nephew returning on his Hobini. Robert was saddled on his war-horse, riding his destrier, nervously surveying the front lines; dispatching some reinforcements to the schiltrons on the left flank. "My lord the king," James proclaimed with a broad grin, "that I have come with news of great cheer.

Those are not reinforcements, but deceptive movement of the armed foot to bolster morale most as you surmised; a strategy to trick us that we are fearful of more men at arms to come where there are none!" he boasted.

The King of Scots was elated with the intelligence James gathered but not surprised. De Lindsay wanted to know how he discovered the ploy. "My own kin Bernard de Cathe in that camp most near de Clifford's men," he explained. "The good and faithful James of Lothiane told him in quiet earnest that he begged to come to the king's peace," he chuckled at the ruse. Sir Alex chided him. "The son of le Hardi to surrender to the pagan despot; how could such a lie be taken for the truth?" he begged to know with a bemused countenance. Robert asked if Bernard was kin to the knight James met at Linlithgow Palace, just before the battle of Methven. "Aye, the same," he scoffed. But quickly his bravado returned. "The good and just James of Lothiane," he teased them, "came to join the English; to sooner pledge his fealty; to be promised lands reseised so in return."

Figure XCVIII-Part Two; Dalserf mains near the kirk of the old manor once held by Willelma Douglas de Galbrathe, then by her daughter's heir Bernard de Cathe

Robert Brus drew a big grin. "That this king has no lands to offer any vassal; why did you not so seek that proffer?" he taunted the squire good naturedly. James' expression grew solemn; his face contorted into a menacing grimace. "That any agreement with dear Edward would be breached; this lad could never trust one king who broke the truce at Berwick with Lord Douglas," he told them icily. There was a long pause of silence before Sir Alex broke the tension and jovially replied. "Aye, look there; we are winning now the field! Good that you turned down that fair exchange of wealth for the life of the rebel." Robert and James looked over towards the front lines; the tide had clearly turned against the Earl of Pembroke's forces. And with the knowledge that de Valence had no further reinforcements, Robert changed his strategy quickly to bring the battle to fast victory for the Scots.

DOUGLASDALE MID JUNE-Before reporting to de Valence and the muster called for Loudon Hill, Robert de Clifford had taken leave in late April to return to his barony in Lanarkshire. Finding the foul rumors of the castle raid from Palm Sunday true he set about plans for rebuilding the stronghold and establishing another garrison under the command of someone he trusted. He requested and was granted £100 from King Edward's treasury for the restoration of the damage done by one James of Douglas. The English king also allowed him the use of twenty-one royal masons. The payments for these stone craftsmen ceased abruptly however after only nine days, on 7th July 1307; their job not nearly done. A tragedy for England took place at Burgh on Sands that day; precluding any further assistance in rebuilding Douglas Castle. De Clifford was undaunted; perhaps the efforts to remove him from Douglasdale were finished as well he speculated. Fool heartedly the English lord believed the raids would not continue. Yet the son of William le Hardi was only just beginning his harassment of Edward's vassal.

Figure XCIX-Part Two; Castle Hill in Ayr; on the south bank of the River Ayr, just east of the harbor

On the heels of yet another victory in Ayrshire, James headed back to Douglas Castle. It was an older, more confidant lieutenant to his king that returned to Douglasdale; emboldened by the Scots' successful routs of the English, most recently against the Earl of Gloucester, Ralph de Monthermer, and his army, forcing them to seek refuge at Ayr castle. This time he had more than just his yeomen from Girvan; the squire and his larger retinue, increasing everyday in number, were camped near Broken Cross Muir. After several days, the Douglas squire called a small muster for Sandilands, late in the night that the local villiens might come in secrecy. The lang days of summer gave few hours for the cover of darkness to shield their plans. So James called for men to join him at this farm situated a few miles from the park of the castle, near the ferry landing at Crookboat, where the Douglas

Water met the River Clyde. James had been scouting de Clifford's men at arms; watching closely as loyal Douglas tenants played their roles with false alarms, testing the response and readiness of the new captain of the garrison. The squire decided the time was never better; commander Thirlwall was vulnerable, underestimating the Scots with the usual English arrogance, he surmised.

Some few hours later as the first glimmer of dawn streaked sunlight across the moorish lands of his ancestors, James of Douglas led his retinue towards Happendon. Here he dispatched a few of his armed horse to drive the cattle pasturing in the shadow of the castle motte towards their position near Happendon Woods. Thirlwall's men perceived the theft immediately; the drawbridge lowered in a lumbering descent while the portcullis creaked and rumbled as it was slowly being raised upward. With little time for ceremony the trusted vassal of de Clifford bolted forth leading his small retinue. James spotted the English in pursuit of the Scots and their herd. He chuckled when he saw Thirlwall spurring his destrier forward, his head covered only by the flowing locks of thick yellow hair, a handsome profile strangely out of place in wartime; the knight was riding into battle without a coif of mail or bassinet to protect himself.

Figure C-Part Two; view from the park of Douglas and Park Castle towards Happendon

James recalled le Hardi's words of warning to his son; telling the lad of his near-miss at Fawdon. The Douglas squire spoke softly, barely audible to anyone. "Dear father, that he has not the benefit of your good teachings, to don his mail or helm first before he so attacks," he observed, pleased with the Englishman's folly. "Sorry knight, for there will be no next time to so put on your armor; foolish fellow not to know" James scoffed, "that the battle waits for the warrior!" As he spurred his Hobini into the fray James shouted the menacing war cry, A Douglas! A Douglas! Then he grabbed the horn with his right hand and blew into le Hardi's oliphant to sound the strange instrument's ear piercing death rattle to rally his men at arms. Holding his battle axe in the ready, the squire repeated his dreadful cry as he drew closer to the knight; with his left hand he made a swift decisive strike from the high guard. The garrison commander took a mortal wound to the head and was unhorsed immediately.

The garrison was being assailed from the front and back; the Scots were having another successful rout. Few English escaped but those that did made their way back to Douglas Castle safely. James noted the larger forces assembled by de Clifford since spring; gathering his intelligence well before he decided on the raid for that day. He heard of the many masons and wood workers sent to help rebuild the edifice. He decided to forego another attempt to take the castle this day. "That we will come again, and bring more men," he vowed to his Douglas adherents. He chuckled some as he realized that de Clifford was building another tower; overlooking the morass lands towards the outer bailey and the Douglas Water that formed the second and furthest moat of the castle's defenses. "This tower is most a folly," he scoffed. The English lord had determined the need for a forth tower; to give his men at arms a better view of any who might approach the castle perhaps. But to the Douglas squire, this edifice was imprudent; wasteful of good resources. James knew that no one could pass through the swamp lands from that direction; a tower built there was most redundant. What did interest the lad was that de Clifford was rebuilding the palisade; choosing stone walls to replace the wooden timbers James burned to the ground in March. "That my father would so approve," he sighed remembering how le Hardi had always desired a more permanent barricade to hold off intruders to their castle.

BURGH-ON-SANDS 7TH JULY 1307-Hearing more foul rumors of King Hobbe's victories over de Valence in Scotland the old curmudgeon king set aside his litter and mounted his destrier for the last time; to settle the matter with Scotland once and for all he vowed. But God saw fit to end his life before the fate of Alba had been determined. The pagan despot rotted from the inside out; he died an ignominious death befitting his despicable crimes in life. On the 7th of July in the sixty-ninth year of his life, thirty-fifth of his reign, Edward Plantagenet, yet in the Marches of England outside of Carlisle, died of the squirts. Scotland was still in revolt to his attempt to conquer that kingdome; with a brave King of Scots yet leading his countrymen to freedom. Word of the dead king's procession returning to

Westminster, contrary to his deathbed command to his son and heir, Edward Caernarvon, barely flew through the shires. Many men flocked from the Highlands; rode in droves through the Lowlands; coming from villages and glens and especially from the Forest; all to pledge to Robert Brus. Edward, the Hammer of the Scots was dead and there was hope again for National Independence: a free Scotland. De Valence's days as the lieutenant in Scotland were numbered; the dragon raised by Edward was vanished; plunged at last into the seas in search of another demon master.

Some time after Plantagenet's demise, Robert Brus and James Douglas paid a call to Douglas Castle. They brought a larger contingency in preparation for another raid; but the reinforced garrison would not leave the fortress, correctly fearing for their lives they stayed inside. Without siege engines the Scots would have to wait. "That we shall have to beckon them to do battle another time," the king scoffed. James was already planning his return; he would devise a simple ruse to flush them out he vowed; most the strategy of Thomas Dickson, he would create a deception to gain entry or entice the English from their safe quarters.

Figure CI-Part Two; cattle grazing at Castle Dangerous as viewed from the edge of the motte of the ruined folly tower

One sorry English valet serving in the king's household found himself in peril as he was present during this attack. Upon returning home to England he petitioned the king's chancellor for relief. Four years later the request for compensation by Lucas de Barry was still being bandied about the king's council. He prayed for some recompense for his long service relating this story: when under the command of the late king, the very time King Edward died, that this loyal yeoman was at 'Douuueglas Castle' he told them, accentuating the Gaelic name; when Sir Robert de Brus and Sir James of Duglas so attacked that fortress. The council took their time with the request. Some four more years passed after that petition when an aging de Barry was finally permitted his redress for a stipend; granted relief at last.

DOUGLASDALE EARLY SEPTEMBER- The relentless warrior had returned to his homeland with a larger force; determined to bring the Douglas barony under his control at last. The Lanark Fair was approaching so there was much activity of good Scots in Lanarkshire, should he need some reinforcements he mused. After few days in the hills of Douglasdale gathering intelligence, James quickly determined that the new garrison commander was his own worst enemy. Sir John de Wanton was perceived by the good villiens of Douglas as flaunting of his authority with little understanding of the dangers that might be lurking in the countryside. The castle was well garrisoned but surprisingly not well provisioned. The cooks and cellarers were now local tenants of the barony as others of the small folk of de Clifford were yet on campaign. Foul rumors of a shortage of coinage for the castle; rents were yet unpaid and the larder close to barren the servants told the Douglas spies. James was quick to devise a stratagem that would work well for the circumstances.

Figure CII-Part Two; the ruined tower on the remains of the motte for the grand fortress that was Douglas Castle in the late 13th century

Little did the squire know that he and de Wanton held something in common however. The English knight was recently a guest at Berkeley Castle; attending as one of the many suitors of the widowed and unmarried heiresses, the daughters of Lord Thomas and his wife Joan de Ferrers, Lady Berkeley, Ellie's sister in law. On the last night of the festivities a minstrel was heard to play a merry tune, singing of one James of Douglas, a warrior in Scotland known for his prowess and great bravery; in a fortress known to all in England as the Adventurous Castle, the garrison fearing most the return of the vengeful soldier. The lady turned from her suitors, begging the minstrel to sing his words again, that she might be sure the name was James, an odd name for times. Could he be her honest squire and dear friend from five years ago she wondered? Lady Alice de Berkeley could not believe her ears; the forthright young man with the charming lisp who rescued her and saved her sister Isabel as well from the ennui boredom of English knights prancing to their attention was now one of the most feared warriors in all of Scotland! She quickly devised a plan; no chivalric knight worthy of renown could deny her request she mused. Lady Berkley told these English nobles that to win her hand they must meet the test. She would bestow herself in marriage to the brave knight who stayed a year and a day as the captain of the garrison for Douglas Castle. Only Sir John de Wanton was stalwart or perhaps foolish enough to accept the challenge.

Figure CIII-Part Two; artist's concept of Douglas Castle in 1297

The Douglas muster was set for the Park of Douglas where le Hardi once called the men of Douglasdale to his retinue. They would gather near the old Ash tree next to the earth and timber keep of Park Castle, presently deserted and much damaged; no one was living there. In the wee hours just before dawn James' loyal vassals arrived eager to do battle; joining friends and neighbors from as faraway as Ettrick Forest. As James watched the warriors report for service he was sitting under the protection of the magical Ash of the Celts. Looking upward at the outstretched branches of the magnificent tree James recalled the happy times he spent with his father when Lord Douglas carefully explained the importance that their ancestors held for the Ash: the symbol of universal order. "That the ancient ones most know this truth: for all we do here in this world so begets our future in the next life of the Otherworld; we can not escape our actions of this place most like an endless chain that can not so be broken," le Hardi told his son. "To be in perfect harmony with the Universal Truth this day; beginning our raid in God's good pleasure," James said in whispered tones. "This humble squire does give his pledge to all the Celtic warriors that have so gone before; a promise to restore the harmony to Douglasdale, ridding our homeland of these men with tails who would seek to destroy our ways."

It seemed to James that the old Ash tree stood to remind him of his deep sense of belonging to these lands and the need to defend them to his last breath; the roots of the old tree were deep as were his own he mused. Looking downward towards the Park Burn and his assembling armed force he reflected on the days when he was but a knave and the Park witnessed a different entourage; the abbot and his monks, the white monks making their way from Melrose Abbey to Mauchline. These Cistercians with the blessing of Edward came to use the Park of Douglas as their gate, their road in seising; angering the laird to erect a sign post, directing the churchman in the wrong direction. Le Hardi had no recourse to their impetuous trespass once Edward became Lord Paramount; he could only remind the monks to take heed that he was lurking there, *scaring them*, as was their complaint to the English king. James chuckled to think that Sir William was probably about, ready with his most sinister grimace to frighten the churchmen should they return to his lands.

Figure CIV-Part Two; view of Park Burn with the terraced cart path that led to the Park Castle motte in background

The squire rose from his seclusion beneath the old Ash and turned to his men at arms as he began to explain his scheme to rout the English garrison. "That we will fill these sacks," he said, showing the Douglas vassals plain cloth bags he secured for this purpose. "With these rocks from Park Burn and the dried grasses of the glen here, we will prepare our ruse. To carry these burdens for twenty of our number, presenting to the garrison as peddlers with their beasts and grain on the way to Lanark's fair this day," he proposed.

Figure CV-Part Two; a Plane tree or Sycamore on the motte of Park Castle grows near some older ash trees; the insidious tree was often confused with the Sycamore tree of Egypt that provided foliage for healing

As the men carefully gathered the dried grasses of the late summer James came to notice some lingering Bluebells on the wee brae near the burn. Without mentioning it to anyone, he grabbed some of the flowering stalks; kneeling unobtrusively he stuffed some of the fading Bluebells into one of the sacks; *just for luck*, he mused. Soon their pack train of peasants was assembled and making their way around the Mainshill Wood down past Brown Hill, continuing around by Springhill Farm before going through the village of Douglas and past the Douglas Kirk. It was a roundabout way but necessary; the new outer wall-walk though not yet complete provided de Clifford's men with almost a panoramic view of the approaches to the fortress. James wanted to convince the watch that the impostor peddlers came from the village, possibly the Douglas Kirk where they stopped to leave offerings before going to Lanark. If the garrison thought they came from any other direction they might draw suspicion. The supply train moved slowly; waiting for the signal from James. The older son of Thomas Dickson appeared from behind the kirk; riding towards the disguised retinue, only to continue, never to stop. This casual action was their unspoken word to begin their ascent towards the castle grounds, riding below the fortress, traveling along the banks of the second and furthest outlying moat directly in line with the drawbridge of the stronghold.

These would-be peddlers wore peasant garb over their hauberks and mail; their swords and shields carefully concealed under the looser tunics of peaceful villiens. The larger cavalcade of thirty armed horse was led by James, with Thomas Dickson at his side. They proceeded undeterred; quietly and carefully they made their way along the Douglas Water, coming from the direction of Braidlea Cottage. Dickson watched with wonder as the twenty-one year old son of William le Hardi took on the appearance of his father; transformed into that knight of renown. James rode tall in his saddle, conveying a bold demeanor with his eagerness to do battle. His face was contorted in the furled brow of Douglas determination; frozen in the stern grimace as he watched the ambuscade develop before him. Behind him rode the aging vassal of le Hardi; now fully recovered from his wounds incurred at the Douglas Kirk on Palm Sunday. The older knight reflected on the day and the brave young leader before him. The son as the father was a consummate warrior on the field of battle; never leaving much to chance with a well thought out strategy; both leaders of men to inspire great confidence, mused Thomas Dickson.

Figure CVI-Part Two; ruins of the the13th century rubble and stone walls below the folly tower in Douglas

James' eyes were ever vigilant; searching the countryside as they rode nearer the village and the gates of the castle grounds. His perfect knowledge of his family's lands, his understanding of their ancient ways prepared him for this day; if anything was amiss he would know it and could alter the attack midstream as required. Would they take the bait he wondered? Certainly the word of garrisons around the shires was true; supplies were few, larders most empty for their stores. Perhaps this squire has over anticipated the greed and arrogance of this de Clifford vassal, he said under his breath; second guessing his plan.

But James did not have to wait long for an answer to his concerns; the drawbridge was being lowered; the portcullis was lifting, an English knight in full armor of the times, wildly and flamboyantly spurred his destrier from the wooden planks crossing the moat to the grazing lands below. Sir John de Wanton led his men at arms, nearly all the garrison, in hot pursuit of the pretenders, viewing the train of provender his very own to capture. James motioned to his followers to unsheathe their swords; hold their weapons in the ready for their attack; the battle was eminent. He had directed his six archers to ride towards the cart path, the main gate from Uddington for higher ground; this ambuscade would be a three sided attack. Nearing the Gallow Knowe, the Douglas men at arms awaited the signal from their captain.

Figure CVII-Part Two; ruined cellars under the folly tower of Castle Dangerous; flood waters from local mining flow in the background below the tower motte

Thomas Dickson was filled with nervous energy; his horse snorting his displeasure for the wait as well, as he brought the veteran destrier to stop beside the squire. His feelings were familiar, like old times now lost when James turned to him spouting the well known look of le Hardi; the strange smirk that always preceded the guttural, frightening war cry: A Douglas! A Douglas! The squire bellowed his first call to battle; the vision of the mighty Sholto filled the hearts of his followers. The English looked behind them to see James and his armed horse on temporary wait; in their distraction the soldiers missed the approach of the bowman. These archers from Ettrick appeared unnoticed until the English heard the foreboding sounds; the menacing swoosh of arrows flying into the air; followed by an ominous thud as they begin to hit their mark. The bowman picked off two or three of the garrison quickly; then James grabbed the oliphant as he gave Thomas Dickson a knowing look. He shouted his angry call again; A Douglas! A Douglas! He yelled his chilling war-cry the third time and followed the words with the blood curdling sound of the Crusader's horn spurring his Hobini, his men close behind as they moved fearlessly into the fray, to take on de Wanton's retinue.

At the same moment, the peddlers dropped their sacks; the booty the English garrison greedily sought spilled before them: dried grass and silk topped thistle lang gone to seed fell about the field. The pretenders threw off their cloaks; turned to unsheathe their swords. The Douglas men at arms having removed their disguises were now in command; in position to expel the English from Douglasdale. De Wanton had never expected the ruse; he deftly maneuvered his war horse to avert the fight and flee only to discover the Douglas squire and his retinue face to face in front of him in his retreat.

Figure CVIII-Part Two; the outer defensive walls of Douglas Castle as viewed from the motte of the folly tower; the Douglas Water runs behind these manmade walls that would have supported the wooden palisade surrounding the outer bailey

The bowmen were successful, performed as planned; pandemonium ruled as the English garrison was confused by the sudden charge from every direction with nowhere to turn for safety. From each corner they feared assault and had to fight the ravenous Scots. De Wanton was unhorsed by Dickson; a former peddler ran him through when he hit the ground. The three way attack of bowmen, armed horse and foot was a successful strategy.

When the battle was over James was confronted by one of his yeoman from Girvan; they had found a letter on the body of the garrison commander. James took the parchment, noted a female hand and as he read the words his eyes moistened with anger and hatred for a war that was not his doing. He turned from them; walked away from the battle site. "Dear St. Bride," he began in low tones that no one could hear him, "why must this life I live to be so difficult; that those we know and love most suffer for the rightful deeds we must so do. My truth is here in Douglasdale; my heart not healed from the many losses too painful to recall; my dear father that I miss him so; what shall I do here?" he poignantly put to the patron saint of the Douglases; seeking in earnest the guidance from the Celtic saint. James had read the fair words of Lady de Berkeley pledging her hand to the brave knight who would hold of the Adventurous Castle, Douglas Castle for one year and a day; the garrison commander, her betrothed was dead at his command.

Figure CIX-Part Two; a motte similar to the one supporting the remaining folly tower would have supported the postern angle tower of Douglas Castle; a tree grows where the tower once stood

Thomas Dickson noticed James' sad countenance and came quietly to his side. "What is in that document that saddens your heart so my laird?" he asked le Hardi's young son. "That I do know this lass; Lady Alice so trusted me and was my friend; that I have destroyed her plans for love with this foul deed we so contrived this day," he said sorrowfully. Gilley's loyal valet hugged the lad to him. "Your father was a noble laird and knight; he wanted not of war; to write his poems and live in his Douglasdale was his rightful intention. That Edward shamelessly stole that life from us; de Clifford and de Percy too, in their unholy scheme; now others suffer for their greed and dishonor to God's word." James thanked Dickson for the comforting reminders. He looked about and decided they must proceed to take the castle. "That this task will never come again; to take another life of any man, I will raze my family's home to do no further harm to those I love and care for!" he promised his father's vassal, now his own lieutenant in Douglasdale.

The garrison that remained in Douglas Castle surrendered the fortress quickly. James entered the great hall of memories of a life time that would never be again. He looked about him and recalled his promise to Hugh that he would not destroy their family's home before he saw it. "Dear Hubicus, forgive this lad his deed to do; I know you will," he spoke softly to himself. "That I must end this madness as no other can; to build another home for our family; but how will it ever be the same dear father?" he asked le Hardi, demoralized for what he must do. His men at arms inquired as to the disposition of the garrison that surrendered. "Would this be another Douglas Larder as they called our deed of that Palm Sunday last?" asked Richard, the son of Thomas Dickson. James shook his head. "Bring me the coffers that you find; the coinage will I disperse some to the English left so here that they will return to England unharmed." James demeanor was solemn, though somewhat wavering from the determined warrior that first led the raid from Gallow Knowe.

Sitting at the table in the great hall James had his retinue bring the sergeant of the watch to him; he explained his sadness for de Wanton, told him he knew the lady. The English knight thanked the squire for sparing their lives and was stunned when James gave his men coinage for their return to England. "Take of yourselves homeward to Essex, Hereford and Yorkshire," he commanded them. "For if this Scot finds of you again near his homeland I will finish the deed most started here today," he promised. James next turned to his own men at arms and instructed them on how he planned to raze the fortress. Dickson and many of the older vassals of le Hardi knew how deeply the lad cared for Douglas Castle; sharing the love his father held for Douglasdale, his own true paradise they knew. The dour countenance of the youth told them their thoughts were correct; this day was the saddest to come since the passing of that noble and martyred laird, William le Hardi.

FAWDON-James rode through the day and night; stopping only to eat of bannock and drink of wine. He did not sleep; his eyes were swollen and deeply reddened from the tears that flowed profusely as he watched the homestead he promised to restore to Douglas lairds razed before his eyes. As the frightening flames shot up in red and yellow spires, curled around the memories of a life that he would know no more James cried; sobbed till his tall, muscular frame shook with anger and despair. In the darkness of the final hours of Douglas Castle the squire commanded his men to a rendezvous for Ettrick ten days later; then alone he mounted his Hobini and departed Douglasdale. The rough black stubble of a clean shaven face just two days before was now covered with the soot from the burning fires of Douglas Castle; streaked in misshapen lines by the copious tears that flowed uncontrollably down his face.

James knew that September was too early for Ellie and his brothers to be in Craig Douglas so he continued on towards Fawdon hoping to find them there. He made his way east then south towards Jedburgh where his exhaustion brought him to seek shelter in the forest along the Jed. He noticed a cave hovering in the outreach of a craig near a place called Lintalee. "This squire to stop and rest for some few hours," he assured himself out loud, too tired to resist slumber for the cool night's air. Before settling down to nod off he made his rounds of the countryside. Even in his confused state from lack of sleep and the emotional drain of the deeds behind him, James' instincts for survival kicked in; the squire knew he needed all his wits about him before continuing the journey south to Fawdon. Northumbria was a dangerous place for James of Douglas but the only home he could think to run to in his overwhelming sorrow. Satisfied with the safety and seclusion of his perch high above the Jed, he headed for the cave. It was dry and provided him good lookout, with ample space to hide his horse discretely nearby. "Perfect," he summed up as he fell off quickly to a sound sleep.

Figure CX-Part Two; cave near the Jed at Lintalee

Just a few hours had gone by when the squire awoke; jolted by an owl sitting not far above him on the limb of an old birch. "You have my gratitude," he saluted the owl, "for I must journey east again this night." He mounted his Hobini and vowed to return to the safety of the secluded spot someday. On and on he rode until at last he arrived in the comfort of the Cheviot; the growing darkness fell upon him as he made his way up the hill to Fawdon manor. He was heading not for the stone tower house and primary residence of the estate, but the smaller dower house, the fortified house near the mains that was the only portion of the estate yet awarded to Ellie for her dower. "Even our Fawdon is not truly ours," he said out loud in disgust; knowing their wee castle in the Cheviot as le Hardi called it was yet held by de Umfraville, the corn and hay saved for the king to pay his father's fine for marrying Eleanora nineteen years before.

The light from tallow torches was still glowing though burning low; yet no one was in the great hall when he arrived. He took his Hobini to the stables in the rear of the mains buildings and smiled when he noticed his Fortis in the next stall. Patric was staying with the horses and stirred when he heard the squire bring in his pony. "Good James," he exclaimed. His father's valet was cheered to see the lad. James quietly told him of the dreadful siege at Douglas Castle. Patric was about the age of James, growing up with the family, he understood the squire's sentiments and tears welled in his own eyes. He took the Hobini from the Douglas son and began to ease his own sorrow through his work; grooming the horse for the night. James went to Fortis and greeted his old friend; sharing stories of adventure that only his palfrey could hear. Patric and James had an understanding that words could not convey. The ensuing silence and knowing glances told of their shared grief and anger for a war that was not of their choosing or device; only theirs to suffer through with losses unrelenting.

James made his way quietly up the turnpike stairs to the family chambers. He heard no noises that indicated anyone was in the manor house; but from Patric's words and the scattered possessions of his brothers he knew the Douglases were in their Fawdon. James remembered this smaller dwelling from his youth; staying there when le Hardi was having the masons build an addition to the main keep of the manor. He tapped lightly on his mother's door; she answered thinking it was Ana for her final check and bid goodnight. As she looked up she gasped in delight to recognize her James, his tall, slender form outlined by the dim light of her chamber. He closed the door and slowly came to her side. "Dear mother," he blurted out, "this lad most needs your welcome arms this night." As he made his way across the laird's chamber Ellie was able to distinguish his features more clearly in the candle light. His face was encrusted with dirt and soot yet strangely streaked; tear stained, she mused as she hugged him hard to her breast. "What has so saddened you to come to us like this?" she asked, still holding him tight in her embrace.

Then she pulled abruptly back from him. "And of what is that smell?" she asked with an impish twinkle in her eye. It was the Douglas way to comfort then tease with humor when confronted with a family member in despair. James gave a slight grin. "Not just a sorry sight but one of soily odor most as well; like to smell of dear Edward at his foul end," he scoffed sarcastically. Ellie chuckled. "This lass will call of Ana; to bring a bath and I shall clean my son and warrior," she said happily. "No mother, this lad is much too old for such a bathing!" he exclaimed. But Lady Douglas was hearing none of his protests and began stripping him of his hauberk and coif. James was resisting but to no avail as Ana arrived and received her orders; but first she grabbed her lad and kissed him hard. "What a welcome sight," she chuckled. Then in came Hugh. "What a sorry figure of a knight you are," he chided his older brother and hero. "Dear Hugh, the saddest of news to share with you," began the squire as he was relinquishing his armor to his mother. Ana had returned and reminded Ellie that it was dangerous to have the servants see James in her chamber; some of them were not known to the Douglases and might be loyal to the English she cautioned.

The next knock on the chamber door announced the cook and cellarer bringing the tub and buckets of steaming water. Ellie shoved James into the latrine closet, throwing his armor after him as she grabbed the Deerhound that he would not give her son's hiding place away. "M' lady," the cook began, "this water is the hottest that we have; more is heating over the fire in the kitchens but will take some time to warm for you," he allowed. Ana told him that such wait was necessary and would be no trouble to her lass. The servants left and James was allowed out of his confinement. "Our father once warned this lad that for such hiding there was a punishment to come: *that spies were hanged*," he chuckled, spouting an amused grin. Ellie and Ana were roaring in laughter to remember the story of James and his sisters; hiding in the garderobe in attempt to discover what caused all the giggling in their parent's chamber. "That our Shamus gave you all away; taken captive when you so hid in the latrine," Ellie added jovially. Ana explained to Hugh that Lord Douglas was more than just annoyed with his children's intrusion and promised consequences most severe should they dare repeat such transgressions against their laird!

Another knock on the door, yet barred to entry for the discovery of their squire, and the wee Archie was permitted to join them. "James!" he shrieked, the excited scream was squashed immediately by the outstretched hand of Hugh covering his mouth. "That we must keep the presence of our James a secret," Ellie whispered; admonishing the lad. "Our rebel squire is most sought by English knights; looking for reward from our new king to be," she added sadly as she reminded them of the future coronation of Edward Caernarvon, the successor of his father. James looked up from his undressing and asked her if the dismal end of the 'pagan despot' was true. "That we so heard from Carlisle he died of the squirts; is that true?" Archie blurted out the answer. "Of course so trivial an end would come to such a hated man that Edward rotted from the inside out, spewing his foul humors from both ends," he chortled, explaining that the king died of an acute case of diarrhea. "When will this lad be allowed to join in the fight for our homeland?" Archie continued. James looked over at Ellie for a response; she had none. Lady Douglas realized the futility; only she would remain in England; her sons would return to Scotland in support of National Independence. "It is done," she admitted quietly to herself.

James told his youngest brother that he had seen Uncle Alex and that Beatrice was asking for him. The lad's face lit up; beaming in true love for the de Lindsay lass. "That laird has told me that you can return," the squire began, "but only when we have a truce with Edward." Archie was despondent until Ellie interjected her words. "Dear lad, your mother will insist that you return as the squire to your brother when he is dubbed," knowing that his exploits and the success of King Robert meant knighthood was coming soon to James for he had earned the right she told them all proudly. "My Beatrice most waits for me; her one and only love," he sighed. Ellie chuckled. "Fortunate for you to feel the same; there is not a greater gift than the true love shared as I so had with one named William," she added warmly; recalling her own dear knight and the true undying passion that they shared.

The bathing tub awaited the warrior as Ana brought out Ellie's small compact mirror that James might take a look at himself. "This warrior can not so lead his men that he should show emotion on his face with rivulets of telltale tears to run down my cheeks. That I will grow a beard so thick that no one will suspect, this knight to be most has his tender side," he proclaimed. Then he lowered himself in the steaming hot water. Ellie began to wash his back; he tried to fend her off but she would hear none of it. "This lad is most a man; I do beg of you to stop!" he commanded. "That I have washed a man before, my dear Gilley," she chided him for his shyness. "You are but a child to this lass; a mother will wash her son. It is done!" Archie was in hysterics. "Your retinue would find of folly seeing their captain overpowered by an Essex lass," he said teasingly.

Then Ellie gave him a scowling look. "Your mother is a Scot," she shot back in terse words, holding up her left thumb exhibiting the scar from the cuts that William made ten years before with this dagger when they mixed their blood in a Celtic ceremony. "This lass was most fearful that night; your father had consumed much wine and little food that he brought about his war sword for the deed," she chuckled. "Mother, you did not tell this lad that part of the ritual," James responded, laughing at the thought of William using such a weapon for such a small incision. Ana reminded him of how angry and despondent Gilley was to pledge fealty to Edward, a demeaning gesture after Berwick's trickery she mused. "But he told my girl she had earned the right to be called a Scot with his noble Celtic blood to join with hers," Ana said proudly. Hugh and Archie looked at each other in amazement; their father had the strangest ways they mused. "Perhaps there was even more for us to learn about one named le Hardi," Hugh whispered to his brother Archie.

Figure CXI-Part Two; wine baluster, medieval pottery on exhibit at Caerlaverock Castle, a castle managed by Historic Scotland

"There," smiled Ellie proudly as she finished washing off the stench and grime from her son for the many weeks on campaign. "Now you are free to finish your bathing that I may fetch a cloak for your use." Ana was already prepared for that as she handed Ellie a blue velvet chamber cloak and a white and green silk cote that once belonged to Gilley. "Our laird of Douglas does demand his finery," she chuckled knowing James' deference for fine garments just like his father. Archie took the clothing from her hands. "This page will serve our knight to be; to help our brother dress," he proclaimed, laughing at his own silliness. Ellie ordered food for feasting and they adjourned to the other chamber where James and his brothers would sleep. "Good brother, that you can rest to know you are quite safe this night," Hugh told him. "A noble churchman and a bowman of renown, one to stand guard of men and the other to say prayers for your safety, are both staying here this night." James breathed a sigh of relief; being home in Fawdon was just what he needed. He inhaled the food on the platter and was asleep in his own bed before he finished his first carafe of wine.

Ellie and Ana had quietly set about hiding the squire's Hobini; they also sent Sir David with the English servants on an errand to nearby Billesdone, to keep them occupied should they discover Edward's enemy, James Douglas in their midst. The lands in Billesdone included the territory and village that were granted to the heirs of Nicholas Puncharton in 1270; given in a charter from Willelmi, Lord Douglas, le Hardi's father when he was raising coinage for his son's Crusade. Near the village was an additional carucate adjoining the territory that became the dower lands of Lady Constancia, le Hardi's stepmother. This messuage was now held by another Douglas widow, Lady Eleanora; the income hers to have as well as the service and fee of Billesdone of one penny. Ellie was taking these extra measures to insure safety and anonymity for the squire; that he might move about the manor hall freely and without concern for discovery. Sending Sir David on the errand also resolved some of Ellie's plans to collect rents during her trip to Northumbria.

When James woke from his slumber, Archie was sitting on a bench beside his bed. "Good that you are now awake," he snickered. "That this lad does not have to rouse you from your sleep." James responded with a silly grin. "What method were you choosing?" he demanded to know. From behind him Archie brought out a baluster filled with water. James looked at him, then at the container of water, then back again at the mischievous page, the wee Archie. "This laird of Douglas has need of a squire soon," he began. "Perhaps you have brought that water for my morning ablutions," James suggested with mocked intent. "Of course Lord Douglas, this was certainly my plan," Archie replied, readying himself for the dousing of his brother when suddenly he was interrupted by Ellie who was entering the chamber. "Saved by your mother," scoffed the younger lad. Eleanora looked about quizzically. "Never mind Lady El; the over zealous bowman was about to lay siege on this warrior until your entrance prevented such attack," James chuckled. "Henklebaldicus," she addressed her youngest son. "You will cease such activity the noo!" Ellie then ushered him out of the chamber.

"Mother that I must speak with you; tell you of that dreadful siege; the many memories so lost; the family chapel, the deftly painted decorations by my sisters; the wood carvings, all gone. Our once proud home but an oval mass of cinders around charred rubble and hewn stone," he told her mournfully. Ellie sat down next to her son and took his hand. "Dear James, many lang years ago this lass first came to Douglas Castle," she began slowly, trying to comfort him with her words. "Our home now is destroyed; and only you and I so recall that loving place we shared with our William, and our sweet lasses Mura, Martha and Amy with dear wee John, all now with God. Pray, continue; and spare me nothing of the sights you saw before the deed was done."

James started by telling her that he went through the castle carefully; stopping to take inventory of anything he might salvage. He brought with him whatever he could from each chamber; large wooden boxes, some over four feet lang, he explained, were filled with tapestries and other fineries; then packed up and taken to places of safe keeping. "This lad commanded the removal of the wooden carvings and adornments from the withdrawing room and the old platt-and-scale stairs," he told her; describing how he tried to save as much as he could. But in each chamber he felt overcome with emotion. "There were so many memories," he confessed. "That sadly those dear thoughts I was forced to leave behind." James looked up at Ellie and noticed she was deep in a reverie of her own, perhaps there in the past with his father he suspected. As she felt his eyes upon her she returned his gaze and beckoned him to continue telling her about those final minutes before Douglas Castle was razed. "My thoughts so stirred in every chamber; the *Three Headed Monster* in the withdrawing room; the elegant fireplace in the great hall where one morning the wee Fortis greeted this lad on his birthday; and the chapel where the Douglas children decided spying was better than praying." James was laughing now with Ellie as the mother and son recalled their happier, yet poignant days in Douglasdale.

"Then at last this lad had made his way to our father's special place; the wall-walk of the parapet, to look upon my Douglasdale for the last time from that sacred place," James said alluding to Gilley's private sanctuary. Ellie smiled to recall the many times she found him there; how he welcomed her to his personal abode with open arms. "That you dear James would know of this," she sighed softly. He understood; only his mother held of these memories; the tragedy was not so much about a stronghold razed but of a home so lost from them once filled with memories, children's voices they could no longer hear; smiling faces that were no longer visible to them, having passed to the Otherworld of the Celts. "This lad must build another castle; but it can never be a better one. That I ran my hands most over the fine hewn stone, noticing the mason marks for the first time in many years as I made my way down the left sided turnpike stairs," James said reminding her of the special stone steps his grandfather built for left handed warriors to defend. "This squire did his best to recall most every detail; to never forget that I might create another in its place."

"Perhaps to make some memories for yourself," suggested Ellie, inferring it was perhaps long overdue that he thought of starting his own family. "Of these days such thoughts are not possible," he scoffed. Lady Douglas was not deterred. "Love comes at the strangest of times dear James; that you will know when it is true and right. But children bring a sense of hope; a knowing that the future can only be better from the work we do on their behalf most now," she concluded. He realized that she was speaking for herself as much as she was for him. "That Lady El so wants to be a grandmother," he grinned. She shook her head and started to giggle. "To hold a wee one lad or lassie makes no difference as my Gilley would say; a child to carry our good name of Douglas; more heirs for Douglasdale!" she proclaimed giddily, mimicking his father.

"Come, these clothes do we have for you," she offered as she rose from her seat; changing the subject. She handed him some fine mantels and surcotes that she had intended for him since the spring, whenever she saw him again. "You have fashioned fair work to alter these garments," he said as he ran his hands over the new embroidery on his father's former finery. Ellie then quickly advised him that she sent the two English servants not known to James on an errand with Sir David; that he could join the family in the great hall without concern. "This lad will be most there and quickly," he assured her as she took her leave of him. James reflected on Ellie's words; perhaps it was time for him to visit Lady Joanna in Logan he mused. Then he quietly dressed himself and joined the others in the great hall. Hugh was already finished breaking his fast but waiting patiently for the arrival of James.

Figure CXII-Part Two; chapel of Queen Margaret at Edinburgh Castle, a premier site operated by Historic Scotland; smaller family chapels were common in medieval castles

"Beware the thieving hound," said Archie solemnly as Lindsay lurked about the large trestle table next to the fireplace where a small peat fire crackled playfully in the background. "How many times has this mother so warned her son?" scolded Ellie. Archie was dour; the Deerhound had scoffed a cinnamon cake from his hand as he was talking to Hugh; a luxury, there were but a few left for James to enjoy. "Henklebaldicus," his mother said forgivingly, "that there are enough for you to have one more." Ellie knew her youngest son shared his father's passion for the sweet pastry and decided to relent this time on her scolding.

James was laughing at his wee brother. "Perhaps the hound can be persuaded most to share," he teased Archie. Hugh was growing impatient; he wanted to know about the state of their home; was there anything left that he could see to remind him of a life he really did not remember. The squire's face fell as he recalled the promise made to his brother. He quietly began to share the story of his saddest day as he described the tragic event. "All that remains of that once proud fortress, most now an empty relic are the scorched stones and burned timbers of devastation. Many of the loving paintings of our sweet sisters and dear mother destroyed," he continued as tears welled up in his eyes. Ellie felt the warmth of tears flow down her own cheeks as Ana sitting next to her was wiping her face as well, trying to mask the sadness she felt. "The pride of generations now stands empty as my heart; devoid of feelings," said the squire looking more a troubled lad than one of Scotland's most feared warriors.

"Most again we set fires to raze the remains of the former residence where our father held baronial court; this lad watched the old earth and timber hall burn completely, razed to the ground. Then we set fires in the newer tower of stone. That I so followed the flames rise and engulf the supporting structure of the scale-and-platt stairs of our grandfather Sir William; to disappear into smoldering ash; the floors soon caught and the tower was ablaze. As the smoke filled the air I forgot to take my leave; only the persistent cries of Thomas Dickson awoke me from that strange reverie in time to remove myself to safety," he continued. "Did you not save anything before you set the fires?" asked Hugh. James shook his head yes. "This lad took out the old tester of Lord Douglas," he affirmed as Ellie gasped remembering the bed that belonged to Sir William, le Hardi's father. "And the portcullis was saved along with the large oak doors of the great hall with those beautiful carvings of the Douglas armorial bearings; the elegant oak staircase most as well, that you so know, this lad insisted must survive. These and other treasures we brought; dragged with many beasts harnessed for the task, to secure them all to a place near Park Castle. Thomas Dickson and his son Richard covered the great iron gates with goose fat to keep them right till I return to build another fortress there."

Ellie wanted to know if his grandfather's tapestries and other treasures were yet about. "Many had gone missing but those most there were saved; stored safely by the vassals of our father," he replied. "Most as well that I so kept from the destruction of the fire was the elaborate mantel in the withdrawing room; the paintings on the wooden paneling and carvings near the capitals as well; but little more," James said painfully. Hugh walked over to his brother and put his arm around him. "That someday you will build us another home," the lad reassured him with that sweet smile and kind voice that was always his demeanor; his stuttering indiscernible as he spoke. The squire hugged Hugh hard as he sobbed into his chest. Archie was confused; he demanded to know why James felt he had to destroy the castle now. "The worst story yet to so describe," he responded, drying his tears. James recounted the details of the raid; how he set upon the garrison with a successful three point attack including the use of bowmen from the Uddington gate. "The garrison commander came out in pursuit of the warriors most disguised as peddlers on the way to Lanarks' fair," he told them. As he elaborated on his strategy, everyone became engrossed with the exciting details.

"When the battle was most over, one Douglas yeoman found this letter on the body of captain," James said as he gave the parchment to Ellie to read aloud. She quickly scanned the writing and noted the signature of Lady Alice de Berkeley and understood at once. Silently, Lady Douglas experienced the same vanquished pain and devastation that James felt when he learned John de Wanton's true identity; the reason for becoming the garrison commander at Douglas Castle. "Oh James, no," she moaned in grave sympathy. "Please mother, read aloud her words; I can not bear to do it," he sighed deeply, shaking his head in disgust for the irony; the tragedy that fell upon him for circumstance of a war that was not his to choose, only his to fight.

Ellie explained that the lady was betrothed to Sir John de Wanton; giving her hand for his bravery in accepting the challenge she proffered at a party given by her parents: Sir Thomas de Berkeley and his wife Lady Joan de Ferrers of Berkeley Castle. Archie and Hugh were stunned; they recalled the happy times they shared there in Gloucestershire as guests of Ellie's kin. How could this misfortune have occurred they demanded to know? Ana could not contain herself; she burst into tears. So lovely a lass; one who most befriended the lads; another victim to Edward's avarice and cold ambition, she mused. Ellie returned to reading the letter out loud to her sons. "That you have so chosen to lead Sir Robert de Clifford's garrison in defense of the Adventurous Castle," their mother continued, adding that the English were calling Douglas Castle by that silly moniker because of the successful exploits of their James. "That this lady promises to accept of your proposal; the license for this marriage to be heartily approved." Lady Douglas had finished reading the letter, as sorrow and silence filled the great hall.

"Mother, this lad is most distraught," James told Ellie. "When warriors are bred to fight we are never told of the heartbreak that we might cause to others of our kin and friends," he said ruefully. "And now our family stronghold where for generations Douglases have lived is most gone from us; destroyed by fires this lad so set upon our home," James scoffed almost viciously. Archie reminded his brother that le Hardi was also a knight of renown and sadly missed. "Most bred a warrior but a poet knight he preferred to be; one laird who loved his Douglasdale, his true Paradise," he said confidently. "Remember our father's words you so often shared with this page, 'the lands of our Celtic ancestors are God's sweet gift; not the fortresses we so create upon them.' There will be time left for us to build another castle," he reassured his older brother.

James listened in silence to Archie's words; the comfort of his family nurtured him while the enduring sentiments of his father's teachings revived him once again. "This lass knows strongly the disgrace we must endure; the false face we wear; forced to live in fear that our treasonous thoughts are most discovered," Lady Douglas said softly. "Only those so here know of our truth. We are Scots; hiding from our hearts to keep ourselves alive, far from the Tower prison that stole our father and dear husband from us, that we might fight another day."

Eleanora reminded them all that their ancestors were of noble birth and that they must never forget the sacrifices of Douglases gone before them. For her, the war was even more debasing: the only man she ever loved was William le Hardi; yet his proud family name of Douglas threatened her very life that she might never chance to use it again she feared. "War came upon us unwillingly at Berwick but fight the invaders is we must now do. Our Celtic way, the heritage from the ancient ones, entrusted to us by Willelmi, Lord Douglas, we must bravely defend. That, my sons, is our charge to keep," Lady Douglas proclaimed solemnly. She paused for a moment then looked directly at James; her face took on a proud countenance, as her next words caused a hush to fill the room. "With de Clifford's men most routed from our homeland, the first battle has been won. Dear James, we wait for your word my son, for you have earned the right to lead us Lord Douglas."

Part III
1308 to 1320

THE FOREST JULY 1308-It was nine months since James took his leave of Renfrewshire for the valley of the Tweed. On the Ides September last after just returning from Fawdon and a visit with his family the Douglas squire had found his way into the Passelewe Forest and the manor of Paisley. Here stood the impressive Paisley Abbey and the proud kirk of the Stewards dedicated to St. James the Great, for whom he and his Uncle James were both named. James knew the village and surrounding countryside almost as well as he recalled Douglasdale. And he was surprised to find English soldiers lurking about; with their old foe from Edirford, Philip de Mowbray in command. Just before de Valence was recalled from Scotland he had dispatched a company of soldiers to do damage in Renfrew where rebel sympathizers were suspected to be hidden there; possibly staying at Paisley Abbey the English knight was told. It was true that James and his men were in the district but they were safely in their normal domain: the forest of the shire.

Figure I-Part Three; Paisley Abbey

The English set fire to the abbey to persuade the abbot to relinquish their protection of the Scots de Mowbray believed were being sheltered by the churchmen. While the intelligence de Valence's forces received was wrong, James' spies had accurately alerted him to the approach of the English, even to identify the opposition by name. Once again he found himself engaged in warfare with some of his mother's kin; Alymer de la Zouche and Robert de Hastings were two knights in Pembroke's retinue, distinguished only by losing their horses in pursuit of James that day. The squire had planned his attack again in a sheltered glen staging his archers from one direction, his armed horse in another, taking advantage of de Mowbray's overconfident approach. The result was another success for the men of the Forest and more entries in Edward's Rolls of the Pipe: losses of destriers, chargers forfeited for combat with the Scottish rebels by knights, their squires and other men at arms. This time Philip de Mowbray made his way to Inverkip where he would increase his number, taking men from the English garrison to return in search of the insurgents to his lord the king.

Figure II-Part Three; Borders rainbow seven miles southwest of Kelso; part of the old stomping grounds of James Lord Douglas

Back in the Borders some months later James of Douglas and his ever growing force of freedom fighters were enjoying their summer days; making their presence very unpopular with Edward's garrisons. From Moffat to Selkirk they roamed; from Hawick to Jedburgh they rode, then winding their way north to Kelso, these marauders patrolled the Forest; the eastern Marches becoming the Douglas domain. He held of three counties for the Scots; *his stronghold* he boasted. Edward Caernarvon responded in his frustration by dispatching John of Brittany to put down the rebellion. This English lord took over de Valance's fortress, garrisoned Selkirk Castle to gain foothold in that region; yet to no avail. The men of Ettrick were now solidly behind the Douglas squire. These good men were reputed for their great prowess with a bow; their fair stature and good countenance the mirror image of their leader. While James was making inroads to the English control of the old Caledonian Forest, Robert was uniting the north. Victories and submissions were weekly for the king that he had dispatched his brother Edward with Alexander de Lindsay to bring Galloway under their control. James had joined them briefly, bringing with him his growing force, now a retinue comprised of over two hundred men. But after several sieges, James was making his way back to Ettrick.

Figure III-Part Three; view of Selkirk village from the graveyard adjacent to the ancient Kirk in the Wood

    The Douglas squire felt relief in returning to the Forest. He could easily follow the lead of the king's own brother but preferred another course. James took quiet umbrage with the knight who foolishly, time after time, led his men into wanton peril when another strategy seemed more prudent. He fervently believed that Edward Brus was more a knight of vainglory than a true commander of good Scots that he found a way to take his retinue elsewhere without appearing to desert the king's brother. He withdrew to Tweed-dale, feigning need to take flight in pursuit of the good men of Lothiane. As truth most often follows such pretense, James and his men found themselves afforded such an opportunity while taking the main road east towards the moorlands of the Tweed Valley; passing through the region by means of the old Roman cart path. Lord Douglas and his men at arms had deliberately traveled further north of their normal haunts to avoid an encounter with English sympathizers believed to be in the area. Knowing this vale well, he planned on taking refuge in a safe house on the banks of the Lyne near where it meets the Tweed, some few miles outside of Peebles.

    But upon approach James noticed with great surprise that the wee fortress seemed occupied. Happily no watch was posted to notice of our good arrival, he mused. Quietly the Douglas adherents and their leader made their way down into the glen to the bed of the Lyne Water. Unobtrusively they surrounded the tower house. As James crept cautiously nearer the doorway of the keep he listened to the conversations to determine the identity of the occupants. To his surprise and great pleasure the knights were from the Lothianes; on determined campaign in search of one James of

Douglas! Two voices that James heard he knew quite well; his own cousin, Alexander Steward of Boncle, the son of John who perished at Falkirk and Thomas Randolph, the king's own nephew who was captured by the English at Methven. Sir Thomas was also James' kin having married his cousin, the sister of Sir Alexander Steward; descending of Carrick kin as well. Perhaps this lad might come to persuade these fair knights of their folly in allegiance to Edward, he chuckled at his thoughts.

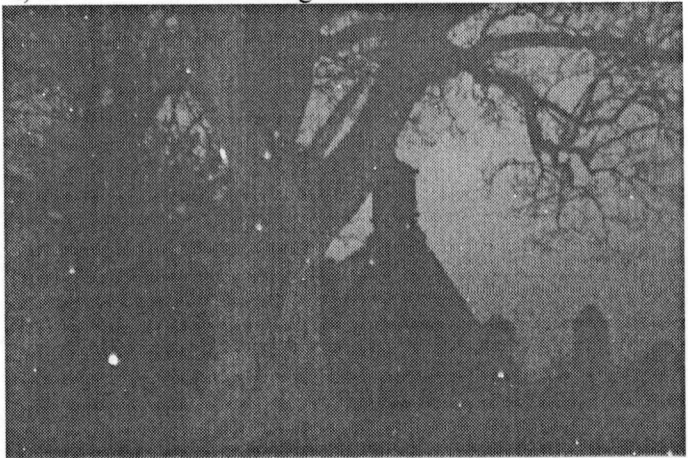

Figure IV-Part Three; Lyne Kirk in the gloaming; a large tree in the graveyard perhaps date back to around the time of James' raid at Lyne Water

"That we will aid these good men in their search, to end it most quickly; welcome their good hospitality as well," the squire declared in his normal undaunted manner as he explained his plan to his sergeants. James had been given fair warning as well not to venture to his own stronghold of Blackhouse Tower just eight miles to the south of their location. During a brief stop in Glencorse, loyal Douglas vassals informed him that some de mischef was about. A Lothiane baron by the name of Adam of Gordon had dispatched spies to the district near Craig Douglas hoping to locate the whereabouts of an irreverent squire who had been lurking in the Forest, making raids upon their tenants in that shire. This heeded caution was the very reason he chose to be in Lyne that night. What luck, he mused, that I have most found them instead; congratulating his good fortune for the chanced discovery. He motioned his men to take their positions, to cordon off the keep, blocking the escape routes. James then mounted his Hobini and took the charge, giving the perilous war cry; A Douglas! A Douglas! Then he valiantly blew that terrible, shrill sounding battle horn his father had brought back from the Crusades. The oliphant reverberated in an ominous cry; invigorating the men of the Forest to do battle for their laird. The fight was on! The encounter was fierce; while Gordon and his men took their fast escape, the other knights were not so quick to give up, taking a ferocious stand against the squire and his retinue.

Sir Alexander took two wounds though neither of them was mortal; the one to his right hand came from a left handed cousin smashing back with his small shield, a parry to his thrust. Having lost his sword when his right hand went numb, the Steward knight yielded, surrendering to his cousin. When the ordeal was finally over, James had two noteworthy prisoners: the nephew of the King of Scots and the knight's brother in law Sir Alexander Steward. He beckoned his kin, these two Lothiane knights, to join in feasting; offered them their own good wine to drink as well. James reflected on his plan; to present Lord Robert with his prize. They would take their leave of the Lothianes for the Highlands; beginning their journey the day next to rendezvous with the king who was now moving towards Argyll. But unlike Sir Adam Gordon in his laxity James posted pickets; the watch would insure their safety for the night he surmised correctly.

"That you have caused much trouble to our peace with Edward," scoffed his cousin Alexander all the while enjoying the feasting and wine. James looked at the knight quizzically. He could not understand how this Scot might ever join the English. "Good cousin, this lad was so at Berwick; to see a king betray his word and bond; slaughtering the good citizens of that Royal Burgh after giving of his promise that should my father Lord Douglas so surrender he would spare the town such peril," James explained earnestly. "With my uncle your dear father perishing at Falkirk refusing his submission to dear Edward, how is it that you so pledge of loyalty to the English lord?" he asked. Alexander replied in a condescending tone that was startling to James. "Your father and my own with our Uncle James so broke their pledge of fealty to Lord Paramount; their lands seized for their rebellion, rightly so this knight will so attest," he said smugly. The Douglas squire deferred to do battle in his words with the foolish knight at another time that he turned to Thomas Randolph. "And you good sir, that you might have so escaped in Methven, would you be now in the camp of those fair men with tails?" James begged to know.

"This sorry knight can only so reflect that he is once again a prisoner of my enemy. My uncle, your king," he said sarcastically, "is most a fool to carry out a war with Edward. With few men at arms and a treasury of paltry measure dear Robert has no chance to turn true victory." James reminded them both that now another king had been crowned in Westminster. "With not the prowess of his father, that he and his lions both un-caged could not stand in comparison," he joked referring to Edward Caernarvon's penchant for traveling with his pet lions in a gilded cart, spending some 14d a day on their feedings.

Randolph cracked a grin and laughed slightly at the thought of the strange son of one of the most ferocious commanders he had ever seen, Edward Plantagenet. James realized that there was some chance to win these Lothiane knights over to his cause; but he would leave that final persuasion to Lord Robert. "Dear cousins that you will be most comfortable this night is my desire; just let this squire know if your needs are not so met that I will right the wrong most quickly." Alexander was feigning his boredom. "That you could free us from the most strained arrest; held as prisoners of the noble King of Scots," Alexander snidely replied. "There will be no chance of that," James chuckled in his response.

Figure V-Part Three; Neidpath Castle a mile west of Peebles is on a craigy cliff overlooking the Tweed, once the location of the castle of Simon Fraser, the brave patriot and adherent of Robert Brus; this tower dates to the 14th century, residing about two miles east of Lyne Water

GLEN LOCHY-James had received word of the king's successes in the Highlands; that Robert was moving south and west towards Glen Lochy, in a place a day's ride from Tyndrum and Dahl Righ. As the squire rode the cart trails north, leading his retinue with two distinguished prisoners in tow, he recalled how bleak the circumstances had been just two years before. Lord Robert's dwindling forces were on the run from de Valence then, recently defeated by Lorne at Dahl Righ, the king sought refuge in the Hebrides. At that battle this squire so received his first injury, he signed. Now the seasoned warrior was leading his own retinue to rendezvous with his lord the king; the situation had certainly changed, James reflected. With Robert Brus intending to do battle with John of Lorne, repaying a debt long overdue and James of Douglas joining him with his own retinue, the landscape of Scotland was much improved for Scots in search of freedom. The tide was turning against the English and their stranglehold on the Scots and with remarkable speed, it seemed to the squire. De Valence had been recalled from Scotland in defeat; replaced by John of Brittany. In the Highlands, the men of Moray had joined the Scottish king. And even though the Lord of Lorne commanded many men at arms, this traitorous Celtic Chief was about to fall; James was certain of it.

Perhaps this squire can now earn his knighthood James ventured; making his plans to take on more responsibility, a warrior of rank leading his men at arms. As merely a squire among the many knights serving Lord Robert, James was commonly outranked; even by those that followed him into battle, fighting their guerilla warfare in the Forest. Arriving at the king's temporary lodgings near Glen Lochy, James of Douglas and his men at arms from Ettrick and Selkirk and Douglasdale were greeted warmly by Robert Brus. Upon seeing the prized captives the squire had escorted to his camp, the king openly proclaimed his praise. "That you have earned your spurs this day dear James," he hesitated slightly here for emphasis to his next words, "Lord Douglas!" Robert Brus was obviously pleased; heartily acknowledging the lad's accomplishments with the noted salutation.

James grinned broadly; it felt good to hear the King of Scots address him with the honor he so coveted, to bear his father's noble title of Lord Douglas. Brus so highly valued the squire's personal successes that two celebrations would follow in James' honor he told the lad. With that cherished title he would receive another: chevalier. James was almost overcome with emotion as the king announced he would be dubbed. Lord Robert was giving him public ceremony for not only capturing his noble prisoners brought to camp this day, but also for his exploits in Douglasdale: permanently evicting Lord Clifford from the Douglas barony, opening much of Lanarkshire to the Scots. "After your last rout of de Clifford's garrison, that you razed the castle in Douglas, my good vassal took back his lands and title of inheritance," Robert cheerfully exclaimed. "No more to be James Douglas of Lothiane?" the squire inquired with his silly smirk.

King Robert told him no, that he had justly earned his worth; to carry on the noble heritage of his family, kin to his mother's own Carrick blood. "That your younger cousin will hold of that sobriquet from this day forth," the king declared. James retorted that he could live most happily with that change. While his words were filled with bravado, his eyes were tearing; hidden only by the thick black beard that covered his face disguising his very emotional response. James of Douglas had at long last achieved the one recognition he steadfastly sought; freely granted this day by his king and true lord paramount. "That we shall have the ceremony in your honor in the prime, a dubbing for my new knight, before we venture north to set up camp nearer to our prey: the good John of Lorne," King Robert announced.

Figure VI-Part Three; James, Lord Douglas with full beard to conceal his tender side; shown here with the fur helmet adornment of Sir Thomas Richmond that he acquired some years later at a battle on the Jed

James offered his own congratulations to Lord Robert; the rigorous and impressive campaign led by the now seasoned commander beginning last fall brought the Scots many successes, opening the Highlands to embrace their king. Robert described how they overtook the garrisons of Inverlochy Castle and Urquhart. He then detailed the march into Moraydale, the Black Isle as well. "That we fired the inside of Duffus Castle; then demolished it," offered Robert, giving his view of their assault on the fortress then held by Edward's warden in that district, one Richard Cheyne. "That castle this lad knows well; the ancestral home of my Highland kin," said James. "The great fortress of de Moray built by one named Hugh then passed to Cheyne by way of the female line. This lad so visited that stronghold many years ago with le Hardi," he allowed. "Such victories restored the health most quickly to this laird," Robert replied, referring to his grave illness that winter. "That nearly left Scotland without a king again," interjected the king's chancellor, Abbot Bernard, who had just joined James and Robert in their feasting. "That your own kin, our brave David, the Bishop of Moray, has joined again with us returning from his self appointed exile in Orkney," added the Tironensian priest, once the abbot of Kilwinning in Ayrshire.

Figure VII-Part Three; ruins of Inverlochy Castle, successfully taken by Robert Brus in 1307, a former Comyn stronghold

"That good bishop preaches war most like Robert Wishart; that the English are the Saracens; our war for National Independence the Crusades," he chuckled. "He demanded that the Earl of Ross do penance; that he laid waste the bishop's lands the year he fled to the islands of his ancestors," said the Master. "For excommunication he most threatened should that laird not make good on the damage." James chuckled at the bishop's audacious commands to the earl; how very like the noble men of Moray to take their stand and boldly so he reflected. "So pleased to hear such fair reports from our great warriors of the Highlands," he told them. "More rejoicing too for this lad; to hear that my de Moray kin are back in the fight," he said with bravado. "Our Celtic heritage the rule for others to so follow; to free the lands of our ancestors from the invaders, these men with tails," scoffed the chancellor. James was startled by Bernard's frank words; his usual eloquence was seldom as base as that. Robert smiled; it was this plain honesty combined with the churchman's superior command of verbiage that endeared the Ayrshire abbot to the king. Brus rose from their feasting; he was intending to have some discussions with the captives he allowed. "Your words are true," the king praised his cleric. "The brave battle that we do here is not one for Scots this day but for our very way of life so dear to us that Englishmen most disregard," he said with thoughtful conviction.

James interrupted his departure to ask a question that was most on his mind. "My lord, this lad has heard foul rumors; that our king was most taken to his bed from a poisoning intended to do more than harm; to send Lord Robert to the Otherworld," James said, adding his concern was for the identity of others close to his king; perhaps a traitor was in their midst he suggested. Robert gave a knowing look to his chancellor. "Your observation was not one this king has overlooked. Yet sadly this illness was not a poisoning but the sickness of my body that yet endures; comes and goes with little hope to so control it," he admitted quietly. "Few men will ever know the truth of this but you and our Chancellor Bernard here; my brother Edward most as well." James thanked him for the confidence he shared. Robert then took care to acknowledge his gratitude to young David, son of Sir John and the new Earl of Athol for giving him refuge at the castle of Strathbogie when he took ill at Inverurie. "That laird's sister will one day soon make a good wife for my brother Edward," he announced displaying a more festive mood. The king began to talk now with almost a hint of bravado; he pronounced that there were more victories now before them.

Figure VIII-Part Three; Duffus Castle ruins; site of the motte and bailey castle of the descendants of Freskin the Fleming in Moray, also known as Hugh of Moravia

Then Robert turned his mind to the matter of the prisoners that James had brought to camp. Brus intended to enlist the loyalty of the Lothiane knights; sadly his plans were not readily accepted. The king was surprised by the response of his prisoners, especially the resistance of his nephew Thomas who gave little regard to his proposal. The younger knight was the grandson of the Countess by her first husband Adam Kilconquhar. Disappointed but resolute, the King of Scots ordered Edward's adherent to be taken to more secure confinement, committing him to incarceration until Thomas Randolph changed his mind. Fortunately for the Scots this brave knight did alter his opinion of his uncle and rejoined the fight for National Independence, submitting and pledging fealty to Lord Robert. For his more prudent choice, his uncle rewarded Sir Thomas by making him the Earl of

Moray. Years later this brave and daring soldier redeemed his lapse for his unpatriotic stance; at Bannockburn and later as the regent serving Scotland unfailingly until he made his passage to the Otherworld. James' cousin Alexander held for the English however; not won over to the Scottish cause; he ransomed himself and was later set free.

Figure IX-Part Two; Strathbogie castle was later called Huntly Castle; the ruins above are a site managed today by Historic Scotland

ESSEX-In the midst of the summer heat Hugh had been out tending his healing garden. He had built the square terraced enclosures next to the cook's small planting confine adjacent to the manor kitchen. The aspiring canon had been spending his mornings at the priory farm of the Hospitallers in Stebbing; learning of herb healing and the properties of herbs. The priest at the farm that was in charge of the spicery was very helpful to the lad especially after Hugh shared with him some of his father's writings. The records of Gilley's work in Alchemy and healing were noteworthy, but it was the second journal, the leather bound book that interested the old infirmarer the most. Gilley had encountered a physician while on Crusade; a schooled healer who was traveling in Prince Edward's household and held for a poem; some writings on the properties or resources of herbs, the well known composition of Bishop Odo of Meung. Whenever he could, le Hardi copied sections from the old text into his journal adding his own drawings of plants and other descriptions and conclusions as he went along. The invaluable journal was the one that James had found discarded in the vaulted cellars of Douglas Castle with Gilley's old pestle.

The Crusader seemed captivated by Odo's work and wrote copious notes and comments on the physician's assertions. In reviewing the well respected treatise De Viribus Herbarum, Hugh was extremely impressed; his father was speaking to him from the Otherworld, sharing his knowledge with his son. Hugh reviewed every word that Gilley wrote to accompany

Odo's writings. As he read through the old transcripts with the Hospitaller, he concerned himself with the use of many spices that were not available in Scotland; Arabian oil of myrrh, ginger, clove, aloes and similar commodities could only be obtained by trade for use in the kitchen as well as the apothecary.

Gilley had made notations of suitable substitutions, combinations of herbs common to Scotland that could be used in place of the more exotic and imported herbs whenever possible. His diligence in such entries was an exhaustive effort that fascinated the Hospitaller. He was eager to assist young Hugh; help him to learn what he could from the ledgers. He decided to show the lad how to grow his herbs, helping construct the terraced gardens at his mother's manor. As the one who had purchased the exotic spices and other provisions for his monastery, he was also able to share information on obtaining sources for those items that were not indigenous to their climate. Hugh was excited by the prospect of these new found skills; determined to learn more about healing and incorporate that knowledge into his future work as an Austin canon. Working in tandem with the old Hospitaller, Hugh studied diligently to develop a full understanding of herbal treatments, believing that such information would make him an asset to his brothers, future knights and warriors who would certainly need of his healing ways he mused.

Hugh learned of mordants; mineral salts that would bind colors to cloth so that they were wash-fastness; would not bleed when wet. He poured through lists of healing elixirs, herbal poultices, and blends of spices with alum and honey for even such mundane remedies as the whitening of teeth. "These herbs have such power at their centers," he exclaimed. "So much is there to learn about their many uses and combinations for fair cures!" The aging churchman was pleased with the lad's eagerness to master the knowledge of plants and their properties; seldom does one find a student with such enthusiasm, he reflected. Father John looked forward to their days together and he shared eagerly with the lad. Their friendship grew as the old infirmarer saw joy and purpose return to his quiet life; pleased to be an instrument in the education of a young lad whose intentions were to serve God with his many gifts and talents. The old healer was also hopeful to help inspire the young Scot was his personal dedication. The happiness gleaned from their studies, the excitement shared between the Hospitaller and the young lad, provided each with much needed healing. While the priest taught, Hugh readily absorbed the teachings; their self esteem grew, each filling the void of the other in their daily studies on herbs.

As Hugh led his palfrey around to the stables of Stebbinge Park he encountered Archie. "Dear brother; a challenge to you!" he boasted, trying to get his older brother to meet him in the ring set up by Sir David for competition. The Alchemist in training was turning the age of squire, becoming fourteen this month. Ellie had insisted early on that her Hubicus would be taught the regimen of a knight to be. Fortunately her son's idol and example had become the Bishop of Glasgow; a prelate not adverse to wearing armor when circumstances called him to such duty. "This lad has so many studies," he said, shaking his head wearily, trying to avoid such an encounter right then. But Archie was not easily swayed; his morning was spent learning Latin and Norman French; now he wanted to compete; whether by lance or bow, he did not care he told Hugh. The youngest son's enthusiasm fell on deaf ears; his brother begged him to take back the challenge for the day, he was too tired. Archie could see the strain on Hugh's face; he was trying too hard to learn everything at once he told the aspiring churchman.

"Perhaps tomorrow then," he allowed as Hugh walked off with his horse. "This lad will speak with his mother about our Hugh," Archie told Sir David; the aging knight agreed with his concern, but understood the older lad's relentless compulsion to grasp the knowledge of healing. The time was coming very soon when Archie would join his brother James in Scotland. Hugh was afraid he would be left behind; unable to contribute as a warrior, he needed to find his niche so he too could participate in the family's clandestine support of the war for Scotland's National Independence.

Strange how this knight so lives Sir David reflected with a bemused expression; no longer concerned that he was training warriors to be for Scotland. Archie beckoned him to a chase; riding the aging destrier of Sir David, he would challenge the old soldier to lance the ring, that he might learn more of tilting in the process. Sir David accepted the ploy; he loved teaching his skills to these aspiring squires and knights. As they rode round to the training enclosure Sir David built behind the stables they encountered Maudie's son Andrew. He was finishing his chores as groom for the day. "A contest of lance the rings would be just the thing," he replied excitedly to Archie's invitation. True to her word, Ellie insisted young Andrew be trained with Archie to become a squire, then a knight as was her promise years ago to the loyal Douglas nurse. Lady Bagot could not pay in coinage for their service but she could offer what no other would; an opportunity to elevate his station to a freeholder and knight.

Sir David was riding a new charger today; recently able to relinquish his own war-horse to Archie in favor of another destrier. James had acquired the noble horse last spring on one his of daring raids. He sent the war-horse to Fawdon as a special gift for his mother's loyal and long serving knight, Sir David, hoping he would accept the animal as his own. James was grateful to the English knight; Sir David had found the squire several Hobini, the horse of preference for his guerilla warfare in the Forest. This charger was his way of thanking the old knight; repaying him for the kind effort.

The irony fell upon Sir David now that he began to chuckle out loud; this Essex knight so acquired mounts for the enemy of Edward that now he rides the war-horse once of de Clifford. A charger lost most reimbursed; paid for with coinage from King Edward's treasury; his vassal so rewarded for his loyal service, all in the pursuit of one name James! So this is what the war is most about, he laughed; finding humor in the situation. James was making his name well known to Edward these days; that the new laird of Douglasdale was filling the king's rolls of the pipe: horses lost to *James Douglas;* chargers killed in pursuit of *James of Duugelass*; destriers and beasts of burden lost to those lying with *Sir James Duglas*. Yet what Edward Caernarvon and Robert de Clifford did not know was that some of the spoils of these Scottish victories were finding their way to Stebbinge Park!

Ellie was calling to them now; beckoning them; *come the noo*! When Hugh, Archie, and Sir David with Andrew in tow were all in the great hall they recognized the recently arrived guests; Thomas Chaunceler, the son of Sir Thomas, the vassal of Willelmi. He had ridden down from Fawdon with another lad from Northumbria. Ellie led them all into the withdrawing room, including Ana who was bringing in good wine and some platters of food. Closing the heavy oak door behind them, Ellie's smile broadened as she excitedly began to read aloud. "Our James is most a knight!" Sir David's eyes moistened; Hugh's face beamed; while Archie proclaimed loudly, "Saor Alba!" His mother stopped reading to quiet her youngest son; to quickly subdue his youthful enthusiasm, cautioning his words, "That we are still in Essex," she said with an admonishing grimace.

Ana was thrilled and begged to learn more of the details of the adoubment. "That our James writes there was little time for great ceremony. He barely found a white robe to wear; perhaps the one he found was even the robe of a Cistercian monk he writes; teasing us this lass is sure of it!" she chuckled. Everyone in the withdrawing room was laughing at this admission; they could vividly see James' smirk as he related the tale. The Douglas' nemeses over the years, the mischief making monks of Melrose were called the white monks, Cistercians who wore the simple white robes. To picture James wearing such a robe in ceremony, a substitute for the normal white tunic of a knight to be in such adoubements, was hilarious to everyone.

Ellie continued with James' regaling of the solemn event. "Bathing was most limited to the wee burn near our campsite; to cleanse this humble body as best I could." His mother giggled, remembering the scented bath she gave him at Fawdon; far more in likeness to the ablutions for a dubbing she mused. She continued to read as James had written more. "That this lad followed his father's ways, prayed the night through; asking God for his blessing that this humble servant might be worthy of the honor." Archie wanted to know why he had to bathe in the burn. Sir David explained that the ceremony was of great importance; "to wash away the felony of life before this day; to open his heart most chaste and true, to defend his God, his king, and his family with strong mind and true conviction."

Ellie continued carefully, using James' own words and not her own. "That this lad did fast and pledge his faith that night. To the wee hours of the prime I spoke with God; our father too. I said my words proudly to Sir William; to give my thanks for his good writings as well: The Art of Chivalric Warfare, that so prepared me for this day." Ellie had to pause; her eyes were overflowing with tears to recall William's treatise that he wrote for James on a knight's responsibilities the first day he began his training as a page. "The dubbing took place in the presence of a good priest and many supporters of our king, prayers were said as Lord Robert gave this lad a new sword; perhaps from an English noble as it was quickly fashioned from some booty for the very purpose of this fine ceremony, so this lad was told." Ellie was laughing heartily from his last words; she could just picture his silly smirk as he wrote down the last sentence. "For such a solemn ritual with so serious a charge, our good James has found his time for the joys of humor," she said knowingly.

Sir David told the younger lads about the use of a new sword; not often given but an option for a king to so decide. The remaining ceremony was always the same; that James would gird himself, and then sheath the sword. Ellie read the rest of the description, still giggling; to think of James trying to be circumspect; knowing he would respect the ritual but with the circumstances of wartime, everything was makeshift at best and often humorous. "That this lad can so assure you; I was discreet in every effort; proper in all degrees." He then elaborated further; told them how he kneeled and received the blow; a cuff of hand from his king to proclaim him a knight. "Then my cousins were allowed to put the spurs upon me." In James' typical fashion he allowed as how the origin of these spurs was rather dubious as well; perhaps to come from an English vassal of Lord Edward, now with God he speculated wryly. Archie interrupted them. "Mother, pray what so happened with the spurs of our dear father?" he asked. Ellie sighed and solemnly told them that when William was first imprisoned by de Percy, his spurs were removed to put his legs in fetters; then stolen from him by the vassals of that English lord. "Life has its fair way," she told them wistfully for now James had spurs from another knight; a soldier who no longer needed spurs.

The proud mother thanked Thomas and his fellow squire for coming all the way to Essex with the letter. Such messages were gratefully received she told them and rewarded the lads with coinage and some gifts for his father back in Fawdon. Archie was excited as he blurted out his plans. "Our knight will need a squire now; three horses and more armor that this lad can so provide," he boasted. Ellie was not surprised nor upset by his response. The good news of James' knighthood surely meant the promotion of Archie to his squire in Scotland was eminent. As she looked around the withdrawing room at Stebbinge Park she realized that Hugh's departure was not far behind Archie's leaving for Scotland. The canon would be in the kingdome of his homeland before long. She looked down at Gilley's seal ring and just held it to her breast as she silently prayed to her loving knight in the Otherworld. "Protect our lads dear William, for their mother can no longer do this. That they will be in our Scotland; our sons carrying on the fight of le Hardi against the son of the murdering pagan despot; I know you will my Gilley, dear knight most loved and missed," she said quietly as Ana followed with a definite "Amen."

Figure X-Part Three; an antique engraving of Little Dunmow Priory church in the author's collection

"That there is still some daylight left, this lass will go tell father of our good news," she said intending to ride to Little Dunmow Priory and visit her husband's grave. She invited the Northumbrian lads to stay for a few days; that she would have a letter to send back to her son; gifts for their father for his kindness to send them to Essex. What she did not reveal to her lads was that she was writing a response to another letter that arrived this day; a missive from Alexander de Lindsay suggesting that Archie come and join them in Ayrshire, to serve their household. Ellie had a lot on her mind and needed time to think. She had the groom saddle her old mare, Winter Rose; her favorite palfrey had not been available for riding for some time as the strains of age nearly bowed one of her tendons. Today the two old friends were happily making their way along the familiar cart paths of Stebbinge Park.

Ellie noted with approval as her mare resumed her proud and nearly perfect gait of years past. They ambled together to the priory church with the silly Deerhound tagging along. Ellie was in her glory; the day's sun was warming her face and made her feel happy. Riding the familiar gait of her Winter Rose, Eleanora recalled those early days when she and Gilley first took their amblers out together as *Sir William and Lady Eleanora of Duglas*. They were staying then at Bothwell. Their cousins the de Morays had left Lanarkshire and returned to their manors in the Borders to give the newly wedded Douglases some private time together at that glorious castle on the Clyde in Lanarkshire.

Figure XI-Part Three; Bluebells in an ancient churchyard, Isle of Mann

It was the late spring in 1288 and the couple had stopped one day to rest and enjoy their good wine and meat pies. William drew her down from her horse, bringing her close, face to face that their noses almost touched as he held her up in the air. "You know dear wife that you are my own sweet Winter Rose; your love for this humble knight so treasured, to bloom in the winter time of my life," he said softly. "That I will love you always and most true, my pledge to you." He drew her closer still and they kissed deeply and for a very long time, like the newly married couple that they were. Ellie remembered how she loved his caring ways; listening to his words and his sweet sentiments; they were shared almost in ritual followed by a special memory to cherish. "That I will always think of you when I see the Winter Rose," he promised her. His kindnesses she treasured so; but alas she had a dream last night and it was very real!

Lady Douglas smiled discretely to herself; remembering every detail of the vision, the true visit that she had; the brief but poignant encounter with her Gilley. Her husband was as vibrant and alive to her then as he had ever been. She held his hand as they sauntered through the Park in Douglas and she felt the warmth and power of his physical embrace. She realized with surprise that she was not afraid; Lord Will had told her they would not be trifled with, on a special journey in God's safety. Ellie sighed deeply, back in the present as she rode her Winter Rose to the priory. But in her mind Lady El was enveloping herself, filing her senses with her memories of William. The love she felt from that vivid dream engulfed her; the touch of his caring embrace felt like a mantel of soft ermine about her nakedness. How sweetly the vision stirred her to recall his comforting ways. As she arrived at the priory she turned to notice that her two sons had been following at a small distance behind; her escorts. Ellie chuckled, realizing that she had not even noticed them, being so involved with her reverie of her own sweet knight. She was turning forty this year; eight more years is all that Gilley had in this life she mused; wondering what her future held.

Figure XII-Part Three; interior courtyard Bothwell Castle; once the stronghold of the de Morays it was held by de Valence for Edward until October 1307

PASS OF BRANDER-Robert Brus was moving his forces slowly westward into the territory of Lorne's Highlanders and Loch Awe. The lairds of Lorne held of three castles there, Dunstaffnage on the sea where Loch Linnhe meets the Firth of Lorne and two other fortresses on Loch Awe. From the successful Moraydale campaign the King of Scots had been gathering followers by the hundreds to where he could count his men at arms now in the thousands. His brother Edward had taken his leave for

Galloway some weeks before. The king's army had become some eight thousand strong; joined in smaller numbers by the retinue of bowman from the Ettrick and the armed foot and horse from Lanarkshire, all under the command of Sir James of Douglas, his newly dubbed knight. Douglas vassals were a hardy lot. The archers traveled in light armor; wearing gambesons and hauberks of mail, sometimes leather. These men at arms were hunters of the Forest turned warriors for Scotland; bare legged soldiers riding the smaller agile horses like the Hobini. These brave Celtic warriors who read the lands like huntsmen searching their prey could traverse the braes at lightening speed; climb to the mountain tops like sheep; move through the glens with stalwart agility that they seemed to vanish in the sea mist when pursued by the enemy.

The king had received word that the laird of Lorne was setting forth a surprise attack as he and his men made their way down Glen Lochy through Dalwally to the imposing view of Brander. With his scouts and lieutenants the king decided that the pass was the obvious location for a rout; the very method of his victory at Glen Trool, he mused. "That this southern route is most convenient for our Lorne to set his ambuscade for unsuspecting Scots," he told them. James agreed and offered to take some men at arms to the formidable slopes of Ben Cruachan. "To find the location of Lorne's Highlanders; that we will go most higher like the wild goats of Arran," he said with a grin. "Perhaps to chase them down into the seas," he suggested with boyish enthusiasm for the arduous task in front of him. This warfare was to James' liking; he enjoyed the demanding strategy; the treachery of the challenge. But unlike the king's brother, James was not one to accept outlandish dares. He would bravely lead his men to do the most stirring of feats but never without first sizing up the alternatives for a safer method.

While the Scots were reviewing their strategy, John of Lorne was convalescing on his vessel in the Loch Awe; arrogantly planning to watch his Highlanders assault Lord Robert's contingency and destroy the rebels. He had sent many of his Argyll men into the shoulders of Ben Cruachan, overlooking the footpaths that narrowed to such small distances to only allow single file advancement through the track. While Lorne's armed foot were well entrenched on the southern slopes, Brus dispatched some of his Moray Highlanders along with the men of Ettrick under the command of Sir James of Douglas to move in the early hours of the prime. Under the cover of sea mist these brave Scots moved to still higher reaches of the mountain to lay in wait on a vaulting craig imbedded in the defying outstretched cliffs. With him James took several good leaders and knights, including the redoubtable Sir Alexander Fraser; Sir William Wiseman, a good man of Moray and old recruit to Robert's cause; and another knight Andrew Gray. As the newly dubbed Lord Douglas lead his men up the winding slopes, they found the location of John of Lorne's soldiers; stationed in wait; ready to surprise the King of Scots.

As was their plan, the men of the Forest rode further, following the sheep tracks up the face of Ben Cruachan. When they reached their position they set their fires for their griddles. The Scots grabbed their iron cooking utensils once secreted under their saddles and cooked their bannocks, unobtrusively feeding their hunger in preparation for their impending battle. When the sea mist lifted from the warmth of the sun's glare Robert could detect their position by the wafting of smoke rings from their camp fires. When sure of their location, the king would sound the horn to battle and begin making his way into the pass. James did not stop to set camp with his men; he continued to move stealthily, confidently to even greater heights that looked down upon the Argyll warriors. He set out the watch and dispatched some good men of Moray to detect the armaments and positioning of Lorne's would be attackers.

Figure XIII-Part Three; rugged Highland view; Loch Linnhe looking south to Glen Coe

Waiting for the sunrise James Douglas talked of his philosophy; shared his wisdom with the soldiers that followed him up into the wilds of Ben Cruachan. "This lad so knows our purpose here is right and true," he began. "Most like our Bishop David, who preaches of the importance of such battles that we do; *the Crusade for Scotland's king and law*." He elaborated on the reasons for war and when such encounters were justified. "Our God does so expect us all to have great courage; to fight for what is ours to have, that was so wrongly taken from us. Our charge to keep that we must so direct our minds and hearts to follow with our sword in mighty search of God's own truth for us. That we have been most sent here to protect where other's fail to so defend; we are Scots and honor those who have died supporting our great cause with our own brave course." James explained freely his own driving force; he told those who did not know about his father, that his martyred end was the son's incentive to do better, exceed his own accomplishments with others more astounding than the first.

Figure XIV-Part Three; medieval village reenactment at Linlithgow Peel by Fire and Sword; battle sites included camp followers, workers who performed tasks such as preparing food or repairing armor for the knights, their squires and other men at arms

    James made his rounds in the camp of his followers. He shared in their ritual of bannock and joked with his men at arms to keep them relaxed as they waited anxiously for the sound of the king's horn; Robert's battle cry to begin their siege on the men of Argyll. His men at arms trusted him; followed the knight for his core values. James epitomized a leader who knew the necessity of loyalty up as well as down the rank of command.

    When he had spoken with everyone he retuned to his private council and reflected on his strategy for battle. The brisk mountain air piqued his senses; the sound of the mavis overhead reminded him that he was not alone; those in the Otherworld that had fought and gone before him were watching, perhaps to offer some guidance he mused. His mind wandered but not to the battle so shortly at hand. Instead his thoughts turned to the blonde haired lady, disguising herself as a soldier in the pheasant woods of Ayrshire. James surprised himself; in the many months since first he joined with Lord Robert, more than two years ago, he had never considered the private life of a soldier: a bride for his bed, a family of his own he thought were unobtainable.

    Then his thoughts turned to another time, lang ago, when on hunt with his father, just before le Hardi was arrested by de Percy and taken prisoner.

They were discussing Sir William's decision to escape to Brabant or France with his family, taking them to safety. His father had explained that he would rather a knight-errant be than to seek the refuge of foreign soil; *'but I found true love with Eleanora'* the old Crusader confided. James had determined that to stay alive and remain an adherent of Scotland's king and law, he must never allow himself the luxury of falling in love. Now as his gaze became lost in the sea mist he felt a stirring, deep within him a yearning for a simple touch; a feeling so alien but so desirable that it almost made him giddy. He watched the hovering clouds of heavy dew seep over Glen Nant, enfolding their gentleness about the jutting shores of Loch Awe; James was in a reverie with the fair Lady Joanna at his side. Then a distant groan of an aging horn jolted him to the present: King Robert's first signal was being sounded! What foolishness is this daydream, he sputtered reproachfully.

Figure XV-Part Three; the wild Highland landscape before entering into the Pass at Brander along the River Awe

The three knights sent by Robert to assist James and his archers in their enterprise approached his secluded position while his squire was bringing his Hobini, saddled and ready. For the first time since Methven James was riding into battle without his usual preparedness. The Douglas knight had made it his practice to review the battle plan and traverse the site in private reconnaissance. But this time he was lost in a fool's dream of enchantment, he chided himself. But the vision of the Ayrshire woman filled his nostrils with a scent he could not seem to shake and it baffled him. As the first knight spoke, he quickly regained his warrior's demeanor and forgot about the lady he had been visiting in the Lowlands of his reverie.

"Sir James," said Sir Alexander Fraser with quiet concern, "that our good king proceeds yet towards the pass!" James told him to ready his armed foot yet hold his flank until the archers took their positions; word would be given when to descend against the enemy he cautioned. "Be patient good knight," he said in full battle mode. "We are fortunate to yet have surprise to our advantage." The second knight under James' command was William Wiseman; late the sheriff of Elgin for Edward, he was a tenant of the de Morays and now firmly back in Robert's camp. "These Highlanders are too confident for their position," he observed. "Unsuspecting of our attack we will meet a frightened army if we wait the moment," Sir William added, agreeing with James' contention that hurrying into the fray would be a mistake. They must await Robert's second call before giving away their position, he allowed.

Figure XVI-Part Three; another view of Brander Pass looking back towards Loch Awe; James' charge would have been from the upper left of the image down the shoulder of Ben Cruachan

    With unobtrusive movement the Douglas men at arms mounted their horses; some rode destriers, others Hobini while many bowmen were yet on foot. Looking down the hillside James could see that the sound of battle horn had rousted the Argyll soldiers from their hiding places. Turning towards Loch Awe he noted how the sunrise was melting through the mist, revealing several cogs and other galleys pulling up anchor from their positions near the shore. The Lord of Lorne must be on one of those vessels James surmised. Good that he will see how fast we foil his plans for victory he said under his breath. The second signal of attack was given; Robert's battle cries were heard echoing through the glen as his armed horse began to make their way through the narrow pass of Brander.
    The men of Lorne responded; armed warriors appeared where the willow herb had sauntered peacefully on the shoulder of Ben Cruachan. The purple flowered greenery once pointing majestically to the skies, dancing softly to and fro in the Highland winds was now being trampled; the onslaught of Lorne's Highlanders, soldiers loyal to King Edward were seeking vengeance against the invading King of Scots. The English adherents began to propel their stones and boulders towards their captive rivals in the pass. There by the waters edge of the River Awe these Argyll

warriors sought to detain their victims and begin their perilous assault, riding confidently down the shoulder of Ben Cruachan, to finish them off.

Victory at hand was what the band of Argyll attackers surmised as they made their way towards Brus' retinue; until another shrieking horn bellowed unbridled fear into their hearts. James had reached for his father's oliphant; as he blew on the ornately carved ivory the old Crusader's battle horn voiced terror from the depths of the hollowed tusk. Lorne's Highlanders were stunned; some braver souls turned to ride up the hill and do battle with the Scots. "A Douglas! A Douglas!" shouted James; his men began the fevered chant as well. The swooshing sounds of arrows taking flight paralyzed the Highland armed foot; holding them strangely in their place until the thud of successful strikes shook them from their reverie. The deafening sounds, pounding hooves of ascending armed horse and the Douglas war-cries resounding through the glen were demoralizing the Argyll men that they panicked; many riding to the south and west, crossing the only bridge that led to the other side of the River Awe. Some of Lorne's men at arms riding towards their assailants met the fierce warriors face to face. James' nimble retinue undaunted by the steep incline and treacherous bearings, with swords held in the ready was glad to do battle with the enemy. Knowing their archers had prepared the way, felling some and scattering others of their opposition in frightened confusion, the Douglas men at arms were confidant in their attack.

Figure XVII-Part Three; these stones near Brander Hotel are believed to be the location where the dead were laid to rest after the great battle

James was leading the way, the first to come in contact with a sorry knight trying hard to maneuver his destrier on the craigy cliffs of Ben Cruachan. The gallant horse was no match for a crafty Hobini and the young Douglas knight. Hollering the war-cry, his old standard held in the middle guard the warrior fearlessly made for the Argyll soldier. As the two combatants grew closer James sensed the advantage and with a strong left to left cut he made contact with the shield of his opponent only to watch the charger lose his footing in the rubble of the hillside. He quickly turned the agile Hobini to face the knight in a second attack; this time his sword met a forearm; the blood spurting out from under leather armor indicated a serious injury had been rendered. The battle was fierce around them; soldiers were fighting for angled ground, chargers stumbled and took injuries before their riders felt the contact of an opponent's weapon. The undaunted Highland hills had seen such combat before and barely yawned for the experience; but the Scots were storming their opponents in a cacophony of war whoops and clanking iron. Screams of injured warriors reverberated; Lorne's men taking more of their share of severed limbs and life threatening cuts from the relentless swords of Douglas men at arms.

Figure XVIII-Part Three; Dunstaffnage Castle ruins; a castle of enclosure with a massive curtain wall, held by the laird of Argyll in 1308; managed by Historic Scotland

Far below this battle line the blur of retreating Highlanders in flight could be seen making their way westward. They were hoping to take the only bridge standing on the River Awe and destroy it before King Robert and his men could use it for their crossing. As James rode above the fray to sense the progress of the battle he saw a flash of Lorne pennons, Argyll men at arms rushing the banks of the waters below followed by the hot pursuit of Brus' armed horse and foot crossing the Awe fast at their heels. Many of the Scots were already across the bridge by now. James smiled broadly; Robert Brus was leading his men in splendid glory through the Pass of Brander, no longer detained by the enemy they made their way in symbolic gesture, opening all of Argyll to the King of Scots. As James and his sergeants rode through the pass towards the bridge they stopped to supervise the burying of their dead; stones were brought to cover the graves to insure their sanctity from wild animals.

The marching army continued towards the heart of the laird of Lorne's authority besieging Dunstaffnage Castle and taking it for their king in the best of all ways. Sir Alexander of Argyll seeing the Scottish army approach sent an entreaty of surrender which Robert Brus readily accepted. The Argyll lord came to the king's peace and pledged his fealty, happily agreeing or so he said to attend a council with the lairds so present in the king's retinue. Sir John of Lorne the son of this aging nobleman took flight on his cog and made his way to safety in one of his other fortresses nearby; to meet with Brus another day he vowed to the English king.

Figure XIX-Part Three; Ardchattan Priory ruins under the management of Historic Scotland; site of the last Parliament where Scottish Gaelic was spoken

The battle at Brander was at an end and the Scots were in triumph. Sir Alexander was allowed to keep many of his vast estates except for the strategic fortress of Dunstaffnage. This stronghold was now deemed a royal castle; provisioned with the king's own garrison. The successful campaign through the fall of 1308 meant that the civil war in Scotland was drawing to an end. Robert and his army would remain in the Highlands but before James and his retinue took their leave for the Lowlands the king held a council; a meeting of his lairds and cleric leaders yet with him in Argyll at the Ardchattan Priory. Here Robert Brus granted charters and took pledges of those who came to the king's peace. A truce followed with King Edward so Robert ordered a Parliament to convene the following March at St. Andrews. Sir Alexander of Argyll promised he would so attend there as well. As the Scots spoke their Gaelic and tended to the business of the realm the council marked the last recorded session where the language of the court was spoken in that noble tongue.

BLACKHOUSE TOWER MID OCTOBER-James, Lord Douglas arrived at the stronghold of his ancestors near Craig Douglas expecting to find his mother and brothers waiting his arrival. But except for the household servants and the farrier and grooms, the manor was deserted. He brought with him some of his Douglasdale adherents and posted a watch with some of their number as soon as he arrived. A few of the squires in his retinue had only heard tales of le Hardi and his stronghold near Selkirk; this was their first excursion to the Forest and the wilds of the eastern Marches. James endeared himself to his men for his kind ways and generous spirit. But his largess was not limited to the spoils of battle; he shared his private time with them as well.

This day he decided to take the younger lads with him on a leisurely course of travel around Craig Douglas towards Yarrowford. He told them of the Celtics ways, showing them the Douglas stones, a stone circle left by the ancient ones near his family's stronghold; then to the Yarrow Stone some miles further east. There were other sacred sites in the area he boasted, but these two were particularly satisfying for him to share with his special followers, many of whom lost their own fathers at a very young age. "My father le Hardi would take us to these monuments of the ancient ones; teaching Douglas sons the ways of our ancestors that would serve us well in the future days."

Figure XX-Part Three; Yarrow Stone

Two days had passed before anyone else joined James at the tower stronghold. He had just returned from the morning hunt, leaving the stables when he noticed four riders under the familiar banners of de Lindsay. A broad smile crossed his face as Uncle Alex greeted his kin. "Is it most true, Argyll has come to peace with our king?" asked Sir Alex. James told him about the campaign, the battle in Brander Pass as he beckoned the old warrior into the great hall of Blackhouse. "What brings you here dear Alex?" asked the Douglas laird. "A matter of a squire to join now our household," he said with a silly laugh. "One Archibald of Douglas, my son in law to be!" he exclaimed, a mischievous grimace dominating his countenance as he spoke.

James looked perplexed by the pronouncement; he had no word of a proposal let alone an impending marriage for his youngest brother. Sir Alex shook his head as he explained the willful actions of his daughter Beatrice. "This lass has so called for his compliance with a strange practice; to ask him for his acceptance to a scheme of marriage, the Leap Year holding her true in this proposal to become his bride." James recalled his mother mentioning to him of a lawful practice some twenty years now in effect in Scotland; permitting a woman to propose of marriage, but only in the leap year when the second month held of twenty nine days and no fewer. "Your Beatrice has so given herself in marriage to the wee Archie?" he asked in utter disbelief. Sir Alex was laughing that full hearted barrel laugh that he enjoyed doing as much as others liked hearing while he nodded in agreement.

"This old knight is most old fashioned in his ways; the words of Dame Beatrice when her contrived assertion was most questioned by her father; the proposal to her Henklebaldicus, her 'love for all eternity' as she so informed me," he continued finding humor in the arrangement even now. James ordered wine and feasting as he sat in the great hall; his head was spinning with the news. As his squire poured the wine from the baluster he grinned at his private thoughts; the lady Joanna is a fair lass, perhaps she might accept the hand of this Scottish knight and baron he mused; surprised at his sudden interest in such matters. "Another Douglas wedding will chance to follow in one more year as well," he allowed as he brandished a silly smirk. Uncle Alex expressed his startled response then relinquished a knowing grin. He knew that James had been frequenting the manor of Logan near his Ayrshire manor at Barnweill, but his nephew had seldom spoken of his ultimate ambitions in that endeavor.

Suddenly the heavy oak doors of the tower burst open to the ebullient entrance of the new de Lindsay squire, the wee Archie. The Deerhound followed, quickly finding his way to the feasting table; as Hugh escorted Ellie into the great hall. The two were already talking excitedly about their plans returning next spring to Scotland. "James!" shouted Archie. "Good knight, we are most here to listen to your words of great victories. Saor Alba!" he shouted. Ellie shook her head; but they were safely among other patriots so she decided not to suppress the exuberance of her youngest son. "Mother," exclaimed James as he went to hug her. "Good sir," she said giggling as she addressed him with his new titles of esteem, "our dear knight and laird." Ellie was cooing as she held her son in her arms, she was so proud. She pulled back only to look at the black beard that had grown over his face; a thick mass of curly hair that tickled her nose that she teased him. "My son the menacing terror to the English," she chided. "Do not worry; this lass knows your tender side." Archie was interrupting her. "James, this lad is betrothed!" he declared with a manly strut. The laird of Douglas offered his blessing on his brother's future plans with Dame Beatrice; while keeping his own matrimonial endeavors secret for the moment.

Hugh was bringing in some of their personal belongings, including his father's healing box and manuscripts as he came to greet his older brother. "Good James," he said smiling ear to ear. "Fair news do I so have as well. Soon will this lad embrace the teachings of the Augustinians; to take my place with other noble Douglas men devoted to the kirk." Ellie elaborated further on his bold pronouncement; "That so well has our Hugh acquired the knowledge of divine literature that the priest at Little Dunmow Priory suggested he might take his vows at an early age." James congratulated the youthful canon to be on his tenacity at scripture. "And a healer too I hear," he added with a hearty embrace. Hugh regaled him with the journals of their father including the notes he had written on the *De Viribus Herbarum*, the writings of Odo. "Our Hospitaller at the priory farm in Stebbing has gleaned anecdotes most interesting including many cures that our dear father's inscriptions in this good ledger so revealed," he explained with pride. "Father writes with humor most as well," Hugh added with his own version of the Douglas smirk as he opened to the text where Gilley had recorded his convalescence at Fawdon and the methods of healing he felt were valuable, noting others he discarded.

James read his father's words so everyone could hear, beginning with le Hardi's first surprising determination that ran contrary to the widely accepted practice of bleeding. *"Leech-craft has been found faulty from this lad's experience,"* Gilley wrote. James interjected that le Hardi first put forth his conclusion then he backed it up with his first hand evidence:

"Each incident of being bled has left one William questioning the need for such a practice; this squire had most decided to eliminate the use of it for true recovery. With eleven days gone by since last this patient held for such a purpose, strength in great quantity has most returned to me. This event is not mere coincidence but rather an end devised of faithful watch of my fair activity. No longer will this healer hold for proper leech-craft as a cure. The Celts have not contrived such practice so says the speywife; this humble squire most agrees with her from such recording of my days here. A fair experiment's results declare no more use of bleeding that it fouls the body; a squire most weak that he succumbs to **take his passage to the Otherworld; the cure more deadly than the sickness it was sent to remedy, I do fear."**

Ellie was listening attentively; she chuckled at Gilley's last words of sarcasm; how so like him she mused. And she also took time to reflect on his valuable assertions; she had not known that her husband had recorded his studies of healing in such deliberate detail. "How so like our father to conclude his observations by proclaiming of an outcome most different from the given truths accepted by the learned ones," she said; amazed yet again by his ability to effect their lives in the present though gone from them and their world for more than ten years.

Figure XXI-Part Three; view from Fawdon Farm, part of the old barony of Fawdon; William le Hardi recovered here in 1267 after nearly having his head cut off in a violent raid led by Gilbert de Umfraville with his marauders from Redesdale

"What other knowledge has Lord Will to share with us?" she asked. Hugh told her that Sir William wrote down details of the food and sustenance he craved as his wounds healed; how he wanted to devour rare commodities of fruit from foreign lands such as oranges from Spain. "Lord Douglas described tasines that made him ill; others that worked to clear his nausea," he continued to elaborate. James was extremely impressed. "That our Hugh can proclaim his most gracious and honored respect for our father that he so continues his studies of his healing ways," said the Douglas knight, in awe of his brother's choice for his life's work. Hugh gave him an impish grin and added his teasing words. "Our good brother and fair chevalier will need an infirmarer to watch over him; better than a bowman in battle," he declared alluding to Archie's prowess in that choice of weaponry. "A good priest so trained can serve his knight in both virtues: spirit and body."

The wee squire took umbrage with Hugh's inference that his work was more valuable to their older brother; he blurted his indignation out loud in a verbal assault on the aspiring canon. "Dear Hubicus that for this squire's protecting of his knight would you not have a breathing man to heal!" James rolled his eyes upward in mocked indignation as he threw Ellie a knowing glance. "Good Sirs, this knight is through with strife between his brothers; there will be a truce this laird has so determined. You are most residing on the lands of Douglas and I your lord paramount command it so! It is done!" Ellie was roaring in laughter as she watched her older son discipline his younger siblings; each one competing for their laird and brother's attention at the expense of the other.

Ana came in with the kitchen servants, bringing in more wine and platters of roasted pheasant that wafted with delightful scents. "Perhaps some game will quiet you good lads," she chuckled. Sir Alex was chatting with Ellie about the war; he wanted to know what was going on in England. "That dear Edward's choice for regent in his absence shall be his beloved Piers Gaveston; so much gossip and foul rumors at Westminster," Ellie said with a deeper meaning in her voice. "This Earl of Cornwall though married to Lady Margaret, the cause of much resentment; the barons of England most united to rid themselves of this silly fool, now the king's new lieutenant in Ireland. That Edward had this lord to carry the very crown for this new king; paying more attention to his clandestine lover than his queen and lawful wife; this grievance the contention of most nobles at court."

Sir Alex thought that Edward Plantagenet had dealt with such a problem before. "Was not this strange fellow banished from England?" he asked. Lady El responded that indeed he was; his very return the king's own rule in dire defiance of his lords. Ellie also told them that Edward Caernarvon had begged the pope to intercede with the English bishops on behalf of the excommunicated Gaveston. "The petty fool this king asks of favors of the Holy one yet he will not so entertain the pope's request to release our good Scots, the bishops Lamberton and Wishart, that they might yet come home," she scoffed. "That we know of Lamberton; most practiced in the well known virtues of your family," Ellie teased as she turned to Sir Alex. "Brandishing the golden tongue of good persuasion like a knight with sword; that bishop has yet gained his enlargement and without the help of others it would seem!" she said wryly, adding that William Lamberton renewed his pledge of fealty to Lord Edward. "That our good friend and patriot Robert Wishart held of such a talent to convince the king of his fidelity; sadly he yet remains held in the confines of Porchester Castle," she concluded.

"You should know as well; the good sound of coinage jingling in a coffer full accompanied the good Bishop's ceremony of kissing the gospels, promising his loyalty to Edward," observed Archie. Hugh chuckled and shook his head at his brother's plain words. "This lad will most explain. Bishop Lamberton has so agreed to pay 6000 marks in a bond to Edward, to gain his freedom while he yet remains in the bishopric of Durham for some time." James eyes widened in hearing the grand sum the bishop pledged yet admitted he would have paid the same to gain his own liberty. "This knight is most encouraged; that we had only learned that Lamberton was seeking enlargement to the confines of Northamptonshire; to have secured himself to the bishopric of Durham is exciting news, a short excursion on the Tweed and he is home!" James said, ebullient at the thought. Hugh then advised him that there was still some hope for Bishop Wishart; word had come to the Austin canons at Little Dunmow from their brethren priests at St. Mary's, the priory at Southwick. The Scottish prelate told them he expected to gain his freedom within months; taking his leave of prison walls for France where the Pope had moved his court from Rome. "Then for this dear friend and prelate of renown, to Bishop Wishart that he might gain his freedom quickly; my prayer this day," James proclaimed.

After some time at feasting James excused himself and beckoned Ellie into the withdrawing room. "Dear mother as most every day now the lord de Ferrers loses more of his manors in our Scotland, would you allow this humble knight to so provide a dower?" he asked. Ellie told him no at first. "Our father's Fawdon has just recently afforded more in payments on the balance of our fine. Richard de Umfraville was forced to remit another £10!" she said, glowing with pride for her success. "And de Ferrers has granted me some carucates in the manor of Frating for my own in dower rights for the rents from lands most lost in Scotland," she boasted. James did not accept her cheerful retort; he knew she was in need of funds, noticing her surcote was an older one refashioned for the times. "Lady El, what were the words of your dear husband?" he asked lovingly knowing her pride in such matters. "To share your burdens truthfully with one named James," he responded not allowing her to answer.

Ellie bowed her head and her eyes began to tear. "This lass has fought so long and hard and now there is another Chamberlain of Scotland is what I hear." James interrupted her tears. "That King Robert when he so finds a treasury to guard, he will secure a true chamberlain for Scotland; issue writs and assign baronies to his loyal vassals." Ellie replied through peels of laughter; teasing her son for his foolish thoughts. "King Hobbe is going to issue charters; assign dower to an Essex lass?" she asked rolling her eyes in disdain. "Mother, more respect is so required," he said pointedly. "Our first Parliament will so be next March in St. Andrews; then and there will I approach Lord Robert on your behalf should you so desire it."

The widow of le Hardi wanted to accept this offer; with all her heart she wanted to say 'yes' but she could not bring herself to such bold action. To risk all her Essex lands and income was nearly frightening should their country fail; then too, there was the matter of William Bagot. "That I could so address for many reasons to refuse this fair proffer and all of them could be thrown out save one; this lass is married to an English lord," she said sadly. James had strangely forgotten that one point; for Ellie to even receive the income from her dower lands she must come to pledge fealty to King Robert he told her reluctantly; her husband would be required to do the same. "Lord Bagot would be most pleased with that request," she chuckled. James shook his head and chided himself out loud for the thoughtless idea.

"Dear son, that you have been most generous in your kind ways; this lass does so forget herself that she is married to that knight; most foolish to have married so I fear," she whispered. James held her close and told her that her only choice at the time was to accept that marriage contract. Feeling her despair he held her out from his chest that she might see his grimace, the famous Douglas smirk. "Unless you think this lad can so persuade that knight to join with Robert?" he teased her. Before she could respond he said he had another plan. He reached for his coinage and counted out many coins, nearly £3 of them in silver. "The largess of de Valence and Sir John of Argyll has brought much bounty to this knight's coffers," he allowed. "That you will take this and come again in spring to collect the others of your rents most due?" he inquired. Ellie's eyes overflowed in tears as she shook with emotion, sobbing into his manly chest as she thanked him. "Perhaps to buy some finery for the widow of my father," he suggested and she agreed she would. "But such a large sum," she tried to protest the amount but James would hear none of it. He covered her mouth gently with his large rough hand; the gesture reminded her of how Gilley handled such discussions that she began to giggle. "Beast Sholto," she teased and they burst into laughter together.

Returning to the great hall with Lady El on his arm, James was excited to hear Sir Alex telling stories of the raids they held in Passelewe Forest. Archie called out to him. "Come tell us about your battles!" he demanded. "Yes, please entertain us with the tales of the great descendant of Sholto!" Sir Alex quipped. Archie had not heard about this brave warrior and was now very insistent to learn more. "A brave Douglas knight?" he asked. "Why has this squire not so found him among the names of those who held of Douglas charters?" he asked revealing the fact that he had been reading those documents Ellie secreted away for more peaceful times. James told him that every family had their heroes and great myths.

"Our Sholto is not a story so made up!" declared Ellie. "Though many in our clan have told stories of that brave Celtic soldier in service to his king; through the years have some of those tales become entwined, confused with those of other Douglas lairds," she confessed. James drew up more wine and began the tale of Sholto of Duglas as his father had once told him many years ago. He spoke about the great warrior fighting in the Highlands near the lands of Sutherland in Aussinshire. "That he brought a goodly number of his closest followers to fight along side the overlord of Moraydale; though not a king, this laird was very powerful. Men under the leadership of a rival laird and invader to their lands so arrived brandishing spears and maces in their hands to do great harm." For once Archie was too enthralled to interrupt. "Our father told us that the evil laird was called of Bane; but not the Donald Bane that fought against a king of Scotland, some several hundred years most after Sholto lived. This laird was another enemy with a similar yet different sobriquet." Ellie explained how Sholto was unrivaled in his fierce leadership; his combat skills equally impressive that he won the day and praise of the overlord.

"So tell this lad I pray you; why is there no charter with the name of Sholto?" Archie asked again. "Perhaps because the document was lost or never written," James suggested. "Six centuries have passed since then and writing for those early ones was most a chore and not in Latin or in Norman French as we use in our current courts." Ellie assured the lad that Gilley told her that the story of Sholto was true. "Alas he often told us that without the charters for his lands the tales had made their way to legends without substance, confused and amended by the story tellers," she said. "But know this: Sholto lived as the bravest of warriors and you my son so descend from that great soldier." Ellie was adamant that Sholto of Douglas was their true ancestor and great hero. "Yes, this knight is most sure of it as well; if only for your rounded size," teased James, poking fun at Archie's growing girth and extreme height for his twelve years. "This lad will be most taller than you Lord Douglas," he responded readily, "looking down his nose at one named James!" Hugh had enough of Archie's boasting. "Yet kneeling will you be for he is your lord paramount and benefactor," he said wryly. "Enough good sirs!" demanded Ellie.

"Were the lands of Sholto in the Lowlands?" inquired Hugh. Ellie shook her head no and told him that Gilley said he never lived but in the Highlands. "Others of our Douglas ancestors most settled around the Borders; the reason for our charters here in Craig Douglas and in Traquair," she told them. "Family lands with deeds and records dating before the Conqueror, in 1057 are stored in our Douglas charter-chest," she boasted. James was amazed that Ellie knew so much of the history of their lands. "Lady El, our father had most taught you well," he praised her.

She threw off the compliment with a silly grimace and continued. "That the first laird of Douglas was a soldier named William residing near Kelso and the Abbey there; given lands for his service to his king. Our father always told us that the Duffus Clan, powerful barons in Morayshire were our kin as well. The name so taken from the Gaelic much like our own to mean the same as Douglas with slight difference yet about it: black water." James told his brothers that remembering the history was important;

someday if the charters got lost or destroyed there would always be tales for others to hear, told by Douglas storytellers to continue their family's heritage in oral history. "And boast of one Douglas knight feared by all the English, with raven hair and the grey countenance of one Sholto, our dear James?" asked Ellie with a twinkle in her eye. "That brave knight of renown, sure aye!" he chuckled.

Archie still had other questions about their family documents. "And what of Fawdon then?" he asked. "The charters speak of Batayle; was that our father's mother?" he innocently questioned. With those words a huge explosion clamored from the fireplace; a loud crackling noise smacked the air, emanating from the logs burning nearby. Sparks from the disheveled wood and peat seemed to fly everywhere. Squires grabbed for liquids to douse the flames from the burning embers that had taken flight. Ellie and Ana were bent over in laughter; only they were privy to the joke it seemed to the others. "Your father has most spoken to us from the Otherworld with his noble roar," she said still laughing. "The mother of Lord Will was dear Martha; her family was kin to the Earl of Carrick, one named Duncan and well before the Brus family married into that noble line. That lady brought a dowry of the lands in Girvan; some bovates too in Northumbria that you see in our charters." Ellie said. She told them she was surprised this information had not been shared before with her younger sons that she would continue with the story. "Lady Constancia was a Batayle widow who married your grandfather after this lady, she was his second wife. That Sir William had purchased more lands in Northumbria at the encouragement of his king. He now owned lands in Warndon and others in Redesdale including a carucate of Fawdon that he acquired in 1225 from the father in law of Constancia," she explained as she dried her eyes from all the laughing.

"But these lands were not then of English rule; not until a decade and some years later when the pope's court declared that the English king should hold Northumbria as his own," James interjected. "Our poor father had many troubles with the Batayles and the lands they once held. His most relentless opposition was his sorry stepmother and her heirs. She brought a suit of dower most against him, demanding more from our Douglas lands than the one third so allowed to widows, alleging all the while that some lands were being hidden from escheators," he told his younger siblings. Ellie also said that when Edward seized their father's land until he fined for marrying their mother, Constancia's lands were inadvertently taken from her as well; her sons filing a suit of dower posthumously as Constancia was dead, tweaking their father all the more with their greed. Ana chuckled and added, "That dear Sir Gilley most reminded us this night of his foul opinion of the Batayles; his outburst from the fire so burning there. Most amused is this lass that he was overhearing our good conversation from the Otherworld!"

The Douglas squire seemed satisfied at last and now turned his attention to the war. Sir Alex added that he too was eager to hear more about the battles, especially about the one at the pass beside the River Awe. "This knight has turned his eyes to shorter engagements; closer now to the barony of Barnweill," he chuckled. James smiled at his uncle; but he knew the truth of his reticence to join with Brus in Argyll. Sir Alex was still recovering from his last encounter with Robert de Letham in Carmunnock three months ago. The de Lindsay knight was also feeling the pain upon a soldier's body that comes from years of campaigning; his bones ached that some days he could barely seat his palfrey. "And what of your lands of Byres?" interrupted Ellie. Sir Alex told her that all his lands in the Lothianes were now held of Robert de Hastings, "Your own dear kin is laird of that fair manor should you most desire to visit there," he said morosely.

James told his mother that for every manor she lost in Scotland her de Hastings cousins were taking more than double in their wake. "And the others of your lands," she asked quietly, "are they now held by English lords?" Sir Alex added hopefully that the success of Brus in Dumfries had brought him rents again with more to come from the manors that he held near Langholm and Barntalloch. "Yet to regain these lands was too high a price," he said sadly. "For now this knight and father has three sons in Edward's prisons; my David at Devises, far south in Dover, while his younger brothers Reginald and Alexander are yet in Carlisle." Archie was stunned; Hugh and Ellie gasped in shock and despair. "You had not written of their fate," Eleanora said painfully. James told her that good Scots so sentenced and confined were seldom able to notify their families of their location for months, sometimes a year or more.

Their pensive silence was broken by the entrance of Sir David and Maudie's son Andrew. "And who might the lad of great stature now be?" James kidded, knowing that Andrew was joining his own brother Archie in service to Sir Alex. The young Scot was shyly circumspect and bowed appropriately as he respectfully addressed 'Lord Douglas' his long time friend. James rose and embraced the laddie; invited him to join his men in their feasting. Andrew was elated; the generosity of the Douglases was overwhelming, filling the lad with heart-felt emotions. He dare not show his tender side with all these knights of renown sitting now before him Andrew decided as he walked quietly to the other end of the great hall. "Where are you most going and what of that teasing smirk we know so well?" asked the laird, realizing Andrew was holding back, uneasy with his new found status. Archie beckoned the lad to join him. "Come here good friend; you are family to sit with us," he said instinctively. Archie had been taught to know that the Lowland Douglases were feudal lairds but they were also Highlanders in their blood and held for Clan and family as one.

Sir David pulled up a seat near the Douglas sons; eager to enjoy the feasting that yet continued. "What of these foul rumors of a 'Black Knight' that scared de Valence from his seat of power, that Edward called him home again and replaced him?" he quipped. James grinned ear to ear as de Lindsay interrupted, "that you mean our good James?" he asked teasingly as his nephew was laughing to think of Edward's ruthless vassal fleeing Scotland. "That foolish lieutenant of the English king," scoffed the Douglas laird as he grew more caustic thinking of de Valence. "Once to have fallen for his trickery at Methven Woods was enough and more for this lad. For my amusement now I so seek of him to chase his knights of vainglory; confusing and surprising his English men at arms," James said interspersing his terse words with sarcastic tones, "only to spill of their blood and take of their chargers."

Figure XXII-Part Three; parish kirk of Langholm, Dumfries; a de Lindsay manor

The de Ferrers knight was chuckling. "Most happy is this old soldier to have that fair horse," he allowed with an impish shrug. The laird of Douglas' countenance turned into a broad smirk. "Fair justice for our family is it not?" he replied. Ellie told her sons that war had certainly changed her perspective on things. "Our morality most tested; to steal from one and give to the other, forced to disguise our feelings with false words. How sad it is to become what we most hate; as others that speak so falsely, act so with pretense and now we are most like them I fear," she said bitterly. Archie was not content. "Most like the brave Robin Hood of Essex," he said mischievously, "to steal from the English lords yet give to poor Scots from whom they had appropriated it in the beginning, is it not?" Ellie was not so sure anymore she allowed.

James cleared his throat for emphasis; he was speaking softly now that others would listen attentively; to hear his every word. "Our father spoke to us of his truth; God's own truth held here in his heart. That love of his family took him from us in his martyred end; all here most mourn him still." Ellie bowed her head; Ana moved to sit beside her and hold her hand. "We asked only to live in peace; farm our lands and rule our barony with fair administration. But Edward Plantagenet wanted more; he stole from us our lands and chattel, destroyed our father's life. With brave indignation we became his silent opposition. Now we are able to speak out; we do so in our words as well as in our actions. From prayers each day I beg our God for understanding, fearing only the Lord of Heaven; this knight knows our lies are seen for truths in the Otherworld. Forgiveness will be given us; an alliance with our souls and God's own universe will free us from the sins we must commit to survive in this peril."

James looked away and drew in another breath. "Mother, it saddens me so to see you living there in false testimony to a life you most despise. Forgive us all that we have not relieved you of that fate; soon you must come home to live with us; to enjoy the spoils of freedom, to breathe in the very joys of Scotland: feel the sweet dew dampening your fair feet; to relish in the soft embrace of mist laying lightly on your face as you saunter joyously in the prime at Douglasdale. If God does so allow us in our fight to say what we must say and do what it feels most right to do then all will be forgiven in the Otherworld. The second half for each and every life of those most here will be spent in God's own Paradise with our dear father, I do know it."

The great hall became filled with silence as James completed his speech. A hushed stillness flowed through the air while tallow torches flickered in embrace of the young laird of Douglas and his words of eloquence. Ellie thanked her son for his understanding; she confessed her dread of returning to Essex, more each time she took leave of Scotland. "My English friends and kin share none of my feelings that I must keep them to myself. One day we all will be most free again but only from the toil of brave knights of renown and their squires too as you and dear Alex with our Archie, and good Andrew. And dear Hugh to say the words of God for all of us to hear. Thank you James; my heart's desire will I suppress until divine love deems us worthy of the peace we all most seek. This mother and the others here are comforted by your words and secure in your noble deeds that what we do is right. God bless us all." Hugh added an appropriate 'Amen' and most everyone in the great hall that evening quickly followed his example.

DECEMBER 1308-James had ridden west towards Douglasdale with his smaller retinue; two squires and some bowman from the forest with some loyal vassals from Lanarkshire who were returning home with them. The doughty Scots had another victory to celebrate; the recent taking of the castle at Rutherglen had further solidified their control of Lanarkshire. James and his vassals were intending to stay the next few weeks until Hogmanay in the barony of Douglas. But as he drew nearer to the marches of his family's lands James abruptly changed his mind about stopping at Park Castle, turning south towards Logan. He felt his heart nearly skip a beat as he rode into the manor of Lady Joanna and saw her standing in the courtyard with her son Walter. And when she responded warmly to his arrival he knew he made the right decision. Walter's unrestrained jump for joy to see his 'friend Sir James' summed up his own feelings on the matter; he was home in his heart. "That you startle us with your good arrival," she acknowledged as he came to put his arms around her and give her an affectionate kiss in view of everyone. "You are most a rebel and a beast sometimes," she scolded him, indicating that her son was watching and she was embarrassed by his public show of affection.

James gave her a smirk and left her side to greet young Walter who was turning eight in some few weeks. "And how are you most doing with your studies?" he inquired with true interest. James had provided a tutor for the lad and wanted to hear of his progress learning to read. Walter told him that his days were filled with words and nights with chores to do. "This lad is very busy," he explained. As they entered the great hall of the small manor house James asked Joanna how long would it take her to pack up her things to join him at Park Castle? The lady was surprised by his impetuous bravado that she begged him to come and speak with her in the withdrawing room alone. "Dear James my affection for you has not faltered; but follow you with my son, abandoning my lands and the few fees I have here, to yet live in your castle without the sanctity," her words trailed off as he interrupted her with another kiss upon her lips. She looked quizzically at him; he had always been affectionate but something had clearly changed between them. "This lad is planning on a wedding; that you are the rose of my heart, the brave and fair Joanna. Would you so do this humble knight the honor and agree to be his wife?" he begged to know, allowing his slight lisp to become more pronounced, an endearing trait he held for women.

Lady Logan's eyes flooded; she felt her heart barely leap from her body, pounding uncontrollably within her. "You do take my breath away James Douglas," she began, almost shaking with excitement. "There is nothing in this world that I would most prefer to do than to be your bride and lady of your barony, to share the most solemn of vows of sacrament." He asked her with an impish grin if she was saying yes. She replied with a smile that 'lit up her face like the morning sun falling on the moors' he reflected to himself, giddy in his new found poetry of thought. Then in his victory he let out a war whoop, picked her up like Gilley used to do with Lady El and swung her around in some exaggerated dance that made her giggle. "Put this lass most down!" she demanded half seriously, realizing quickly that this strange action was some sort of Douglas ritual.

"Sweet girl, my bride to be; please tell me, how long will this most take for you to pack your dearest of possessions and come with me to our Douglasdale?" he asked her. She told him that on the morrow in the prime would she be ready. "For now will you and your men join us for one last feast in this humble manor," she asked rhetorically as they rejoined the others in the great hall. "Are we to go with Sir James and live?" asked the laddie. "It is done!" said James. "Now young Walter, it is time we had a talk," he told him as he knelt down to meet the lad's eyes with his. "This knight has proposed of marriage to your mother and she has happily accepted. Would you so offer the same, as I would come to be your father in every way I can?" The younger Logan's face beamed. "A father of my very own; most yes is my reply!" he said, sighing deeply, utterly amazed for his good fortune he allowed. "Good! And now it is time for feasting and fine wine sure aye!" James replied. Pleased with himself he began directing his squires to bring in the food and wine cask that they brought with them from the Forest.

PARK CASTLE THE FEAST OF STEPHEN-The earth and timber tower house once occupied by Gilley and his older brother Hugh lit up the hillside overlooking the Douglas Burn, beaming light from tallow torches lining the cart path that wound its way down and around the terraced motte of the fortress. The brilliant illumination emitted a warm glow that seemed to permeate throughout the vale; the gonfalon of the laird of Douglas was unfurled; the noble baron of Douglasdale had returned to the home of his ancestors. The night air was heavy; the stars clouding over, portending snow by the morning. Along the cart paths on the journey back to Douglas several days ago, James had gathered more of his supporters; to stand the guard, perform patrols of reconnaissance about the stronghold he told them. Now that James would have his family living with him, he was even more relentless about such preventive measures.

Inside the great hall of the tower James and Lady Joanna were seated at the trestle table feasting with the Douglas household when the watch entered quickly to interrupt; to speak of four riders approaching from the south, behind them an escort of perhaps six men at arms he noted. James was excited; tingling inside as he awaited the arrival of the wee Archie and Maudie's son Andrew. Tonight he would introduce his betrothed to his youngest and most outspoken brother. His thoughts were racing through his head for no one in his family knew about Joanna; how would he respond he wondered?

The Ettrick squires announced the arrival of James' brother and guests with great pomp and flourish; sounding trumpets then calling out in name: 'Henklebaldicus of Douglas, squire and his betrothed Dame Beatrice de Lindsay' as Archie explicitly requested. James was bent over in laughter as his brother strutted into the great hall, but abruptly stopped when he beheld the fair lass at his arm; the oldest daughter of Sir Alex had become a very striking and beautiful woman, he reflected. Following the regal couple almost unobtrusively was young Andrew, Maudie's son; announced simply at his request as 'Andrew of Carmacoup'. Lady Joanna sat in awe and admiration as she noted Archie's attire. He was wearing a super tunic of green lined with an iridescent blue silk, trimmed in ermine; his cote and surcote were of silk brocade and velvet respectively and both in varying shades of lavender and blue. Upon his head was a dramatic red chapeau with fur as well. This was hardly a wee lad turning thirteen she whispered to James, noting the imposing stature of nearly six feet tall with a large, rounded physique. Her fiancé nodded that he was indeed that age, but growing fast he said rolling his eyes in feigned ill humor.

As the couple turned their gaze to Dame Beatrice they were equally taken aback by her exquisite presence. She was attired in a surcote of crimson velvet worn over a green silk brocade cote; ermine trimmed her cloak and surcote creating a soft swishing sound as the two made their way gracefully through the birch rushes that were scattered across the flooring of the great hall. James rose from his chair; he had been seated at the laird's seat; the carved oak chair once fashioned for his great grandfather Archibald. This famed sit-upon was the wooden throne as Sir Archibald once called it, the ceremonial seat of power that James saved from destruction before he razed Douglas Castle to ashes. The wee Archie noted the remarkable design of the carved oak; he was thrilled to see the Douglas heirloom he had only heard about. But he would save his comments for a better time he mused; continuing to happily take note of such things.

It is now our Archie's turn to be surprised, James said under his breath. The laird of Douglas just twenty-two himself greeted his brother and Beatrice; then he turned to Joanna with a fixed grin, "May I so present the future Lady Douglas, Lady Joanna of Logan." The young squire boasted he already knew. "Uncle Alex can not keep a secret," he allowed. "A fair lovely lass and brave too this lad so heard," Archie said, praising Joanna as he held her hand politely in his. Then he introduced 'my Beatrice'. James was chuckling; how silly of this lad to think that my brother would not approve, he chided himself. He turned now to Joanna's son. "And this lad is Walter, my own son yet to be," he added warmly. "Welcome to you good sir," said the squire heartily. "Our family rejoices to add in number to our clan; a knight to be of renown most guaranteed."

The quiet and introspective son of Lady Joanna smiled warmly at the squire. "Your own good brother has seen to this lad's tutoring in Latin and of other languages; studies most agreeable for this Scot," Walter boasted. He further allowed that he had not decided on his future; perhaps the church was more his liking he added quietly. "This squire has wrongly stated; it is our Hubicus who will be most happy to meet you! That he is studying for the canon's life," Archie replied joyfully undeterred, as he gave the Logan page one of the famous Douglas smirks. "Another churchman to so outnumber our good Douglas knights," he teased with feigned remorse and everybody laughed. Then he turned to James, sighing deeply as he reflected on their number; he had become strangely quiet in his thoughts; his eyes reflecting the substance of heavy, heartfelt emotions. "That I only wish our mother and dear Hugh could be here with us to enjoy our family celebrations this fair day." James nodded that the laird of Douglas shared his sentiments.

Archie and his entourage with Dame Beatrice on his right had taken their place at the feasting table. "Dear brother, where does a landless squire come to obtain such coinage to afford attire most grand as this?" James began, suppressing his smile. "The gift of my betrothed," he said glowingly. Then Beatrice explained her father offered the garments and she wholeheartedly accepted; that her brothers were finding little use of their finery as they were yet held in Edward's prisons. Hearing those last words brought a pained grimace to Lady Joanna; some of her own kin had lost their lives during such incarcerations, then too, there was le Hardi she reflected.

James felt the shift in Joanna's mood that he changed the subject quickly. "In the prime this lad is giving tours of Douglas Castle," he suggested festively. Archie's entire face lit up. "Is it safe to go there?" he questioned. The youthful laird of Douglas told him yes; though getting into the fortress was not easy without the drawbridge, they could certainly arrive there without harm going slowly up behind the palisade near the Douglas Water. "It is done!" Archie said as Beatrice giggled; she remembered well Sir William le Hardi and his grand castle. She also enjoyed it when her *dear Henklebaldicus* imitated his father; right down to famous Douglas smirk. "Such a visit would be most pleasing to this lass," Beatrice allowed. "Excellent; Joanna has not ventured up there till now. Your good company will add to our adventure," James concluded as he commanded more wine to be poured for them.

Archie had finished his second platter of roasted game and began to take in the details of the old earth and timber tower that formed the central structure of Park Castle. "That our father had most lived here with our Uncle Hugh makes this stronghold a special place," he began. "This lad is proud to enjoy your good hospitality and cheer dear brother in a place Sir William once called home. But it does puzzle this squire some; how did he come to live in this wee fortress that it is quite primitive?" James chuckled to think of le Hardi living at Park Castle. And he knew exactly what Archie meant; their father being a large man demanded an expansive stronghold and one without a chamber pot that he most loathed! "The latrine most stands behind that drapery," he said pointing to a wee door leading off the great hall. "Our father so insisted on the amenities of a garderobe," he confided to Joanna. "That he had such chambers built into the Essex manor houses Lady El held there in dower most as well."

Figure XXIII-Part Three; the wee Archie depicted two years later, at an age of fifteen

Beatrice marveled at how cozy the great hall felt to her; the two fireplaces providing not just heat but light as well, she observed. "How lovely to have this hall most standing for your use good James," she said cheerfully. Her brother in law told her that the fortress was seldom used after le Hardi's time as laird; the access frequently flooded and the gorge of the Douglas Burn became impassable to even livestock for many months of the year. "The wee cart path on this tiered structure of stone had most washed away; only to be repaired by Douglas men at arms some few months ago," he explained. "Our good fortune that the English did not try to stay here; holding out to the assault of James," chuckled his brother coming from behind the screened entrance to the latrine. "Might then the very chamber where we most sit be open to the skies; James would have razed it!" he said boasting of the knight's resolve in such matters.

Joanna began to turn her attention to sparsely decorated walls of the great hall; she was startled to perceive some small paintings that appeared to be of cherubs, beautifully enhancing the simple doorway to the withdrawing room. "Who so painted these fair faces?" she inquired. James' face beamed in excitement and pride. He stood up and beckoned everyone over to take a look at the delicate artwork adorning the carved wooden pieces newly placed around the arched entry. "This cherub here the work of our sweet sister Martha; without instruction she just began to paint with the breath of an angel," he gushed. "And these are of our dear Mura; Lady El painted all of these lovely angels flying fast and upward towards the capital." Archie was thrilled; his brother had made a huge effort to preserve the artwork of his sisters and his mother too. "That you never spoke of this before," the squire exclaimed. "You surprise this lad so James," he told him. "Lady El will be most happy to see of your good effort." Joanna was standing a step away from everyone; taking in the conversation and trying to comprehend the loving and thoughtful man that stood in front of her; a knight of many good deeds but few words she reflected.

Figure XXIV-Part Three; the laird of Balgonie Raymond Morris painted the ceilings of the great hall at Balgonie Castle, Fife in the manner of a medieval tower

"There is a portcullis too that came from Douglas castle," James said with the impish enthusiasm of child sharing his great treasure. He marched his family to the far side of the great hall where he had a slanted desk covered by some parchments with crude drawings on them. "These then are my plans; to so construct a tower of good stone, bigger than the one so here." James went on further to explain that he would then take the former portcullis from the old castle and build an archway for it between two protruding towers on a conical mound he was constructing for that purpose. "See the rise of the motte?" he asked pointing to the drawing. "There will be the towers; the bottom of the hillside is most here, opening to a cart path that will lead up to Park Castle." Archie's mouth was hanging open in wonder for the moment at hand. For once he did not know what to say; the squire was in awe of his brother's plans.

James' enthusiasm was obvious as he pointed out where he would construct the vaulted cellars of the first floor with three more levels of living space to follow. "And a wall-walk with a cap house for the watch," he further explained. "Our good Hugh would be most pleased as well to see of your good intentions here," his brother said quietly. Archie realized as he marveled at the tower plans that he regarded James very differently now; the laird of Douglas was more to him than just his hero knight. As he watched James elaborate on the rest of his plans for the park of Douglas Archie knew he beheld a true man of core values; relentless in his desire to restore their world of Douglasdale as best he could in the image of their martyred patriot and father. Astounding, he mused. "This lad is most impressed," he whispered to Beatrice as she shook her head in full agreement.

Figure XXV-Part Three; model for building medieval vaulted cellars using staging formations built of wooden construction, courtesy of Stuart Morris of Balgonie

DOUGLAS CASTLE-The slow currents of the Douglas Water had receded by the ford where the Douglases and future Douglases crossed over the stream and then the shallow moat. They continued their ride up the steep banks of the earthen motte that supported the ancient stronghold of their ancestors. "Lord Clifford had so built another smaller dunjon there; a folly," James said, indicating the charred timbers of a razed stone tower of four levels comprised of sturdy oak; the rubble and stone exterior built within the palisade of the castle. "The two corner towers in the front and the one looking out toward the Douglas Water were built by our grandfather Sir William," he acknowledged.

Beatrice was wiping the tears that ran down her face; she remembered Douglas Castle and the glorious edifice that it was so lang ago when she used to stay here learning languages, under the tutelage of Lady Eleanora. She dismounted her palfrey crying openly as she turned away from everyone, embarrassed by her emotional response. "This lass is most displeased to see this fine home in such sad condition," she said aloud. Archie had not noticed her distressed state until then, that he quickly bolted from Audāx, running fast to her side to comfort her. "My Beatrice; that my brother had to do this," he explained, prying up her chin gently with his thumb and forefinger, so she would look at him as he soothed her with his words. "Our once mighty fortress stands here yet defiantly; a permanent reminder that we are yet at war. But as our father had so told his sons, his words passed down to me, the lands of the Celts are yet here to so protect us from the invaders. Our Douglasdale is not the castle but the grouse heather and the pheasant woods of the ancient ones that surround our fortress," he told her quietly but firmly.

Figure XXVI-Part Three; portcullis at the entrance of Edinburgh castle

James was surprised by Archie's understanding and ability to convey his thoughts into words. The knight considered the time he spent away from

Essex while this lad was growing up and how Lady El had become both mother and father to his brother. The widow had kept her word most true to our dear father he reflected; teaching my brother the Douglas ways and Celtic heritage of our ancestors. He got down off his own palfrey and helped Lady Joanna dismount. "Perhaps someday our good king will allow this lad to rebuild our family's stronghold," James told them wistfully. "But sadly we can not stir to that endeavor now; until the peace with Edward is fulfilled and lasting." The youthful laird beckoned his family inside the ruins. He showed them where the original earth and timber structure, their ancestors' first home, once stood. Archie's eyes were wide in excitement. "That this castle is even larger than this lad imagined," he said in amazement. As they strolled through the courtyard he asked his brother many questions and James became the storyteller; sharing tales of the escapades of his father and Lady El when he was but a knave himself.

Figure XXVII-Part Three; moat around Caerlaverock Castle similar to the one that shaped the outer defenses of Douglas Castle; courtesy of Susan Shane

"Most here is where we had a pell where men at arms could test their skills with swords; the very place this lad trained so as a page. The archers practiced daily there," he pointed to the rear of the courtyard. "A butt constructed yet survives," he told them. "That one day this lad so hit the target twice and our father went to find Lady El to so come out and praise this son for his prowess with a bow." Archie's competitive spirit was tweaked; when he saw his moment, he took full advantage. "Fortunate for you dear laird of Douglas, this lad was later to join our good family; for that pathetic work with bow and arrow would not merit such attention with one Archibald about!" he boasted. James took the bait and went in search of more arrows for the bow he carried with him. "A challenge to you then good squire," he proclaimed.

The ladies were chattering away; their husbands to be seemed exuberant in their play they agreed. The Douglas brothers were taunting each other; teasing in their claims of heroic actions and exaggerating their achievements gone before. "This lad will have his justice," Archie declared and he proceeded to hit the target the first try. James followed and tied his mark. Archie held the lang bow in the right hand; the wooden frame held straight up, end to end it towered some above him. He pulled back the string held between the two top fingers on his left hand. With a whoosh and thud, he placed the arrow's iron head right through the wooden shaft of the first one. Young Walter was astounded; such marks he had never seen before he told them with breathless wonder to the event. The knight looked the target over; he would try to meet the same advantage he surmised. James shot the second arrow, but it hit only near the target center; his third arrow narrowly split of that. "That you have clearly won the match this day," he said to his younger brother. "Le Hardi's son with bow, sure aye!" he continued, congratulating Archie.

As was the Douglas way, with the competition concluded, the winner acknowledged, James went on to finish telling the tale he first began. He described his father's impatience; how Sir William had insisted Lady El join them, *the noo*! "That when she proclaimed *most later would she join him*, he scooped her up in his broad arms and carried her most out to the courtyard." Joanna was taken aback by his father's bold ways. "Did your mother allow such bandying about?" she asked with great concern. James replied that while Lady El was most independent for a lass she enjoyed his silly humor and let him do it. "Le Hardi was forever whisking her here and there; dominating her with his physical advantage but always in a loving if not teasing way. Lady El would chide him for his larceny of person, calling him 'beast Sholto' in her defiance," he told them, brandishing a bemused look. Archie was laughing to hear the story as Beatrice interrupted. "Beast Sholto," she teased her betrothed; telling everyone that such activity was not alone reserved for Sir William. Joanna's face broadened into a grin; so that was the reason for his picking me up those days not long ago, tossing this lass around, she mused as she threw her Douglas knight a knowing look.

James continued marching everyone through the castle grounds as he finished telling the story, sharing the happy ending with his entourage. "When upon my mother's true congratulations and much ceremony given to this knave, our Lady El nearly had the lay-in for our sweet sister, the wee Amy there and then!" he chuckled. James was in his glory; this was his Douglasdale and everyone with him was enthralled by the history he shared with them. Recalling those happy days so helps this lad feel the joy of those fair times again, he mused. Walter was walking up ahead of them when he came upon the low, circular walls of the great well. He leaned over the stone masonry surrounding the top of the deep shaft; then suddenly he pulled back. "There is a man's face most there," cried the startled lad, pointing inside the well.

James rushed over to view the apparition but all he could see was the water surface below. He knew that the carnage of the Douglas Larder, the bodies of the horses, had lang been removed. What could it be he wondered to himself? "Tell your mother about the man you saw," Joanna demanded from her son. "A knight with long black hair and pleasing eyes, a big grin, he seemed most large," he told them. Then he added more details. "He so had a great scar that ran down the right side of his face." Beatrice gasped; she knew the face was Sir William's. Archie and James exchanged knowing looks and burst into laughter; their father was about! The knight kneeled down to be at Walter's height. "The Celts have so taught us good page that we can see to the Otherworld through the bodies of water so about. My dear father was a powerful laird and true to his core values who loved his wife and children very much. That you have seen the face of le Hardi, our good father and brave patriot of Scotland," James explained. Walter told him he was not surprised; he and his mother had seen his own father back in Logan from time to time.

Beatrice was not amused. "What if he comes to see me?" she asked. Archie told her not to be afraid. "My brother Hugh saw my father when he first passed to the Otherworld. If you are most frightened to see his Spirit, Sir William will not be seen by you; that is what my mother has so told this lad." James was strolling arm in arm with Joanna; she was beaming in her contentment with the day. "That every thing we so share, learning of our ways together is most endearing to this lass," she said sweetly. James was surprised how much he was enjoying her company. He had been worried that he would not know words to say to fill a winter's worth of talking.

"When did you know you loved me?" she asked him. James gave her an impish grin. "Will you most promise to never tell our king of this?" he asked her sheepishly. "When I was in my private council just before we began our battle charge in the Pass of Brander, this lad was in a reverie of you, feeling the innocence of your sweet touch, the softness of your golden hair upon my naked shoulders." Joanna turned to look at him, face to face. "Thank you most for that," she said softly. "You have never before said that you loved me." James realized her words were true and resolved to change his clumsy way; not telling her his feelings could cause great harm he knew from his father's teachings. They continued walking and talking until the approaching rains beckoned them all to return to Park Castle. "A good day then," said Archie to his brother. "Sure aye," admitted James, referring to le Hardi's appearance as they shook their heads in sound agreement.

ST. ANDREWS 16 MARCH 1309-The abbey was filled with lairds of the realm dressed in the finery of the times; it seemed more a social gathering than a Parliament the Douglas knight surmised. James, Lord Douglas had arrived in full armor, his silk tabard brightly bore the Douglas arms over which he sported a super tunic that resembled one that Gilley had some decades ago: crimson velvet trimmed with ermine and lined with gold silk brocade that barely shimmered over his shoulders. He used a closure brooch of Sir William; his grandfather's bronze and silver clasp of an ancient Celtic design that Ellie had given him last fall at Blackhouse Tower. He had just arrived in St. Andrews having ridden east from Douglasdale to Craig Douglas with his lady and her son some few days ago. James had offered to bring them both to St. Andrews but Joanna preferred to remain at their manor near St. Mary's Loch until his return.

Figure XXVIII-Part Three; the Borders looking north to Craig Douglas from above the winding serpent of the Yarrow Water

The lady was shy about their arrangements. The couple had agreed to have their wedding in the fall; a time when Hugh and Ellie would have ventured north from Essex; to be married in the Douglas Kirk with his family present. But for now she was Lady Joanna of Logan, not his wife; she would be waiting his return at Blackhouse tower she promised cheerfully. Walter was disappointed; he looked upon James as his hero; to accompany him to Parliament was his greatest dream he told the knight; but Joanna insisted that he go another time. James understood; it was barely seven months ago that he even considered marriage; a family and a wife were still an image and some words to him. Time will resolve these concerns he assured himself.

As James entered the great hall he recognized at once his Uncle James across the chamber. The elder statesman was sitting among some other men of note that the Douglas laird knew as well. "Good nephew," exclaimed the Steward. "Ready for Parliament I see from your attire!" James grinned knowing that his uncle was referring to his fur hat and the velvet and silk finery fashioned deliberately after le Hardi's 'robes for Parliament' as he had called them when he was but a knave. "That it was only last year you pledged yourself to Edward," James teased the old ambassador. The Steward wrinkled his nose, and with a twinkle in his eye replied, "An annual occurrence that so ends with this good council I do pray; too costly for the bond that I must promise to that foolish son of Plantagenet!" The uncle was referring to an agreement he signed in 1307, pledging 500 marks to the king for his freedom with 'good behavior' implied as well. Turning round now to greet James was his former prisoner and cousin by marriage, Thomas Randolph; newly titled Lord of Nithsdale. "Greetings good sir," Thomas said. "An apology most owed to you dear James," he began, referring to the trouble he caused the lad at Lyne Water. "Such words are not required. That you have chosen well to join with us again; to support our good king; a knight of true renown are you my kin, coming to defend our Scotland now," James praised him. "That my prayers have so been answered; welcome to the fight for freedom from Edward's tyranny!"

Figure XXIX-Part Three; St. Andrews Cathedral ruins

"Praise be is that my cousin James of Lothiane?" spouted Robert Keith, now the Marischal of Scotland. He was reminding the Douglas knight of their strange encounter three years ago at Linlithgow Palace when he was in the service of the English. In 1306 Robert Keith had then recently gained his liberty, released from the confinement of Edward's prisons for which he pledged his loyalty to Edward in return. Now with the success of the king's campaign to unite the kingdome, Sir Robert had returned to claim his rightful place on the side of Scots and Robert Brus. "That I am James, Lord Douglas at your service," he replied with a smirk. "Our king has so proclaimed that sobriquet to be used only by my younger cousin, my dear father's God son." There were greetings all around; excitement filled the air as knights and barons and earls of Scotland were exuberantly celebrating their business at hand; to declare themselves a sovereign nation with Robert Brus their true and only king. It was to be a solemn affair overall; but the atmosphere was electric. Nobles and clerics greeted each other emotionally as long lost friends reminisced of days of another and more timid king, John Balliol. But the day had finally come; Scotland was at last on a path with freedom at her gate; under the hammer no more.

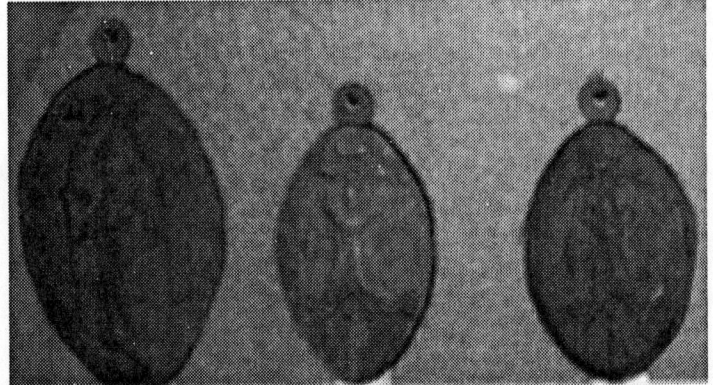

Figure XXX-Part Three; seals of William Lamberton, Bishop of St. Andrews on display at the abbey ruins managed by Historic Scotland

These lairds of Alba had come to this council for two purposes; the first to reply to a letter from King Philip of France. The French monarch had penned a curious missive the previous year and was the first to designate Robert Brus the true King of Scots. His strange communication also included an invitation to the Scots to join with him on Crusade; this they graciously declined for the time being. The second reason for their gathering was to boldly declare their support and loyalty as representatives of the community of the realm and affirm Robert Brus' right to the throne. Now as these magnates and clergy of Scotland were gathering; to throw in their lot with Brus and make their desires known, everyone was filled with excited anticipation. James continued to make his rounds of the great hall; he was amazed at how many of these honorable and worthy men he knew, many more gathering this day than the number who came to Scone three years ago he mused.

Then suddenly from behind him came the well appointed voice of Lamberton, his former employer. "Sir James of Douglas is it?" asked Bishop of St. Andrews, chortling as he spoke. James smiled broadly to acknowledge the prelate's welcomed visage. "That my brother Hugh had so informed us of your good news; to buy your freedom from Lord Edward. When you so found your way to the bishopric of Durham, this lad prayed for your fast escape!" Excited as well for the bishop's arrival the jolly Ayrshire laird came to greet his old friend speaking with his nephew. "The short voyage over the Tweed, just another afternoon for Lamberton!" the Steward observed with his well known wit. "This humble knight is pleased to lay his eyes upon his benefactor," James admitted as he embraced the prelate in genuine affection. "Though correctly am I here on business of the king; the granting of safe conduct just received from *dear Edward*," the bishop boasted tongue in cheek. He pulled out the document for everyone to see. He read out loud the greetings from the king, 'that our most loved and trusted William of Lamberton is traveling under the protection of Lord Edward' he concluded in sarcastic tones. Everyone was laughing at the ruse played on Caernarvon. "A rascal priest with a golden tongue," chided the Steward, laughing so hard that his rounded girth shook with every word; he grabbed for the parchment to read for himself. "That I have come to Edward's peace," Lamberton chuckled. "But that pledge was many months ago in England. That this bishop is in his Scotland, most faithful to another king, Lord Robert," he assured them with a twinkle in his eye.

Figure XXXI-Part Three; view of St. Andrews Bay from the ruins of the abbey

Then from across the room making a grand entrance was another survivor of Edward's tyranny with his new and very young squire in tow. Though Archie was only in his thirteenth year, thought generally not old enough to squire to his knight, his true passion for Scotland and his great height and figure made up for what he lacked in years. "To be in the great presence of one clever bishop of fast banter, my good cousin," said Sir Alexander de Lindsay in his most booming voice. "James!" shouted Archie as he spotted his older brother. Giving little deference to decorum he marched right for the laird of Douglas. "That the garrison so permitted the likes of you in this fair hall?" asked James with an impish grin.

"This squire will so behave," he replied quietly. "Our father must be so proud to see us here," Archie shared with him. The remark caught James off guard; his eyes teared some. He reflected on his gratitude for the heavy mask of curly raven hair that covered his face nearly to his eyes. The Steward had overheard the lad's remark. "Good Archibald, come greet this old laird," he commanded. "This lad is pleased to see you have returned from Paris," Archie began politely. But the Steward had some words to say and interrupted him. "Le Hardi was a brave knight and true; a martyred patriot most missed. His sons are forever welcome here. Sir William's great wit and bold ideas now lost to us; a tragedy for Scotland was his passing. Only his presence could make this day complete for this Steward," he told Gilley's youngest son. "Thank you most kindly," replied the squire, almost inaudible in his words; his eyes were welling with tears and he was chewing down on the inside of his cheeks to keep from showing his true emotions.

Figure XXXII-Part Three; St. Andrews was the site of the first official Parliament of Robert Brus; James Lord Douglas was in attendance as a baron of the realm

James quickly came to his rescue; recognizing the look on his brother's face he beckoned him outside, "to meet more of our kin and friends of le Hardi," he said, excusing their quick departure. As the knight led the squire through the narrow halls beyond the courtyard of the abbey James saw they were alone and abruptly stopped. For some moments he just stood in silence, running his eyes over the vast and compelling shoreline of St. Andrews Bay. "This day is one of strange feelings to this laird of Douglas most as well," he began; then he turned to look Archie in the eye. "Your brother is most happy to have you here to share this fair occasion, an event of true history is unfolding so before us," he confided. As James took in another breath to calm his own words he spoke again. "This lad misses his father more today than any yet so far." Archie just nodded; he understood he said. The brothers then went quietly about the Abbey walking with their silent thoughts of one named William.

Figure XXXIII-Part Three; Dunfermline Abbey corridors returning from the dormitories of the ruins; a site managed by Historic Scotland

As the two Douglas sons stood perusing the shoreline they heard a commotion of riders coming from behind them and heading for the castle of the bishop. "That would be the king," James said excitedly. Archie pulled out his velvet and ermine hat and placed it carefully on his head; another gift from 'my Beatrice' he allowed. His brother did not tease him; he understood remembering his first visit to see the council chambers with le Hardi. "Come," beckoned James. Archie noted there were several riders in the king's entourage. "Those lasses so with King Robert; who are they?" he asked James. "Friends," the knight said sheepishly. "Lasses who enjoy the hunt," he added cryptically. Archie was upset; he considered Robert Brus a great man, the King of Scots; why should he do such a thing he asked James. "Dear brother our lord the king is but a man; with his queen yet held in Edward's prisons, he is prone to such activity as was his father and his before that," he informed the squire. "Not a man of core values like our father?" Archie questioned. The laird of Douglas shook his head; he understood his brother's protest. One concern this lad shares most as well he mused.

Robert Brus was leading his party in the direction of the Douglases; spotting James he decided to stop to inquire on those present for the council. "My lord the king; how good it is to see you most again," he said with true affection. Archie's deep brown eyes darted from the king to his brother and back again; an amazing moment he mused. "Have you seen the Lord of Argyll; has he most come as promised?" Robert inquired. James told him that Sir Alexander had arrived some time ago. "And gratefully most as well the silver tongued Bishop of St. Andrews," he replied cheerfully. "That he has crossed the Tweed is good news indeed!" Brus acknowledged. James told him that Sir Alexander de Lindsay had brought with him another Douglas son, a squire to pledge his fealty to Lord Robert; then he introduced his younger brother. Archie bowed and greeted the king as they exchanged amenities. Then lifting his chapeau in a sweeping manor of great pomp, Arched added: "A message from your other bishop soon to be in France," he said referring to Robert Wishart. "Saor Alba!"

Figure XXXIV-Part Three; view ov St. Andrews Bay from the castle of the bishop adjacent to the cathedral ruins; managed by Historic Scotland

James and Robert were laughing loudly at the squire's words; they could plainly visualize the old prelate in his relentless chant of freedom for his beloved Scotland. "This lad has come to serve you most as well my king; a bowman of great prowess from the Great Forest of Essex," he boasted. Robert Brus threw a teasing glance at his Douglas knight. "Fair competition to the good men of Ettrick?" he asked. "That this squire has most surpassed the laird of Douglas; just some months past when in our Douglasdale this Archibald so bested this most humble knight in contest with a bow," James told Robert in feigned embarrassment. "News most pleasing to this king, more archers for his army; welcome to our good fight Archibald of Douglas." And just as quickly as the king arrived he departed for the castle where he was staying during Parliament.

By the end of the council session good men had staunchly stood in support of their new king. The earls of Ross, Lennox and Sutherland all attended with the earldoms of Fife, Menteith, Mar, Buchan, and Caithness in wardship represented as well; these magnates put their seals to a declaration in favor of Brus, followed by many other barons, lairds, knights and clergy of the realm. James put his new seal to the warm wax dangling on the string; when fastened to the document his name became forever linked in history with these most powerful men of the Kingdome of Scotland: James, Lord Douglas. For the decades of service that followed with the many charters he witnessed and documents he signed, all in service to his king, the eldest son of William le Hardi never deviated from this, his true identity. Even when an earldom was in the offing, he refused. Faithful to his original ideal, James only wanted to be known as Lord Douglas like his noble father and grandfathers before him, chiefs and barons of their homeland.

STEBBINGE PARK MID AUGUST-Ellie and Hugh were feasting in the great hall with Ana and Maudie; Sir David was yet returning from the mews when he noticed the approach of riders under Northumbrian banners. "Greetings to you good sirs," smiled the aging de Ferrers knight. "That we are about our feasting hour; come join us in the great hall." Thomas Chauncelor and his men at arms were coming to Essex to escort Lady Eleanora and her son to Fawdon; their semi annual event. Only this time they were planning to return home to Scotland for a wedding; the ceremony of Joanna and James. Ellie was looking forward to the festivities; many of her husband's kin and friends were expected to attend. The Ceilidh that would follow the vows of sacrament might even last for days she reflected; she certainly hoped for such good times again! As their guests entered the great hall they were warmly greeted by the lady of the manor, beckoning everyone to join in the lavish repast. "Lady Eleanora, a letter do we have from young Archibald and some news from Lord James as well," they told her. The folded parchment bore the new seal of Henklebaldicus of Duglas; she chuckled as she noted his formal ways.

Her eyes scanned the even writing; a good escheator's hand she reflected with pride for Archie's penmanship. But as she read the words her eyes filled with tears; Sir Alex de Lindsay had passed to the Otherworld. "Dear Alex," she sobbed, as she turned to Hugh, "has fought his last battle with Edward; old wounds so slowed him down but it was a strange infection on his leg that fought the healing; he most left us some several weeks ago," she sighed ruefully. Ellie explained that Archie had gone to Parliament with him; the aging knight had complained about the continuous pain in his right leg; confused that it would not clear up; it grew black and sickened him to take his life Archie's words conveyed. "Mother, this lad felt so helpless in his fate," her youngest son wrote. "That our brother and good knight has so postponed his wedding till the spring when most again you return to Scotland." Ellie was crushed; all her plans were thwarted by yet another great loss. "Dear Alex we will miss you so," Lady Eleanora said out loud. As if understanding who they mourned the silly Deerhound Lindsay came to her side to comfort her. "My sweet hound," she said, petting the animal; grateful for the affection he brought to her heart and the memories of Sir Alexander de Lindsay.

"Dear mother, is that the letter then?" Hugh asked. Ellie shook her head no; there was more. "Alas our Archibald has decided to make the celebrations a double wedding!" she said pausing to take in all the words. "My Beatrice is most saddened by the difficult loss of her dear father; to comfort her we will be most wed the April next and I will take her to live with James, serving him in his retinue." Ellie closed her eyes and held the letter to her breast; both her sons might find themselves in the same and desperate battle that they might fall at once together. "Dear God, please protect my sons," she prayed. Ana reassured her; told her not to fear. "Sir Gilley will look out for them," she offered.

Figure XXXV-Part Three; Deerhounds from St. Hubert's Hound Sanctuary romp freely in their retirement at Balgonie Castle in Fife; the laird of Balgonie and his family have supported Deerhound Rescue for over thirty years

Hugh seemed distracted; he wanted most to return to Scotland and join his brothers, fighting Edward in his way, serving God and doing healing for the warriors. Ellie continued reading Archie's letter. "Sweet mother, please do come this fall; with the sadness of the news you know we need our mother here with us," he begged her. She put down the parchment and looked at her middle son; he was fumbling with the ties on his tunic and seemed very far away. "My Hubicus; you mother requires your fair counsel," she began. "With heavy heart we must go to Scotland; but this mother needs you to return with her. Will you so favor this lass with that request?"

Hugh looked up at her, biting his lip to restrain the stuttering that came when he was upset. "This lad most understands," he said quietly. "In truth my time for leaving Essex to reside in Scotland has not come; though surely you do know my heart is there in our homeland with my brothers," he confessed. Ellie went to hug him to her. "My son, this mother so appreciates your candor; soon enough I promise you, our Hugh will be in the kingdome of his ancestors, defending Scotland's warriors with the word of God and the healing of the Hospitaller you are trained to be." Ana was wiping her tears; Sir Alex had been a special favorite, kin and friend, he was always there for her lass. "And what of the words from James?" she asked. Ellie was surprised she had forgotten they had news from her oldest son.

"The laird has sent tidings of another sad passing," Thomas informed them. Ellie gasped and shook her head; what more must we so bear she asked in silent counsel. "Sir James, the High Steward, the renown uncle of our James, he too has made his journey to the Otherworld. My father is most sad as well; serving so in Irvine with the great laird of the Kyle," the squire told them with sympathy. Ellie turned to bury her head in Ana's arms. "Too many losses for this lass to so accept," she moaned. Hugh's eyes filled with tears as well. "That he was in Parliament with Sir Alex is most gratifying to this lad," he offered. There was a long silence before his mother could respond. Then quietly Ellie told him his words were true; the only consolation from all this grief was that these two old soldiers, friends and kin of her dear Gilley had lived to see their Scotland hold a Parliament with Robert Brus as their king. "And freedom from Edward's tyranny increasing with each day and every castle and fortress falling to the King of Scots," added Hugh consolingly.

BLACKHOUSE TOWER OCTOBER 1309-Joanna and Walter were sitting in the great hall of the family stronghold near Craig Douglas. James and a small retinue had left Blackhouse Tower early in the prime on hunt in anticipation of great feasting on the arrival of his mother and brother from Fawdon with the dozen or so of her household that accompanied the lady. He also made sure there were other men at arms left to defend the fortress should the enemy come about; though the Scots controlled the Forest the times were yet uncertain, the English unpredictable. A watch was set and a patrol was assigned. The onfoot walked the lands in the immediate areas as James instructed them; their reconnaissance took them as far west as Kirkstead Burn, south to Dryhope and eastward to the cairn at the Mountbenger Law. These boundaries took them north again and west by the Douglas Stones and up the Brakehope Rig before turning back to Blackhouse Tower. The footpath was one his father traversed with him many times the last years they stayed there. James left the manor confident of his family's safety; eager for the joy of the hunt as well.

Figure XXXVI-Part Three; the romantic cleugh of the Douglas Burn at Blackhouse

As the sun rose on another beautiful fall day in the Borders the lady and her son decided to venture out themselves to survey the bounty of the Ettrick Forest. Before leaving Joanna and Walter took with them a small escort. "Our good knight would chastise us sure," she allowed with a smile, "if we rode out without the company of some Douglas men at arms." Walter told her he preferred to have others worrying about their safety. "My son is most wise and true; this lady so appreciates the protection and the concern as well afforded by our laird in his good care." Joanna let him choose the route for their wee adventure and the page suggested riding to St. Mary's Kirk to pray; he was nervous to meet Lady Douglas and James' other brother Hugh he confessed. "This lad is most concerned; does this lady tell our laird what he should do; does the Essex woman rule this family? Will she find fault with us?" Lady Logan was startled with her son's ideas. "Lady Eleanora is a brave lass; our James has told us so, that she held their family most together when his father was taken from them," she reminded the page. "That James is Lord Douglas now, the head of this family. Most certainly this lady would support him in his happiness. With few words of strife to ever pass between them why would that so be different now?" she begged to know. Walter did not have an answer but he wanted to go to the kirk he affirmed.

The small entourage made their way west towards Kirkstead near the ford of the same named burn racing down the cluech-brae. As Joanna looked north towards Drycleuch Rig she became immersed in nature's splendor, a palette of blazing colors streaming before her. Clad in elm, oak, beech and rowan, the wild cleuchs of the Borders were draped in breathless hues of reds, yellows and deep oranges of the season. Looking down towards the loch below Walter noticed the heavy mist of hovering of clouds spreading eastward towards the Yarrow. "The storms draw up quickly here," he observed. The riders dismounted their palfreys and Lady Logan and her son entered the wee kirk. She lit a tallow candle hanging in the nave and gasped at the primitive beauty of the kirk. The small windows allowed little light but of what she saw, the chapel was exquisitely detailed in paintings of great saints and depictions of the Passion; well cared for and recently adorned with fresh rushes to welcome strangers seeking God's word, she reflected.

Then suddenly the Logans heard the loud pattering of rain hitting unexpectedly on the roof of the kirk; the doors slammed open and entering from the shelter of the porch were their escorts. "Lady Joanna; the rains have come in flooding downfalls; this squire most suggests we stay and wait out the rage of the storm." Joanna agreed and beckoned everyone inside. The winds whipped up the hill towards the kirk, lapped the rig behind them and ran down the pathway of the gorge carved in intricate patterns by the flash floods of the burns racing through the shadows of the braes. The beautiful fall day and blue skies were now hidden behind the darkness of the blue-white rising mist from St. Mary's Loch. "Good that you suggested that we come here," she allowed. Walter smiled for the kind words as they sat in the darkness of the sheltering chapel.

Figure XXXVII-Part Three; view of St. Mary's Loch from the kirk site of the same name; the low clouds of portending rain hang over the loch

Lady Eleanora and her household had arrived within the hour at Blackhouse just before the rains; James was right behind her bringing in the fresh game of his successful hunt. Along the Ettrick Water the lands of the Forest provided well for our family's reunion he reflected. "Lady El; good

Hugh!" he exclaimed. "And Lindsay; least this lad forget," he added as the Deerhound put his paws upon his chest. Then James looked around and not seeing Joanna or her son he spouted his own foolish grin and turned to address the hound again. "Have you already scared away my lass and the wee Walter?" It suddenly occurred to everyone then that the lady and her lad were indeed missing. The doors of the tower burst open to some very wet men at arms yet returning from their patrol. "Have you seen my lady?" asked the laird of Douglas. "Aye, they took themselves a wee escort and made their way towards St. Mary's Kirk when last this squire saw them. That they will so require shelter there for some hours I do fear; the burns are taking water at a rapid speed, washing out the wee bridge at Whitehope Burn."

Figure XXXVIII-Part Three; the rippling flow of the Tweed where it meets the Ettrick Water winding through the Forest in Selkirk

"That they will be safe there," the squire assured his laird. James agreed. "This knight will venture forth and find my lass with the others should they not arrive here within the hour of a lighter rain," he told them. Ellie and Hugh were visibly excited; they could not wait to meet their new family members they told James. "That we have so brought gifts for your betrothed and young Walter too," his mother said cheerfully. But James responded strangely; he seemed nervous and unsettled that Ellie decided to speak with him alone in the withdrawing room. "What troubles you so?" she asked him as she shut the door behind them. He tried to turn away, mumbling some platitudes about the weather; but that response would not do for Eleanora; something was very wrong she knew that she pressed him harder. "This lad is not so fit to marry," he said gravely to her continued questioning. As he turned to look at her his eyes began to fill with tears. "Mother what is so wrong with this lad that his heart is carved in stone most days?" he begged to know. Ellie moved towards him and held out her arms; he barely fell against her sobbing. "The more this lad so thinks of having this family do I want to take flight into the Forest. This war has made me fearful so to love!" he stammered uncharacteristically.

Ellie understood she told him. She sat him down and began to tell James about his own father, when they were first together. "My Gilley felt such overwhelming thoughts when first his brother Hugh passed to the Otherworld that he informed me he must take his leave for some few days; to go on hunt or some other journey; just away from us is what he finally told this lass." James was stunned to hear her words; his father never seemed to falter from his love for his family he replied. His mother explained that his love was not in question only his resolve in what to do; what decisions were the right ones with so much responsibility at hand. "That you have had your share of loss these last few months as well; our beloved Alex and our dear James the Steward; good knights and kin so gone from us, that others so remaining have never known our William." The youthful laird acknowledged her words were true; he felt apart from everyone who did not know le Hardi. And he fretted that he had so many concerns with no one to advise him. "Were my father so here," he began, "this lad would have of many questions for his good counsel."

Ellie smiled; concurring with his sentiments. She also confided the same lonely trepidation, a raw terror sometimes that filled her; that only James could possibly comprehend. "But Mother; this lad would rather not a wife to have; a child could be a burden most as well to this warrior that he might be distracted from his task of battle to worry for their safety," he protested but his words were becoming less angry, no longer holding true conviction for the knight. "Your father feared as well for our good purpose; that he so wanted once to roam the forests as a knight-errant we both know," she paused for emphasis as her words became more pointed. "But marry is what a true soldier of renown and great laird must do; not to live in sin with out the blessings of the kirk," Ellie shot back in reproach of his plans. James was taken aback by her indignant tone; she had never before disarmed him with such words of near contempt. "The children should you have them will be most a blessing for you I do promise; as you have truly been to me," she added more gently, as she tried to hold him again.

But James was not persuaded; he turned away from her. "What can I most do for this lady? Should this knight so fall in battle; another funeral hatchment would be her grieving end once more," he sputtered. "This lad is fearful to bring more sadness to her life than joy; I will not marry her." Ellie grabbed his arm and spun him around; James was so startled by her daring actions that he did not pull away. "James Lord Douglas!" she shouted angrily to get his attention. Then she spoke in more modulated tones, yet firmly for emphasis. "Listen most careful to my words; this lady you most love I do know it; your brother has so written of the sentiments you shared with him. The feelings that chill your heart to stone are formed of fear; do not forsake the brave lass who cares for you and the wee lad who so worships you as well," she told him.

The young Douglas laird grudgingly reflected on her advice as he looked away in silence. "Lady El," he began some moments later, "had you most known Lord Will would so be taken from you; his martyred end in only few short years together, would you have most agreed to marriage with our father?" he asked her candidly. Ellie did not hesitate in her reply. "No man could so replace my Gilley; the love we shared is my heart's reverie. Those years most shortened by Edward's treachery gave me a lifetime full of love, one for all the ages that few have ever known." James thought long and hard on what his mother told him before responding. "Some days this sorry knight feels anger towards our father," he confessed in a voice barely above a whisper. Ellie bowed her head and softly shared her own admission. "Many nights this lass so cried herself to sleep; with calloused thoughts of my dear Gilley. Most deserted and unloved I so felt when he first was captured by de Percy," she said as her eyes filled with tears. "Why was his love for me not enough to keep him with us? These sad questions I sought in answers from my prayers, seeking God's good guidance to understand. Then years later those sad sentiments turned sometimes to anger and even rage. I miss him so; too much to not forgive his stubborn ways now."

James put his arms around his father's widow and hugged her to him. "Thank you for your fair words of honesty. This lad has felt most guilty for those thoughts. I hold the same sentiments as my mother," he told her. James sighed deeply, relieved that he was not alone in his feelings. "Lady El your words are more than comforting," James allowed as he moved to sit alone seeking time for his soul searching; a deep contemplation on what he must do. He thought about Joanna and Walter; reflected on his loneliness and unpredictable life as a rebel in service to his king. In the quiet of the withdrawing room he came to realize that his concern for what might come in war, the battles yet unknown, had overshadowed the love he felt for the lady. Ellie watched his face change, the uneasy scowl from fear and anger relaxed to a calmed resolve; he was listening after all, she mused.

The silence that settled between them was interrupted by the sound of light knocking from outside. "The door unbolted to your entry," they both said together; laughing out loud as mother and son realized they both considered Blackhouse Tower their own domain. "Lord Douglas," Ellie said quietly, "this lady begs your pardon for her words; this is your manor now." James interrupted her seeing Joanna enter their chamber. "Lady El, this lad is proud to so present my sweet lass, my Lady Douglas," he boasted, "if she will so have this knight as her fair husband," he said brandishing his well known smirk; his demeanor clearly transformed from his mother's council. "Welcome dear Joanna; that I am proud to meet the beauty that has stolen my son's heart," she offered with a warm embrace. Arm and arm the ladies went, heading for feasting and good wine in the great hall.

Walter had made his way over to speak with his 'friend James' he told the knight, beckoning him back into the confines of the withdrawing room. "Good lad, that I will be your stepfather soon; not just to be your friend," he chided the boy good naturedly, sharing a broad smile that cheered young Logan. "We heard some angry words and this page so feared your mother was not happy with us here." James felt heartsick that his conversation might have been overheard; he loved Joanna and her son, these were trying times and most confusing he mused. "Walter dear lad, know this: I will be your father if you will so permit me; in the spring when my family can so join us once again we will go to Douglas where your mother and this humble laird with my brother Archie and Dame Beatrice will take our vows of sacrament together at our kirk in Douglas," he said as he led the boy back into the great hall. "It is done!" James continued, proclaiming his last words in the jubilant bravado of another Lord Douglas that Ellie turned around to add, "Sure aye!"

Ana had taken over supervising the kitcheners and cellarers; ordering the platters of food to be brought while instructing the page and squire in James' retinue to pour the wine and bring the ale. It was like old times in Douglasdale she mused. Ellie and Joanna were becoming fast friends James observed and no wonder, they were most alike he said to himself. "So many stories has this lass so heard of your bravery Lady Joanna," said Ellie. "My dear Archie has written flowing verse of your good deeds and valor." James chuckled to add that both of 'his ladies' were knights of renown. "Only that your armor is of cloth not leather or mail of men," he added praising them for their courage in the face of despair. "Like our ancestors, the ancient warriors of Alba where both men and women fought side by side in battle!" Ellie joined in the storytelling as she remembered Gilley's tales of the painted warriors of the Highlands. "And running naked in the wind, brandishing a spear in one hand, a dagger in the other these brave people fought the invaders to their homeland, their bodies colored in bright hues to shine in the sunlight blinding their opponents," she told them, pleased to share their history as her husband used to do. Everyone was feasting and enjoying themselves; healing in their sorrow, sharing in their joys together as a family.

The festive mood and sounds of laughter were interrupted only as the doors to the great hall opened to more guests; Henklebaldicus and Dame Beatrice with their de Lindsay entourage had arrived; even Maudie's son

Andrew was with them. "Dear lad!" exclaimed Archie's former nurse, upon seeing her son again, "just to set my eyes upon you!" Ellie looked up to see the well dressed squire. "That this sight most pleases me as well," she praised Maudie's boy. Then Ellie turned to speak softly that only Ana could hear. "This lass had good notion to educate our Andrew that he now rewards us now with good cheer and comfort most as well. Our Gilley so approves this day for Douglases I know it." The tower was crowded with little room for everyone to sit around the tables but they managed; happy for the challenge of increasing numbers to their family.

"Mother!" shouted Archie as he came running for the dais where Ellie sat. He threw off his supertunic and ran to her side; Dame Beatrice in tow. Ellie beamed; she was in her glory surrounded by her family, new and old alike. Hugh had been chattering away with Walter, sharing his stories about the first priory of Austin Canons in all of England as he boasted; telling Joanna's son about the history of Little Dunmow Priory and his studies there. "Good Hugh; this lad is pleased to see his brother most as well," Archie proclaimed. The canon to be looked up at his younger sibling; a strange grimace flooded his face. "Can this be the wee Archibald?" he asked. "That lad of contentious nature has most vanished; what ever has so changed you?" Hugh teased. "My Beatrice," he responded unabashedly.

"That love has taken a fevered reign upon this humble squire; to feel as wild as the Douglas Burn racing through the cleuchs of the Forest for the sweet words of my betrothed," Archie chuckled in reply as he took the hand of Beatrice, kissing it with a flourish for all to see. "You are most your father's son; the poet knight yet lives!" proclaimed Hugh to peels of laughter from Ellie and James. "And what news is there of Essex and our Stafford?" Archie queried Hugh and Ellie. The aspiring canon rolled his eyes; feigned his indignation. "That Lord Bagot, your good stepfather, fared well in tournament," he scoffed as Archie wrinkled his nose for the information. Ellie explained that many of her kin appeared on the rolls of that tourney in Dunstable; that it was her sad duty to attend. "Though not the excitement we once shared in Newmarket, this tournament brought knights from several shires. Better to retain their interests there in England, competing in the joust than to have these soldiers in our Scotland waging war against our knight and squire," Ellie observed. The homecoming continued well into the night; Joanna and her Walter melded into the family as if they had always been with them, while Beatrice celebrated renewing her ties with all the Douglases.

LIECESTERSHIRE MID MARCH 1310-The mild winter allowed Ellie and her son to begin their trek towards Scotland's Borders earlier than normal. As they made their way north to Groby, stopping briefly at the de Ferrers manor they were informed of some stunning news. Her stepson William was returning to Scotland with forty men at arms in the retinue of Nicky's brother, Sir John de Segrave. The new Guardian of Scotland was replacing Robert de Clifford taking his own good men at arms north with de Ferrers in six weeks. Ellie was agonizing over the last postponement of the Douglas family wedding; fearful that something dreadful might happen to disrupt their family plans again in Douglasdale. But she was unable to share her worries; no one in Groby knew she was venturing west to Lanarkshire let alone attending nuptials in Douglas!

Sir William blithely added another caution to her travels north to collect her rents in Scotland; rumors of a muster being called by Edward. He told her that another invasion of Scotland was being planned for late summer. Ellie replied indifferently to de Ferrers that she shared no true interest in Edward's war. In truth she was scared. But sharing such feelings with her kin was unrealistic. Ellie forced herself to not seek the advice or sympathy from her English kin; she only discussed her travels to Fawdon and the Lothianes with vague imagery. Eleanora sat quietly in the great hall of Groby manor realizing that with each passing year it was getting easier for her to be elusive. Lady Bagot was strangely finding herself more adept at hiding her true whereabouts from family and friends in England; disguising her real motives in traveling north from everyone that thought they knew her.

The English household of Lady Eleanora Lovaine de Ferrers Douglas Bagot made their next stop briefly in Staffordshire to partake of Ellie's share of coinage from the rents. Lord Bagot was in Wales but sent his regards she was informed. Eleanora, her son, the Deerhound and the rest of her Essex entourage stayed the night then moved quickly north again, finally reaching Fawdon. The spring air breathed life into her lungs; as she rode through the comforting shelter of the Cheviot she realized that she never fully relaxed until she reached the vale of the Breamish and their Fawdon. Here she received word from James; messages about a Scottish prelate in service to King Edward. Traversing the Marches Bishop Lamberton had been sent to secure a truce with the Scots. Ellie chuckled when she was told that William Lamberton was appointed one of the commissioners to achieve a peace with Robert Brus; though Edward feigned to recognize King Hobbe as the true sovereign of Scotland.

Lady Douglas as she fashioned herself when in Northumbria had some news herself about the prelates to share with her son and the Douglas vassal. She told Thomas Chauncelor that the Pope had been interceding on the behalf of bishops Lamberton and Wishart for over two years, most recently with good success. As Lamberton was allowed to return to Scotland with safe conduct of Lord Edward; that the same king began to partially relent on

Robert Wishart as well. "Edward Caernarvon delivered 'the evil bishop' to Arnald, bishop of Poitiers to be taken to the pope in Avignon," she explained to her late husband's vassal. "A good man and patriot; who preached for war with Edward with his every breath," admitted Thomas, recalling his days at the Irvine muster thirteen years ago.

Ellie then asked Sir Thomas to accompany them to Douglasdale. "A new guardian for our Scotland; my dear kin Sir John de Segrave and young de Ferrers as well to bring their retinues to our homeland in some several weeks is what I hear." The Northumbrian knight grew concerned; were they facing another tragedy he wondered with a wedding in few days? Sir Thomas quickly dismissed his fears; this family to have suffered so much, God's will should hold more for them this time, he assured himself. The knight told Lady Eleanora that he was pleased to be of service to his laird's good widow; "honored to be invited for the festivities in Douglasdale as well," he proclaimed happily.

Figure XXXIX-Part Three; the marker points out 'Fawdon one mile'

"Fortunate for us de Clifford has returned to Wales," Ellie chuckled; but she was uneasy she admitted, informing Sir Thomas of the muster for King Edward's forces that would be invading Scotland no later than the fall. "That we will be home in Essex," Hugh consoled her. But Eleanora was thinking of her two sons, a knight and a squire, who would be celebrating their marriage and love one day to put on their armor the next to do battle with her kin. "How this war so pains this mother; more for the irony of kin and friends that hold of love for me but hatred for the enemy, my own dear sons," she said mournfully. Ana could offer few words of support; she had said them all before she mused. Hugging her girl stroking his hair; Ana wondered to herself, how does one comfort such a mother? What can be said to a lady who must stay in England to struggle to collect her rents while her heart was clearly in her Scotland with her sons and their families and friends, to share in memories of her Gilley?

Hugh decided he would try to change the subject. He told Sir Thomas more news about his favorite bishop; how Robert Wishart after taking leave of England and his prison at Porchester Castle had filed suit. "In the court of Rome the bishop sued the Pope for his release to return to Scotland," he explained; conveying to everyone as well his confidence that his prayers would be answered; his wish granted by the pontiff before too long. "But as Edward pleads with the Pope to excuse 'our dear and most loyal Bishop Lamberton' from the general council in Vienna, the same English lord commands his writs opposing reinstatement of Bishop Wishart to his see. This is what this lad has heard from the Austin canons in Essex," Hugh confided.

Figure XL-Part Three; view from Park Castle earth works of Park Burn

Sir Thomas told Hugh and Eleanora how pleased he was with the news. He was not surprised that the wily Bishop of St. Andrews had won the confidence of Lord Edward but was clearly stunned to learn about the successful escapades of Bishop Wishart. "This is exciting!" he allowed. Hugh and Thomas kept talking but Ellie was in a reverie; ignoring their words intended to deflect her worries. She was very aware of the dangers for her family and their future. How could she yet remain in England; something had to change she knew, but what? The peace that had prevailed the winter with England was portending change; Edward Caernarvon needed to prove his prowess as a warrior to fend off the revolt from his discontented nobles. He was making plans to load the cages of his lions onto carts and call for a muster to do battle in Scotland.

DOUGLASDALE-Arriving in the valley of the Clyde brought back a rush of feelings to Lady Eleanora. Turning to Ana the two old friends shared a knowing look; this was their first time in Douglasdale in thirteen years. Riding the Uddington gate they would arrive at Park Castle long before the turn that would have taken them to the ruins of the once mighty fortress they had called home. Gillerothe and Patric had ridden a short distance ahead of the household to alert the sentries of the Douglases' approach. The varlet of le Hardi was barely giddy for an old warrior nearing the age of sixty as he rode the well traveled cart paths he remembered as a child growing up in the barony. Gillerothe had served three lairds of Douglas and now there would be a forth he reflected, Sir James of Douglas. The loyal vassal was coming home for the last time. Lady Douglas understood; making it right with the young laird that Gillerothe could join his household. How many years the old Celtic warrior had left he did not know; but he would put his bones to rest in Douglasdale he had promised himself. He met laird James' patrol even before he was in Rigside. "Good and noble men of Douglas, it is I Gillerothe and our Patric here," he boasted, "come to bring Lady Eleanora and the laird's own brother Hugh for the wedding."

The armed horse reconnaissance numbered six; but only a younger squire in their party seemed to recognize these Scots returning home from Essex. The rider moved forward out of concealment of their formation to greet le Hardi's varlet. "Proud to be the first to welcome you most home dear Gillerothe," Richard Dickson cried out happily. "Good to see our Patric too! And where is the lady with her entourage?" Le Hardi's loyal vassal told him that they were just approaching, pointing to the large number of riders now appearing on the rig behind him. Lady Douglas smiled and waved as she saw the banners of Douglas displayed by the patrol; she spurred her palfrey forward with Hugh lagging just behind her as they went to greet James' men at arms. "So early to encounter such a force of armed guards," she commented somewhat anxiously. "Is there trouble here about?" Richard introduced himself and Ellie beamed as she recalled his noble father Thomas. "My dear husband's most loyal soldier," she proclaimed. The squire thanked her for the kind words and told her that James ordered two such patrols of the valley; his standard requirement while in Douglasdale he told her. Ellie felt a little more relaxed to know the reason for the extra watch was her son's over-cautiousness. Better to be safe, taking little chance for danger that might ruin our happy plans, she mused.

The wee clan from Essex rode in escort of the Douglas men at arms for the remaining short distance to Park Castle. As they took the final turn in the direction of Parkhall, Ellie looked sadly on the old fortified manor house that was once the proud domicile of le Hardi's seneschal. The earth and timber edifice was in need of repairs; I will speak to James about that she chuckled quietly. A light snow began to fall as the Douglases made their way up the small cart path by the Park Burn. The marsh land running along the side of the stone laden waters was still frozen by the winter temperatures even though spring was yet upon them. Ellie looked to her left as she guided her palfrey up the terraced entrance of Park Castle; the Bluebells that graced the banks of the burn were not yet in bloom she noted dreamily. Just then Lindsay spotted Archie and Beatrice coming towards them with their own wee hound; his loudly barked greeting startled Ellie out of her reverie.

"Mother!" Archie cried out happily as he hugged her, while helping her down from her mount. Then he began twirling her around like le Hardi once did. "Put me down the noo!" she teased him, "Beast Sholto!" Beatrice was close behind them calling Ellie's hound, introducing Lindsay to her own Deerhound Minerva. "Perhaps a third wedding will we have," she chuckled as she supervised the furry playmates romp in the courtyard of the stronghold. Joanna was just opening the heavy wooden carved door of the tower house; Walter and Maudie's son running out behind her barely knocked the lady over. As Ellie gave her palfrey to the groom she greeted the future Lady Douglas. "Most grateful is this lass to be here. And so lovely do you look this day," Eleanora cooed in fond embrace of James' betrothed.

Then Ellie took her leave briefly to look behind Lady Logan; curiously surveying the wooden door of the keep. "Ana, come most here; is this not the same door from the castle?" she asked excitedly. Joanna was chuckling as she watched Eleanora look over the details of the carved oak. "Lady El, our James told us that you would be the first to take notice of his good work. That he brought the doors out of hiding some few weeks ago for that very purpose; to fashion them for Park Castle." Ellie was thrilled; then she realized that Joanna had indicated two doors. "And where is the second one?" Ana was standing by the old oak panel; running her hands over the intricate carving that included the Douglas armorial bearings as if admiring the handiwork of an old friend. "The two together were too large to fit and sadly one had been altered to include the checky pattern of de Clifford's armorial bearings." Ellie sighed; at least this door is most complete she mused.

Walter and Andrew were with Hugh; the lad had promised to teach them about healing this visit; a clear bribe to induce them to study harder at their Latin. "This is the healing box of the laird of Douglas, my dear father," he explained. The middle son of le Hardi had found his place at last his mother observed; a teacher priest and healer was certainly his proper calling. Archie interrupted her private thoughts telling her of the plans for Saturday; the double ceremony where both couples would say their vows at the Douglas Kirk. "Our priest is coming all the way from Glasgow, our kin John de

Lindsay," Archie told her proudly. "Your brother seems to have everything most organized," Eleanora replied. Beatrice was beaming ear to ear as Ellie came and hugged her as well. "That you dear lass have been most patient for this day," she praised her. "Some many years ago this mother so recalls a great beauty with a mind for the financial dealings of a household; that you have only grown most taller from those times," Ellie chuckled. "Our Archie will rely strongly on your good sense as well." Beatrice was quiet in her response. "My dear Henklebaldicus, my love for all the ages; that he has a mother I can love as my own most pleases this lass, in her great loss," she told Ellie, referring to her father's passing nine months ago.

"The snow is not to last; but it is growing cold. Are you most coming inside or shall this lad erect a tent for the court you are holding here dear mother?" growled the laird of Douglas, feigning discontent with the time Eleanora already spent in her greetings and salutations. With a silly smirk James chided her that she was forgetting her manners to always seek the presence of the laird most first! "My lord the baron," she replied in teasing retort; "are you quite finished with the business of the manor to so greet this Essex lass?" James saw his opportunity; he came to her side but not to hug Lady El; he lifted her above his head like his father used to do.

Figure XLI-Part Three; Monty plays in the courtyard of Balgonie Castle in Fife; a harrier or mixed breed including a lot of Deerhound, the wee hound came to the laird and his family by way of the Scottish charity: Home A Dog Association

"What has so come over you and Archie that you must show your prowess by lifting this poor mother here and there so like a trophy of good boast; chattel won in the spoils of the battle?" Ellie demanded to know. Joanna was giggling. "The Douglas ritual; the Sholto greeting of the laird to the ladies of his court!" she offered brandishing a silly grimace that made Ellie giggle as well. As James set her down in the great hall Ellie noticed the familiar face of Sir Andrew de Fleming and a younger lad sitting next to him that from his manner had to be his son she surmised. "Good that you have listened to your mother," she teased the young laird. "That you have found yourself a seneschal!" Sir Andrew greeted the widow fondly with a bear hug and a kiss on both cheeks. "Your son has promised to return our family to Park Hall," he allowed. "And this must be young Andrew?" asked Ellie. Le Hardi's steward said no; that alas his daughters had to find him a son through marriage that he could tutor in his financial skills. "But this lad is learning fast," he chuckled. "Soon this old seneschal will take his seat in grateful retirement; to have his son in law so manage the quarter days for our Douglas laird. It is done!" he proclaimed to the resounding laughter of everyone in the great hall at Park Castle.

The feasting began; squires came with balusters of wine as kitcheners brought platters of food in huge quantities. Ellie was looking at the tableware with a quizzical expression. "The largesse of Sir Robert de Clifford," James allowed with a silly grin. There was so much food that Ellie had to refuse some courses. "Our Lady Joanna has most impressed you then?" asked her son; knowing his mother's eager appetite for good fare. "This lass feels like a goose most fattened," she chuckled. "Dear Joanna, a fine hostess you have shown yourself to be this day!" Archie was telling his mother that James and his men captured so much game that the cook was threatening to find another laird to serve if he brought in any more for two more days. Hugh was laughing; he had never known such bounty he told them. "This is the way of our Douglasdale," James said boastfully. Ellie looked at Ana as they shared a private moment; there was always a larder full in Douglas Castle. "A true homecoming for this lass," Eleanora said. "Not since the days before rebellion have we seen of feasting grand as this."

The door of the great hall opened; the Douglas men at arms announced the arrival of the canon from Glasgow Cathedral that was coming to perform the wedding. The newly reinstated parson, Aylmer de Softlaw, the rector twenty years before when le Hardi was Lord Douglas, was yet in Kelso on business of the abbot. His presence was not required this day; Lady Beatrice had arranged for her kin to perform the sacraments for the couples at the Douglas Kirk. The de Lindsay churchman was wearing an exquisite supertunic, shimmering jet black trimmed in ermine all around. His robes were of a finer cloth than any Hugh had ever seen for a priest. John de Lindsay held a commanding presence as he embraced the family in the great hall. James made the introductions and the secular canon joined readily in conversation. "Greetings to one and all," he began, "that I have words and salutations from one bishop that you must all know." Ellie and James looked surprised, they knew the canon beckoned from the prelate's See of Glasgow, but Robert Wishart was in France last they knew.

"The word will most be heard, but from this priest you will have heard it first," he boasted. "The brave and noble bishop, our dear Robert Wishart, has just most recently arrived at the port of Antwerp, returning safely from his clandestine journey to Dundee; dear Edward none the wiser to it." There was a low hush of stunned gasps and whispered words; how could that be, they wondered; Dundee was still under English control. The loyal canon and friend of the Bishop of Glasgow told them that the prelate had grown restless waiting for the Pope. "That we know about the suit he brought to the court in Rome," Ellie told him. John de Lindsay explained that there were many delays with that request; several letters of protest came from King Edward that had to be considered. "The good bishop realized he was running out of time. He desired with all his heart to so attend the Ecclesiastical Council Bishop Lamberton was convening for February last; once postponed in hopes of freeing the noble patriot from Edward's grasp," the canon told them. "The day was finally set; this canon was commanded to meet a Flemish cog already landed in the night at the hidden cove near the castle of Bishop Lamberton." James excitedly told John that he recognized the place; he had served in the household of William Lamberton. "Do continue," the young laird said.

Figure XLII-Part Three; Porchester Castle ruins; an antique engraving in the author's collection; Bishop Wishart was held prisoner here from 1306 until 1310

Then the canon's voice lowered, slowed for emphasis for what he intended to say next. "Even in the shadows of St. Andrew's bay I realized at once who was now approaching. My heart so leaped to see the brave patriot last arrested by the English in full armor making his return to Scotland. Coming up the shoreline path was he, wearing not his bassinette from Cupar but the bishop's miter and carrying the crozier of his office most defiantly, his elegant robes denoting his eminence wafting in the shoreline breeze. As our bishop strutted forward, brandishing his investitures of office, it most occurred to this canon, our most blessed Glasgow kirk no longer was a widow; Robert Wishart had come home!" the canon happily declared. "Our dear Robert was older both in face and gait for his four years as Edward's reluctant guest; he walked tall but not without some help," he said sadly. "The noble bishop was eager to look about; taking in 'the very breath of Scotland' he proclaimed though being February it was very dark with little to be seen, though he relished it. He was at peace he said to be home again, this I know most certain!" John said confidently. The great hall filled with talk of the prelate; how like him to once again defy Edward; coming home to Fife!

Hugh told the priest that he had seen Bishop Wishart in Porchester. The canon's face lit up in a huge grin. "That when I told our good prelate that I was coming here to perform a marriage for two Douglas men, one marrying my dear kin Dame Beatrice, he inquired of the names of those to say their vows." John replied. "I proudly told him James and Henklebaldicus and our good bishop responded with a look not unlike relief. Dear Robert asked that I deliver this lad a message: 'Tell one Hugh of Douglas his friend has not forgotten his promise' and we embraced and he was gone from us, back to France is what this canon has been told." Hugh was stunned by the thoughtful words of the bishop and thrilled to know that his prayers were answered: Robert Wishart was able to return to Scotland, if only for awhile.

"And what about the council in Dundee; did it so take place as planned?" asked James. The laird of Douglas had advance knowledge of the secret conclave of clergy but until his next meeting with the king he was unsure of the outcome. "The bishops came from all of Scotland to put their seals upon the great document. Bishop Lamberton had chosen the Franciscans' priory, the Greyfriars' kirk most there for their clandestine meeting." James reflected on the irony; the bishops and other noble churchmen of the realm were gathering in February, in another kirk of the Greyfriars; as King Robert and the Comyn of Badenoch had met four years before, for what heralded the rebirth of their country.

John told them that he traveled with his bishop all the way to Dundee arriving at the Priory of Friars Minorites on the Tay within a few hours. "In some short time our good prelate so insisted to take his walk through Dundee in prime. This humble priest and canon was fearful for his safety; most grateful for the convincing words of Bishop Lamberton to wear the coarse grey robes of the Franciscan friars, to leave behind the crozier of his office as he traversed the gates of Dundee," he chuckled. "That he saw his Scotland most again," sighed Hugh. "Aye, but how clearly is unknown; his sight is most afflicted from lang days of captivity and his advancing age," the Austin Canon allowed. John de Lindsay explained that when it came time for Wishart to append his seal to the warm wax he joked that he hoped his good chancellor, referring to the position Lamberton last held before becoming bishop, had not mislead him in the wording as he could not read much even with his spectacles.

DOUGLAS CASTLE RUINS-Their feasting lasted lang hours into the night as the Douglases, their kin and many friends and vassals of their laird packed the great hall of Park Castle, celebrating the return of a true laird of Douglas. Even though the charter for the Douglas barony had not been seised to James; re-confirmed in a new charter by King Robert, the family, his villeins, and tenants, kin and vassals all, knew that Douglasdale was his barony. Only de Clifford might have challenged that contention but he was yet in Wales Ellie told her son. Little did she know that Robert de Clifford would be recalled to Scotland by his king; to parley a meeting for a truce; sent to Selkirk to entice the peace with the King of Scots, months later, by December. But today the Douglases were going as a family to visit their old home; returning to the "site of great treachery by King Hobbe," Ellie teased James. "Mother, this lad must caution you most again. My lord the king is a not the same young earl most pledged to Edward," her son corrected her. Ellie threw a look of reproach until she spotted his well known smirk; then she broke out in laughter.

"When King Hobbe grants you most a charter to our Douglasdale, will I frame my mind to call him by that rightful title you so bestow; but not the noo!" she said with a playful tone; her eyes twinkling a challenge to his pompous words. "That your great laird most removed this lass from her home; only he can so undo the curse, reseise us to the Douglas barony in chief as it was for your ancestors, generations now most gone." Ellie and James were in their glory; bantering and teasing as they mounted their palfreys for a ride over to the castle ruins. They were led by an armed escort; James insisting such precautions necessary for the times he offered. As they rode the cart path down into the glen it was not very long before Ellie spotted the desolate, stone specter that was her home. Ghost-like the ruins stood above the moat that spilled into the Douglas Water winding behind the outer defensive walls. "Oh my dear sweet God," she exclaimed; a sickness gripped her abdomen that she had not felt since the horrible day in Berwick when she unknowingly watched the prison ship with her Gilley sail from Scotland for the Tower of London. Lady Eleanora could never have imagined the devastation that was once her home. Ana was right at her side; watching Ellie's every move and grimace. But Eleanora was determined to remain composed; for James' sake she vowed to suppress her inclination to break down in tears for the dreadful sight before her.

"This mother so regrets her son's most thorough ways," she said softly. She looked over at James and found him staring not at the castle ruins but at his mother. "My lord the king forbids rebuilding of such fortresses," he told her, his deep voice quivering in sadness for the deed he was compelled to do. "Our brother has most driven out the English," proclaimed Archie as he rode up boldly, his exuberance contrasting to the moods of Ellie and James. "Such small price to pay; to rout the men with tails from Douglasdale and gain the freedom for our lands from English lairds. Do you not agree?" he asked his mother. Archie peered deeply into her eyes; he hoped with all his heart that she would applaud his brother's actions, not chastise him for razing their home to the ground. James had confided to the squire how heart broken he would be if Lady El dissolved in tears of sorrow. Eleanora blinked back her tears as she listened to her youngest son's words. "My Dear Henklebaldicus," she began; "that you have much to learn from our laird, Sir James of Douglas," she said with bemused look. "To destroy in one short night this once great edifice; that took of many years to build, the hard work of generations of Douglases during the lang peace of Alexander; a remarkable deed of fair accomplishment for one named James!"

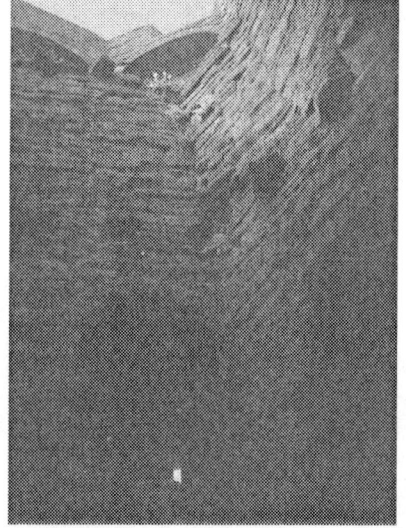

Figure XLIII-Part Three; the murky interior walls of a ruined tower at Bothwell are covered with mold and plant growth; a castle site managed by Historic Scotland

As le Hardi's widow ran her eyes over the once majestic site she felt a strong shiver leap through the core of her body. The cut stone of the walls was left barren; proud mason marks of the artisans fading from exposure. The cold rains and pelting sun diminished their stalwart stance that they now lay naked to the mist, their grey and red patches peaking through; speaking only of their origin. The outer walls were once glowing in pastel washes of yellow with pale rose; chosen both for beauty and to retard the growth of mold, a castle's dreadful enemy in time. Now the palisade and walls of the tower were scorched in black soot, pitted by the weather and surrounding sand that swirled in wild torrents from an unchecked wind. The corner towers lost their caps she noted sadly. The thatched peaks were gone; the dramatic blues and reds that adorned the roofs were long forgotten as were their proud banners once waving the armorial bearings of Douglas and Lovaine. The defiant donjons that stood guard to the castle entry now opened to the skies as well; the floors below had fallen into the pit of stone cellars, their jagged and charred timbers rotting in the sun.

Eleanora looked over to her oldest son, summoning all her courage of composure she added, "One brave act this lass so knows was of true courage." Ellie was trying valiantly to assure James that what he did was right and seemed to regain her control for the moment. "Thank you Lady El," he said emphasizing his lisp and endearing grimace. "Most like your father with that fair smirk!" she replied to his obvious ploy. "This lass will lay down her challenge to a race!" she boasted. Eleanora turned her palfrey and spurred him fast down the wee brae, over Gallow Knowe then up the embankment of the outer defensive walls, along the ruined palisade to arrive at the postern of Douglas Castle; ahead of James and Archie.

Figure XLIV-Part Three; ruins of a corner tower at Caerlaverock as the Douglases might have seen Castle Dangerous in 1310; an Historic Scotland property

"This structure is yet unsafe," James cautioned his mother. "Can we not enter by the tunnel?" she asked. Her son frowned sheepishly as he described how he burned the wooden structure that once secretly provided an escape from the protruding tower past the morass lands along the palisade to the

Douglas Water. Ana was overwhelmed by the devastation; she teared up as she walked up the temporary planks James constructed for their entry. She and Ellie were walking together, arm in arm, more for emotional support than for any other reason.

"That we will use the stone from the unfinished curtain wall dear Edward so constructed for his loyal Clifford; to build two gate towers on the entrance and smaller motte at Park Castle," James elaborated for Ellie while he motioned in the direction of the partially erected masonry. "Built by English masons, this work was stopped when dear Lord Paramount so died of the squirts at Burgh on Sands," he added, always happy to include the ignominious end of the king when referring to him. "That this was most completed before this lad so razed the castle," he explained. "We have fashioned sleds like the Manx men used to harvest their crops for market," James added. He looked over to Ellie as he shared a poignant memory of their first travels together with le Hardi to the Isle of Mann. Ellie beamed as she recalled those times exploring that isle and another village named Douglas.

Figure XLV-Part Three; interior of a ruined tower at Bothwell, three levels above the cellar; each compartment held a fireplace, a window and perhaps a latrine as well

Lady Douglas then walked quietly about the courtyard; breathing in the memories as she made her way down familiar paths. Before she even left Essex, she tried to anticipate what she might see here, how she would feel when she beheld the tattered and demolished walls of her former home. But Eleanora never expected the glowing warmth; the cheerful greeting she experienced as she roamed the charred rubble of the castle ruins. It was as if her body felt a semblance of belonging there; the energy exuded from these weathered grey walls of stone was not of despair as she had imagined; but of powerful enrichments enfolding strength and truth. The ruins seemed to beckon her to a higher realm; she drifted off for a moment in her private world. Then as she returned to the reality of her surroundings Ellie realized what this strange sense of omnipotence was all about. "This is our Douglasdale; proud and mighty so, standing in defiance of both Edwards," she began. "I know my William is beside me this day; telling me to so remind you all of his love for his family and the lands of our dear ancestors; to take courage and continue the fight for Scotland and our freedom. This is our charge to keep," she concluded.

Figure XLVI-Part Three; the folly tower; rubble and stone defensive walls protrude from the motte where the impressive castle once stood

Coming to the entrance of the large keep that held the great hall and family quarters, Ellie and Ana exchanged more somber looks. James led the way with torches to light their path until inside the tower. Here the sunlight streamed in from the floors above that were no more. As the Douglases crept into the old keep, the wind whipped through the open archway whistling an eerie greeting to the former residents sweeping upward through the opening that once formed the roof and wall-walk of the tower. Until now Eleanora had sustained her resolve; controlled her emotions. Walking into the barren hall, she became gripped with fear of what she might yet see. Hanging from the walls were some tapestries she did not recognize; they yet remained surviving the fire, diminished now to tattered strings of grime and colored silks and spun wool. The gallery where Lord Will had played the wee pipes in celebration of their wedding was gone; the only indication of where it stood was the rubble formed when the flames engulfed the large timber supports that ran the width of the chamber.

Ellie forced herself to look at everything; glancing frequently at Ana as if to say she still had the courage to continue. She moved her eyes upward and was suddenly struck by the bleak degradation of the outer shell of the tower that once formed the exterior walls of the laird's chamber. Eleanora gasped to see the exposed stonework now covered with the green growth of gnarled plant-sculptures pointing to the bright blue sky above them. Her head moved slowly, her eyes curiously investigating the mangled appearance of the ruins. The latrine closet appeared strangely hanging off the walls and the lay-in where most of her children were born was barely visible. Ellie tried to fight the tears as she ran her eyes across the carved stone to the former location of the family chapel; indiscernible but for the uniquely shaped window on the exterior wall.

Lady Douglas felt strangely numb then as her entire body became very hot; the great hall was spinning about her. She grabbed James' arm for support as he caught her fall just in time. In her overwhelming sorrow Ellie was stifling her normal breathing; suppressing her grief she caused herself to swoon and faint. When she woke from her unexpected slumber she was surrounded by her three sons and Ana. Hugh was administering to her from Gilley's healing box. "By St. Bride," Ellie sputtered at herself in anger. "This lass is most foolish in her ways," she scoffed. James shook his head. "No Lady El that you were trying most to deceive your James; to let this lad believe you were content with his unholy deed; the destruction of our home." Tears flooded her eyes and ran down her cheeks as he held her. "So sorry is your mother," Ellie began. The laird of Douglas smiled and put his large, calloused hand over her mouth, silencing her as Gilley would have done. "Shhh," he told her. "It is allowed that you should mourn our loss; together we will rebuild this fine stronghold most again," he promised

DOUGLAS KIRK APRIL 1310-Lord Douglas led his family down the cart path towards the village of Douglas and the kirk of his ancestors. In front of him was a large contingency of armed horse; an equal number brought up the rear of the grand procession. Lookouts and watch patrols were everywhere in the Douglas barony: monitoring the road towards Ayrshire, lurking in the Douglas hills; riding in tandem down the well traveled gates that reached south to Crawfordjohn and patrolling the braes and rigs that formed the western boundaries then north to Lesmahagow. A surprise attack this day was unacceptable James resolved; he would take no chances that the English might have heard of his presence in Douglasdale, coming to disrupt this most sacred of days. Ellie and Ana were riding with the other ladies in the middle of the caravan. Even the weather was cooperating; the sun shining in a bright blue sky as the mavis sprang above, swooping down to belt out a raucous melody at the parading Scots.

As the Douglases arrived at the door leading to the nave of the family kirk they were greeted by the sweet sound of the Lowland pipes in a serenade of familiar tunes. Dry eyes were not meant for Douglases James chuckled to himself upon hearing the music of the Celts that beckoned them inside their ancestral chapel. This fair day I do share with you dear father for I know you are most with me, he said under his breath. Ellie greeted the priest, the secular canon from the see of Glasgow. "And what beast do I see hiding behind you," scoffed the Augustinian priest good naturedly. "Good sir, this is Sir Lindsay, named for your dear kin and mine, Sir Alex," she allowed, whisking the Deerhound into the kirk. The Douglas tradition for weddings Ana noted wistfully. She chuckled as she recalled leading the noble Deerhound Sir Shamus down the aisle; taking their seats to witness Gilley and Ellie renewing their vows some twenty-one years ago. Lady Douglas looked around and was surprised that few things were missing or out of place. "Our brother took great pains to so insist that any sign of de Clifford be removed," Archie whispered to her. Most like his father; our James takes care of our every need she mused.

Figure XLVII-Part Three; 13th century window in the wall remains of old St. Bride's, formerly the Douglas Kirk, in Douglas; maintained by Historic Scotland

The priest had the two couples exchange their vows in the nave; then concluding that part of the ceremony the four Douglases, James, Joanna, Archibald and Beatrice walked among the rushes laid on the floor toward the altar where they would partake of the sacraments of marriage. The ladies were in cotes and surcotes of contrasting greens, the outer garments delicately trimmed in ermine. Beatrice had worn her curly auburn hair loosely draping over her shoulders to her waist. The shimmering blond hair of Lady Joanna was covered by a simple veil of white that she wore with a wimple; her filet was covered by the rosemary Ellie had given her and

Beatrice just as they departed for the kirk. "For good luck," she told her new daughters.

As Eleanora watched the brides take their places she noticed happily that each lass wore the jewelry she had presented them the evening before. Joanna had a lovely brooch once worn by Elizabeth; a Steward heirloom Ellie found tucked away, hidden among Lady Martha's ring and simpler brooches. Beatrice was wearing her smaller gold brooch with pearls and rubies; the de Hastings piece Ellie received from her mother Helisant, honoring the occasion of her own marriage to Gilley. The de Lindsay lass had protested the extravagance; but Eleanora insisted. "Only that you must provide this grandmother with many grandchildren," she teased her new daughter.

Figure XLVIII-Part Three; 13th century stone from capitals, old St. Bride's, Douglas

Ana elbowed Ellie as James and Archie were now standing right next to them; how handsome they looked she whispered to her girl. James' mane of curly black hair caressed his shoulders; pulled aside on his left side only to reveal the silver buttons Ellie had given him on the occasion of his marriage. These shiny adornments were the very ones she presented to Lord Will that he wore on their wedding day at Kelso Abbey. Archie wore the brooch and matching buttons Lady Helisant had given Gilley in Little Easton. Standing beside his older brother Ellie was startled to see how close they were in height now. Archie's eyes glistened; his straighter locks of deep brown accented with red hues were tied back in a silver clasp. His simple hairstyle made him appear older than the fourteen full years of life he was approaching, Ellie reflected as he walked past her.

Both brothers were dressed in velvet cloaks; tunics in glowing hues of the deep Douglas blue trimmed around the hems and closures with fur.

Peeking from beneath the flowing velvet were exquisite surcotes of silk brocade; the knight wore one of deep azure, the squire had his in warm green, to match his eyes he told them all with a smirk. Following closely behind in this procession was Hugh; wearing the black velvet and fur mantel of le Hardi over a purple surcote with gold trim, his specific choice to honor his father's memory this day. He held the traditional swatch of woven cloth, the ancient Douglas Chiefs' designate of black and grey, carried on the white silk cushion with 𝔇𝔘𝔊𝔏𝔄𝔖 embroidered in azure; the double sets of rings, four in all, that the couples would exchange he balanced carefully on top of the ancestral woolen symbol. The words were said and the sacraments satisfactorily completed as the de Lindsay canon pronounced the names: James Lord Douglas and his bride Lady Joanna Douglas; Archibald Douglas and his bride Lady Beatrice Douglas. To the sounds of the fair Lowland pipes the Douglases, their friends and kin began to make their way back to Park Castle.

Figure XLIX-Part Three; view from above the Lintalee earthworks adjacent to Lintalee Farm, seen right middle of the image

THE MARCHES SUMMER 1310-The new Douglases and their husbands had removed themselves from Douglasdale for the safety of the Forest. James left a garrison of men at Park Castle to defend the region, protect the Douglas tenants and secure the new stronghold being built for their laird. Sir Andrew had returned with his family and son in law to Parkhall; his daily tasks included supervising the construction of a new tower at Park Castle. The foul rumors of Edward Caernarvon's muster; his army expected to march north to Scotland by the fall had the Douglases making haste for their strongholds of the Ettrick. The forces of Brus were scattering; on his orders not to engage the enemy, his lieutenants were going with their retinues into the hills.

When the King of England finally arrived he would not find a single battle; no army of the Scots could he locate anywhere. James preferred the safety of the Marches; Lanarkshire might become a target that they should leave he told his family. He desired to build a fortress at a place near the Jed Water. "This fair Lintalee will so provide us with a most excellent view into the north of England," he explained to Archie and their wives; then he told the ladies of how the nearby cave afforded him shelter the day he razed Douglas Castle and fled to Fawdon for moral support. "That we should venture there to take a look where Douglases shall live; a place not far from Fawdon," he added with a smirk. Archie smiled too; he understood the choice of location as it was near the military road, St. Cuthbert's Way. "When our mother hears of this new fortress, she will be most pleased," he said confidently.

The Douglases and their household stopped at their strongholds in Craig Douglas. It would be a few days before they would continue their traveling, going further east towards Jedburgh. The ladies had become close friends; their slight differences in ages was of no concern to them. Joanna had confided a secret; on her wedding day she knew she was with child already. Now with her forth month upon her, the lay-in was planned for late December. "My Archie's birthday as well," giggled Beatrice. Joanna was a woman of tall stature; her body rounded in curves was muscular, from her days surviving as a widow raising her young son in Ayrshire alone. "That our James does not yet know?" asked Archie's bride incredulously. Joanna shook her head, smiling in the ruse. "That I plan to tell him this night," she said as they were helping supervise the kitcheners and cook.

Scotland was having its worse season for crops growing in decades. A severe famine was coming that would last an entire year; few fully grasped the seriousness of the situation; most Scots were yet complacent about the coming scarcity as they could do little to prevent it. "Our stores are dwindling too soon I fear," Joanna observed. "My Archie says that without the crops, producing their abundance as we hoped, trouble may come to our homeland this winter. We may have more to fear from our own dear Scots trying to find food for their families than the English soldiers," she told her sister in law ruefully.

"Perhaps this is the wrong time to bring another wee one into the world so troubled," Joanna offered. Beatrice told her not to fret. "God chooses when we are to have these children; we can only do our best for them." Then Joanna made an admission that surprised her. "I wish so that Lady El was able to return with us this fall," she said wistfully. Beatrice told her that since her own mother and now her father had passed to the Otherworld, Eleanora had become her true parent. "That this lass so trusts her good judgment most as well; her calming self does so improve the temperament of James when he is worried for his Scotland," Joanna confided. "And you should know that Hugh has become a healer like his father," Beatrice reminded the older Lady Douglas. "That my Archie's mother experienced no pain from her lay-ins; Sir William was a clever healer of renown, an Alchemist Healer is what this lass was told." Joanna was stunned; she had never heard of such a claim. "Her husband was the midwife for the lay-in?" she blurted out. The de Lindsay lass told her it was strange but true. They both started laughing together; to think of their own husbands in charge of the lay-in was profoundly humorous to these new brides.

That night after feasting, Beatrice took her cue from Lady Joanna to take their leave from the great hall. She beckoned Archie to their small chamber; actually a corner within the family level; their small but private quarters in the tower separated from a hall passage by a wooden screen and draping. Henklebaldicus had his father's appetite for romance; his shyness in such matters as well. But his wife, his Beatrice had ordered a scented bath; a trap for love he teased her, that he followed her quite happily. He ordered extra wine and sweet cakes brought to them and he got out his book of poems he was writing to read to her as they sat together in the steaming tub of sensuous aromas and soothing oils. Archie pulled her to him and she snuggled into his manly chest; a characteristic Douglas trait even at his young age.

Archie and Beatrice were granted the right to wed even though he was not technically of age. A young man had to reach the age of fourteen; this year he would, but not until December. When Ellie provided his information she was careful to say this was his fourteenth year so they could be married in the kirk; considered close enough as most births were only recorded by the season or nearest Saint's day. Gilley had insisted they observe dates by calendar and number; Ellie knew exactly when he was born.

"My dearest," Beatrice whispered, "this lass has a secret to so share with her husband." Archie's eyes darted to look over her rounded frame, but she shook her head no, not me she told him. "Joanna has timed her lay-in to so be around the anniversary of your own day!" she told him happily. "But until tonight, our James has not been told." How like my brother to not take note of such things, he sighed to himself. "Promise this lad, that the very first moment that you know, you will so tell your husband and love for all eternity," he said lovingly, engaging her with his eyes. Beatrice smiled at his response and swore faithfully that she would. "We hold no secrets between us," she reminded him. "The strength of our great love since first we met lang years ago is truth." Archie kissed her on the forehead, and smiled as he moved his mouth lower to give her a passionate kiss on the lips. Then suddenly as if distracted he pulled back from their embrace. "Perhaps this lad should dispatch a message to Essex; request the presence of our Hugh." Beatrice was thrilled with the suggestion. "Please," he begged her, "do not share this idea with the others; if he should not come," his words trailed off. "Oh he will come; but I will not reveal our plans," she assured her husband as she cuddled closer to him. They relaxed into the comfort of each other's body and Beatrice giggled as they began the ritual of fond lovers.

The peace brokered between England and Scotland had been extended through the spring but by summer further talks had failed forcing Edward's hand; his nobles were losing faith in his leadership that he decided to unite the magnates of England with his father's well known formula of going on campaign. The earls of Cornwall, Gloucester and Warwick followed his banners, showing their support for their king. On June 15 the first ships and men at arms were dispatched to Perth. In August the king sent letters to the mayors of the Cinque Ports and some three dozen other ports of England to provide him ships for the fall campaign into Scotland. Within three weeks the king himself and his caravan of carts including the ones to hold his lions, made their way to Berwick. From there he marched to Roxburgh following the Tweed west towards Peebles then stopping at Biggar. Here word came to Edward Caernarvon that King Hobbe and the Scottish army had been seen camped on a moor in Stirling. Edward responded by moving the army further west to Lanark continuing through the valley of the Clyde north of Douglasdale, finally winding their way to Glasgow. Now it was mid October when Edward and his army had marched to Renfrew but still there was no sign of Scottish resistance. Robert Brus and his army had vanished it seemed.

STEBBINGE PARK LATE OCTOBER 1310-Because of Caernarvon's muster and the arriving forces of other lords such as John de Segrave with William de Ferrers and his forty men at arms, Lady Eleanora had decided to remain in Stebbinge Park through the fall and into the next spring of 1311. She had planned to dispatch letters to her sons and their wives by messengers; now with the arrival of Archie's letter, she was sending Hugh to take her communications to her family in person. "My son, this mother would fear less if you would travel as a friar or a canon," she protested. Ellie wanted Hugh to wear the tonsure; cut his hair in manner of a monk who had taken his vows so the English might not trouble him on his journey into the Marches of Scotland. "Lady El," he began thoughtfully, "this lad is English born, traveling under the banners of de Ferrers and Bagot. Should I see your kin Sir William from Groby, will I turn another way and so avoid him," he boasted with a twinkle in his eye. "That you so tease this mother!" she chided at him in return. Then softly she continued. "Do take care to so arrive without fearful incident." Sir David had just entered the great hall; he was excited about the adventure, embarking on a journey into the wilds of the Forest with a Douglas brother in tow, through the lines of the English. "It is done," he vowed cheerfully. "Another knight to so dismiss this lass for worrying," she said, cracking a slight smile of embarrassment for her fears.

Figure L-Part Three; miniature 12th century effigy of the Lovaine ' Heart Crusader' Knight in Little Easton

Ellie had packed up many things to send to her family in Scotland. She also brought out the Douglas cradle for Hugh to take with him. "Dear mother, only the cruelest of men would attack our wee retinue to steal a cradle," he chuckled. "There is more that you must take," she said unmoved by his continued mocking of her concern for their safety. "And here; some letters that I have written to each of my four children," she said happily. Eleanora was nearly overwrought that someone might intercept her missives that she had devised code names for each one of her sons to conceal their identity. Beatrice and Joanna were names used often in England and their specific relationship to Lady Bagot was not commonly known. But writing a letter to James Lord Douglas or Archibald of Douglas was another matter she told Hugh. She called James 'Sir Shamus' and her youngest son the wee Godfrey, referring to his great uncle the Duke of Lovaine. Hugh was laughing uncontrollably as he read of her silliness. "Our Archie will resent such sobriquet," he challenged her. "Before the letter is most read our James will be addressing him as the wee knight of Lovaine," he chuckled, referring to the tiny effigy of the Lovaine heart Crusader at Little Easton Church. Ellie flashed a furled brow in the direction of her son. "Inform our oldest son for me that if he taunts our Archie at the fair expense of our noble heritage, he will have to answer to this lass!" she told him pointedly.

CRAIG DOUGLAS NOVEMBER-Joanna had grown large with child and was expecting her lay-in as late as Christmas she told James. The four Douglases with Maudie's son Andrew and many other men at arms from Ettrick had gathered in the sheltered haven of Craig Douglas. Some onfoot from James' retinue were staying in Traquair; others in the smaller tower; the former earth and timber fortress of his grandfather adjacent to St. Mary's Loch. This fortified manor was not far from Blackhouse where Lord Douglas and his family were staying. James was nervous; his child was coming soon into the world while any day he might be called into service for his king; the very worst of circumstances that this lad so feared might be, he mused. "Your brother is fearful for his family," he confided to Archie as they broke their fast in the great hall of Blackhouse Tower. "Dear James, the speywife and the others are most close here; the glen undisturbed, is most secure; the English roaming through the Forest are quite few, not to be of threat to us," he reminded the knight. "That Lady El could be here is my only wish," he allowed. James smiled and told him that he would certainly feel a lot better to see her face.

While the brothers were discussing their plans for Hogmanay the doors to the tower opened to James' men at arms serving watch. "Six Armed horse from Northumbria approaching; the banners of the Chauncelor knight are what we see. "Perhaps to have news from our mother and dear Hugh!" Archie exclaimed. The squire bolted from his seat to see who was in the party of riders. Dear St. Bride he began softly to himself. "Hugh!" he shouted from the open door of the great hall. James' eyes lit up to see his brother with Sir Thomas and Sir David and their squires. The loud shouts of greetings and the sounds of swords clanking at the heels of knights brought Lady Joanna and Lady Beatrice into the great hall; they had been working since early in the prime to complete the small closed-off area near the laird's chamber that they planned to use for the lay-in. "Our dear Hugh; he will help now with the speywife when your good time has come," Beatrice boasted; beaming in the successful plan of her husband. James was stunned by Hugh's arrival and begged his brother to explain how he persuaded Lady El; coming north in the middle of Edward's campaign was very daring, James told them.

"The letter so sent by the wee Godfrey," he chuckled, "requesting the presence of a healer. That she could not turn down the appeal of her youngest son," Hugh said. "This is her response to you, Sir Godfrey," he said mysteriously as he handed the first parchment to a very confused squire named Archibald. "These are sweet missives written by our mother for her children," he said with a hint of folly. "And for you Sir Shamus," Hugh continued mischievously, handing the second one to James. It was obvious from his tone that something was afoot James observed. The aspiring churchman calmly took the other two letters and presented them to his sisters in law. "These fair parchments are for two sweet lasses," he said. "And what names are so written upon the missives to our brides?" James asked beginning to realize why Eleanora was addressing him as Sir Shamus. The aspiring canon summoned all his might to present a straight face. "Most the same, Lady Beatrice and Lady Joanna," he allowed. Hugh finally could not contain the ruse any longer; he started laughing as he told the silly story. "That Eleanora felt most frightened to pen a letter to Sir James of Douglas; most as well to her wee Archie that she thought up careful names; like spies as she so told this lad."

Figure LI-Part Three; looking north from Stow towards the Moorfoot Hills on the Lugate Water.

But why Sir Godfrey, James kept asking himself? Then suddenly it came to him as he recalled the name written under the tiny Lovaine effigy: the Heart Crusader. "The wee knight," he chortled. "Most perfect," he began, when Hugh quickly interrupted. "Careful with the words you are about to say; our Lady Eleanora has sent bold warning to any son that disparages the noble house of Lovaine, the effigy for the entombed heart; the brave descendant from the House of Brabant," he said brandishing the Douglas smirk. "Her words were these, that any who might choose to take in jest that noble figure be forewarned that *they will have to answer to Eleanora*," Hugh admonished them. James reflected for a moment. "This lad has seen the dagger that she so conceals about herself; this sorry knight will not chance such peril to reflect on brave warriors of Lovaine," he teased, and then added his grateful words. "This brother is in debt to one healer named Hugh; thank you most for coming, to help in the birthing of a new heir for Douglasdale!" James proclaimed to rounds of cheering.

The feasting was upon them; wine was being poured when another announcement came from the watch: three riders from the king," they told him. James eyes darted towards his brothers; what peril was about? The king's men at arms told James that others were being commanded to rendezvous near the Pentland Hills; to send a message to dear Edward. "Round up sixty of your best men; archers from the Forest and armed horse, Lord Robert has so stated here," they told the knight. "When?" James begged to know. "In three days or less," they said quietly. The laird of Douglas looked sadly at his bride; put his hand gently on the roundness of her belly. "Dear wife; the times we feared most are now here," he said sadly. Joanna smiled and put her hand at his chin, pulling lightly at his curly lang beard. "My husband most forgets, this lass holds true for Scotland. Our child will be in the good hands of Hugh and the speywife from Sundhope," she resolved calmly. James held her hand and stroked her hair. "A true Douglas are you my sweet lass," he said meaning every word of it.

Figure LII-Part Three; ruins of the Kirk in the Woods, Selkirk; near the motte believed to be the site of Selkirk Castle

Archie was eager to go along. "Not this time," James quietly told him. "But only because my brother is most needed here for the arrival of his dear niece or nephew," he reminded Archie. The outspoken squire was silent in his protest; strangely grateful that James had remembered the family event almost upon them. As he reflected on the decision of his laird, the squire realized that James was not at all cold hearted or aloof as others might observe. Only that for the circumstances of their lives was he forced to show little emotion; his disappointment to not be home with his wife for the birth of their first child was plain to the squire. The young laird of Douglas was a most trusted vassal and loyal knight in service to his king; a higher calling Archie phrased it later when he explained it all to Beatrice. And somehow he knew this one occasion would not be the last time; the king's requests and the demands of Scotland came first, before the needs of James' family. Not surprisingly, the weight of his personal life came to bear on his younger brothers. "And happily, this lad is here to help him," Archie proudly told his bride.

Figure LIII-Part Three; the gloaming, Loch Whitmuir; a working farm today near the site of Whitmuir Hall, Selkirk

DECEMBER-The raids into the Lothianes, burning the villages and farms of the English sympathizers went on for several days. Before the campaign concluded, the Scots had encountered a foraging party of Welsh and English foot and armed horse; surprising them at a ford. It was a fierce battle that ensued; nearly none of Edward's patrol made their escape. Those few soldiers who returned to the Berwick garrison, begged for reinforcements. By now three hundred of their own lay dead beside the ford and the Scots had vanished once again back into the hills or deep into the bogs, safe havens from the English soldiers. Robert Brus was satisfied with the delivery of his message to Edward's adherents in the Lothianes that he ordered the Scots to scatter once again. Back into the Highlands, north of the Forth the Scots withdrew on the king's orders. The large contingency of Brus disappeared in the mist like ghost riders across the moors. The safety, the protection of the English sympathizers was now in doubt; Edward sent his army to confront the King of Scots but again he was too late. Out of frustration Caernarvon decided to entreat of peace and set up a meeting with Lord Clifford and Robert Brus in Selkirk.

Brus had retained Douglas and his retinue to join the king's escort as they moved south towards Traquair and the former royal hunting lodge nearby. James was anxious to send word to Joanna that he was but a half day's ride away; but the secrecy of their arrival was required so he thought better of it. They were there only for short hours when word came of the proposed meeting at Selkirk. "This knight looks forward to such greetings," he said with a broad grin. "Perhaps that English vassal will give reason for my sword to make him sicker of the fight," he joked. Lord Clifford had requested Lord Robert to come to Selkirk Castle; a fortress under Edward's control; garrisoned by the English. Robert and his advisors were not familiar with this part of their kingdom so relied on James' knowledge of the burgh; to find a suitable site for the meeting with the lord who formerly held Douglasdale from Edward.

Figure LIV-Part Three; Borders bridge over the Yarrow near Philipbaugh

"Perhaps to stay at the fortified tower at Whitmuir; hold our discourse with the English there as well. Selkirk's abbey is most in ruins but the manor house is yet maintained by Tironensian monks for the Abbot of Kelso," he suggested. "Early in the 12th century these monks so established their monastery of Selkirk on the Ettrick where it meets the Tweed. But within few years they found it necessary to move to Kelso; the entire monastery to locate there and that structure near Lindean was most abandoned." The king's chancellor had joined in the discussion; he approved of the site. "The abbot's good stronghold in Whitmuir will be to our benefit for these discussions; that I may know some of the monks to our advantage most as well."

The meetings in Selkirk were tedious. Edward was relinquishing little in the initial offer though the king's envoys made it clear they were eager to come to some good conclusion. Finally the discussions were adjourned; another parley was set for some several weeks later in Melrose. James quickly took his leave of Brus. "My sweet bride awaits her husband and new father," he boasted. James headed home to Craig Douglas; it was almost Christmas he mused. As he rode west towards the Yarrow he reflected on his family, crying out inside: *to be so near to them and not be able to take my leave*; how frustrated this knight has come to be! "A struggle grows within me; more than I can bear some days I know it," the laird yelled loudly as if to reach the Heavens with his cries. On and on he rode; spurring his Hobini faster, home to Blackhouse went James, Lord Douglas.

Racing down the cleugh-brae, he turned his Hobini homeward; following the winding path of the Douglas Burn he rode like a blur of azure past the watch, his supertunic flowing wildly behind him; the young laird was more than eager to reach home. He bolted from his horse and threw off the supertunic to his squire. As he reached for the latch of the tower house doors he was greeted by another Douglas: Hugh; the healer and now experienced midwife grinned as he beckoned in the new father. Seated by the fireplace was Joanna; she had just finished nursing "the wee William," she said proudly.

Figure LV-Part Three; a tranquil Borders scene, Torwoodlee northwest of Galashiels; the Moorfoot hovering in the background on the scenic A7

"A brother do I have," shouted Walter as he ran to James. "He is a very lang laddie; all covered with black hair like a little bear," marveled the Logan page. Minerva the Deerhound came up from her warm place beside the cradle and nuzzled James hand; trying to get his attention it seemed. But the knight just stood there helplessly for a few moments, with his mouth hanging open unable to say anything, taking it all in; all he could do was smile now. Archie had enough of his brother's hapless delay. "Kiss the lass," he commanded impatiently. James ran to his bride and kissed her and then kissed her again. He grabbed the swaddling of baby and lifted him high over his head and danced around the great hall. "A son, I do have a son!" he proclaimed over and over; as if daring himself to believe it.

In the spring Edward sent his men into the Forest; to command the good men of Ettrick and Selkirk to pledge their fealty. The laird of Douglas and his family knew of the king's every step; watching the procession from the safety of their stronghold. The knight who called the Forest his domain was not concerned for the pledging; these men would be ready to forsake their praise for Edward when Lord Douglas called them back to do battle for their true and rightful king, Robert Brus. James had moved his family west; Lord Robert was planning to invade England from the Solway.

The second meeting scheduled for Melrose to entreat of peace did not occur. The king had been forewarned; de mischef was about. The English had planned to attack him at the abbey; to end the life of Scotland's titular king. In retaliation Robert Brus was taking his army to burn all the land of the lord of Gilsland, the town of Haltwhistle, as well as a good part of Tynedale. When the Scottish army returned north they brought with them large booty including many head of cattle; strangely some of the English herd made their way to Douglasdale

DOUGLASDALE SUMMER 1312-Eleanora and her household took advantage of the political climate of unrest in England to leave for the north; making her way to Lanarkshire to see her children and grandchildren. Hugh had returned for Hogmanay six months ago and would accompany her; 'escaping England' she gleefully proclaimed with Sir David and the rest of her household and men at arms in tow. They planned to join up with the usual Northumbrian entourage at Fawdon and then cross the Marches, over the hills into Scotland. After a brief stop in Blackhouse Lady Bagot was making haste for her beloved Douglasdale; it had been over two years since she had seen her sons and daughters. Now there were wee grandsons about; dear William and his cousin John, named for John Crawford, the great grandfather of both parents, Beatrice and her beloved Henklebaldicus. When John Crawford's daughter married another Archibald, the Douglases came into possession of Crawfordjohn. The de Lindsay laird had married the eldest Crawford daughter; bringing with her Crawford castle as part of her dowry for the marriage. Now the families were united once again and the young couple found it fitting to honor their mutual ancestor with naming their first son John.

As Ellie and Hugh rode into the vale they marveled at the prosperity that seemed to be returning; not that every farm and villein were affluent but once again there were crops growing; cattle could be seen grazing on the moorish lands of the barony. "Aye, the Bluebells have come to greet us

Hugh," she sighed to see them gracing the banks of the Park Burn. Then she turned to look between the trees growing on the motte of Park Castle; the new tower was really taking shape and the first few levels appeared occupied! The wall-walk was incomplete and the battlements were not yet constructed; still there was a roof. Out from the double doors of the new dunjon bounded a squire and his bride; Archie was carrying his infant son, a huge mass of swaddling cloth and reddish brown hair that stuck out from all directions. "A wee hairy beast like his father; le Hardi most as well," Ellie cooed as she jumped off her palfrey to take her newest grandchild into her arms. Maudie had made the journey as well; she was thrilled to see Ellie holding another baby. "The look upon your sweet face," she marveled. Ana could see it too; her lass had not looked so fair since the lad's own father was first born their last year in Douglas Castle she mused.

Figure LVI-Part Three; view from the folly tower towards the location of the postern tower motte of the ancient Douglas Castle

Joanna was walking out with young William; his fine, black hair glistened in the sun as the wind tossed it about his face. He was squinting, cupping his left hand over his eyes in a serious effort to check out the visitors. "The very face of one named James," Ellie exclaimed. "Come meet your grandmother," she beckoned the lad. He ran full tilt that he almost fell flat on his face. Ellie grabbed him and pulled him up to her. "There, you bold wee warrior," she teased the boy, "you've been captured!" Joanna embraced her and Ellie pushed her back. "You are with child again?" she asked. "Our James must keep you locked in chamber; most like his father in so many ways," she chortled happily. "And where is Lord Douglas?" Eleanora inquired. "Parliament in Ayr," Archie responded with a hint of exasperation. "This lad preferred to remain at Douglasdale; guarding our home and waiting for our mother and good Hugh to so arrive," he told them plainly.

Hugh greeted everyone and was especially delighted to see Walter who beckoned him to see the pell and butt James had constructed by the stables. "Our father wants all the men of Douglas to know how to buckle on their armor like a baron and fight with sword; even those who seek the word of God," he explained excitedly. Hugh understood; his own father's influence was everywhere he reflected. "And did you see the sun so disappear?" asked Walter. Hugh told him that he did. "The moon eclipsed the sun that it appeared most like a horned-moon to return again to its normal sphere in three hours is what we saw." Walter asked if Hugh knew the one who did that; to have such great power in the skies. "Only our God can do such things," he told the page. "Not Edward?" the lad asked. "No. Edward although a king is but a man; tales of his great powers as a healer, his father most as well are false. My own father Sir William was an Alchemist Healer, trained on Crusade; but he could not make the moon so cover the sun."

PARK CASTLE LATE JULY-James finally returned from Ayrshire; having remained longer than anyone to discuss the strategy of the upcoming campaign in greater detail with his king. He would be home 'for a stay of few days only' he told them. Much feasting followed in the great hall of the partially completed tower; the larger chamber was very comfortable even though as Ellie put it, 'everything smelled new' and was not yet homey. The laird was laughing and telling stories of the raids the Scots had been making into northern England; how he returned with much booty of coinage and cattle too for their trouble. "And what came of Parliament?" Archie demanded to know. "More was this a war council than a Parliament. Our king has proposed of plans to secure more revenue for Scotland; increasing our control of strategic fortresses in our kingdome most as well," James replied.

The laird of Douglas told everyone how Brus sought to take the castles of Dumfries, Caerlaverock and Buittle with his own forces, men at arms from north of the Forth. "With Edward's troubles now in England," James continued, "our king has so decided that the north of England has suffered little in these bitter years of war. That we will take our front in battle off to Cumbria; then through Northumbria as well," he allowed. Ellie was frightened; Sir Thomas was also concerned for Redesdale and Fawdon and for his family there. James explained that it was not by accident that Fawdon was avoided when the Scots swept through the Cheviot last fall. "Our Fawdon holds a special place in this lad's heart. Then most as well the crops growing so reduce the fine for marriage yet not paid," he added teasingly to

Ellie; knowing her dower rents were still held to pay le Hardi's fine from over twenty years ago

Hugh wanted to understand how King Robert felt it safe to invade England when not too lang ago Edward was in Scotland and Brus avoided such encounters with English. "My lord the king so understands the troubles Edward has created for himself with these nobles," James began. Ellie interrupted. "That this lass so told you of the excommunication of Piers Gaveston; that dear Edward fled with him, leaving his Queen behind. Then with oblique defiance returned the sorry fool to England against the consent of Parliament; his nobles angered to organize against their king." James told Hugh that even more important, the Earl of Lancaster with his new inheritance as the Earl of Lincoln and Salisbury, already holding the titles of the Earl of Derby and Leicester had become the most powerful baron in all of England. "This lord and many others have sought to rule over Caernarvon; to proclaim themselves the lords Ordinaners they control his revenue now while upholding the banishment of Gaveston." Ellie said that that only Nicky and few others supported Edward; the de Segrave knight did so for the pardon he received from Edward for his conviction of treason eight years ago.

Figure LVII-Part Three; Lanercost Priory church was burned in 1311 under orders of Robert Brus; services are still held for the parishioners in the old church today

"The moment has come for Scotland to remind the English of what they so allowed with both Edwards, the horrors and great sufferings inflicted upon the Scots. But we are seeking only to put fear into their hearts; not revenge for the killing they set upon us," James allowed. As he continued, he explained the king's strategy. "He would dispatch his brother Edward, to join this noble laird of Douglas in raids in the Marches of England." The laird described the full of his assignments; to extort as much coinage and other goods for protection and his assurance that the Scots would not burn their villages and lands. "So the next months on into winter we will spend roaming the Borders; riding into the north of England, marauders into Cumbria and east into Northumbria as well," James explained, elaborating on the broad spectrum of the king's plans for campaign. As he looked at his bride sadness crept over him that Ellie sensed immediately. "This lass will do her part for Scotland; to stay with our Joanna until the birth of another Douglas heir is so confirmed," she interjected, hoping to allay some of his worries.

The knight realized his mother had once again read his thoughts; he hated being gone from his Douglasdale especially when such important family events were about to occur. But he was not just any soldier; Scotland and his king came first he knew; only why was he always forced to choose between them and during such strenuous times he wondered to himself? "Your own dear father was once so meeting at Carstairs; planning secret strategies of true importance with the bishop and other patriots," Eleanora reminded him. "Then a young squire came to the rescue of his mother as the wee Archie wanted to be born." James' face lit up as he recalled that early morning when he and Ana brought Ellie to the lay-in so he could ride out to Castle Torres and bring le Hardi home before his brother arrived ahead of the midwife, his father. "Your brothers are most here; Hugh and this humble squire will so preside," boasted Archie. Then James realized he had forgotten the rest of the news. "Our Hugh and dear Lady El will have to do without you squire," he said with a smirk. "Our king has called out all his followers for this campaign; your lord paramount so commands your presence in Cumbria!

Archie's eyes grew huge; his mouth dropped open in astonishment; he was finally going into battle! Ellie trembled; sitting next to Joanna, she grabbed her hand instinctively. The ladies looked at each other; the importance of the moment was both exhilarating and frightening for now two Douglas brothers, the squire and his knight would be fighting for Scotland together on the same battlefield. "Dear St. Bride," Ellie blurted out unconsciously. "Lady El do not fear; this lad will be most careful to not allow Lord Douglas to take injury," the squire proclaimed with bravado. James burst into laughter. "It is your sorry self that this lad will most worry for in battle; to protect my wee squire when it is he who should be defending this knight." Archie demanded justice for his brother's words; a competition he declared. Before Ellie or Joanna could protest the Douglas brother were in the courtyard of Park Castle setting up the archery butt; the disagreement would be settled by trial of bow they declared!

CORBRIDGE LATE AUGUST-Robert Brus had led his armies plundering and burning their way, moving through Tynedale with horrific ease; little resistance intercepted them as fear paved their way. Taking the old gates of the eastern Marches the king led his men by way of Harbottle and Redesdale burning the district and destroying everything in their path as the Scots made their way south to Corbridge. Feverishly the army moved through Northumbria leaving death and destruction in their wake; but strangely their determined path into the Cheviot lay far west and miles south of a small manor called Fawdon. The Scots burned Hexham Priory again; the tomb of Gilbert de Umfraville barely shook in fear; the alabaster effigy taking on an odd cloak of black and grey from the charred remains of flames that engulfed the priory. The old nemesis of le Hardi and aftertimes his widow must have wondered what he did to deserve such desecration to the mark of his remains. "Greetings and salutations," cried Lord Douglas to the late Lord of Redesdale as his retinue threw liquid fire upon the wooden supports and carved seating within the holy structure, to nearly raze it. James reflected as he rode out of Hexham that sometimes war had a strange way of equalizing things.

Figure LVIII-Part Three; Corbridge today

Razing English manors, defacing the countryside of King Edward's vassals, became a way of life for Scottish warriors invading the Marches in 1312. By such show of force, Brus' raiders were symbolically undermining Lord Edward's strength; his heretofore, powerful protection for his nobles was made impotent. Such raids were necessary for Scotland's very survival Lord Robert determined, but to James, burning villages and destroying crops of villeins to cower their lords into submission was not very much to his liking. While putting the blade of his sword through the belly of an English knight was acceptable; killing women and children reminded him of Berwick, sickening his victory to a gruesome end.

James and Edward Brus now made their way south through the barony of de Umfraville at Prudhoe. With Durham their final destination, the Scots moved under the cover of night. Ten miles north of Durham they arrived at Chester-le-Street, routing the sleeping citizens from their beds. The savage war cries reverberated through the night air as the Crusader's screeching oliphant was sounded by a Douglas squire; putting fear into their very souls of the town's inhabitants. Some of the people rose from their confused state to seek refuge in the castle and cathedral church; others were not so fortunate. The reports that reached Westminster told of an army thirsting for revenge, cruelly killing everyone who crossed their path. The sight of the dying affected Archie greatly; but he refused to acknowledge his repudiation for the deeds. As he rode his Hobini in formation with his knight and brother he blamed his confusion, his compelling concern for the English citizens on his inexperience.

Figure LIX-Part Three; Hexham Priory remains today one the best examples of medieval religious houses in Northumbria

Later the Douglas squire was sitting alone in the Scots' camp; trying to comprehend the gruesome slaying he just witnessed. James noticed how introverted and reflective the lad had become. "So foolish for this sorry knight to have not prepared you for this fight," he began quietly. Archie looked up and the light of the camp fire caught his eyes that James realized he was crying. He began to tell Archie about his first battle. "Most fortunate to see only soldiers so in combat; such treachery as we beheld today is most revolting to this knight," he quietly confided. Archie kept silent; his eyes searched his brother's face; he wanted to know why so many had to suffer for the foolishness of Edward as he deemed the reason for their war. James continued. "Only from the memory of our dear father slain most bitterly, dying that he did for his core values; these thoughts alone have kept this knight most focused on his work to do. Know this dear brother: your James recognizes those feelings of regret; to feel not pain or sorrow for our actions this day is not to breathe of life. Feel the pain; then let go of the memory. It is the only solace for a soldier's shallow ways in war," he counseled the squire. Archie shook his head in somber thanks for James' understanding. It was not cowardice or lack of resolve that caused Archie sorrow James assured him; it was the stark reality of war in its most grueling definition.

Arriving on Market Day in Durham the next morning, the Scots surprised the good citizens of that bishopric. The plunder resulted in great booty; the townspeople yielded to surrender with a treat of peace purchased at great cost in coinage. From this successful raid the Scots increased their stores and added to their treasury. A huge sum of £2000 was promised; some payments were raised immediately and hostages, sons of great lords were taken for guarantee of the remainder due. The price was only casually protested; paying for protection was preferred, that the Scots would avoid their town in future raids. The word spread throughout the countryside; fear preceded the arrival of Brus' raiders in every English village. For all of Cumbria, Durham and Northumbria the specter of one black knight took notice; even the word that he might be about sent chills of terror through the English villeins. This frightening soldier became well known to the good citizens of the Marches giving the blood thirsty marauder as they described the Scottish knight a special name: The Black Douglas. The knight's appearance was swarthy and hirsute, brandishing a frightening grimace of destructive resolve. The threat of his arrival spoke horror to the English; he could be lurking anywhere, to find them without warning, to strike them dead they feared. Mothers rocked their wee ones to sleep with words of the comfort: "hush now, do not fear, the Black Douglas will not find us here." But for James and his brother Archie the good knight and his brave squire were just Scots following the orders of their king; trying to keep alive the fight for liberty; National Independence for their wee country, their beloved Scotland.

DOUGLASDALE OCTOBER 1312-Eleanora, Ana and Hugh assisted the speywife from Douglas village as they welcomed into the world another Douglas; a beautiful lass Joanna named Elizabeth. "She has the Steward eyes of beauty," remarked Ellie as she handed the newborn to her mother. "Such lovely red hair," admired Joanna. The lady was exhausted but fairing well from the ordeal as Ana termed the lang lay-in. Hugh was putting away his vial of Holy Water. He had taken the opportunity to baptize the new Douglas within minutes of her birth as Gilley had instructed in his notes on being a midwife and healer. Joanna begged to know what they were doing; she had slept through the last such ritual with the wee William. "My husband did not hold for ceremony of the kirk; he would christen each child at the moment they were so born to insure safe passage to the Otherworld when that time most comes," Ellie replied. Hugh explained that the way of the Celtic church was more practical; an innocent child should not be condemned because he might pass before a priest had time to say the words of baptism.

Before James and his brother returned home Ellie and Hugh were forced to take their leave to make their way back home to Essex before winter. "That we will await your good word," Ellie said referring to the uncertainty of James' and Archie's whereabouts. "Lady El thank you most for staying with me; you too dear Hugh," Joanna told them. "Know this; were there trouble with our men we would know of it most quickly. When Walter's dear father made his passing, his body was brought to me within few days." Beatrice ran to Ellie and hugged her as tears ran down her cheeks. "This lass is frightened for my husband and our James," she admitted between deep sobs. "A warrior's family suffers each and every day their loved one is off on campaign; the soldier himself only falls once to his end in this world," Ellie said quietly. "You have married a knight to be; my own sweet William most reminded me of my duty: to pray to St. Bride for his safe return. I bid you that good advice most now." Beatrice wiped her eyes and kissed Eleanora and Hugh goodbye. "Our children the only solace for these days spent so in worry and fear," Ellie reminded her daughters in law.

BLACKHOUSE-James and Archie were returning from campaign, crossing paths with Hugh and Ellie in Craig Douglas. "Your daughter Elizabeth is well," she boasted, "baptized by our Hubicus as our father would have wanted." James turned to Archie and commented that Beatrice must next have a son or they would be outnumbered. Ellie chuckled to recall le Hardi's sentiments when their three daughters were born all in a row. "Are you to stay in Douglasdale and be there for Hogmanay?" Hugh asked. "That we will remove our family to Lintalee for the winter; to keep watch of the eastern Marches for our king," James told them. "In the spring months this lass and our Hugh to make our way to Fawdon;" she predicted, "though later for some business I must attend to in Stafford."

Archie teased her about their Northumbrian manor being in the path of blood thirsty Scots. "That messuage should yet be there unless the Black Douglas forgets his bearings; to come with fire and sword to the parish of Ingram," he said wryly. And who is *'the Black Douglas'* she demanded to know? Archie rolled his eyes and told her, "The sorry knight you so see before us," he said pointing to his brother. Ellie sighed; to think her son was becoming a legend of terror, bringing fear to northern England. Then she remembered her concern for Fawdon and warned them should de mischef come to the Ingram parish. "That le Hardi will be there to remind you both who holds of that messuage," she retorted playfully. "Do not fear Mother; this lad loves our Fawdon as much as any Douglas laird. That there is little coinage for our coffers there so insures our good intentions!" James added with a smirk.

Figure LX-Part Three; a misty view of Dryhope Tower ruins near Craig Douglas lends mystery to the landscape of the Borders; photo from Susan Shane

"That there are others who could offer richer payments for protection," she allowed. "The Lord of Alnwick might be about," she teased them referring to their sworn enemy Henry de Percy who now held the barony and castle near Fawdon. James' face brightened; he had forgotten the news he planned to share with her. "Some words of great regret for that lord; that he is now an unwilling guest in Edward's prisons; the escheators so ordered to take his lands and chattel into the king's hands," he said sarcastically; nearly gloating in his pronouncements. In all the years since their bitter enemy had falsely accused Lord Douglas of treason, sending Gilley to his certain death in the White Tower, Ellie and James never dreamed Sir Henry would fall out of royal favor. "While passing time in Hartlepool this knight and Douglas squire came upon fair rumors of great interest." Ellie was stunned to hear that her sons were raiding English towns that far south. "This squire must assure you; we rode that far and further, taking booty and burning villages to the ground," he said in matter of fact tones. The war had finally spread to England; but Ellie could hardly blame them she allowed;

having seen the devastation Edward reaped in Scotland they had years to go to just make even the score she reflected.

Figure LXI-Part Three; Alnwick Abbey ruins, an antique print in the author's collection

James continued telling Hugh and Lady El about the demise of one lord named Henry. "That as he took part in a conspiracy of his own to find the king's favorite in Knaresburgh; to join with others in support for the execution of Piers Gaveston. Though Lord Percy was not the one to order the beheading of that sorry lord he was the one nobleman dear Edward chose to punish." Ellie and Hugh were taken aback by the news. "But not one bit remorseful for that dreadful lord," Ellie scoffed.

A year later de Percy was pardoned and received back many of his lands. But during his brief imprisonment, another king saw his advantage. While the lord was Edward's prisoner, Robert Brus judged Lord Percy to have overstepped his charge in another matter. Sir Henry had been ordered by King Edward to take Brus' daughter into custody in 1306. De Percy did so; but piqued Lord Robert's ire by imposing his own views of imprisonment on the child, to woeful extremes beyond the imaginative requests of King Edward. Brus decided to return the favor; to remind Edward's vassal of his imprudent deeds. He reseised de Percy's holdings in Scotland, awarding the earldom of Carrick to his brother Edward. Now the tables were turning; the years were closing in on de Percy for his vile overreach of power and there was no king to protect him from the Scots.

LINTALEE 1ST DECEMBER-Joanna dispatched a letter to Lady Bagot; a newsy missive about their winter days near Jedburgh, adding words from the noble Sir Shamus and the wee Godfrey of good cheer for event of Hogmanay approaching at month's end. One of their men at arms was going to ride to Fawdon with some gifts to Sir Thomas and his family; his son would then travel south to Essex with the salutations and greetings from the Douglases of Lintalee. Snow was falling over the valley of the Jed as the family gathered in the great hall with their household for the day's feasting. Men at arms were coming in and out of the partially completed tower house of earth and timber extraction.

Figure LXII-Part Three; Glendouglas near Lintalee

The watch was changing for the hour when one of James' most loyal vassals entered the great hall with a strange package wrapped in coarse cloth; so heavy it was being carried by three men. "The siege engine for our good laird of Douglas," pronounced Sym of Ledhouse. The older soldier had joined James when he was but a squire during the second siege at Douglas Castle. Sym was from the parish of Lesmahagow; his father had been a loyal vassal of le Hardi from Crossford. Now this jolly, even tempered warrior from Lanarkshire was going to demonstrate his other talents for warfare he told them. The ladies and their husbands gathered round the soldier, known for his valor and good ability with sword they were surprised to discover he was quite a technician as well. "When we so returned from doing battle in the English Marches the fall that my lord the baron most mentioned the need for better distractions of warfare more suited to our calling," Sym began. James remembered telling le Hardi's vassal about his desire to right the wrongs done to his father when held prisoner in Douglas Tower in Berwick on Tweed. "Perhaps to devise a way to take back that castle for the Scots," Lord Douglas had suggested half heartedly. Ledhouse had suggested building a siege engine. But James did not think much of the idea. "That this laird has little use for such contrived warfare, waiting out a starving garrison; nor coinage for such extravagance as well," he told Ledhouse. But the old warrior was undeterred; he decided to build the ladder and pressed his knight for details on the fortress which James albeit grudgingly supplied.

Sym was determined to surprise the knight. He worked secretly on his plan for weeks, while James had given little more thought to his vassal's idea. But now as he pulled out the maze of two hemp ropes, *'as lang as the walls of Berwick Castle are most tall,'* his eyes grew wide in eager anticipation. The required dimensions had been drawn out by James' own hand; his memory of the fortress when le Hardi was garrison commander was still etched clearly in his mind. Archie excitedly looked over the two ropes; each was knotted at intervals of eighteen inches apart, he noted. Here the craftsman had placed a board, a hand-hewn log with two holes one carved through on either side for the rope to pass through. At one end of the lang expanse of rope was an iron hook that could grasp the enclosure walls of a large castle or the crenelles of a smaller battlemented tower. At the bottom of the *'wondrous construction'* were some rings where the Scots could attach a lang spear and move the ladder upward until it reached the top of the wall.

Figure LXIII-Part Three; Lintalee earthworks; Borders fortress of the Good Sir James

"That this laird does have his siege engine, sure aye!" James proclaimed. Everyone was cheering and laughing; the wee ones John and William had wandered over as well, bringing their Deerhound to investigate. Minerva as if protecting his children grabbed the end of the rope and began shaking it to and fro as if the strange ladder was some kind of treacherous invader. "Silly hound; release your captive!" ordered Archie. "Now may we begin to set our strategy," James announced happily. "To our success then; that we will return Berwick Castle and Douglas Tower to her rightful kingdome!" Wine was being poured in great quantity as the knight and his sergeants sat down at the trestle table in the great hall at Lintalee to plan their attack on the great fortress on the Tweed. Little did James realize that were he successful in gaining entrance to the castle he might encounter an English yeoman; a soldier holding a position of great prominence in that stronghold. The knight in question was Sir John de Wysham, the one time suitor of Lady Douglas; heiress and widow of Sir William le Hardi.

BERWICK ON TWEED 6TH DECEMBER-Under cover of darkness sixteen men at arms were carrying two siege engines of the Lord Douglas. Their captain and his vassal Sym lead the way as they proceeded to move stealth-like up the approach to the walls that comprised the stone palisade of Berwick Castle. They had worn dark cloaks and super tunics over their armor as they quietly moved into position. The Scots laid the ladders out in the darkness that enshrouded the fortress; the murky mist flowing up from the Tweed covered their clandestine activity completely in a vaporous cloud. They did not speak but for hand signals previously arranged. James carried his scaling ladder and with Archie's help they began to move it into place. The air was heavy; not a sound could be heard except the rolling of the tide; rippling in retreat over the rocky bed of the inner harbor below. Deftly the Douglas knight moved the spear-point to attach the hook over the wall of the castle. Sym followed in perfect unison; his length of roped steps securely hanging in place as well.

Figure LXIV-Part Three; the walled burgh of Berwick on Tweed; later defensive structures built in and around the ancient protective enclosures

An eerie silence surrounded them as James nodded his signal to begin their ascent. Sym was going first on his ladder; the laird would lead his men up the second as was their plan. Silently they rose in perfect step when suddenly from above they heard barking. A foolish hound either spotting their movements or gaining their scent began to pace feverishly, back and forth, barking incessantly. The animal's disturbance alerted the lone member of the watch to the presence of intruders. Panic prompted the startled guard as he went to rouse the rest of the night patrol; some he found asleep. The party of Scots began to retrace their steps in an orderly retreat. James was not one to risk his men; this siege was aborted he told them quickly. The small unit of English guards did not know how many were in James' retinue, calling loudly for the assistance of the rest of the garrison. "The King of Scots is attacking the castle!" they shouted. The late hour of the attempted siege meant that many of the soldiers within the fortress were sleeping; readying the men at arms for battle would take time. Unfortunately for James there was not enough delay to allow the Scots to take back the scaling ladders in their retreat. "Abandon our work here!" Lord Douglas commanded, as he called to the squires to bring up their horses.

Figure LXV-Part Three; defensive walls and moats at Berwick on Tweed sought to protect the Borders burgh from invaders

    Into the night rode the men from the Forest, following their laird toward their stronghold on the Jed. The Scots dared not look back until they reached a ford they trusted to be safe from ambuscade; one of forty crossings they had to choose from to cross the Tweed. Here James and his men at arms stopped to catch their breath before proceeding past Coldstream and on to Swinton where they camped the night before returning to Lintalee late the next day. "We can build two more by Hogmanay," Sym suggested. James was laughing by now; at least they escaped without injury or loss, save only their 'wee siege engines' he quipped. "That we must plan for better cover; some contrivances to disguise our armor most as well; seeking of a quicker way to gain admittance too," he determined. "Build the Douglas siege engines again good Sym; we will try another time; perhaps a different fortress most as well."

The Douglas knight sent word of their failed encounter at Berwick to his king. Lord Robert was still north of the Forth having held a Parliament in Inverness two months before; he was heard to have moved south to Perth. The king's messengers brought great news; Perth had fallen to the Scots! A wall of stone surrounded the burgh; several large towers were strategically set along the massive structure and the final defense was the very deep moat encircling the fortress. Ironically it was the gallant knight William Oliphant who was in charge of the town's garrison. He was the same brave soldier who held Stirling Castle for the Scots when it was under siege of Edward's Trebuchet in 1304. The warrior had gained his freedom from the Tower of London to take this command and he was not going to capitulate to the Scottish army without a struggle, Lord Robert determined.

The story of the King of Scot's successful siege arrived in Lintalee by the end of January. The details of the taking of Perth came to be the legendary tactics of Robert Brus. The king had withdrawn his army to sneak back eight days later. Then Lord Robert took forth his own ladder and in full armor waded into the moat of the fortress; the water was starkly cold as it was only the first week of January. His men watched anxiously as their king walked into depths up to his neck before making it safely to the other side of the moat. Brus' men at arms were thus stirred to follow his gallant lead and soon the entire retinue had made their safe entry into the walled burgh. With little resistance the town and garrison commander William Oliphant obligingly surrendered. Soon afterward Sir William appeared in England where he arranged for his ransom to be sent to the Scottish treasury. Robert Brus, King of Scots grew into greatness; the legend became the man this day. On the 8th January 1313 Lord Robert, the great leader of men, the fair knight of chivalry, and the superior strategist won a huge victory on the Firth of Tay by his bold spirit and true deeds of renown.

STAFFORDSHIRE SPRING 1313-Eleanora was making her traditional trek north to 'collect her rents,' as she framed her traversing of the Marches and bold escape to Scotland. Lord Bagot was joining her at the manor of La Hyde in anticipation of signing some important documents that would settle their Staffordshire estates for the future. In the last years Sir William had been in Wales almost exclusively and more recently he became custodian for the Castle of Aber Conway. Conway Castle was given to Sir William Bagot for his life by Edward Caernarvon; directing his royal Chamberlain to pay the knight substantial fees for his service there. Arriving today at the Staffordshire manor Ellie and Hugh and her traveling household from Stebbinge Park made themselves at home; waiting for the English knight to make his appearance.

Lady Bagot was reviewing the charters she held with her husband; the changes would bring an inheritance to Archibald and define the remainder of the estates of the Hyde and Patshull including Coppenhall for his younger brother Ralph. She planned to settle the manor of Wilbrighton Hall, a messuage and carucate, upon her youngest son. The trust would be devised to terminate at the time of her death or earlier if Lord Bagot predeceased her or when Archibald reached his majority.

Figure LXVI-Part Three; Ranton, abbey ruins, church and adjacent manor; a deed in trust was issued by Eleanora Lovaine Bagot and William Bagot 29th April 1313 to Richard the chaplain of Little Dunmow for lands in Ranton

Another tract of land in Ranton Parish would be conveyed to Richard, the Prior of Little Dunmow. The Austin Canon's fastidious teachings to prepare young Hugh for his life in the church would be rewarded, she determined. For Sir William's part in disbursing these charters Eleanora offered to resign her claim to their manors of La Hyde and Patshull. Should she become Sir William's widow and rightful heir to all their estates, Eleanora agreed to relinquish her rights of dower in favor of her brother in law Ralph Bagot with the signing of the new documents; to which Lord Bagot happily consented.

Ellie came to these decisions to amend the status of their holdings after word reached her from the Bagot seneschal, albeit accidentally, that Sir William was borrowing from the quarter day fees not yet collected. She had always held suspicion regarding her husband's proclivities towards games of chance; now she had the frightening evidence of heavily mortgaged lands despite Lord Bagot's extra income from Conway Castle. Nicky had forewarned her of the knight's forays with Edward Caernarvon, gambling away the income of his family's estates; much like his father who was the sheriff of the shire, squandering his income, incurring debts of over £1000 on La Hyde, Coppenhale and Patshull. The consummate survivor, Lady Bagot decided now was the right time to secure income for her own use before the estates were wagered away.

Figure LXVII-Part Three; Bagot manor of Coppenhale from the church yard adjacent to the manor house of the old estate

Her squires announced the approach of two knights and their men at arms 'with the armorial bearings of three gold eaglets, a red bend with ermine,' they told Eleanora; Lord Bagot and his friend Sir William Martyn were arriving at La Hyde. It had been nearly four years since she had seen the knight at the Dunstable tourney; the campaigns that ensued during those years had taken their toll Ellie observed. "Sir William; that you recall my son Hubicus?" The couple sat in the great hall of the manor; Ana ordered wine and feasting, keeping a close eye on her girl she intended to remain at her side. Hugh greeted his mother's husband with respect, hiding his true sentiments. My noble stepfather, one of Edward's favorite knights, he said ruefully to himself. Pleasantries were exchanged between them but for the hours they were together no mention was made of the Scottish wars; no discussions came about regarding Ellie's dower lands in the north and no one mentioned Lord Bagot's well rewarded friendship with Lord Edward. When the couple affixed their seals and the two knights and witnesses appended theirs to the documents, Eleanora begged to take her leave to chamber for an early departure the next day.

CRAIG DOUGLAS SPRING 1313-Ellie and Hugh arrived in Fawdon where they stayed three days. "To dry our clothes," she allowed. The last week of their journey was spent traveling short hours of the daylight in determined downpours of rain. They had continued to trudge further north despite the weather. Eleanora was anxious to visit with her children and grandchildren; learn of the latest battles and conquests from her warrior sons. Hugh was eager 'to return home at last' as he would remain in Scotland when it came time for Ellie to journey back to Essex in the fall. The aspiring canon had completed his studies at the priory in Little Dunmow; his knowledge of healing had developed just as rapidly with the Hospitaller in Stebbing. Now Hubicus was the latest Douglas to repatriate in Scotland. As mother and son rode the old cart paths that took them by the Yarrow Water Ellie reflected on her own desire to remain in the land of Celts; her true home if her heart had its way.

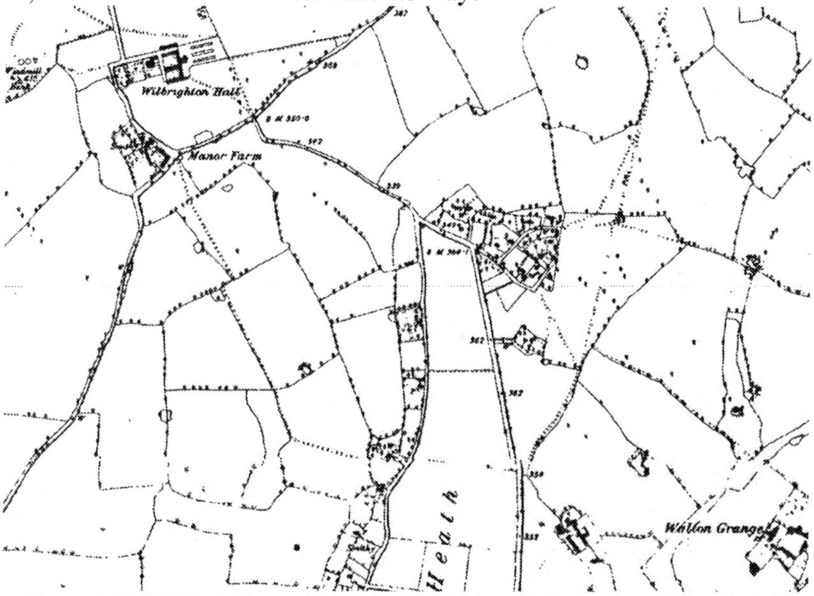

Figure LXVIII-Part Three; Map of Wilbrighton Hall courtesy of Landmark Information Group

Three year old William and two year old John were running their nurses ragged in the courtyard of the stronghold at Blackhouse as their grandmother and uncle arrived. The Deerhound Lindsay was thrilled to have the children to play with and Minerva as well. "Grandmother, we are to have pups," William told her proudly. Ellie chuckled. "My wee grandson; how did you learn of that?" she asked him. "My mother told me so," he beamed. Ellie's daughters in law were standing in the doorway of the tower house. Beatrice and Joanna were thrilled to have their company they told her. "Dear James and my sweet Archie are most always on campaign," Beatrice allowed, pouting in disdain for all the times they were forced to spend alone without their husbands. "Hiding us deep away in the Forest," she scoffed.

"This lass is lonely for her husband most as well," added Joanna; her reticence to complain made her words startling to Ellie; curious as well.

Lady Bagot and Hugh sat in the great hall as they feasted and enjoyed their wine. Ana had taken her now usual place beside 'my lass' at the trestle table; taking in every word from Beatrice and Joanna. She also noted the strain on Joanna's face. Ellie was aware of everything; each sentiment and aside as she listened attentively to the wives of her warrior sons. Sadly they had little word of their husbands' whereabouts. "Somewhere south of Hexam," Joanna said a little impatiently. Ana and her lady exchanged uneasy glances; they had just come north from Fawdon and saw little sign of the invading Scots; perhaps they were in England collecting tribute Ellie reflected. Trying to change the subject and bring some needed cheer to the conversation Ellie asked about Elizabeth. "That she is very sickly," Joanna replied almost inaudibly. Hugh and Ellie expressed their immediate concern as the canon went to get Gilley's healing box. "Where is my niece?" he asked his sister in law. Joanna got up and took the lad to her bed chamber. Ellie and Ana were not far behind. The wee lass was burning up with fever his grandmother announced. "The same fair illness once threatening the life of our wee Hugh," Ellie reminded Ana.

Figure LXIX-Part Three; the Yarrow winding through the beautiful Borders near Craig Douglas

"Bring Maudie here the noo!" she ordered. Within two hours the healers' efforts of Hugh, Ellie, Ana and Maudie, using herbs and soothing tonics had driven down the temperature. "A wonder that all of you most do," sighed Joanna gratefully. "That our Hugh is staying now in Scotland," Ellie consoled her, "our healing priest has the good training of le Hardi, my dear husband." Ana told them how Gilley and Maudie had saved Hugh's life with their herbs and healing rubs. "Aye, wee one; your Maudie is here for you dear Elizabeth," the old nurse said. Ellie watched Archie's former nurse holding her youngest grandchild and realized that the time had come to leave Maudie in Scotland as well. "Fewer still will be returning to Essex," she told the faithful servant. Maudie's eyes sparkled; her fondest wish had been to remain in her homeland near her son Andrew and now her dream was becoming a reality. "Thank you Lady Douglas," she replied gratefully, "to all three of my ladies," she chuckled realizing that Eleanora, Beatrice and Joanna all held of that title. Everyone was laughing; the mood at Blackhouse had certainly improved with the arrival of their Essex family Joanna allowed.

Two days later the watch announced the arrival of twenty men on horseback; the laird and his brother were returning home. Ellie and Hugh stood back from the ladies at first, allowing the brides to greet their husbands. "Oh my dear Henklebaldicus!" shrieked Beatrice. Archie was brandishing a wound on his forearm; blood was oozing from the bandages. James was also no longer riding his favorite Hobini Ellie observed. "We met with some strong resistance south of Durham," James concluded somberly. He was walking with a limp. "The old injury from Dahl Righ," he quipped as he noticed Ellie following his halting steps. He allowed grudgingly how it gave him discomfort from the lang ride some days especially when it rained. "Dear mother," he grinned, "this knight could use one of your healing baths." James told her teasingly that he remembered with great fondness the time she scrubbed him clean when he returned from campaign. "You have a wife to so take care of that duty James Douglas," she retorted gleefully. "And as for you dear Archibald; your mother has a healer of renown to serve you; pay close attention and follow his every word," she said mocking her own motherly tone.

Ana was chuckling as Hugh went to tend Archie and within moments their well known bickering began. "Be careful what you do there churchman; this squire is in the service of the laird of Douglas!" Hugh furled his brow with feigned lament. "This healer can not repair what is not injured," he replied. Hugh realized Beatrice was taking the injury very seriously and wanted to downplay the sober extent of the wound through humor. "Perhaps to apply good leech-craft," he began. "And most here!" he added playfully pointing to a very sensitive area on his brother that Beatrice let out a scream. "Not on my poor Archie; please not there, I pray you!" Hugh and James were roaring in laughter at their sister in law's expense when Ellie interrupted. "This lass will make quick the repair," she said mischievously as she brought out Gilley's dagger, hinting at the need for drastic surgery. Beatrice realized now that she was again the victim of the well known Douglas humor and began to laugh at her overreaction to Archie's injury. "I am most alive dear lass," he snickered. "Soon to take my pleasure with my bride, as my right of husband!" he boasted. "That you will have to catch me first," she dared him. "Stop!" ordered Hugh. "Give this humble healer time to complete his task; there will be no chase or capture until my work is finished. Mother; stand guard that these young folk most behave here."

Later that evening Ellie presided at the feasting; she wanted to make some important announcements. First she told them about her changes in her estates; how both Archie and Hugh were able to benefit from some of her holdings, settling in trust the manor of Wilbrighton on Archie and the income from her Ranton parish bovates on Father Richard at Little Dunmow Priory. "Lady El our seneschal," James praised his mother. "Your good work deserves a toast," he proclaimed. "That this lass has more," she replied, motioning to Hugh to bring the packages from her chamber. With great ceremony Ellie proudly presented a large, long package to James. "Your father had this war sword made for him the last year he was Lord Douglas. This lass has decided to relinquish it to another laird, most deserving of the honor, earning the right to bear the noble weapon of my dear husband," she said solemnly.

James face was frozen; he was trying hard not to allow the tears welling in his eyes to flow openly down his face and beard. "Lady El that someday this great sword will I wield in battle; to defeat the English king and bring a lasting peace that only comes from true victory; this is what I pray," he replied as he stood up and hugged her in a long embrace. He then whispered in her ear, "Only you would know of such treasure that means more to this humble knight than any purse of coinage." Thank you, she replied with her eyes to his touching sentiments. Then she turned to Archie. "This package of great weight is the mail of le Hardi; that you could favor this with a body growing quickly to his manly form," she added with a smirk.

"And my Hubicus; these are the Douglas Charters; now your responsibility to keep as the Scribe for Lord Douglas." Hugh looked to his brother James as if to ask him if the new position within the barony was his to have. "Good Hugh; a secular canon within the see of Glasgow must first prove himself to be a man of substance with an income before a bishop will most chose him. Lady El and I decided your good hand and ability in Latin make the choice quite simple for a laird in need of such services for his growing barony," James explained. "Do you accept of our good proffer; to be the Scribe for this laird?" Hugh's grin covered his entire face. Ellie watched her son; the same look when he got his first palfrey she sighed happily. Then she looked about and noticed that Walter was sitting quietly observing everything. "Come here to your grandmother," she told him. Taking out a small wrapped package she presented him with her gift. "That you have suffered great loss at the hands of Edward I know my dear Gilley would want you to have this," she said as she handed him one of her husband's small and well worn shields. "This one he used in battle at the side of William Wallace." Walter's eyes were open wide in wonder; he could barely speak, only managing to say 'thank you' as his eyes began to fill with tears of humbled emotion.

Figure LXX-Part Three; view from near the motte believed to be the site of a royal castle in Selkirk

SELKIRK LATE SUMMER 1313-Castles held by the English were declining steadily in number for the year 1313; by Lord Robert's continued strategy of patient progress. When the summer solstice arrived the Scots had successfully taken three more castles: Buittle, Dalswinton, and Dumfries. The king maintained his plodding strategy to take each stronghold one by one either by surrender or siege. To support his war financially he continued to extract tribute from the English Marches. James fanned the flames of fear for those living in Cumbria, Northumbria and Durham by returning often to remind them of their promises to the Scots. Whether by raids, bringing fire and sword to the districts or through the now normal process of extortion for a period of truce, James and his armed marauders came collecting; as if they held for rents in England's northern shires and it was quarter day. And when he was not in England the laird of Douglas was resting briefly in Traquair before descending upon the Lothianes. Since the expiration of the truce in that region, this last major English holdout in Scotland became the victim of James' new aggressive tactics; burning and plundering south of the Forth.

On this occasion however, James' assignment was closer to his domain in the Forest. He and Archie moved their family back to the shelter of Craig Douglas with a suitable garrison for protection. He was now ready to take the castle at Selkirk and then destroy it. Ellie had finally returned home; she told them that she would await the reply of Edward to the challenge put forth by the Scots and communicate by letter her intentions to return next year. Around the time Lady Bagot was just beginning her journey to Scotland in 1313, Edward Brus was beginning a siege of Stirling Castle. The king had left him in charge of that continued assault as he made his way to the Isle of Mann. Without the prior knowledge of his older brother the king, Edward Brus made an agreement with Sir Phillip de Mowbray, the constable of the castle that not only infuriated the King of Scots, but also guaranteed an invasion of Scotland by the English within a year or eight days of St. Johns Day the next: 24 June 1314. Heretofore Lord Robert had been making great inroads; conquering more territory for his kingdome by not engaging the English in a major battle. Knowing that their forces were superior both in number and the armaments they wore, the Scottish king was loathed to discover that his brother had committed the Scots to just that: a large engagement with the English army for the rights to garrison Stirling Castle.

But for now it was still the summer of 1313. The King of Scots had landed at Ramsey, a port James recalled from his youth. Brus' captain had remained in the eastern Borders; setting his sights on Selkirk Castle. James developed a plan similar to the successful strategy last fixed on the garrison at Douglas Castle when de Clifford's men held the fortress for their English lord. He used a ruse to gain entry to the castle. Little resistance greeted the laird and his small retinue of Foresters as barely eleven men remained in the garrison, one was but a knave. When James and his squire Archibald descended to the cellars to survey the stores of the stronghold they were stunned to find them nearly empty; barely enough grain to feed the men at arms for another week. "That we have so arrived in time," he scoffed. "To set free these sorry soldiers to save them from starvation," he said sarcastically. "Allow all except the archers to take their leave of Selkirk; give them escort south towards Redesdale," James told his sergeants. "Then bring the English bowman before me in the great hall," he commanded solemnly.

James' penchant for thoroughness led to an obsession. He believed that by eliminating the threat of prisoners who might return to take up arms again in Edward's service he could set them free to return home. The laird of Douglas was sadly mindful of the hundreds of Scottish lives lost to English and Welch soldiers armed with bows that he devised a practice that struck at the very heart of bowman. James commanded that before he set free any archer or crossbowman, they must relinquish their first two fingers on their right hand. Then he gave them coinage for their journey home. "God speed; but never to return again to Scotland," he warned them, "or this knight will so finish the work we started here."

STEBBINGE PARK NOVEMBER 1313-For the first time in over twenty-five years Ellie was alone in Essex without any of her Douglas family. She, Ana, and Lady Elizabeth were making gifts for Hogmanay that Sir David would take back to Fawdon for Sir Thomas to then carry the distance to the stronghold where the laird of Douglas and his family were staying. They were all sitting in the withdrawing room of the manor house when Patric announced the arrival of the prior from Little Dunmow. Father Richard was smiling broadly as he entered the chamber, "Good news to share with you my lady," he began. Ellie ordered some wine and her favorite sweet cakes and then begged the prior to please sit down and 'bide a wee.' The Austin canon told Lady Bagot that his friend the Master from the priory in Ely had sent him some note of interest in a missive. "Robert Wishart has been remanded to the custody of the good bishop there to be held at the Priory of Barnwell." Ellie's eyes radiated her joy; that meant the old prelate was residing in the more relaxed atmosphere of a religious house and one much closer to Stebbing than the southern coastal site of Porchester Castle.

Figure LXXI-Part Three; the Prior House, the oldest part of the monastic buildings, Ely; Bishop Wishart was confined here upon returning from Vienna

"That the good bishop has now returned from Vienna; the king released him to the Ely priory with its the chapel by the spring so dedicated to St. Andrews," Master Richard explained. Ana was setting up the wine and cakes. "Perhaps there should be two vestments for us to work on now," she quipped. The ladies had been embroidering steadily for three weeks to create a chasuble for their future canon Hugh; a fine outer robe with fair embroidery that he could use when he said mass. "Dear father would any of your priory so dare with the good escorts of my knight and his squires to take our friend in Ely our letters and some gifts for his Hogmanay?"

The prior's face clouded some before he responded. "There is the matter of his difficulty now to see," Richard explained. "That the good Master has confided: our dear Robert no longer reads from the gospels; his eyes diminished so in sight for age and days he spent as Edward's guest in Porchester is my conjecture." The canon from Little Dunmow Priory had become rather fond himself of the old bishop. During the long hours he spent in preparing Hugh for his life in the church, the two had shared many stories about the prelate from Glasgow. "That our Bishop of Glasgow has attendants with him that he most trusts to read from scripture or our good missives that I know," Ellie replied. "We will send him gifts and news of Scotland; it is done," she vowed. "This prior will so arrange for two canons most trustworthy to your cause, to take their leave for the Priory of Barnwell whenever my lady desires them to go," Richard assured her.

By the last week of December Ana and Elizabeth had completed the second and more ornate vestment for the venerable prelate Robert Wishart. Ellie had filled her days copying from the old Gaelic Psalms that William had provided her twelve years ago when she told him she wanted to learn the tongue of his Highland kin. Their gifts and writings were ready and she sent Patric to arrange for the canons' travel with Master Richard. As she read back through her Gaelic transcriptions Lady Bagot noticed that she too needed glasses now. "Good that I have kept the spectacles of my dear Gilley," she chuckled in acceptance to her own 'advancing age' as she styled it. "Dare I not to see my face in a mirror wearing these fair assists; that with the years of forty-five upon my visage might I look to be a crone; I'm sure of it!" she moaned in feigned protest to growing older. "Younger than any grandmother we most know," Ana retorted.

"I do wonder sometimes what Lord Will would have said when he looked upon this face," she confided anxiously. "Oh how this lass most misses that good knight; *'and most of all I miss a kiss upon my lips from you.'* Oh to be so loved," Ellie said wistfully. As her words trailed off she slipped into a reverie about Gilley. Lady Elizabeth asked her if her words were fair verse of poetry she found in a book. The question jolted Eleanora to the present; bringing her back to the withdrawing room at Stebbinge Park. "Oh none that I have read. They are Gilley's words to me; a dream recurring time to time that now I so remember his fair sentiment of verse," she told them. Ana giggled as she noticed Ellie smiling that wondrous gaze of young bride when first in love; that my lass is forever thinking of her Lord Will she mused.

"Do you see your husband sometimes, perhaps so in a dream?" asked the widow from Fife. Ellie nodded yes; adding sadly that the image never lingers for very long. Elizabeth shared that she too had seen her own husband; but he was so young and handsome in appearance, that she felt almost embarrassed to look at him. "Do you believe they know we yet think of them?" she asked. "The Celtic teachings of the ancient ones tell us that they are always with us. I do believe it's so; hearing our good words and knowing of our sentiments," Ellie replied knowingly. Ana reminded both widows that the lads had seen Lord Douglas too; it was not their imagination that brought visions of their loving husbands, the dreams were real!

Ellie looked down at a small oval locket that she wore on a velvet rope; inside she had painted a likeness of Lord Will. "This Hogmanay is the loneliest of all dear Ana. Not to have our family most with us; this lass must change our travel plans to journey into Scotland and most stay," she declared impatiently; twisting le Hardi's seal ring in her frustration. Ana knew already what Ellie was truly feeling; her appetite was feeble and the only activity she allowed herself was a daily ride to Little Dunmow Priory to speak with Gilley and tend to the knight's grave and those of her daughters Mura and Amy and grandson William; having moved the casket of her youngest daughter from Woodham Ferrers to Little Dunmow last fall. "Perhaps to visit with your kin; your brother has been asking for your good company," Ana suggested. Ellie vowed that she would visit Thomas; he was twenty-two and getting married in the spring. It was her duty to accept his invitations Lady Bagot reflected, though somewhat listlessly.

ROXBURGH FEBRUARY 1314-More than a year had passed since their failed attempt to take Berwick Castle. Their losses that night in December were nil except for the personal embarrassment of having their ladders on display on a pillory in the Royal Burgh the next day. Now the Douglas laird decided to try their luck again. This time James set his sights on a castle not a half day's ride from his stronghold on the Jed. The women and children with their nurses had been sent to Craig Douglas for their safety; a small garrison was left for their protection at Blackhouse. With a combined force of sixty men at arms, followers from both Douglasdale and the Forest, the laird of Douglas moved towards the town of Roxburgh.

The village was wedged in between the Teviot and the Tweed, guarded by the fortress which sat on a brae overlooking the rivers where they converged at nearby Kelso. Pasture lands ran forth along the other side of the castle; allowing little chance of passage through that area without notice of the watch. Shrove Tuesday was fast approaching; the garrison would be feasting and consuming great quantities of wine and ale; dancing to music in great celebration James surmised. Such an occasion could be to the Scots' advantage he explained to his sergeant. "That we will be outnumbered if the words of our fair spies are true," he explained. A trusted villein from Roxburgh provided the latest figures for the English garrison; the retinue of the constable Guillemen de Fiennes held for fifty men at arms, a dozen crossbowmen, two dozen hobelars and another fifty archers with some ten others he told the Scots.

The Douglas men at arms held high hopes of taking the castle that night; yet when they arrived at Roxburgh they discovered they had mistakenly brought only one of the two 'wee siege engines' with them. James realized that such an opportunity might not come again so he decided to go forward with their plans. He commanded three dozen of his men at arms to set watch around the town and await his signal for reinforcements. Lord Douglas selected some sixteen others who would accompany him into the castle by means of the siege engine. The band of would be invaders slipped quietly into their disguises; the black costumes of loose cloth, mantles camouflaging their armor. The objective of their ruse was simple; moving about the pasture land below the castle they would travel on all fours, appearing as cattle to the watch. Lang past the gloaming of the day these brave Scots moved about their mission without discovery of their true identity. Ledhouse had the honor of carrying the ladder strapped on his person. When he was crawling on all fours the great girth of the sack hung down in such a manner causing the ever observant Archie to take notice with a wry comment. "That you most appear like a cow ready to calve than a bull," he whispered loud enough for the retinue to hear his words. This vision of the rugged, round soldier lugging his *calf* across the pasture nearly foiled their mission; everyone was struggling not to laugh.

The herd of Douglas cattle milled about until they finally arrived together to take their places hidden in the shadows of the castle walls. Sym had been the first to reach the fortress. He laid out the siege engine, unwinding it carefully; meticulously he checked each knot for security. Standing below the garrison in the comfort of darkness James and Archie exchanged amused looks as they heard the watch comment on their ploy. "A herd of oxen mistakenly left out; that foolish husbandman must blame no other than himself should the Douglas find his herd before morning to steal it off." Their plan of deception had succeeded the brothers agreed; the garrison patrol was convinced the Scots were cattle mulling about not knights with blades and bows set to destroy their celebration.

When everyone had been accounted for the soldier from Lesmahagow took the nod from James and began manipulating the ladder to move it into place. Sym then pushed the square iron hooks over the crenelles of the battlements of the fortress walls and began his quick ascent. But the maneuver of the metal spear engaging the iron hook made a wee sound barely audible but heard by one of the watch. As Sym reached the top of the ladder he found himself face to face with an English soldier! He leaped at the man; surprising him with the recklessness of his courage. His stalwart reaction overpowered the guard. Throwing his entire weight upon the Englishman Ledhouse grabbed for his dagger and ended the fight. He shoved the body over the wall; with a thud it hit the ground drawing yet another on patrol.

Figure LXXII-Part Three; the ruins of Roxburgh Castle sit opposite Floors Castle today

But Sym was ready for the next attacker. He made his way stealth-like, moving quietly around the inner walls. Finding a secluded vantage point he leaned into the stone edifice; his large frame falling into the cover of darkness. Hurried steps warned him of this second member of the garrison moving towards the parapet. As the soldier ran unknowingly in front of Sym, the Scot leaped from the shadows and stroked the man's neck from behind with his small, sharp blade. The English yeoman was unable to cry out; his throat was slit through to his vocal cords. He crumbled in death as Ledhouse let go of him.

The disciplined soldier now went about his business to check for others of the guard. When none were found he returned to the body of the second soldier; the poor diel was so heavy that Sym could barely lift him up. So the Scot wedged the yeoman against the parapet, then shoved him through the crenelles. The effort took two attempts as the opening between the merlons was almost too narrow for the girth of the guard. Ledhouse then provided the signal for James: the path was clear. The Douglas knight quickly made his way up the scaling ladder with Archie close behind him. But suddenly as the laird grasped at the edge of the stone wall to bring himself over the top, a well hewn brick of good size partly crumbled loose and fell perilously below hitting Archie squarely on the face. Even in the darkness James could see that his brother was bleeding profusely; his nose was obviously broken but the brave lad did not cry out.

The knight leaped over the parapet and then turned to assist his brother. Archie's sight was perilously hampered from the large amount of blood that seemed to run in every direction from his injured nose; obscuring some cuts

439

and small scrapes on his face. James gripped his brother's right hand and gave one strong pull, bringing Archie onto the wall-walk. With Sym fifteen feet away on watch for the rest of the castle's garrison, the laird moved his brother to face him and ripped the bottom off his own silk tabard to wipe Archie's nose and bruised skin. "The silk will treat your injury without infection that you must hold it there to quell the bleeding," he whispered to the squire. The lad winced and pulled back slightly from the touch as the shooting pains were unbearable; still he kept his silence to protect them from discovery. "You are truly le Hardi's son," quipped his older brother. James knew that not only was Archie in huge pain but also the squire was inhibited in his breathing by the injury. "This knight is humble to your courage dear brother," he added sincerely. Archie smiled in gratitude and then winced for the grimace that caused him more discomfort. "Can you continue?" James asked; the squire nodded his affirmative reply.

Figure LXXIII-Part Three; the exterior walls at Rushen Castle, Isle of Mann; merlons separated by crenelles, or open spaces as they would have been at Roxburgh Castle

    The rest of the whimsical herd of cattle had thrown off their disguises and made their ascent. Joining with Lord Douglas, Archie and Sym these brave Scots now slipped unobserved into the courtyard of Roxburgh castle. Music and laughter could be heard coming from the great hall. The entire garrison seemed in attendance; except for the patrol who were now safely dead. It was the Shrovetide festival; the Tuesday before Lent and everyone was making merry in the castle. All but the Scots to celebrate tonight; yet our time approaches, observed the laird of Douglas with solemn determination.

Dubbed in 1311, the Gascon soldier de Fiennes was already considered a warrior of renown. But tonight he was celebrating; dancing and feasting with the rest of the garrison, unsuspecting of de mischef about. James led his men through the quiet of the courtyard; he knew the castle layout from one of his own vassals who had served under his Uncle James the High Steward, the garrison commander of Roxburgh Castle in 1296. The old Kyle soldier preferred staying with the garrison in Craig Douglas on such raids; his limbs no longer supple he could not make such daunting climbs, he admitted. But his memory was still in tact and he drew up the plans of the old castle as if he had been there but a month ago. James was grateful for the map; it was accurate and gave the Scots another advantage to the larger English presence in the fortress.

Figure LXXIV-Part Three; artist's concept of a medieval carved ivory horn, around sixteen inches in length, it would be similar to le Hardi's Oliphant

The Scots were making their way to the entrance of the great hall. James gave the signal, the heavy wooden doors swung open to his terrible cries, 'A Douglas! A Douglas! The eerie shriek from le Hardi's oliphant was sounded; the Douglas knight and squire were upon the English quickly, the laird's retinue was close behind. The startled English soldiers looked about; they could barely comprehend what was happening; the Scots were sounding the war cries from *within* the great hall! The unarmed and inebriated garrison was no match for knights and squires sober and alert; in full armor for the times. James bolted forward. His old standard held in the ready he attacked a knight seated on the dais, cutting across his chest. The surprised grimace on the Englishman's face went blank with the second thrust as the point of the Scot's sword pierced through his rib into his heart. Archie had never raised his sword in such close confinements of battle before with intent to kill a foe; but he seemed to respond instinctively. Not the swordsman of his older brother he had been concerned for the encounter.

An English squire was pouring wine when Archie moved his sword from the middle guard. He made a left to left diagonal cut and the squire offering no resistance met his death.

Screams of pain emanated from the injured and dying; cries of fear from the ladies in attendance resounded in a cacophony of bloody slaughter. Swords clanked and rattled; men shouted their defiance, throwing the tops of trestled tables in the path of the charging Scots. Benches were emptied; lifted in the air, in attempts to shield them from the onslaught of cuts and thrusts from the blades of the attacking men from Lintalee. Barely every defense the unarmed English seized upon was to no avail. As James and Sym forced their perilous weapons through the crowd the floor beneath them became a slick sea of dark red blood blending eerily with the watered wine from a broken baluster. The fluids of death joined together beneath a trestle where a knight lay motionless; draped across the wooden support.

Figure LXXV-Part Three; ; an older Archibald Douglas as depicted in a sitting by Spirit Artist Rita Berkowitz, author of *Empowering Your Life with Angels;* note the broken nose and the indication of a tartan that is represented as green and blue

James moved wildly through the crowd of the startled celebrants. He was fierce; showing no mercy as he wielded his father's sword in fluid movement with his body. Then he abruptly turned; James spotted one of de Fiennes garrison taking a wooden platter filled with the venison and capon bones of his feasting. To distract the Douglas knight the soldier threw the contents at him. Then he used the emptied platter like a small shield, grabbing for a table knife to attack. James' eyes were focused on the folly; the cross of his sword made a thud on the platter splitting it in half. The Englishman thrust forward with his knife as the laird parried with le Hardi's small shield; moving his old standard from the middle guard James made a sheering cut into the bared abdomen of his opponent. The platter warrior fell helplessly to the blood soaked floor, to join the discarded bones of his former feasting.

Knights and squires were cut down in rapid succession. James's iron weapon continued to thrust through flesh and cut through sinew in rhythm to his body, moving slowly and confidently through the crowded hall. Then he adjourned carefully to one side of the chamber as he sensed the fight was abating; to observe the course of the battle above the fray. To his left he saw Sym wiping his blade; beyond him was a squire with a fierce grimace enhanced by two black eyes, the results of his fractured nose. Archie too was quickly subduing his last opponent; an older knight with more experience it seemed, had pulled a hidden dagger in his final defense but the lad caught the weapon on the edge of his shield and thrust forward with his own.

James noticed three other battles, all coming to conclusion. The Scots were making their deadly strikes in rapid motion; using their weapons from the half-arm or wrist. When a knight faced an opponent in full armor he was taught to strike using the full arm in a wider, higher position. A slower pace but one required to penetrate full armor of mail. But today the garrison was dressed for dancing and frivolity; allowing for the quick destruction of their number in combat with sword. Archie and Sym made their way to their laird's side. James hugged his younger brother; smiling his approval for the valiant fight the lad waged under the encumbrances of a broken nose. The Douglases and the rest of the Scots began making their way about the great hall for a final tally. Sym took some others outside to post a watch.

"A countenance most frightening; your Beatrice may not know you," he teased Archie. "Good Hugh will make me well again," he retorted. "But not pretty!" the knight scoffed playfully. "This lad will wear his injury as a brooch of courage; to remind all that like le Hardi my dear father this squire walks through fire and yet lives," he proclaimed with the bravado of a poet knight. Then Archie gingerly applied his fingers to his swollen nose and cried out loudly; screaming an unholy sentiment, shouting his anger at the tower where de Fiennes and his men were holding out. "To all who are yet waiting for this fight to so conclude; this squire is committed to run you through most quickly to go home," he bellowed; the pain angering him all the more. During the heat of the battle de Fiennes was heard above the din, yelling fiercely to his men. He ordered the members of the garrison who were able to fall out in retreat. These seven men took over a corner tower for their defense; they were the lone survivors save three others in the great hall.

The festival of Shrovetide ended in an unholy rout; Roxburgh Castle was nearly fallen to the Scots. Few Douglas men at arms sustained injuries; but for Archie's nose there was only the peril of broken wine balusters thrown at the invaders that caused much harm. Now James turned his attention to the tower; mulling over his strategy for the assault. "Do you think you could climb up there with little trouble?" he asked Archie, pointing to earth and timber buildings near the stables. "Aye, little effort for that deed were there cover to our scheme," he allowed, suggesting that his brother have bowman attack the tower from the front as he moved to the roof of the adjacent structure. James then sent Archie and two others to climb atop the thatch. The rest of the Foresters had arrived from their wait in the village bringing a goodly number of archers in their number. They were instructed to keep de Fiennes and his men occupied while Archie and his compatriots moved to higher vantage point slightly hidden from the enemy's view. The brave men of Ettrick fired swarms of arrows, in waves of flying peril that descended upon the English who were trying to hold the tower. And every time an English bowman tried to send an arrow towards the stables he was met with a rushing assault from his right.

For hours as the darkness moved into dawn the English held off the Scots' attack. Then de Fiennes took a painful injury; a noble squire had hit his mark penetrating the knight's cheek and eye socket with the deadly iron of his arrow. "That is for my father," he groused. "This one to remind you that Scotland is for Scots," he spouted indignantly as he fired off another iron volley. Archie continued pelting the tower with arrow after arrow; in rapid succession he launched his deadly assault from the thatched roof top with the two bowmen from the Forest. Many arrows were hitting their mark, noted the commander with pride; how is it that he can be so cunning with a bow yet with his sword he seems almost hesitant James wondered aloud. He knew his brother was fearless; his bravery not in question. Then suddenly there was activity from the tower; a truce of surrender was offered by the English as their constable was dying. James accepted their terms of life and liberty; he himself escorted de Fiennes with his men to the English lines.

The castle was eventually razed; Sym Ledhouse was dispatched with a small band to alert their king to the good news from the Borders: Roxburgh was now held for Scotland. The citizens of the surrounding villages and into the Lothianes were grateful to have Sir William de Fiennes and his marauders removed from Scotland. For the last several years his reputation had grown for his own treachery. The knight had sent his garrison to attack the citizens; stealing from them and imprisoning those that did not pay their ransom. The Bishop of St. Andrews then currently 'on the business of King Edward' had been *menaced for life and limb* going to Berwick. He complained bitterly in letters to Caernarvon how de Fiennes' garrison fell upon him and stole eight tuns of wine. Other lords holding for the English sent letters of their disenchantment with Sir William's tactics in the region. In formal missives Sir Adam Gordon, the Lothiane knight James encountered six years before at Lyne Water, informed Edward of de Fiennes' continued larceny; that instead of protecting the king's lieges he was plundering and imprisoning good merchants for his own gain. Routing such a villain from the Borders reminded the Lothiane citizens that it was Brus and the Scots who could defend them from dishonest constables; not Edward Caernarvon.

STEBBINGE PARK MAY 1314-Ellie was reading from a long letter from Lady Beatrice of Douglas. Ana and Lady Elizabeth were quietly seated in the withdrawing room as she spoke aloud of the news from Scotland. "That my 'wee Godfrey' was valiant in his glory; but sadly he returned with his lovely nose most flattened by a rock falling from the battlements." Beatrice was faithfully using Ellie's codes for her sons' names. Ana sighed and shook her head. "That our lads all three of them are most alive; my prayers have all been answered." Ellie chuckled; "Like le Hardi with his scars of bravery for all to see!" Then she screamed gleefully as she read further; "Our Beatrice is yet with child! Though dear 'Godfrey' does not know it for he is off on muster with Sir Shamus, near Castlecary; in Somerset where Lord Lovel has his manor," Eleanora read; then she looked up to explain that Beatrice must be referring to the ancient Roman road near Stirling; Castle Cary being the location of a Roman fort along the Antonine Wall, built to defend that military way and the northern outposts of that empire. "The war; the battle we most feared is so coming," Ellie said sadly.

Elizabeth asked about the rest of the letter; encouraging Lady Bagot to return to reading what else Beatrice wanted them to know. "Archie let me help him clean Sir William's mail. We thrust it into a leather bag so filled with sand and vinegar; rolling it about most roughly. Surprising to this lass it came out brighter; the orange rusting gone from the wee rings, oh how marvelous!" Ellie and Ana were laughing; trying to imagine Beatrice assisting Archie at that 'manly task' as he fancied such chores. "Why does he not have others to do that for him?" Lady Elizabeth inquired. Ana said that Gilley instructed James that a squire was in charge of such things. "And this mail is of le Hardi; our Archie treasures his good armor as a trophy that he wears in battle proudly." Ellie suddenly put the letter down and solemnly reported that Hubicus was also going to the muster; all three of her sons were going to be in Stirling she told them mournfully. "Our good healer will be most needed there writes our Beatrice."

The chamber fell silent; the ladies were at a loss for words. What comfort can this lass so give a mother for such worry Ana asked herself? After some moments of contemplation, Lady Bagot raised her head; her face reflecting a new resolve. "That we will go to Scotland in the fall; this lass will celebrate her birthday in the homeland of my Gilley. It is done!" Ellie told them. And no war with Edward was to deter their journey she proclaimed defiantly. "Lady El," interrupted Sir David as he entered the withdrawing room. "Edward's war will be most over by the fall; it will be as safe as anytime that we have ventured so," he said with an amused grimace. The aging warrior delighted in Eleanora's determined spirit; he would certainly be part of this adventure he boasted to the ladies.

"And we will leave the quarter day collections to my brother Thomas; he has so offered and now we will accept his kind assistance," she allowed. Thomas Lovaine was fast becoming the accountant of staunch reputation like his father Matthew Lovaine; under the guidance of his late mother's brother Thomas de Blakenham, he studied the financial management of manors. With her brother overseeing her manor lands as seneschal, she could safely travel without concern for lost income. Many of her tenants paid their rents not in silver but in crops growing or other chattel. Eleanora's own steward had retired the year last; his 'sight declining faster than her fees and rents from lands forfeited in Scotland' John le Parker teased her as he begged notice to return to Bennington for the remainder of his days. "Another dear friend I will not see again; more of those who knew my husband to be gone from my household forever," she said sadly when she granted his request. Ellie added a small pension to their agreement; for his years of loyal service under many trying circumstances she had told him.

THE MARCH TO BANNOCKBURN FOR JUNE 1314-Lord Edward had summonsed his earls to join him at Wark on Tweed by the 10th of June. Three months earlier he began the extensive call up of infantry, including bowmen and spearmen from Wales and a great following from Ireland with provisions for the English army. But the response from the English nobles was not what he expected. In 1296 there were 60,000 infantry on payroll in Newcastle. Eighteen years later, the Earls in the north were demanding a Parliament to decide if war was even necessary. When Edward cavalierly refused their request four earls, Warwick, Lancaster, Arundel, and Surrey along with Lord Henry de Percy, recently set free from his confinement, refused the call. A fifth earl not present in Wark was Norfolk, the king's half brother and Earl of Oxford; he had a legitimate excuse as he was yet fourteen.

The four rebel earls responded only with their minimum requirement of sixty men at arms; when in the past they would have come themselves with thousands in infantry and hundreds in armed horse. The Earl of Hereford and Constable of England was Humphrey de Bohun. He arrived in Wark with Gilbert de Clare the Earl of Gloucester, Robert de Clifford and his own nephew and name sake Sir Humphrey a rash knight who brought with him cart loads of furnishings in anticipation of acquiring vast estates in Scotland. Only Robert de Clifford seemed to hold an accurate assessment for the outcome of the battle. Before leaving for Wark he entrusted his estates to his closest friends; de Percy and Warenne were asked to hold his lands for his young son should anything happen to him.

The English were heading to Wark; the number of infantry levied to the shires totaled 21,540; with only some 14,000 English and Welsh actually reporting. There were another 4000 Irish archers and armed foot ordered by King Edward; most of them arrived in Wark in sufficient time to begin the campaign to Stirling. The armed horse, English cavalry of knights and esquires numbered some 2500 in camp with another 600 coming they informed the king. And sauntering into Wark reporting for the muster were many of the French. The sometime allies of the Scots; these French knights and Gascon soldiers with their adherents were joining with the English king. The Auld Alliance was but a flight of memory for these warriors were coming for the plunder, the rout of the Scottish army.

Figure LXXVI-Part Three; memorial site Bannockburn with Stirling Castle rising in background; the site is maintained by the National Trust for Scotland

The Scots were armed with a very strong morale; they wanted the fight for their homeland, National Independence for Scotland was their common bond. Lord Robert called for a muster; the Scots were gathering in Torwood. Sir Robert Keith as Marshall of Scotland would lead the contingency of armed horse. But they numbered only five hundred strong when all reported. Their mounts were not destriers; rather they were light horse with none of the equipment flaunted by English knights in huge displays of vainglory. Edward's cavalry consisted of soldiers wearing large quantities of plate and other body armor, riding covered war-horses; destriers armored for battle just like their knights. The onerous sight could well have overawed the Scots; and nearly did the night before the great battle.

The Scottish onfoot counted several thousand; from that great number who came to Torwood in support of Robert Brus, four thousand hoped to be hand picked for the four divisions the king devised. Three Douglas brothers were making their way from the Forest towards Stirling. Two were coming to join the king's muster; riding their palfreys and leading their Hobini. Hugh only brought his one horse, Sir William. The aspiring canon did not require a war-horse as he would not participate in the fight; he did wear armor however. The healer planned to join with the Hospitallers and other healers that would serve the Scottish army; bringing Gilley's healing box and herbs to the battle at Bannock Burn. Hugh was also carrying Sir William's bassinette, wearing his leather hauberk and silk tabard under his dark mantle of fine linen. Though bred for the church the eighteen year old son of le Hardi was proudly dressed in full armor much like his hero the Bishop of Glasgow.

Figure LXXVII-Part Three; the impenetrable fortress of Stirling Castle, under the management of Historic Scotland

The knight and his squire were leading the Douglas retinue of over seven hundred men from the Forest, Clydesdale and Douglasdale with some loyal vassals from Ayrshire and the Cheviot as well. They would rendezvous with James' cousin Walter the Steward who was leading a contingency of similar size, with many men at arms who followed Douglas into battle in Ayrshire in times before. Many freeholders staying with their laird had horses for the journey and some for the fight; but most of the archers, the men of the Forest were expecting to fight onfoot and were either riding a pony or walking to the muster. These brave soldiers were knights and squires, landholders and free tenants. They included names like Dickson, Ledhouse and Carmichael from Lanarkshire; Douglas from the Lothianes; Carslogie from Lauderdale and Fife; and Chancellor from Northumbria. Robert Brus would use his proven captains to lead their men in battle; assigning these seasoned veterans with divisions comprised of men at arms who knew of their valor and followed them into fights before.

Figure LXXVIII-Part Three; the Maiden of Flanders commemorating the Battle of the Golden Spurs, Courtrai; with the victory, French influence diminished, Dutch became the language, July 11th Flemish independence day; photo courtesy Daniel van Buynder

The laird of Douglas was lost in a reverie of strategy; it was early May, the Ides would be the muster, as the fight would come in June. James was thinking of the great battles fought in history when armies were victorious though greatly outnumbered by skilled opponents. He remembered Courtrai; how the brave men of Flanders with their backs pushed to the sea won in fierce combat over the French knights. The knight mulled over their battle plan: a multi-force attack against the weaponry of the French armed horse turning a rout to their victory by decreasing the size of the battlefield; giving advantage to their smaller, lighter army. The only time the Flemish soldiers every beat the French in battle was at Courtrai. In that successful foray they used pikes and armed foot against the arrogant knights of King Philip's armed horse, over confidant in their ability to put down the revolt of unskilled freedom fighters. "Perhaps our king will use again this tactic to create a smaller arena for our warfare; to assist the infantry pike to foil the English cavalry as they did in the Battle of the Golden Spurs," James told

Archie. "This lad so visited the battlefield before returning home to Essex," he recalled aloud.

"And what about the bowman?" asked the squire. "Are we to fight as infantry or on horse?" James told him that such decisions were yet unknown to him; Lord Robert would have the final say for such battle plans. "That you will surely serve onfoot," he postulated. "Our proud history of Scots is for infantry; those of noble birth like our dear father who fought as knights, riding their war-horses into battle number few in our wee army today," he explained. "But more important as Sir William often told this lad, as lairds we treat our noble foot soldiers with dignity and respect for their valor and true courage; often to dismount and fight along side our vassals."

James reminded his brothers of the stories of the ancient warriors; Celtic kings battling their foes, side by side with their foot soldiers. "With their women too they fought in battle," he added with a chuckle. "Good that Beatrice is staying home," Archie replied. "That lass to gasp and moan with every drop of blood this squire spilled; though none have I so planned to give this fight," he added quickly. "That Douglas lass made this brother to so promise that you will come home to her alive and pretty; no more scars or wounds to heal," Hugh told them with a chuckle. James begged to know if Hugh had agreed to her request; he nodded yes as he rolled his eyes in feigned protest. "Perhaps our squire should remain with the Hospitallers," Lord Douglas teased. "No chance of that dear knight; that I have made a pledge as well; a promise to your bride Joanna to watch your back in battle, save you with my bow!"

"Henklebaldicus to give cover to this warrior, provide protection to this knight?" James asked in mocked indignation. "That you might have to do it with a sword," he snickered, knowing Archie's reticence to use that weapon. "This squire allows his bow to do his deadly work," Archie replied softly. Lord Douglas remembered now what he wanted to ask his younger brother; what bothered him so to do combat with a sword; his bravery at Roxburgh defied any to call him fearful or a coward. "To send arrows at great distance or use a deadly pike with others in formation of a schiltron; aye this lad can do such work with little effort. But to run a soldier through and see his eyes lose life, focusing on death; it is too painful to look upon," he said with quiet resolve.

"Our father told this son how he preferred a poet knight and healer most to be; but bred a warrior he was forced to do battle that was neither of his liking nor of his doing to so cause the fight," James began. "Almost with the same words you just spoke Lord Will had told me what he came to understand of war. Bravery comes but not from going into battle without fear. True valor rises in us when we accept the burden; knowing we must end the life of another, one we may never come to know in peace." James paused to make sure his brother comprehended his meaning; then continued. "Our father told me to remember this: fight as if the breath of your sweet bride depends on your successful deed of death; know others would take your own to murder if you relent. This knight takes those words into every battle," he confided to his brothers. "Thank you James, and Lord Will," Archie replied; his voice hesitating with the heaviness of his emotions. The squire acknowledged that he finally understood; no true soldier ever wanted war, but when he was called to fight he would be armed and ready to serve.

Figure LXXIX-Part Three; Bannockburn memorial site near the statue of Robert Brus and his location during the battle

As the three Douglas brothers rode towards their muster at Torwood, a hush came over them; to the man they were struck by the significance of the task before them and the feelings that were building within them. Hugh spoke first. "Dear James, with yearning but not dread does this humble churchman ride to the battlefield against the enemy of our father. Though this lad comes as a healer not a warrior, I feel a strange comfort from the hauberk that I wear and sword I so carry, the dagger so secreted here as well." James nodded; he understood he told him. "Not all men are bred as warriors dear Hugh; but all soldiers know of God and need of healing from their battles. We must keep our churchman safe from harm," he grinned. "It is right and just for our good Hugh to wear the leather hauberk of le Hardi and carry his old standard for defense," assured Archie. "Our father was a healer of great merit; he must be proud to see the three of us most here together in our cause for Scotland's freedom." Hugh sighed. He still felt uncertain for his part in the battle that was to come; hopeful he could contribute in some way.

Then Archie shared a knowing look with him. "This lad is most convinced the Bishop Wishart too would commend your actions most this day. You are a Douglas, trained as a knight, schooled as canon; our mother so insured for you to choose, churchman or warrior to be." James smiled reassuringly at Hugh as he interjected his own thoughts on the matter. "So fortunate a man as you this day, you can be both!" Then he told his brother about the abbot Maurice who would be traveling with the king's retinue. "When you so meet this brave warrior for God and King, then you will understand," he told Hugh. He explained how the abbot was bringing relics from Saint Fillan; the left arm of the monk and his healing stones. "King Robert so commanded him; the relics so protected our good cause to keep us most alive since Dahl Righ that we might fight another day. That day has finally come. Dear Hugh that you are here with us is proof of God's own promise to that martyred patriot le Hardi: a devoted churchman sent by the Holy Father to keep Douglas warriors safe with words of prayer; to tend our wounds of body with your good training, learned from that healer of renown, our dear father."

TORWOOD MAY 1314 -James Lord Douglas and his growing retinue arrived in late May; besides the Douglas vassals from Douglasdale, the Kyle, Girvan, the Forest and some kin from the Lothianes, he brought with him two Douglas brothers: one a squire, an archer of great merit known to all of Essex; the other a canon to be and trained healer. He also brought with him the iron-knobbed-staves of Jedburgh in great quantity. The blacksmiths of the Jethart had fashioned great weapons for their laird of Douglas; stout staffs of good wood with a four foot extension of tempered iron. "My lord the king," James began as he dismounted. "Good men of Douglas have so followed this humble knight, from Ayrshire to the East Marches and the Forest, in service to the King of Scots," he added with bravado. "And from the Forest; good weaponry do I have." Robert looked into the carts carrying the handsome staves. His face broke into a great smile as he praised the smiths for their fine work; promising rewards for their endeavors.

King Robert beckoned his lieutenant to follow him to his tent where he gave him his first assignment: to dig some trenches, the camouflaged pits they constructed at Loudon Hill. Then the Scottish king took James to see the work at a make-shift forge where his Highland blacksmiths were constructing some cruelly spiked booby-traps called calthrops that would be laid within the pits; a device to maim the English cavalry. "Yours to so secure the area most here," said Robert, describing the bog-lands southeast of the Bannock Burn, on the north side of the Military Way. "Randolph and Keith are building their trenches and scattering their calthrops on the north of Bannock Burn at Halbert's Bog." James understood the strategy at once. "That we will force the English to their narrow path most here," he pointed to the parchment chart Robert laid out before him. "Aye, most like your favorite defensive stand at Courtrai," chuckled Robert, alluding to the Flemish battle plan from 1302. James openly favored and frequently drew upon this successful war plan. It was perfect he would tell everyone; the strategy supporting situations for minimal forces against overwhelming odds. "The way of Scots fighting the English in every battle," he would remind them with a disarming smirk for emphasis.

At the campsite of the Scottish army nearly 7000 men at arms including cavalry came to muster; another 2500 camp followers came with them that included cooks, farriers, kitcheners, blacksmiths, barbers and other workers that a large army might require. And then too, there were the rag tag warriors who came with little equipment, save only a big heart and great desire to fight the English; these men and women became part of what they called the small folk of the Scottish army.

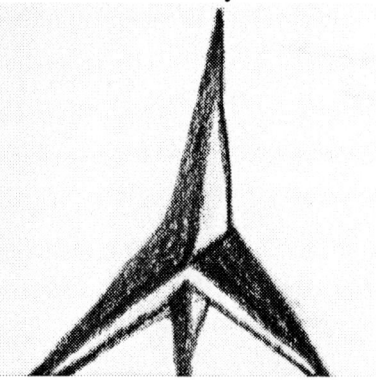

Figure LXXX-Part Three; an artist's concept of a calthrop or eight inch spike that was hidden in trenches to disrupt the English cavalry in their charge

James and Hugh Douglas were making their way now to the village of St. Ninian. There on Kirk Wynd stood a chapel, located near the old Roman road, not far from the carse where the Scots expected to do battle. It was dedicated to the saint of that same name: Ninian. At the kirk other healers and monks had already arrived and were setting up a hospital; a center for healers where during the battle men at arms could come for quick remedy. Further away in Cambuskenneth another more elaborate infirmary was being stocked, already established within the walls of the monastery, it was being readied to accept those with more serious injuries. A wounded warrior would first be brought to St. Ninian's then taken to this abbey nearer Stirling Castle.

Sir James led his younger brother inside the kirk. "This fair chapel is another built in memory of that good saint we so visited in Whithorn," said Hugh, deeply impressed by the coincidence. "That everything most happens for a reason," said James, reminding him of le Hardi's teachings. "The ancient ones would tell us such occurrence is a sign that our battle yet to come is blessed by Spirit, those in the Otherworld most knowing we would come here to wage our struggles with the English army." He then introduced Hugh to Maurice. "This Master for his canons regular of Inchaffray most helped your brother when my leg was badly injured at Dahl Righ," he said, boasting the healing skills of the abbot. "So grateful is this lad to meet one churchman as brave as any warrior," Hugh told the Master. Maurice showed the aspiring canon around the hospital and then took him to the chancel where he stored the relics and the healing stones of Saint Fillan. Hugh held the stones in his hands; felt the energy pulsate from the cold, smooth surfaces. "Such power lies within; I do feel it," he said with wonder for the moment. Maurice chuckled. "Aye, faith is how it works my son. Belief in God and the ancient ways of good healing assists those in the Otherworld to send their good work through the veil of time, from their world of the Holy Spirit to help us here among the living."

Further down the Military Way, Archie was busy building trenches near the bog-lands. The defenses would provide the Scots with the protection to keep the English in a smaller area; minimizing the effect of the larger army by decreasing the size of the battlefield. James' followers were working in this region. When the English chanced to come there with their cavalry, they would find a smaller area to maneuver and probably avoid a charge here altogether near the spring tides of the burn. "Was this the course of preparation for the brave Flemish soldiers at Courtrai?" Archie asked upon seeing James ride up to inspect their work. "The tracks and trenches were so constructed but the calthrops are the design of Scots," he replied. "Our knowledge of the English cavalry, their powerful war-horses like our father's destrier, loaded down with their own armor with their knights in full armaments with mail hauberks and iron weaponry. Such horses will find the going too strenuous. And then when they discover the fatal iron stakes to further disable their footing, it will be too late to turn around; they will be finished in their battle for the day." Just then a small cart was being driven about delivering more of the deadly iron stakes constructed for the trenches. James brought one over to Archie and showed him that no matter how they were placed in the camouflaged trenches the calthrops would show a cruel spike to the invaders. "Most likened to the thistle to the barefooted approach of ancient warriors," Archie said with a broad grin. "Exactly," James replied brandishing a Douglas smirk.

23RD JUNE 1314-The English vanguard was making their way from Falkirk to Torwood; the Scots had withdrawn their forces, taking a position where they watched every movement of Edward's army. The long weeks of monotonous drills; schiltrons training in formations in perfect motion, the porcupines of battle armed with pole axes and lances; their day of truth was here. Would their training be enough Brus wondered to himself? He prayed so. Proceeding in lumbering motion, slowly along the Military Way was the rest of Edward's contingency made up of over two hundred wagons each pulled by eight oxen; a march of onfoot including Welsh archers of almost twenty thousand. The English brought tents and furniture and food; weaponry and anvils to make repairs. Edward's knights traveled with every convenience. Lord Thomas Berkeley, the husband of the late Joan de Ferrers, arrived with a following of over two hundred personal attendants, not vassals to fight for Edward, but barbers and kitcheners and Berkeley farriers for his horses. They were a pompous lot; riding to new riches in Scotland.

Figure LXXXI-Part Three; the Bannock Burn, one boundary of the great battlefield

    As the detachment of English knights and squires crossed the Bannock Burn in the shadow of the ominous dark crags of Stirling Castle they spotted some lone Scottish footsoldiers withdrawing into the woods of New Park. Following the old Roman road they did not encounter the deadly spikes hidden in the bog-land to either side of the Military Way. The small retinue made their way up the hill to the Scot's position. All along their activity was carefully monitored by King Robert and his lieutenants including James, Lord Douglas. Following in the rear of the group was the nephew of the Earl of Hereford, young Henry de Bohun, kin to the de Ferrers; a young knight fully armed with his horse barded, ready to do battle with the rag tag insurgents. As he approached the Scots he noted almost incredulously, that there in the middle on a wee hack and armed with only a battle axe trussed at his side was the titular King of Scots!

De Bohun's surcote blazoned with the arms of Edward's chosen laird of Carrick. The English warrior lowered his helm, raised his lance and charged his destrier; he would end the war with Scotland with one brave and successful assault on King Hobbe! But as he approached Brus, the king stood his ground, but to move aside at the last moment on his agile hack, stand strong in his stirrups and swing his battle axe down at the knight's helm. The thundering gallop of the war-horse abruptly stopped; the axe slugged hard into the warrior's armor, making a gruesome thud, the deadened sound of metal piercing metal when it hit bone, sinking into soft grey matter. The shaft of the battle axe split as it 'clove skull and brain'; young De Bohun was dead prompting his squire to ride out and stand protectively over his knight's body. In but a moment he too finished his war with Scotland, the fight that ensued about him took his life in the first advance. The Scottish infantry was in an uproar of celebration; their king victorious against great odds; who now would not so follow one named Brus into battle, they demanded to know?

Figure LXXXII-Part Three; the Pelstream Burn met the Bannock Burn near the English campsite not far from the battle; it is but a drainage ditch on a single track road today

Recovering quickly Brus made his way to a good vantage point to watch for the rest of the English cavalry as they proceeded to move towards the Scots. Here he was surprised to see that de Clifford and Beaumont were leading a larger contingency along the carse, passing not far from the village of St. Ninian. His nephew Randolph, Earl of Moray, was standing beside him; reeling from the actions of his uncle, he admonished the king for foolish deeds that might have ended his life before the battle began. James told Robert it was too early to be searching for heirs to take his kingdome had he fallen. Robert Brus dismissed their concerns. "That I have broken my good axe," he said with disdain, silencing his critics for the moment. As he continued to view the English men at arms moving northward he called his nephew to take notice. Randolph mounted his horse and flew to his schiltron.

The charging English cavalry came unguarded like the French against the brave Flemish freeholders; their Welsh archers were in the rear of the slow moving caravan that comprised the onfoot and two hundred wagons of supplies. The Earl of Moray's brave footsoldiers held their ground; they kept their lang spears thrust forward for the fight. The dust of the hot June day swirled and chocked them; the sweat poured down their faces as the close confinement and physical exertion beaded in perspiration that oozed through their quilted gambesons and dampened their wool surcotes. The ominous attack of barded war-horses ran full tilt towards the Scots, turned their course right at them; the destriers' thundering charge making the ground beneath them shake. All the while the brave Scots of Randolph's schiltron stood their position; valiantly they would not yield.

James watched, pacing as was his way before he engaged in battle; eager for it all to begin, he bore the impatience of le Hardi waiting for a fight. "My lord, de Moray fails; the English will be breaking through I fear," he said, worried that Randolph's foot were not gaining any ground in repulsing the enemy. Brus told him to hold off; then moments later he relented and sent James to take his men to join in battle with his cousin's contingency. With him came a squire; a bow and quiver on his back yet carrying a lang spear. "Good Archie; I will need your cover," he chided his younger brother, beckoning him to join his schiltron. "That we are going to fight the Clifford!" Archie shouted with glee. He was excited to take on Edward's vassal who had a hand in his father's foul end in the Tower. But as the Douglas men at arms rode out, the knight and squire squarely in the lead, James abruptly stopped. He moved forward on his own and there from the hill top overlooking the Earl of Moray's position he noted the battle had shifted. "Good Randolph is winning the field!" he exclaimed; holding his men back, they later returned to their position to wait for further orders, not to engage the enemy. The Lord Douglas was not one to steal a victory from a lieutenant when the field was already won; he would wait to do his battle with the English.

That night in camp Archie and Hugh were cooking their bannock on their griddles. "Most the same as when we took our fight to Durham," boasted Archibald to the churchman as he regaled his brother with his war time experience. "Though we could not see the English destriers, the kirk walls shuddered to the rhythm of their hooves; what a tremendous sound they made. And what great noise must it have been to be so close, to hear and see their charge!" Hugh exclaimed. James approached his brothers and told Archie to mount up; they were going on a reconnaissance. "Will you so fight a battle at night?" asked the healer. "No, we are but a force so small that we can travel unnoticed, to slip behind their lines and count their numbers is our intention," James explained. "Will you be rested for the battle on the prime?" Hugh inquired, concerned for them both, riding all night then fighting in combat the next day. His brother looked away; he was distracted by what he had to do; how many English onfoot had been in the call-up and did they all report? Archie told Hugh that before a battle James slept very little; he was often out scouting with his men, making sure of his opposition before engaging in combat the next day.

"This churchman will so pray for the safe return of his brothers," he told them. Then James added curtly, "And for the soul of Sir William Airth." Archie was stunned; whatever could have happened to the knight guarding their king's baggage. James pulled his brothers to him and whispered what he knew to be the most unholy of acts. "Dear Edward, King Robert's own brother decides this night to bed a lass in the camp of the small folk not far from the king's own tent. The young Earl of Athol, one David, the son of John, our father's friend and brave patriot, was told of such foul deeds; his sister the consort of that sorry Brus, bearing his child." James was seething; he felt that Edward was bringing harm to their cause with his selfish and impetuous deeds. "One man not worthy of such a lady to so wed," he shared with Hugh and Archie, telling them that Edward Brus made scathing remarks about young Athol's sister. "When Earl David faced him with strong admonishment he cowered. That most vile of knights, the king's own brother spit upon the earl; turned his back refusing any duel of chivalry the lad proposed." Then James paused and said quietly, "The words he added only tormented the youth to commit a disgraceful deed, to revenge his sister's loss of honor." Archie and Hugh were stunned; they could not believe that the king's younger brother would provoke a fight on the eve of battle with another nobleman. "He told young David that his sister was but an ugly woman not fit to bed and more a whore than lady holding God's piety," the Douglas laird added, shaking his head in anger.

"Then what happened?" Archie and Hugh asked in hushed whispers, demanding to know more. Their brother told them that to avenge the wrong of Edward Brus the Earl of Athol took his men at arms to desert the Scottish camp. "Yet on their way back towards Stirling he mounted a surprise attack on the king's baggage, killing Sir William Airth and many of his men as they were asleep." A sensitive lad, Hugh turned to look away in sorrow as tears welled in his eyes. "That I will say prayers these few hours so remaining for the souls of both men, Airth and Sir David," he said quietly.

He watched Archie and James mount their Hobini and then ride out of camp. That our James holds much worry inside not to share with others; how alone my dear brother is with his agony for what might be and what goes on here, Hugh reflected.

Before the sun rose on the short summer night the Douglas knight and his squire with the others of their wee group returned to their camp in the woods of New Park. They had reported with Randolph and his scouting party their dire findings: the English were 20,000 strong. "A Scots' battle sure aye," grumbled James, noting that they were outnumbered three to one; the normal odds for such fights he told them in mocked praise. "The men with tails so sleep in bogs," Archie said as he chattered away gleefully. He told Hugh that with the large wagon train to move and secure in camp, the English were up most the night; then to sleep in swamp lands. "A sultry night making their stay even more enjoyable," he added sarcastically.

Figure LXXXIII-Part Three; the Breccbennach which held the relics of Columba depicted in a painting by Marguerite Connolly

"We were in council," James told Hugh quietly. "One more to our number this night from the English camp; Sir Alexander Seton has come to the side of Scots and timely so to tell us that the English soldiers are many but demoralized. We will fight the battle to come after all," he said solemnly. Hugh was startled; he did not realize that the Scots had considered disbanding and vanishing into the hills. "The ways of the Mamlukes," Archie began, "to fight in small bands of men is what we so prefer good Hugh. To make our attack and then quickly take our leave to fight another day." The squire explained that the king realized the greatest successes of Andrew de Moray and William Wallace were in their many, smaller raids upon the English. While their rout of Edward's army at Stirling Bridge was exhilarating, the Scots' next encounter at Falkirk, the massive slaughter of the Scots proved to Brus that to fight the English in a great battle might be foolish. Edward Caernarvon would be gone by fall and the Scots could take Stirling Castle then, rather than risk a fight they might regret. "We are doing battle with the English on the morrow," James assured them both again. "It is done."

THE CARSE 24 JUNE, ST. JOHN THE BAPTIST'S DAY- Hugh began his day in prayer; he promised the saint that he would dedicate a chapel in his honor should he bring them victory this day. Young Walter joined him; concerned for his stepfather and the others, "That they would be in the thick of battle in but few hours," he said. Since returning to their camp James had somehow fallen off to sleep; in less than an hour he awoke and felt revitalized as if he slept the night. Archie too had fallen off to slumber. With a semblance of rest under his belt he felt relaxed and confidant. He also was satisfied with the battle plan as he was to follow James in his schiltron rather than to use his skills as an archer and fight under another command. The king assembled his army; they broke their fast with bread and water and kneeled in prayer.

Up and down the ranks the fast footsteps of the abbot from the Highlands could be heard as he made his path among the Scots. The barefooted and bareheaded Maurice carrying the relics of the St. Fillan made his pleas to the Scottish footsoldiers to fight for their rights against the tyranny of Edward. Chancellor Bernard gave his prayers to the soldiers; mass was said by priests throughout the camp. Father Bernard was also the Deòradh, the Dewar or keeper of the Breccbennach Chaluim Cille, the tiny silver and bronze box that held the bones of Saint Columba who founded the abbey at Iona. This prized symbol of the Scottish Church and her country's independence would be taken to the battlefield this day by the Tironensian monk where he would bless the Scottish army.

Everyone was ready; but there were two more ceremonies to take place. Walter, the young cousin of James and the surviving son of his uncle, James the High Steward, was to be dubbed on the battlefield. Then the king turned to Lord Douglas and took his knight's pennon; slashed through the arrowed tails, the forks falling to the field as the king squared off the Douglas banner with three stars on a chief azure; making Sir James of Douglas a knight banneret, a field commander. James and his cousin Walter would command one schiltron; Edward Brus, Thomas Randolph, and the king would hold the other divisions. And another Douglas cousin, Robert Keith, commanded the Scottish light cavalry as the Earl Marischal of Scotland with five hundred armed horse. The king now went through the ranks of his army. He told his men of the low morale of Edward's contingency. Lord Robert spoke of freedom and Scotland's laws; he told them they could turn and flee or stand

and fight it was their choice to make. Not one man broke rank; Scotland's men were ready to take their battle to the English.

The Scots moved forward, headed down into the carse, not far from where the English army had stayed the night. The first to move into battle was the schiltron of Edward Brus. His men were confidant from weeks of drilling; changing formations in tedious repetitive actions, they knew every move they would have to make. The battle began with this younger Brus taking the initiative and charging the English. Edward's vanguard was leveled to a bloody sea of nobles lying in their death-gaze facing the sun of the hot June day. In the opening moments of battle the young de Clare, the Earl of Gloucester and Robert de Clifford spent their last blood in Scotland; their bodies were returned to Berwick to journey on to England in a coffin covered by a shroud. The deadly schiltron led by Edward Brus moved forward and was anchored against the Bannock Burn; the right flank was now set.

Edward Caernarvon dispatched the next wave of cavalry; there were two thousand in all at his command. Randolph moved his schiltron forward and there were so many armed horse circling these Scots that the barbed formation of twelve foot spears seemed to disappear from view as if sinking into the carse below the surface. But the brave men of Alba held their ground and soon Edward's second group of cavalry was failing. Impaled by spears, many of their horses were mortally injured. They stumbled and fell upon the drying earth of summer's heat. Knights were falling victim to the schiltrons; once unhorsed the forward surge from the grotesque porcupine of men with spears found their mark easily, quickly ending the war for these English soldiers. The bodies of destriers and their riders transformed to a gory defense for the Scottish pikes. Cluttering up the battlefield the dead and dying enemy eerily protected the schiltron of brave Scots from close encounters with the English attack.

Now James and his cousin Walter the Steward moved their spearmen, many armed with Jethart staves, forward to the left of the Earl of Moray. The door was shut on the English cavalry for further advance. It was then Edward moved in his archers with a deadly turn against the success of the Scots. Archie's line within the schiltron was the hardest hit; nearly two hundred of the Douglas followers, good Scots all, would lose their life that day. James was agonized as the sound of Welsh arrows careened over his head. Many armed foot in his retinue were hit, injured by multiple assaults of arrows flying with deadly accuracy. His schiltron would fail without support of cavalry or archers, he was sure of it! The knight banneret spurred his Hobini forward shouting encouragement to his men at arms, "Press on, press on," he commanded.

Then he saw his younger brother take a second arrow in the same shoulder; soon Archie will have to drop his spear he realized. The field commander's heart was pounding fast, his heavy breathing betrayed his anxious concern for his brother, but the young squire stood his ground. What agony he must be feeling James reflected; then from behind him came the comforting sound of Keith's armed horse. The Marischal was leading the Scottish cavalry of light horse to annihilate the left flank of Edward's archers. The fast destruction of the bowman sent the others in their ranks running from the field. The Scots quickly recovered their forward momentum and this permitted James to remove his brother from formation and tend to his wounds. "Squire, that you must seek our healer at the kirk in St. Ninian's parish," he commanded. Archie wanted to stay and began to protest; remaining in formation.

Just then a horrifying exchange of blows took place right near the lines held by the Douglas schiltron. Alan de Clephane of Carslogie for the Scots was returning from the successful cavalry assault on the Welsh archers when a larger war-horse approached him; the destrier carried more armor than that Scottish laird wore as a knight. Clearly disadvantaged, the laird from Fife fought hard against the English chevalier and would have prevailed but his light horse struck the surface of a fallen enemy and stumbled to break his leg. The gruesome sight of the snapped legged as it bent forward was followed as if in slow motion by the nearly fatal unhorsing of Alan. His right arm was crushed beneath the animal and then quickly severed by the swift cut of an English war-sword thrust mercilessly by one of Edward's charging armed horse. James rushed to meet the foe; unsheathed his father's own war-sword before the knight could return for another assault on the defenseless Carslogie laird. With a left to left upper cut le Hardi's sword laid the Englishman to his final rest. "That fallen enemy is yours dear father," James declared proudly. He had not planned on his individual fight in battle this day; but how satisfying it felt and using his father's sword, the recent gift from Eleanora, made the deed the sweeter he reflected.

As the laird of Douglas wielded his Hobini around he saw the squire of Alan of Carslogie rush to his knight's side and pull him to safety; the right arm was now gone from him. Another squire retrieved the arm to remove the prized gauntlet and the laird's signet ring. Then strangely the young lad stood there a moment contemplating what to do with the limb; unable to just throw it back into the fray he put it down, under the wooly saddle cover as if to provide some strange privacy for his laird's now severed limb.

"Archibald; so assist our fallen friend to take yourself with his squires to the kirk, to ride with him to Cambuskenneth when you can!" he ordered. Archie was just leaving the schiltron formation and came quickly; holding the arrows yet embedded in his shoulder, he joined James. The two Douglas brothers led the two Carslogie squires with their laird in tow to move above the fray; here James had them stop. The knight banneret had left his cousin Walter the Steward in command of their division; instructed the young knight to bid their schiltron forward. As the Douglas laird watched from his new vantage point he could see Walter leading his men in perfect formation; steadily, mercilessly they cut their way through the cluttered mass of English knights. The enemy's on horse were a baffled and constricted mass of angry warriors, throwing their weapons helplessly to the center of the schiltron in their overwhelming frustration. With the deadly assault of archers no longer upon them the Scots were turning the momentum to their own.

Then in a brilliant move, King Robert saw his advantage. He gave orders for the onset of a Highland charge. The king's men who waited most impatiently now moved with bold enthusiasm and energy into battle under the command of Angus Og Macdonald of Islay. James watched with satisfaction; knowing now that the forward progress of the left flank would continue he could turn his attention to the wounded squire and knight. "Dear brother that you must allow this laird to look over your injuries," he said quietly. Archie was in a lot of pain; the arrows pierced his father's mail; one was resting near the bone he told James. The knight ripped off the bottom of his surcote and tied it hard around Archie's shoulder above the wounds. Carefully he assessed his brother's injury as one of Alan Clephane's squires was wrapping the stub of arm left hanging from his laird's right shoulder in silk as James instructed.

Behind them, coming from the left flank was an ebullient young Steward spurring on his destrier while leading a liberated English war-horse he brought for them to ride. "To make good speed with this fine animal," he chuckled; then vanished back into the frenzie of battle as quickly as he had appeared. The Carslogie knight was groggy from the pain and injury but managed a grateful smile to his rescuers. He watched with bemusement as his squires ripped the rich caparison of embroidered silks from the charger that said the great animal once belonged to a fallen Comyn. James was concerned for Archie's injuries. He pulled out le Hardi's dagger and grabbed some herbs from the pouch strung on his belt. He gave some to Sir Alan's squire and instructed him on how to apply the salve that would deaden some of the pain; then turned back to Archie to administer the herb concoction to his shoulder.

"Stand without motion," he commanded his brother sternly. The herbs did their best to deaden the area where James made an incision to remove the arrow heads. The armor had impeded their assault; the missiles were not entwined with muscle, cartilage or bone; only imbedded straight-in they withdrew cleanly from the shoulder. "Dear Beatrice will most forgive me?"

the Douglas knight inquired sheepishly. Archie nodded in frustration. "To be most hit by English arrows, one then two, a sorry fate; at least the archers missed the face of this squire," he said sarcastically. "They were Welsh bowman; better than the English, they hit their target. Recognizing your fair beauty they aimed only to keep you from your duty to hold a spear," James teased him as he continued to pry the solid metal head of the arrow from the muscle and flesh of the shoulder. "This one is from a crossbow," he said quietly. "That it could pierce most any armor with this square faced head of four small points; this lad has not seen many of this design before," he explained. "The other arrow was from an archer's bow; a sharper head would find it difficult to penetrate our father's mail hauberk; it was fired to hit you most after the crossbowman's arrow is my fear." Archie told him that the second shaft hit him right on top of the first. "A lucky shot," he scoffed. "Is it not time that you return to you command?" the squire asked his older brother in mocked disdain.

Figure LXXXIV-Part Three; a cottage on the Carmichael estate today; many of the estate cottages are available as self-catering facilities to visitors

    Archie was putting on his gambeson as he turned to help the injured knight onto the war-horse. Then into the quiet of their small group came the pounding hooves of a destrier; an English knight brandishing a lance spurred his great horse onward, he was riding for Lord Douglas! As James turned to meet him, he unsheathed his sword and grabbed for his shield braced to the saddle of his Hobini. He fought off the first attack, standing his ground then moving aside to thrust with his sword. Another run from the English knight might be more successful he mused when suddenly he heard a familiar voice riding up behind him; William of Carmichael had seen the chevalier break formation, heading for the very location of the laird of Douglas. "My lord, allow your vassal to unhorse this enemy from our midst," he boasted ceremoniously.

The English knight lowered his helm and made the return run toward Douglas and his vassal. Carmichael held his sword in the ready, and then glided his lightly armored pony to the side of the charger. William then made a cutting blow that thrust deep into the knight's thigh while his body jolted sideways as he avoided the deadly lance. In the confusion that followed Archie grabbed his pike and thrust at the underbelly of the destrier; the elegant animal whined pitifully, falling in weakness as blood filled his lungs, the war-horse could not breathe. Edward's warrior was unhorsed and the fight ensued on foot. James wielded le Hardi's war-sword, parried with his small shield as the injured knight would not surrender to his wounds. Then Carmichael whisked his Hobini in a tight turn, charged the opponent and felled him in the muddy track of the spoiled farmland.

"Dear William, no words of praise can so affirm your brave action this day; this laird will so reward your valor most properly when this battle has so ended," James promised William of Carmichael. Years later when Brus issued the official charter of Douglasdale to the heir and son of William le Hardi, the lands included those of Kirk Michael. The laird made good on his promise. James Lord Douglas then issued his own deed to William, the first Lord Carmichael of Carmichael; a benevolent recognition of Sir William's timely assault on an English knight at *Blàr Allt a 'Bhàin-chnuic,* Gaelic for the Battle at the Burn of Bannock.

James completed the temporary bandaging of his brother's shoulder and the lad was able to mount the destrier to begin his ride to the hospital with Alan of Carslogie. Archie held the injured laird in front of him seated in the saddle while he stood in his stirrups like a knight in tournament. The two Fife squires rode on either side in escort; each one was seated on a new English mount complete with fancy carved saddles decorated with silver studs and all the luxuries and comforts of a nobleman. Edward's army was leaving many horses in their defeat this day with more spoils for the Scots to plunder when the battle was over. The English had anticipated a quick victory. Elegant silver utensils, fine linens defined with lace from Bruges, carved furniture of beautiful woods, exquisite tapestries woven in bright colors and precious gold, all were brought to stock their new castles and estates in Scotland. The fine assortment of household goods would yet remain in that kingdome but in the homes of good Scots loyal to Brus.

Not counting on defeat the English were now running to the hills for their very lives. Five hundred of their noblemen, all knights, spurred their chargers forward with their king in fearful retreat. The frightened warriors made fast their escape, leaving behind much booty including the king's own

Privy Seal in their haste. No one looked back; wary of capture, they left the Keeper and his clerks most unprotected, at the mercy of the Scots. Many sons of Alba were able to ride home days later with new weaponry; fancy silver studded sword belts, fine armor of mail and great war-horses that before the battle they could only dream about. The next time Edward comes, he will find our Scottish army well suited in fine English armaments they snickered as they packed away their spoils. There was so much plunder that Robert Brus ordered the abandoned baggage train of Edward taken to the abbey at Cambuskenneth; to be divided later among the victors. And to the Scottish treasury came a stunning lift; Edward's abandoned coinage for the English payroll and supplies. The total plunder was estimated at some £200,000.

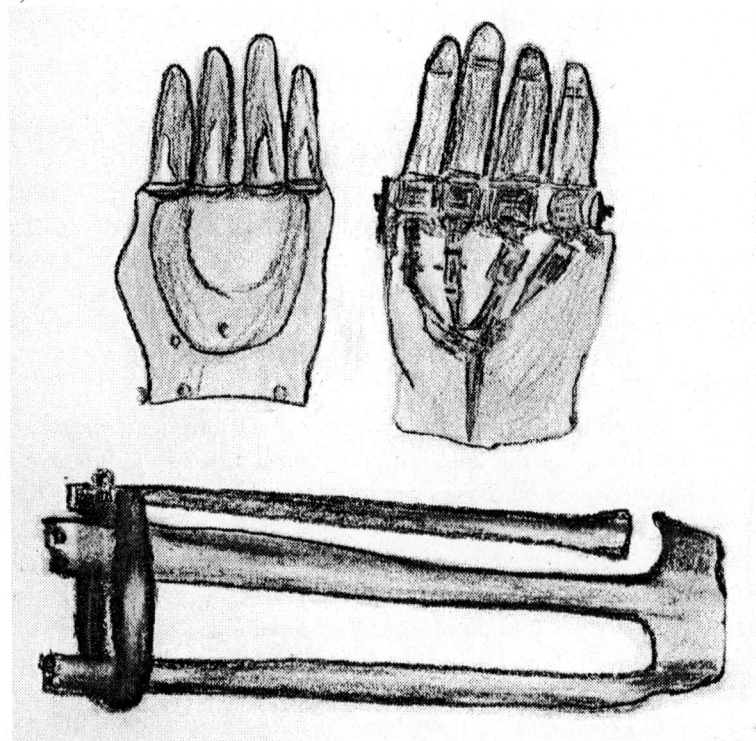

Figure LXXLXXXV-Part Three; depiction of a 19th c. engraving: a mechanical steel hand made to hold a sword for battle; the prosthetic device ordered by Robert Brus for his loyal vassal Alan de Clephane of Carslogie; the laird lost his arm at Bannockburn

Finally Archie, Clephane and his squires had arrived at the hospital set up at the kirk and were greeted quickly by the Hospitallers. The squires helped the laird off the destrier gingerly; the man was weak from the ride and his perilous wounds. Immediately these healing monks decided they would remove the knight to Cambuskenneth and the abbey infirmary; but first there was some work that they would do before releasing their patient they said. Hugh quietly came to tend to Archie's shoulder; young Walter ran for supplies of bandages and maggots that he would administer to heal the wound; the Logan lad was learning healing from his Uncle Hugh as he called him. Hugh looked over his brother's wounds; the flesh was cut badly and required a great deal of stitching the churchman surmised. The aspiring canon was circumspect as he tended to his brother, taking his time to do the surgery with care. "Lady Beatrice will have her words to say should this humble healer not be successful in his work this day," he said feigning fear for her recriminations when the Douglases would be reunited with the ladies after the battle. "More scars for her to look upon; at least this face is most pretty for another day," Archie grumbled good naturedly.

Hugh looked long and hard at his brother. "That our James is fairing well; no English man at arms to touch our laird of Douglasdale," the squire boasted, giving Hugh the answer to his unspoken question, knowing he was concerned for James' safety on the battlefield. Young Walter of Logan returned to Hugh's side smiling, as he heard Archie's report on his older brother. "My father is most well?" he asked hoping the squire would elaborate further. "Aye, the tide has turned against the English they fall out in disarray," he began.

The now seasoned warrior, Henklebaldicus de Douglas, squire had a lot to tell Walter and Hugh. He described in the most accurate of details the gory scene; the strangled commotion of English knights, their injured horses falling, being trampled by the others who followed them. The carnage and smell of death was overwhelming in the extreme heat of the day; the agonized screams and begging cries of the dead and dying English mingled with the snorts from horses and the clash of swords against the iron heads of Scottish pikes in a confused din. "The sounds of battle most deafening at times; this squire's head to spin from all the noise to concentrate the more on the fight at hand, to grip the staff most hard as well to keep my wits," Archie explained.

The abbot Maurice came over to the Douglas lads and asked if they would both assist the laird of Carslogie to the Augustinians at the abbey; they both readily agreed and Hugh went to administer to the laird before they began the short journey to the more permanent infirmary. "Perhaps to make a good hand and arm of strong metal," suggested the aspiring canon. "This lad has seen one so fashioned for an Essex warrior-priest; an old Templar knight that came to our good priory in Little Dunmow," he explained. The laird was fading into an unconscious state; he dreamed from the words Hugh offered that he might be made whole again. And when days later he was recovering at Cambuskenneth Abbey, Alan of Clephane was visited by Robert Brus at the infirmary. In good time this king would order a prosthesis made, with a mechanical hand to hold his sword for battle Brus promised him.

THE AFTERMATH; DUNBAR, THE BLOODY FAULD AND BOTHWELL-
James made his way back towards his schiltron on the left flank; he heard the gleeful chant of his sergeants, "On them, they fail!" He watched with satisfaction the continued progress of the Scottish lines as they moved forward. Then curiously James noticed Caernarvon banners surrounded by a large contingency of cavalry headed for the Roman road; King Edward was making his escape with an escort of knights towards Stirling Castle. He spurred his Hobini to the side of his king. James intended to beg a command of light horse to pursue the English lord. Successful capture of Caernarvon would bring a ransom of enormous measure and recognition of Robert Brus as king of an independent Scotland he reflected; his heart beat so hard as he considered the opportunity that he thought it might leave his chest. But when he met up with Brus, he found the king was less excited by the prospect; concerned for the numbers on the field that still favored the English. "To preserve our presence here, that battle not yet over dear James. This king can only spare of sixty armed horse for your good measure," Robert Brus allowed sadly.

Figure LXXXVI-the Bloody Fauld, a location described in David R. Ross's book, *On the Trail of Robert the Bruce;* Edward's armed foot gathered here in defeat near their supply wagons

The garrison commander at Stirling, Sir Philip Mowbray, refused Edward entry and now the king was valiantly making his way eastward on the Military Way towards Linlithgow, perhaps to stop at the loyal English stronghold of the Earl of March at Dunbar, James speculated. As the knights and their king spurred their destriers onward, the Lord Douglas and his sixty armed horse were nipping at his heels.

While the Douglas contingency pursued Lord Paramount and his knights another smaller battle of importance raged near the old Roman road. Enemy armed foot had gathered there to await orders but their leaders were in flight. The foot soldiers in an English army were expendable; their nobles had left them, deserted their adherents in the wake of the Scottish victory. As they circled the supply wagons stationed on the Military Way they were suddenly surprised by an onslaught of victorious Scots who were eager to do battle with their foe. On a site along a wee burn near the woodlands a great many English soldiers ended their fight with the Scots on Bloody Fauld; to the man not one survived the terrible attack, their bodies writhed and fell to quick decay in the hot June sun.

Figure LXXXVII-Part Three; the ruins of Dunbar Castle on the North Sea

Lord Douglas spurred his Hobini forward, leading the Scots and their light horse. The Scottish cavalry finally caught up with the English in Linlithgow; the Hobelars were making good time in their pursuit. The English armed horse were more nervous for the encounter; they spurred their war-horses eastward with a sense of urgency and fear. The Scots were in full view, closing in on their quarry, taking prisoners of the stragglers. As James rode towards Winchburgh in the West Lothianes he suddenly recalled tales of another hot pursuit involving the enemy and a Douglas knight. Le Hardi and William Wallace were following the English justiciar Ormsby, chasing him from Scone where he had abandoned the king's treasury to the hands of brave Scots. James chuckled as he remembered the stories his father shared of the English vassals and their fear of the wild lunacy of Scots in close chase to their noble escape. "Were there more of us this journey, we would catch your sorry self dear Edward," he scoffed out loud. He looked back at his men following his lead and wished now that Archie was among them so he could share with him the escapades of their father and Wallace. Another time, he mused. He then motioned his men to slow their pace as the English army had drawn up to rest their horses and tend to their care.

Figure LXXXVIII-Part Three; Ayton manor was held by the Earl of Haddington; a Victorian castle stands there today on the site of the 13th century ruins

    James did not have sufficient number to take on the English; but harass them he would and capture those who lingered behind he promised to continue. Along the way the laird of Douglas engaged the company of young de Abernathy, kin by marriage to his Uncle Hugh. The young laird was reluctantly heading to the battle in Stirling; in service to Lord Paramount until he heard of the great victory of the Scots. "Dear cousin that we might surely use of your kind assistance in this endeavor," persuaded Sir James. Showing good sense Sir Lawrence de Abernathy joined with his kin to add twenty to the number of armed horse for the Scots in close pursuit of Edward. It was a grueling charge with little to show for it at the end. Edward was welcomed with open arms by the Earl of March into his fortress at Dunbar. The king secured a wee boat there and sailed to the safety of Bamburgh while his contingency of nobles and other knights continued south to Berwick with the Douglas armed horse in close proximity. To the gates of the English burgh the Scots rode; but they would go no farther. That night some of James' followers returned with their laird to stay at Ellie's manor in Ayton; while others set their course for Stirling to share in the spoils.
    Meanwhile in Lanarkshire a large number of English knights sought the safety of Bothwell castle; the garrison commander, Sir Walter Gilbertson,

held the castle for the English with a small contingency of armed foot and archers. He readily accepted his new guests but upon hearing the outcome of the battle changed sides, making prisoners of the English. Among these sorry knights at Bothwell were the Earl of Hereford and an English lord well known to the Scots, Sir John de Segrave. The ransom for Hereford, brother in law to Caernarvon, came to be an exchange of prisoners. The earl's release brought freedom to fifteen Scots of noble rank held in English prisons including the Queen of Scots, the king's own daughter and one prelate, the Bishop of Glasgow. Sir Thomas de Berkeley, the widower of the late Lady Joan de Ferrers, was another of the unfortunate English captured at Bothwell; he was ransomed for such a great sum that the measure taxed his estates for generations to come. The rest of the English and their adherents including the surviving Welsh bowman, made their way south to England, in grave retreat, under the leadership of Maurice de Berkeley. For some time Scotland would be rid of the English in their homeland; but they would return again, Lord Robert reflected.

THE MARCHES, AUGUST 1314-As the weeks passed after the great battle it became ever apparent that the English would not recognize a king named Robert much less a free and independent Scotland. The Scots had but won a battle at Bannockburn, but not the peace. The king sent his lieutenants James Douglas, Thomas Randolph and Edward Brus with a large army leaving from their muster near Berwick to ride southward, back into the north of England. Amid much burning and destruction except to the castles of the region, the Scots secured more booty for King Robert's treasury and spread more fear in the English villages. Barely had James and Archie returned to days of celebration with their wives and children that they were once again on the trail in search of English tribute. As Lord Douglas, his brother and the Douglas vassals from the Marches and Douglasdale were making their way south they were joined by the king's brother. "A bloody course will we most drive," observed James as saw the impulsive Edward Brus leading his men at arms to join with the Douglas contingency. Archie understood; the king's brother held for himself, a crown upon his head was his ambition. A ruthless and careless man in every endeavor, James knew he would have trouble containing the foolish enthusiasm of this reckless earl.

The Douglas laird and his men rode through Northumbria following the coastline and bypassing the parish of Ingram for their pilferage; they headed east to Alnwick and the fortress of de Percy. "We have a date with le Hardi's foe," James said sarcastically. Archie asked him if he felt they might goad the English lord into battle. "Aye, such contest he must accept or lose the confidence of tenants he is paid to so protect." Having avoided the fight at Bannockburn, Sir Henry was little eager to take on the Scots just now. He was demoralized by Edward's treatment of him, the imprisonment and loss of estates though temporary had destroyed his self esteem. "Our father's life was brought to an early end for the treachery of that greedy lord," James continued. He then explained his strategy to Archie: they would feign attack of the abbey there and draw out the small garrison.

Sir Thomas Chauncelor, the son of le Hardi's vassal, had done much work of spying in that village. He discovered as well the low morale and few numbers of the garrison at Alnwick and reported these with his other findings to Lord Douglas. "Your mother is expected to arrive within few weeks; to return again to your Fawdon is her plan," said the newly dubbed knight from Northumbria. James was surprised at first to hear that Ellie was coming north just now. "Our mother not to wait for another of Edward's musters," quipped Archie. "She will so insure that my fair Beatrice has her good hand to so deliver another Douglas heir," he boasted, speaking about his daughter or son that was due to be born in late fall.

Figure LXXXIX-Part Three; Alnwick Castle, Northumbria where Sir Henry de Percy spent his last days in 1314; he purchased the manor lands and castle under dubious circumstances from Anthony Bek

James chuckled at the prospect of Lady El making her way through Yorkshire then to Fawdon and finally into Scotland's Borders. "No war to stop our Lady Douglas," he said smiling. They rode towards Alnwick and began to strategize their attack. De Percy had received word of their presence in the Cheviot, moving near his fortress. When he heard it was the son of his old enemy le Hardi, an old glow of confidence returned. "That we will show dear Edward; to destroy the Black Douglas, a feat unknown to my lord the king, this knight will demonstrate the way of warriors not fools in battle." But Sir Henry was not successful in his encounter with the followers of the young laird of Douglas. When James led his men at arms into warfare it was always his habit to seek out the captain or in this case the lord of the manor to do battle with him personally. But before he even spotted the armorial achievements of de Percy, the English knight had charged ahead of his own garrison and took on a late patrol Douglas had sent out on reconnaissance. At forty-one Sir Henry made a poor showing for his ambitious deeds; the foolish encounter nearly cost him his life that day. He barely made his way back to Alnwick Castle with the assistance of his squires only to expire there some eight weeks later. The greedy, vengeful Sir Henry de Percy, the evil and foul accuser of the most honorable of knights, William le Hardi Douglas, was finally dead; the earldom he most coveted eluding him in the end.

The Douglas knight and his followers continued south as they brought fire and sword to Northumbria and further still to Durham; they burned and pillaged, leveled the countryside to waste. These brave men of Alba would seek tribute when villages feared more the flames of Scottish armies than the starvation brought by paying huge sums for protection. The crops of 1314 failed and now the winter was coming; the English from Northumbria and south as far as Essex were facing the grey, stern skies of late fall to spring with few crops stored or growing. The choice between hunger or home and hearth was chilling and where villagers could not save their homes they made off into the hills taking with them what livestock they could manage to lead to safety

The Scottish raiders under James, Randolph and Edward Brus split their forces to rendezvous much later at Richmond they decided. James took his men south where Archie though yet a squire was given a small command to continue more raids, burning crops and forcing the inhabitants to pay for their immunity to save their homes. The slaughter continued; the fires burned fiercely carving the night air with funnels of black soot, gasping streams of grey smoke and yellow-red flames twisting in the wind. The Scots were sending Edward a stern message: recognize our king and kingdome or the north will fall to ravaged fear and pillage; scorched beyond all recognition for your folly.

DOUGLASDALE NOVEMBER 1314-The cooler days of autumn beckoned Ellie as she, Ana and Elizabeth rode up the steep grade that led to Park Castle, her Essex household following close behind. The Tinto were fading in their purple glow of heather gone by for the season. The Park Burn was rushing through the gill, swollen from the heavy rains that fell late summer into fall, spoiling any hope of harvest, the crops rotting in the soil. As the Douglas-Bagot household rode into the outer gates of the palisade of the fortress, the comforting barks of Deerhounds greeted them coming from the courtyard of the newly expanded stronghold. Young William was outside playing with the hounds and his cousin John; under the supervision of their nurses, they were enjoying the few remaining days of good fall weather.

Suddenly they spotted their grandmother on her jennet riding towards them. Squeals of glee were followed by the chattering of wee ones as they ran to Ellie's open arms. "Where is your sister Elizabeth?" asked Lady Eleanora. William pointed to the large oak doors opening to two Douglas wives; a two year old red haired beauty was walking between her mother and aunt, each lady holding one of her wee hands to assist her movement. Ana dismounted and stood to one side; Ellie the grandmother was surrounded by her three grandchildren with Deerhounds lapping her face and jumping all about. "If only her William could see her happiness this day," Lady Elizabeth from Fife confided to Ana. "Somehow I know he must be here; this is his Douglasdale," chuckled Ellie's companion of thirty three years, "he would will it so!"

Figure XC-Part Three; view of Park Burn from from the smaller earthworks on the cart path to Park Castle, looking towards Coalgill

"Hubicus!" Ellie yelled heartily when she spotted her son walking her way. "Dear mother that you are here most pleases this lad!" Ellie held him close. "Just to see my son and hold him so," she cooed. "And what of your brothers?" she demanded. Hugh explained that Archie would return soon; he accompanied James to Cambuskenneth for Parliament. "But our Archibald went there only for short days; not to linger with the business of state he will be in Douglasdale by the lay-in, so he promised his dear bride," Hugh said with a wink towards Beatrice. Ellie turned to her daughters in law, hugging them one by one in a long embrace. "We made good time to travel north; arriving none too soon that your lay-in fast approaches," she said teasing Archie's wife. Lady Eleanora laughed as she beheld the great girth of

Beatrice hidden by her large surcote. "This mother so remembers carrying one Archibald that I wobbled all about," she chuckled. "That this lass most wants to see her feet," Beatrice moaned wearily, "to appear most like myself before my brothers so arrive. That they will not so recognize their sister is my fear."

Ellie had not heard the news about the release of Scottish prisoners; she begged to hear more about the de Lindsays' homecoming, how and when the exchange was arranged. "Let us all adjourn to the great hall," beamed Lady Joanna, giving her daughter to her nurse Maudie. "We have much news to share first." As they sat around the great trestle table Ellie looked around and giggled. "That this tower looks more like Douglas Castle; the grand old tapestries, this lass had no idea our James had saved them from the fire." Joanna explained that some of the tapestries were new to them; plunder from the wagons of English knights in retreat. "But that one there," Ellie pointed to a special wall hanging of blue and gold she knew for certain had been in the withdrawing room of her former home. Hugh grinned. "Our James had just returned from chasing Edward to his wee skiff in the North Sea," he began. "That when he returned to the abbey at Cambuskenneth, to give our lord the king his fair report, he found one Richard Dickson standing guard over this tapestry. Found among the banners and household goods of de Clifford, to lie there in the knight's own wagon he was told."

Hugh said that the laird of Douglas was ebullient for the treasure he thought was lost. "That our James calls Park Castle his fair tribute to le Hardi." Beatrice added with bravado, "A recreation in wee splendor of our Douglasdale; most as our Scottish knights mounted on Hobini not destriers, with their army of sixty armed horse not 60,000 men at arms; everything we do as Scots much smaller in comparison, yet we do it!" Ellie told them that the great hall was remarkable; she felt so at home there. Lady Joanna had wine poured and ordered great feasting as Hugh began to relate his stories of the great battle at the Bannock Burn. Sir David sat at the end of the large trestle table; he was eager to hear about the fight. A sense of pride rose within him, strangely so for his English heritage he mused; but he had trained the Douglas knight and squire, the victors of this 'Bannockburn'.

Before Hugh was able to elaborate and describe the scenes of warfare, his mother was already interrupting. Ellie's concern was for the old foe of her husband, the man responsible for her Gilley's imprisonment at the White Tower. "This lass so heard that de Percy is now with God; that vile and greedy lord who took our sweet knight your father from us," she said with little sorrow for his passing. "Sir Thomas told me of the wee skirmish of the summer; was he not at Edward's muster most as well?" Ellie asked. Hugh said that de Percy refused the call, sent only his feudal requirement so James and Archie set their sights on Alnwick before continuing their raids south towards Durham. "Our James so promised to be the laird that brought him to his death certain; to avenge our father, killing him in battle was his pledge," Hugh elaborated. "Not being at the muster of his king meant James had to devise another way to meet de Percy; so moving south our Douglas warriors stole their way to Alnwick," Joanna excitedly related. She and Beatrice had lingered on every word when Archie had first related the details of the Alnwick attack; now they wanted to share the tale verbatim with Ellie; mimicking the sentiments of their knight and squire as they told the story.

"Our James sought to meet Sir Henry in combat; to send him to the Otherworld on the point of his sword. But our God had other plans. An ignominious charge that foolish knight so made, riding out alone, attacking three Douglas men at arms at once. These startled warriors were just returning from reconnaissance, fought him fiercely until he could move no more," offered Beatrice. Emulating Archie's bravado as she spoke made Ellie and Ana giggle. Joanna added more details of the skirmish; then brought the tale to its celebrated conclusion. "Sir Henry was badly injured; to linger many months in tormented misery, he died quite recently." Hugh said that the defeat of Sir Henry de Percy was a family affair; everyone felt the need to hear the story; to relate it over and over again. "To release our anger and send forgiveness to that treacherous lord is very difficult to do," the churchman allowed.

"And what of Edward's former prisoners that are now returning to their Scotland?" Ellie asked. Satisfied with the details of de Percy's demise, Lady El was eager to change to a happier subject. Beatrice told her that Sir John de Segrave was captured at Bothwell and was being exchanged for many good knights. "My brothers, David, Reginald and Alexander will be waiting in Carlisle for their release to Scotland, so Edward has agreed; we only wait for the English king to sign his orders, command his writs to another of your kin, the son of that knight, Stephen de Segrave." Ellie was stunned; her English relatives were being exchanged for dear Alex's own sons. "And there are others," Hugh began, "young Andrew de Moray captured some ten years ago will now return to Scotland. And another brave patriot our James so tells us that you would know: Sir Thomas de Morham." Ellie gasped and felt chills go up and down her back. Ana grabbed her hand; this was a painful memory for Lady Douglas to recall.

Sir Thomas had been held at Berwick Castle the same time as Lord Douglas in 1297; his squire had heard of a scheme of escape that Gilley's squire shared with his knight. Lady Douglas was suspicious and with her coffers dwindling she refused to give her husband the coinage for the intrigue. Some few days later Lord Douglas and Sir Thomas de Morham sailed for London; both admitted to the Tower of London on 12 October 1297. But when the Scots left Berwick on Tweed as Edward's prisoners in the English cog, Lady Douglas did not know the plot for escape had been a ruse; a squire for de Morham murdered for his compliance. Ana was concerned for the memories. Ellie lived for many agonizing weeks before she saw Gilley again and he told her his captivity in the White Tower was not her fault; the scheme in Berwick was a trick to steal the little coinage they had left, not to free her knight. Her instincts had been valid. As Lady Eleanora sat in the daze of those haunting memories she finally was able to ask Hugh more about de Morham. "That he is still alive?" Ellie stammered.

"Yes and most happy to come home to his Scotland," he smiled in his response. "Our James has told us that this fair exchange he calls the Douglas-Lovaine treat of peace; where your English kin de Segrave is allowed to return to his England as Edward so returns good Scots and Douglas kin to their homeland: three brothers of Lady Beatrice and our good kin Andrew de Moray most as well," he boasted. "Sir Thomas Morham that he knew our father and suffered with him it is only right that he should so return with Douglas kin." Ellie agreed but the awful memories of the tower were upon her; she was twisting her ring as tears filled her eyes. Every time someone spoke of the time her beloved knight stood prisoner in the White Tower her response was always the same: a great overwhelming sadness and sense of excruciating loss seemed to envelope her in every way.

Ana was stroking her hand and rubbing her back; she gave Hugh a familiar grimace, a signal to change the subject. "Dear mother, more news this lad has for you; Bishop Wishart is coming home the noo, if he is not here already!" Ellie lifted her head and wiped her face, apologizing for her 'silly ways' she begged him to continue. "This lad was so planning to attend him, to ride to Carlisle and bring him north with the sisters of the king, his wife the queen and his daughter Marjory," Hugh elaborated. Then he paused to look over at Lady Beatrice; brandishing the Douglas smirk for emphasis. "But our wee William or Eleanora had other plans for this good healer," he snickered. Ellie was startled somewhat; she had never before considered the prospect of her grandchild bearing her name. The wee Eleanora she kept saying under her breath; chuckling at the idea.

Beatrice interrupted her thoughts to explain what her brother in law meant; that she had false feelings of a birth most coming that she sent for Hugh. "How foolish this lass most felt when nothing happened after that; the wee one so deciding to most wait!" The feasting began and continued into the late hours of the night as Hugh spun his tales of great warfare. The churchman became the story teller like his father and had everyone including Sir David riveted by his exciting descriptions of the great Scottish victory at Bannock Burn. During their conversations of great battles, their thoughts turned to the tragedy of Caerlaverock. After these many years of being part of the Douglas household it was only now that Lady Elizabeth the lad's tutor realized that she and Lady Joanna shared the same sad memories for that cruel siege; both their husbands died at that battle on the Solway Firth in Dumfries. "So many lives were changed that dreaded summer, fourteen years now gone," lamented Elizabeth. Joanna shook her head in agreement. "That we are all one family and safe now; our God so answered all our prayers but one that day," she reflected; wondering if that husband would be the last to leave her a widow from doing battle with dear Edward.

Ellie was out riding in the prime some days later with her escort and in the company of Elizabeth and Ana. They had visited the Douglas Castle ruins and were returning when they encountered a frantic Archibald riding for them; he had just returned from Cambuskenneth. "Dear mother, our wee one most comes the now!" he exclaimed. "A hello would be most welcome," she admonished him with a grin. Then she gave her jennet a kick and off she flew with Archibald following behind her. Ellie made her way up the steep turnpike stairs, running backwards to the natural curve to favor the left handed Douglas warriors. She made haste into the chamber for the lay-in on the family level within the keep and found Hugh preparing to make a cut to ease the birthing. Beatrice was very nervous and chattering away anxiously that Ellie went to her side immediately to calm her. "When my Gilley so delivered our dear Muriel he first thought to grab his dagger to so prepare the opening that I screamed in fear he did not know what he was doing," she said, laughing in such a contagious manner that Beatrice began to giggle. "This lass is most fearful of such things as well," she confided. Hugh did not have the intimate bedside demeanor of his father; he was just learning how to deal with emotional women as they were giving birth. The rhythm of the contractions and the mother's breathing flowed easily now and suddenly Hugh was guiding out the head, then body of a lovely baby girl with a full head of jet black Douglas hair and the milky white skin of Lovaine.

The aspiring canon said the words: "I baptize thee Eleanora Douglas, in the name of the Father, the Son and the Holy Ghost." Archie had been waiting in the doorway, now bolted to the side of his wife. "A daughter do we have my Beatrice," he said softly as he wiped her brow. Hugh had wrapped the child and put her on Beatrice's breast for a few moments; he knew she would fall off to sleep before long. Beatrice looked at the wee one then at Archie and began to laugh. "Archibald of Douglas, remove that armor from your sorry self before you hold our daughter!" she scolded him with feigned indignation. Ellie was laughing, exchanging glances with Ana; his father le Hardi had forgotten to remove his armor when he came into the lay-in that December day eighteen years ago to deliver one named Archibald. "Perhaps you so remember your own birthing," Ana teased him, "to wear your mail and gambeson most now, like our brave knight and midwife Sir Gilley, to honor his dear memory." Everyone was laughing at Archie's impetuous ways; he was certainly his father's son Ellie acknowledged to Ana.

On a signal from Hugh the speywife removed the infant; taking the wee Eleanora aside to clean the lass as instructed with the salves and oils Gilley had described in his healing journal. Beatrice was exhausted; Archie was frantic that his bride looked so pale. "Henklebaldicus! Your bride is most weary from a trying birth; it is normal to feel such need of slumber. This lass so slept from the none to the day next when you finally chose to arrive into this world," his mother teased him. Beatrice smiled and squeezed his hand, then fell fast asleep. By now the speywife had completed her work and returned the infant to Archie who barely flew to the great hall to show the other children waiting there excitedly with their nurses to see their new sister or young cousin. "Does this lad do anything with patience?" asked Ellie out loud. Ana shook her head. "Archie is Archie," she agreed. "He has the innocence and joy with such things as Lord Will," Lady Eleanora sighed.

GLASGOW CATHEDRAL, JANUARY 1315-In a small ceremony in the bishop's great hall at his private residence one Hubicus of Douglas was to receive his ordination from Robert Wishart. Ellie, James, Joanna, Beatrice, Archibald, Ana, Elizabeth with Walter and Sir David and many Douglas vassals were all present. The cruel winter that year gave good cover for an Essex household to remain in Scotland in search of their lady's rents. Eleanora Douglas watched with pride and humility as her dear friend Robert, Bishop of Glasgow took the pledge of fealty from her son. Hubicus touched and kissed the gospels as he gave the good bishop his solemn oath; his long tresses falling to his shoulder now surrounded the naked crown of the tonsure on his head. Hugh of Douglas, Canonic was now an Austin Canon for the see of Glasgow. "Rise good canon and bid this old bishop your fair eyes to assist me here," Bishop Wishart grumbled good naturedly. He was going to put his seal upon a very important document; to declare null and void the office usurped by Thomas de Durram who wastefully spent and likely too embezzled the funds of Kelso Abbey and the Priory of Lesmahagow. "A day for Douglases to rejoice," James declared. "To right the wrongs of English in our favored abbey and the good priory of our dear St. Brice; to be rid of such alienations that stole from us. And celebrate as well the treasured homecoming of our beloved prelate and the ordination of our humble canon, Hugh of Douglas." A jovial mood prevailed as everyone hailed the old churchman and the new canon for his see.

The Bishop then allowed Hugh to guide his hand and seal to the declaration. "The first day of many more to come to rid ourselves of Edward and his greedy vassals," boasted Archie. Ellie took the prelate's hand and led him to the feasting table set for the occasion. "Dear Lady Douglas; that I wear this fair chasuble in your honor this day," the old bishop said proudly. "Your good handwork of embroidery here," he continued; indicating the inside of the neck closure where Ellie had spelled out *'Soar Alba'* in small letters that only he would know about. "This mother is most grateful for all that you have done for us and our Hubicus," Ellie told him.

"Would you find that lad who wears fur hats to Parliament," he asked her, meaning James. "That I am here," said the laird of Douglas. "Has our dear king, our good Robert given you leave from his side this day?" asked Wishart with a humorous chuckle in his words. "That I have not laid my eyes upon my lord the king since two days hence Conception Day," he said whimsically, meaning the 10th of December. Then he took out a rolled parchment that Brus intended for the bishop. "Such gift of charter do I have to so present our good Robert Wishart," he declared ceremoniously. Hugh read the grant of deed from Robert Brus, King of Scots, to his beloved and most wise Bishop of Glasgow, Robert Wishart, for his faithful service: lands in free barony in Fife that he might grant to heirs of his device or sell for profit at his pleasure. The smoky blue eyes of the old bishop filled with tears; the gratitude of Robert Brus to remember his part in the coronation nine years ago overwhelmed him. "That our king does so recall a bishop's last memory of his Scotland, with failing sight, yet present at Dundee in Fife," explained Hugh. Everyone began to laugh as they remembered the extraordinary effort of Bishop Lamberton to smuggle Wishart into Scotland in 1310; a bishop temporarily freed from Porchester's prison to attend the Pope's Council in Vienna.

BLACKHOUSE TOWER MARCH 1315-The crowded fortress on the Douglas Burn was the scene for many goodbyes this day. Ellie was riding home to Essex and James was going to Edinburgh on business of the king. "This lass would rather stay in Scotland," Lady Douglas said as tears welled in her eyes. The Douglases enjoyed nearly four months of peace in Park Castle; spending a joyous Hogmanay together as a family for the first time in many years. Yet their Scotland was still at war; James and Archie would be riding into the north of England within weeks. "My wee grandchildren," she chuckled as they gathered around her. "Grandmother," began little Eleanora, "that you should stay!" declared the child gleefully. "Nothing would so make this lass happier that I could," she replied with heavy heart. But Lady Douglas had to return to England; she had a sometimes husband in Staffordshire and rents to review in Essex, Stafford and Hereford. Lingering any longer in Scotland might set tongues to wag in question of her loyalty to Edward. "Someday will your grandmother so return to live in her Scotland; it is done!" she declared. James looked away; he had something on his mind; a strategy was brewing; he would secure her income and a manor in Scotland for her purpose he decided.

As Ellie and Ana gave their Douglas men and their wives their last embrace, they could not have known they would not return for two more years. At the Parliament held in November at Cambuskenneth, Robert Brus had taken certain measures to insure allegiance among his nobles; issuing an ultimatum that all Scottish landowners who had not come to his peace within the year would forfeit all their lands. Most all of those not pledged came forward in support of Scotland's king. Eleanora Lovaine Douglas Bagot would have given this king her fealty for her de Ferrers and Douglas dower lands most willingly. But she could not bring herself to do so and not because she was married to Lord Bagot or would forfeit her Essex lands in her pledging.

Ellie's income in Scotland would rise and could sustain her and her household that only one concern kept her from turning her back on England. What of her Gilley and the others she wondered? William le Hardi was yet buried with her daughters and grandchild at Little Dunmow. Declaring her allegiance for Scotland meant she would be forbidden to return there to the priory. Forfeiting her Scottish lands was one thing but she would not lose her knight again to Edward's wrath, even if his bones were all that remained there, she promised herself. Her decision sealed her fate with her Scottish holdings. From the Parliament in Cambuskenneth the de Ferrers lands with those of the de la Zouches were lost to the English heirs, Ellie's dower so included; being the largest single land holdings in all of Scotland to be reseised to others more loyal to Brus.

CARLISLE JULY 1315-The new *Custos Marchiarum*, Warden of the Marches, was James Lord Douglas and now his king was calling him to do battle in Carlisle. Lord Robert intended to take the town; revenge for the savage atrocities waged against his brothers Thomas and Alexander was on his mind. James and Archie, now his brother's permanent partner in such matters, had just returned to the Douglas manor in Lintalee, rejoining Joanna, Beatrice, and the children; examining the construction that was still in progress. The reunion was short; the orders from the king took precedence James informed them stoically. But even the laird of Douglas was growing tired of the constant need to ride off to do battle with the English. When will this end, he wondered to himself? Then he realized this was the first time he ever could remember feeling a resentment to attend his king when called to service.

Beatrice was crying openly when the Douglas laird and his squire were set to ride off to their muster; she had her fill of wars and battles she told them. As James mounted his Hobini his young daughter broke the hold of her nurse and she went screaming to his side, "Fad' er do not leave your Lil'Beth" she begged him. James got back down from his horse and comforted his daughter. "You must be brave and keep your mother company," he told her as his own eyes welled in tears. Beatrice wiped her eyes, she did not want to be a burden to her husband; but her sadness was overwhelming she told him. Archie took her aside and confided his feelings; he too resented the constant churn, the calls for muster, followed by lang weeks on campaign with few days to spend in the comfort of their home, in the arms of his Beatrice. "That this lad so promises to spend some months and more with his sweet bride; it is done," he told her wearily.

Figure XCI-Part Three; Carlisle Castle

The ladies and their maids in wait with the children's nurses were all busy packing; shuffling their household once again to the safety of the Douglas Burn. "When will this lass so stay in one place for some time?" moaned Beatrice. Joanna came to comfort her friend and sister in law, sharing her thoughts on a lady's responsibility to her knight and husband. "These campaigns, the raids they take into the north of England are difficult; the days hang heavily on our warriors I fear; we must try to shield them from the truth of our feelings." Beatrice confided her loneliness; her plans those many years ago to share her love and life with Archie had somehow become lost among the fierce attacks and terrifying assaults as the Douglas brothers rode into the Marches of England. "This lass so prays for peace," she said, her words muffled in fearful sobs as Lady Joanna held her in a generous, caring hug.

Robert greeted James circumspectly as the Douglases and their entourage arrived near Carlisle. This was England; reinforcements for the enemy were likely he warned. They must act swiftly if the Scots were to meet with success the king advised his Warden of the Marches. James agreed and set about a reconnaissance of his own to assess their situation. There were three gates to the town; should they attack them one at a time he wondered? One of the walls had a particularly difficult access and seemed undefended he noted. When he returned to Robert's side he found the king already planning a full attack; ready to explain his strategy to his lieutenant.

The siege began with the Scots out numbering the English; their equipment equal to the task at hand. But each day and every night that followed, the torrential rains fell; never to subside. The wet weather created impenetrable mud, cavernous ruts where cart paths once ran along the fortress walls. Never before had the weather been such a factor in their battles James reflected. The relentless downpours were befriending the English as they hampered the Scots mobility, deterring their lumbering siege engines as well. The slogging assault continued for eight fatiguing days with no success to show for their gritty determination; the garrison of over five hundred men at arms were standing firm against the Scottish aggressors.

The governor of Carlisle was a knight of renown, a seasoned warrior of many campaigns; Sir Andrew Harcla from Westmorland. His garrison respected his leadership and fought tirelessly for their commander. The long battle continued but the Scots were losing their resolve. They had not expected the foul weather to annihilate their siege, nor had they anticipated the brutal fight Harcla surmounted. Each time the Scots shifted their attacks, moved from one front to another, the governor countered perfectly. The Westmoreland knight shifted his men at arms with great alacrity, rushed his well trained soldiers from one barraged gate to another in little time, to demoralize Brus' army for their efforts. The English knight was strutting his prowess as if to say to Edward I am your commander in the Marches; follow the lead of this soldier to great victory!

The Scots' sad predicament was obvious to all; their assault tower or berefrai that Brus so proudly commandeered becoming the symbol of their failing mission; mired in mud, unable to mount the siege. Yet King Robert was on a mission of revenge; determined to not give up. When frustrated by the constant hail of darts and arrows and stones that the Scots constructed a catapult of their own. They volleyed huge rocks across the walls intending to break the morale of their enemy. But the Carlisle citizens were undeterred; suffering but one casualty to the stone throwing war machine.

On the ninth day James and Robert commiserated. The king put forth a strategy to gather crops growing into bundles. He intended to fill the moats and ditches with the dryshod to gain access to the stronghold but the floods washed away the materials; their dreams for taking the town and castle slipped through their hands into the unleashed flow of Carlisle's swollen streams. At every turn the Brus' army seemed thwarted in their fight.

The Scots still did not give up; they fashioned small bridges on wheels operated by a system of pulleys. But once again these fine engines of attack were fruitless, useless for the relentless deeds of the Carlisle garrison and the muddy impassable tracks that once were sturdy gates. On the tenth day of their paralyzing siege, the winds whipped through the burgh with a raw chill embellished by sheets of the ever constant rains. The Scots began a multiple assault on two gates; but the governor was not fooled. He commanded his archers to a frenzied pace; ordered his garrison to pommel the Scots with large rocks that seemed to multiply each hour in number. "What kind of machine lies behind these walls?" James wondered out loud. "Aye, these stones are more in number again this day," said Robert angrily. James was growing more restless and impatient; determined to initiate a fruitful assault upon the fortified town he offered a plan to wage an attack on the undefended gate. Brus championed the idea and added some strategy of his own. James was to lead his force up the west wall; Brus would then take the larger retinue and lay forceful siege upon the eastern gate, diverting attention from James' warriors in their advance. Lord Douglas agreed to the plan, announced his departure and bid his commander God speed.

James and Archie rode with their Foresters into the night to arrive at the western precipice that protected Carlisle from grave assault. They gave their horses to the younger squires and pages to hold should they require fast escape. The Scots set their wee siege engines, the Ledhouse ladders, in place; all three were now readily secured to the high walls of the western gates. James instructed Archie and the rest of the bowmen to give the Scots cover; arrows should fly in swift succession whenever Harcla's men appeared on the wall-walk above them, Lord Douglas told them. As was his habit, James was the first to climb his ladder; to lead them into battle and successful siege he promised his men. But when he cleared the wall, thinking the bridgehead secure he came to a rude discovery: nearly the entire garrison was waiting for him hidden in the alcoves along the wall! He made haste to retreat; yelling for his men to stop their ascent. Archie realized at once they were in great peril as he saw the English men at arms now lifting small catapults to shower heavy rocks upon the invaders. He shot his arrows swiftly, one right after the other, with grave accuracy. But the fury of his actions and those of the other archers was not enough to protect James and the rest of the Scots stuck halfway up the steep edifice; they would certainly take injury and in great measure he feared.

Scots making their escape down the ladder were encountering those trying to scale the wall; their momentum clashed causing as much mayhem to themselves as the Carlisle garrison with their furious assault of rocks and arrows now upon them. James in his escape caught his right leg on the ladder as one plank gave way; his calf was impaled by a metal skewer that once held the step in place while the tangled rope held him fast. Frozen in place by his predicament the knight took an arrow deep, one that penetrated his right shoulder in such a way to restrict his motion. As he hooked his injured right arm around the ladder he cut his way loose with his dagger in the other. Good that this lad is left handed he mused.

The laird of Douglas began again to make his descent, but slower now for the injury that kept his right hand almost useless for the moment. As he was just about to take his final steps and break from the wall, rocks rained down from above. Archie and the other Douglas vassals sent rapid response in a frenzied hail of blistering arrows. Whooshing sounds filled the air followed by resounding thuds as the Scots were hitting their marks perfectly; yet the new assault from the garrison to the side of the bridgehead was gaining momentum. Then tragedy befell them; James suddenly slipped, plummeting past the last three turns of the ladder and not on purpose. Archie watched in abject horror as his brother was sent to his death certain by the heavy stones that put a fair dent in his head-armor. The Douglas squire yelled at the others to cover him while he ran in a zig-zag manner to the side of his unconscious brother. The burley squire threw the injured knight over his back careful not to dislodge the arrow in his shoulder. Arrows flew from the wall-walk creating the fearful sounds of peril spinning, buzzing around the squire; but Archie was unrelenting. Panting hard, his chest heaved in heavy exertion; his own armor now inhibiting his breathing. But Archie kept running. As the weight of his brother was cutting the circulation in his own shoulder, the squire felt shooting pains; still he did not stop. He carried James far from the outer walls of Carlisle to the wooded area where the younger lads, their pages and squires were holding their horses in ready wait to depart.

Finally arriving in the safe haven of the trees he slowly lowered James to the ground with the help of two squires. Taking the herbs from his pouch to deaden the pain, Archie began the treacherous process of first removing the imbedded arrow. James bolted to a semi state of consciousness from the piercing pain; held fast by the other squires, he was unable to move. "Hold him steady," barked Archibald. With one swift tug, the arrow finally departed sending spurts of oozing blood all over his hands and arms. "By St. Bride," he muttered, remembering the tourniquet he needed to apply before removing the arrow. The squires tore some strips from the silk tabard of the knight and gave it to Archie. He then treated the wound with the salve Hugh had prepared some weeks ago and pronounced his brother healed. "Go tell our king that James met peril on the wall." It was then that he noticed the wound on the right calf of the knight. "More work for this squire," he muttered good naturedly as James was showing more signs of consciousness. "Our days of warfare will be most over for sometime," Archie informed him. "Good Hugh will so see to the rest of your injuries; this healer is quite through with you," he teased James hoping to see him smile, but the knight was drifting off again to a dazed awareness.

Figure XCII-Part Three; the ruins of Hadrian's Wall and the major Roman fort of Camboglanna; an historical site in Cumbria today called Birdoswald; some speculate this was the site of King Arthur's Camelot

    With the injuries James sustained and the Scots' siege quite repelled by the garrison of Carlisle, Robert Brus decided to disband his army. Archie took command of the Douglas vassals; with James' sergeants he led them north and east towards Lintalee. They fashioned a litter for their laird and leader; carried him homeward. Past the lands of Lanercost Priory they rode, following the path of Hadrian's Wall, then into the haven of trees and stone enclosures of the old Roman fort at Camboglanna where they stayed the night. The next morning they rose to a clear day; the first since beginning their siege at Carlisle. "Where might you have been these lang days?" asked Archie sarcastically as he sneered up at the sun in the bright sky. He looked over at his brother; James' weakened state had not improved and when he came to a brief consciousness he complained of great pain in his head. "We must get our laird to the shelter of Lintalee," Archie told the retinue.

    When they arrived at the fortress on the Jed the Douglas squire dispatched an escort to retrieve their healer from Glasgow or wherever he might be. "Bring most my Beatrice and the Lady Joanna too; with the children and their nurses. The Douglases are to remain in Lintalee for some time I fear." He was still concerned for James; his headaches were unrelenting and he was not showing any signs of recovering. "Dear Hugh;

that you must hurry," he prayed. Four days later the ladies and their Austin Canon arrived with children, nurses and Deerhounds all in tow. James began his convalescence quite slowly; his weakened state was to keep the Douglas warriors at home for many months, just as Archie had suspected.

"St. Bride most answers our prayers in the strangest of ways," admitted Beatrice as she and Archie shared their love that night. "My sweet lass, that I am home and held by you is the most precious gift this squire could so have," he admitted. No, Beatrice shook her head to his reply. "That this lass so fears she bears a blame for the injury of our dear James," she said, telling her husband how she prayed that her warriors would remain at home some time before their next campaign. "Dear Beatrice; our God and dear Saint have not time for such trifling; pray as often as you might, this lad enjoys his days at home with his dear bride!" he said brandishing the Douglas smirk as he grabbed for another embrace.

Figure XCIII-Part Three; the site of the Auld Roxburgh Kirk; Hugh Douglas held this prebend of the see of Glasgow

"Dear Henklebaldicus this lass so misses you," she said adamantly. "My Beatrice; a poet knight much like my dear father would I prefer to be; but James is called to do battle for his king and I must follow." Then he told her the details of the failed siege; how James was impaled by his own ladder then assaulted with rocks and arrows. "This lad was certain he might meet his peril of foul end at Carlisle," he admitted ominously. "You most saved him from that fate," she praised him, looking up into his grey green eyes, her own eyes as wide as saucers for the story he just shared with her. "How this lad could carry that large warrior, most the size of this squire," he said with amazement for the miracle that happened, enabling him to save James. "Perhaps that you had help," she giggled. "Aye that must be so," Archie admitted thoughtfully. "That I had a true dream of my sweet father that very night; the tall warrior with the lang scar on his face; he praised me for my valor." The squire's face was one of wonderment as he recalled the vision; he knew he had his father's help that day. "Sure aye!" giggled Beatrice.

ROXBURGH 26 NOVEMBER 1316-Hugh of Douglas was working in the hospital near Roxburgh kirk, Maison Dieu. He had recently been informed that he would finally be given the prebend for the parish, convenient to James' stronghold in Lintalee. The income from Roxburgh as well as the allotment as a Canonic would permit him to hire others to preach and give the sermons in the kirk. And the extra coinage allowed him precious time to pursue what he knew best: treating the infirm and healing his brave warriors. Two riders approached with Douglas banners and Walter barely bolted from his horse, gasping for breath, he was almost too excited to give Hugh the message. "My father begs you come immediately; our dear friend Robert Wishart has left us for the Otherworld." Hugh's face went ashen; he had hoped to visit the bishop before the Holy days next month; now there was no chance to see his benefactor again. Tears filled his eyes. "That we should stop and pray for his soul before we return to the manor on the Jed," he said quite sadly.

Figure XCIV-Part Three; the headless effigy of Robert Wishart, Bishop of Glasgow, lower church, Glasgow Cathedral; no marker designates the remains of Scotland's patriot; ironically he lies under a banner he would certainly oppose: a Union Flag

"And what of your lessons in Latin this day," he asked Walter. The lad said that he was truly sorry; but for this day he was asked to join his Uncle Archibald and his father James in the courtyard of the manor, "for tilting," he said circumspectly. "That you must learn of warfare most as well," advised Hugh. "Our Lady El so promised my good father as it was his intention: all Douglas men must learn of warfare. The just and very brave patriot, the Bishop of Glasgow stormed castles in Fife; overtaken by Edward ten years ago in full armor at Cupar Castle," he explained. "The bishop was a knight?" Walter asked. "No; a prelate with the training of a warrior," he chuckled. "And the fair mind of a brilliant cleric and astute solicitor. Our Robert Wishart knew both our Canon Law and Civil Law that he would so defend us in the council of dear Edward years ago when my father was Lord Douglas." Walter reflected for some time. "That I will train to be a canon like Robert Wishart, ready to do battle or to teach the gospel most as well. To do so in his honor is my promise this day." Hugh and Walter entered the kirk and prayed for the soul of the prelate, the souls of a knight named Logan and a laird named le Hardi.

LINTALEE EARLY 20 April 1317- The construction of the manor on the haugh of the Jed was progressing nicely James reflected as he walked the meadow lands of his fortress. "This knight is truly happy to so have our Ceilidh now," he shared with Hugh who had joined him on the morning constitutional. The silly Deerhound James was training as a gift for Ellie was scampering playfully about, bolting here and there before launching himself to a flight down towards the banks of the Jed. "Hound," he called to the wee marauder. "Come!" Hugh was laughing as the Deerhound went ambling off in the opposite direction paying no heed to his laird. "Have you no name for the lad?" asked the canon. James thought for a moment. "Perhaps to call him Robert after the good bishop," he replied thoughtfully. "Our mother to find that most amusing; her wee hound to carry the good name of both of Edward's greatest enemies," Hugh suggested chuckling at the thought.

Archie came running from the tower and told James that word had come from his patrol; the English were marching north with a fair contingency. The peacefulness of the quiet spring day, the warmth of the sun upon his brow and the sweet song of the mavis flying from tree top to tree top were now lost from Lord Douglas, shattered by the prospect of another encounter with the English invaders. James was making his way to the great hall his head bent low in deep concentration as he listened intently to Archie's words, the grave findings of their daily reconnaissance. "That the Earl of Arundel with many knights with banners that we know, are moving a large force of men at arms with armed horse into the north. Yet their intentions are most unclear; many of the earl's followers are armed with hatchets," he explained. James and his brothers shared looks of troubled concern. "That they are coming to clear the Forest, our Douglas domain for concealing our escape from raids against the English," James said anxiously. "We will have to stop them then," said Archie, resigned to their course at hand for another campaign. "Do they come as well to fight us?" asked a worried Hugh. Lord Douglas allowed as the earl would certainly attempt an attack on the Scots; believing it safe with King Robert absent in Ireland.

In the great hall the vassals of the Good Sir James presented their findings on the English forces; the number in the muster, how many of them knights and cavalry, all details they had gathered over the last two days. And some special news they had for their laird: there was a banner, one of three armorial bearings they were most assigned to look for on their watch, to take note in their report; it was being carried by a small following. "The knight banneret with the armorial bearings of ermine on a bend gules three eaglets or," they informed Lord Douglas. "Bagot; dear Eleanora's sweet lord," James said sarcastically. He had instructed his men to take heed of three specific English banners; Nicky de Segrave's lion rampant argent on sable with label of gules; William de Ferrers' armorial bearings of the same red with seven mascles voided in the field; and William Bagot's ermine with three gold eagles, a red bend. Now James knew that Staffordshire lords were in the retinue; others of Ellie's kin could thus be with them as well. "Such favored soldiers so among them that they most seek of plunder as their goal here," Archie surmised.

With only two hundred followers near and around his manor on the Jed, James thought it best to send the ladies and their children west to the sheltering stronghold on the Douglas Burn; the Ceilidh would have to wait. Archie quietly excused himself from the great hall; he had some more bad news for Beatrice and wanted to tell her privately. There will be trouble on this accord the squire mused, heading for their chamber reluctantly. As he entered through the large carved oak door his somber countenance told his bride what she already suspected; something was about to happen to ruin their plans for feasting and dancing. "This lass is so resigned to never have a happy day again with my sweet husband," she said wistfully, as Archie held her in a deep embrace. "You are not angry with your Archie?" he asked her, knowing her brothers and their families were expected any day now. Lady Douglas shook her head no; realizing that the English came on their own calendar not hers she would not blame him for their troubles. "Perhaps to so plan another Ceilidh when Lady El comes north," she said quietly. Archie was so relieved for her response that he picked his bride up and spun her around in gleeful play. "My sweet lass," he whispered in her ear, then brought her close to sit upon his lap; they began the rituals of their lovemaking, knowing it might be many months before they would see each other again.

When Archie returned to the great hall Hugh told him that he made the arrangements for ladies and children to depart in the prime on the morrow. And he added with concern that James and Joanna were not in agreement for the arrangements at hand. "Our brother and his sweet lass and dear wife are having discord; she is more angry than this lad has ever seen our Lady Joanna," he said ruefully. Archie nodded; he understood only too well the concern of a wife for her husband going into battle. "And for more than the fight at hand; the Ceilidh to so cancel is a terrible occurrence." Archie wondered where the children were; he wanted to take them riding to Glendouglas while it was still safe to do so. "Their nurses took them quickly out to the courtyard as the shouting between the laird and his Joanna most continued and quite loudly," Hugh said slightly embarrassed. "You did not hear them?" Archie said that he and Beatrice were too busy making plans for another Ceilidh in the fall; then gave his brother a big, teasing Douglas smirk.

Figure XCV-Part Three; near the site of the ambuscade in Glendouglas

"So many things to talk about," the youngest Douglas son said whimsically. "Perhaps to teach our brother of such ways; that you keep your bride most happy and content," the canon suggested wryly. "Is it that you so command her and she obeys?" Just then Lady Beatrice entered the great hall; dressed and ready to go riding on her jennet she announced happily. "But in answer to your question dear Hugh, my Henklebaldicus would never order this lass about; he just reads me his poetry and I but swoon," she said in mocked tones of trite compliance. Archie rolled his eyes and grabbed her up again, swinging her over his head. "Sholto beast!" she chided him playfully, then seeing the twinkle in his eye: "Again?" she asked with a shy grimace. Archie answered her query by carrying her up the turnpike stairs, barely running, taking her to their chamber, "to make more plans for the Ceilidh," he chuckled.

JEDDART 23ʳᴰ APRIL-James' call to muster was lean; he had only his normal garrison from his manor on the Linthaugh Burn: fifty men at arms and only one hundred thirty archers as they set south for Jeddart. He told Archie to be prepared to lead a fair contingency of bowman; they would be greatly outnumbered if what his spies had told him was true he warned the squire. A desolate cart path from the Carter Bar was the road the English Warden of the Marches chose to travel. He had with him a large callout of men at arms; many knights including Earl David of Athol and Sir Thomas Richmond. South from Glendouglas the Scots rode, toward the old gate where the forest closed to a much narrowed opening. The cleugh was thick with the thin saplings of birch; the array reminded James of a time when le Hardi was alive and they plaited the small trees together for their use, in the way of the old Celts. "Archie, we will have to work quickly," he said, dismounting his Hobini. He called the others to assemble; instructing the warriors on how to build a screen to inhibit the English cavalry while giving the Scots good cover but not blocking their sight; to set the battlefield.

Figure XCVI-Part Three; the striking views from Carter Bar in Northumbria on the A68 noting the Scottish Borders ahead

The laird of Douglas watched with satisfaction as the good men of the Jed Forest followed his instructions well. Then he carefully explained to Archie and the other sergeants his plan; when to come upon the English armed horse with their streaming arrows. Lord Douglas then took himself with his armed foot and on horse to the other side of the open meadow; well hidden within the trees they waited. His oliphant he held in the ready; giving a prayer to St. Bride for their success this day. "Once again dear Saint does this humble knight so ask of your fair protection. Our wee army most out numbered by the enemy; as by now you have come to so expect." James laughed quietly as he continued his petition to the Heavens. "Do protect your faithful servants in our most fearful hour; the woeful men with tails will soon be most upon us," he pleaded to the patron saint of Douglases.

St. Bride must have heard the prayers of her loyal servant Lord Douglas and surely brought with her an army of many thousand warriors from the Otherworld for the English found themselves in great difficulty and quite quickly as they maneuvered their way into the open glade of the Forest. "A Douglas! A Douglas!" cried the laird as he signaled the archers to let fly a swarm of vicious arrows into vicinity of the approaching English vanguard. The knight then led his light horse and armed foot in bold charge, deep into the fray they bravely went in search of victory. James spurred his Hobini forward towards the English commander; the weight of the strong, solid thrust of the old standard cut flesh and splintered bone. Lord Arundel's vassal felt a punishing blow quite squarely between the shoulders; surprised and injured he was unhorsed.

The English noble was wearing a strange fur hat over his metal helmet; a taunting treasure for a Douglas knight James reflected. Le Hardi's son turned his Hobini quickly to the right, to return to the site of the fallen warrior. In a dashing show of physical prowess Lord Douglas dismounted his Hobini in one swift, gliding motion to meet his foe face to face. Before the English commander regained his sensibility James stabbed the warrior with his dagger. Ceremoniously he doffed the dead man's hat and took it for his own. Sounding the retreat on his oliphant James led his men towards the protective woods where Archie and the rest of the Douglas bowmen waited their return, well hidden from the English.

Wildly they rode their light horse across the English front then quickly vanished into the wooded solitude of the Forest. As James found his perch above the Jed near Dolphinston he saw Arundel with his field commanders and sergeants leading their retinue towards another clearing. Overwhelmed by the surprise attack; the staggering number lost to the Douglas Foresters' first assault, the English were in disarray. "Lord Douglas," cried a young rider coming towards him; a lad he recognized at once as the son of one of his tenants at Lintalee. "What brings you here?" he asked as Archie was returning to his side as well. "My father so sent me my lord; to tell you of unspeakable occurrences at your tower house," he said breathlessly, his excitement and the strenuous ride showing in his halted speech.

"Good Hector; calm yourself; what has happened to our Lintalee?" asked Archie. The lad told them that the English had invaded the stronghold; perhaps to kill those so guarding the Douglas fortress he feared. "Fear not good lad; that we most needed all the men of the garrison, to spare none in defense of our wee manor," James assured him. "No member of our followers remained behind, needing all to muster for our deeds this day, none were lost at Lintalee. Thank you for your bravery to warn us," he praised the lad for bringing him the news. James took the fur hat from his head and stuffed it under his saddle. He threw a knowing glance to Archie.

"Later," he snickered meaning he would explain the strange, furry acquisition at a better time.

Mounting his Hobini he ordered the others of their retinue to his side; told them of the invasion, the uninvited guests most supping on their larder for the Ceilidh that was planned then cancelled. James then shouted the war cry and beckoned all to follow. Archie instructed Hector to stay close to the squire; they would escort him safely home he promised. North through Kersheugh they rode; crossing the Jed near Glendouglas they made their way to the woods near Hundalee where they could approach their fortress undetected from the north. The drawbridge was in place and the portcullis opened to their entry. The anger felt by one to the violation of his home was multiplied two hundred fold inciting the Douglas warriors to barely swarm their prey seeking their revenge.

Figure XCVII-Part Three; the banks of the Jed near the site of the ambuscade

Lord Douglas and his vassals had entered the tower quickly. They surprised their uninvited guests under the dubious command of a brigand called Elias. Once an English cleric he had turned to thievery for the devastation of his homeland in the north of England. Archie held his sword in the ready; he moved from the high guard almost in tandem with his brother. The fury of these two Douglas warriors fired their desire and embellished their already great strength; at a fevered pace their swords and knives made fatal thrusts and cuts. Their reinforcements followed; the laird's wee army of archers, on foot and light horse enveloped the followers of Elias. Those soldiers in the employ of Arundel were mostly slaughtered; some escaped while few others were taken prisoner but later freed after the careful interrogation of Lord Douglas.

James commanded his squire to retrieve the fur adornment secreted under his saddle. "And who held of this fine chapeau?" he demanded to know, brandishing his fur trophy hat. The English vassal responded that it belonged to Richmond. James' heart barely leaped when he heard the name; to believe that Sir John of Brittany, the Earl of Richmond was the owner would be most fortunate. Quickly the laird caught himself. He recalled the banners of the knight: the red and gold of a Yorkshire family he guessed, the earl had armorial bearings much different of checky or and azure, gold and blue. "Not Sir John?" he asked, though he knew the answer before the squire spoke. No he was told; a noble named Sir Thomas Richmond. "Another time," James scoffed. The two prisoners were released; warned not to show their faces again near Lintalee for the next encounter would spell their deaths certain. The anxious young warriors rode off; fearful to look back they met up with Arundel's army in quick order. The squires entered the English camp with wild tales of great numbers in the Douglas retinue, crazed Scots with swords thirsty for English blood they told their lords, embellishing their own stories of brave escape from the gory clutches of Lord Douglas. With the chilling news and his army demoralized for their defeat the earl disbanded and headed home in quiet retreat.

"Who were these sorry fellows?" asked Archie. The knight told his brother that the leader was a priest, the one they called Elias, "a schavaldur, a renegade warrior and one time cleric of poor conscience brought forth to join the army of the English." As James and Archie looked around to assess the damage to their newly furbished abode, they beheld a morbid site. There on the hearth next to the trestle table of the great hall was the headless corpse of Elias; the face of his severed head in a macabre contortion now pointed to his arse. "Better that we remove this foolish warrior before the return of the fair Beatrice," teased James. Archie was repulsed by the cadaver's gross spectacle and he ordered whoever had the ill humor to effect the stratagem to remove it, "the noo!"

STEBBINGE PARK MID SUMMER 1317-Ellie was reviewing her fees and rents from the previous quarter day; the continued famine of the last three years had taken a grave toll on her finances. "Dear Ana; to travel north to see our family will take much coinage," she said sadly. "The loss of fees in Scotland most damaged our coffers as well." Elizabeth suggested that Lady Bagot consider holding off on the payment of their wages. "Another winter with our weepy Eleanora for not seeing her dear children and grandchildren would be unbearable," she said firmly. Ellie was fearful to take the chance; to venture north with little hope for coinage meant taking too big a risk she cautioned them. Their discussion was interrupted by the arrival of Sir Thomas the younger from Fawdon; with good rumors from

Scotland he proclaimed. The letter from Lady Joanna was as uplifting as it was long, six full parchments in all were sewn together. But it was the short penned note of Sir James or Sir Shamus as he portrayed his identity that caught her attention. He pleaded for her presence in the fall for a Ceilidh, adding a curious sentiment. "This knight has most gathered a surprise to settle upon his mother; a fair manor of her own to replace those lost for the *rebellion* of Lord de Ferrers, with no pledge of fealty so required." Ellie was roaring in laughter when she read his words about her stepson's diminished status with the King of Scots. "We are once again rescued by a Douglas knight; to travel north to Scotland and our home is my intention now," Ellie told them triumphantly.

She returned to the detailed accounts of her sons' encounters that Joanna had carefully disguised in her seemingly whimsical missive. Having been limited in their communications over the last year, she decided to venture forth in carefully concealed detail of the Douglases' adventures in the last year. Joanna wrote a lengthy story of James' injury at Carlisle and Archie's heroic rescue of his brother. In flowing words she described the demise of Arundel's vanguard near Lintalee. Ellie gasped. "Lord Bagot was most in that retinue," she said alarmed for the encounter.

Figure XCVIII-Part Three; Stebbing cottage

But as Lady Douglas Bagot read further she understood that Sir William was to the rear of the army with others of Staffordshire; never even seen on the battlefield by either Douglas warrior. "What relief for this Scottish mother and English lady," she sighed. The constant peril and daily fear Ellie lived with was that her sons might fight her kin; this near reality overwhelmed her. In the quiet solitude of her chamber on many nights she imagined the horror of burying one for the victory of the other. She looked down at the parchment and forced herself to continue reading Joanna's words. "Then a battle most ensued bringing us much booty for Sir Shamus and King Hobbe," wrote Joanna. She told the story of Sir Robert de Neville known as the Peacock of the North. Ellie looked up from the letter and explained the story of de Neville in Westminster. "Such perilous desires this foolish baron so had to regain the favor of the king; Edward holding much displeasure when Sir Robert killed his rival Marmeduke."

Ellie was speaking quickly, filling in her knowledge of the pleas set before king and council for this family as she went along. Sir David and Ana found themselves both on the edge of their seats, listening intently not to miss a word of it! The foolish Neville went to Berwick to openly challenge the Douglas knight to do battle. "Or Sir Shamus as Joanna writes here," Ellie began, then stopped. Frustrated by the subterfuge of hidden names, she forthrightly started using her son's true moniker. "Our James to take offense to his silly words; he marched his retinue at night, planting his banner in full view of the citizens at Berwick in the prime: Sir James of Douglas so accepts!" Lady Douglas read Joanna's vivid description of the battle with animated gestures; told of the treacherous exchange of attack and parry in a lang fight that ended with victory for the Scot, the Peacock dead and his three brothers held for ransom.

Figure XCIX-Part Three; Lintalee earthworks on the Jed

Eleanora herself was enthralled by the writings. She looked up from the letter and saw that the griping tale held everyone's attention, waiting for the outcome. She added her own details, told her listeners about the mortgaging of the Neville estates to pay off debts; their father Sir Randulf impoverished for their demands of coinage to obtain their freedom. "But this lass so thought the damage owed was from the battle three years ago at the Bannock Burn; not from this recent capture at Berwick, their ransoms most

497

due to the coffers of Lord Douglas and his king," she chortled at the news. The more Ellie read, the more she was astounded; so many battles, wee skirmishes and terrifying events had transpired since she left Scotland two years ago. "Good this lass did not know of these fair happenings," she said with relief as she read Joanna's final words that everyone was well and safely home, including Hugh and a special Deerhound named Robert. "Robert?" questioned Ana. "That is her way to tell us that she received my last letter and the sad news of our dear Lindsay, passing to the Otherworld, I do guess," Ellie offered sadly, remembering with heavy heart the loss of her wee hound last year.

LINTALEE EARLY FALL-Riding her jennet through the High Hills to the fortress on the Jed brought a sense of calm and belonging to the Douglas widow as she led her household to the newly completed stronghold of Lord Douglas. The crisp air of autumn brought special scents that warmed her with memories of William and their family traveling in the Cheviot, staying at their Fawdon with the children; in happier times of peaceful prosperity. Now she traveled with a large escort with three knights in full armor; two from Northumbria and one from Fairstead. Sir David was also training one of his squires to take his place soon; too long in the tooth he told her for such travels every year.

As Ellie made her way through the gates into the inner protective walls of the fortress she found herself gleefully surrounded by barking Deerhounds and joyous grandchildren all coming to greet her. Lady Douglas dismounted her jennet and embraced them all one by one; the Deerhounds taking their turn as well. James was coming from the tower through the oak doors, arm in arm with Joanna. "Mother," they cried in unison. "That this lass is most happy to set her eyes upon her family!" she exclaimed. "And where are Archie, Walter and Hugh, and Beatrice?" James explained that the churchmen were most likely still at the hospice in Roxburgh.

"Our Henklebaldicus and his lady are enjoying a ride to Bonjedward," he chuckled. "Come inside," beckoned Lady Joanna, "there is much good wine and feasting to be had!" Then James gave his wife a feigned admonishment as he looked very seriously to Lady El. "But first dear mother, you must meet the newest member of your Essex household," he said, then brandishing a silly smirk he called out, "Sir Robert!" to get the attention of the Deerhound he had been training for Ellie. A streak of grey flew by; but did not give his master as much as a brief acknowledgement when away he went in the other direction towards the glen. "Trained him yourself did you then?" asked the taunting Archie as he rode through the gates of the palisade. "Dear mother, how wonderful it is to see you!" he continued as he jumped from his palfrey, helping Beatrice from her jennet.

Then he went to Ellie and swung her high over his head; handing her to James who did the same. "Most a Douglas tradition is this now?" she begged to know. "Put me down the noo!" Everyone was roaring with laughter; it felt right, very right indeed and they almost drowned out the war in their happiness this day for their reunion.

Then through the gates came the playful Deerhound, hearing all their laughter he was returning to the fold. "Come here Sir Robert," Ellie ordered and the wee hound ran obediently to her side. "See of that Lord Douglas; one command from Lady El and the beast is tamed!" teased Archie as James rolled his eyes with indignation for the Deerhound's silly ways. "Our father has worked for many weeks to so train that lad," said the wee William. "That you are here but few minutes and he obeys your every word!" Ana was chuckling. "That he must know her plans; where the wee Robert is to sleep now," telling the laddie how his grandmother insists that her hound share her bed as Sir Shamus had done when she first met his grandfather, her dear Gilley so many years ago. "Grandmother," asked a bewildered Elizabeth, "that you are forced to sleep with the hart hounds?" Ellie threw back her head in joyous laughter. "That this lass prefers it so!" she exclaimed proudly. Then more seriously, Lady El explained to her granddaughter that in Essex she was lonely for her family and enjoyed the comfort of having a hound close by; to alert her if there were any strangers about as well.

Figure C-Part Three; ruins of Blackness in Linlithgow; this castle is a later structure built by Crichton but lands in this manor were once held by the Douglases of Linlithgow descended of Andrew Douglas, uncle of William le Hardi

In the great hall at Lintalee the laird of Douglas sat at the head of the table and pages poured good wine; on his right was Lady Joanna, to the left Lady El. Archie and Beatrice were seated next to Ellie as platters of steaming game and fish were brought before them. "Such feasting has been so scarce in Essex," their mother explained as her eyes widened for the prosperity of table. "Much famine so persists in Edward's kingdome; unspeakable and foul rumors of cannibalism in the north so resounded as cattle writhed in pain to die; sheep so fell over with disease and crops growing were washed away in rains that would not stop." Ana was busy filling her bread bowl with fine stewed beef and beans with onions and a caramelized sauce. "Aye, the Scottish households speak of bounty we can only imagine with hollow rumbles of our stomachs for Essex feasting." Archie proclaimed that it was lang time for Ellie and her wee clan in Essex to return to live in the north; in their Scotland, permanently! "Soon though would I most do that," she allowed. Then Ellie looked up and down the wee page that was coming now to pour her wine. "This lad looks much a Douglas," she said recognizing the darker countenance and raven hair.

Figure CI-Part Three; Bonjedward, a sign in the road, a few buildings and some farm lands now designate this former manor given to James Lord Douglas in charter by Robert Brus; adjacent to Jedburgh, not far from Lintalee

"Mother, may I present William, son of James Douglas from Linlithgow?" Ellie gasped. "That I remember the day your father was so christened. Did you know my William was God father to your own father?" she asked the page. The lad shook his head with a quiet yes for his reply. "That I am named for my grandfather William of Hermanston and Linlithgow," he told her with a broad grin covering his face. "Welcome," Lady Eleanora told the lad. "More family will so arrive for our Ceilidh," James announced excitedly. Joanna started providing the list, ending with James Douglas and Walter the Steward. "Walter?" questioned Ellie. "That he is the son of dear James?" meaning le Hardi's brother in law and James' uncle. "Aye, the same," said her oldest son. "That with this laird we are the wardens of the Marches." Ellie shook her head in disbelief. How much responsibility the Lord Douglas carried on his shoulders; that there is no wonder why he is seldom home with more wee ones about, she mused.

James was in his glory; chattering away about their accomplishments in Lintalee; the plans for three outer towers for the stronghold. "Most a smaller Douglas Castle," he chucked. Then as he looked around the great hall of the tower he pointed out the contributions of others in the laird's household. "Our good Henklebaldicus is training all in archery; a butt he so constructed most as well that all men of Douglas practice their skills each morning in our courtyard," he boasted, praising his younger brother for his work on the assignment. "Sir David," began Archie, "that I so lift this wine in toast to you for all that you instructed me to do and well!" There were others joining in the acknowledgement. The aging knight, an Englishman from Essex smiled in quiet acceptance: Sir David of Fairstead, his legacy now deeply entwined with the Foresters of Scotland. "My greatest wish is that someday the English king will treat of peace with Scotland and we can all live again as friends and neighbors," he replied in chivalrous sentiment. "I will join in this toast, sure aye!" said Ellie.

The squires from the gate towers entered the great hall to announce the arrival of the churchmen; the Austin canon and the priest in training, young Walter now seventeen. "Hubicus!" Ellie exclaimed as she rose to meet him. "And dear Walter; how much you have grown," she chided him, pointing to the rounded girth hidden by his surcote. "This lad is spoiled by the largesse of our good laird of Douglas," he said referring happily to James. "That it is often said with some great amazement how the cattle of Northumbria most follow this mischievous baron, the Black Douglas and his bewitching sounds, the melodic calling of the Crusader's oliphant to lure the beasts to Lintalee for our good feasting. Praise be to God and the good St. Bride for that!" Walter chortled.

The next morning James was up early, eagerly awaiting Lady El's arrival in the great hall. His face lit up when she made her way down the turnpike stairs into the lower levels of the tower. "This lad most knew you would be the first to break the fast with this laird," he said happily. "Dear James, what excitement is brimming in your heart this day; your face is aglow in wonderment," Ellie chuckled. Ana had followed her down into the great hall and was marveling at how happy her girl looked this day as well. "Dear mother, we are to ride to Bonjedward this prime; Ana you too must come," he commanded jovially. "This lass will have her porridge first," Ellie said with feigned affront to his orders. "Your jennet is saddled and ready," he replied with the determined speech of his father. "Most like le Hardi," she retorted, "when our Lord Douglas has something on his mind, his impatience is most comical to this lass!" James seemed to relent; he knew she was just as stubborn as he was; pushing her would not be a good choice. Then a silly smirk crossed his face. "Remember now, when Lord Douglas does ask a third time, he waits not for the answer," he said, mimicking le Hardi as he went to pick her up and carry her out into the courtyard. "Beast Sholto!" Ellie chuckled knowing he was determined for their adventure to begin the now!

Figure CII-Part Three; site of Jedburgh Castle where King Alexander III was born and later married; this later building was used for a jail

    With their normal escorts James Lord Douglas, Lady Eleanora Douglas Bagot with Ana and Sir Robert her new Deerhound now all together headed north to Jedburgh, past the castle there that James pointed to say was to be his, granted in charter by the king. "These lands dear Lady El are Bonjedward," he proclaimed when they arrived at a manor not far from his stronghold on the Jed. "Since our Parliament in Scone the June last this lad so holds these lands and many others," James said humbly. Ellie gave him a look, a teasing gesture of disdain she meant for Robert Brus. "King Hobbe does not see fit to grant you yet a charter for our Douglasdale, but rather these lands of the Marches?" she asked in her best sparring tone. "Our king has seised of this fair manor and many others to this laird; our Douglasdale included when he is so recognized as our rightful king," he retorted, then sighing ruefully he added, "when that time so arrives, this lad could be past the age for tournament." He looked back at Ellie now to share with her his surprise. "This manor will belong to my mother," he said softly. Ellie questioned him with her eyes; he knew she could not pledge fealty to a Scottish king yet married to William Bagot. "No kissing of the gospels or vows taken to be most loyal to our King of Scots is so required. This knight will hold these lands for your good use; an agreement so between us," James reassured her. "These carucates, this wee land with tenements and villiens, the fees and rents are to be most yours my dear mother! Your laird paramount, James of Douglas does will it so!" Ellie was taken aback; tears flowed from her eyes and she found herself unable to reply.

    Her oldest son then dismounted his palfrey and took out a small purse filled with silver pennies. "This fair expense is but a trifle due to one Lady

El," he said quietly as he put the coinage in her hand. Ellie opened the velvet pouch and ooh'd and ahh'd. "My son, a fortune is most here; I shall not accept this tribute," she started to say; then noticing the disappointment in the lad's face, she stopped. "This mother thanks her son for his fair generosity. Such coinage will allow me to return to Scotland and my heart's own home more often," Ellie said poignantly. Ana was drying her own eyes; no mother could have a truer son, a man most like her Gilley in his devotion she sighed to herself.

"Good! Now you will most have our Hugh to manage your rents on quarter day; to come and stay at Lintalee whenever it is safe. But you may fashion this manor as your own; tenants and servants will be provided for your good use and management. It is done!" James mounted his palfrey and brandishing the well known smirk he added, "That you are finally silenced! Le Hardi could only dream of such a day!" he teased her. "James Douglas; this lass was only speechless for one wee moment! From this time forward will I most fill your days with words and many, not to take leave of my Scotland for lang times most again!" And she challenged him to a race home to Lintalee and off they flew; mother and son riding to a breathless pace that the others found difficult to follow!

Figure CIII-Part Three; the ruins of Jedburgh Abbey; an Historic Scotland property with many displays and an educational exhibit on medieval monastic life

The Douglases abandoned their competition in fast order upon reaching Jedburgh; James wanted to show Ellie the castle there that would be part of his estates in the Borders. "More lands to change hands in these years to come," James told his mother. "But for young de Ferrers his manors are most forfeit." Ellie wrinkled her brow; the mention of her stepson prompted her to relate a strange conversation she overheard at Groby on her recent journey north. "That Sir William has granted his manor of Groby to his vassal and cousin, Sir Murdac de Mentethe, to be held in capite," she said curiously. James surmised that de Ferrers must be in need of coinage for the loss of his fees in Scotland; most like his mother. Ellie shook her head in disagreement. "No there is something afoot here I do know it." She went on to explain that the night she stayed there several gentlemen remained in the great hall long after the feasting; consuming much wine and ale they were quite inebriated she told her son. "This lass was right above them, in a chamber with a chimney most the same; what most they spouted in their wild humor was quite frightening and confusing."

James' interest was piqued and he begged her to continue. "These barons all lost lands for writs of Robert Brus in your Parliament in Ayr," she reminded James and he nodded his understanding. "Then this Murdac in slurred words of drunken fools proclaimed loudly yet in the clearest of sentiment: 'the mortal soul of King Hobbe to reach God's Heaven most quickly with the success of our fair strategy.' These sentiments were followed by great cheers in hearty agreement." Ellie added that several of de Ferrers' guests and their kin served with him a decade before in the Scottish wars; speaking the names of Mowbray and de Graham. "Whether they were there that night I do not know; several of these knights and soldiers arrived quite late; leaving before the prime."

James told Ellie solemnly that there were foul rumors about; some English nobles, the disinherited were plotting to revenge the taking of their lands. "That they want to murder our king," he said ominously. "Did they have more to say?" Ellie told him no; but de Mentethe is certainly behind the plot. "This knight will so alarm King Robert; de Mentethe may have others to join in his scheme, but his is the first name we know certain, thanks to 'out little spy from Essex' as Bishop Lamberton most called you." Ellie chuckled to recall that time when she took her sons to the Isle de la Cité; meeting with Baron Wishart and James the Steward there with the bishop of St. Andrews. The prelate gave her that famed moniker for all the information she garnered on the war with Scotland from English social occasions. "Pray be careful," she cautioned him, "tell only dear Robert of his name; that others yet among you might have joined in the conspiracy, as yet unknown to you." James assured Ellie that he would be most circumspect with the information.

The Douglases were riding down the cart path towards Lintalee when Ellie took note of the once beautiful abbey. "That your kin Sir Richard de Hastings detained the lead dear Edward restored to them for the roof," James began telling her; detailing the difficulties for the monks and abbot since the invasions began over twenty years ago. "Though now some monks and the abbot have returned, it is most deserted for the great number of brethren that once stayed there. "This lass recalls another time when the abbey was a haven for Lord Douglas and your mother," Ellie acknowledged, sharing an old memory she had of the monastery when Gilley was alive. "That your father and I were on our way back to Mosstower; the skies broke open in shearing sheets of rain that we could barely see the path; Lord Douglas decided to ride for the abbey."

James had never heard this story so he was listening intently. "We arrived most as all seemed to be at their sleep; our men at arms in escort taking our palfreys to the mews while my Gilley led this lass to the cathedral kirk." She explained that it was nearing time for vespers but that not even the Hospitaller was there or perhaps not yet awake to greet them. "We walked throughout the kirk; from the nave towards the choir, the silence made us feel like we were lost in time, wandering about. The abbey too was a magnificent structure but without a single member of that order most around; it was a ghost like place," she said describing the strange feelings that had walking through monastery, that next they went into the chapter house hoping to find an Austin canon there. "Again we found of no one. But in the quiet serenity of our aloneness there, we were able to take in all the loveliness afforded to few outsiders. Gilley and I marveled at the beauty of the vaulted ceiling; the solid but graceful lines of the column that supported the arched roof and the walls of understated elegance to exude of peace," she said wistfully. "If we were to end of our journey there most now," James offered, "we would find that Augustinian house half empty most again I fear with many of the monks and canons living on their lands in the south for the disruption of the wars." They shared poignant looks and sighed almost in unison. "No one escapes the English king; the pains of war he brings to everyone that this lad so wonders where is our God in all of this?" James reflected ruefully.

STEBBINGE PARK HOGMANAY 1318-Ellie had found it difficult leaving Scotland this year; with coinage no longer a problem for her she wanted to stay in the north with her family. Sitting at her slant desk in the withdrawing room, she became aware of a raw, damp, prickly feeling about her. Ellie looked around to see if the fire had gone out but it crackled and hissed as the flames licked the sap from the pine logs. It was snowing and the day had actually become warmer to allow the flakes to fall. A beautiful winter scene enveloped the manor house, but Ellie was feeling anything but calm. As she sat re-reading her latest letter from Joanna another brisk, chilling draft swept through her chamber. What could this be, she mused? Then she called to Ana to bring her a warm tasine and something to cure her winter chill as she tried again to read the letter from Lintalee.

"Another heir for Douglasdale," she chuckled reading the news that James longed to hear; Lady Joanna was due for lay-in by late March or early April. "Our laird will celebrate his thirty-second birthday with another wee one on the way to warm his heart so!" she sighed happily as Ana appeared in the arched doorway of the withdrawing room. "What evil wind blows through here?" she asked as she came to stand beside the slanted desk where Ellie was reading. "You feel it too?" she asked. Then Ellie told her that the odd sensations began as she started to read Joanna's letter. "Best to say some words in the chapel; pray to our dear St. Bride to take good care of our new Douglas heir and his good mother," Ana offered with a strain of concern that an omen was being sent to them. "This lass will not allow such evil to enter into our lives; we must burn some sage and clear this chamber," Ellie told her, reminding Ana of Gilley's remedies for such things.

Ellie began writing her letters to her children; each one received good words and cheer, even her grandchildren had a missive that Joanna or Beatrice could read to them; it was her manner of staying close to her family while in 'exile' as she termed her time in Essex. Eleanora also told them that she planned to return to Fawdon in the fall; her way of saying she would see them in Scotland around her birthday. She was still using coded names and masking her intentions ever wary that some enemy of Scotland might happen upon her words. "When this lass shall so be fifty you will all be in my presence," she proclaimed. "Know this my children your mother has relented on few feats but one in her fair dotage, no longer will I try to vault my horse," she chuckled, "but coming north will Lady Douglas do unless a muster of dear Edward postpones the journey!" It is done she resolved. Ana was laughing; knowing that going to Scotland was no longer in doubt through the generosity of James that only Edward's army might deter her lady in her travels. "That we should beg of Edward not to do battle with the Scots once the autumn has approached," Ana suggested wryly. Ellie flashed her dark eyes in mocked horror. "This lass should not set eyes on any king named Edward most again, if God is in his Heaven!"

PARK CASTLE EARLY WINTER 1318-Lady Joanna was in the nursery sitting with her wee daughter Elizabeth when James came in to tell her that some riders had brought news from his king. "That once again must the knight take his retinue into the Marches," he said quietly. Lady Douglas looked up with a blank expression. "Dear Hugh has found no remedy," she told him; their only daughter was growing weaker by the day with an ailment that gave her fevers and pains in her stomach that she refused to eat. "Where is my brother," the laird inquired, noticing that the canon was not with them. "That he has ridden out the prime; to seek of a physician from Soutra," Joanna explained, meaning the hospice not far from Selkirk that even King Edward sought for cure when on campaign in Scotland. James frowned in self deprecation; his detached state since the wee lass had become ill had kept him focused on his duties to his king but now separated him from his wife. "My sweet bride let us go to the chapel that we might pray together for our daughter." He offered his hand and she accepted; Elizabeth's nurse taking her place at the child's side.

The couple knelt in prayer together for some time. Then James reached for Joanna's hand and drew her near. It was then that he noticed how frail she too had become though her lay-in fast approached in just ten weeks. "That my fair wife is filled with worry," he said looking into the beauty of her face. She bowed her head; told him that she was having pains in her belly that Hugh was giving her tasines with ginger and other herbs, a remedy le Hardi had written down in his healing journals. "That this lad so recalls another of those fair treatments," he said leading her to their chamber. She looked up at him with a countenance of a wee lass in total wonderment. He told her to call her maid in wait; he was preparing a surprise for them. Then James bolted down the turnpike stairs to find his varlet; ordering a scented bath with oils of lavender and roses. "Just like my dear father would have done," he boasted. Satisfied with himself, all the arrangements made, he quickly returned to the laird's chamber, followed by a cellarer with mead and sweet wine. "More to follow for my sweet lass," he said with the Douglas bravado. Joanna was smiling by now and told him of her embarrassment of a woman's body late with child. As James dismissed their servants he graciously drew her to him. "Have I not so said, with child is how I love to see you," he whispered. Then he helped her into the warm water of the large tub. "The fair scent of roses and sweet lavender," she cooed. For the first time in so many months that he could not remember, James of Douglas and his bride enjoyed the solace of their love, in the warmth and comfort of their bodies.

BERWICK 28 MARCH 1318- The King of Scots was camped not far from Berwick with his Marischal, Sir Robert Keith. James Douglas and his brother with their retinue from Douglasdale and the Forest were returning from their raids into Northumbria with the Earl of Moray, Thomas Randolph. To their surprise the king sent word to report immediately to Duns Park for a muster in Berwickshire; Lord Robert was ready to take Berwick on Tweed by siege. The Sheriff of the Lothianes, Sir Robert Keith was offered a betrayal of the royal burgh currently held by the English by one of his own kin, a burgess by the name of Peter of Spaulding. This citizen with many others of the burgh had taken opposition to the cruel treatment of their English governor Sir John de Witham. Spaulding held of one wall and gated entrance to the burgh; on the 1st of April he would lay open Cow Gate for the Scots. Lord Robert's strategy once they gained entry to the town would be to set a final siege to Berwick Castle. "Such a plan is not easily done," he cautioned his lieutenants. "Sir Roger Horsley holds the castle as garrison commander for Edward."

By the time Archie and James rode into the Scottish camp it was already the 28th of March just two days before the anniversary of Edward's brutal genocide during the broken truce with another Lord Douglas: William le Hardi who was forced to watch the butchering from the large donjon tower that now bore his name. James was nervous; he had been away from home for nearly two months and had not received any word from Joanna. He had hoped to get a message from Walter or his brother Hugh; but they were not in the Borders he was told. Robert Brus noted his grave countenance. "Dear James; what ever is most troubling to your good self?" The knight banneret was uncharacteristic in his reply; providing many details about his bride's frail health, her lay-in most due and the sickness that was infecting the wee Elizabeth. Lord Robert realized at once the seriousness of the situation as James was never one to reveal such personal concerns just before a battle. The most stalwart and consummate of soldiers, Lord Douglas was always focused on the fight. Yet standing at the gates of Berwick, two days from a siege to regain the castle lost when his own father was garrison commander, James' thoughts were of his family in Douglasdale. The oldest son of William le Hardi so consumed by revenge for his martyred father, ever focused on the recapture of Berwick was not the lieutenant before him today, reflected Robert Brus.

The king decided to dispatch the Douglas squire, young Archibald with a few good men of Lintalee to bring word from Douglasdale. "Our good fight here should most continue for some days," he said assuring the lad that there would be a battle left to wager when he returned. James was circumspect; grateful for a king who understood such things and almost embarrassed for his concerns. The well respected lieutenant of Robert Brus had never allowed his personal life to interfere with his duty to his king. This time something felt very different he mused; why was he so on edge James wondered to himself?

PARK CASTLE-Archibald was just arriving in the vale of Douglas when the royal burgh of Berwick surrendered to the control of Scots. While Sir James of Douglas and his king celebrated the first stage of their victory, the Douglas squire was being greeted somberly by the men at arms of Park Castle. Left to defend the fortress hovering above Park Burn, these older armed foot could recall many battles fought for their laird. They knew as well the many sorrows the Douglases had endured; the countless members of their family that were sent to the Otherworld so early in life. As he dismounted his palfrey Archie at once noticed a funeral hatchment covering the heavy carved oak doors of the stronghold. The doors creaked slowly open; first came Hugh and Walter, followed by Lady Beatrice. Tears were streaming down their faces as they shared the passing of the wee Elizabeth; then the tragic tale of Lady Joanna's struggle to save herself and the unborn child she carried from the illness that took them both to God. Archie was overcome with emotion; he choked on his words as he held his wife close to him, wrapping his arms around Walter and Hugh. "How is this lad to tell our James?" he asked them, sobbing openly himself. "What God would do this to such a noble laird; that he could not be here to say his soft words of goodbye to his dear bride and child?"

Hugh led them all inside then took his brother to the chapel to pray with him. "That I will come with you to Berwick to tell our James of this tragedy; it is only right to do this together as brothers," he said grimly. "And what of Lady El?" asked Archie. How were they going to tell their mother; prepare her before she rode north in the fall he wondered aloud. Walter entered the wee chapel and said his prayers then asked to come along to share his grief with his father for the loss of his mother. "That you most certainly will join us in our lamented hour dear Walter; so sorry for the loss of Lady Joanna," Archie told James' stepson. "This lad worries most for the wee William, my dear brother," Walter confided. Archie threw Hugh a quizzical look as the canon explained that James' surviving son was confused by all that happened even wondering if his father were truly yet alive. "This lad will so assure him; Lord Douglas is at Berwick and will return most quickly," Archie explained as he headed into the great hall to find his nephew William.

BERWICK ON TWEED-The King of England was furiously issuing writs to his bailiffs and the Mayor of Berwick on Tweed; forfeiting the goods and chattel of his careless subjects; admonishing them for allowing the Scots into the gated town. Edward was enraged; justly incensed he proclaimed. It was now mid April, just two weeks after Brus, Douglas and Randolph made their successful raid on the royal burgh that the English king was quickly assembling large supply ships to transport wheat, corn, swine and other victuals with iron and steel for the munitions of the castle at Berwick on Tweed, that it might not fall as well. But Edward's writs and supplies were fruitless; eight weeks later the garrison commander would finally surrender; taking his soldiers with him to Newcastle on Tyne where they would remain waiting safe conduct to return to Westminster.

For this day the King of Scots was reviewing his plans for successfully taking the castle; they would starve out the garrison, then after the surrender set up government within the burgh. "That we not destroy this fortress; to fortify the castle for our use that Edward may march north again to seize our Scottish burgh," he allowed. Brus planned to stay at Berwick for as long as it took to break the will of the garrison commander Roger de Horsley. He was now busying himself with devising a strategy for further raids into Northumbria. "With our goods and stores of armaments acquired here," he told Randolph and James, "our army will be strengthened. We must now bring other burghs into submission." The king told his lieutenants that he wanted them to press further south into Newcastle; explaining that Edward would try to bring supplies for the garrison through that port. "When the castle is most ours will this king appoint good Walter here, our Steward to be the garrison commander; a fair number shall we leave of armed foot, bowmen and horse to complete his retinue."

While the king continued his discussion James looked up as he heard a commotion of riders entering the courtyard of the abbey. The laird of Douglas smiled as he saw Archie, but his heart barely leaped in torment from his chest when he recognized the somber gait of Hugh followed by his stepson close behind. "Dear St. Bride," he whispered aloud. King Robert looked up; he too noted the serious countenance on the three Douglas faces. James bolted to the side of his brothers and Walter; their looks betrayed his biggest fears come true. "Dear James," began Hugh, "that we must speak with you in private chambers," he said softly, but Lord Douglas was hearing none of it. "Do tell me first, what of Joanna?" Archie begged him to step in the withdrawing room. "More sorrow here that we can only speak in quiet solitude; please my brother." James relented, went to Robert and requested a few moments alone with his brothers and stepson, excusing himself he led the three Douglases to the private chamber.

"Pray, tell me what tragedy" he began but was interrupted by young Walter. "Far worse than any evil so imagined. Our sister is most with God; my dear mother too," he blurted out sobbing openly, running to James he hugged him hard. Lord Douglas looked first to Hugh then to Archie; each nodded yes, this was the truth of their sad tidings. "What God could be so cruel as this!" James shouted. "By St. Bride I swear this laird will so revenge the perpetrators of this foul crime!" His eyes bulged from their sockets, the veins in his neck protruded as if to break through to the surface at any moment. "Sit down good sirs and tell this laird of what has happened," he demanded of his siblings. Archie started to describe his arrival at Park Castle but was interrupted by Hugh. "This lad brought a physician from the Soutra," he began. The doctor insisted to bleed our Joanna; but I most stopped the practice as le Hardi spoke against it. This physician left in anger," he said sadly. The canon explained that they were left to their own devices and even with help from the speywife from the Douglas village and our Maudie the wee Elizabeth did not thrive. Then her mother failed as well, her symptoms similar that he feared she must be sick from attending the sweet lass.

"It is my fault," Hugh said ruefully. James went to his brother and held him in a strong embrace. "Good Hugh, of the Douglas men so here, it is you our God would favor most; the blame is not due the canon and our good healer. But truly the anger of our God is so directed at this laird for what we do to free our Scotland. Of that I am sure." James was certain that the Heavens were reaping revenge for his raids of fire and sword into Northumbria. "Good brother, my Lord Douglas; this lad has followed orders of our king most as well and dear Beatrice, praise be to God and the good St. Bride, is most well as are the wee ones that she bore," Archie reminded him. "Eleanora would tell us..." but James cut him short. His anger overwhelmed his very being; how could he believe in a loving God when everyone he cherished had been taken from him. "My sweet father; my dear bride, her unborn child and our sweet daughter gone; what God would do this wrath without a reason?" he sneered. Walter tried to comfort him, but James was filled with such rage that he stormed out of the chamber. "This knight is ready for the fight," he proclaimed. James told Robert little of what transpired in Douglasdale; just that he was eager to leave for Northumbria, the noo! The change in his demeanor was reminiscent to his king; was this knight before him not the youth of sinister countenance who with the very mention of one named Edward flew into a rage that few had ever seen?

James returned to the withdrawing room to grab Archie and tell him that they were heading south. "Not to stop until every village and town between the Marches and Newcastle lay waste in flames we set!" he said seething in his rant. Hugh and Walter looked on in horror; what was happening to the laird they loved most, the good and just Lord Douglas was transformed before their eyes to a vengeful warrior. As James was taking his leave he bellowed to his brother. "Do not bother to say prayers on my behalf." But Archie was hearing none of it. "Pray for me and say vigils for our laird; do not stop for feasting that we will need God's good grace to see us to return!" he said in rueful anticipation for their task at hand. Three weeks later the Douglas knight and squire would reenter Berwick; their raids into Northumbria successful; much booty and tribute returned with these Scots as they crossed back from England into Berwick on Tweed.

HARBOTTLE, MAY 1318-James was leading his retinue of marauding Scots south from Netherton, bearing westward towards Harbottle. "That our grandfather was so held here most against his will some fifty years ago and more," the knight told his younger brother. "De Umfraville with one hundred men of Redesdale that sultry night in July on the Eve of St. Margaret invaded our Fawdon as you know to carry off our grandfather to his castle in Harbottle." Archie grinned. "This day we most avenge our father and grandfather for that fateful raid!" he boasted. "Sure aye!" James replied emulating le Hardi.

The village of the manor was not well fortified but it was populated with men and woman of various ages except for men not too old for duel; those citizens mostly resided in the Otherworld, tragic reminders of the lang time spent fighting in the Marches. The terrifying war cry was given; the oliphant sounded as the Douglas men at arms entered the village promising to drive the residents from their homes. Archie noted with concern that since leaving Berwick his brother's face had a strange look, vacant of expression; all the while they mechanically burned and pillaged their way through the Northumbrian villages and towns. It was as if the knight wore this cold visage as a mask to his soul. What is this squire to do about our James, Archie wondered to himself.

Villiens and tenants of Harbottle were fleeing from the squalor of their homes; the garrison of the castle finally surrendering to Douglas. But before the village was theirs James and his men at arms fought through the throngs of common citizens; farmers and laborers who worked the lands not trained warriors with armaments and mail. Archie detested these raids; he would almost turn away, trying to avoid the eyes of these untrained foes as he ended the lives of tenants and farmers, loyal supporters of their lord. He looked back as James was wielding his weapon; thrusting and cutting with his old standard. They were battling their foe onfoot; searching the village for resistance when suddenly Archie called out and grabbed the hilt of his brother's sword. "James stop; look what you are about to do!" James had drawn his sword, holding it in the high guard he whirled around to begin a thrust on a figure that startled him coming from behind. "A wee lass my brother; she is but a girl!" The laird of Douglas looked quizzically as if comprehending the true action of his impending strike for the first time. James' countenance bore the look of someone coming to a conscious state from sleep-walking. The knight threw down his sword in disgust. "That this once great warrior for his king and country has come to this?" he scoffed; horrified by what he was about to do: to murder a helpless lass; unarmed and carrying her baby at her breast. "Get on with you!" Archie told the girl; clinging to her wee one she ran quickly to her hovel for safe haven.

James turned to his brother; tears streamed from his eyes, down the thick of his beard and onto his tabard. "What monster dwells so in my soul to take a life of that sweet child and her wee one?" Archie picked up the sword and gave it back to his brother. "Dear James; there is no braver knight than you. And no hero that this lad so worships that has endured more in loss for the sake of king and kingdome," he whispered as he grabbed him; holding him hard in a strong embrace of true compassion for one who held such sorrow and self blame. James was incredulous; he told Archie he felt like death walking, a ghost perhaps. "That you most stopped this lad would I have much penance to give for such a woeful deed." Then as if in a fog of controlled confusion he commanded the others to carry out the surrender of the castle. James stood away from his retinue; in somber silence, by himself, the knight was lost in his own thoughts. Nor far from the laird stood his younger brother; waiting for James to return from the isolation of his reverie. Finally the Douglas knight gave Archie a knowing look; beckoning his brother to join him. The Douglas warriors moved to the remote palisade, set apart from the stricken castle; their silence spoke their pain. "Revenge for a dear father taken from his family; a sweet bride and wee ones now lost from us as well; this war is painful most enough without the killing of more innocents," James said thoughtfully. "Thank you good squire for sparing this knight any further sorrow for his deeds this day."

FAWDON EARLY FALL- Ellie and her Deerhound were leading the way up the cart path past East Hill to Fawdon manor and her small messuage there. She was followed closely by Ana and Sir David with Lady Elizabeth and another dozen armed horse and their grooms in escort to their lady. Ellie was startled to see Hugh and Walter come from the fortified residence; she had not expected them to meet her in Northumbria. As the two churchmen came to greet Lady Douglas, the look on their faces forewarned her of some terrible news they had come to share. Ellie was trembling as she dismounted her jennet. "What sadness compels you both here?" she asked them quietly. "A tragedy of the most perilous nature," Hugh began with a circumspect demeanor; his stuttering was almost indiscernible. Walter was too emotional to hold back; he ran to Ellie and blurted out the tragic news. "My mother is with God; baby Elizabeth most joined her. This lad is now an orphan!" Ellie held him to her. "Shhh dear Walter; that you are a Douglas our James has told you so." And she held him out in front of her and looked him sternly in the eye. "Never again is this lass to hear of such nonsense; you have family, we are your kin!" she proclaimed. Walter told her that James was changed; something about him was very different. "Our Lord Douglas blames himself for this great loss," Hugh explained, "that he takes his anger out on others of our household."

"This mother beckons all inside our manor house; we will talk more on this sadness that has come into our lives." Ana shook her head; the more our Eleanora endures the further our God so challenges her, she mused. Ellie had wine and ale brought to everyone as she sat down quietly at the old trestle table in the great hall of her manor. "And what of the others?" she asked them. Hugh told her that Beatrice, John and the wee Eleanora were all well. Walter was more emotional; providing many details of the others in the household. "And my brother William now seven misses his wee sister and dear mother; this lad is most concerned that he stays in chamber and speaks little," admitted the aspiring canon.

Hugh elaborated on how he even called in physicians from Soutra; but nothing seemed to change the outcome. Ellie held Walter's hand. "That you are training as an Augustinian?" she asked him. The lad nodded yes. "Then my churchman, do you so recall the writings of Ivo of Chartres when he spoke his truth in the Decretum? He wrote: 'Love and do as you will. Most as sick people are not always cured when the law of medicine is applied; they are cured when the laws are suitably put aside' and there is more," Ellie said, quoting the Augustinian for emphasis in answer to their queries, questioning God's Will. She continued to explain that sometimes even when they were the most disciplined and did their best in any situation, always acting in love, even altering procedures for a chanced opportunity, the outcome was not always to their pleasure. "We are not forever successful and we wonder why. This lass so recalls my Gilley's words: we the living can not be responsible for the outcome when we act in love; it is God's will not ours that so decides our fate." Walter told her that he understood but admitted that God's plan was most puzzling.

"That my good husband, William le Hardi often told us of the Celts; that our good souls but take their journey to the Otherworld, yet to remain most near to us, waiting for our return as well," she offered compassionately. Walter told her that he appreciated her good counsel. Hugh smiled; he remembered that he often found Ellie reading from the writings he brought home; his studies in training as a canon. Now Ellie was using her knowledge to help her family overcome another great tragedy and loss. Would she be able to assist James through this time of great sorrow he wondered? Then Hugh suggested that they leave for Douglasdale on the morrow. "Our Lord Douglas needs most the loving counsel of our sweet mother," he admitted. Ellie agreed and assured everyone that they would stay at Fawdon much longer on their return. "This lass so loves her days in the Cheviot; we will yet take our days in leisure before returning to Essex."

LINTALEE-In the mist of the gloaming a small group of travelers from Northumbria was making their way up the winding cart path. Trees shrouded the way as the gate followed the Jed into a clearing centered by a motte and the growing Douglas fortress at Lintalee. With heavy heart and grave concern for how she might find her son Ellie dismounted her jennet to take the final steps inside the manor. Archie was the first to come and greet her; Sir Robert bolted from her side to place his paws on his shoulders. "Down wee hound; it is my mother's arms this lad so seeks, not yours," he chuckled. As he held Ellie he realized how important her being there was to him; to have her calming influence in Scotland meant so much. "Our James is in the great hall; Lady Beatrice is in the withdrawing room with William, John and the wee Eleanora," he whispered. Ellie realized that Archie must have seen her coming for some distance as he had everything arranged for her arrival, so she could meet with James alone.

Figure CIV-Part Three; the gallery above the arched doorway peers down into the great hall at Craignethan, a castle in the care of Historic Scotland

    As Lady El made her way through the carved oak doors she peered inside the darkened hall; though it was sunny and bright outside a gloomy, dark shadowing prevailed inside the fortress. The fireplace was cold, the tallow torches not lit and the gallery where the minstrels once played was empty and silent. James looked up and sarcastically bid the Deerhound to come; to his chagrin Sir Robert came obediently to sit at his side. James could not restrain a laugh; the hound had won his amusement. "Dear wee grey hound; this lad so needs your kindness," he began, scratching him behind the ears and up his broad chest. As James rose to hug his mother tears filled his eyes and ran down his nose to drop on her face. Ellie was crying too; they had no words, just a love and understanding that bridged the lifetimes of sorrow they shared. When James could finally speak he whispered softly in her ear. "Only my Lady El holds greater sorrow in her heart." Archie decided to remove the others of Ellie's entourage from the great hall; directing everyone to leave as they made their way to the withdrawing room.

"Dear James there are no words to convey such despair for your great loss," she began. James pushed away from her; not in anger, but rather for his own grief. "This lad finds his solace in a bitter feud with God; to call our Creator names and shut my heart to love is my soul's desire," he admitted. Ellie listened; gave him time to share his feelings before she spoke again. "Your mother was most angry first with le Hardi; for taking me in marriage that he did, then to die defiantly in the Tower, leaving us too soon. And when I reflected on his goodness and great love, I fought with God and cursed the Blessed Virgin; to take my sweet Amy and baby Douglas; then allow my Gilley to be wrested from our lives by greedy enemies of bitter hatred. What God so allows of this I questioned in my heart."

James was listening; he followed her with his eyes as she moved to sit at the large table in the great hall. "Oh my dear son; how often has this lass most questioned: what did this mother and faithful wife most do to make her God so angry?" The Lord Douglas approached the table to sit next to Lady El; he took her hand in his and just held it. "Pray what revelation came to you that restored your faith?" he asked earnestly. Ellie explained that one afternoon she was visiting Little Dunmow Priory and the Douglas graves including Gilley's. "This lass had fury in her voice and daggers in her heart as she sent words of spite to the Heavens. Then from behind me I heard the most calming and sweetest of words from a canon coming from that priory."

James was curious and begged her to continue; her words were coming slowly through her own tears of emotion. "That as this priest was speaking words of comfort he told me his name was Robert. He shared with me the most beautiful of thoughts: 'it is not the length of time that we so have to show love but the depth, honesty and unconditional way we are allowed to express love,' he began," then Ellie stopped abruptly; the heaviness of her heart brought sobs to her throat, blocking her words. James encouraged her to continue when she could. "That this dear Robert the kindest priest that I have ever known save Hugh then shared these final words with me; 'your knight was the most fortunate of men; to so experience sweet love in all its glory with you his wife and true love and that he most taught you how to love as well. Bless him and thank your God for such a gift my daughter' and then he turned and left me there with my Gilley. I never saw that priest again," she said wistfully.

James was moved by the canon's sentiments; the rage that he felt for the loss of his wife and daughter was transforming within him; changing to the deep sadness of a grieving laird. "That our days were not so spent without a purpose?" he questioned his mother in wonderment for the thought. Ellie shook her head no. "That knowing this truth: the time this lass so had with my sweet William was God's gift; a sentiment to make his loss much easier to bear. And upon my sad reflection those same words of Father Robert to comfort me as well for the loss of Mura; baby William too." James wrapped his large arms around her smaller frame. "Do you ever wonder if our father sent that priest to speak with you that day?"

Ellie looked up at him, startled by his questions; gazing deep into his eyes, her own swollen by tears that streaked her face, she surveyed his countenance. "Most often when I go there I think of that priest. This widow went to find him the day next; to give him thanks for the reprieve he gave my heart and soul. That the Master seemed surprised by my inquiry; no canon named Robert was a resident of the priory he told me." James suggested that perhaps he was a pilgrim passing through Essex. "Only this is truly known; that canon comforted me with his words and sentiments that day most as Gilley would have done." James put his calloused thumb and fingers around Ellie's chin to tilt it up. "Lady El, our father le Hardi is most an amazing man," he said chuckling. "That he has spoken to us; comforted this humble knight most as well this day with the words from that fair priest."

The next day James rose in the prime and rounded up his family; commanding his sons, nephew, and niece with his brothers and mother; they were going to Blackhouse he told them. "This laird will show the wee ones the ways of the Celts," he grinned. "Like le Hardi, we will venture forth to seek the wisdom of our past; sit among the Douglas stones and share stories and songs from another time," he boasted. Archie was stunned; his brother had transformed to the boyish lad he remembered from their youth just overnight. "Good James; are you to show us how to fish, taking us to the Tweed as you once did this lad?" he asked enthusiastically. The Lord Douglas told him yes; once they held their sacred ceremony at the stones, there would be plenty of time for such adventures. Beaming ear to ear James began regaling them with their times at Blackhouse when le Hardi was alive; he would emulate the traditions of his father he told them; healing them in love and respect for the ways of the ancient ones he promised. Then he dispatched the children with their nurses; told them to make ready for the journey.

Beatrice had been silent; stunned by the abrupt change in James' demeanor, she finally found her voice to ask him, *what happened?* Lord Douglas replied in unsuppressed delight. "That this lad so had a dream last night; most like the time when my dear father had come to me in Essex. My beloved Joanna held my hand and kissed me on the lips; to tell me she yet waited my return to the Otherworld of the Celts," he said in quiet jubilation. Ellie understood. When James' anger had abated, he experienced God's most precious gift to the living: to see his fair Joanna among the Heavens. This was no dream; Ellie knew that quite certainly for James could truly feel

Joanna's sweet presence, most like she had experienced with her Gilley when he came to visit his girl.

"And like our father, this lad will set about a ceremony at the Douglas stones to celebrate the ways of the ancient ones," he informed them, then adding quietly, "and express our mourning respectfully to our God, singing to our loved ones lost to us." Ellie looked up; surprised that she had not thought of it before. Gilley had taken his family to the stones to organize a tribute to the Otherworld for the loss of the wee Martha, their daughter who had then recently drowned in the moat of Woodham Ferrers. "A splendid plan Lord Douglas!" she said, her face aglow in anticipation for the sacred rites; the loving sacraments of ceremony of the ancient Celtic religion: to heal their losses in songs of tribute, sung in the ancient tongue of Gaelic to those loved ones now with God.

Figure CV-Part Three; artist's drawing of the Douglas Stones between Blackhouse and Mountbengerhope; eleven remain today but only a few are still standing

BLACKHOUSE TOWER- James led his family in an orderly procession from the tower house up the cart path to the Douglas stones. All the Douglases including Ana, Sir David, and many others of their household entered within the protection of the ancient circle to sit quietly as the sacred event began. Archie had brought the white wand; the one James entrusted to him nearly a dozen years before, the very same staff William le Hardi used to mark the baronial court and the healing circle of the stones. James instructed Archie to assign the boundaries of their temple, stretching the depth of the protective stone circle to the trees. Then when the squire was finished he presented the ancient wand of a Scots Ell in length to Hugh who would first lead the group in song, the verses to be given in Gaelic, the language of their Highland kin and ancestors of these Lowland Douglases.

518

Before they began, Ellie passed around the baluster that held the Holy water. Each participant poured a little of the liquid to cleanse their hands; wiped them dry with the same woven cloth of grey and black used in the wedding ceremony. Hugh began with a small prayer; opening their sacred rites with a tribute to God in His infinite wisdom and grace. Then he started singing, almost chanting his first verse, a tribute to Lady Joanna. The depth of his emotions stirred the others to follow their reply all in unison and await the next call of words sung by the canon. Hugh led them in more verses, speaking of Joanna and the great love she showed to all of them; while the Douglases and their kin followed, repeating his words in chorus. Hugh then drew in his breath for his final words; his concluding sentiment for his sister in law: "*'S mi fo bhròn 's tu gam dhìth,*" Hugh sang softly; his voice crying out *I am sad without you* in Scottish Gaelic. The others followed lamenting Joanna's loss, expressing their own deep sentiments. Then the canon handed the wand to James who stood up to take the center call while Hugh sat down in the place once held by the grieving husband and father.

James was visibly emotional, singing his words of love for Lady Joanna; of how he mourned her passing, missed her fair touch, lamenting her lonely departure while he was on campaign. The ceremony continued as the laird expressed his anguish; the weeping husband and father was conveying his sentiments through the language of his ancestors, using the expressive tones of Scottish Gaelic in song. He sang of his children, the wee Elizabeth and the unborn son or daughter now lost to him. Then James drew in his breath for a final crescendo; his last verse sung in tribute to his bride. "*Mo thasgaidh; mo leannan,*" he proclaimed loudly to the Heavens that she might hear: *my treasure, my sweetheart*, the compelling, final words to Lady Joanna from her knight and loving husband. Ellie was choked by her emotions; she could barely reply to his verse, so she mouthed the words of tribute. As she looked around the circle she noted that some of the wee ones were not singing at all; why she wondered to herself?

The Douglas children were given a choice to attend; they all accepted the invitation, but something was amiss Ellie noted; perhaps they do not know the words she mused. But she had little time to consider their Gaelic language skills for now as James came to stand in front of his mother; it was Ellie's turn to lead them in verse. For every ceremony of the ancient ones, Lord Douglas, her Gilley, had reminded everyone that women served as equals in their ways. While their Douglas Kirk of the bishop's see held for male priests to celebrate the sacraments, the ancient church of the Celts permitted women such equal status to their men. Ellie reveled in the task at hand; standing and singing loudly she expressed her mourning of Joanna; then too she added her grief for the loss of the wee Elizabeth and the unborn Douglas carried to the Otherworld with Joanna's tragic passing. Her words were healing to her family and to this mother and brave widow who knew such loss herself.

When the Douglases were later feasting in the great hall at Blackhouse tower Ellie begged to know the reason the younger Douglases did not participate in songs of the sacred circle. "Why were there quiet looks and few words chanted by our wee ones?" she demanded to know. Young William told her that save only for her visits Gaelic language lessons were seldom given. "Our father has most told us that even in our Scottish Parliaments the Gaelic has not been said in ten years or more," he allowed. Ellie shot a look at James that made him sit up and take notice. "Lady El, we shall honor the traditions of our father and engage a tutor in the Gaelic tongue at once," he told her acknowledging her concern immediately. "Such lessons shall commence the noo! For the prime all Douglas children will join their grandmother in the withdrawing room; by the first light this lass does so expect to see each and every one of you!" Ellie informed them. Not one of her grandchildren protested; they realized trifling with Eleanora was something even the laird of Douglas would not chance. "Lady El, perhaps to wait for Morning Prayer," quipped James with a broad smile. Ellie began to giggle; realizing her stern reply was not necessary. She told the wee ones that first they may visit their chapel in the manor to give their thanks to God; then all should break their fast in the great hall. "And once prepared for the day, to then join with this lass, your grandmother in study for the language, to sing and speak the words of our proud ancestors." Ana was wiping her eyes; she was overcome with emotion: another generation of Douglases was to be schooled by her girl, carrying on the traditions of that proud knight and laird, Sir William le Hardi.

SCONE 3 DECEMBER 1318-Robert Brus had called a Parliament to determine succession rights to the kingdome as his brother Edward had recently died in Ireland; the younger Brus killed in battle, his army destroyed there. Lord Robert's first concern was the Act of Settlement invoked in 1315; it was recalled. The king spoke with grave concern for a Scotland that could fall prey to the same dilemma of thirty years ago when King Alexander died, if he passed to the Otherworld without a male heir or one in majority. His only daughter died giving life to a male heir two years before. This younger Robert was born at Paisley Abbey, his father yet living was Walter the High Steward, James' own cousin. Robert Brus surveyed his most loyal followers and kin; stalwart Scots who would defend their country from Edward as he had done. There were two knights he signaled out: Sir Thomas Randolph his nephew, great, great grandson of Earl Duncan of Carrick and Sir James of Douglas, the grandson of Martha Douglas, kin to the brother of Earl Duncan. The king proclaimed the succession: his grandson Robert Steward would be his heir; Randolph Earl of Moray, then James Lord Douglas should Randolf die before his grandson reached majority would hold his ward; the two knights and lairds designated as tutor or guardian for his grandson.

In a ceremony of great solemnity, both Sir Thomas and Sir James kissed the gospels and vowed upon the relics of the saints to uphold the wishes of their king. Twelve days later in Arbroath Lord Robert issued charters to Sir James of Douglas for lands in Annandale known at Polmoody in celebration of the royal designation. "No truer knight could there be than our good servant Lord Douglas; that he has most endured deep sadness and great hardship second only to his king," Brus said addressing his loyal vassal. The king felt a genuine connection to James and his heavy-hearted loss. With his last surviving brother dying overseas and his daughter dying in child-bed, the King of Scots shared an empathy with the knight that few could comprehend.

Since Lord Robert began his long road to kingship he suffered the agony of sending his brothers to their gruesome deaths. Now his lang-time adherent while faithfully on campaign, valiantly leading raids into Northumbria, had endured his greatest personal loss since the death of his father William le Hardi: the passing of his wife and unborn child and his wee daughter. Robert Brus wanted James to know he understood and Lord Douglas acknowledged just that. "Good and most generous king that you have suffered great tragedies most as well; this knight is most humble for your kindness and good sympathy this day," he said circumspectly. The looks exchanged between the two warriors and friends were not lost upon any in the king's council that day; Robert Brus, King of Scots and Sir James, Lord Douglas were linked in Spirit as well as sentiment and deed most done.

CHARTLEY SPRING 1319-Ellie was on her way to the Hyde in Staffordshire to settle some disputes on fees and rents concerning one of the Bagot manors. She was planning to continue on to Northumbria and if it was safe, to make her way in secret across the Borders to Lintalee. This day she decided to stop at the de Ferrers manor of Chartley to visit with her sister in law, the widow of Sir John who resided there with her young son and daughter. Robert de Ferrers, the son and heir of Sir John, was not yet the age of majority; his interests were held in ward by his mother's older cousin. His older sister was Ellie's namesake, Eleanor de Ferrers. Born in 1305 the de Ferrers daughter was the God child of Lady Eleanora Bagot and her husband Sir William Bagot; one of their first official acts after their marriage in Bildeston that year. In the great hall of the grand castle Ellie was feasting and enjoying fine wine; gossiping with her kin Hawise, Lady de Ferrers on the affairs at court. Ten year old Robert was gallantly holding up his end of conversation with the ladies while fourteen year old Eleanor was bored by all the talk of war and politics, excusing herself to the withdrawing room.

Figure CVI-Part Three; Chartley ruins, a motte and bailey castle that was once the seat of Ellie's father in law, the Earl de Ferrers before he forfeited his lands for his rebellion

    Then suddenly the de Ferrers men at arms opened the large doors of the great hall; with great ceremony they announced the arrival of Sir Nicholas de Segrave, Baron of Stowe. "Nicky!" Ellie screamed with delight; she had not seen her cousin since the funeral of his wife, Alice de Armenters two years ago. "That you are here!" Nicky exclaimed. "You have come to even greater beauty," he sighed as he kissed her gallantly on the hand. Then he abruptly turned to Lady de Ferrers and young Robert; throwing some rolled parchments on the table. "Lord Edward plans to call us for a muster," he said angrily. The de Ferrers squire was incredulous; his mother horrified. "For Newcastle on Tyne!" he explained. "Our king does so regret the loss of Berwick; that he will call us out in numbers to repel the rebels from that burgh," Nicky sneered. "Is this the writ?" asked young Robert. Nicky told him no; only the rough draft as he must wait for Parliament.

    Ellie was listening intently. A muster meant she must delay her travels north; more than an annoyance she hissed under her breath, ignoring the possibility of Edward doing battle with her sons. "Lord Bagot will be most called to attend my lord the king as well," Nicky explained. Ellie grabbed for the document that Nicky brought, to read it for herself. "This lass must go to Pattishall the noo!" she declared. Ellie was at once furious and scared; angry at Edward for his continued wars with Scotland and frightened that her husband might use all of their income for the muster. So if Sir William was going on campaign she realized she must get to the steward of their manors before him or there would be little left in their coffers for her share of the rents. "On the morrow will this knight so give you good escort for that end," Nicky offered to the obvious dismay of Lady de Ferrers of

Chartley; Hawise had grown quite fond of his visits as they were both widow and widower now, his late wife her own kin as well.

But the de Segrave knight had other thoughts on his mind; his favorite cousin was seeking good escort. And he was more than ready to provide for her needs. Nicky's lands of Stowe were not far from Ellie's other Bagot manor of Pattishall; a day's ride south of Great Ashby, the former Bagot manor once held by Lord William's father. Hawise interrupted his thoughts; she was nervous she told him; espousing caution to Nicky, a knight she perceived as exciting albeit reckless in his ways. She advised him to be careful with his words; his loyalty to Edward might be questioned. The de Segrave knight was growing restless with his political ties. Since becoming a widower, his only child and daughter married to a de Bohun knight, he had speculated for the first time on his future. Perhaps to be a knight-errant he reflected. Nicky knew his days of loyalty to his king were coming to an end; if the Earl of Lancaster leads us in rebellion this warrior will follow he vowed to himself. "Take no heed of my raucous ways this day dear Lady Hawise, my good kin and friend; this knight will heed your good counsel," he promised knowing his course was already chosen.

Figure CVII-Part Three; Wilbrighton Hall lies vacant and boarded up today; the manor held by Eleanora Douglas Bagot, then by her youngest son Archibald Douglas

WILBRIGHTON HALL- Ellie and Nicky stopped for a day at her manor of Wilbrighton; these lands were hers alone now she explained to her cousin; staffed with her own servants, those she could trust. "That this lass so intends Wilbrighton manor for my wee Archie to have in freehold," she confided; speculating that peace would someday come between the two countries. Entering the great hall of the manor with her cousin and his small party of men at arms in escort they were greeted by Sir William Bagot's seneschal; he too was on his way to Pattishall. "That it is my desire and plan to complete my twice yearly task; to find of freeholders and inhabitant householders of the lordship for the list. Then to collect the fees and rents most due," he explained. "My husband shall expect to raise a retinue to do battle for our king," Eleanora explained. "But this lass has many expenses on my Essex lands that must be settled first. My due in coinage is most necessary that as Lady Bagot I must regretfully not share the burden for this campaign," she told him in matter of fact tones. The Bagot family steward understood at once; he realized that the knight banneret, Lord William Bagot was prone to overestimate his needs to include funds for his greatest passion: games of chance. And for the last call to muster he stripped the manors to their very base of sustenance. "That we shall all proceed to Pattishall is my intention," he agreed. "The rents in silver are the first to come; the crops growing less plentiful, those harvested are small, but rents and fees for your fair use Lady Bagot are most there," the steward assured her.

That evening Ellie and Nicky dined alone together in the withdrawing room of Wilbrighton Hall. Nicky was uncharacteristically solemn. Lady Bagot knew her cousin well; he must be struggling with a grave concern to keep him so quiet she mused. Finally he broke his silence. "Our king's muster is a sad choice I fear; to drive his loyal nobles to choose sides between the foolish war or treason." Ellie's heart seemed to skip a beat in her shock. The only English nobleman she truly trusted was her kin Sir Nicholas de Segrave; if he became a traitor she would have no safe confidant in all of England. "That some years ago you were most forgiven by Edward," she said in a flustered response, reminding him that he was pardoned once, reprieved from a sentence of death in the Tower. "That such grace might not come again," she cautioned. In very low tones, almost in a hushed whisper, Nicky told Ellie what she most feared. "This humble knight will not wage another war against the Scots," he said ominously. "Sir Thomas, the Earl of Lancaster is gaining the loyalty of many nobles with like sentiments; this knight will join with them," Nicky said. "Perhaps to treat with the Scots and a knight you know most well," he added alluding to James. "The Black Douglas and his squire, Essex trained, these men true masters of their craft and warfare," Nicky said with a twinkle in his eye. Ellie shook her head wearily; she knew what he said was true; her sons had told her of such discussions; the earl most yearned for a peace in a countryside made desolate by war.

De Segrave took his cousin's hand and grasped it to his chest, then looked into her eyes with a deep intensity. Ellie was taken aback; she had never seen this side of him before. Nicky spoke again. "That we are kin, but not of such near degree," his words trailed off as he brought his mouth to cover hers in a passionate and powerful kiss. Ellie's body shook in response; twenty years without a lover's fond embrace flamed fire to her very soul. But the feeling lasted only for a moment; she realized it was le Hardi's kiss she desired not Nicky's. "This embrace is false; filled with a passion that I hold for another," she whispered as she gently pulled herself away from him. The gallant knight banneret pushed back and fumbled for an apology. "Nicky, my sweet cousin and dear friend, that this lass is married to another," she tried to say, but he was hearing none of her excuse. "No; the truth is this: the Scotsman most buried in Little Dunmow Priory yet holds your heart," he smiled, mocking his own futility. "More times than this knight so cares to admit do I sigh in envy for that love le Hardi and his bride most shared," he said as he boyishly pinched Ellie on the check. "Friends?" he asked sheepishly.

Ellie nodded yes. "And were there no memory of Gilley in my sad heart, your sweet self would be the one I would so dream upon in my lonely hours," Lady Bagot confided to her cousin. Nicky took her hand again and asked for her promise. "If ever you have a change of heart you will call for this humble knight, your cousin; yours for the very asking I pledge my heart to one Eleanora. Until then, we shall not speak word of this to anyone," he said with his well known bravado. The cousins resumed their wine and feasting, but used only words to express their sentiments; no lover's kiss or affectionate embrace passed between them again. That night lying alone in her chamber Eleanora Douglas Bagot dreamed of her sweet William: his long dark locks were flowing wildly in the wind as he rode fervently towards her. Then as he drew near he reared up his war-horse and gallantly bolted from the saddle; the gleam in his eye portending the impassioned embrace that followed. Ellie woke abruptly, feeling jolted to her bed; the light of dawn filled her chamber ending her sweet reverie. But as she reflected upon her dream she swore she had truly felt the warmth of her Gilley's lips upon her own. Lady El chuckled to imagine le Hardi; coming to visit in a dream just to remind her that she was still *his girl*.

BERWICK AUGUST 1319- Nicky's information from court was accurate and Ellie reluctantly returned home to Essex. At nearly fifty-two her stamina for long journeys was not what it once was; outrunning Edward's army was no longer feasible. When she returned to Stebbinge Park her fears for the muster were realized; her brother Thomas told her that Lord Bagot, now a knight banneret, was called by writ of 20th March to meet the king at Newcastle on Tyne with horses and arms to proceed against the Scots. Ellie took Nicky's heed; not knowing when she could return to

Scotland she decided to conserve her coinage, not even venturing forth to Fawdon. Edward's muster in Northumbria was too close for comfort she sighed; instead a resigned Lady Bagot sent messengers from Essex to her manor in the Cheviot with her letters that would then be taken into the Marches of Scotland for her sons before the summer solstice.

In July from York Edward commended further writs; ordering his powerful army to a march on Berwick. By August he was at the gates of the town; thwarted by the cunning commander Sir Walter the Steward, James' own cousin and son in law to the King of Scots. Edward was so incensed by the Scots' being entrenched at Berwick on Tweed that he wrote the Pope to condemn the actions; he was ignored. Then Caernarvon issued orders to the Earl of Lancaster to levy 2000 foot for his muster. Surprisingly, Sir Thomas reported with the requested contingency and more. Then Edward begged the Duke of Brabant and Robert, Count of Flanders to repel the Scots; they refused with Sir Robert openly acknowledging Robert Brus as King of Scots. Edward was aghast in horror for the lack of support from the Papal See and the nobility abroad. He responded in anger at his own nobles; defiantly ordered all English lords who did not fulfill their call of men to pay their fines to the Exchequer without delay.

With extreme effort, Edward marched north; with only 10,000 men at arms, no more and a small naval force he planned to take Berwick back from the King of Scots. But King Robert had other plans. He fortified the town and garrisoned the castle with many archers and armed foot. He provisioned Berwick with substantial stores and then set about organizing his own army to distract the English forces with raids into the north of England. Following the summer into fall over eighty towns in Cumbria and Northumbria were met with fire and sword while Berwick held for the Scots. In disgust for Edward's ineptness as a commander, yet again out maneuvered by the King of Scots, the Earl of Lancaster withdrew his forces compelling Edward to disband his army in retreat.

STEBBINGE PARK EARLY NOVEMBER- Ellie and Lady Elizabeth were waiting for Ana to join them in the withdrawing room; a letter from Beatrice had been delivered by Sir Thomas de Chauncelor's men at arms from Northumbria. "Come Ana, sit here," Ellie said happily; it had been months since they had received word from Scotland's freedom fighters. They only knew that Edward was forced to raise the siege at Berwick and retreat home. "Now might we read of the gallant knights of our blessed Scotland," Ellie proclaimed. Sir David's arrival was announced; having just returned from Fairstead, he broke into a broad smile when he noticed that Lady El held another parchment in her hands, undoubtedly from Scotland by the look on her face. "Our Black Douglas knight has brought fear to the hearts of Yorkshire men," Sir David sighed. The aging English knight was now too old for tournament; disabled in his early years all he lived for now it seemed was the success of his most favored students, ironically fighting the very king he pledged fealty to for his Essex lands.

"You know of the battle at Myton on the Swale?" Ellie asked him. Sir David nodded; not much of a battle as a rout he told her; nearly three hundred men of the cloth died there. Ana gasped, Lady Elizabeth shook with horror; priests had taken up arms against their Douglas men! "Oh dear St. Bride," Ellie moaned as she began to survey the letter quickly. When satisfied that her family was not among those who suffered for that fight she relaxed; ordered wine from the cellarer and began to read aloud for her wee clan in Essex, those she trusted with the news from Scotland. "Lady Beatrice writes first that we should travel to Scotland in the spring; to arrive no later than late March!" Lady Douglas looked up, her face beamed to know she was going home; by the Vernal Equinox she would be in the Marches! "This lass agrees; the wait much sweeter now, that we will join in celebration with my sons, our sweet family most soon," Ellie cooed. Ana was thrilled; to venture north was what her lamb most needed she mused. "Our Archie and dear James; they are both well," Ellie continued. "We knew of that before such reading had begun," scoffed Sir David good naturedly.

"Good kin that our brave Douglas men were sent with the Earl of Moray to York to provide distraction to Edward's siege, they feigned to capture Queen Isabella!" wrote Lady Beatrice boasting of their deeds. Ellie read further and informed everyone that a brave Scot allowed himself taken prisoner as a spy; revealed 'secret plans devised of the Black Douglas' and from his words the queen was taken safely inside a fortress to wait out the Scots' invasion; "fearful of our Archie and dear James!" added Beatrice. Ellie was chuckling; the letter was obviously penned by a doting bride; treating James the equal to his younger brother in their prowess at battle and social status. "Our warriors fought bravely, our king's lieutenants led their men some 15,000 in number to Yorkshire where they encountered the fierce opposition of English armed foot in great numbers," Archie's wife continued.

Ana wondered aloud if Lady Beatrice understood who was squire and who was knight in this army; chuckling as she spoke. Ellie read on; the words told of an untrained army led into the fight by greedy bishops in pursuit of Scottish benefices. "The king's own Chancellor, the bishop of Ely with the Archbishop of York denied the Scot's story. These foolish prelates decided most to seek in battle our Lord Douglas. Lay and clergy took the field; monks and sheriffs, canons and other regulars carrying axes and simple arms, wearing armor of banded mail and cuir bouilli; few trained soldiers formed the contingency of English armed foot this day." Sir David shook his head; peasants and clergy wearing the boiled leather armor were no match for the experienced and now well armed marauders under James' leadership.

"The Scots so took the field, in the manner of trained warriors," Ellie continued the tale. "The foolish English gulped of air; their fierceness withdrew from their very souls to hear the perilous war-cry: A Douglas! A Douglas! The sorry army of our enemy barely fled in fear for their lives before the battle even started." Beatrice was writing in a rapid, looping hand Lady El noted to her audience of listeners. "Her breathless excitement apparent so in her every word!" Ellie told them, to set the scene properly. "Three thousand men of Yorkshire were put to the sword; our Scots taking many prisoners for good ransom while others of the enemy drowned in the Swale for their desperate flight," Lady Beatrice exclaimed. Ellie kept on reading; her sons sustained small injuries and took home much booty. Lady Elizabeth and Ana were enthralled by the story; Sir David was saddened by the loss of so many untrained soldiers; the hopelessness of inexperienced warriors against the open field tactics of the experienced Scots gnawed on the conscience of the old knight. He denounced the prelates who foolishly spurred the rabble to confront a well trained army. "Such greed these clerics have; that they should be protectors to their flock. Their desires for victory have outsmarted them I pray."

Figure CVIII-Part Three; site of Newbattle Abbey

More details of the battle followed but they were written down in another hand; the Douglas canon's words continued where Lady Beatrice's writing left off. "The commanders of this English army of churchmen and burgesses had been tricked; duped by a smokescreen of burning hay beyond the river where the untrained army came upon the Scots. Their eyes reddened and streamed tears from the haze of smoke, these brave men came to a startling circumstance when they crossed the Swale: the Scots were waiting their arrival in tight formation to do battle!" Hugh explained that the bravado of these foolish warriors turned to fright and quickly. Expecting to find a scattered, rag-tag contingency of Scots these monks, priests, and townsfolk and peasants came face to face "with our brave schiltrons; the disciplined armed foot of the greatest army to grace our kingdome or any other!" boasted Hugh.

Ellie wondered if what her canon had said was true; one look at Sir David told her volumes. "No bigger fool could there so be to pick a fight with the skilled warriors under the leadership of one named James," the old knight scowled. "For now the battle was over; the tide so turned that the English cleric leading his flock to peril that foul day has been turned out, reduced to begging for his folly." Ellie sighed; another lesson put upon the English by her gallant warriors. "This lass is most grateful to our God and dear St. Bride for the safely of our James and Archie and their retinue of good men, all. To ride to Little Dunmow is my choice this hour," Lady Douglas announced to her household as she rose to request her jennet be saddled; her escort rounded up for the ride to the priory and a visit with Lord Douglas.

NEWBATTLE ABBEY MARCH 1320-A parliament was called to respond to Pope John XXII; matters having worsened in the past year. The continued stream of papal bulls for Lord Robert's excommunication and those of his loyal subjects ended with a summons of four Scottish bishops to attend the curia and give cause for many breaches with the papal see including breaking the Pope's peace. The prelates were requested to appear in Avignon by the 1st of May 1320. Edward's continued pleas were finally being addressed; the charges being brought against Scotland's king once more included the suspicious death of the Comyn in Dumfries some fourteen years ago.

King Robert's army under the joint command of Randolph and James had returned again in November to Cumbria and Northumbria, about the time Ellie received the letter from Beatrice and Hugh of their September successes. The Scots laid waste all of northern England, arriving just after the harvest, they burned crops, leaving many dead in their wake and demanding more in tribute. Now nearly one fifth of Edward's kingdome was in tributary to Lord Robert. The ferocity of the invasion, the increased flow of coinage from English coffers to the Scots brought Edward to a more conciliatory mood that he treated of a two year peace with Lord Robert. The pause in the war and the growing conflict between Scotland and the Holy See portended an opportunity Robert Brus determined; it was time to take another step: to write a letter to Pope John. The King of Scots decided that if Scotland was to ever gain her freedom from Edward he must do everything in his power to align himself with the Papal See; a stroke of brilliance that marked his statesmanship for centuries to come.

In the great hall of the abbey a huge crowd of Scotland's nobility had assembled. James Lord Douglas and his entourage including his younger brother and squire Archibald of Douglas made their rounds, talking to kin and friends alike among these magnates of the kingdome. Archie took his role very seriously and was unusually circumspect in his demeanor as he followed James around the hall. He was attired in a fine mantel of ermine with a red velvet hat adorned in matching fur; his surcote of black silk brocade was trimmed in gold and red. Lord Douglas did not pale in comparison; his own deference for fine attire bore a strikingly similar stroke. Though of different colors, he too wore a distinctive mantel and elegant surcote; the brooch that secured his supertunic was le Hardi's worn on the occasion of his marriage to Lady El.

As the Douglas men entered the withdrawing room of the abbot's domain they were greeted by an aging Bishop Lamberton. "That le Hardi himself has come to court this day," he teased the knight and squire. "Lady Beatrice with her good hand has so restored this fair garment," Archie boasted to the prelate, adding that his father had worn the ermine mantel once at Scone before he was born. Eying the now familiar attire the bishop's eyes began to water; he recalled his many friends and kin, lang years gone from us he mused. "Your father was one laird this churchman so respected," he told the squire quietly, attempting to conceal the strong emotions of loss that overwhelmed him. "Thank you for those fair words," Archie replied biting back tears as well.

The session was being called to order; nobles were taking their places as others were preparing their words to speak. When James' turn arrived that he might provide his input on the letter's contents he emphasized his support for the phrases the Chancellor proposed. "That my dear father, that noble laird William le Hardi so often impressed upon his most humble son: had the Bishop of Glasgow's fateful words some twenty-nine years ago, in 1291, been heard we would not have entertained any Lord Paramount. Let us so include Robert Wishart's bold sentiments as our fair abbot of Arbroath most stated," James began, plainly alluding to the bishop's taunt, quoting the prophecy of Gildas, that Scots *would nobly uphold their right.* Then the soldier cleared his throat, took in a deep breath that he might continue with his own thoughts for the council to consider. "But for this humble knight, no truer sentiments can so be written without a word for those good citizens, men, women, and children most massacred at Berwick on Tweed in the year of our Lord, 1296. Few men lived to tell the tale of the Butcher King, his vile and most despicable of deeds; but this Douglas laird was there to see with my own eyes." Again James had to pause; something was clogging his throat, his words were being muffled as tears began to fill his eyes and spill down his beard. By St. Bride I will continue he swore to himself!

When his voice returned, it sounded to James as if someone else was speaking for him. "As my brave father stood from his confinement in Douglas Tower there at Berwick Castle, this grave slaughter he was forced to so behold; the unspeakable horrors inflicted by the benevolent *Lord Paramount*. That *dear Edward* broke his promise of a truce. To stop the massacre of the citizens of that fair burgh he assured; intentions feigned in subterfuge just to glean my noble father's fair surrender; then only to resume the senseless murders." James continued; he spoke quietly but each and every Scot could hear his words; the silence within the great hall of the abbey reverberated with only the sound of the knight's voice relating his personal account of the first genocide in recorded history. "That for lang times after that my sweet sisters woke from nightmares of that dreadful day. Most with my mother and good sisters we had ridden to our safety, only to never truly escape that foul deed. What we saw that day we will carry to our graves! While others of our kin, good friends and fellow citizens, defenseless and unarmed, remained to be so captured for the hanging, seven at a time; or to be chased down like vermin and run through by the point of an English sword."

Archie had never heard the entire story of the Butcher of Berwick and his destruction of Scotland's most prestigious port. In March 1296 he was the unborn Douglas son carried within the womb of his mother as she rode through the gates of the burgh. After her husband's brokered surrender, Lady Douglas was free to take her leave that day. With her children and the castle garrison, in the escort of her Douglas men at arms, she made her way past the banners of her father Lord Lovaine and others of her kin, overwhelmed in guilt for what the English wrought that day. Hearing his brother's words brought Archie to tears; the injustice festering within him to nearly burst. "Spare not word or sentiment for these most grotesque and barbaric deeds. That we must so include in this fair letter to the Pope the atrocities we suffered at the hands of such infidels and their pagan despot king!" declared James to a round of heartfelt support from Scotland's nobles and Lord Robert. Archie shouted an unrestrained, "Saor Alba!" but was barely heard above the roar of his countrymen at Newbattle Abbey.

ARBROATH ABBEY 6 APRIL 1320-The nobles were being called forward in somber ceremony to append their seals to the official document. The letter to Pope John had been finalized from the draft devised at Newbattle Abbey; Bernard the Chancellor of Scotland and his brilliant clerics at the abbey in Arbroath completing the task with great skill and close attention to the prose. At the end of the declaration were lines of small slits to which strings of silk could be threaded; looped into the wax made ready for the impressions of seals from the magnates of Scotland. James Lord Douglas was one to affix his seal through a slit on the first row; the red wax depicting his highly regarded status within the Community of the Realm; the others following in a green wax for the next two rows as was the king's intention for his nobles. The ceremony took place in the great hall of the bishop; the king insisting rather forcefully that seals must be affixed to the document, even sent to Arbroath in absence of a laird too ill for travel.

Figure CIX-Part Three-the annual reenactment at Arbroath Abbey where nobles affixed their seals to the letter to Pope John in 1320: the Declaration of Arbroath

The first to put his seal upon the fateful letter was Duncan, Earl of Fife; with his younger cousin, Archibald Douglas intently watching. James introduced the earl to his Lovaine kin. "That you are both the great grandson of Sir Matthew de Lovaine," he chuckled. "Cousins of de Percy most as well," Archie added sarcastically, spouting his boyish grin. The earl remarked at the honor; thanked James and Archie both for their father's brave stand to behead the de Percy culprit, one of his father's murderers, to le Hardi's dreary end in Edward's prison. "That I was most present at that Baronial Court," James explained; providing the details of the event of thirty-two years ago; one he had committed to memory. The earl bid his adieu; it was now James' turn; his would be the tenth Scottish noble to affix his seal to the document.

And as the warm wax was readied, poured onto the silk strings waiting for him to impress his signet, James scanned the letter to Pope John, noting with pride the references to the Berwick atrocities of 1296. Then his eyes fell to the words he most revered; the essence of the declaration: 'For as long as but one hundred of us remain alive we will never subject ourselves to the dominion of the English. For it is not glory, it is not riches, neither is it for honor; but for Liberty alone do we fight, which no honest man can so give up but with life itself.' The Lord Douglas added, "Sure aye, dear father, sure aye," as he appended his seal: Sgill. Jacobus, Dni. de Duglas with three stars on a chief, just like his father before him.

Figure CX-Part Three; the ruins of Arbroath Abbey, in the care of Historic Scotland

6TH MAY 1320- Within the walls of Arbroath abbey the king had set up court; in a private withdrawing room where he was accepting visitors only by his express invitation. The heavy oak doors of this royal chamber opened with somber decorum; through them strolled a family a younger Robert Brus had once encountered in Douglasdale. The king looked up to see James Lord Douglas escorting Lady Eleanora Douglas Bagot on his arm. Following the couple were more Douglases: Archibald Douglas and Lady Beatrice de Lindsay Douglas; Hugh of Douglas, Canon see of Glasgow; Walter and William, the sons of Lord Douglas; John and the wee Eleanora, the children of Archibald; and finally a small group of the private servants of these lairds and ladies including Ana. "Dear Lady Eleanora, we meet again under better circumstances I do pray," began King Robert. Ellie curtsied and kept her head bowed in deep respect. "Our Lady Eleanora wishes to speak," James said gaily. "Lord Robert," she began quietly; but the king was already interrupting her. "Not King Hobbe?" Brus asked with a bemused look. "You do flatter me with your fair words, addressing this king as 'Lord Robert'!" he said mimicking the lady.

Ellie flashed a somewhat glaring look at James. "That my son has shared my foolish words most said in confidence," she replied; her jaw slightly clenched in feigned pique that Lord Douglas had revealed her private name for Robert Brus, the same moniker that Edward Plantagenet placed on him years ago. Robert smiled broadly and then it was James' turn to interrupt. "That Lady El so promised this laird, *when King Hobbe to seise our James to our Douglasdale will this lass address him most as King of Scots and not one day before!*" Ellie flushed; she felt these knights were having too much fun at her expense. "That Lady Douglas, must so remind you kind and gentle men that to be in your very presence here and not under your arrest is the highest act of treason to *dear Edward Caernarvon*; risking my very life for this good council does this lass demand of your respect!" she told them pointedly, then raised her head brandishing the well known Douglas smirk.

Robert's laughter was boisterous and genuine; le Hardi's widow and her sharp tongue had caught him off guard. But now it was his turn to venture a surprise of his own. The king motioned to his squire to bring one of his personal daggers to them, carried ceremoniously on a silk pillow marked with the king's armorial bearings, the lion rampant. "Lady Eleanora, it is lang time due that this king should offer his deepest of condolences for the loss of Sir William le Hardi; his martyred end in defense of Scotland's freedom will now be recognized by Robert, King of Scots." Ellie's eyes filled with tears immediately; her body shook with emotion that she could not speak for some time as she marveled at the sentiment. She leaned into the strength of James' chest for support; feeling weak from the words of Lord Robert for her Gilley The king handed her his dagger. "One that was carried into battle at Bannockburn," he told her quietly.

When Lady Eleanora regained her composure she began to laugh at herself. "That this lass will be doubly safe when in Essex; to carry not one but two such daggers, from brave Scots both," she chuckled as she pulled back her surcote to reveal le Hardi's sheathed dagger hanging hidden on the belt of her cote; the one she had given him on the event of his fortieth birthday. "Mother!' exclaimed James, "no weapons are so allowed in the presence of the king save mine and few others," he said incredulously. Ellie looked her son up and down and scoffed at his concern. "No truer subject is Lord Robert most to have!" she proclaimed indignantly. "For by his grace and true generosity we are seised again to Douglasdale, your father's true paradise, sure aye!" his mother reminded him. Ellie was referring to the charter the king issued to James, as the son and rightful heir of Sir William le Hardi Douglas; one month before at the Court in Berwick. Then Ellie turned her eyes to look directly at the King of Scots as she quietly thanked him. "Most grateful is this widow; your good tribute for my husband, my dear Gilley the only man that I have ever loved."

"That some credit so belongs to you as well dear Lady Eleanora; three sons you have given to our Scotland; all now in service to their king," Robert said. Then he told her that for her anonymity he had arranged a safe departure through the postern gate of the abbey. "Most grateful too is this laird for you good words of warning. The conspiracy you most heard; the sentiments most spoken by your stepson Lord de Ferrers with his vassal and kin, that rascal Murdac proved most true." Ellie was stunned; she had almost forgotten about the plot of treason she had theorized to James, overhearing Murdac, Sir William and the others in their plans. The bold scheme of the disinherited English lords to murder Lord Robert was accurate after all; the traitors would be brought to justice by summer's end she was told. "Pressured to reveal the conspiracy our dear Murdac came forward with the names of many; he was told our knowledge came from another; a Scottish widow with Comyn sympathies; a woman who truly did confirm what you had most told us," James explained, assuring his mother that the information could not be traced to her.

Then Lord Robert presented the charters that had been witnessed by other Scottish nobles of rank including Duncan Earl of Fife, Randolph Earl of Moray, Gilbert de Hay, Robert de Keith Marshall of Scotland and many others; their seals affixed at the end of the official documents. "To our most loyal knight and true servant to this king, Lord Douglas," Robert proposed as he gave the parchments to James. The manors bestowed upon the laird included Jedburgh with the castle, the town of Bonjedward, the Forest of Jedworth and finally the manor of Stabilgorton in Eskdale. The Eskdale manors were those recently resigned by John de Lindsay a canon; the future Bishop of Glasgow, the kin of Lady Beatrice, withdrawing his claim to these lands; waiting for his confirmation from the Pope to fill the vacancy of that see. "These lands shall add in great total to your holdings in Polbuthy of Moffatdale." James smiled broadly. "Good king, that you most know of all such charters only one does this lad so covet: the barony of my dear father, given to this lad on that fateful day, one month now gone," he said; admitting that only the lordship of Douglas truly mattered to him; the other holdings were superfluous.

CLACKMANNAN-The Douglases were making their way south from Arbroath towards the Firth of Forth, on their way home to a Ceilidh in Douglasdale. Ellie was in her glory; explaining the significance of every monument and ancient stone they passed along their journey. When they stopped in Clackmannan she led her grandchildren to see the great monolith standing near the old kirk. "First founded by St. Serf seven hundred years now gone, this ancient place of worship was the center of the village for this great port," she explained, giving them many details on the construction of the holy place. James then told the wee ones about the monolith of the ancient ones; the stone named for Celtic God Manau. "Many kings were so crowned near this great site."

But it was Archie, acting like a wee lad himself, who had the most questions for his brother. The squire was very curious for the identity of Manau; wondering aloud how the ancient ceremony proceeded when great leaders were proclaimed king. James took the time to explain everything clearly; Ellie reflected that he truly reveled at his father's ways. "The religions of our noble ancestors included many gods; this Manau was the great God of the Sea. Our father had so told this lad before; this same Manau so revered for all his glory on the Isle of Mann as well," he boasted.

Figure CXI-Part Three; the ancient monolith at Clackmannan; the top boulder was placed on the great stone in a more recent century

The wee ones were riveted to their latest discovery; the size and shape of the old boulder intriguing to youngsters who grew up with farm animals sharing the courtyard of their home. Young William demanded to know the significance of the monolith. Archie's son John chimed in as well; brandishing the Douglas smirk, for he knew the answer before he asked the question. Ellie blushed; James saved her from embarrassment as he told the wee ones the story behind the great stone. "That very long ago a great king's prowess was most measured by his many children, brave sons to follow him in battle. Such shape conforms to his great stature; his true maleness," James explained expecting his words to end their queries. When his nephew John pressed the matter further it was the wee Eleanora who ended the discussion. "That lang times now gone the women of this great land were most to be quite large!" she reflected, her eyes wide in wonderment for the thought. Ellie gasped then chuckled; her granddaughter had quite a way about her, wanting to make sense of everything.

Figure CXII-Part Three; standing stones, on Torry Bay near Oakley; photo by Susan Shane

    The next day the family traveled to the shore, towards the ferry where they would make their crossing of the Forth. They rode their palfreys along the coastline westward and stopped to admire a great stone circle not far from Oakley. "This spring weather," Ellie cooed, "to remind this lass of her most favored time surrounded by the fragrance of the Bluebells!" Ellie and Ana were exchanging glances; recalling memories of other times when both ladies were younger and le Hardi was with them. Here again they were at the banks of Torry Bay, resting their horses and enjoying meat pies with ale and sweet wine. "Grandmother," squealed the wee Eleanora as she ran towards Ellie. In her hands she carried a fist full of Bluebells. "Where did you so find these?" Ellie asked her six year old namesake. "Uncle James," she said; revealing the ruse of Lord Douglas. "That you should know our father is most with us; to travel to our home again, a charter in our hands that proclaims our Douglasdale is for Douglases again!" he told her.
    James was making his way towards Ellie as he spoke; carrying in his hands the Douglas charter chest. Ellie giggled and thanked him for his words. "The Bluebells most as well; that this lass should know my Gilley, your sweet father is with us most this day." It was his way she told herself; she was turning to get up, but James stopped her. Lord Douglas was not content; there was more he said. He opened the ornate lid of the small chest. Ellie noticed the coffer was now engraved with a design of cloisonné. "What splendor!" she cooed looking over the inlays. The carved leather covering of the outside she recognized; decorated by the hand of Eleanora when she painted the Douglas armorial bearings thirty years ago; the arms of the Chief

William le Hardi; in bright colors of azure, silver for the mullets and red for the three salamanders that walked through fire, as Gilley used to say.

"That I must allow us all to hear the words again of our most beloved king: *to Jacabo de Duglas filio et heredi Willelmi de Duglas, militis*; that he most grants our Douglasdale to this proud son and heir of Sir William de Duglas," James proclaimed for all to hear. Ellie's eyes filled with tears as she hugged her son in a strong embrace; thanking him again for all he had sacrificed to make their dream a reality. They shared the silence in private prayer before Lady El mounted her jennet to continue the journey to the Douglas barony. She sighed audibly, breathing in the soothing sea air; they were finally returning to their homeland, held again in chief by a royal charter of their king. "A promise made and kept," she reminded Gilley, knowing he was listening to her thoughts this day.

Part IV and Epilogue
1320 to 1330

DOUGLASDALE SUMMER 1320- The laird of Douglas was in the withdrawing room of Park Castle; several knights of the kingdome were with him to witness a charter. James was granting lands to his youngest brother Archie for his service; sufficient that he might be presented to knighthood, a freeholder and good soldier of the realm. The next day it was planned that the entire Douglas clan, along with many of their friends and kin would attend the sacred ceremony in the family kirk where Archibald of Douglas would be dubbed by James Lord Douglas, Knight Banneret. On the eve of the adoubment, Ellie and Beatrice stayed up until dawn in the great hall of Park Castle; chattering away about how much their lives had changed since first they met twenty-five years ago; what miracles had come to them, tragedies as well. Beatrice's son John and young Will, the son of James and the late Lady Joanna sat with them; eager to hear the tales of their grandfather le Hardi; Sir Alex as well, grandfather to one, great uncle to the other; how these brave knights fought Edward Plantagenet; the ruthless king and fearless campaigner that everyone most loathed. Ellie was sharing her memories of William Wallace visiting Douglas Castle. Just then Lord Douglas joined them, in time to retell stories of le Hardi's battles and especially those fought with Wallace. "Scotland's brave patriot and hero of Stirling Bridge," he reminded them.

Archie was in the kirk; he had been bathed earlier in the day in ceremonial fashion by Lady Beatrice and Lady Eleanora. A white silk cote never worn before was brought to cover his nakedness, followed by the deep purple surcote of rich velvet, trimmed in gold, once belonging to his father. Sequestered in the Douglas kirk he made his way towards the altar where he would stay the night. The ornate floor tiles felt slippery and cold on the soles of his silk slippers, made expressly for the special occasion by the fair hand of Lady Beatrice. The squire prayed for hours in plaintive vigil as was his requirement. At one point he nearly fell asleep but for the howling of a Deerhound at the door of the kirk. Archie felt jolted from his apparent reverie. He looked out the door from the porch of the kirk; a swift shadow, a black form resembling a Deerhound shot past the squire in the dark of the night. For some silly reason he thought of Shamus; the wee hound who was his first friend. Then the squire, soon to be a Douglas knight, returned to his prayers.

The next morning Sir James performed the solemn rite; Hugh the canon and designated priest said the Holy words, while young Will and John with

Beatrice's brothers performed the other roles required for the ritual. James dubbed his brother dutifully in "God's good grace and service." James' son adjusted the golden spurs to fit the right foot of the knight, while John did the same for the left foot of his father. Two de Lindsay knights girded on the new sword belt appropriately on Archie's right side for his left-handed manner, while Hugh spoke. "This sword has two sharp edges to so remind our good knight: loyalty and justice are now one." Archie then unsheathed his father's sword; given him by Lady Eleanora on the occasion of his knighthood.

Sir Archibald's wife cried her tears, her eyes red with joy for Archie's greatest accomplishment; Lady El smiled, glowed in satisfaction; Ana wiped back the tears flowing freely down her cheek while Sir David beamed with pride, his own tears streaming from his face, staining his de Ferrers tabard. The day was glorious; the sun shining brightly to herald in one more brave, Douglas knight for Douglasdale. Lady Beatrice proudly announced as well that yet another Douglas heir would be born to them in the spring. Archie grabbed his bride, held her up for all to see, amidst her shouts of defiance, 'Sholto beast!'

When he brought her down again, Sir Archibald placed her in a chair as he knelt before his bride. Taking out a small scroll, he opened it as he took her hand in his. "Lady Beatrice, from your Poet Knight," he began. He told her that while in the midst of a strange reverie during the night as he prayed a vision of his dearest love and wife appeared before him; that he almost felt her presence in the kirk. "That you were in the great hall with the others I most knew; perhaps to write some words for you this knight so decided," he said softly. He declared his love for her before everyone; then read the poem.

Forever yours in time...
Eternal majesty
Sweet bliss of perfect gentleness

Oh Spirit of my heart
Replete with hardy sentiment
And golden voice

To you I pledge my essence

To great cheers Sir Archibald presented the scroll to Lady Beatrice. The Ceilidh was beginning in the great hall of Park Castle. James led his followers and kin to a splendor of great pageantry. The stately trumpets sounded their arrival; Lord Douglas was announced; on his arm was Lady Douglas; "our dear matriarch and sweet mother," he said jovially. Lady El wrinkled her nose in feigned disdain for his words. "Matriarch; such sentiments to cost you dearly," she teased. "Perhaps to add more water in your wine before you speak again Lord Douglas!" Ellie added with a smirk. The Douglases, their kin and many vassals took their seats around the trestle tables for the feasting and good wine. The calls came from the gallery; pray, would Sir James of Douglas join with them to play the wee pipes? "That this lad would be most proud to do so!" he exclaimed happily. He played three tunes before retiring from the performance. The knights, squires and their ladies danced and sang and celebrated; laughed at the minstrels and gossiped with their friends during the entremets. Great trumpets sounded songs; the drums beat through the melodies; as a merry night of entertainment rained down from the gallery.

Figure I-Part Four; the terraced cart path to Park Castle motte

    The kitcheners were bringing more of their steaming platters up from the cellar ovens; pungent fragrances wafted up the turnpike stairs to the delight of all. Ellie and Lady Beatrice had planned the menu with Ana's help. There were roasts of lamb stuffed with salt pork, covered with a sweet mint-green sauce and roast kid served with the mouth-watering sensation of the golden glaze of saffron and cloves. Ellie beamed while the guests expressed their excitement. As the next courses were being carried into the great hall, many game birds graced the tables, including Squab smothered in almonds and exotic spices brought forth on smaller platters made of seasoned breads for each guest to enjoy. Then larger wooden service plates, one delivered to every table, arrived filled with pheasant and grouse; some were seasoned with garlic, others simmered in red wine with cloves, ginger and cinnamon to enhance the flavor.

And of course Eleanora included her favorite: eels in a dark sweet sticky sauce. She devoured her personal platter of the specialty almost immediately! The pages poured sweet wine and mead in great quantities; bringing ale as well. When the desert was served several hours later the guests were surprised to see so many choices with delicacies that had not been served in Scotland in such quantities for many years. In addition to the many puddings, there were poached pears in seasoned syrup; sweet cakes with spiced honey; and marzipan tarts. James recalled the Ceilidhs of his father le Hardi as he looked about the great hall; reflecting with satisfaction that Lady El had outperformed herself again. "Thank you dear mother and Lady Beatrice for the splendor of this feast here," he said happily. The laird of Douglas was truly home in his Douglasdale at last; surrounded by his family in loving harmony of generations past.

SCONE, THE BLACK PARLIAMENT AUGUST 1320-The de Soules conspiracy to assassinate Lord Robert was foiled without grave incident to the King of Scots. Murdac Menteith was ingeniously persuaded to reveal his knowledge of the plot. A countess came forward to provide more evidence as well. But no mention was ever made of a lady from Essex who overheard the words in Groby manor many months before of a vallet named Menteith and a lord named de Ferrers. The names suspected in the scheme included those of Graham and Mowbray. Many of the perpetrators were executed; others fled in their great fear, seeking Edward's asylum. Ingram de Umfraville successfully persuaded Lord Edward to reseise him to his English lands; renouncing Scotland and her king forever was his claim. And all the while Lady Douglas had returned to Essex well before the trials began; her identity kept secret for her part in exposing the plot. What Ellie had not been told was that conspiracy included other Scottish lairds destined for the point of a treasonous sword. The English sympathizers planned to murder not only Robert Brus, but also Lord Douglas, the Earl of Moray and Walter the Steward to insure against another insurrection when Lord Robert's death was proclaimed throughout the realm. Fortunate for Scotland de Soules and his rogue conspirators were not favored in their gain; many hanged cruelly for their foolish intentions.

NEWBATTLE ABBEY SEPTEBMER 1ST 1321- There on the oak clad banks of the South Esk James Lord Douglas was collecting his witnesses for a charter of lands he was conveying in gift to another one of his loyal adherents: 'Roger de Moravia, son of the lately deceased Archibald of Moravia'. The charter was careful to define the boundaries of the grant of Fala, in the barony of Heriot, lands once held by their Flemish ancestors. "The de Duglas and de Moray immigrants who first settled in these Borders," he reminded his cousin. "That you are of my own blood, a true and loyal soldier in service to his laird, this land is gifted you in freehold," he told Roger. And as with everything James did, he recalled well the lessons of the past, learned at the knee of le Hardi. "This Lord Douglas made sure to obtain the water rights for the manor in perpetuity," he advised his cousin. He used his influence, pressing his case upon the abbey with lands residing near the manor to issue another charter for a rent of 3 shillings annually to guarantee the rights. "That the abbot has pledged to secure for one Roger de Moray the privilege of drawing water from the moss, west of the Derestrete way; the Roman road most there," James assured his cousin.

Figure II-Part Four; a farm on a single track road in the Moorfoot near Heriot Water

During the course of several years James had acquired many charters from King Robert. He then would seise manors to his kin and vassals; repaying their allegiance over the years by gifts of lands. To his brother Hugh he granted the canon's request for a bovate of land in Crookboat; that he might build a chapel there dedicated to St. John the Baptist, fulfilling his vow of seven years ago at Bannock Burn. Hugh would begin building the chapel he promised; but these plans were thereafter delayed, the small kirk was not completed for nearly two decades. By now the Lord Douglas held lands in many shires; in Douglasdale, Moffatdale, and in the broad scope of The Forest, which included Jedburgh, Selkirk, Ettrick, and Traquair; adding manors in the barony of Bedrule in Teviotdale; the constabulary of

Lauderdale including part of the de Quincy barony that Ellie and le Hardi held of her dower; lands of Cockburn in Berwickshire, with many more to come to him.

WILBRIGHTON HALL LATE SUMMER 1321- Sir William Bagot was serving in the retinue of his king but not in Wales, Ellie was told; that was where Humphrey de Bohun was leading an uprising against Lord Edward. The Earl of Lancaster was poised ready to assist him but he drew up his army, hesitating to begin the strife. Nicky de Segrave had been staying with de Bohun and in his loyalty came face to face with the king's forces. De Bohun and others made fast their escape, joining with Lancaster in the north their plan they told the de Segrave knight. Nicky was supposed to be in that retinue, but he was unable to make the journey. Two of his varlets were killed by Edward's loyal vassals; the knight was badly wounded, dragged by his servants and one remaining squire to a secluded tenement until he could be moved to a more secure hiding place.

Figure III-Part Four; armorial bearings of Nicky de Segrave the younger from the 19th century translation of the Roll of Arms of the Princes, Barons, and Knights who attended King Edward I to the siege of Caerlaverock 1300, by Thomas Wright

Nicholas de Segrave determined that his fugitive status meant he could not return to Stowe or any of his other manors. Led by his squire the servants carried him in a litter to another place Nicky deemed was safe for his recovery. The strange caravan traveled by night; secretly bringing their lord to Wilbrighton Hall. Lady Bagot bid her cousin and his small entourage into her manor at once; taking charge of the situation she was barking orders in a clipped delivery. "Take Sir Nicholas to my chamber," she told them. The weakened warrior managed a smile. "That this knight has so achieved his fair privilege," he teased Ellie as he was brought to the privacy of her apartment. "My Ana will be here to watch over your recovery!" she hastily replied brandishing a smirk. "But before you heap your good self upon the linens of this tester, a hot bath and clean garments are my intentions here," she told him pointedly.

Ellie's cellarer and Nicky's man-servants were bringing in a large wooden tub; trailing behind them were kitcheners with buckets of hot, steaming water. Ann followed with oils of lavender and rosemary. Nicky was too weak to protest as Ellie began to take off his coif and mail hauberk. Then as she removed his surcote, she gasped. A gapping wound was oozing blood in a mass of greening flesh, coming from under his right arm, running through to his back. Ellie had seen many injuries before; but never one so infected as this one. "Ana, summon Sir David to bring forth the Hospitaller from Stebbinge Park," she said quietly, but firmly. Ana understood; the priest was the only one Eleanora knew that shared of Gilley's healing knowledge having read his writings with her son Hugh. "And bring our healer's coffer; the maggots most as well," she said. Leaning over her cousin she now knew from where the awful smell originated: the putrid flesh of the poorly treated wound. Nicky looked up at her wistfully. Her eyes moistened as she bent forward, intending to kiss him gently on the forehead. The old soldier was not wasting his chanced opportunity; he summoned all his strength to move his head at the last moment that she found herself kissing him on the lips. "Rogue; this lass is most a married lady," she reminded him.

Nicky watched Ellie intently as she removed the remainder of his clothing with the help of his squire. To the warm water of the bathing tub, Ellie added boiled barley water to stimulate his health; it felt good he mused as she gently washed his body. "An angel in my midst," he sighed aloud. "Hush with you; conserve your strength for you will need it," she instructed. Then Ellie told him what she must do: after applying a poultice of herbs to deaden the pain she would press him with a cautery iron; a hot piece of metal to cleanse the injured tissue. "Then to take the goose fat, with some deer and goat tallow as well; added with a wee tinkering of belladonna, all that I have this day for pain." Nicky nodded; he expected as much he told her. "No blood letting," she calmly informed him, "my William said such practice did not serve him when he was near of mortal injury at Fawdon."

Several hours passed as Nicky slept. Ellie was patiently sitting in a chair beside her bed that was now occupied by the handsome knight. Her Deerhound Robert was lying beside her on the floor, with one eye open, watching the intruder to his bed. And when Nicky began to stir, coming to a conscious state the wet kiss he felt was not from his cousin, but the wee hound who understood his weakened state. "Who is this?" he demanded. Ellie was laughing so hard that Ana came running thinking something had happened. "Sir Robert is most hoping for your fast recovery dear Nicky," she exclaimed. "For you good sir yet rest on his side of the bed!" Nicky wrinkled his brow. "Robert?" he questioned. "Named for the good bishop; my dear friend, Robert Wishart, the dreaded enemy of dear Edward!" she proclaimed, telling him as well that James thought it might amuse her to have a hound bearing the moniker of a great Scottish rebel.

Ana stood chuckling in the doorway; Nicky's squire at her side. She offered to bring a tasine; perhaps some food. The knight accepted gratefully. "That you must tell of no one that this knight is here," he whispered to Ellie, confiding his status as a fugitive. "This lass does her part most well; taking in good traitors to our Edward," she teased him. "That I am most returning from my Scotland," she boasted. He smiled; admitting he already surmised as much. "This knight knows of your fair flight: that each spring you travel to Northumbria, to slip through the pass into Scotland then return unnoticed to our England," he teased. "And most as well this cousin has so heard of others to meet with your James; to treat of peace in true conspiracy to Lord Edward to join of their forces against our common foe," Nicky added. "De Bohun is going north to stay with Lancaster by this very day." Ellie nodded her understanding; Nicky had become the knight-errant after all she mused.

Several days later the healing priest arrived with Sir David; he marveled at the recovery of the injured soldier. "A wound as this might mark the end of most," he stated calmly. "But fortunate for you good knight you found this healer of renown to mend your tattered self." Ellie was grateful for the priest's arrival; exhausted from the days and nights of tending to Nicky, she begged to take her leave; sleeping nearly an entire day before returning to his side. "That you are sitting up this day most pleases this lass," she told him as she sat down beside him on her bed. Nicky took her hand and held it tightly in his. "The priest most tells me that you saved my life," he said quietly. He looked into her eyes and surveyed her face, his gaze traveling down past her shoulders. "That you no longer wear the wimple," he sighed as he drew his fingers to touch her chin then move them gently to caress her uncovered neck. Ellie blushed; she had only recently decided to no longer wear the full veil and wimple. Discarding the neck covering was a big step for her as only Gilley saw this area uncovered.

"Were your cousin a lad and not this haggard knight approaching the age too old for duel," he speculated only to spasm in coughs; wince in pain for the dislodging of his injured chest. Ellie immediately brought him thickened honey with herbs. Then she called for Ana to prepare a special remedy she wanted for Nicky. When it arrived Ellie administered the tasine of water mint with sage and cinnamon. "To remove the phlegm and suppress the cough" she told him. Nicky frowned in exasperation. "That most each and every time this knight so tries to caress your fair self, my affliction so betrays the effort," he scoffed. Ellie chuckled; reminding him her chamber was only his until he recovered from his wounds.

Weeks went by; Ellie was surprised how quickly time was passing for them. Nicky was showing signs of improvement; but he had lost a great deal of weight so that his stamina was still threatened. His wit and sense of humor were not deterred however; he constantly teased Ellie about everything. "That you must spare this lass your words this day," she told him. "For I am putting forth a challenge to you, my Lord of Stowe: a game of Merels." Nicky was holding in his laughter, trying not to put pressure on the deep wound still healing in his chest. "That you would know of strategy?" he asked feigning his indignation at the offer. "This lass has bettered such knights of renown as the Black Douglas," she admonished him playfully. "Please; pray you now; do not continue with this teasing," he begged her, with tears streaming down his face in his struggle not to laugh. "That your pain does serve you rightly; to make fun of this fair cousin is a sin, I do know it!" she said in mocked disdain. It felt like old times only better to Sir Nicholas as he and Ellie sparred. Friends, kin, and nearly lovers the knight and his lady were enjoying a day in the shadows of war and unrest; hidden from Edward and Lord Bagot, they celebrated a life long love affair that could not be for them in any other way.

The days of fall were fading into the raw chill of a portending winter. The fields of villiens were barren; the crops growing harvested. Lord Bagot was in Wales; Lord Segrave was in Wilbrighton with his cousin, unable to return to Stowe as he was a rebel to his king. Enjoying a feeling of exuberance Nicky suggested they take a walk out of doors. "To stroll about as lovers should," he suggested wryly. Ellie was no longer protesting his insinuations; she slept in a separate chamber with her Deerhound in her bed and that was that. But the lady certainly enjoyed his company; the doting attention of her knight and cousin. Ana beamed as she saw the couple come into the great hall of Wilbrighton. "For the walking and the talking are you both to venture out?" she asked them good naturedly. "That our Lady Bagot allows this knight little more," he chided his cousin.

By November Edward was issuing writs; prohibiting Humphrey de Bohun and other nobles including Nicky to attend the meeting called by Thomas Earl of Lancaster for Doncaster. The king instructed the earl as well not to hold the meeting. He had already issued other writs that prohibited these rebellious nobles from collecting assemblies of men. But Ellie and Nicky were untroubled by Edward and his attempt to thwart the uprising of his nobles. The couple strolled arm in arm; they spoke briefly of the war but only to remember times of peace when their youthful enthusiasm marked their days with tournaments and parties. They took time to marvel at the countryside; the undulating hills of Staffordshire. The couple discussed the merits of the crisp, clean air of late autumn; speaking as lovers often do of many things, some pertinent, others frivolous. "This lass is most content this day," Eleanora finally admitted as she smiled up at her cousin.

Nicky stopped abruptly upon hearing what he considered to be inviting words, turned her slowly to him and kissed her warmly on the lips. Ellie returned his embrace; but as she held him to her she winced to feel the frail skeleton that was once the muscular frame of her handsome, robust cousin. His beautiful mane of golden hair was thinner, scraggly on top and turning grey; his gait was slow; halted by the many injuries of war. Was this how my Gilley would have aged she wondered? He interrupted her thoughts as he whispered into her ear. "Thank you dear Ellie for loving this foolish knight." She feigned a protest then giggled. "You have waited long enough; this lass will not renounce your claims to my fair sentiments this day. I love you most as well, though differently from," she began to say. But Nicky stopped her; he understood he said and he was satisfied with however she came to love him. "That we must celebrate our fair pledge of love with fine wine and feasting," he suggested happily as he led her back towards the manor.

Nearly three months had passed since Nicky first arrived, injured and weak from his encounters in Wales. Yet it seemed to Eleanora that he barely held his own; the knight was not gaining much weight, even as his stamina improved she mused. Then Ellie noticed something that made her nervous; spots of blood appeared on the linens of the bed; stains lingered in the chamber pot as well. "This lass will speak with the priest. Perhaps the old healer can put my worries to rest; I do pray so," she confided to Ana. Ellie had grown so accustomed to having Nicky around that she found herself surprisingly making plans for a celebration of Christmas and Hogmanay as well. She was chattering away in the great hall when the Hospitaller interrupted her cheerful discussion. "Sir Nicholas has collapsed," he told her solemnly. By the look on his face, Ellie and Ana knew he meant that Nicky was relapsing; possibly dying as well. Lady Bagot had been denying the significance of the signs; his fluctuating stamina and his inability to gain back the weight he lost from his once beautiful physique were indications of a lingering infection.

Ellie ran past the Hospitaller and to her cousin's side. He seemed to sense her presence and briefly opened his eyes. Through the rest of the day and night Ellie remained at his side until his body began to shiver in a spasm of fever. He awakened to a conscious state as he moaned, crying out for his pain. A knight who experienced excruciating injuries in battle must truly feel of agony to call out so, Ellie surmised. "Sweet lass, this knight feels the very warmth of life most leaving me; pray, keep away this dreadful chill," he pleaded. Lady Bagot took off her veil and removed her surcote; wearing only her thin cote she joined him in her bed, wrapping her body around his thin frame. The spasms and cramps subsided as the knight's fever broke into a comforting damp sweat. Ellie dared not leave him, leaning softly against his emaciated body; she kept vigil over her cousin. Nicky survived the night.

Figure IV-Part Four-view of a motte in the open field at Wilbrighton Hall

Ellie was still cradling him in her arms as he woke the next morning. He smiled up at her and she giggled. "Such a ruse you play that I might share this bed with you," she pouted playfully. "That my dreams have now been most fulfilled to have you here," he said triumphantly as he tried unsuccessfully to wrap his arm around her. "I truly love you my Nicky," Eleanora told him. The knight shook his head. "That this soldier most loves you more; for I am bigger," he teased. Ellie laughed again; he was joking in a silly way as Gilley would have done. "No; that this lass…" her words trailed off; she could not profess stronger feelings; they would be untrue. Nicky was her favorite cousin and beloved friend, but he was not the knight she loved with all her heart. After twenty three years, that man was still le Hardi. Nicky noticed her pause but made light of it. "To be most truthful is your cross to bear my sweet Eleanora; this knight most knows the Scotsman's words are the ones you long to hear; not the loving sentiments of one named Nicholas," he chuckled. "Fetch me a baluster of wine that I might drown my sorrows, good cousin!"

Ellie bounded from the bed, promising to bring him a warm tasine instead to soothe him. "Then this lass will so come back to warm you most again," she teased. But when she returned Nicky was not moving, his eyes were open but she knew at once, he was gone from them. "How like your boastful self to be most gallant in the end; to leave my side when my eyes were gone from this chamber," she sighed softly. Then feeling Ana at her side, she began to sob. "He has taken his final leave from us," Ellie whispered, as she carefully closed his eyes. She begged Ana to bring the de Segrave squire and servants to assist the priest in his duties. Weeks before Nicky had been given the last rites, only to recover. Today the Hospitaller would prepare the knight's body for burial at Stowe. Ellie retrieved the letter the knight had written to his only heir and daughter; Lady Maud de Bohun, his other children having predeceased their father. She was yet at Peasenhall in Suffolk; he did not want to burden her, he claimed; that she might never know that he was in hiding at Wilbrighton Hall. Ellie commissioned Sir David to ride with his escorts and bring the lady back to Staffordshire. "She must come to know the man who saved my Gilley; the knight who held his truth above the greed that marks of other English lords," she vowed.

Several days later, after breaking her fast Ellie was seated in the withdrawing room of the manor; one by one Ana was to bring in Nicky's squire then his two servants. She began by telling the older man at arms her concerns. "This lass most needs to know your heart," Ellie confided reminding him of her ties to Scotland. Then she offered him a carucate of land should he decide to stay with her. "Good lady that we three once in Lord Segrave's service desire only to remain in your good household. Sir Nicholas had spoken to each one of us some weeks ago now," he admitted. Ellie was initially surprised then realized that Nicky was a lot like her William in many ways and would have arranged this for her. "To follow you; protect you Lady Bagot where ever you might chose to journey for we like our beloved and most missed Lord Segrave are rebels to our king. We pledge our good selves in service to you as most we did Sir Nicholas." Eleanora smiled sadly; sharing her feelings of loneliness for the knight's recent passing. She thanked the squire for his honesty; offered him the land again should he desire one day to be dubbed a knight of England. "Good lady; this squire wants nothing of such service for King Edward. His vile writs the very reason for the death of our beloved lord," he told Ellie adamantly. Lady Douglas replied; the land was his whenever he was ready; welcomed him to her household and he graciously accepted her kind offers.

LINTALEE LATE IN THE WINTER OF 1322-During the months following Nicky's passing, Maud de Segrave and her husband Edmond de Bohun were seised to the manors of Chrishall and Burleigh; as the rightful heir and daughter of Nicholas de Segrave, militis. His manor of Stowe he held of his late wife's dower, returned to the heirs of that family. But where Nicky never made the muster of the earl, his son in law later proclaimed his rebellion and joined those in the north. The Earl of Lancaster's army had grown to large measure with many nobles riding north to join with him; other's staying with that lord out of sheer desperation: their king was not protecting them from the Scottish raids. But Earl Thomas was hesitant to begin action against Edward. His indecision would eventually prove fatal to his cause and to the nobles who yet stayed with him; even his own life would be forfeit in the end. While the earl could agree with the stipulations of an agreement with the Scots, he was demanding a direct meeting with Lord Robert before confirming his treat of peace. But the king could not entertain such a meeting. Robert Brus was convalescing; the grave illness that beset him thirteen years ago was rearing its ugly head again.

During the interim of peace Harbottle Castle had been destroyed by the English as was required. James was writing a letter to Ellie though he realized it might be weeks or even months before the missive could be delivered to her; such correspondence might fall into the wrong hands he feared. So he took the time to write down the details of the Harbottle incident with pleasure. "For your eyes soon dear mother that you might know this: the fortress held of de Umfraville that once held prisoner of my dear grandfather is no more!" He reminded Ellie of the horrible attack; the one hundred infidels of Redesdale that rode the Cheviot in search of Douglas doom that treacherous day in 1267. "That most scurrilous of raids on our beloved Fawdon nearly bringing death to our sweet father and your dear husband; that grave assault is now revenged!" James wrote noting that Harbottle Castle's demolition was included in the treaty at his behest. "That *dear Edward so complied* has most pleased this Lord Douglas," he concluded to his mother. James and Archie celebrated; chortled openly for what they deemed was a great accomplishment. "That your revenge is most plotted far ahead; so patient is Lord Douglas, his strategy to take of many decades to complete," teased Archie. "Success so often follows a most relentless laird!" James boasted. He smiled; admitting his great pride for having a hand in that decision.

Few days passed from the expiration of the truce that James, Randolph and the Steward were again taking their retinues into the northern Marches of England. They brought fire and sword to the villages and towns. Lancaster was still procrastinating; he had not committed to an agreement with Lord Robert's 'lieutenant' as he fashioned Randolph, but he did agree to meet with another of Brus' trusted vassals, James Douglas, to discuss the treaty further. Archie was reluctant to leave Lady Beatrice; sending her back to their stronghold on the Douglas Burn was not to his liking either. With false bravado he assured her of what she must do; resigned to travel with James into Yorkshire he made her plans for the journey with the children, Hugh and Walter. "The winter travel back to the safety of our Blackhouse is most important," he told his bride. "That you will surely meet with peril traveling to Pontefract," she moaned.

Pontefract was the seat for the Earl of Lancaster; a half day's ride from Leeds in Yorkshire. Archie, James and their men at arms were traveling under the cover of darkness. "That we were taken to the castle at Knaresburgh; when this lad was but a knave," he began. Then he told Archie how he came to meet Nicky there. "Johannis de Hastings most as well." Archie always appreciated the stories James told about the times when le Hardi was alive. "Your words most help this humble knight to keep the memory of our noble father most here," he said, pointing to his heart.

James had sent two letters in code *to the bearer*; to be delivered to Earl Thomas. At their secret meeting that followed James presented a draft of an agreement from Lord Robert. Sadly when the Douglas entourage returned to Scotland, they arrived at Lintalee unharmed but with little else in closure for their efforts. As they broke their fast in the great hall at his fortress on the Jed the next day the Lord Douglas shared his concerns. "Lancaster is promoting folly I fear," he told Archie. Then James abruptly ended his repast before he had finished even half of it. He was visibly nervous this day and began pacing back and forth. The laird of Douglas had sent his spies to the Marches; the word returned was of growing trouble in the guise of one he knew: Andrew Harcla. "That noble commander at Carlisle; a true soldier who understands of battle," James scoffed fearing that Earl Thomas did not comprehend the peril he might be up against. "A fierce fight, sure aye!" Archie commented as he recalled their unsuccessful siege in Cumbria three years ago when his brother was almost killed. James was growing intolerant of the delays until Archie reminded him of words James himself once shared with a young squire years ago. "Our father so told us, all such occurrences come from the Divine; the timing most His for the Heavens to so complete." James solemnly agreed. The he cracked a smile. "That your knighthood has improved your good memory!" he teased his younger brother.

BOROUGHBRIDGE 16 MARCH 1322-Despite Edward's many writs de Bohun had ridden north to join with the Earl of Lancaster to take up arms against the king of England. Edmond de Bohun was also in his retinue; leaving behind his wife Maud de Segrave in the safety of Chrishall. The English nobles met in battle at Boroughbridge; the Scots could not come to their aid for Lancaster's own folly. The earl's continued insistence on a private meeting with Lord Robert sealed his fate in the end. The solemn word of the English nobles that they would welcome the Scots' support for their uprising; not take up arms against them ever again; and to seek a final peace with Edward on their behalf, never materialized. When they pledged their fealty to Lancaster the document the Scots most coveted was not included. For Edward this meant he would have his victory. De Bohun was killed in the battle; the proposed treat of peace with Lord Douglas was found on his body. Andrew Harcla was victorious again; Lancaster surrendered only to be tricked, that he did not flee in safety to Scotland. Edward's vassals posed a ruse; Earl Thomas put down his arms only to find himself under arrest for treason. The earl and his adherents were hanged cruelly, drawn and then beheaded; knights once staying with Lancaster were found hanged from village toll booths in most every shire. Lord Bagot's king was successful in suppressing the uprising of his nobles and Andrew Harcla was rewarded for his victory: Edward proclaimed the knight the Earl of Carlisle for his brave deeds.

DOUGLASDALE APRIL 1322-Hugh was in the chapel at Park Castle baptizing the new son of Sir Archibald and Lady Beatrice. "That you are baptized William in the name of our Father, the Son, and the Holy Spirit." He held the infant up near the tallow torch that lit the chamber so he could really take a look at his new nephew. "A Douglas lad sure aye," the canon chuckled. His eyes cast over the wee William, his body was thin and very lang in length; dark in countenance with the raven hair covering his head, running down his back. "That your grandmother will most believe you are le Hardi to come back to us!"

Archie watched from the doorway; he was mesmerized by the size of this hairy beast that was his second son. "Our cousin William Douglas with his father James to be the God parents for this lad," he quipped as Hugh handed the boy to his father. "Lady Beatrice your sweet mother is sleeping most already dear one; but soon to see her most again, I do promise you my wee laddie," Archie cooed to the child. "That we must write at once to my good mother and tell her of my latest son and heir!" he chortled. "When you meet our Lady El will you know of trouble," he scoffed. "To learn of Latin and fine dancing you will do or entertain her ire," Archie warned the wee one as if he understood. "And that you do not forget the Gaelic of our ancestors and good cousins," snickered Hugh. Archie rolled his eyes; he had just found someone to teach his children and nephew the languages; finally fulfilling the promise he made Ellie when she was last in Scotland. "Fear not my William for this good knight has found a lass to school you with your brother, good sister, your cousin Will most as well," he assured the boy. "None too soon," added Hugh teasingly.

LAUDERDALE AUGUST 1322-Edward had marched into Scotland again; bolstered by his great suppression of the uprising through his victory at Boroughbridge. But when he arrived in Lauderdale, he could not find an army to oppose him. Lord Robert had seen fit as well to remove the cattle and other beasts from their path; driving them into the inner lands. Then the King of Scots removed himself and his contingency north of the Forth to Culross; leaving James to monitor the English army's movement from his vantage point in the Marches. Edward and his adherents were estimated to consist of many thousands of infantry; a muster of armed foot with 2000 Hobelars or more; six thousand Welch men at arms and many soldiers from Ireland were also ordered to his muster. Levies were made on nearly every shire; to report with sixteen days of food per man. Edward was ready to do battle with the Scots!

The English rode through the Borders of Scotland not only unmolested but also all alone; neither beast nor man appeared along the way. Finding no animals to butcher or corn to seize they looked gratefully to the fleet of supply ships sent from England up the Firth of Forth. But the Flemings had other plans for the English cogs; stopping many, stealing their cargo before they reached the Forth. "That these traitors most aided our enemy the Scots," berated Edward. In total some fourteen ships with supplies were lost at sea; an equal number taken by the scurrilous thieves: the Flemings. The wasteland Lord Edward and his army found in Scotland coupled with the loss of many of their supply ships forced the English to a grim decision: retreat back into England or starve. On their way out of Scotland the English army set grave destruction upon Holyrood Abbey, burning the monastery; portending more devastation to come to God's houses.

Secured in his fortress in Lintalee the Warden of the Marches was listening to a group of his informants just returning from the Lothianes; the patrol sent to determine the movement of the English army in their retreat. The Douglas men at arms informed their laird that the English sacked the abbey in Edinburgh. "These men with tails are so inclined to retrace now their steps through the Lothianes, to come south," his sergeant said. "The army is spread out in search of food; that there is none, many of Edward's Hobelars with some of his armed foot are moving up ahead of his true course. We fear it is to the Abbey of Melrose they must go to find refuge for Lord Edward that he might bide a wee." The circumspect laird was looking away from his men at arms, already contemplating his strategy for a siege; this latest news intrigued him. "How many in their number?" James asked his sergeant. "If my laird would tell us three hundred you would be no a wrong in saying it."

"Prepare our leaving most at once," Lord Douglas commanded. Archie knew his brother was eager for a fight and these Foresters had brought him the battle he was waiting for; their shrewd observations the remedy for their disconsolate laird. To Archie, the preparation for warfare almost felt like a relief. "We will go to Melrose; to greet these English invaders and provide them the very best of hospitality we Scots can so devise!' he boasted. Lord Douglas' spirits had improved. For months he had mourned the opportunity lost with the Earl of Lancaster; delays and hesitation were not his manner once he decided to do battle. Fool hearty was the soldier who procrastinated once committed to a fight; such opportunities are seldom given, he reflected ruefully. "More lives are lost when a leader so hesitates than for one who might so blunder in his planned response; to lose of lives, but fewer."

Figure V-Part Four; the beauty of the Eildon Hills

North and west the Douglas men at arms rode their Hobini; towards the Eildon Hills, keeping themselves hidden within the confines of the Forest. James was chattering away with his brother. While his eyes were ever alert to their surroundings his words were filled of sentiments from other times. "That we are to share our destiny with that abbey and those foolish monks," he scoffed. Archie pressed his brother for more stories of the churchmen that plagued le Hardi so in Ayrshire. James obliged him happily. He told of the signage that their father had the farrier paint for him; directing the clergy to take the opposite direction than to their fortress in Mauchline. Archie was laughing boisterously; their father had quite a way about him he sighed. "And what is the history of this fair monastery he inquired. James told him that the prior holds the status of an Abbot and has for many years. "Yet he is an aging man; that laird most destitute for his holdings; many of the brethren most gone, forced to flee their devotions. There are not many in their number so surviving there for the wars," he offered sadly. "To say then this: we offer penance for our dear father for his vexed ways with these poorly monks that we have come to save them now from the wretched invader Edward," Archie replied. "Amen," James agreed; the sentiments were true he told his brother.

In the valley of the Tweed, beneath the shadows of the Eildon Hills the secluded monastery seemed to rise before them. "The wizard Scott, some say his bones to rest there at that place for God's good service," Lord Douglas offered jovially. Then James told Archie about the Queen of the Fairies, Queen Elfhame who was said to live in the fair Eildon Hills. "Known to us as well as the Trimontium for the ancient fort that lies there; those days lang gone when the Romans were invaders to our lands," Lord Douglas continued; intending yet again to explain everything in great detail just as le Hardi would have done. As he most did for this laird when but a knave, now grown James reflected. "That Thomas the Rhymer would come to this broad glen in search of that fair queen; seeking his refuge and retreat nearby at Huntly Burn; there in a grove surrounded by the strength of the oak and the mysteries of the ash, beside the beauty of the waterfall that flows into that wee burn." Archie listened intently. He always tried and with good success to commit his brother's stories to memory; to share them with the wee ones when they returned to Lintalee or wherever they were staying then.

The Tweed was fast approaching in their view; stretching wide before them to the east and west as they descended into the glen; riding for the abbey. James was perusing the countryside; looking for an advantage to each and every site for his ambuscade of the English. His mind was working feverishly Archie surmised by the intensity of his countenance. As they road down the craggy hillside James noted the location of the main ford that Edward would use in his approach; his hobelars too if they continued to proceed ahead of his entourage as they were doing two days ago. "To find the abbot and most quickly; then to set our camp so, over there," he noted. Within two hours James had sent out his patrol and was receiving the intelligence on the location of the king's army. He conferred with the priest; set his plan in motion; dispersing his bowman under the command of Sir Archibald while he would take the armed light horse, his followers on Hobini and lead them from the opposite direction; their onfoot, the remaining men at arms to follow when the signal from the oliphant was given.

In these Border raids the initial charge was not made by schiltrons but by a combined attack of their commander's available strengths. James sought a different objective than a standing army like the one at Bannock Burn. He devised a method where a continuous flow of armed men using several fronts and multiple types of warfare would engage the enemy in nimble formations that could change quickly. These small units were flexible and able to move throughout the battlefield should the need arise to change the attack strategy during the siege. James as always was to lead the charge; to give the war cry when he received the signal from his special lookout that the English were approaching.

Lord Douglas trusted this assignment to very few but today he put the task to someone new. His vassals would all be engaged in the fight so he accepted the kind offer of assistance from a strange volunteer to his wee army. A brave monk from the abbey offered to stand at the tower waving his spear high in the air to warn of the advance. When this brave Cistercian, a true patriot for Scotland gave his loud call, rang the church bells for all to hear the battle would begin. Surveying the inside of the abbey James felt overwhelmed by the stark beauty of the once exquisite chambers; the intricate carvings on the capitals and vaulted ceilings had sadly fallen into decay for repairs not made. He also noted with concern the condition of the few priests and monks in residence and for the two lay brothers who were blind. He ordered Archie to select from their good Foresters a small number of men at arms to stay within the walls of the abbey; to repel any English that might break through their lines. Archie knew immediately who he would choose to protect the defenseless monks and laymen held in the infirmary. Without another word he quickly went about his assigned tasks.

More Douglas scouts returned; the battle not far at hand they told James. Everyone took their positions; the friar mounted the turnpike stairs to the bell tower. James was waiting the ambuscade; his Hobini was sensing his nervousness with his own; but only snorted once as if to say: there, that is out of the way. Then from his vantage point Archie witnessed their approach: ten abreast riding the lighter armed horse just as they had been told. In the expanse of the glen these soldiers headed for the gates of Melrose Abbey; then they spied the monk brandishing his spear. "You have taken such stance to so frighten us good friar?" scoffed the English sergeant as he called out to the monk.

"Nay; but my friends might so accomplish that brave task!" he boasted waving the sword like a magic wand to call Lord Douglas and his wee army. The monk quickly retreated as was agreed to ring the monastery bells. The peaceful tranquility that wafted through the valley; the sounds of light summer breezes as they rustled through the Forest leaves followed by the soulful lament of tolling bells from the abbey church abruptly ended; the serenity jolted by the war cry of the Black Douglas! The trees began to shake, bending to the charge of armed horse as the frightening screams of an angry laird ripped through the glen: "A Douglas! A Douglas!" James called out as he led his men to take on the English. Then his squire and cousin, young William of the Lothianes sounded the old Crusader's oliphant.

The battle raged upon the English from every direction. From the rear these riders heard the swooshing sounds of arrows unleashed in their menacing flight by Archie and his bowmen. The paralyzing sounds made worse as the sharp heads pierced the warriors' flesh, hitting their marks with great regularity in ominous thuds. Men cried out their warnings for the ambuscade; others shrieked in abject misery for their painful injuries. James rode in front of his light horse with his sword carried in the high guard; his small shield in his right hand that also held the reins for his Hobini. He immediately attacked the English sergeant; unhorsed him; moved through the lines in lightening speed; taking full advantage of the surprise and confusion James was able to end the lives of seven English warriors himself that day.

Figure VI-Part Four; Melrose Abbey ruins; the Presbytery and vaulted ceilings

Archie called out for his men to move to higher ground; adjust their position, sending their arrows into flight to intercept more of the now retreating English. At one point James was engaged in battle with not one but two of the English warriors. He parried a blow with his small shield, attacked from the middle guard as he turned his Hobini away from a knight the very moment a second warrior onhorse, a younger squire charged towards him in the attack. Lord Douglas noted that the right arm of his opponent was holding a battle axe. Just then his own squire, his cousin William moved forward and intercepted the first knight; carrying his larger shield low the Douglas squire parried the cutting blow of his opponent. Then he swung his pony to the left as he bravely moved in for his charge. Young William's sword was held in the high guard; parried once by the

Englishman's shield, his second thrust was true; ending the battle for the warrior.

During his squire's able fight James deftly moved his Hobini to observe the attacking, younger Englishman and simultaneously catch his breath; suddenly he spurred his horse to the counter side of the axe wielding squire. Perfectly balanced as befit his well honed skills, James slowly threaded his shield on his sword belt freeing his right hand and as if part of the same motion he grabbed for his battle axe. Naturally left handed he was also ambidextrous as most knights were though more so for the insistence of le Hardi. James avoided the squire's weapon in the charge, turned his body and his horse in unison as he swung his weapon fiercely; striking his opponent; unhorsing the younger man by the solid strength of his blow. Just like my father showed me in his training lang ago, he reflected. Edward's vassal was injured in the fall, his final battle over as he met a Forrester's pole-axe.

The fierce fight was not over for Lord Douglas. He moved his horse above the fray to inspect the field. There raging before him came his next opponent: an English knight on an aging destrier; unusual for the contingency of light horse. James made his stance to accept the charge; he parried the knight's sword and quickly responded with a strong thrust moving from the high guard to the middle guard position. James' smaller sword cut the knight; the sharp edge of his blade sank into the warrior's flesh as James was hit by a small spray of warm blood from the Englishman's arm.

The knight was not ready to surrender; returning for a second attack. James readied his Hobini to take the charge again, parry the sword from its deadly thrust. As James made his counter attack the guard of his sword hit the Englishman's shield with a thud sending shock waves up his arm. "By St. Bride," he sputtered for the miss. James deftly spurred his horse back to the perimeter only to move forward again full tilt, his Hobini running at the wounded knight. His father's old standard hit hard against the warrior's mail hauberk then slipped off the armor to cut the knight's arm a second time. The Englishman turned in retreat; no longer able to wield his sword with any strength he was finished for the day. The rest of Edward's Hobelars scattered; some ran for the ford to withdraw from the field. The Scots on their Hobini did not pursue; Sir Archibald had the Tweed crossing well covered, their arrows hitting their marks to a deadly number.

The few English that escaped returned to the rest of Edward's army with frightening tales of the Scottish raid. The king, his nobles and their army were filled with anger and dismay at the success of Douglas that as they made their haste to the safety of the English Marches, the army stopped only to lay waste the Abbey of Melrose. James had tried with all his might to convince the priests to come with him to a place of safety; but the abbot

William de Foghou would not hear of it. "Lord Edward is most pious as was his father; to not molest us will be his choice," the abbot assured Lord Douglas. The laird was dubious of the priest's good faith; but there was no changing his mind he mused. "This knight must take his leave and quickly; here is coinage that you might say some prayers for the souls of the warriors who died here. And that you give proper burial to all as well," he said graciously. De Foghou thanked him; assuring James again they would be safe.

The English king and his army arrived the next day to rest at Melrose. Dear, pious Lord Edward, the king Abbot William so entrusted with his life chose to punish the clerics; to ransack the abbey, tear the sacred vessels from the altar; pillage and burn the church. Then Edward's army proceeded to slaughter two lay brethren, blind and sick that were housed in the abbey infirmary, killing the aging abbot and another monk as well; scattering the rest with vicious injury. Four years later the Good Sir James was given the task to monitor the payments for the abbey's restoration where Robert Brus commended many thousands of pounds for the rebuilding the magnificent structure destroyed during this villainous attack. Edward Caernarvon had achieved a coveted goal this day: to be most like his father; emulating in perfect degradation the butcher king, Edward Plantagenet.

RIEVAULX ABBEY YORKSHIRE OCTOBER 1322-Ellie reluctantly decided against her trek north to Scotland; Edward's invasion into her homeland kept her travels limited to Staffordshire and Essex. She had more family members to consider she prudently counseled herself. The daughter of her beloved Nicky and wife of Edmond de Bohun was stripped of her possessions; her manors seized into the king's hands. Sir Edmond was in one of Edward's prisons; his lands and those of his wife Maud de Segrave were taken for his rebellion. The lady and her household were now the invited guests staying with one of Edward's loyal subjects: Lady Bagot of Woodham Ferrers, Stebbinge Park and Wilbrighton Hall, Essex for the two former and Staffordshire the latter.

James and Archibald had barely returned to Lintalee when they were summoned to a muster with their king; eighty thousand Scots including a large numbers of Highlanders and Islesmen made their way to Yorkshire. Edward was resting in Rievaulx Abbey, issuing more levies for his army and waiting for new members to assemble. Lord Robert upon hearing of the king's location began moving his army swiftly; proceeding through the secrecy of the most rocky and inaccessible region in Sutton Bank known as Blakehoumor. Desolation marked the Scot's path of course; fire and sword the signature of their passage through the countryside. The Scots proceeded without stopping until they came upon the Earl of Richmond, Sir John of

Brittany and his command of a large force of English armed foot and horse entrenched in Yorkshire near Biland.

"To delay our march; take another path would allow Edward his fair chance of escape," Lord Robert told his council of Scottish commanders. Then he explained what needed to be done; a bold and dangerous plan he conceded that he asked for volunteers. James Douglas was the first to step forward; he would lead his men up the face of the rocky brae or entice the English to come down to fight him. The king accepted and the bravest of Scotland's men at arms volunteered to assist him.

When James returned to his own retinue he told them all including Archie of the king's intentions. "Lord Robert asked of volunteers to come most willingly; that this laird most stood first," he boasted boyishly. Archie rolled his eyes; scoffed under his breath. Then Sir Archibald rose from their group and went directly to his horse. He saddled the beast himself and started loading up his belongings; looking as if he were going to take his leave of them. "Just where are you most going?" asked James incredulously. "Home to Lady Beatrice and my sweet children. You most said our king to beg of volunteers; this knight has of no such intentions," he said plainly. James told him he had to go; but Archie replied *no;* he would fight another time. "This lad is nay a coward; you most know it. That this foolish husband has not seen his bride in most seven months or more; to fear of Lady Beatrice more than Edward is my truth," he confessed. Lord Douglas started laughing; his brother was the bravest warrior he knew; but to fear a lass, he would not hear of it. "You will most return to that sweet wife in three weeks or less; this laird makes his promise to you good brother." Archie looked at James, breaking into a broad grin. "This lad will stay; if only to save your sorry self from grave injury or trouble!" he chided.

The battle began early in the prime; a cold brisk beginning with the sun rising later for the fall day. James led his men to the terrible raid; up the rocky face of the pass to where Lord Richmond staged his army. King Robert dispatched his Highlanders to the rear guard. While James shrieked his fearless war-cry, 'A Douglas! A Douglas!' the brave men of the Celtic northlands and their good cousins of the isles ran nimble as deer; climbing the great cliffs to block the other side of the pass. The English tried to pommel the Scots by rolling boulders and throwing rocks in their path. As arrows glistened through the first rays of sunlight the Scots kept coming, faster, higher; suddenly they were upon the English. James had been joined by Randolph in the fight; taking in surrender Henry de Sully; the French lord and Butler of France. James with Archie's alert assistance surprised another group of knights with their squires; overwhelming them in the battle the three French knights surrendered with their vassals to Lord Douglas.

The armorial bearings James seemed to recognize from their shields; but he dared not hope he told himself. "That this humble knight and your good prisoner, is most known to all as Robert of Bertram; there by my squire is Sir William of Bertram; the third of our fair party is most Sir Elias de Anillage." James doffed the fur hat that he wore on his helmet since the battle near Lintalee where another soldier named Richmond had perished in support of Edward. "A fair ransom," Archie chuckled when he heard their identities. "Nothing of the sort dear brother; to trade in more than riches with our king; that you and others of our retinue will share, I do swear it!" James told him.

Lord Robert was pleased with the siege; though King Edward made fast his departure. In pursuit of the English king was Walter the Steward with five hundred horse. Edward once again abandoned his Privy Seal to the Scots and many other treasures; leaving the protection of the fortress in only his bed-clothes, the king later made his escape, passing through Beverley to a ship on the Humber. Many English were slaughtered and those who were captured marked quite a prize. The Earl of Richmond took two years to collect his ransom, held in confinement for a tidy sum of approaching 14,000 merks sterling. But Lord Sully was set free without a fee. The prudent King of Scots instead put forth a treat of peace that this French lord most championed; acting as the emissary with the English.

James and Archie released their prisoners to the king; the ransom earned totaled some $4400 merks, including the sums established to free the French valets. Eventually these fees were set aside, granted to Lord Robert for a designation prized by many and held by none. The King of Scots would present the Emerald Charter to Lord Douglas for his charity with the three French knights and their squires this day. The Douglas laird, his brother Archie and their men at arms returned to Scotland by early November; James had sent ahead a small escort quite secretly to Blackhouse; returning their children and Lady Beatrice to Jedburgh Castle where they were staying. Archie was summarily surprised in the courtyard of that great fortress; greeted by the outstretched arms of a loving Lady Beatrice, ten year old John, seven year old Eleanora and his infant son the wee William. "That you are most safe," she cooed and Archie knew at once he was forgiven for the long absence.

THE HYDE STAFFORDSHIRE FALL 1324-Ellie and her household had returned to the Bagot manors for a funeral at the Coppenhall church. Lord William Bagot had fought his last battle; Eleanora Lovaine de Ferrers Douglas Bagot was again a widow. "This lass is too old for marriage," she scoffed at Lady Elizabeth's suggestion that she might have to take another husband. Approaching the age of fifty-six Eleanora was almost relieved to be making the funeral arrangements for her third knight named William. The de Grendons attended; the de Ferrers and some de Segraves too; the ceremony was not lavish but circumspect, recognizing a noble soldier who served his king. Ana was feeling ill herself and did not attend. Ellie at first dismissed her ailment; hoping it would pass quickly; certainly when they reached Fawdon she would be better, the widow reflected.

By the time Eleanora's household arrived in Northumbria, Ana was still complaining of discomfort and uncharacteristically admitting that her illness would keep her from traveling any further. For the first time in their forty-three years together, it was Ana who was ill and gravely so by her words and countenance Ellie mused. Lady Douglas as she fashioned herself now, requested Sir Thomas to go at once to Roxburgh. "Find our Hugh and bring him back to Fawdon, the noo." The priest arrived within a day and began his work at once. But Ana did not thrive; she became weaker that she asked Ellie to stay the night with her. "Not to leave your Ana's side I pray you," she begged helplessly; unaccustomed to such desperate illness. Ellie searched the healer's face; Hugh's eyes told her there was nothing he could do.

Lady Douglas remained with her Ana the night; holding her hand and wiping her brow trying to make her comfortable as the lady had done for her all her life. "My sweet Ana; this lass so loves you," Ellie whispered, kissing her on the forehead. The woman opened her eyes and spoke faintly as Hugh entered the chamber. "My dear Eleanora, my sweet lamb; this ring you most gave this lass so lang ago, the jewelry of Lady Martha, please give this to the wee Eleanora, my sweet pet." Then she drifted off into a sleep, deeper than any before. As the dawn rose over the Cheviot Hills Ellie's dearest friend and sweet companion, a woman she cared for and loved longer than she knew her Gilley, was gone from her. Ellie sobbed into her son's chest; her body shook uncontrollably as she cried for Ana. "My son; she loved us so; she lived only for our welfare, to take care of us in her life." Hugh held his mother; sitting her in his lap, staying there for hours as he rocked her. The loss he understood; Ana had always favored him over all the others. "This lad is most grateful that you called for me," he sighed as Ellie woke from her slumber. He helped her up as they made their way from the laird's chamber.

"Your good priest feels most a stranger here," he told his mother sheepishly as he looked around the great hall of Fawdon. Ellie called forward Nicky's squire and man-servants to introduce them to her son the canon. "Sir David begged to remain in Essex; he too no longer journeys to our Scotland," she added ruefully. Hugh asked the two servants Richard and Stephen to join him in Ellie's chamber; to begin the sad task to prepare Ana's body for burial at Fawdon. Ana made as her final request that she be laid to rest in the Cheviot; a place that was yet in England, in sight of her beloved Scotland as well. The funeral service was held in the Ingram church three days later as required. But the other Douglas sons could not attend for reason of Edward's war, that they were outlaws. Another but much sadder burial behind them, Ellie and her household began the rest of their journey; slipping into Scotland but without her Ana for the first time in nearly four decades.

RATTRAY OCTOBER 1324-Archie was just returning to his fortress near Rattray Head; proudly showing his mother some of his elegant and extensive holdings seised to him by Lord Robert for his service. "That these are lands once held of the Comyn," he boasted. Ellie chuckled to ask him which one. "There were forty knights named Comyn in our Scotland when your father was born!" she reminded him. "The one so married to your cousin," he replied with a smirk. Ellie giggled; her son had paid attention to her teachings after all, she mused. Lady Beatrice wanted to stop at the kirk. "First to give our thanks for a most generous king and for our God who so returned our Lady El to us for some time," she told them, leading her children up the gate past the sea outlet where her new home stood proudly facing the open waters.

Figure VII-Part Four; Rattray kirk near Loch Strathbeg, the silted port site

"You so admit that there are other manors here as well?" Ellie inquired. Archie went on at length to list the lands that he now held in chief, including Crimond and the smaller estates residing between Rattray and that manor. "This lad to have of many charters; vast holdings including the carucates and messuages, once belonging to the Comyn are now held of this Douglas laird; to have of Cairnglas and others most as well," he stopped to take an exaggerated breath for emphasis as Ellie giggled for his ploy. "That in some weeks this lad will take you to our Morebattle," said Archie; telling his mother that the Borders manor was not far from Lintalee. "But a short ride of few hours from the beckoning call of Lord Douglas; to come do battle for our king," Beatrice chided. "And not far from good Hugh, his prebendary at Roxburgh Kirk," Archie reminded her.

In the great hall of the fortress that evening James joined his family; returning from Arbroath where he was with Lord Robert on business of the king's court. "Good mother! "So happy to see you," he exclaimed, running like a lad to grab Lady El in his exuberance. "Yet so sad for our grave loss; dear Ana, so much a part of our wee clan from Essex," he said poignantly. "That this lass so expects to hear of her good words; see her walk through the doors most there to greet us; I miss her so," her words trailed off. "And for Sir Nicholas most as well," he added. "Lord Bagot too; that our mother is a widow most again," Beatrice reminded them. By now Ellie was unable to contain her tears; she tried to introduce her new squire and servants, once in the household of the de Segrave knight. "These lads are new soldiers to our cause," Archie proclaimed trying to turn Ellie's attention away from her mourning. "Saor Alba!" he declared loudly. Ellie was trying to laugh; ease her pain of loss. "Our wee Archie; most silly in his ways," she chided him, pretending her admonishment for his behavior; "unbefitting his new position as a great laird of Scotland." Then she giggled, looking over to her oldest son. "Imagine James; our Henklebaldicus of Douglas squire, Lord of Crimond, Rattray, and Morebattle!" she said, brandishing a smirk. Archie just smiled; his diversionary tactics had worked; as James threw him an approving look for his successful strategy.

"Our grandmother has told us that our Gaelic lessons will now continue," ten year old Eleanora offered. Archie winced; the tutor he hired had decided not to travel with the family; something Ellie discovered the first hour of her stay. "And we will all be learning new dances from London!" she boasted. "Your mother has returned good lairds; to insure the schooling in good manners for our future Ladies and good Knights of Scotland," she told them with a wry smile; then she continued. "Our English knight to be and good squire here will build a new quintaine in every Douglas fortress; to begin the training of our Douglas men, as my Gilley would have done." James chuckled. "Welcome home Lady El; your son takes pleasure that you are here to stay. Set about your business with our good children and their training," he assured her; sincerely adding not to spare herself any expense for what was needed to complete her task.

Early the next day Ellie was with the farrier in the mews having her young mare saddled for a morning ride on the dunes of the Rattray coast.

She was startled to look up and see James about to join her. "Shall we go then in search of Bluebells," he teased her. Ellie smiled warmly and happily accepted. As they made their way through the fortress gates and over the drawbridge Lady Eleanora began to speak. "This lass is pleased to return home again; but with one regret; my Gilley is yet in our Essex with your sisters and my grandchild," she sighed wistfully. They rode over the sinking drifts of white soft sand that marked the coastline of Archie's manor as it flowed into the North Sea. "Dear mother; that promise this knight so made may yet come true," he reproached her. "By St. Bride this son will most bring back those Douglas bones; if only dear Edward would treat in peace that I might so return there," he said angrily. "Your father would disapprove of your swearing; my grave influence upon you I do fear," she said thoughtfully. James laughed heartily. "Those words of vile contempt this lad most uses every day and more when on campaign. If le Hardi does protest such sentiments he has not shown it," he replied. Ellie wondered aloud what his father might be thinking now. "That you have driven out Lord Edward; restored us to our lands and more," she praised him.

Figure VIII-Part Four; a motte is all that remains of the fortress of Rattray

James shook his head. "I often think on that myself these days; if he regrets most leaving us," he paused, glancing over at Ellie. The looks they exchanged no others could comprehend. As much as they both loved William, mother and son still held a grudge for his stubbornness that brought him to the Tower and his lamented end. "When this lass yet greets him in God's good Heaven; while I most ask!" she proclaimed, her face covered in a broad smirk. Then she sighed and poignantly added, "I miss him so; even when my dear Nicky was at Wilbrighton Hall; to fill my days with loving sentiments and his good words of comfort; all I thought about was Gilley," she confided. "Did he know?" James asked. Ellie shook her head yes. "That I could not hide my true feelings; the great love I yet hold for your dear father is my cross to bear he so told this lass," she offered. "Mine as well, dear mother; mine as well." Then Lord Douglas stopped his palfrey; got down from his horse and took her hand that she might join him for a walk along the water's edge. "This lad treasures your good company," he told her. "A special bond," he whispered. Ellie knew exactly what he meant: the lives they shared were forever changed with le Hardi's passing; neither feeling free again to live a life of love, that he was gone from them; leaving a wife and son with so great a burden; that to fill the void they soldiered on to their separate destinies, together but alone, without him, raging in their loneliness for William le Hardi Douglas now with God.

"He was so thin," she mumbled. James questioned who she meant. "My Nicky" she replied impatiently. "That his magnificent physique most vanished," she sighed. Ellie described in great detail the scars he bore; the painful gait that characterized his walk; one knee that was much bigger than the other. "And most as well, his hands were gnarled, one finger but a stump," she said sadly. "And the beauty of his hair most gone from him; the color now of grey, in wisps that topped his head where beautiful thick hair the color of the sun once lay; he was so proud of his great beauty; to turn many a fair lady's head," she reflected out loud. James chuckled at her observations. "You wonder if our father would have aged so?" he asked her. Yes she said shaking her head. "This lad knows most of injuries; my headaches that continue; a knee that most locks up when least I do expect it; a hand that deadens to no feeling; these foolish troubles to threaten me to grave harm someday," James prophesied. "Yes; this warrior most knows such discomforts and has such scars though years younger than that brave knight, your cousin." Ellie admitted that his fading looks did not detract from her affection for him. "His eyes and teasing manner still boasted playfulness," she told him. "A rogue of a knight," she chuckled.

MOREBATTLE EARLY NOVEMBER 1324- While the household of Archibald Douglas traveled south with Lady Eleanora to his manor in the Borders, James Lord Douglas with his two sons, William and Walter went on to Berwick on Tweed for business of the king. Lord Robert was confirming a great honor on his trusted Warden of the Marches. For his part in foregoing the ransom of the three French knights two years ago, James Lord Douglas was to receive the most coveted of royal grants; thereafter to be known to all as the Emerald Charter. The document detailed a gift not of lands but of the criminal jurisdiction over all his extensive holdings; baronies and lands that he held of the King of Scots. The grant further decreed that James and his heirs were forever exempt from the usual feudal services such as the warding of castles and suits of court. Only the common aid to the realm in times of war was withheld by the crown.

To signify the coveted decree, Robert Brus took an emerald ring from his own hand and placed it on the finger of his most loyal soldier. "This humble knight will forever think of his most generous Lord Robert, our good king," he said admiring the ring that he now wore. Turning to his sons, James showed them both the exquisite gem. William could only manage a great gasp as his eyes widened in wonderment; Walter, most recently ordained as the second Douglas canon managed a wry comment. "To kiss the bishop's ring?" he teased his father for the ornate designation of his new status.

Figure IX-Part Four; Morebattle kirk is situated along St. Cuthbert's Way

The trumpets bellowed their announcement; the laird of Douglas had arrived at Morebattle. "Is there a king among my wee party?" asked James for the grand greeting to his entrance. "Aye; word has so preceded my fair brother; a ring of gold with blazing emeralds from a generous king," Archie teased his older sibling. "Where are the wee ones?" James asked, looking for the children. The younger Douglas knight made a grimace, indicating that Lady El held them captive in the withdrawing room. "Latin and the Gaelic for their lessons this day," he scoffed. "This lad will so report on your disdain for language lessons," James teased. "Bribery for your silence good sir," Archie proposed as he had a page pour his brother some of his finest wine. "What conspiracy is this?" Ellie demanded, feigning her disdain as she entered the great hall. "Grandmother," young Will exclaimed. "Look at this!" the lad said showing her James' emerald ring. "This lass has never beheld of such finery," she cooed. "Our father was most granted treasured status with his king," boasted Walter as James told them all about the great ceremony and his most coveted award. "And this brother so reminds his laird, such finery is part mine for our clever capture of those fair knights at Biland," Archie prompted James.

"That you might wear the ring; this laird will so consider it," James spouted in fun. Then he quietly explained the plans he had; to present Archie with more charters when others had arrived to witness his seal to the documents. "Mother, do join us in some feasting; that you are working far too much in your good tutoring," Archie said; a little overwhelmed by his brother's generosity. "Perhaps that you should know the truth; our Henklebaldicus' good trouble with the teaching of our ancient tongue." James' words were obscured by his brother's swift reaction and intended distraction. "Here mother, this fair chair is meant for your sweet self," Archie offered. He threw his older brother a scolding grimace; interrupting his tattle-tale remarks about 'language lessons'. James just rolled his eyes. "You good sirs are up to mischief I do know it," she playfully admonished them. "Pray, what about the tutoring does amuse you so? From the withdrawing room Lady Elizabeth was joining them. She noted a smiling, happy Lady Eleanora before her. "This lass has never seen your good mother more content than she most is today." James elbowed Archie as he snickered, "Saved again." Just then the doors of the great hall burst forth with another noble visitor; the trumpets blared their grand tribute; "Hubicus, Canonic, See of Glasgow," the squires proclaimed. With great ceremony they each bowed in unison; in broad sweeping motions they doffed their wee caps, to denote their great respect for the latest guest.

Ellie was chuckling, demanding to know: what pomp is this fair foolery? "Our king does not employ such measures," James chuckled at Archie's exaggerated style. "That he might consider it," his younger brother replied in quick retort. "This humble canon had most thought our king proclaimed another lofty title on a Douglas son; his loyal servant Hubicus to become the bishop! Perhaps Lord Douglas is most here to so inform this lad?" he humorously questioned, joining in the fun. Then Lady Beatrice burst into laughter. "Good James; at your fair expense we play this ruse," she admitted. Archie had devised the format to insure that his brother retained his humility for the great honors recently bestowed on him with the Emerald Charter. "Pax?" he asked Archie, brandishing a silly grin. With a deep sigh of feigned resignation Archie replied, "Well, all right with that; but this laird was beginning to enjoy such pleasures," he joked to the great uproar of laughter from the rest of the Douglases in attendance.

The younger Douglases were being brought into the great hall including baby William. "That I might hold my grandchild," Ellie cooed. "Certainly mother; the wee one has been warned about his grandmother to come here," Hugh said referencing Archie's first words to his son in the chapel when he was first born." She wrinkled her nose; perplexed by the sentiment.

"Warned?" she asked furling her brow like le Hardi. "Yes mother; armed with the knowledge that you would someday keep him captive in drills of Latin grammar; Gaelic for our history in songs as well," Archie confessed. Ellie handed young William to his mother and she ceremoniously rose to stand behind Sir Archibald as she addressed her youngest son and the rest of her family.

"The wishes of your father were to have each son and every daughter tutored in the languages of Norman French, Latin, Lallans, and the Gaelic of our cousins in the Highlands," she began quietly. Ellie told them about her last day with le Hardi in the White Tower. "This lass so pledged her word; to give each child the power of great knowledge, each lad as well to learn the art of war in training for his knighthood." Everyone in the great hall was listening intently as Lady El continued. "Your mother did her best to so insure that each and everyone of you would be prepared for every challenge; to be educated in the finer accomplishments of dance and music most as well. Lord Douglas, your dear father knowing he would not be here to see you grow to manhood, your sisters to become great ladies that from his fair insistence on your schooling you might choose on how to use your skills when you were grown: you would be armed and ready for any task." James' eyes were tearing; Archie was wiping his tears as well but it was Hugh who spoke first.

"Good mother that you have fulfilled those promises to le Hardi and greatly so; accomplishing these brave feats for Scotland's future, the legacy of Lord Will and Lady El," he praised her. Sir Archibald told his son John and his nephew Will that there was work for them with the farrier beginning in the prime. "To train as well with the de Segrave vassal using the newly built quintaine by the week next," he proclaimed emphatically. Then he turned around to his mother who was still standing behind him; he tweaked her on the chin. "This lad will insist on archery as well," he boasted. "And the fair sport of dancing," he chuckled, and then he quickly stood up, surprising Ellie that she did not escape him. "Put this lass most down, the noo!" she spouted in mocked fury, as Archie swung her up over his head. "Le Hardi taught us this fair act as well," her youngest Douglas son reminded her; brandishing a silly smirk as he let her down. "Lady Douglas has returned to her beloved Scotland; to train more knights and daughters for our cause!" proclaimed Lord Douglas to a round of thunderous applause.

BERWICK ON TWEED FEBRUARY 1325-James and his family had spent the last several weeks since Hogmanay in Douglasdale, before returning to the Marches and his castle at Jedburgh. It was late winter, when the laird and his squire William with some other of his men at arms returned to Lord Robert's side in Berwick Castle. Archie and Hugh remained with their children and the ladies near the stronghold on the Jed. By mid February Brus awarded James the lands of Buittle including the castle situated there that once belonged to John Balliol, 'toom tabard,' James recalled under his breath when he took the charter. By March the royal household had moved to Scone for a Parliament. Here James was granted the position of super-auditor over the collection of fees to restore Melrose Abbey.

The times felt strange to a warrior who had been called to muster so often every spring, most summers and late fall; even in the winter Lord Robert would lead them on campaign. But this year was different. In England unrest was keeping Edward busy. When the King of Scots moved north to Arbroath, the rest of the Douglases visited in Crimond and the beautiful fortress at Rattray Head. For weeks at a time James was able to leave the king's side and journey with his family and the Douglas entourage. They even visited his new castle in Buittle. "The birthplace of King John; toom tabard as our father would most say!" he boasted. The castle had been partially destroyed in 1313 when the Scots returned control of the fortress to Robert Brus. But for today it provided another place for Douglases to explore and enjoy together. Occupying a much older site dating to ancient times, there was much to do there. James was in his glory sharing the stories and teaching the history of the lands of Buittle that were now part of his vast estates.

Traversing the countryside with his family invigorated Lord Douglas. He found that he thrived in the company of his loved ones and was stimulated by the interest the Douglas children held for his teaching ways. Surprising himself James felt that he was being transformed. He experienced hope for a time without war; an interest in the future for a peaceful Scotland; this all seemed possible to the knight. Perhaps it was the lack of campaigning and Ellie's prodding that presented this idea to him today; something this lad had not dared to entertain, even in thought, he mused as he began to share his private counsel with Ellie. "To find another lass to warm my bed and fill my heart with song," James told his mother, his face spouting the famous smirk. "You quote my Gilley with those words!" she teased him; for she knew le Hardi told that story often of when they first met in Ayrshire and a wee hound named Shamus, Gaelic for James, found Ellie for his bride. "This lass is pleased that you show such interest; more heirs for Douglasdale," she goaded her son affectionately.

Hugh was planning to join the Douglases in Galloway; most soon he assured them. But not until he took care of his growing list of other obligations the canon noted with bemusement. He was often away from his family these days; forever traveling back and forth between their households and his prebend in Roxburgh Kirk for his lands and income he held of the see of Glasgow. Now the canon was called for an important meeting at the chapter house in the diocese of Glasgow by the new bishop John de Lindsay. The notice commanded that Hubicus, Canon of the Cathedral Church of Glasgow so attend; to confirm the ritual and constitution of Sarum as had been adopted in 1258. Because of the unrest from decades dominated by wars, the canons had not met to renew their obligations with Sarum or Salisbury as it was also known. It had been Hugh's intention to represent himself at the chapter house in person for the 16th May. He had left the Douglases in the Highlands to journey first to Roxburgh, then to Glasgow. Arriving in the Borders he discovered a very ill Austin Canon named Walter. "Dear Hugh, this lad is sorry to most burden you; that you must journey to the cathedral and not to worry." But Hugh would hear none of it; dispatching a letter to his friend and fellow canon Richard Small that he might act as procurator in his place. "For the grave illness of my kin, my nephew Walter," he wrote. There were several hospices nearby but Hugh argued for more prudent measures. "We will take you to Jedburgh; call for others of the Hospitallers to most join us there at James' good castle."

Two months later, by the end of July, both canons were able to travel again. They joined the train of Douglases, wagons and carts and many horses in Galloway. "Good mother; that these many coffers; wee chests of clothing filling up these carts are yours most certainly," Hugh teased. "This good churchman does recall from times we journeyed north never to have left one thing behind!" He was entering the great hall when James joined in the teasing. "Lady Douglas frets the night before such departures; to wonder if she brought with her everything she needed!" Ellie chuckled; giving no heed to their words. "Enough of this fair chatter; help the others to bring in this lady's things," she replied in quick retort. "Le Hardi put this lass to shame for her meager possessions when we traveled," Ellie reminded them. Then seeing Walter coming through the doors she ran to the younger canon and hugged him. "We were most worried for your recovery," she told him. He smiled at her; spoke his gratitude for the healing he received from Hugh.

STEBBINGE PARK MAY 1326- Ellie had reluctantly returned home to Essex, taking nearly a month to journey south from the English Marches in the north. "Old age," she grumbled when they finally arrived; maligning herself for the slowness of their travels; tiring more quickly the trip took her much longer than she expected. Ellie sent for her brother Thomas, to join her at Stebbinge Park for some feasting right away. He had written her about some agreements he had drawn up with her tenants in Staffordshire. After Lord Bagot died she was allowed by their agreement to hold some lands in dower; the rest of the estates passing to his brother Ralph and his heirs; save Wilbrighton Hall which Ellie granted to her son

Archibald. Now she was to write several contracts where her tenants agreed to pay her in silver coinage rather than crops growing in return for a reduction in half of their rents and fees due Lady de Ferrers as she fashioned herself in Essex.

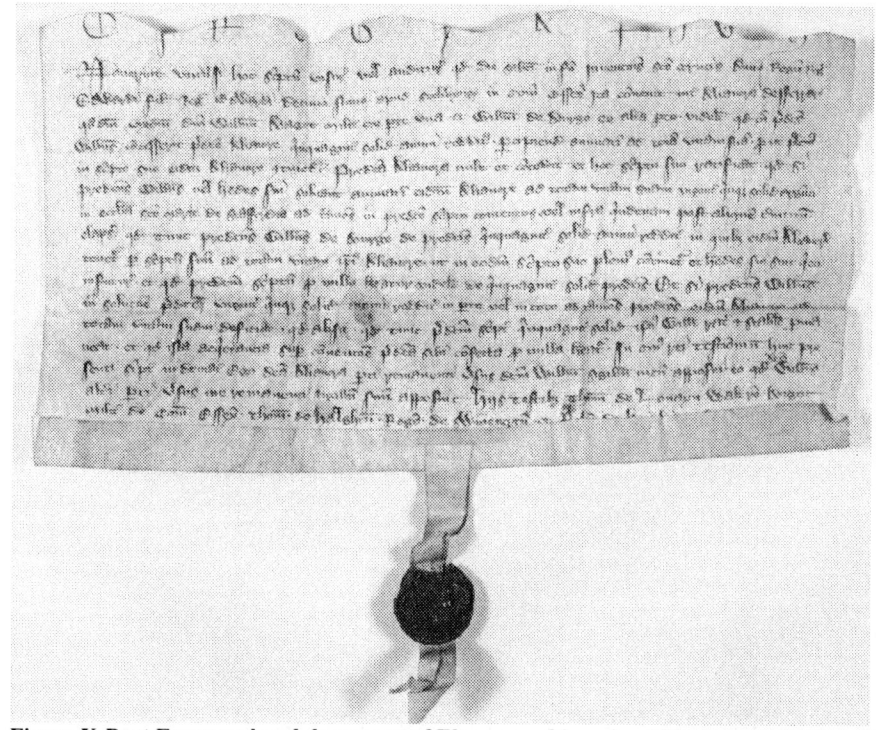

Figure X-Part Four; seal and document of Eleanora of Lovaine 1326; by permission of the British Library, Add. Charter 19988; seal with three eagles representing a knight's love, her three knights named William; horseshoes for de Ferrers impales Lovaine Gules billetty Or with a fesse argent; the indenture is one half of a duplicated charter, torn along a wavy line with the word Cirographum written through the line to guard against forgery as the seal of each appeared on the other's half of the charter

"And when might you be returning north?" Thomas asked her. "In three weeks or less," she replied to his astonishment. "You are not to be in Essex for the summer?" No, she told him. "For now it is the unrest in England that does make this lass so fearful," she confided. As soon as the witnesses arrived with several of her tenants the ceremony began. Each one came forward; Eleanora de Ferrers, formerly the wife of William Bagot, on this Saturday the feast of the finding of Holy Cross in the 19th year of King Edward, son of King Edward, granted to each the reduction of rents in lands of Staffordshire for payments in silver of half what was due. Their annual rents were to be delivered to the church of St. Mary in Stafford, all or in part as specified in their indentures.

There were four knights besides her brother who were present to affix their seals in witness to the indentures. Three were from Stafford and kin to the de Hastings and de Ferrers; Thomas de Haughton, Roger de Swinnerton, and Robert de Knightleie. The forth chevalier, Walter Wigot of Essex was kin to her brother. After the business of her estates and income was settled Ellie invited all to feasting in the great hall of Stebbinge Park. "Thank you good sirs for your kind assistance here and dear brother most as well," she told them. And in the footsteps of her husband William le Hardi she made sure to include her tenants and freeholders for the celebration. Unknown to all of them, this bounty of good wine and fine food was her final tribute to Essex. Lady Eleanora Lovaine was returning to live out her life in Scotland with her family and the memories of her sweet knight.

Figure XI-Part Four; St. Mary's church, in the shadows of the Stafford Castle

Ellie and her household made their way north three weeks later in June; the foul rumors at court of an ensuing invasion by Queen Isabella and her lover Mortimer prompted her hastened departure. Two years before in 1324, the year Lord Bagot died, Edward's queen had returned to the French court; bringing Prince Edward with her on a ruse to have him give homage to her brother King Charles of France for the duchy of Aquitaine. The unrest in England had been escalating. It had been two long years since the battle of Boroughbridge yet the bodies of Lancaster's followers were gruesomely still hanging from the gallows in the shires. King Edward had taken another male lover, elevating this younger Despenser and his kin to higher status within the realm. At the insistence of the nobles and commoners alike, the bodies of the rebels were being given Christian burials at last. Miracles were attributed to the Spirit of their fallen heroes contributing to more dislike for Edward Caernarvon. The nobles of the midlands joined with many in the south; by September Queen Isabella had landed back in England. On the 1st of February of 1327 a new king was crowned, the day known as the Feast of St. Bride.

DALHOUSIE SUMMER 1326-Returning from Clackmannan where he had been with the king, James was traveling south towards the Borders. As his small retinue made their way towards the Moorfoot James had another notion; they would make a stop at Dalhousie Castle. "Perhaps to see of that sweet lass Lady Mary Ramsey," he said out loud, to the delighted ears of his squire. "A fair night of feasting; is that your good intention?" he asked Lord Douglas with a hint of other matters that might be at hand. "To search of many fair amusements there I promise you," James replied, his uncharacteristic lightheartedness surprised his squire. A mood of merriment this lad has not so seen in our laird for many years, William reflected. The band of Douglas travelers crossed the farmlands of Bonnyrigg to the ford of Dalhousie Burn.

James had the occasion to be introduced to Lady Ramsey a few years before; to bring some sad news of her brother, killed in a battle in the northern marches of England. Then early last summer they chanced to meet again. Lady Mary was now a widow; her husband, a brave warrior had not survived his last campaign. James and the lady shared their sentiments of loss and that night they shared their love. Lord Douglas would not entertain thoughts of marriage again he told Lady Mary forthrightly. Their first night, their interlude of passion was to be their last he determined. "For the dear memory of my sweet Joanna is too much upon this knight," he confessed. Lady Mary accepted his honesty and expressed her own resistance to a more formal relationship with James. She admitted being too fearful to remarry. "Too soon in my mourning to be most forced to take license of a husband; even for reasons of my dower, time is what this lass so has to resist such notions," she told him.

Then weeks later James was in Galloway with his family where he revealed his desires to open his heart to love; telling Ellie of his plans to find a lady to be his bride. When his mother championed his sentiments he determined a visit to the Ramsey lass was in order. Perhaps she might hold some similar thoughts for this knight, he ventured. Fate opened the door to his destiny. Just after leaving Scone in October of 1325, heading for the Jed, the torrential rains and flash floods of the unusual fall weather beckoned him to seek shelter at that very castle in Bonnyrigg. Lady Mary was evident in her strong feelings; gracious as the hostess and warm for the intimacy they shared in her chamber that night. They rekindled their relationship and decided to allow for cupid's arrows to take hold though with no hurry to that end as they mutually agreed to be patient. From that fall meeting James found himself in the company of Lady Mary more often. Was it coincidence he wondered for the moment; that he would be invited to a Ceilidh or other such event by some friend or cousin and this Lady Ramsey would be there most as well? Each fair night of feasting and celebration would end in the privacy of her appointed chamber; Lord James and Lady Mary sharing their love and intimacy to the wee hours of the morning.

Now as Lord Douglas led his small escort into the great hall at Dalhousie Castle he began to open his heart to the possibility of asking the lady for her hand in marriage; to begin a formal courting. "This humble knight so accepts of your kind invitation," he began as she beckoned him and his men at arms to join them for their feasting that evening. She called her servants to prepare three chambers in the tower keep; ordered fine wine and good quantities of fresh ale brought to the great hall. Mary's face beamed as she sat them all around the table. The laird was not about Dalhousie; he was on feudal business and would not return for some days she told them. "That this lass is most pleased for your sweet company," she flirted. James was washing his hands in the vessel brought by one of the pages. "This laird has found himself to recall of your sweet face and often," he shared softly; though somewhat clumsily he felt. Not to have the fair gift of Archibald, his poetry of love, he scoffed silently to himself. "That we so found ourselves riding for the Forest; our business for Lord Robert now complete; perhaps to stop at Dalhousie," he suggested with a boyish grin.

Figure XII-Part Four; Dalhousie Castle; view of the Pentland Hills from the William Wallace suite and the wall-walk of the 13th century tower

There was much feasting of good fare; the entremets enchanting, filled with the entertainment of a minstrel and sweet music of the dulcimer and pipes. The Douglas entourage indeed found of fair amusements in this castle, James reflected happily as Lady Mary's maids in wait performed their singing in the gallery. Then circumspectly the lady excused herself for the evening; Lord Douglas followed to his chamber soon afterward to find a trap for romance set, waiting his arrival. A large double bathing tub filled with scented water was placed before the cozy fireplace of glowing peat set among some catching logs of pine; his chamber floors strewn with the boughs of birch; and the sweet scent of lavender fragrance filled the room. His eyes roamed through the chamber lit only by two small tallow torches; upon the tester bed was an elegant robe of silk and velvet in a shade of midnight blue awaiting him. "My sweet lass so planned of everything," he chuckled. Then his thoughts were interrupted by a quiet knocking; in walked Lady Ramsey dressed in a flowing robe of silk brocade trimmed in fur; but nothing else.

The morning arrived bringing with it a golden sunlight streaking through the small windows of the tower chamber; Lord Douglas woke first. He watched the calmness of her breathing, the peaceful countenance and sweet smile of her pretty face. He gathered his resolve and decided what he wanted most to do: to declare his intentions, to seek her hand in marriage, begin his courting of the lady in the proper manner. When she awoke James shared his sentiments; apologized for his ineptness with words of love. But her response was not what he expected. "This lass most appreciates you kind words; yet my heart is held fast to another." James was shocked; if she was in love with someone else, why did she share his bed he demanded to know. She started to cry; then admitted she did not understand herself. "When you first told me you missed your Joanna and could not entertain such thoughts of a permanent liaison this lass believed of our arrangement as most perfect." James stammered; tried to explain how he felt, that he had changed his mind and thought she had as well. "That you agreed with this knight to allow of cupid's arrows," he began, almost incredulous for what seemed abruptly different from their mutual consent last fall. What foolishness is this? A lass most in confusion he allowed to his great frustration.

"This lady most loves her husband now with God," she sobbed. James reached around to bring her closer to him, comfort her, but also to tell her pointedly of his intentions. "Ours is not a love affair for all eternity," he began. "This lad is fearful to begin a marriage; but we can not continue to be lovers and not wed." She told him that she needed time to consider his proposal. "Dear James; that I most worry to marry you; in fear that something might so happen and a widow would I most be again, perhaps the cause of it as well."

James suddenly realized that she was not turning down his proposal; the lass was frightened to ever love again, as he had been when Joanna passed. "This humble knight knows your fears," he said softly, as he stroked her hair gently with his large calloused hands. "We will most discuss our plans again. For now I give you this," he said brandishing his Douglas smirk. He grabbed her, held her tightly in his firm grasp and kissed her solidly on the mouth. She giggled and promised to consider his fine offer. "Of all the knights in the realm this lass would give her hand to only one, James Lord Douglas!" she proclaimed jubilantly. Six months later, at the celebration of James' forty-first birthday she agreed to marry him; for the solstice, in June she promised him. What Lady Ramsey did not share was that she was carrying his child within her; the lay-in due by September. Sadly when the summer solstice came about, James was not in Scotland to fulfill his pledge. Brus had dispatched him with Randolph into the north of England and the wedding was reluctantly postponed.

WEARDALE LATE JUNE 1327-Walter the Steward did not join his cousin James on this campaign. After witnessing a charter in Stirling in March he took a grave illness and died before the summer; the young man who held such promise as a great soldier and leader left his young son Robert without a parent; to reach his manhood in the household of others of his kin. James and Archibald had now raised their army and were following the lead of the Earl of Moray as they entered the District of Weardale. Smoke billowed from rooftops, flowing in cloud like clusters over the stone walls of enclosed towns marking the path taken by the Scottish army. Numbering some twenty-thousand men at arms the Scots rode south under the leadership of de Moray as they burned and pillaged Northumbria; taking their wave of devastation far south into Durham in the district of Weardale. "That we will march most to Appleby is our desire; you my brother to take your good spearmen, mounted on their light horse to travel further east towards Durham," James directed Archie. It was the first occasion where the younger knight was being sent out on his own with a large contingency of armed marauders; to reap havoc among the towns and villages of the English Marches. "But not to venture into the burgh of Durham," James cautioned. Weeks later the younger Douglas knight returned; his retinue mostly intact. Archibald rendezvoused with the rest of the Scottish army bringing much booty and tribute, leaving behind in their wake such slaughter and destruction that Durham shook in fear for many weeks for his return to their shire.

By mid July an ailing King of Scots had sailed to Ulster; issued an indenture with de Maundeville the seneschal there; structuring a truce in exchange for wheat and barley. The consummate leader had been too sick to venture forth on the Weardale campaign; the lingering palsy, the hereditary illness debilitated him from the strenuous muster. Undeterred he made his way to Ireland to take pressure off his lieutenants marching south through the English Marches. Successful in obtaining this agreement, Robert Brus then requested King Edward's approval for the indenture; achieving that on the 12th of July.

Now it was the young English king in the company of his mother's lover Mortimer who was deciding on a muster; to bring a great army to face the Scots. He fortified the city of York and he proceeded to Barnard Castle. James came to speak with his brother; he and de Moray had decided that Archibald's recent success portended more feverish assaults. "Perhaps to take another wee army; move your fair retinue of onfoot most towards Darlington," Lord Douglas said outlining his plan for his younger brother. While Edward marched for the Hayden Bridge on Tyne, Archie was ravaging the towns and villages further south; bringing fire and sword to grave destruction. The luck of St. Bride most with him as he would later describe the encounter near Cokdale, Archie surprised a band of English armed foot, mostly common folk, on their way to join Edward on the Tyne. Directing his spearmen with fierce confidence, he sounded the war-cry, 'A Douglas! A Douglas!' and led his men in gory slaughter of the English soldiers nearly to the man.

"That these men with tails must now consider another Douglas knight, with more Douglas sons to come I swear it," he boasted as they left the burgh smoldering in wasted glory. When he returned to the Scots' encampment he brought forth the great wealth he found in coinage; more cattle than they knew what to do with; and stories he heard of an English army that brought peels of laughter to his leaders. He repeated the tales of knights and squires adorned in fine cotes and hoods with intricate embroidery. "Floral forms with stately branches; colors of the most delicate of hues covering the supertunics of these strange warriors, like peacocks at court." he chuckled. "That they nourish of their lang beards so fondly," Archie scoffed imitating them in exaggerated form, to the great uproar of laughter from James and Randolph.

BLANCHLAND AUGUST-Near the smoldering ruins of the small priory near the Derwent Edward's army was approaching the location of the Scots, high above them on a great hill. The English decided to encamp there. Within a few days the king's lieutenant decided to break the Scot's ranks. He dispatched a thousand archers fortified with much wine; taking with them a large number of men at arms for protection, to encounter the Scottish rebels. The reputation of the Lord Douglas had preceded him; the king's archers feared any such encounter with the black knight, requiring liquid courage before they would join the fight. The policy James employed, Archibald to emulate as well, was to permanently remove any of Edward's archers from future assaults upon their countrymen. He made a concerted effort to round up as many of the bowman he could find; before releasing them to freedom he would remove two fingers or an eye; their choice.

James noted the activity of the English below them and devised a stratagem to counter the attack. He sent Archie with the Earl of Mar to lead their mounted spearmen to a place of ambuscade. "Wait that I give word," he ordered. Then James pulled a plain robe of disguise over his hauberk and rode to the English lines. As he began his retreat to where Archie was hidden with his command, the archers obediently followed him. An English squire assigned to their escort noted something was amiss and riding up on his charger called out a warning to them at once. "It is the Douglas you follow; that he is to play a trick!" James turned and gave his signal; shouted his battle cry "A Douglas! A Douglas!" and Archie's men fell upon the English to another successful rout.

Some days later the Scots moved their army to another hill in Stanhope Park. That night James led about two hundred men at arms into the camp of young Edward. The Scots struck down many English in their slumber and James cut the ropes of the king's pavilion. Lord Douglas narrowly missed the king, almost capturing Edward save only for a servant, who sacrificed his life that the young monarch might escape. Archie had moved through the camp in another direction; garnering many victims to his sword; losing track of time for all the carnage that he leveled. As he paused to assess the damage he looked around for his brother but could not find him! Nearly panicking he thought he heard the alarm calling their retreat but for the turmoil and din of battle he was uncertain. And for all the confusion Archie could not even determine the direction from where he heard le Hardi's oliphant sounding the Scots to fall back; it seemed very far away he mused. How did he let James get out of his sight, Archie muttered to himself? Had Lord Douglas removed himself to safety or was he calling out for help?

The rest of the Scots rode to the banks of the Wear and found Archie there before them; looking around in great distress for his brother. "That James has not been seen?" he asked them incredulously. Just then the vibrant sounds from the old Crusader's oliphant were heard above the clamor of the English mounting a pursuit. Through the darkness James suddenly appeared before them; gulping air, his chest heaving hard in deep, halted breaths he barely stopped to tell them. "This laird was nearly most done in," he admitted looking at the huge dent and missing edge on his small shield, "a warrior of fair size swinging of a club to almost end the war for this humble knight." Archie looked at the damage on the shield and noted that the English soldier suffered more. "Aye, and where were you? To follow your laird not lead him!" James chided his brother playfully as they made their way to the safety of their camp.

JEDBURGH FALL 1327-The Lord Douglas and his Foresters were finally returning home from their Weardale campaign with few men lost to their number. James and Archie were ebullient with their success only to be greeted by a sadness that few could comprehend. The laird's gonfalon was barely unfurled when Ellie and Hugh presented James with another tragedy. Lady Ramsey was never to be his wife; dying in child-bed, giving birth to a son. James was incredulous; she had not revealed to him her condition. "That this laird would have most insisted on a marriage," he told them as tears streamed from his eyes. "That when you were called to muster, this lass sent word to Dalhousie Castle for the postponement of the wedding," Ellie explained. "Then some six weeks later the tragic word was sent to us by young Alexander, the lady's kin; a child to come into a world with a mother passed to another. Hugh and this lass traveled north to retrieve the wee laddie. That we have given him the name of Archibald," Ellie said hoping her son would approve, to honor his brother, great grandfather as well.

"Here is the wee one that we have brought to stay with us," Beatrice told James as she entered the privacy of the withdrawing room with her new nephew. James held his son and clasped him to his chest. "By St. Bride," he sputtered, "that you are most a bastard for the world to so proclaim; what ill will has this foolish laird so forced upon you?" he asked invoking his anger at himself not God for the travesty. "That war has caused another one so innocent as you to come into this life without the benefit of being born of wedlock." Ellie and Beatrice watched as James sat with his new son. "That he is most certainly a Douglas," Lady El chuckled as James admired the dark head of hair. "Is he as lang as this?" he asked; the child being wrapped in the tight swaddling for protection appeared nearly a Scot's Ell in length. "No," said Beatrice, scoffing at his silliness. "But the lad is most the size of le Hardi," Ellie boasted recalling Lord Hugh's often told tales of the day Gilley was born. The child began to cry so Ellie took him from James. "Come Beatrice let us find the wet nurse for this hungry laddie," she said beckoning her to leave the brothers alone.

"That you are certain for this wee one to be most you son?" asked Archie. James shook his head adamantly. "You so heard our mother, that he resembles the laird they called le Hardi," he replied. Just then another Douglas brother entered the withdrawing room; Hugh was returning from his work at the hospice of Maison Dieu. "You have heard the news by your grave countenances," Hugh said observing the solemn expressions on both his brother's faces. "The child is mine," James admitted before the priest asked. "How is it that you did not know about the lay-in?" Hugh inquired. James looked up with almost a glaring frustration. "The lass kept many things so much a secret! But to deny this laird his son born in the sanctity of marriage is most puzzling to me."

Archie was getting irritated with Hugh's insinuations. "Lady El is most correct; this wee one a Douglas sure aye!" The Austin Canon apologized for his manner; the rumors of a child most born without a father certain had clouded his thinking. "Others speak of a trick most played upon Lord Douglas," he cautioned. "That you have been most talking with our cousin William," Archie argued. "That squire has a spiteful tongue some days that makes this humble knight most angry." James could see that tempers were escalating between his brothers. "There will be no further discussion on the wee Archibald and his true father; this laird accepts responsibility, to ask his penance from his God for this foul deed. It is done!" Then James excused himself as he went to the chapel within the fortress to pray.

Figure XIII- Part Four; Balgonie Castle; the tower where the family resides looms large above the exterior walls; though similar in concept Balgonie Castle represents almost a miniature version of the once grand stronghold of the Douglases in Lanarkshire

FAWDON NOVEMBER 1328- Months before, in January, Edward King of England issued writs of protection for one hundred nobles coming from Scotland to treat with him of peace at York. The principle administrators for each country were Mortimer for England and James Lord Douglas for Scotland. Two months later on the 1st of March 1328 Lord Edward renounced his pretensions to the dominion of Scotland; ordered Sir Henry de Percy, son and heir of the infamous lord and Douglas enemy, along with William de la Zouche of Ashby, both kin to Lady Eleanora Douglas; that each to swear to the renunciation. The two nobles affixed their seals to this most important document and to another that day where Edward agreed to withdraw his charges against Robert Brus, King of Scotland, yet waiting the Pope's sentence in the court of Rome.

James Lord Douglas was the knight banneret and baron of the realm of Scotland bringing back this most coveted deed to the King of Scots. Another agreement was made to arrange the marriage of Edward's sister Joan with Lord Robert's son Prince David to insure a lasting peace. Lord Douglas rode home from Yorkshire reflecting on the climatic end of his life long struggle; free at last of Edward, Lord Paramount. The English king was finally defeated; the Douglas estates were restored and there was peace in their kingdome at last. James recalled to mind on his humble pledge of fealty to Lord Robert at Ericstane twenty-two years ago. "That more than two decades have so passed since then; the importance now of such a simple deed and the lang war that followed that fateful pledge never to portend a quiet end as this," he whispered out loud as he crossed into the Borders of a free Scotland.

Now it was the fall; nearly eight months had passed since peace had come to Ellie's adopted homeland. She was just returning home to her manor house in the Cheviot knowing that victory finally prevailed, bringing peace to her beloved Scotland. Soon the entire manor would be theirs again without the interference of de Umfraville; the first time since 1297. James had requested special favor from King Edward: to be seised to all the lands in England held of his father William le Hardi including the Northumbrian manor in the parish of Ingram as James Lord Douglas, the son and rightful heir. Edward granted the request on the occasion of his sister Joan's marriage to the future King of Scots, young David Brus. Ellie had been happily drawing up her plans for the reconstruction of their Lanarkshire home; the rebuilding of Douglas Castle that Lord Robert finally licensed to Lord Douglas. She had sketched designs of the towers with details inside and out; the exterior curtain wall and the interior scale-and-platt stairs, counting them out as she had done forty years ago when Gilley carried her up to the family level of the tower.

As Lady El rode out today she reminisced; it was thirty years since she and Gilley rode their amblers by the Breamish. She never really felt alone at Fawdon, believing he was somehow nearer to her there than any place she chose to live. Though Ellie had arrived from her manor at Bonjedward five days before, she was still quite tired from the journey, coming from Douglasdale two weeks before. But though fatigued she still insisted on going to nearby Billesdone to look after her rents and fees. Archie and Hugh were concerned that she rest first but exhibiting her well known stubbornness she announced that she was going; it is done she said with her usual bravado. Ellie had not ventured far from her manor when her horse stumbled, her palfrey's leg seemed to snap in a sink hole and her sons watched in horror as she was thrown down helplessly towards the cart path.

In her attempt to stave off the fall she landed on her back atop a small stone wall. Her body became motionless and slumped in an odd manner.

Archie spurred his horse to her side and bolted frantically from his saddle to where she was lying helplessly now. Ellie started sobbing as he came into her sight; "My head, the pain," she exclaimed, her face contorted in fright to the anguished throbbing she felt above her eyes and below her neck. "That I can not move; my legs and hands I have no feeling in them." Archie knew at once he must not move her without help; this was serious he realized as his mother never cried from pain or physical discomfort. He kneeled beside her and took her hand; she screamed out again in frantic frustration for her folly. "What has this lass so done; foolishly in my stubborn ways that I have ruined all our plans." Archie tried to calm her as Hugh arrived. The look on his older brother's face confirmed his fears; her neck or back had serious injury that when on the battlefield a knight would surely die and soon.

Ellie sensed immediately what was wrong. "That I shall not recover from this injury," she told them frankly. "Get me to my bed," she barked her orders. Archie told Hugh to stay 'with our Lady El' as he called her affectionately. "This lad will bring a litter and some good assistance to our needs. Pray mother, do not try to move," he cautioned, really not knowing what to say or do. "Dear St. Bride our dear mother needs your sweet healing this day," he prayed under his breath.

Figure XIV-Part Four; Little Dunmow church of St. Mary's with the ruins of the priory still standing in the foreground; an antique print in the author's collection

Lady Elizabeth was tending to Eleanora in the laird's chamber when Lady Beatrice, with her daughter Eleanora and sons John and William arrived. "Dear mother," Beatrice exclaimed. Ellie opened her eyes to acknowledge them and smiled weakly. She was still unable to move her body; except for one of her hands which she used to accentuate her words, she was yet immobilized by the fall. Ellie's voice was faint due to her injured state but she could still converse. While she lay motionless her chest was filling with congestion. Hugh realized the fluids would drown her breath eventually. Outside the chamber door he shared his fears with Archibald. "And what of James?" he asked. Archie told him that his brother was in Glasgow. "We dispatched a messenger on our fastest palfrey; that he will most arrive within two days or less." Hugh shook his head, muttering in grave concern; how could he keep his mother alive until his brother had returned to Northumbria? "St. Mungo's work is never done," he blustered as he entered his mother's chamber to be at her bedside. Hugh was despondent; concerned that his healing skills were not sufficient to insure his mother's survival for another four days. "God's love must not desert us," he cried plaintively to himself. Both Will and Walter were in Glasgow with Lord Douglas. "These three most devout and pious men need to say their goodbyes to this mother," Hugh reminded St. Bride in his silent prayer.

Few days passed that Ellie called her family to her side; realizing her strength was waning she summoned all her strength to make her final hours count. Lady Douglas was trying hard to make herself heard as she had her entire family staying at Fawdon now present in her chamber. Everyone was there but James and his sons. She commended a delicate leather coffin to be brought to her; a wee box with cloisonné medallions of gilded birds; her prized possession, a gift from Gilley that held her jewelry. "This brooch of primrose, I give to you my granddaughter and namesake." The younger Eleanora took the gift; her eyes welling in tears. "This lass will always remember…" the girl's words fell into sobs as the fourteen year old made her apologies. Ellie closed her eyes; frustrated she could not comfort the lass. "This comb with the fair initial *'E'* is for my dear friend, Lady Elizabeth." The lady held her hand and kissed her on the forehead, but could not speak her gratitude through her own tears. Other jewelry was given to Lady Beatrice to dispense later at her whim, Ellie instructed.

Then Eleanora called her grandsons to her side; the lads were trying very hard to hold their emotions in check. "To each of you this lass so grants one of her younger palfreys," she stopped short as her throat closed in a spell of coughing. When she regained her voice Ellie was able to whisper softly. "In my life this lass was greatly humbled by my young horse; that these noble beasts will serve you both the same; learn from them and with them in your days to come." She then quietly asked Archie who was sitting beside her on the tester bed to insure that James' sons, Walter and William were given her jennet and the mare.

"For the wee Archibald, my grandson, the remaining sword of le Hardi's brother, Lord Hugh; this lad will need to know his family; this old standard will remind all that he is a Douglas. I entrust that teaching to you dear Archie with our James and others most as well." Lady Eleanora told him to take the other weapons and armaments in William's war-chest and divide them among the others and her *warrior monks* as well, meaning Hugh and Walter. To Beatrice she gave her dagger from Gilley; teasing Archie for a wife now properly armed. "And for the one given this lass from Lord Robert, please present this to Lord Douglas," intending that James should have the gift of his dear friend, given in memory of his father. Ellie had to pause; she was growing so tired; then after a few moments she resumed. "Bring this lass her charter-chest," Ellie ordered, showing signs of irritation for her weakened state. Hugh gave her the smaller coffer. "This charter is for Wilbrighton Hall; my English lord," she teased her youngest son. Archie was sobbing openly now; he had to turn away from her and wipe his face in his embarrassment. "My wee Archie," she began, seeing his distress. "Your father had a softer side most like you, my loving poet knight," she reminded him.

Eleanora was nearly faltering but she intended to finish. "To my Hubicus, this coinage is for you," she said indicating the silver coins packed in the bottom of the charter-chest. "That you will be charged with the most difficult of duties; to ask of Nicky's men at arms to most assist you," she said quietly, referring to the preparation of her body for her burial. Archie reassured her that the de Segrave servants and squire would be most welcomed into his household, anticipating her concern. Ellie blinked her eyes in an attempt to acknowledge her approval. She tried to speak again but could not; feeling more than tired, her eyes were closing. She knew she could not stay to see James and his sons.

With all her strength Ellie opened her eyes again; forced her words out. "Tell my James and Will and Walter that I love them. Take my Gilley's signet ring here," she pointed with her eyes to the ring on her hand, "to give Lord Douglas, for the next laird, his son Will. And the tapestry," Ellie's words trailed off. Barely whispering in audible tones, her strength waning, with so much left to say, Lady Douglas was becoming more than frustrated by her frailty. She prayed they understood as she had to continue with one last message. "Tell our James, his sons too, I will come to visit them in their dreams as Gilley most came to all of us." Her eyes closed; barely minutes seemed to pass that her hand became limp in Archie's grasp. A smile crossed her face and she whispered as if talking to someone standing right in front of her "Sholto beast." Her body shuddered slightly and Lady Eleanora Lovaine Douglas was gone from them.

James arrived in the afternoon of the following day with his sons. The tell-tale hatchment on the front door of the Fawdon keep told him what he feared most. As he walked into the tower house he saw his brothers and sister in law sitting in the great hall. Archie rose and hugged him. "She tried to stay; to say goodbye," he stammered. James asked where she was and Archie took him to the laird's chamber where Hugh had prepared her body; covering it in a shroud, laying upon a bed of lavender and sweet rosemary strewn across a layer of charcoal. James and his son Will stood outside the door of his mother's room; the wee Deerhound lying in silent vigil by the open casket that would carry her to Little Dunmow Priory; 'to bury this lass beside my only love,' as Ellie had insisted.

Several minutes passed; James and Will were still standing in the archway of her chamber door, like staunch statues, unwilling or unable to break the solemn barricade of silence as they stared into the room. Will stood behind his father; the Lord Douglas, a man who saw thousands in their death, many by his own hand now faced another but more poignant passing. He was here to say goodbye to the only mother he ever knew, the last person to share the memory of his father. James finally broke from his frozen stance and quietly walked to the side of the wooden dais that supported the coffin and kneeled before her body. "Dear Lady El; why could you not wait, this lad most needed to say his words," he stammered, slumping over in tears. His father's agony was so compelling to young Will that the lad had to turn away, to give his father the privacy he needed. The young Douglas left the doorway, finding the open arms of his Uncle Archie standing just behind him in the shadows of the passageway. The knight held his nephew as he sobbed and shook in his grief; joining them as well now was Walter, silenced by his sorrow for a lady he came to love as his own grandmother.

DOUGLASDALE SEPTEMBER 1329- Lord Robert had passed to the Otherworld on 7th June; the noble and most wise of kings was buried at Dunfermline Abbey beside his queen in a ceremony with mourners of his kingdome, knights and nobles from every rank, openly weeping for their loss. Before leaving this world for the next, Lord Robert was holding his court at Cardross. Those closest to the king were told that the palsy that he bore was taking his very strength; his body riddled with age and the miseries of lang campaigns could no longer fight the disease. Before he made his journey to God's Heaven, the king demanded to know, "if the Lord Douglas, my most gentle of knights, would so assist this king achieve what his body prohibits him from doing. To acquit my soul against my Lord God?" He explained his desires to this loyal knight and dearest friend; that Sir James might take his heart to fight the enemies of Christ and fulfill his vows to the

Almighty. The weeping laird readily agreed to fulfill the request; to take the king's heart to the Holy Sepulchre, he promised.

Figure XV-Part Four; round church ruins at Orphir, Orkney; modeled after the Holy Sepulchre in Jerusalem

Several months later the Lord Douglas was home in Douglasdale. Three royal vassals, messengers of King Edward approached his fortress at Park Castle; bringing with them two letters from the English king. The first document was in response to James' request for safe conduct to travel throughout England unprovoked. King Edward granted him protection for seven years from this date; that James of Douglas might take free passage throughout England and that no harm should come to him, a knight on Crusade for the late King Robert of Scotland. The second letter bore the seal of the English king and was written to his cousin, Alfonso XI, King of Leon and Castile; an introduction to this lord for one James of Douglas who was 'burning with love of the Crucified,' intending for his mission with the heart of Lord Robert Brus, late King of Scots. "Now this knight can most begin his journey," he said happily.

He thanked the king's messengers and bid them stay the night before beginning their journey home to England. James went out to the courtyard of the fortress and called to his son. "Dear Will these good men have brought answers to my fair request. That we are free to travel most to Essex," he declared happily. Will was instructing his cousin, Archie's son William now a page on how to prepare the cuir bouilli; to make the hardened leather that would be used for armor in a competition of lance the rings. The squire looked up and smiled broadly. With his father going on Crusade for several years he relished the opportunity to join him on a personal journey, a pilgrimage to Essex: Little Dunmow, Stebbinge Park, and Little Easton as James characterized the journey. "That we will so depart in three days," he boasted.

LITTLE DUNMOW PRIORY MID OCTOBER- The Douglas knight and his son Will met with the Austin Canon, the Master of the Augustinian priory. James provided coinage to the priest to say prayers for the souls of Lord and Lady Douglas; their daughters and grandson and to maintain the graves of these brave Scots. "To thank you most again for your good service to my brother Hugh and with the funeral for our mother," he said graciously. "This laird will need your kind assistance most again; when I return from completing the most noble of deeds; to take the heart of my king, Lord Robert, to the Holy Sepulchre," James explained to the Augustinian. "Then will I come back to Little Dunmow; to secure the bones of my dear family to our lands in Douglasdale," he vowed. The prior said he would be honored for the chore; then offered the travelers and their escorts the comforts of the prior's residence. James readily accepted his kindness. "Thomas Lovaine, my good kin is most expecting us; but for this night and next, this humble laird so thanks you for the hospitality of your noble house."

Figure XVI-Part Four; an unidentified 13th century Crusader's stone coffin lid at Little Dunmow Priory Church; the edifice was undergoing renovations at this time

James told his son that this Augustinian monastery was one of the first for the order in all of England and it was where Uncle Hugh first studied for the church. "A place where both my bothers, your uncles learned their early lessons in their Latin," he chuckled. "And here, the stone coffin of the sweet knight and noble father, your grandfather, William le Hardi Douglas," he added quietly. Tears filled James' eyes as his gaze moved to look upon the other tomb, a new edifice of similar design, built next to Sir William's stone burial chamber: 'Eleanora de Lovaine, loving wife of Willelmi, Lord Duglas' read the inscription. "Dear Lady El," he blurted out loud. Will kneeled down by their grave sites to pray for their souls. James just kept staring; trying to accept the reality of truly being here; seeing the stone coffins of his mother and father side by side.

Some time later the Douglas knight and squire rode the manor lands of nearby Stebbinge Park; passing the wee tofts and messuages that once housed the English tenants of Lord and Lady Douglas. "The manor now held of Lord Henry de Ferrers," he scoffed; adding that they would not entertain thoughts of staying there. He then showed Will the farm of the Hospitallers and told the story of Hugh's study of Alchemy Healing; working from the old journals Gilley made while on Crusade first stopping at Acre with Earl Adam. "Did grandfather fight in many battles there?" he asked. James shook his head no; told him that few engagements of importance occurred during that Crusade. "Merely wee skirmishes were had with the Mamlukes; stories this knight has so told you most before," he reminded the squire. Will Douglas watched his father run his eyes over the small hills of the Essex countryside; the focus of a man remembering his childhood days spent at that manor when peace reigned and prosperity flourished. "Why? Why did you do it?" James kept asking; whispering his plaintive cry, his poignant need to solve the riddle. He shook his head in despair for the years that were stolen from his youth; for Edward's vile greed and ambition, wondering for a different outcome had he never invaded Scotland.

Figure XVII-Part Four; the prior's house today from the vicinity of the old vineyard; the canons grew their grapes in great quantities at the old priory, living at this residence

LITTLE EASTON-James and Will rose from their sound slumber to the comforting peels of the church bells from the priory church. They broke their fast with the prior in the great hall; enjoying fine wine from the vineyard and fresh fish from the well stocked pond. Then James' squires saddled their horses for the short ride to the manor of Sir Thomas Lovaine; the younger stepbrother of Lady Eleanora. "To see the tomb of the fair

Lovaine knight as well," James chuckled in anticipation. In his enthusiasm the Lord Douglas decided to stop first at the church that adjoined the manor. Finding the door open they walked inside. "There is the sweet font where Lady El was christened," he said as they walked towards the chancel where the wee Lovaine heart Crusader knight sits under an immense tomb, the armorial bearings in proud display, gathered above and below the arched edifice. The father related the story of a four year old James inquiring about the effigy; inciting Lady El to great ire when he asked, 'pray mother, how does he ride his horse?' Will roared in a great belly laugh to hear the tale.

Figure XVIII--Part Four; the tomb over the Lovaine 'Heart' Crusader effigy

"This Crusader was killed during a great siege in the Holy Lands. As for many knights of his time he so requested to have his heart embalmed most like Lord Robert and returned to lie under such small monument as this," James told his son. "Is our king to have such an effigy?" Will inquired. James replied with an emphatic, No! "And if our God and dear St. Bride do not see fit to return the Good Lord James alive to his homeland; no such small stone carving is to sit upon my bones or heart! It is done!" he declared. "That we are here to record the fair lines and stone work of this great tomb; to build one so like it for le Hardi and Lady El." Will took out the small coffer that held Ellie's paints and quill pens that she once used for drawing faces and designs. He unrolled some parchment and began to recreate the image. "To bring this back to Douglasdale; that we will commend the very best of masons for our work," James said sharing his plans with his son. "Then when the proper shrine to house the noble bones of that great laird and patriot is most done, will we come south again to Essex and retrieve our father, dear mother and my sisters with the small coffin of my nephew too," he said as if completing a solemn vow. "By St. Bride, it is done." he concluded.

FAWDON NOVMEBER 1329-Three weeks later Lord Douglas and his oldest son returned to Northumbria where Fawdon manor was being restored to the once fine estate of his father, reseised to Lord Douglas at long last. "A fair reunion with your uncles, cousins and wee brother," James boasted of his plans. Their journey to Essex had provided the Lord Douglas with an opportunity to get to know his son and heir. In the spring he would begin another journey; but young Will was to remain at home, under the tutelage of his Uncle Hugh the cleric and seneschal. Until that time will this knight include my son to share in everything that I do; most like le Hardi, James reflected as they rode in the shadow of the Cheviot. "Dear father; that this lad is most impressed by all we saw; to hear the stories of your life as well with my grandfather and Lady El. I am so humbled," Will said with a quiet gentleness that was his way. James smiled broadly; feeling for the first time since he first held the wee laddie that he was a father in the image of one named William.

"This laird will show you the fort; to take your cousins with us and explore the ancient stronghold on the Clinch," he told his son and squire. Then he shared the stories when his father took his family for a day of exploration; riding west towards the falls at Linhope Burn. "This lad with his wee sisters, to travel with our nurses and good escort; that this son with his good eyes came to notice our father and dear mother most slipped away with Ana at their side to ride to the falls alone," he chuckled as he began his tale of that eventful day. "This lad seeing their fair deceit began to ride ahead and led the squires of Lord Douglas to the very spot of Linhope Spout; close to the falls. These men at arms stopped to water their horses while this lad rode on ahead, much further to the falls," he continued, brandishing a grin.

"Our father and dear mother were most surprised when this son so came to ride his horse quite near the falls only to find our Ana there at the banks of the fair waters, guarding of their clothes to keep them dry!" Will's interest was peaked; he asked if he actually found the couple there alone and *in a compromising way.* The look on James' face, the broad mark of the Douglas smirk suggested he was correct. "Aye, much distress to pay for my good folly; that our Ana saw me first; called out to Lord Douglas, 'good James is most here' while she warned this lad off with her fiercest grimace." He continued to tell Will that from behind the rush of the waters he could hear his mother scream. "Come no further James; this mother so commands you!" Will was smiling to envision his father's ploy. "And did you take your leave then?" asked his son. James shook his head yes. "This lad knows when to quit a game," he replied. "That our Ana ran by this lad carrying cotes and surcotes and much more; when short time later they came out from behind the falls this lad had made his fast escape on Fortis!" he chuckled at his fair hoodwinking of his parents and dear Ana.

PARK CASTLE ST. BRIDE'S DAY 1330-James was preparing for his departure first to Spain to assist the cousin of King Edward in his fight with the Saracens; then to the Holy Land with the heart of Lord Robert. He was making a charter to Newbattle Abbey; the half of the land of Kilmad, a promise he made to Ellie. When King Robert seised him to the lands of that old barony Ellie reminded him of the bequest of Roger de Quincy for the remainder of the manor that he gave to Newbattle Abbey. As the widow of William de Ferrers, she once held some of the same de Quincy's lands herself with le Hardi. James had promised to give the remainder, his half of the barony to the same monks. He made a conditional gift; that the monks should perform a choral mass at the altar of St. Bride; and feed thirteen poor on this her day as well. Archibald and six other knights of the shire were present; three witnessed the indenture by affixing their seals to the document. "Sir Archibald; that you must so enforce this document; if these foolish monks are careless in their service, they are to forfeit the sasine," he told his youngest brother.

Then he brought out another charter; already witnessed with silk strings pressed to the wax seals of several knights of the realm. "That this is for our good English lord; Archibald Douglas, Lord of Wilbrighton," he teased Archie for his seising of Ellie's former manor in Staffordshire. "For your good service; the lands and wee tower house of our Fawdon; then to be seised to young William your wee son when you are ready," he proclaimed; adding that it was the Douglas tradition for those lands to go to the youngest son. Archie was uneasy; the bequest was certainly unexpected; he had many vast estates of his own. Why Fawdon he wondered? Hugh was standing near him and they exchanged looks of grave concern; Lord Douglas was expecting to not return.

Tears streamed down the younger knight's face; he got up solemnly and hugged his brother hard to him. "That you must come back to us alive," he said plaintively. "Of course this laird is to be at home again and soon; Douglasdale is my paradise. That there is much to do here most as well!" James replied with an enthusiasm that Archie knew camouflaged a different sentiment. From under his surcote the laird pulled out a trophy and tossed it to his brother. "The Order of the Fur Hat," he joked; reminding Archie of the memento he retained from the battle at Lintalee. "That you must keep it; ready to do battle with the English should they return in my absence; to take our father's oliphant as well; that you must defend our Scotland until Lord

Douglas is back home again to address such matters himself," James told Archie as he presented him with the Crusader's horn.

"Now for more serious concerns," the Douglas laird bellowed enthusiastically. "Here are the plans to build the tomb for le Hardi and our mother; the final drawings with Lady El's kind designs and paintings for the restoration of Douglas Castle as well." Hugh reviewed the parchments; enough work to keep them busy for the six or more years Lord Douglas was away, he mused. "When are you to so depart?" the canon asked. James told him that he was having the ship prepared at Berwick that very day; to take his leave in few short weeks from his manor at Hidegate. "But not before a Ceilidh for our clan," he boasted. "One fond farewell to Douglasdale before this knight most leaves on his Crusade!"

Figure XIX-Part Four; ruins of Castle of the Star, the haunting keep hovers over the medieval village of Teba, Spain

TEBA AUGUST 1330- The Lord Douglas and his fellow knights and warriors fought a rough sea journey; putting in to shore quite frequently as they sailed around the coast of Spain up the eastern shore to land at Valencia. The commendation that he bore from the king's cousin brought him a royal reception when he finally disembarked at Seville and for those noble men at arms in his company as well. There were many other foreign knights at Alfonso's court besides the few James brought with him. Among his party was his own squire, young Hugh from Ayrshire; no others from his personal household came along. There were two knights named Logan; kin to his stepson; Sir William St. Clair of Roslin; his brother John; William Keith of Galston; in all there were six knights to join this knight banneret and twenty squires. They were entertained by fine feasting, given royal treatment befitting a king and his retinue.

James agreed to join the young king on campaign in Teba de Hardales; facing the Moors. With him Alfonso brought five hundred Portuguese knights 'on loan' to him from his brother in law the King of Portugal. These Christian Crusaders as they fashioned themselves, came with siege engines; catapults and mangonels they brought up the wee cart paths to the hills where the castle sat in defiance to their siege. They began the assault on the castle where the garrison with few of the town's people tried to repel the attack, until word reached another general.

Hearing of the siege against the castle in Teba held for the King of Granada, the great general of the Granadian army, know to all as Osmin gathered his forces and made his way towards the Castle of the Star. He camped with his soldiers about three miles away from King Alfonso's army, across the Guada Teba River at Turron. In James' camp the Scots were casually waiting for a battle. The other foreign knights from the Castilian court just arrived and they set about putting their tents near Lord Douglas, to follow him in battle when directed they vowed. So here they waited; the Scots, the Castilians, the Portuguese, the foreigners from other European countries and the Granadians; under the shadows of a medieval town in the hills topped by the stone walled defensive structure known as Castle of the Star. For some days the Granadians attacked and harried the Castilian forces along the river. James and his men were not yet engaged with this enemy. But on the 24th of August there seemed to be a change; King Alfonso decided to do battle the next day.

Figure XX-Part Three; view of the battle site from the ruins of the Castle of the Star, Teba; courtesy Susan Shane

As James lay in his tent that night he was his usual restless self before a battle; but lacking an outlet for his nervous energy. In this foreign land he could not venture out on a reconnaissance to soothe his concerns. King Alfonso had explained how he would lead the assault; he reviewed the battle plan in every detail with James. The Castilian army would be led by the king; the foreigners including James and the rag tag knights-errant from the continent would follow the lead of Dom Pero, Alfonso's lieutenant. The Castilian king would sound the charge, the call to arms which James committed to memory; as with each step of the battle plan the Douglas knight then reviewed them thoroughly with his own men.

Since both armies were camped in sight of one another there was little to doubt for the battle to come he assured himself that night as he tried without success to sleep. "By St. Bride; what of these winds that keep me restless so?" he wondered aloud. The night air was dry; the breezes swift, moving unchecked across the flat lands of the arid valley. James peered out the door of his pavilion to see a murky halo moon; the stars twinkling, peaking out from behind the heavy clouds against the darkened sky. "Aye that is it," he scoffed at himself. "To perceive of such black shadows in our Scotland for this hour of the summer's night would be a grave foreboding. This foolish knight is better to put his nerves to rest; three years gone by from doing battle has made Lord Douglas nervous as a lass," James chided himself.

Figure XXI-Part Four; the Douglas monument in Teba in tribute to the Good Sir James; a Scot on his way to the Holy Sepulchre with the heart of Robert the Brus

Early the next day he gathered his men around him; reviewed the plan of attack and reminded them of King Alfonso's signal to begin the charge. His small retinue joined in number by the other foreign soldiers at court in Seville made their way to the right flank of the Castilian army. His destrier was almost uncontrollable; moving uncharacteristically back and forth. "Perhaps my good charger is too lang from battle most as well," James postulated wryly. But truth told, he said under his breath this knight is uneasy to begin. Then he recalled the dreams he had; not sleeping well the reveries seemed quite real he reflected. Just before dawn he felt he was riding in battle; heading for the carse at Bannockburn; but when he looked to see the knight joining in his charge, the face was his father's; only the scar was gone and he was younger. "What foolery is this?" he grumbled as he woke from the vivid dream. James lay thinking in his bed; wondering why he ever ended up in Teba.

He was at the royal wedding of Prince David and Edward's sister Joan, two years ago, taking the place of his ailing king. Queen Isabella was making small talk of conversation with Lord Douglas. She suggested that perhaps now, since the wars were over, the knight might enjoy another fight for glory: in Spain with the king's own cousin Alfonso. James was fumbling for a polite response to the queen's courtly chatter; he said he favored the suggestion. When the official letter came with the introduction along with his requested writ of protection from King Edward to travel in England he thought this commendation to the Castilian lord might be the opportunity he sought to truly fight the Saracens. Now as he looked about the battlefield a strange thought occurred to him. Was this dear Edward's way to finally defeat him in battle? "This knight has truly had his better days to fear such thoughts," he sputtered at himself.

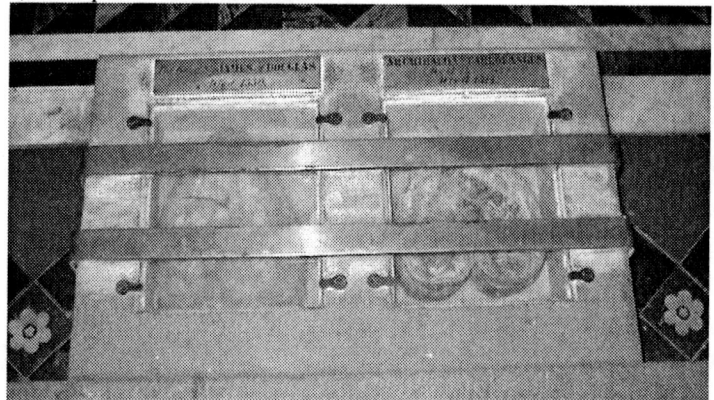

Figure XXII-Part Four; the embalmed heart of the Good Sir James; found in the burial vaults below the ruins of St. Bride's; the other heart belonged to Archibald, Bell the Cat

Suddenly in his reverie; another strange departure from his normal readiness for the fight, the Lord Douglas heard the signal from King Alfonso; the battle was on! "A Douglas! A Douglas!" James shouted to his men as he led the right flank into the ranks of the Moors. His old standard cut and thrust bravely, accurately as the Black Douglas led his Scots and others into the charge. But something did not feel right as he pulled right to move above the fray; to his left no others followed; the army of the king was yet waiting to make their attack! James called his men to the retreat, but from the corner of his eye he saw St. Clair was suddenly surrounded. He spurred his destrier to the knight's side but when he went to hold his stance in his stirrups his right knee locked and he could not maintain his balance. "By God and St. Bride," he grumbled to no avail; the Lord Douglas had no leverage and was unhorsed.

    The Saracens came to surround the injured laird; not knowing of the significance of the heraldry, his three mullets on a chief azure did not reveal his high rank to them. They savagely attacked the stricken knight. James fought back; felling most of Osmin's men, stumbling to their death; they formed a morbid ring of bodies surrounding James in his final passing to the Otherworld. In this last fight the Good Sir James took many of the enemy most with him. But these Moors were successful in their quest where few others had prevailed. They thrust him through; five mortal wounds penetrated the body of this most noble Scot. As James lay dying in the sun of a bright summer's day, the pains that shuddered through his body wafted to the winds, leaving an unfamiliar lightness in his head. He thought he heard the voice of his father, then his king's own words as well, so he responded. "Forever my king, this knight to follow, brave heart," he whispered.

    The words were his last; the formidable knight who fought more than seventy battles, victorious in all but thirteen, had perished. Strangely the battle at Teba was won that day by Edward's cousin. With the body of the Douglas laird left to his vassals to collect, King Alfonso sounded the charge, called out the five hundred Portuguese knights and the rest of his army. The Castilian contingency routed the Moors; claimed the Castle of the Star for Alfonso. But Scotland paid a huge price for the Castilian victory. Lord Douglas, St. Clair and two knights named Logan perished with many squires including one named Hugh from Ayrshire. Adam fitz Hugh, a loyal vassal from Eskdale, secured the heart of King Robert with the body of the Good Sir James; aided by his squire Patrick they carried the knight's body off the battlefield. Outside the laird's pavilion a grim contingency of Scots gathered, just standing with a strange stoicism to their demeanor. They presented a sense of odd finality to a battle that they cared little for the outcome, victory or loss; only that their brave and courageous Lord Douglas was now gone from them. The task at hand was to remove his heart, set it in a lead casket; boil his limbs and body in a vinegar to dispel the flesh and remove the bones to return to Scotland for his burial.

    The final remains of the gallant Douglas knight and the casket bearing his heart were returned to Scotland by William Keith of Galston. The romantic end for the laird of Douglasdale was a bitter one for Scotland. Edward and his vassal Balliol saw an opportunity with his demise as it was followed soon thereafter by another. Just two years from the tragedy at

Teba, Sir Thomas Randolph the Regent took ill; his body writhed with a grave swelling of infection as he passed to the Otherworld; prompting Balliol's return to Scotland with Edward's support. Did Queen Isabella devise such treachery to end the life of the Good Sir James? If he could speak from the Otherworld, might these words be his reply: *you wouldn't be wrong if you said that*? James Lord Douglas, his bones and embalmed heart came to a final rest in Douglas; stored safely in the lower burial vault beneath the altar at the Douglas Kirk. The effigy and tomb he diligently designed to house the bones of Lord Will along side his Lady El were not completed. His promise went unfulfilled; Gilley and Ellie, their shrouded remains with those of their children and grandson yet lie together in a graveyard in England at Little Dunmow Priory.

In the Shadow of My Truth…it is done.

MAP OF SCOTLAND

Figure XXIII-Part Four; Note: place names set to approximate locations

MAP OF ENGLAND

Figure XXIV-Part Four; Note: places shown for relative locations, not to true scale; and in an effort to display Stebbing, the location of the manor of Stebbinge Park, the villages of Little Dunmow and Little Easton were not listed. Little Dunmow and the priory reside one mile south of Stebbing; Little Easton and the former Lovaine manor of that name reside approximately three miles west of Stebbing.

GLOSSARY

armed foot	soldiers on foot
armed horse	cavalry
battlemented	readied for warfare with crenelles, merlons and other devices
Book of Hours	medieval prayer book
brae	hillside
bovate	eight acres or what one bovine can plow in a year
carucate	parcel of land 100-120 acres
cellarers	servants in castle cellars taking care of food provisions, wine, ale or other storage areas
chamberlain	treasurer
charter-chest	small wooden chest securing charters or medieval deeds
cleugh	ravine
coffin	coffer or small box used to store items including coinage (paper money was not used)
coinage	money, coins; silver penny was the common coin
craig; craigy	a crag or a rocky place; rocky
crenelles	a notch in a parapet, allowing defenders to look through to the area below the tower
cuir-bouilli	hardened leather soaked in wax then heated and molded into a shape
d	2d: fourpence; serf earned 1-2 d weekly; 4d a day was a large sum.
destrier	war horse
diel	Scots word for devil
donjon	an angle tower
entremets	between courses during medieval feasting
escheators	exchequers or financial records keepers and tax collectors
freeholder	holding land that may be passed down to heirs, usually for a fee
gambeson	a quilted surcote used under other armorial equipment such as leather or mail
gonfalon	banner of armorial bearings hung from crossbar; indicating the laird in residence
goshawks	kitchen hawks used for hunting for the larder
hauberk	worn as armor over gambesons usually of mail or leather
Hobini	fast and sturdy horses indigenous to Ireland
keep	dunjon or tower house; traditionally of four stories in Scotland
knight	dubbed in ceremony by another knight, ranking nobleman, land holder usually age 21
label	heraldry: figure of three points or ribbons hanging from mitre; to distinguish son from father
laird	Scots word for lord
lang	Scots word for long
larder	kitchen stores
latrine closet	indoor plumbing with a bottomless drop to the ground below; garderobe
lay-in	birthing room or birthing time

Lothianes	Lothians was a district, the older spelling was used
mail	small iron rings strung together in sheets; armor for protection
Mann	Isle of Man using the old spelling
mascle	heraldry: in the form of a lozenge perforated or voided
Merels	a cloister board game
merks	marks, two-thirds of a £; 150 merks in 1296; modern value over $100,000
merlon	the solid part of the parapet between two crenelles
miles	knight
moat	body of water usually man devised that surrounded a castle or castle motte
motte	large hill or mound upon which castles and tower houses were built
nettles and dockins	common to Scotland nettles produce a nerve tingling sting; dockins a numbing remedy
old standard	a sword that could be wielded in one hand
page	generally an eight year old in training for knighthood
palfrey	a noble horse known for his comfortable gait
parapet	a wall or wall-head for defensive position; usually battlemented, it protects the wall-walk
pennon	small flag with a swallow like tail or single pointed end
pit	the lowest part of a tower or donjon, with one entrance; barbaric form of prison
portcullis	large iron protective gate, raised and lowered at the opening to a castle gate or walls
quintaine	wooden post with revolving arm holding a target or shield
rig	ridge
sasine	seising; proof of ownership; an owner is seized or pledged to their lands
scale-and-platt	traditional wooden stair case not often found in medieval towers or keeps
Scots ell in length	about a yard
seneschal	steward or financial manager
squire	usually a lad of fourteen or more in training to become a knight
surcote	outer garment, coat
tasine	fermented concoction of fruit and water
tofts, messuages	lands with buildings and dwellings upon them
varlet	valet
villein	manorial tenant in bondage to the laird or exchanged for a place to live and work.
wall walk	the walk way on the upper level or parapet of a tower
war-chest	larger wooden chest used a piece of furniture holding armor and warriors' clothing
willow herb	a purple flowering long stemmed plant; grows early summer, before the heather blooms

WHO'S WHO
HISTORICAL FIGURES AND WHO THEY WERE

Alexander Steward	Son of John Steward; cousin of James
Alexander de Lindsay	Knight, patriot; kin to William le Hardi, the Steward; of Byres, Luffness, Barnweill, Crawford
Alice de Berkeley	Heiress of Lord Berkeley; another daughter Isabel is often confused with Alice
Amy Douglas	A daughter of William le Hardi and Eleanora
Andrew de Moray Knight	Justiciar North of the Forth; murdered in the Tower of London where he was held after Dunbar
Andrew de Moray Squire	Son of Sir Andrew, Lord Petty; responsible for the North Rising, rebellion in the Highlands
Anne de Spencer	Granddaughter of Hawise Lovaine; widow of Earl Colban 1270, remarried William de Ferrers;
Archibald Douglas	Youngest son of William le Hardi and Eleanora; later Regent of Scotland
Archibald Douglas, the Grim	James' son by Lady Ramsey of Dalhousie per chronicler Froissart, friend of this Archibald
Beatrice de Lindsay	Daughter of Alexander de Lindsay; wife of Archibald of Douglas, brother of James
Bernard de Cathe	Married Joanna de Galbrathe cousin of James, daughter of Willelma Douglas
Bernard the Chancellor	once the abbot of Kilwinning in Ayrshire; a Tironensian, one author of the 1320 Declaration
Colban Earl of Fife	Crusader in 1270; father of young Duncan, he died in Acre
Duncan Earl of Fife	Son of Earl Colban; murdered by de Percy and de Abernathy; mother Anne, kin of Eleanora
Edward III	Grandson of Edward Plantagenet
Edward Caernarvon	Son of Edward Plantagenet, Edward II
Edward Plantagenet	Ruthless sovereign of England; Edward I, responsible for the genocide of Berwick 1296
Eleanora Douglas	Daughter of Archibald who was the youngest son of William le Hardi
Eleanora de Lovaine	Second wife of William le Hardi Douglas, 7th Lord Douglas
Elizabeth Steward (Stewart)	First wife of William le Hardi; mother of the Good Sir James, named for her brother James
Freskin the Fleming	Douglas and de Moray Clans' ancestor Hugo de Freskin, Soldier of Fortune from Flanders
Hawise de Ferrers	Wife of Lord John de Ferrers; sister in law of Eleanora Douglas
Helisant Lovaine	Mother of Eleanora and wife of Lord Lovaine, Steward of Eye
Henry de Percy	Great grandson of Jocelin Lovaine an illegitimate son of the Duke of Brabant
Hubicus Douglas	Surviving son of William le Hardi and Eleanora; Canonic see of Glasgow; 10th Lord Douglas
Hugh 6th Lord Douglas	Older brother of William le Hardi; husband of Marjory de Abernathy

Hugh de Abernathy	Convicted of the murder of young Duncan Earl of Fife; died in Douglas Castle prison
James Douglas	Son of William le Hardi; known to the English as the Black Douglas; Good Sir James to Scots
James the Steward	High Steward of Scotland; Guardian; brother in law of William le Hardi, Uncle of James
Joan de Ferrers Berkeley	Sister in law to Eleanora Lovaine de Ferrers; wife of Lord Berkeley
Joanna Douglas	Wife of the Good Sir James; mother of William, 9th Lord Douglas 1330-1333
Johannis de Hastings	Powerful English nobleman; kin to Eleanora de Lovaine; stood surety for le Hardi
Johannis de Warenne	Earl of Surrey; governor of Scotland under the occupation of the English from 1296 forward
John Balliol	Contender awarded crown 1292 as King of Scots; toom tabard, stripped of his crown 1296
John de Lindsay	Canon See of Glasgow; Bishop of Glasgow 1323
John Douglas	First son of William le Hardi and Eleanora; first son of Archie and Beatrice
John le Parker	Hugh Douglas was in his ward, Stebbinge Park, Essex; held position of steward
John Steward	Brother of James the Steward; uncle of the Good Sir James
John Strathbogie, Earl of Athol	Loyal adherent of Robert Brus; first earl to be executed in 200 years, hanged cruelly 1306
John Wishart	Nephew of the Bishop; Baron of the Mearns; joined le Hardi in the raid of the heart, Fawside
John Wysham	Yeoman of Edward I; awarded license to marry Eleanora, widow of le Hardi; she refused
Marjory Abernathy	Wife of Lord Hugh of Douglas; contract marriage 1259; her brother Sir Hugh de Abernathy
Martha Douglas	Daughter of William le Hardi and Eleanora; drowned in a moat at Woodham Ferrers Hall
Matthew Lovaine	Father of Eleanora de Lovaine; grandson of Godfrey, brother of the bearded Duke of Brabant
Maud de Segrave	Only surviving heir of Nicky de Segrave; wife of Edmond de Bohun
Maud Poyntz	Third wife of Matthew Lovaine
Murdac de Mentethe	Vassal and cousin of William de Ferrers; part of conspiracy of disinherited nobles
Muriel Douglas	Oldest daughter of William le Hardi and Eleanora who later married Richard Lovel
Nicholas de Segrave	Second son of Nicholas the elder; powerful English nobleman, kin to Eleanora; adherent to Lancaster
Patric de Douglas	Douglas household member since before 1267; here he is a squire to Lord Douglas
Ralph Bagot	Brother of William Bagot
Robert Barduff	English knight, nobleman of Staffordshire, kin of Eleanora pledged surety for William le Hardi
Robert Boyd	Ayrshire knight, cousin of the Good Sir James
Robert Brus	Grandson of the Contender; Robert I of Scotland
Robert Wishart	Bishop of Glasgow; the patriotic prelate who supported William Wallace; defied Edward I
Sholto Du-glash	Brave warrior; Douglas ancestor rewarded for service with land in Lanarkshire by the king
Thomas de Blakenham	God father and maternal uncle of Thomas Lovaine, Ellie's half brother

Thomas Chauncelor	Knight in service to Lord Douglas who was captured and imprisoned in Northumbria
Thomas de Lovaine	Half brother of Eleanora de Lovaine
Thomas Randolph	Grandson of Adam Kilconquhar who was then Earl of Carrick; he became Earl of Moray
Walter de Percy	Kin of Sir Henry de Percy; beheaded at Douglas Castle for the murder of Earl Duncan
Walter the Rich	Walter de Moray married an heiress of the Olifard family; started building Bothwell
Walter the Steward	Son of James the Steward; cousin of the Good Sir James
Willelma de Galbrathe	Older sister of William le Hardi Douglas; her daughter married Bernard de Keith
William Bagot	Knight awarded license to marry le Hardi's widow in 1305; Eleanora accepted
William de Duglas	William le Hardi; Crusader, Poet Knight, Willelmi, dominus de Duglas; Guillame de Duglas, ssg
William de Duglas	Son of the Good Sir James, 9th Lord Douglas
William de Duglas	1st Earl of Douglas; son of le Hardi's youngest son Archibald
William Douglas of Lothianes	Cousin of the Good Sir James; son of James Douglas of Laudonia or the Lothians
William de Ferrers	First husband of Eleanora de Lovaine; also the name of his son
William de Foghou	Abbot of Melrose Abbey early 14th century
William de Galbrathe	Brother in law of William le Hardi Douglas
William de Rye	English knight and nobleman of East Sussex who pledged his surety for William le Hardi
William Lamberton	Bishop of St. Andrews; kin of the de Lindsay family
William Wallace	Patriot; valiant warrior loved Scotland more than life itself; executed cruelly by Edward I

Figure XXV-Epilogue; spirit artist's depiction of Gilley, William le Hardi, Lord Douglas on his charger at Castle Dangerous

MY TRUTH A MIST IN TIME

The Douglas Clan, their true saga continues with the third 'Douglas Book' in the series: *My Truth a Mist in Time* ©2004. Accompany these spirited adventurers through the tumultuous years of 14th century Scotland. Read about the travails of young Will, ninth Lord Douglas, le Hardi's grandson; the brave exploits of Sir Archibald, Regent of Scotland. Learn why Hugh the Canon was forced to resign his position within the Glasgow See; succeeding to the Douglas barony as Hubicus, Lord Douglas. And discover the secrets behind the first Douglas earls, Earl William and Archibald the Grim, inheriting their fathers' estates, desperate in their search for truth; the legacy of William le Hardi Douglas…*but a mist in time.*

"This humble knight knows only to follow his truth…God's own truth within him; heid here in his heart." WILLIAM LE HARDI DOUGLAS

Printed in the United Kingdom
by Lightning Source UK Ltd.
102656UKS00001B/235-258